G000097440

STREE

West Kent

www.philips-maps.co.uk

First published in 1994 by

Philip's, a division of
Octopus Publishing Group Ltd
www.octopusbooks.co.uk
2-4 Heron Quays, London E14 4JP
An Hachette Livre UK Company
www.hachettelivre.co.uk

Third colour edition 2005
Second impression with revisions 2008
WKTCB

ISBN 978-0-540-09479-0 (pocket)

© Philip's 2008

OS **Ordnance Survey®**

This product includes mapping data licensed from
Ordnance Survey® with the permission of the
Controller of Her Majesty's Stationery Office.

© Crown copyright 2008. All rights reserved.
Licence number 100011710.

Ordnance Survey and the OS Symbol are
registered trademarks of Ordnance Survey, the
national mapping agency of Great Britain.

Printed and bound in China by Toppan

Contents

III **Key to map symbols**

IV **Key to map pages**

VI **Route planning**

VIII **Administrative and Postcode boundaries**

1 **Street maps** at 2⅔ inches to 1 mile

200 **Index** of towns and villages

202 **Index** of streets, hospitals, industrial estates, railway
stations, schools, shopping centres, universities
and places of interest

Digital Data

The exceptionally high-quality mapping found in this atlas is available as digital data in
TIFF format, which is easily convertible to other bitmapped (raster) image formats.

The index is also available in digital form as a standard database table. It contains all the
details found in the printed index together with the National Grid reference for the map
square in which each entry is named.

For further information and to discuss your requirements, please contact
victoria.dawbarn@philips-maps.co.uk

On-line route planner

For detailed driving directions and estimated driving times visit our free route planner at
www.philips-maps.co.uk

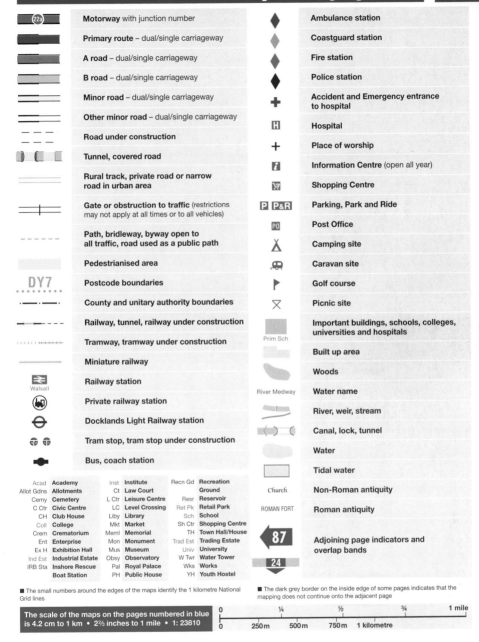

(22a)	**Motorway** with junction number
	Primary route – dual/single carriageway
	A road – dual/single carriageway
	B road – dual/single carriageway
	Minor road – dual/single carriageway
	Other minor road – dual/single carriageway
	Road under construction
	Tunnel, covered road
	Rural track, private road or narrow road in urban area
	Gate or obstruction to traffic (restrictions may not apply at all times or to all vehicles)
	Path, bridleway, byway open to all traffic, road used as a public path
	Pedestrianised area
DY7	**Postcode boundaries**
	County and unitary authority boundaries
	Railway, tunnel, railway under construction
	Tramway, tramway under construction
	Miniature railway
Walsall	**Railway station**
	Private railway station
	Docklands Light Railway station
	Tram stop, tram stop under construction
	Bus, coach station

◆	**Ambulance station**
◆	**Coastguard station**
◆	**Fire station**
◆	**Police station**
✚	**Accident and Emergency entrance to hospital**
H	**Hospital**
+	**Place of worship**
i	**Information Centre** (open all year)
🛒	**Shopping Centre**
P P&R	**Parking, Park and Ride**
PO	**Post Office**
Ⅹ	**Camping site**
🚐	**Caravan site**
►	**Golf course**
✗	**Picnic site**
Prim Sch	**Important buildings, schools, colleges, universities and hospitals**
	Built up area
	Woods
River Medway	**Water name**
	River, weir, stream
	Canal, lock, tunnel
	Water
	Tidal water
Church	**Non-Roman antiquity**
ROMAN FORT	**Roman antiquity**
87 / 24	**Adjoining page indicators and overlap bands**

Acad	**Academy**	Inst	**Institute**	Recn Gd	**Recreation Ground**
Allot Gdns	**Allotments**	Ct	**Law Court**		
Cemy	**Cemetery**	L Ctr	**Leisure Centre**	Resr	**Reservoir**
C Ctr	**Civic Centre**	LC	**Level Crossing**	Ret Pk	**Retail Park**
CH	**Club House**	Liby	**Library**	Sch	**School**
Coll	**College**	Mkt	**Market**	Sh Ctr	**Shopping Centre**
Crem	**Crematorium**	Meml	**Memorial**	TH	**Town Hall/House**
Ent	**Enterprise**	Mon	**Monument**	Trad Est	**Trading Estate**
Ex H	**Exhibition Hall**	Mus	**Museum**	Univ	**University**
Ind Est	**Industrial Estate**	Obsy	**Observatory**	W Twr	**Water Tower**
IRB Sta	**Inshore Rescue**	Pal	**Royal Palace**	Wks	**Works**
	Boat Station	PH	**Public House**	YH	**Youth Hostel**

■ The small numbers around the edges of the maps identify the 1 kilometre National Grid lines

■ The dark grey border on the inside edge of some pages indicates that mapping does not continue onto the adjacent page

The scale of the maps on the pages numbered in blue is 4.2 cm to 1 km • 2⅔ inches to 1 mile • 1: 23810

0	¼	½	¾	1 mile
0	250 m	500 m	750 m	1 kilometre

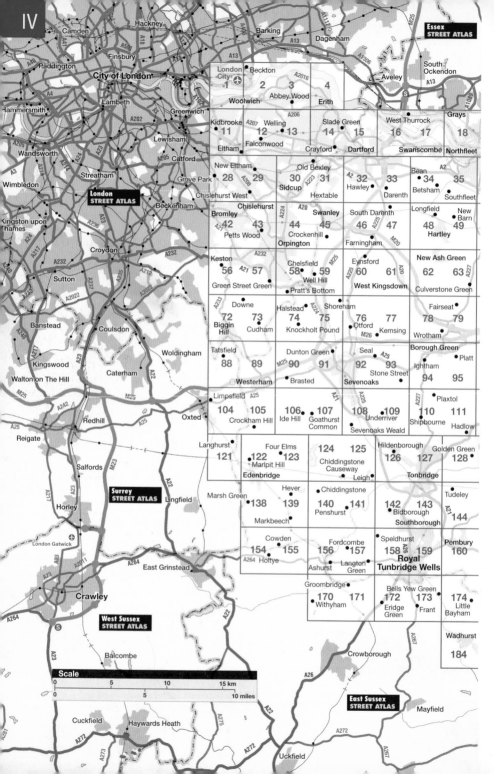

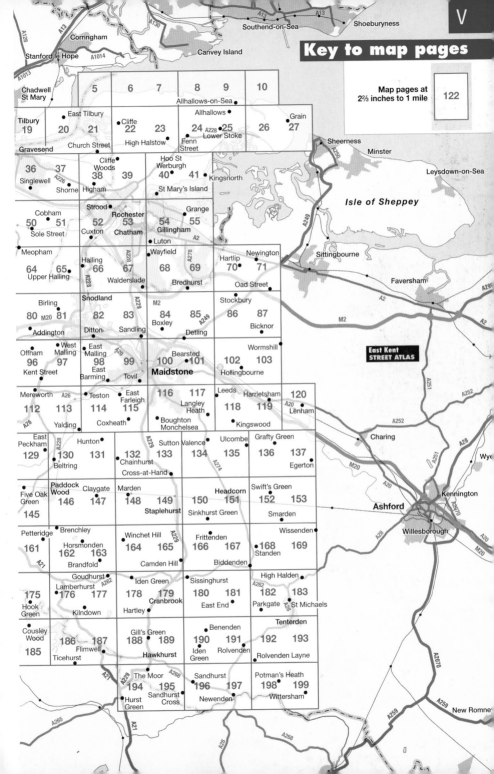

Key to map pages

Map pages at
2⅔ inches to 1 mile

122

Southend-on-Sea   Shoeburyness

Corringham

Canvey Island

Stanford le Hope

Chadwell
St Mary   **5**   **6**   **7**   **8**   **9**   **10**

Allhallows-on-Sea

Allhallows

Tilbury   East Tilbury   Cliffe   **23**   **24** A228 **25**   Grain
19   **20**   **21**   **22**   Lower Stoke   **26**   **27**
        High Halstow   Fenn
Gravesend   Church Street   Street   Sheerness   Minster

Hoo St
Werburgh   Leysdown-on-Sea
Cliffe
36   **37**   Woods   Hoo St   St Mary's Island
Singlewell   **38**   **39**   **40**   **41** Kingsnorth   **Isle of Sheppey**
    Shorne   Higham

Strood   Grange
Cobham   **52** Rochester   **54**   **55**
50   **51**   **53**   Gillingham
Sole Street   Cuxton   Chatham   Luton
        A2

Meopham   Wayfield   Newington
64   **65** Halling   **67**   **68**   **69** Hartlip   **71**   Sittingbourne   Faversham
Upper Halling   **66**   Walderslade   Bredhurst   **70**
        Oad Street

Birling   Snodland   Stockbury
80 M20 **81**   **82**   **83**   **84**   **85**   **86**   **87**
Addington   Ditton   Sandling   Boxley   Detling   Bicknor

West   East   Wormshill
Offham   Malling   Malling   Bearsted   **102**   **103**
96   **97**   **98**   **99**   **100** **101**
Kent Street   East   Tovil   **Maidstone**   Hollingbourne
    Barming

Mereworth   Teston   East   **116**   **117** Leeds   Harrietsham   **120**
112   **113**   **114** Farleigh   Langley   **118**   **119** Lenham
        115   Heath   Kingswood   Charing
    Yalding   Coxheath   Boughton
        Monchelsea

East   Hunton   Sutton Valence   Ulcombe   Grafty Green   Wye
Peckham   **130**   **131**   **132**   **133**   **134**   **135**   **136**   **137**
129   Beltring   Chainhurst   Egerton
        Cross-at-Hand

Paddock   Claygate   Marden   Headcorn   Swift's Green   Kennington
Five Oak   Wood   **147**   **148** **149**   **150** **151**   **152**   **153**
Green   **146**   Staplehurst   Sinkhurst Green   Smarden   **Ashford**
145   Willesborough

Petteridge   Brenchley   Winchet Hill   Frittenden   Wissenden
161   Horsmonden   **164** **165**   **166** **167**   **168**   **169**
    162 **163**   Camden Hill   Biddenden   Standen
    Brandfold

Goudhurst   High Halden
Lamberhurst   Iden Green   Sissinghurst   **182** **183**
175 **176**   **177**   **178** **179**   **180** **181**   Parkgate   St Michaels
Hook   Kilndown   Cranbrook   East End
Green   Hartley

Cousley   Benenden   Tenterden
Wood   Gill's Green   **190** **191**   **192** **193**
186 **187**   **188** **189**   Rolvenden
185   Flimwell   Hawkhurst   Iden   Rolvenden Layne
Ticehurst   Green

The Moor   Sandhurst   Potman's Heath
194 **195**   **196** **197**   **198** **199**
Hurst   Sandhurst   Newenden   Wittersham   New Romne
Green   Cross

East Kent
STREET ATLAS

Scale

0   5   10 km

0   5 miles

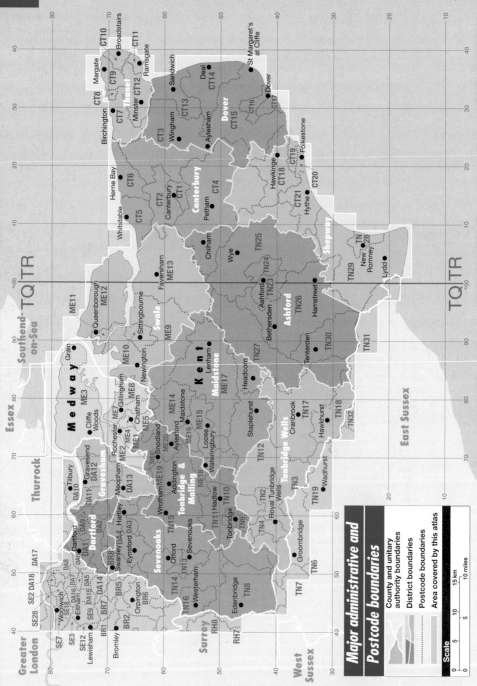

Major administrative and
Postcode boundaries

County and unitary
authority boundaries

District boundaries

Postcode boundaries

Area covered by this atlas

Scale

0   5   10   15 km

0   5   10 miles

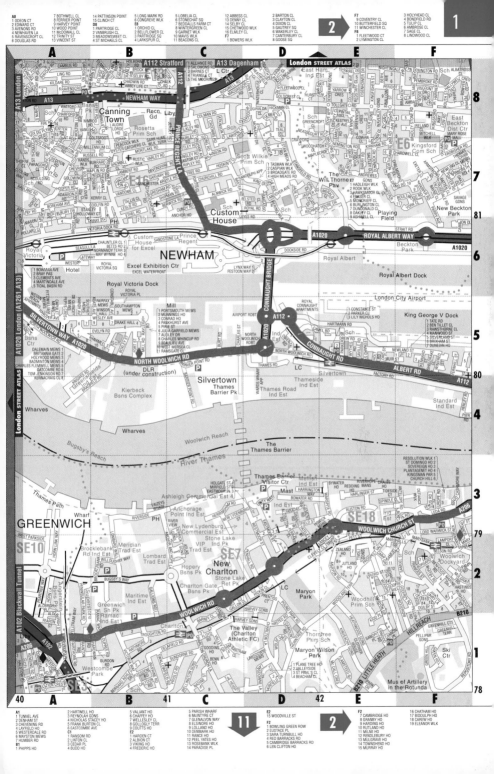

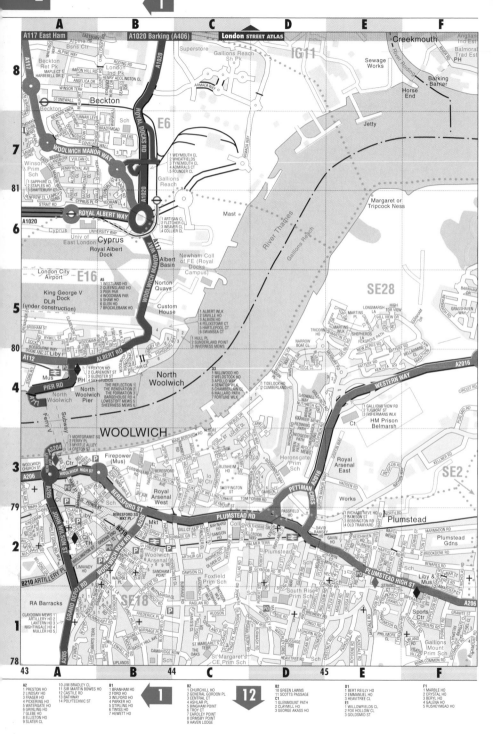

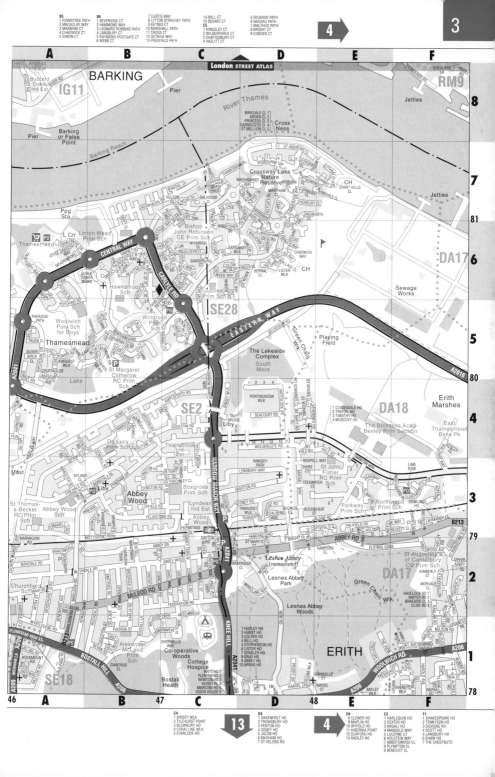

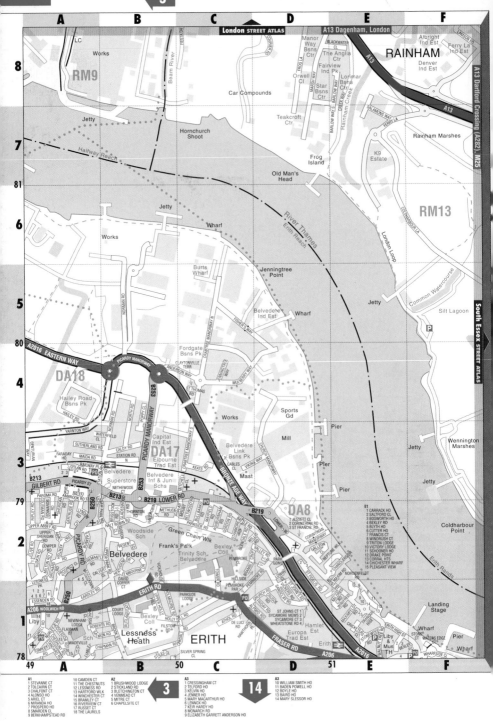

London STREET ATLAS

A13 Dagenham, London

RAINHAM

RM9

RM13

River Thames
Erith Reach

A2016 EASTERN WAY

DA18

DA17

DA8

Belvedere

ERITH

Lessness
Heath

A1
1 STEVANNE CT
2 TOLCAIRN CT
3 CHALFONT CT
4 ALONSO CT
5 ARIEL CT
6 MIRANDA HO
7 PROSPERO HO
8 SMARDEN CT
9 BERKHAMPSTEAD RD

10 CAMDEN CT
11 THE CHESTNUTS
12 LESSNESS RD
13 HARTFORD WLK
14 WINCHESTER CT
15 BRAMLEY CT
16 RIVERVIEW CT
17 RUSSET CT
18 THE LAURELS

A2
1 BRUSHWOOD LODGE
2 STICKLAND RD
3 BLETCHINGTON CT
4 VENMEAD CT
5 MITRE CT
6 CHAPELSITE CT

A3
1 CRESSINGHAM CT
2 TELFORD HO
3 KELVIN HO
4 JENNER HO
5 MARY MACARTHUR HO
6 LENNOX HO
7 KEIR HARDY HO
8 MONARCH RD
9 ELIZABETH GARRETT ANDERSON HO

A3
10 WILLIAM SMITH HO
11 BADEN POWELL HO
12 BOYLE HO
13 BAIRD HO
14 MARY SLESSOR HO

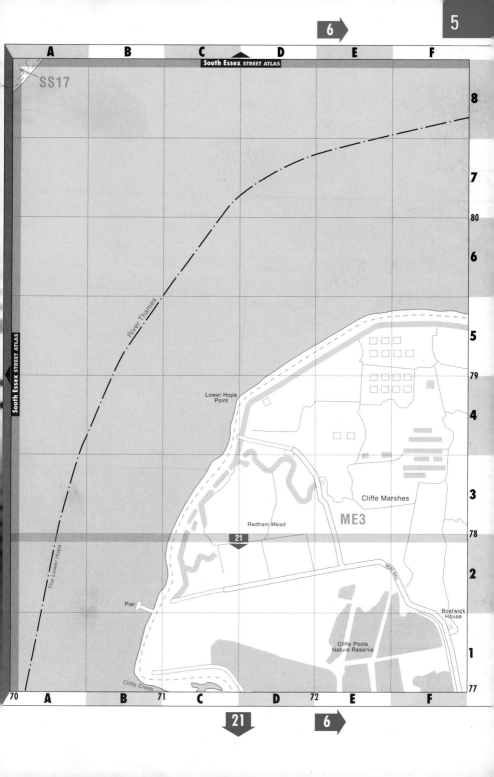

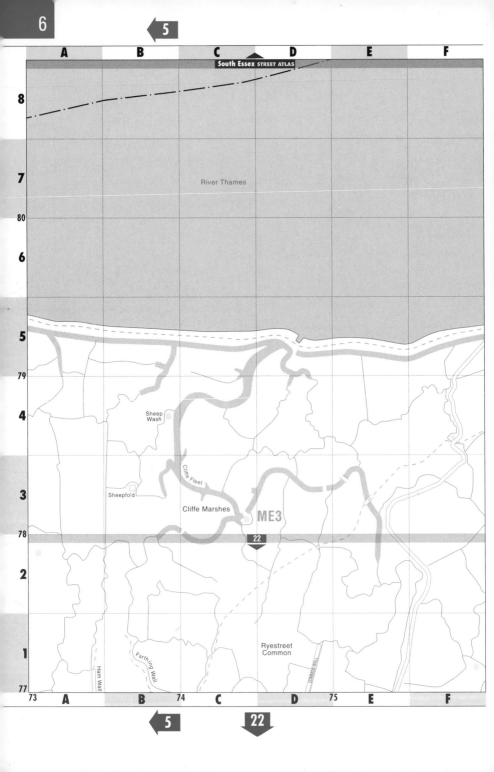

8

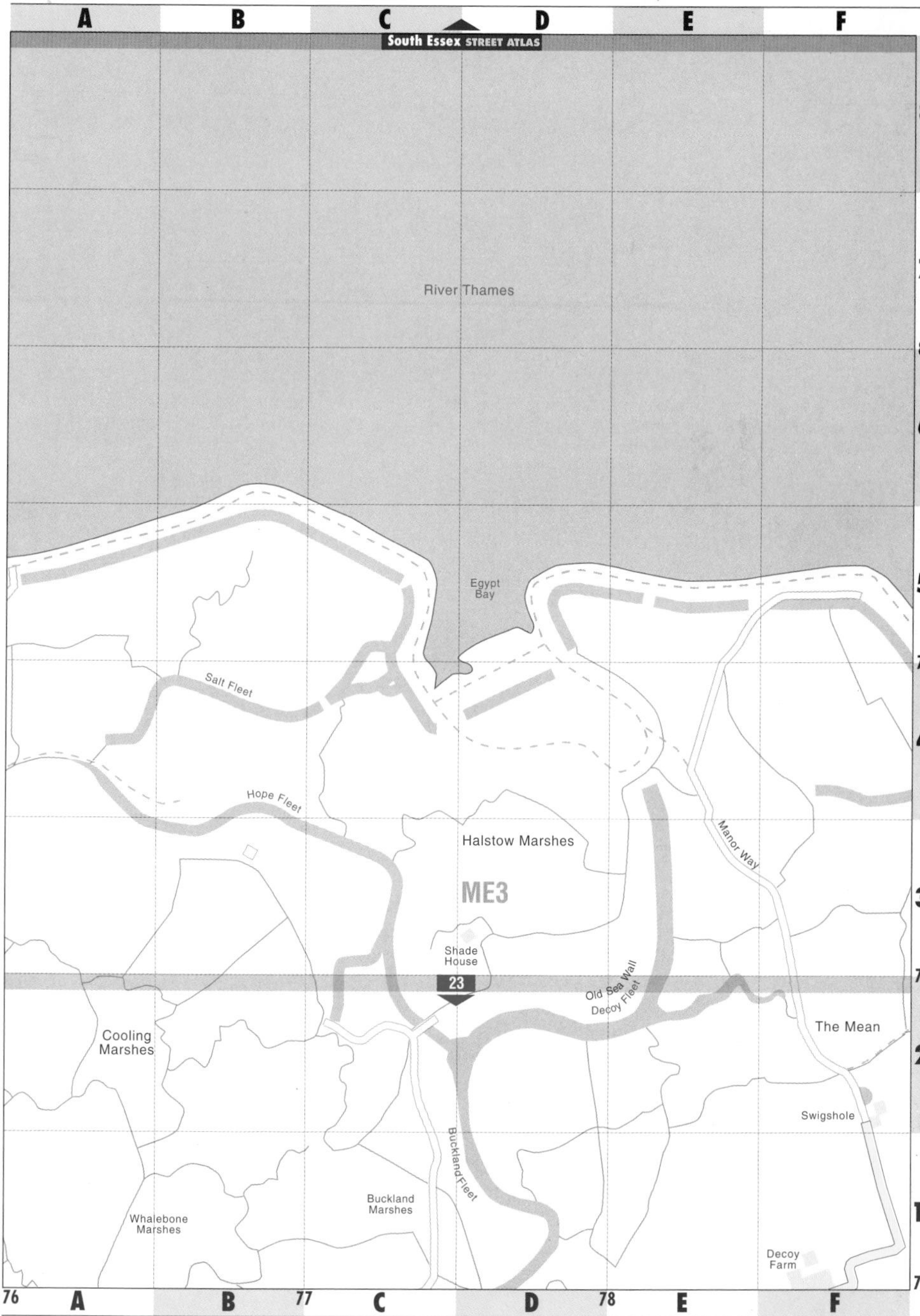
A
B
C
D
E
F
South Essex STREET ATLAS
8
7
80
6
5
79
4
3
78
2
1
77
River Thames
Egypt Bay
Salt Fleet
Hope Fleet
Halstow Marshes
ME3
Manor Way
Shade House
23
Old Sea Wall
Decoy Fleet
The Mean
Cooling Marshes
Swigshole
Buckland Fleet
Buckland Marshes
Whalebone Marshes
Decoy Farm
76
77
78

23
8

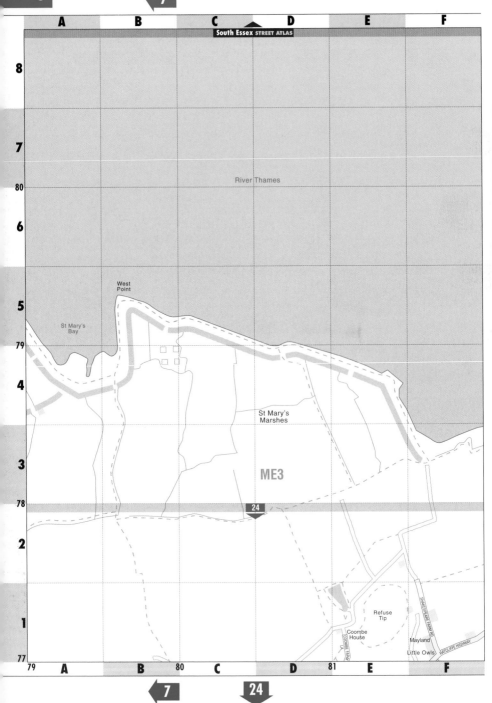

South Essex STREET ATLAS

River Thames

West
Point

St Mary's
Bay

St Mary's
Marshes

ME3

24

Refuse
Tip

Coombe
House

Mayland

Little Owls

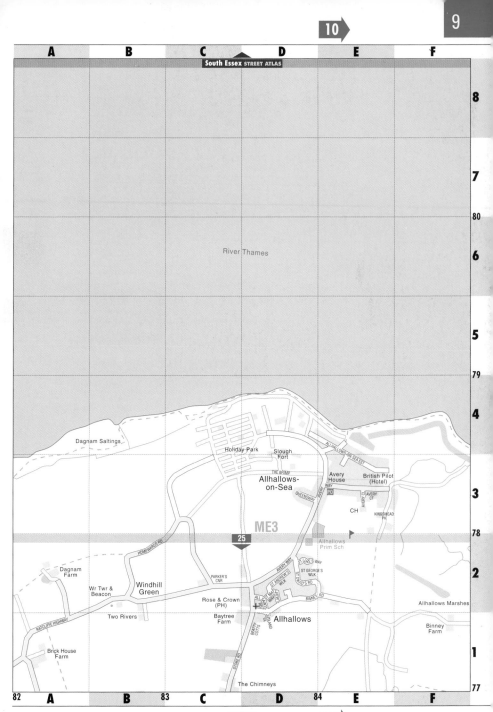

South Essex STREET ATLAS

River Thames

Dagnam Saltings

Holiday Park

Slough Fort

THE BRIMP

Allhallows-on-Sea

Avery House

British Pilot (Hotel)

AVERY CT

AVERY CL

QUEENSWAY

WAY

CH

KINGSMEAD PK

ME3

Allhallows Prim Sch

HOMEWARDS RD

Dagnam Farm

PARKER'S CNR

AVERY WAY

ST ANDREW'S WLK

ST GEORGE'S WLK

ST DAVID'S RD

Wr Twr & Beacon

Windhill Green

Allhallows Marshes

Rose & Crown (PH)

BINNEY RD

RATCLIFFE HIGHWAY

Two Rivers

Baytree Farm

Allhallows

Binney Farm

Brick House Farm

STOKE RD

BINNEY COTTS

The Chimneys

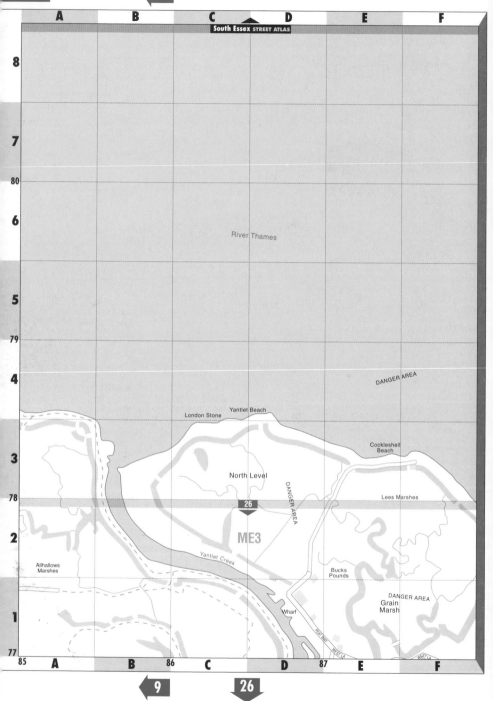

South Essex STREET ATLAS

River Thames

DANGER AREA

Yantlet Beach

London Stone

Cockleshell
Beach

North Level

DANGER AREA

Lees Marshes

26

ME3

Yantlet Creek

Allhallows
Marshes

Bucks
Pounds

DANGER AREA
Grain
Marsh

Wharf

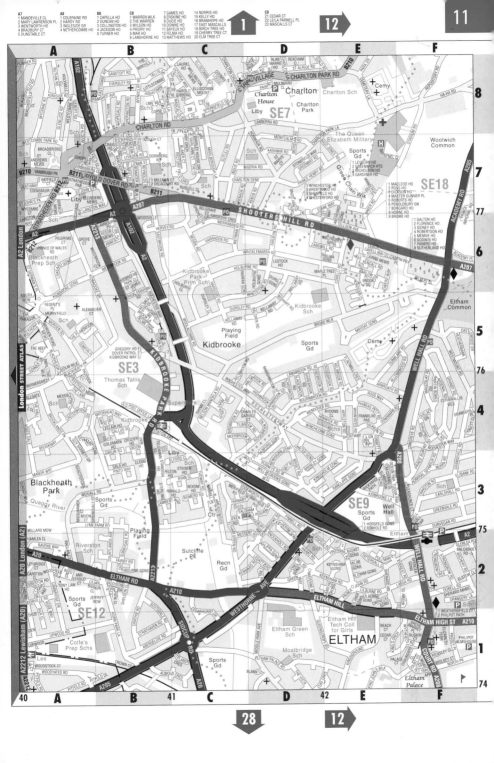

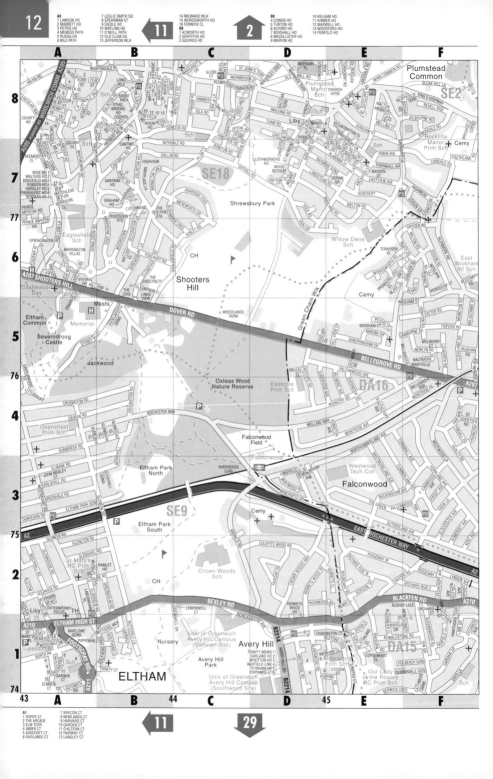

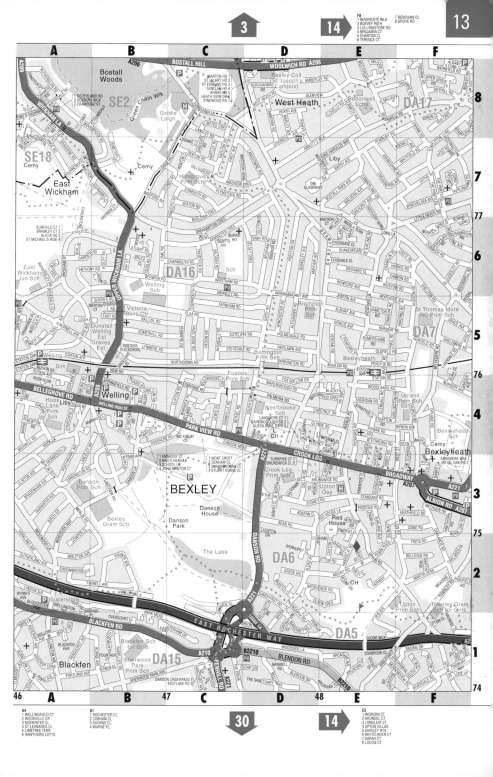

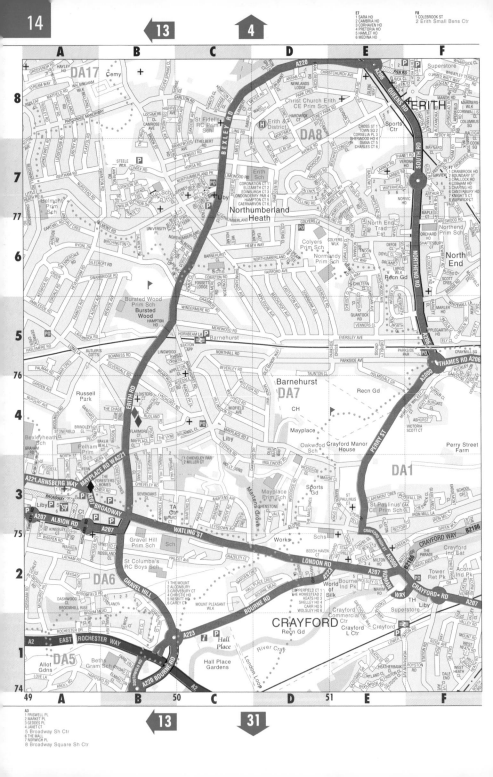

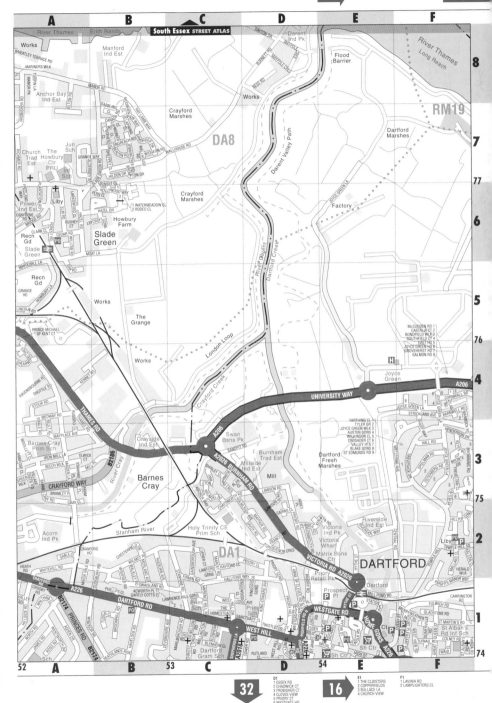

D1
1 ESSEX RD
2 CHADWICK CT
3 FROBISHER CT
4 CLEVES VIEW
5 PRIORY CT
6 WESTGATE HO

E1
1 THE CLOISTERS
2 COPPERFIELDS
3 BULLACE LA
4 CHURCH VIEW

F1
1 LAVINIA RD
2 LAMPLIGHTERS CL

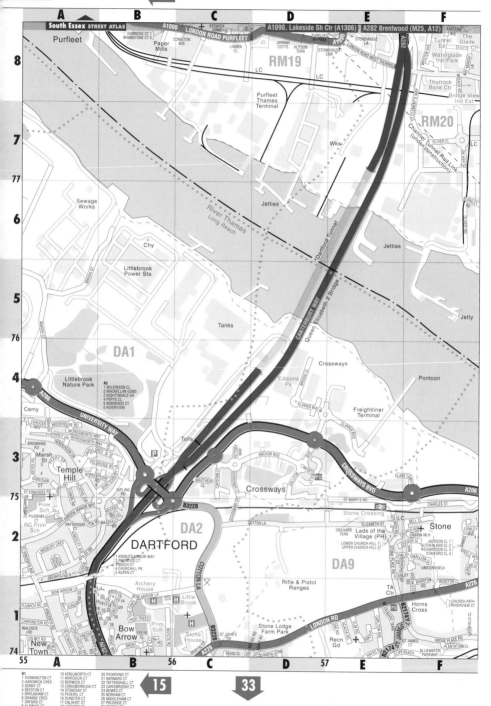

B1
1 DONNINGTON CT
2 HARDWICK CRES
3 DENNY CT
4 BEESTON CT
5 BROUGHAM CT
6 GRANGE CRES
7 ORFORD CT
8 ALNWICK CT
9 BRAMBER CT

10 KENILWORTH CT
11 WARDOUR CT
12 BERWICK CT
13 CONISBOROUGH CT
14 STOKESAY CT
15 PEVERIL CT
16 DUNSTER CT
17 CALSHOT CT
18 LYDFORD CT
19 LONGTOWN CT

20 PICKERING CT
21 BARNARD CT
22 TATTERSHALL CT
23 CARISBROOKE CT
24 BOWES CT
25 NORHAM CT
26 MIDDLEHAM CT
27 PRUDHOE CT
28 BRIDGE CT

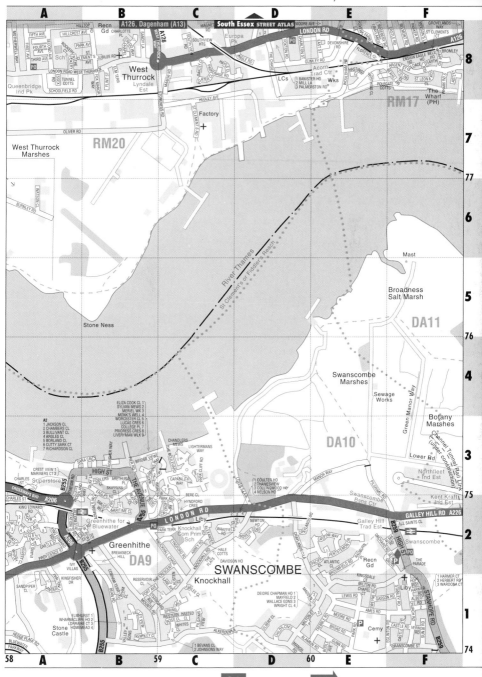

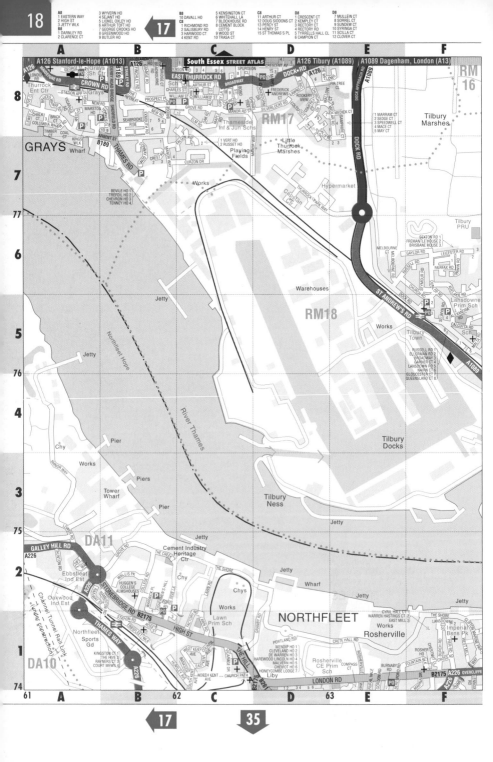

20

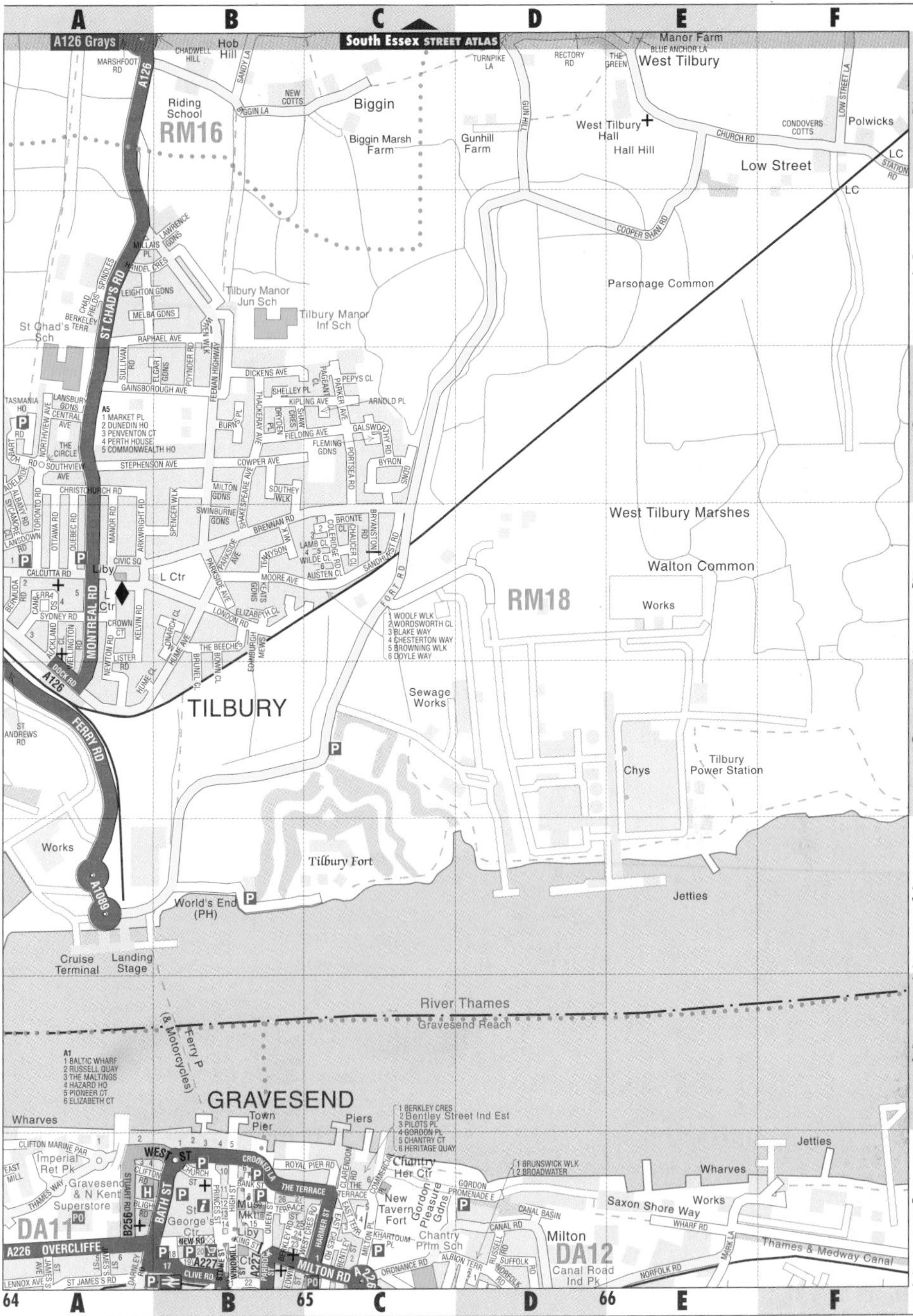

A126 Grays
MARSHFOOT RD
CHADWELL HILL
Hob Hill
South Essex STREET ATLAS
TURNPIKE LA
RECTORY RD
THE GREEN
Manor Farm
West Tilbury
BLUE ANCHOR LA
LOW STREET LA
19

Riding School
RM16
NEW COTTS
BIGGIN LA
Biggin
Biggin Marsh Farm
GUNHILL RD
Gunhill Farm
GUN LA
West Tilbury Hall
Hall Hill
CHURCH RD
CONDOVERS COTTS
Polwicks
LC STATION RD
LC
8

MILLAIS
LAWRENCE GDNS
SANDY LA
COOPER SHAW RD
LC
Low Street

St Chad's Sch
St CHAD'S RD
SPRINGLES
CHAD CHILDERS HO
BERKELEY
LEIGHTON GDNS
MELBA GDNS
Tilbury Manor Jun Sch
Tilbury Manor Inf Sch
RAPHAEL AVE
GAINSBOROUGH AVE

Parsonage Common
7
77

TASMANIA HO
LANSBURY GDNS CENTRAL
P
A5
1 MARKET PL
2 DUNEDIN HO
3 PENVENTON CT
4 PERTH HOUSE
5 COMMONWEALTH HO
DICKENS AVE
SHELLEY PL
KIPLING AVE
PEPYS CL
ARNOLD PL
GALSWORTHY
FLEMING GDNS
BYRON
West Tilbury Marshes
6

THE CIRCLE
SOUTHVIEW AVE
CHRISTCHURCH RD
STEPHENSON AVE
COWPER AVE
SOUTHEY WLK
BRONTE
Walton Common
Works

RM18
CALCUTTA RD
Lby
CIVIC SQ
L Ctr
MILTON GDNS
SWINBURNE GDNS
BRENNAN RD
LAMB CL
AUSTEN CL
MOORE AVE
1 WOOLF WLK
2 WORDSWORTH CL
3 BLAKE WAY
4 CHESTERTON WAY
5 BROWNING WLK
6 DOYLE WAY
Works
5
76

SYDNEY RD
CROWN
LONDON RD
ELIZABETH CL
THE BEECHES
Sewage Works
4

A126
FERRY RD
TILBURY
St ANDREWS RD
P
P
Chys
Tilbury Power Station

Works
P
Tilbury Fort
Jetties
3

World's End (PH)
75

Cruise Terminal
Landing Stage
Ferry P (& Motorcycles)
River Thames
Gravesend Reach
2

A5
1 BALTIC WHARF
2 RUSSELL QUAY
3 THE MALTINGS
4 HAZARD HO
5 PIONEER CT
6 ELIZABETH CT
Wharves
GRAVESEND
Town Pier
Piers
1 BERKLEY CRES
2 Bentley Street Ind Est
3 PILOTS PL
4 GORDON PL
5 CHANTRY CT
6 HERITAGE QUAY
1 BRUNSWICK WLK
2 BROADWATER
Jetties
Wharves

CLIFTON MARINE PDE
Imperial Ret Pk
Gravesend & N Kent Superstore
WEST ST
BATH ST
CROSS ST
Royal Pier Rd
THE TERRACE
Chantry Her Ctr
Saxon Shore Way
Works
Wharves

DA11
OVERCLIFFE
A226
St George's Ctr
Lby
New Tavern Fort
Gordon Pleasure Gdns
P
GORDON PROMENADE
CANAL RD
CANAL BASIN
Thames & Medway Canal
1

A227
MILTON RD
A226
Chantry Prim Sch
Milton
DA12
Canal Road Ind Pk
74

64
A
B
65
C
D
66
E
F

B1
1 CRAWLEY CT
2 MARRIOTTS WHARF
3 REGENTS CT
4 MELBOURNE QUAY
5 TOWN PIER SQ
6 BULL YD
7 HORN YD
8 NEW SWAN YD
9 MARKET ALLEY
10 WHITE HART YD
11 CHURCH ALLEY
12 JURY ST
13 GLOBE YD
14 CHASE SQ
15 BREWHOUSE YD
16 VINE CT
17 BARRACK ROW
18 GARRICK ST
19 ANGLESEA PL
20 Thamesgate Sh Ctr
21 RAILWAY PL
22 MANOR RD
23 WILFRED ST
24 BERNARD ST
25 THE TERRACE
26 ST ANDREWS CT
27 CROSS ST

36
20

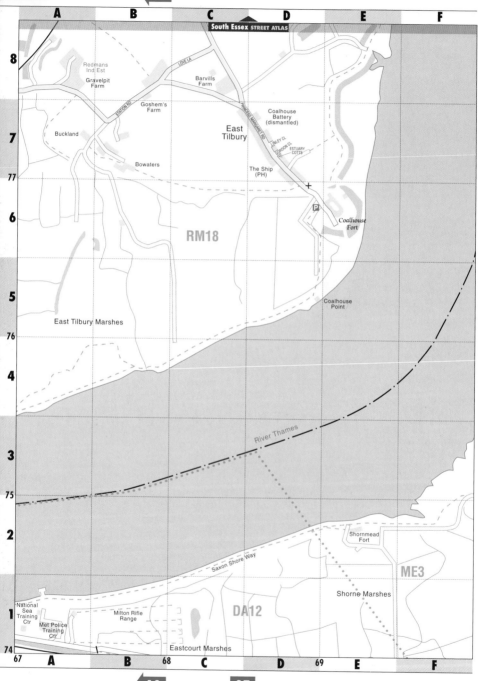

South Essex STREET ATLAS

A **B** **C** **D** **E** **F**

8

Redmans
Ind Est

Gravelpit
Farm

LOVE LA

Barvills
Farm

Goshem's
Farm

STATION RD

PRINCE MARGARET RD

Coalhouse
Battery
(dismantled)

East
Tilbury

7

Buckland

LINLEY CL

LONDON CL

ESTUARY
COTTS

Bowaters

The Ship
(PH)

77

P

6

Coalhouse
Fort

RM18

5

Coalhouse
Point

East Tilbury Marshes

76

4

River Thames

3

75

2

Shornmead
Fort

Saxon Shore Way

ME3

Shorne Marshes

1

National
Sea
Training
Ctr

Met Police
Training
Ctr

Milton Rifle
Range

DA12

Eastcourt Marshes

74

67   **A**   **B**   68   **C**   **D**   69   **E**   **F**

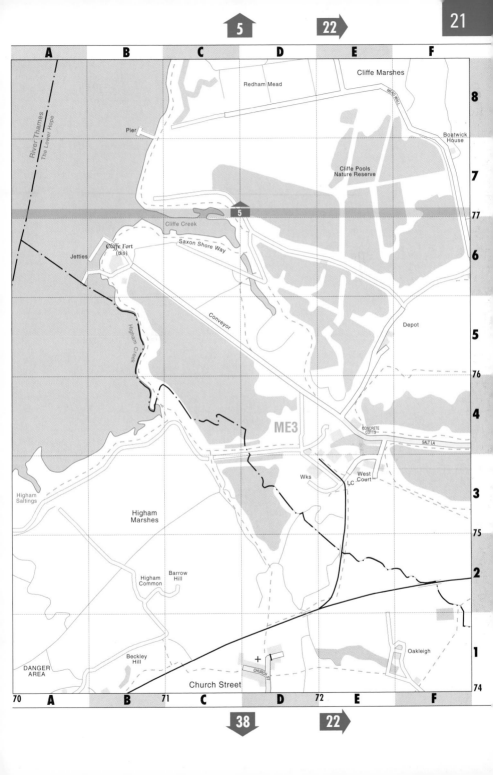

21
6

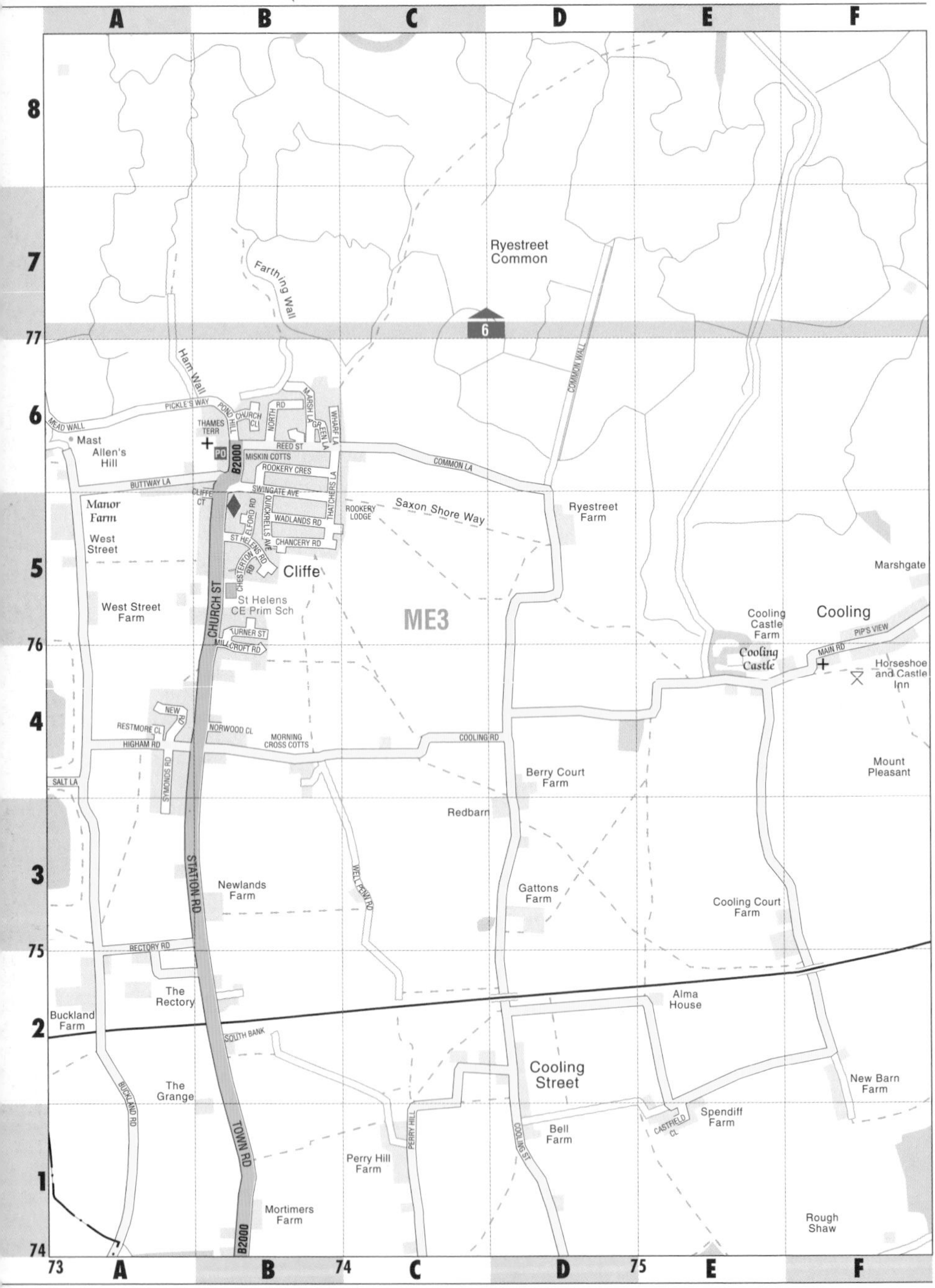
A B C D E F
8
7
77
6
5
76
4
3
75
2
1
74
73 74 75
Farthing Wall
Ryestreet Common
6
Ham Wall
COMMON WALL
MEAD WALL
PICKLE'S WAY
POND HILL
CHURCH CL
THAMES TERR
NORTH RD
MARSH LA
GREEN LA
WHARF LA
Mast
Allen's Hill
PO
REED ST
MISKIN COTTS
ROOKERY CRES
COMMON LA
B2000
BUTTWAY LA
CLIFFE CT
SWINGATE AVE
THATCHERS LA
Manor Farm
ELFORD RD
QUICKRELLS AVE
WADLANDS RD
ROOKERY LODGE
Saxon Shore Way
Ryestreet Farm
West Street
ST HELENS RD
CHANCERY RD
CHESTERTON RD
Cliffe
Marshgate
West Street Farm
St Helens CE Prim Sch
ME3
CHURCH ST
TURNER ST
MILLCROFT RD
Cooling Castle Farm
Cooling
PIP'S VIEW
MAIN RD
Cooling Castle
Horseshoe and Castle Inn
NEW RD
RESTMORE CL
NORWOOD CL
MORNING CROSS COTTS
COOLING RD
HIGHAM RD
SYMONDS RD
SALT LA
Berry Court Farm
Mount Pleasant
Redbarn
STATION RD
WELL PENN RD
Newlands Farm
Gattons Farm
Cooling Court Farm
RECTORY RD
The Rectory
Alma House
Buckland Farm
SOUTH BANK
Cooling Street
New Barn Farm
The Grange
BUCKLAND RD
TOWN RD
PERRY HILL
COOLING ST
Bell Farm
CASTFIELD CL
Spendiff Farm
Perry Hill Farm
Mortimers Farm
Rough Shaw
B2000

21
39

23
8

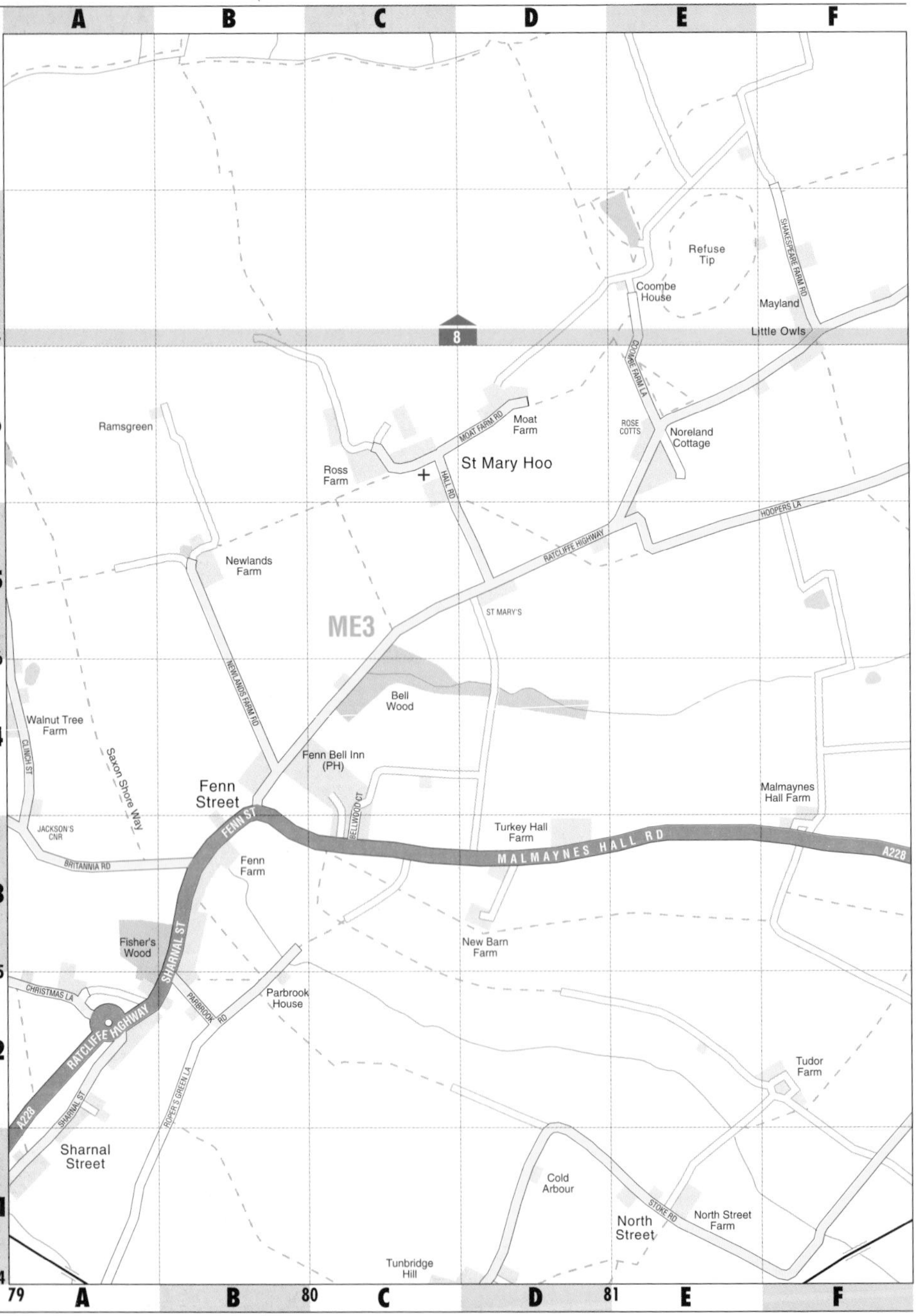

	A	B	C	D	E	F

8

7

Refuse Tip

Coombe House

Mayland

77

8

Little Owls

6

Ramsgreen

MOAT FARM RD

Moat Farm

ROSE COTTS

Noreland Cottage

Ross Farm

St Mary Hoo

HILL RD

ROSE FARM LA

HOOPERS LK

5

Newlands Farm

RATCLIFFE HIGHWAY

ME3

ST MARY'S

76

Bell Wood

Walnut Tree Farm

NEWLANDS FARM RD

Fenn Bell Inn (PH)

Malmaynes Hall Farm

4

CLINCH ST

SAXON Shore Way

Fenn Street

BELLWOOD CT

Turkey Hall Farm

JACKSON'S CNR

Fenn Farm

MALMAYNES HALL RD

A228

3

BRITANNIA RD

SHARNAL ST

FENN ST

Fisher's Wood

New Barn Farm

75

CHRISTMAS LA

PARBROOK RD

Parbrook House

Tudor Farm

2

RATCLIFFE HIGHWAY

A228

SHARNAL ST

ROPER'S GREEN LA

Sharnal Street

Cold Arbour

North Street

STOKE RD

North Street Farm

1

Tunbridge Hill

74

79	A	B	80	C	D	81	E	F

23
41

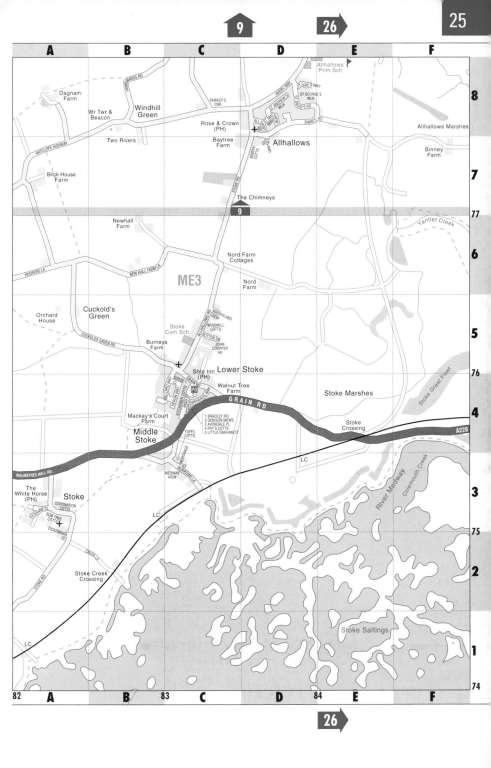

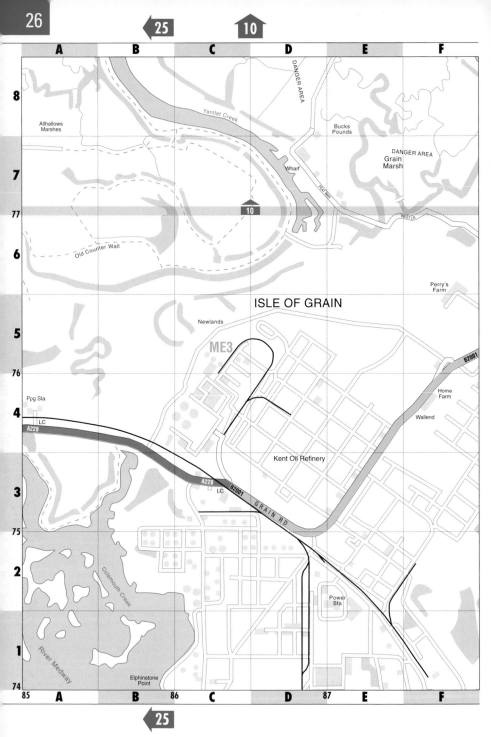

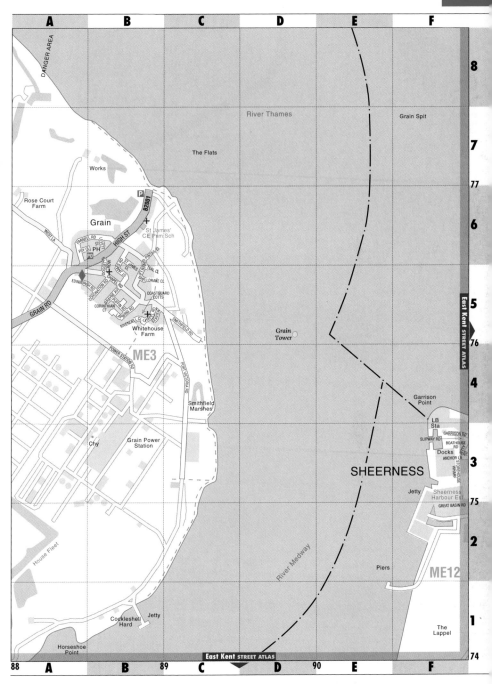

A **B** **C** **D** **E** **F**

8

River Thames

Grain Spit

7

The Flats

77

DANGER AREA

Works

Rose Court Farm

Grain

St James' CE Prim Sch

6

YMBELL RD

HIGH ST

WEST LA

FRY CT

PH

PO

JAMES RD

B2001

P

TEAL CL

SHELDRAKE CT

COASTGUARD COTTS

EDINBURGH RD

CORINTHIAN CT

GRAIN RD

RIVENHALL CT

Whitehouse Farm

SMITHFIELD RD

ME3

5

Grain Tower

76

POWER STATION RD

PORT VICTORIA RD

4

Garrison Point

LB Sta

GARRISON RD

SLIPWAY RD

BOATHOUSE RD

Smithfield Marshes

Chy

Grain Power Station

Docks

ANCHOR LA

STOREHOUSE WHARF

SHEERNESS

3

Jetty

Sheerness Harbour Est

GREAT BASIN RD

75

2

House Fleet

River Medway

Piers

ME12

Cockleshell Hard

Jetty

1

The Lappel

Horseshoe Point

74

88 **A** **B** 89 **C** **D** 90 **E** **F**

A8
1 WILDWOOD CL
2 ROWAN CT
3 SWALLOW CT
4 HONEYSUCKLE CT
5 ST MILDREDS RD
6 HARROGATE CT

7 LINCHMERE RD
8 WAITE DAVIES RD
9 SUMMERFIELD ST
10 ASKHAM LODGE
11 SYON LODGE
12 CHERITON ST

B5
1 GILLAN CT
2 NAPIER CT
3 OAKCROFT
4 ST JOSEPHS CT
5 HOLM ST
6 ROTHESAY CT

7 CANTERBURY CT
8 CHINBROOK CRES
9 BOLLON CT
10 CAMERON TERR

C5
1 BROOK CT
2 PARK VIEW CT
3 LINCOLN CT
4 MERRYFIELD HO
5 PAXTON CT

11

1 POPE STREET CT
2 MOTTINGHAM CT
3 PICKWICK CT
4 ROYAL CT
5 STATION APP

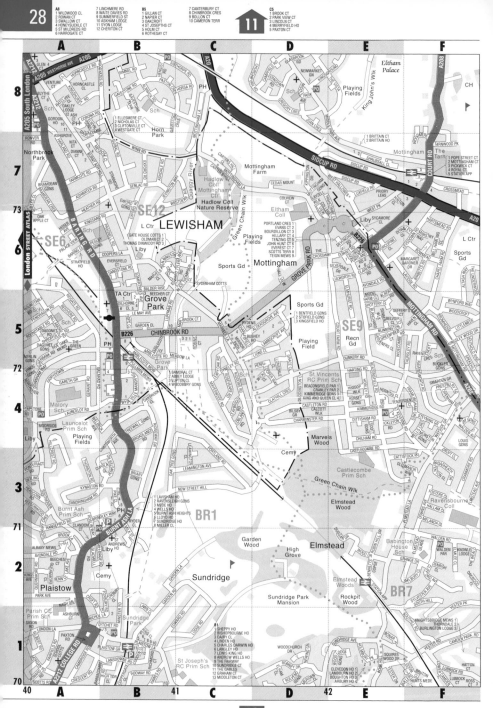

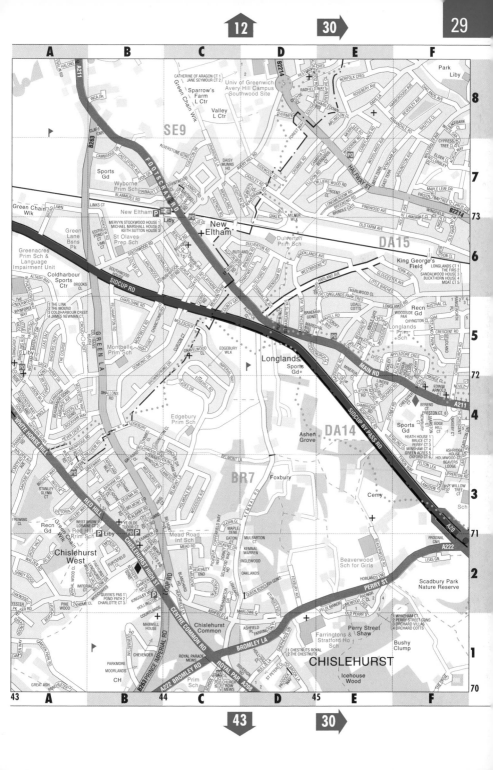

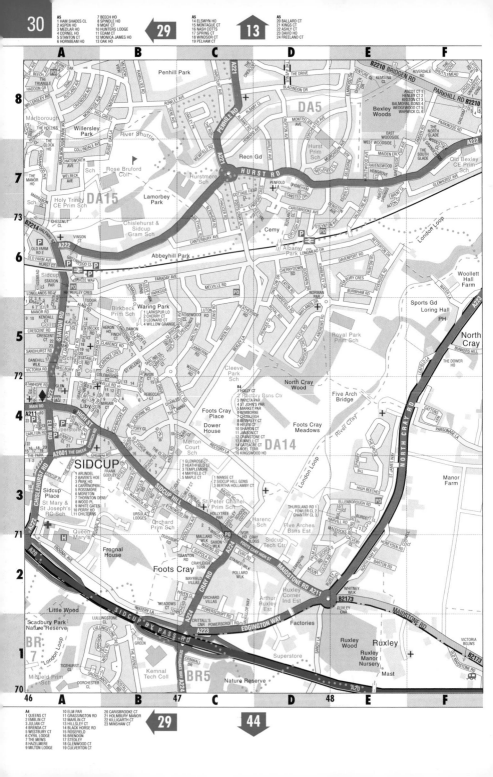

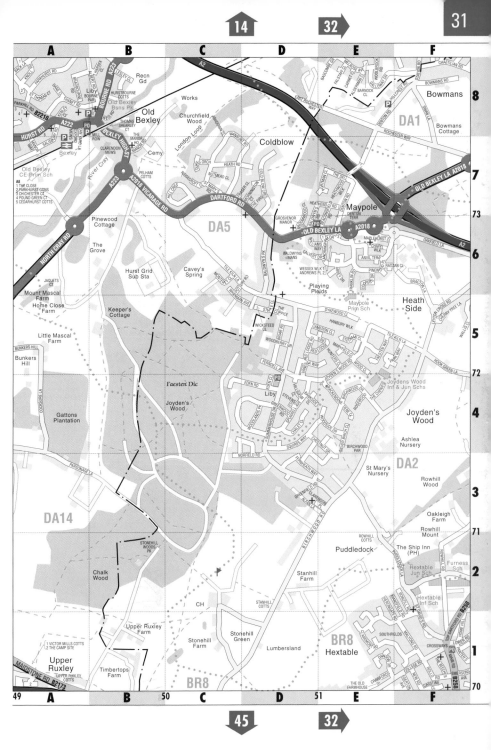

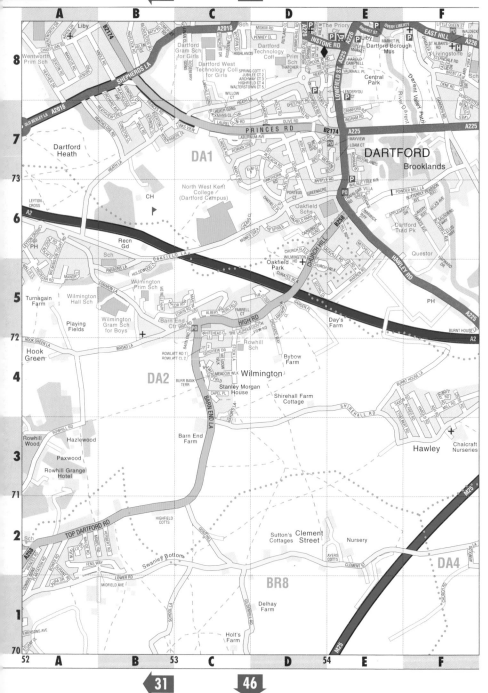

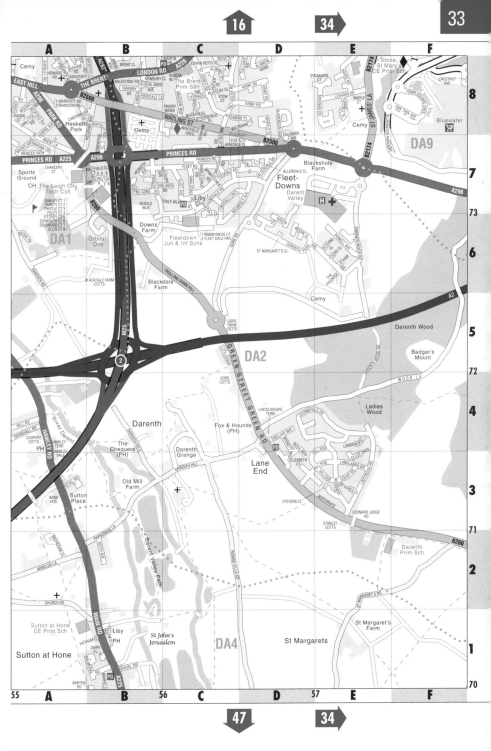

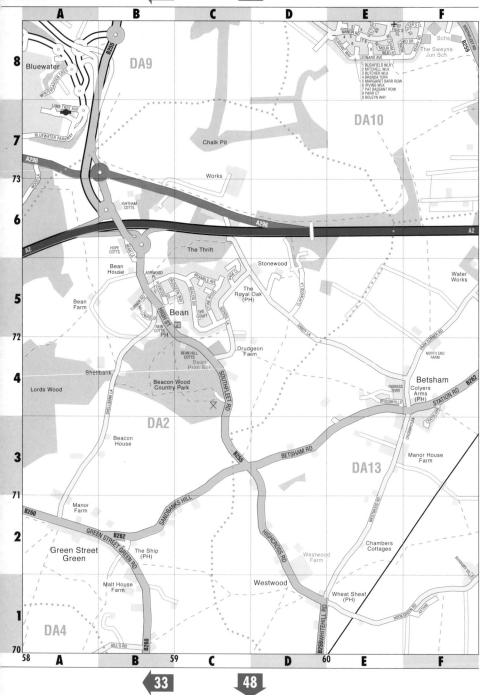

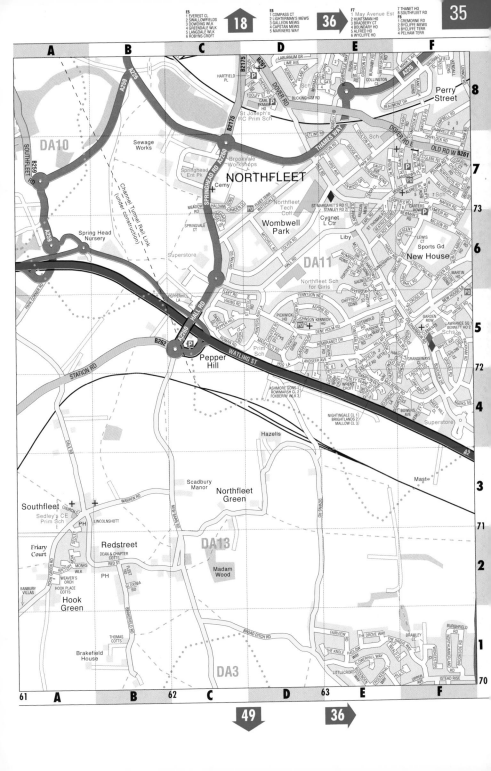

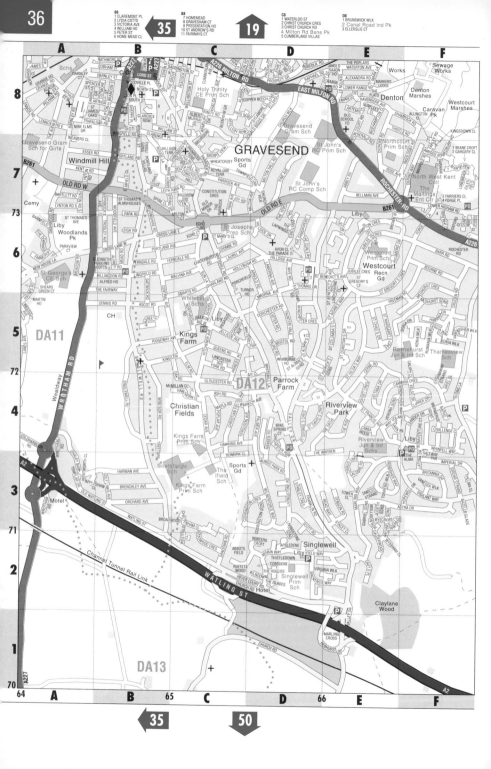

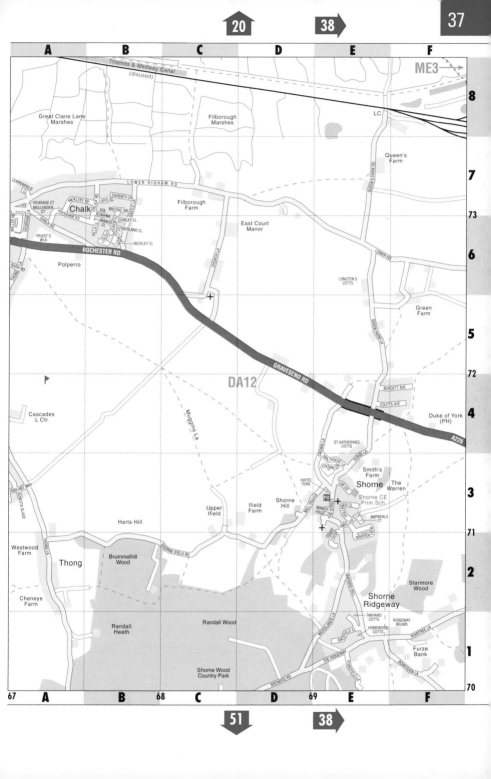

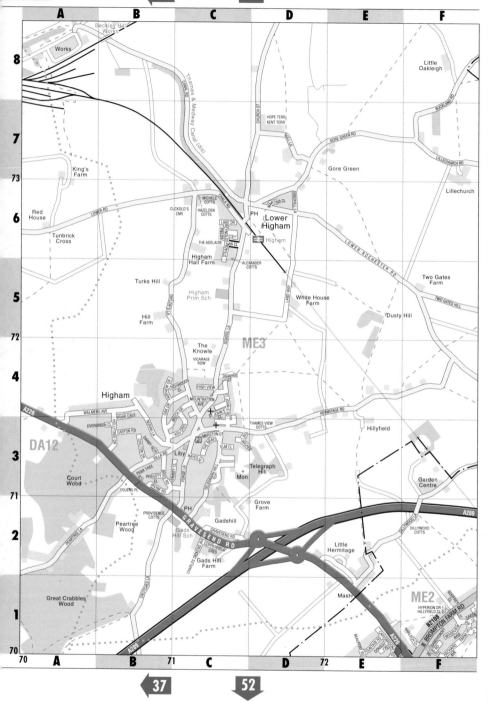

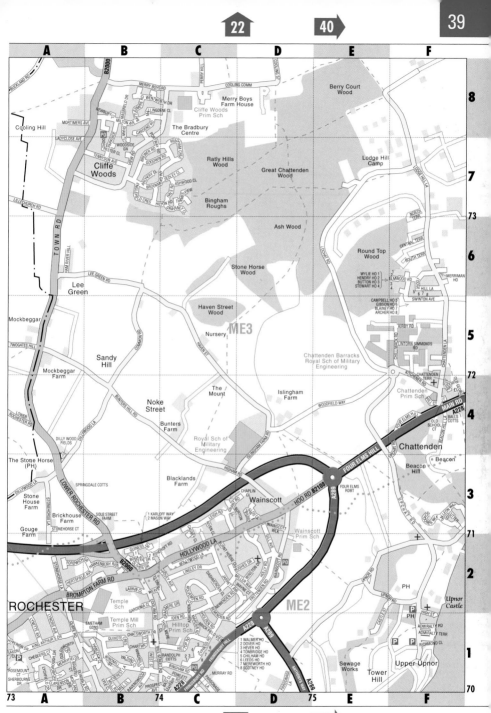

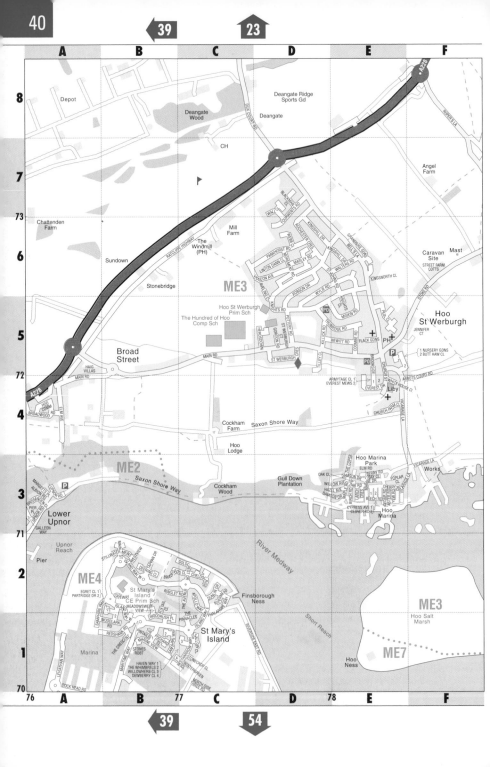

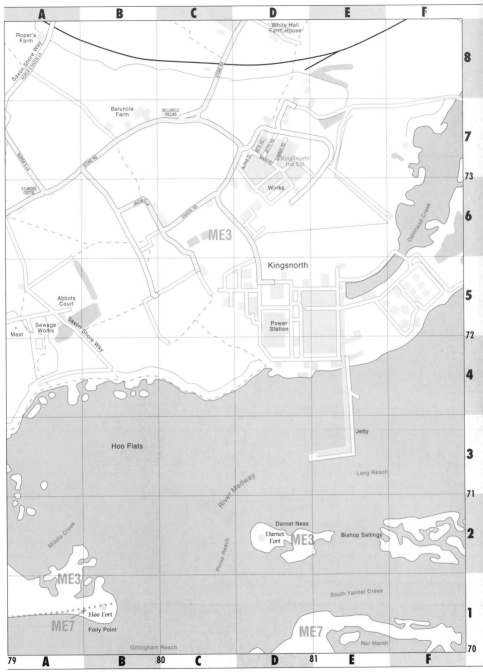

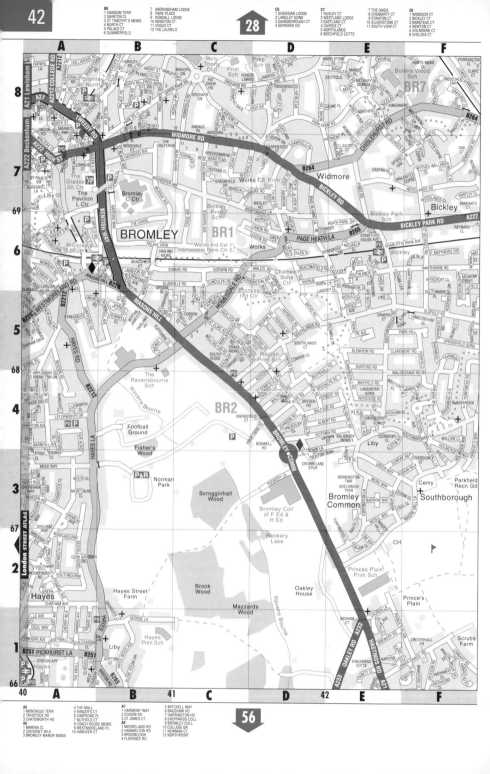

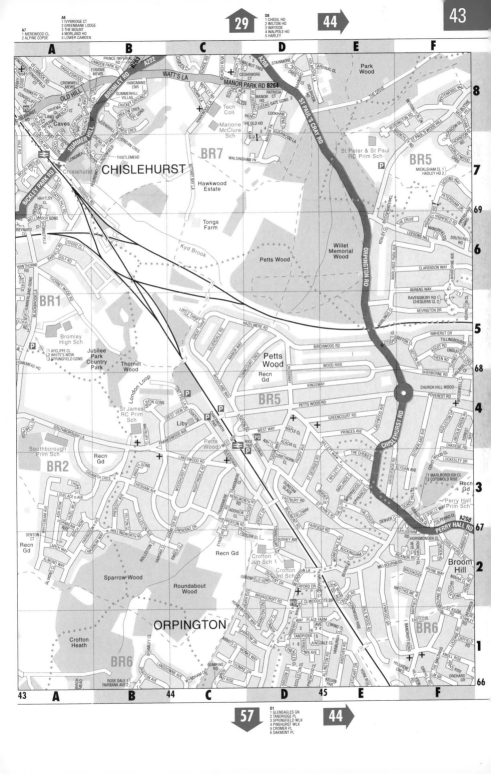

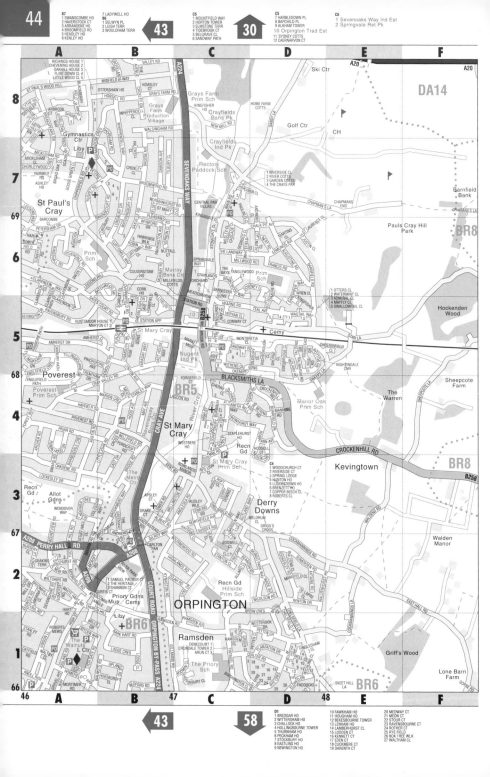

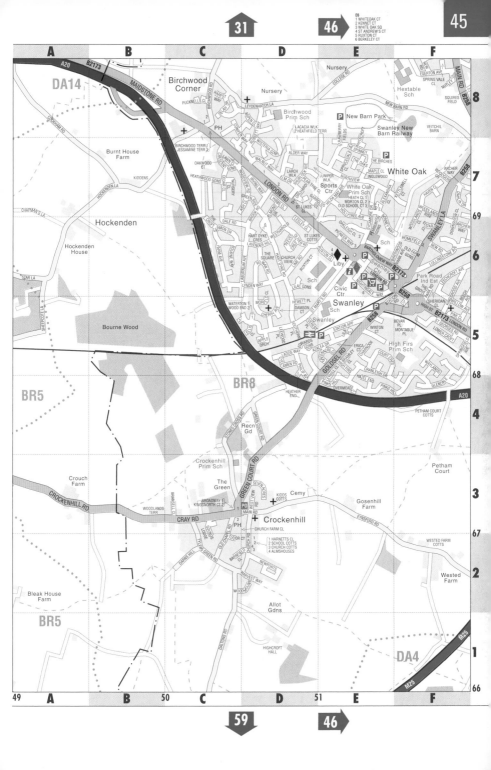

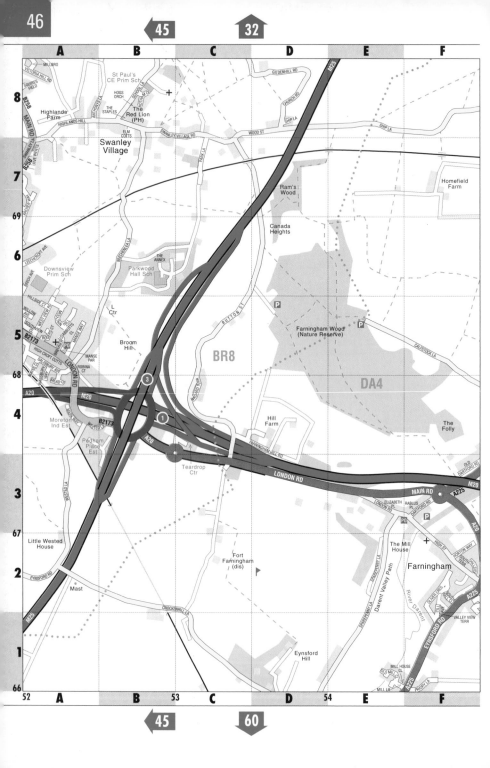

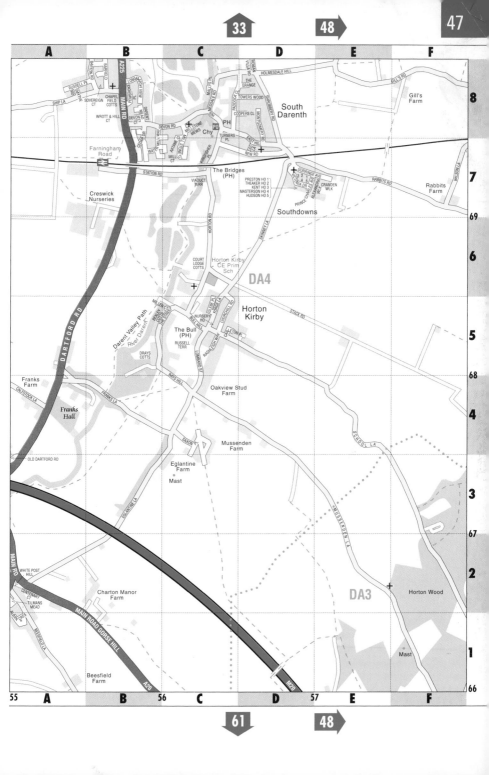

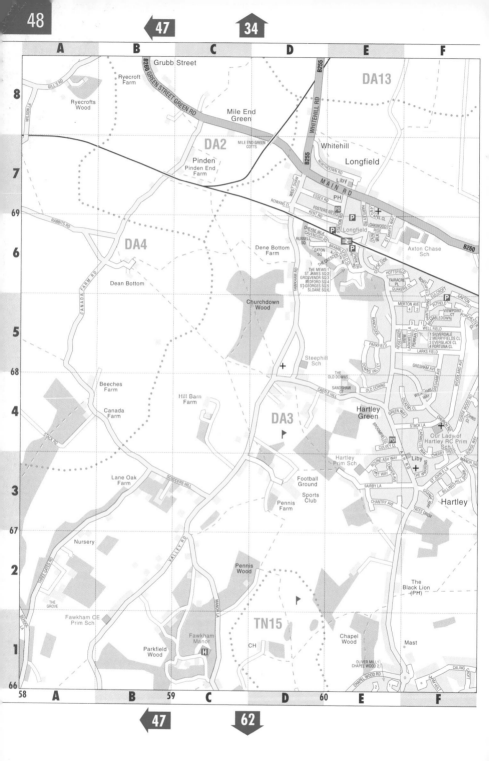

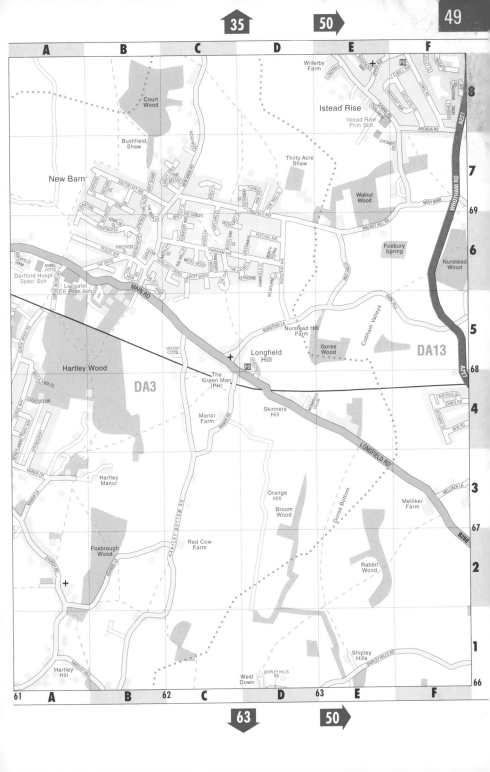

A B C D E F

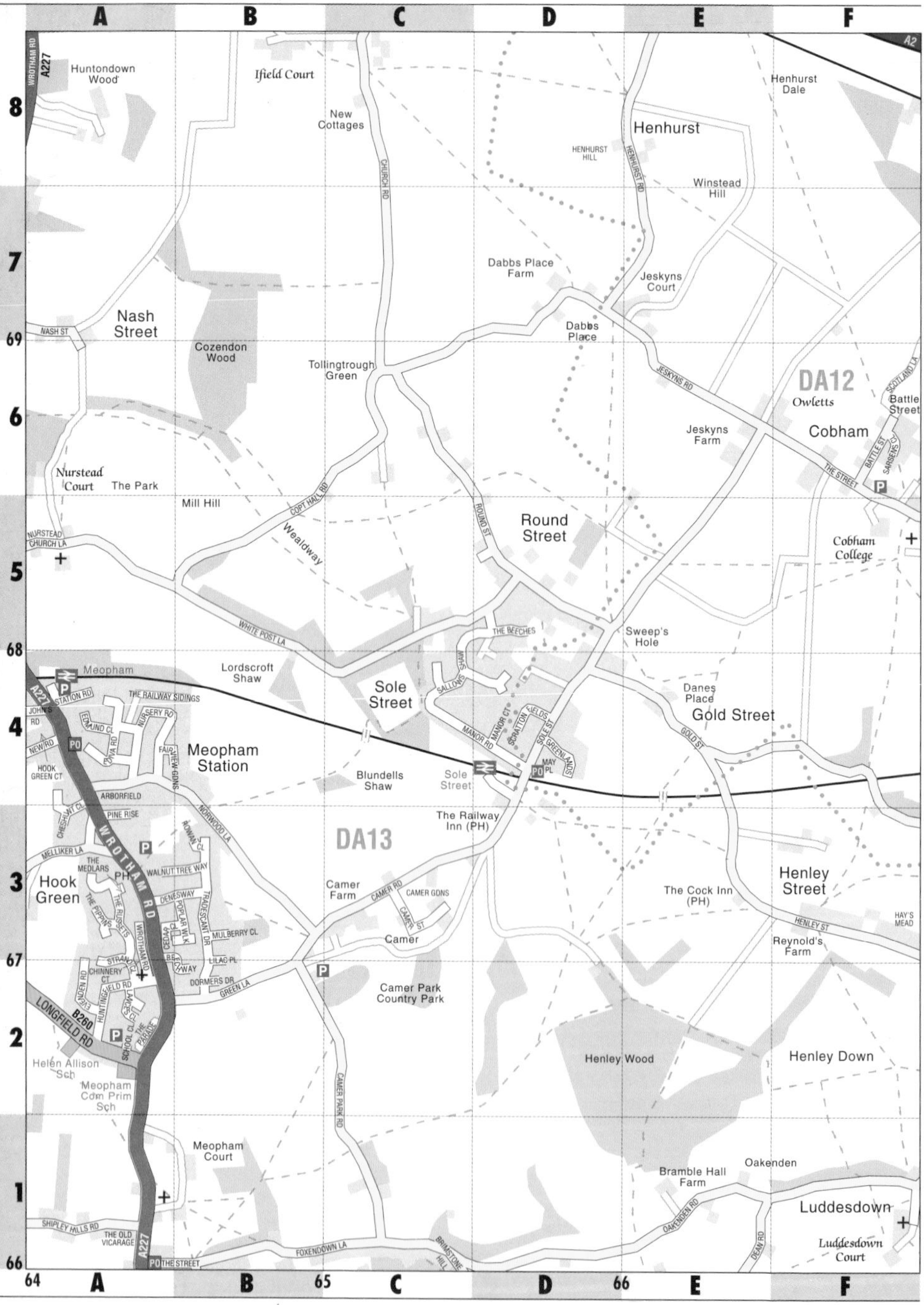

A2

8

7

69

6

68

5

4

3

67

2

66

1

WROTHAM RD
A227

Huntondown Wood

Ifield Court

New Cottages

CHURCH RD

Henhurst
Henhurst Dale

HENHURST HILL
Henhurst Hill

Winstead Hill

HENHURST RD

Nash Street

NASH ST

Cozendon Wood

Tollingtrough Green

Dabbs Place Farm

Jeskyns Court

Dabbs Place

JESKYNS RD

DA12
Owletts

Battle Street

SCOTLAND LA

Cobham

Nurstead Court

The Park

Mill Hill

COPT HALL RD

Weatway

ROUND ST

Round Street

Jeskyns Farm

Cobham
College

BATTLE ST

THE STREET

SANDERS L

P

NURSTEAD CHURCH LA

WHITE POST LA

THE BEECHES

Sweep's Hole

Danes Place

Gold Street

GOLD ST

Meopham

STATION RD

The Railway Sidings

SERY RD

EDMUND CL

Lordscroft Shaw

Sole Street

SALLOWS

MANOR RD

WRANGLING

VELDE

MAY PL

Sole Street

Gold Street

Henley Street

HENLEY ST

HAY'S MEAD

A227

JOHNS RD

NEWFIND

Meopham Station

Blundells Shaw

The Railway Inn (PH)

HOOK GREEN CT

ARBORFIELD

FAIRSEAT GDNS

PINE RISE

RONWOOD LA

DA13

Camer Farm

CAMER RD

Camer Gdns

CAMER ST

The Cock Inn (PH)

HENLEY ST

Henley Street

Reynold's Farm

WROTHAM RD

MELLIKER LA

THE MEDLARS

Hook Green

THE PIPPINS

P

Walnut Tree Way

DENESWAY

FAIRSEAT DR

MULBERRY CL

Camer

LILAC PL

P

The Way

DORMERS DR

GREEN LA

STRAW

CHINNERY

HUNTING

B260

LONGFIELD RD

P

Helen Allison Sch

Meopham Cdn Prim Sch

CAMER PARK RD

Camer Park Country Park

Henley Wood

Henley Down

Oakenden

Bramble Hall Farm

Luddesdown

Luddesdown Court

Meopham Court

SHIPLEY HILLS RD

THE OLD VICARAGE

A227

THE STREET

FOXENDOWN LA

RINGLESTONE HILL

OAKENDEN RD

DEAN RD

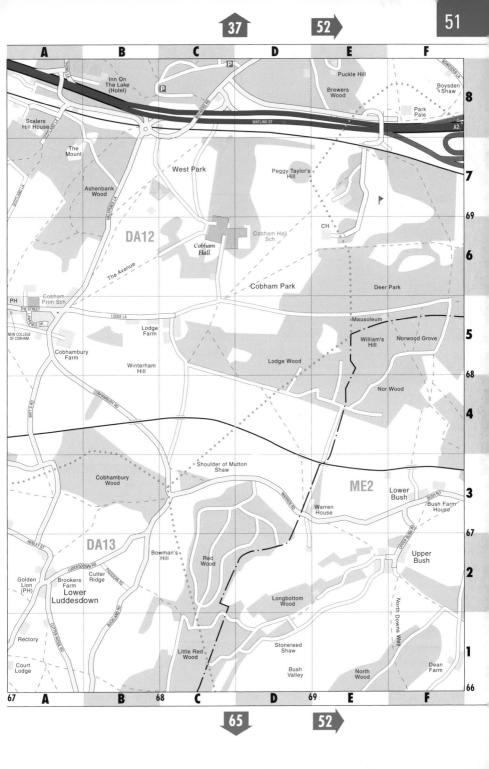

A B C D E F

DA12

Crutches
Farm

ROSE
COTTS

PH

OLD WATLING ST

WATLING ST

B2108

Abbey Court
Speci Sch

White
Gate

Strood

Sports
Ctr

A2

8

A2

M2

A289

Chapter
Farm

THE SHADES

MILLFORDHOPE RD

Chapter
Sch

THURSTON DR

HUMBER
CRES

7

SEAMEW CT 1
SKUA CT 2
SNIPE CT 3
ARRAN GN 4
NIGHTINGALE CT 5

Bligh Jun &
Inf Schs

COBHAM CL

NARVEL AVE

STOUR CL

WITHAM WAY

TINTAGEL DART
GDNS

69

PO

BLIGH WAY

SCHOLARS

HYACINTH RD

GALAHAD AVE

ST FRANCIS

Elaine
Prim Sch
ELAINE

DARNLEY RD

P

Knights
Place

Temple
Wood

COPLEY CRES

WIDGEON RD

PORTSMOUTH

HAWTHORN RD

BEECH RD

CEDAR AVE

Cemy

6

Broad Oak
Wood

Clay Pond
Wood

SOUTHWOLD

ST PAUL'S

CHESTER

COVENTRY

LILAC CRES

LILAC RD

Sherwin Knight
Jun & Inf Schs

NORTH BANK

HEVER CT

POPLAR CL

Great Wood

ME2

GUILDFORD GDNS 1
CARLISLE CL 2
PETERBOROUGH GDNS 3
WAKEFIELD CL 4
LINCOLN CL 5
ST ALBANS CL 6
NORWICH CL 7
NOTTINGHAM WLK 8

CHELMSFORD RD

BRISTOL

WELLS

WELLS RD

MEDWALS WOOD CT

HINSTON RD

BLANDFORD

LABURNUM RD

SYCAMORE RD

5

Birch
Wood

HILLSHAW CRES

ELGIN
GDNS

RANSCOMBE RD

RUSHDEAN RD

CUXTON RD

Ballard
Bsns Pk

68

RANSCOMBE FARM
COTTS

Pit
(dis)

Diggerland

4

Ranscombe

Merrals
Shaw

North Downs Way

Longhoes
Wood

PH

CHARITY WAY

Wickham Reach

Mill
Hill

3

POPLICANS RD

NINE ACRES RD

HAROLD AVE

REGINALD RD

SUNDRIDGE HILL

Caravan
Site

Common
Marsh

Medway
Bridge

Medway Bridge
Marina

CAMBRIA AVE 1
CORDELIA CRES 2
SILVER HILL 3

Kent Cemetery Wks

67

Court
Lodge

HAYLEY

CHARLES ST

LADYWOOD RD

1 WILLIAM RD
2 HOLYCROFT
3 DOWNSLAND HO

Cuxton

STATION RD

LC

River Medway

Factory
Farm

Sch

2

Cuxton
Com Jun &
Inf Schs

PO

LIDY

PH

WOODHURST CL

Cuxton
Ind Est

BRAMBLETREE
COTTS

ME1

Cuxton

ROCHESTER RD

Church
Hill

PILGRIMS

WOULDHAM RD

Borstal
Court
Farm

MEDWAY VALLEY WK

M2

1

Bores
Hole

A228

ME2

Rings
Marsh

Wouldham
Marshes

66

70 A 71 B C 72 D E F

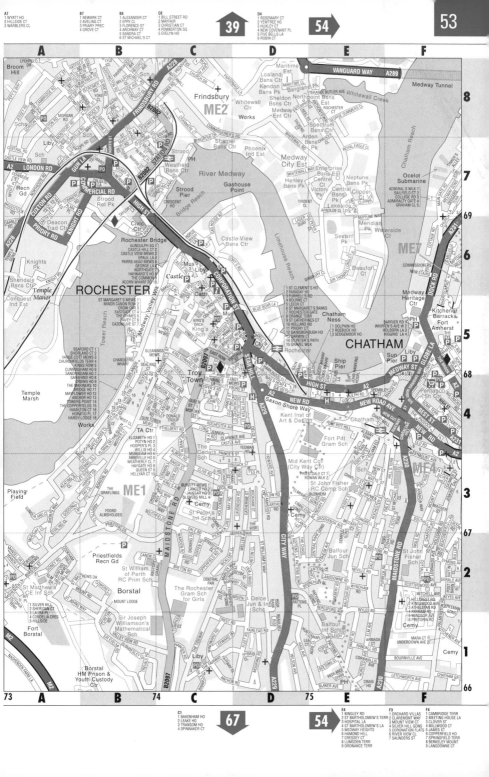

53
40

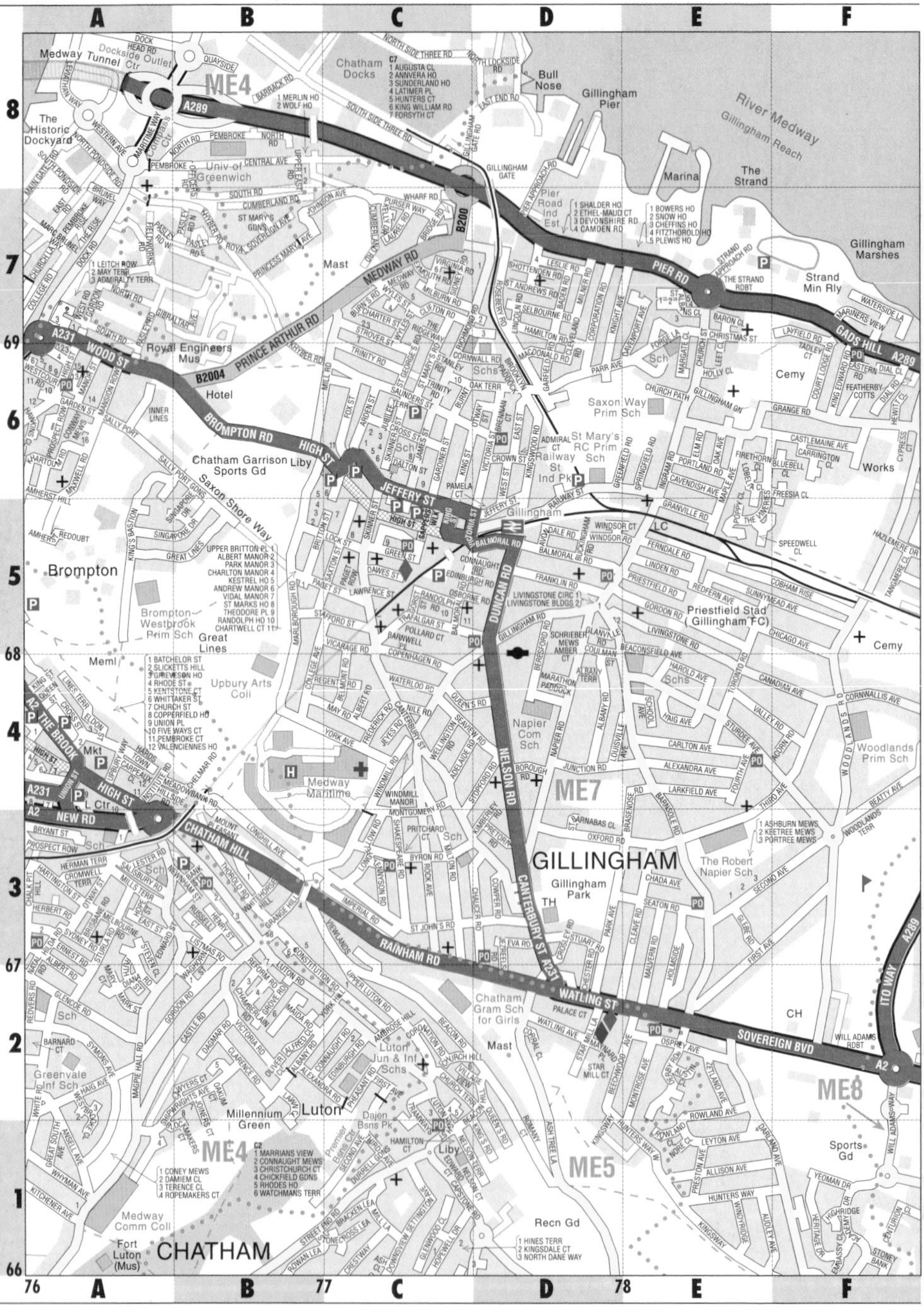

Map

A B C D E F

8 7 69 6 5 68 4 3 67 2 1 66

Medway Tunnel
ME4
The Historic Dockyard
Univ of Greenwich
Chatham Docks
Bull Nose
Gillingham Pier
River Medway
Gillingham Reach
The Strand
Gillingham Marshes

MEDWAY RD
PRINCE ARTHUR RD
Royal Engineers Mus
Hotel
BROMPTON RD
HIGH ST
Chatham Garrison Liby Sports Gd
Saxon Shore Way
Brompton
Brompton Westbrook Prim Sch
Great Lines
Mem
Upbury Arts Coll
PIER RD
THE STRAND RDBT
Strand Min Rly
Saxon Way Prim Sch
St Mary's RC Prim Sch
Railway St Ind Pk

GILLINGHAM
Gillingham Park
ME7
Napier Com Sch
Livingstone Circ
Priestfield Stad (Gillingham FC)
The Robert Napier Sch
Woodlands Prim Sch

THE BROOK
Mkt
HIGH ST
A231 NEW RD
A2
Medway Maritime
Windmill Manor
CHATHAM HILL
RAINHAM RD
CANTERBURY ST A231
WATLING ST
SOVEREIGN BVD
ME8
Chatham Gram Sch for Girls
Palace Gate
Sports Gd
ME5

Greenvale Inf Sch
Millennium Green
Luton
Luton Jun & Inf Schs
ME4
CHATHAM
Fort Luton (Mus)
Medway Comm Coll
Recn Gd

76 A 77 B C 78 D E F

53
68

A3
1 OTWAY TERR
2 LEOPOLD RD

A6
1 VICTORY MANOR
2 TEMERAIRE MANOR
3 BARFLEUR MANOR
4 MIDDLE ST
5 CAMPERDOWN MANOR
6 RIVER ST

7 DAWSON CT
8 MCCUDDEN ROW
9 PERIE ROW
10 PLEASANT ROW
11 LENDRIM CT
12 MELVILLE CT
13 FLAXMANS CT
14 MANOR HO
15 ESMONDE HO
16 CONWAY HALL

B2
1 PORTLAND ST
2 LISTMAS RD
3 BRIGHT RD
4 COBDEN RD
5 SAILMAKERS CT
6 EVORG HO
7 CAULKERS HO
8 THE ENDEAVOUR FOYER

B3
1 SEYMOUR RD
2 HARE ST
3 SHORT ST
4 PICCADILLY APARTMENTS
5 WEALDEN CT
6 OCELOT CT
7 LEONARD HO
8 CONSTITUTION HILL

C6
1 PADSTOW MANOR
2 CAMBORNE MANOR
3 REDRUTH MANOR
4 PENRYN MANOR
5 AUSTELL MANOR
6 TINTAGEL MANOR
7 GRAND CT
8 DEANE CT
9 WILL ADAMS CT

10 CHATSWORTH RD
11 PHOENIX CT

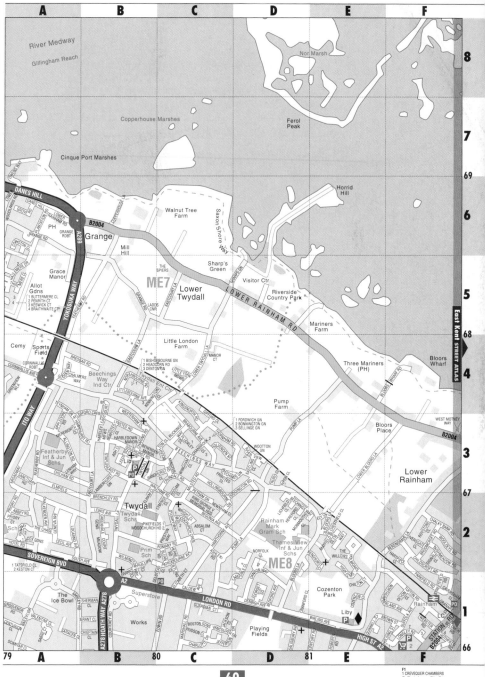

F1
1 CREVEQUER CHAMBERS
2 Rainham Sh Ctr
3 GRESHAM CL
4 HARRISON CT
5 MAPLINS CL
6 SIGNAL CT
7 SUFFOLK CT

42

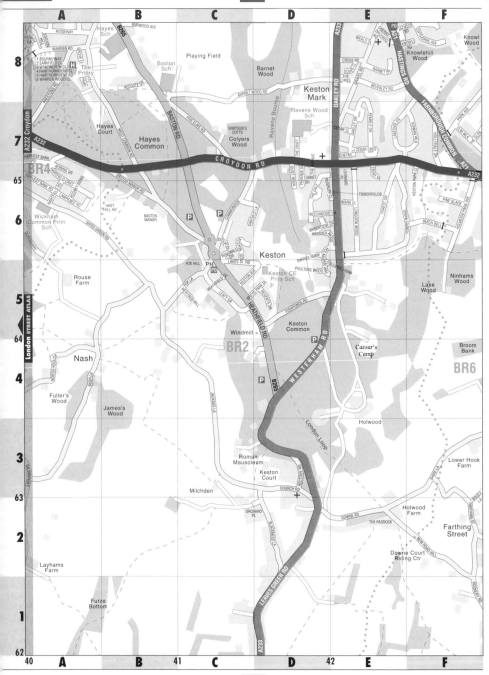

72

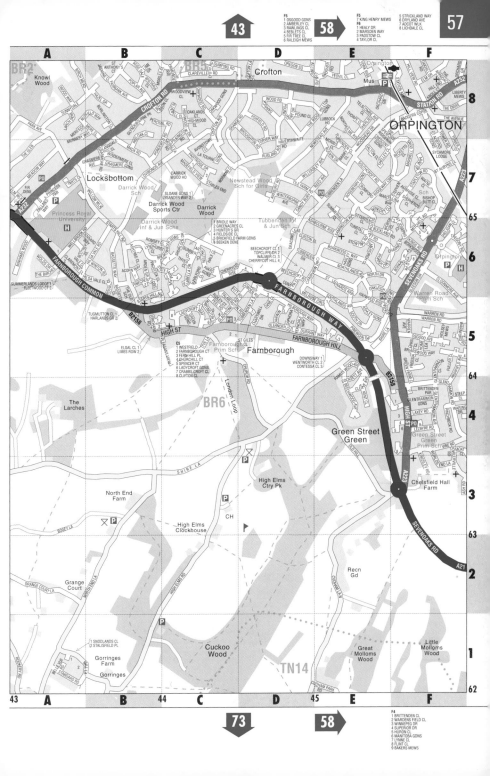

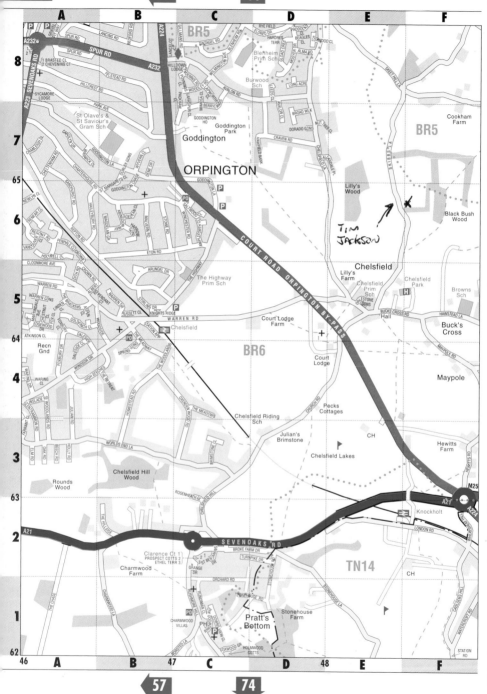

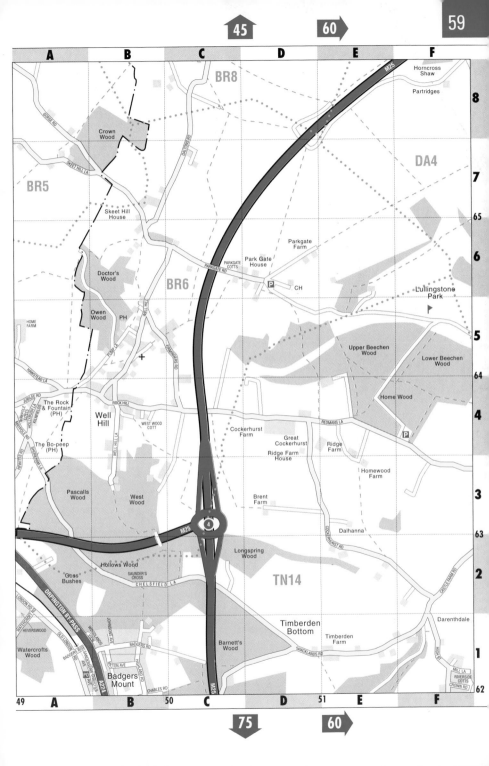

59
46

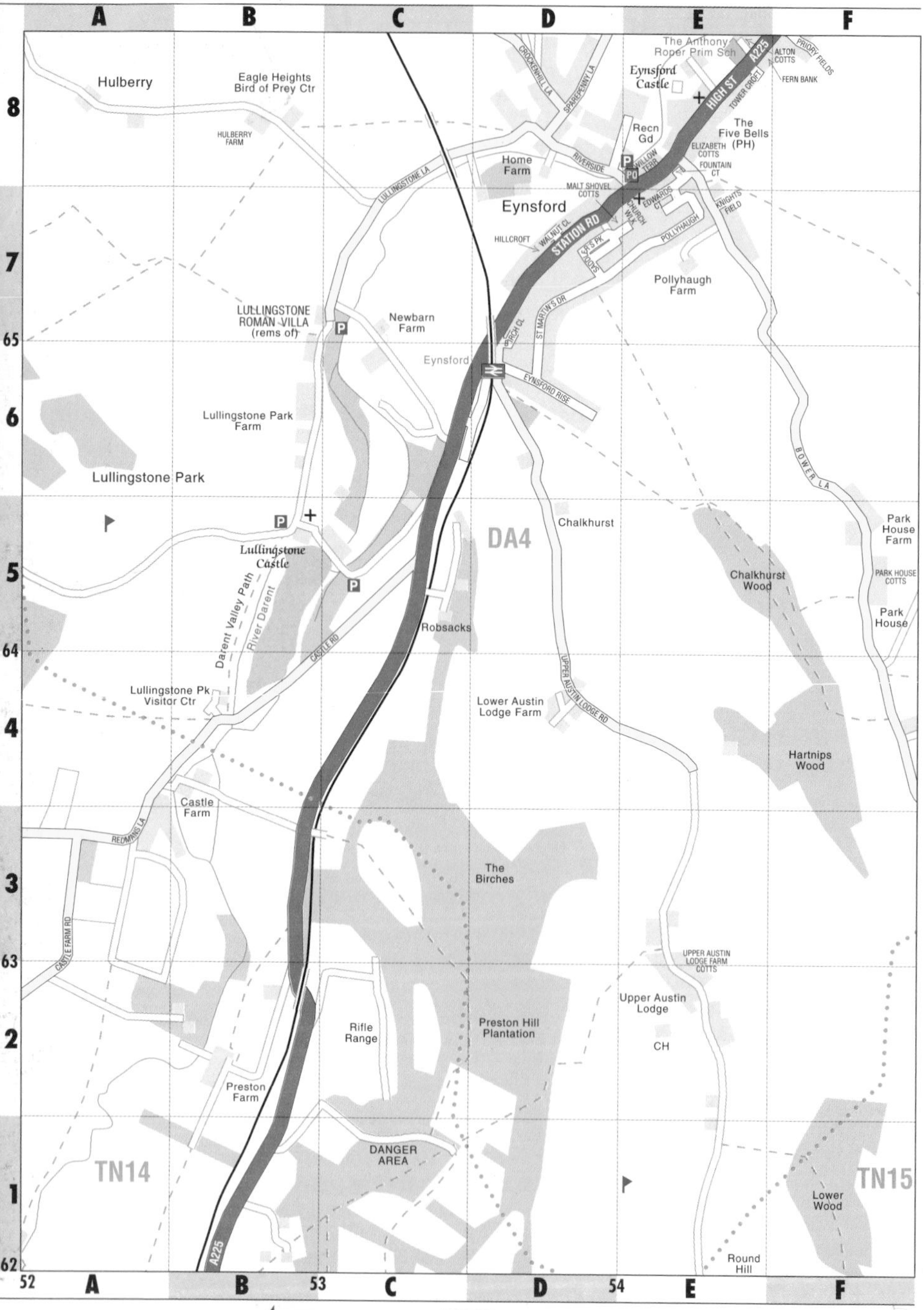

	A	B	C	D	E	F

8

Hulberry

Eagle Heights
Bird of Prey Ctr

The Anthony
Roper Prim Sch

Eynsford
Castle

PRIORY FIELDS
ALTON
COTTS
FERN BANK

HULBERRY
FARM

HIGH ST

A225

TOWER GRO

The Five Bells
(PH)

Recn
Gd

7

LULLINGSTONE LA

Home
Farm

RIVERSIDE

Eynsford

HILLCROFT

MALT SHOVEL
COTTS

STATION RD

ELIZABETH
COTTS

FOUNTAIN
CT

KNIGHTS
FIELD

POLLYHAUGH

Pollyhaugh
Farm

65

LULLINGSTONE
ROMAN VILLA
(rems of)

P

Newbarn
Farm

Eynsford

Eynsford Rise

ST MARTIN'S DR

FINCH CL

6

Lullingstone Park
Farm

BOWER LA

Lullingstone Park

Chalkhurst

DA4

Park
House
Farm

5

P

Lullingstone
Castle

Darent Valley Path

River Darent

CASTLE RD

P

Robsacks

Chalkhurst
Wood

PARK HOUSE
COTTS

Park
House

64

Lullingstone Pk
Visitor Ctr

Lower Austin
Lodge Farm

UPPER AUSTIN LODGE RD

4

REDMANS LA

Castle
Farm

Hartnips
Wood

3

The
Birches

CROFT FARM RD

63

UPPER AUSTIN
LODGE FARM
COTTS

2

Rifle
Range

Preston Hill
Plantation

Upper Austin
Lodge

CH

Preston
Farm

1

TN14

DANGER
AREA

Lower
Wood

TN15

A225

Round
Hill

62

52	A		B	53	C		D	54	E		F

59
76

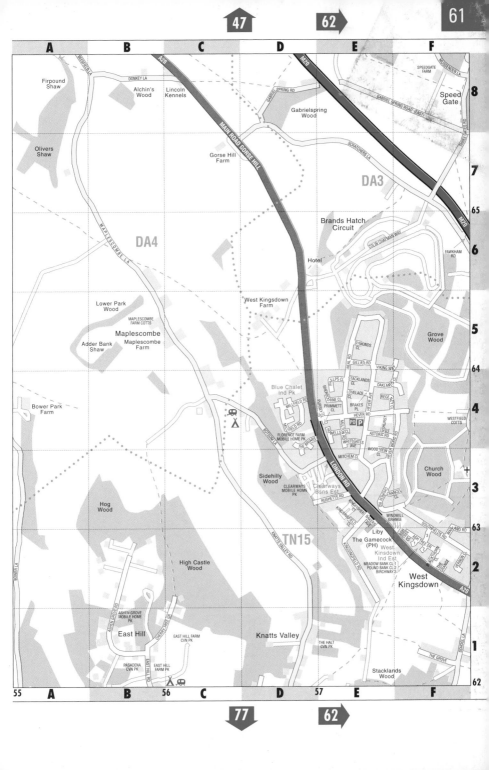

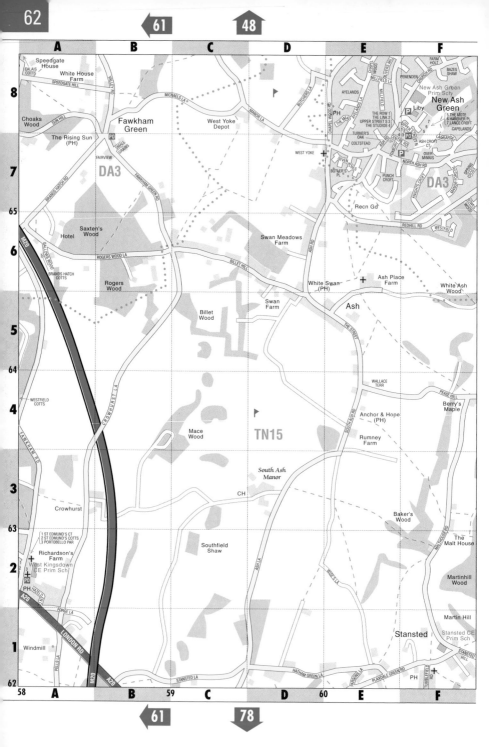

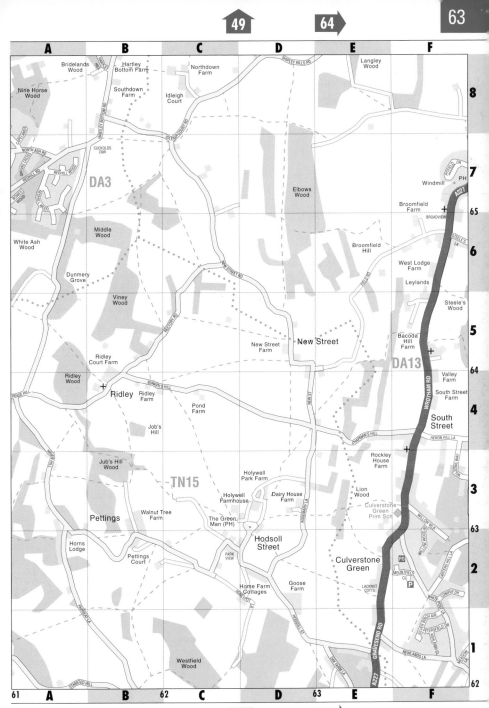

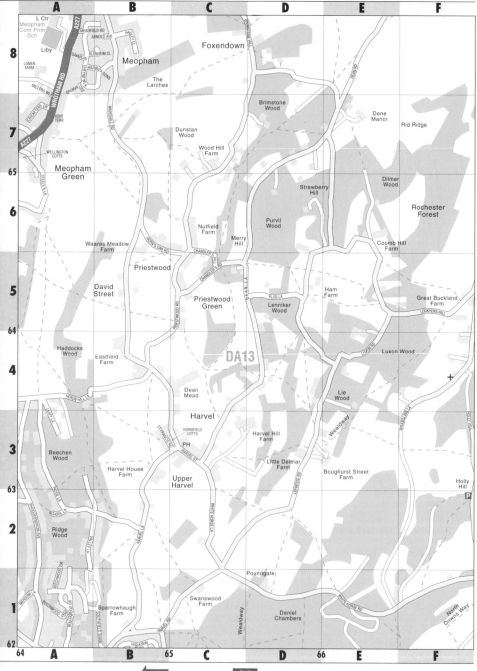

L Ctr
Meopham Com Prim Sch
Liby
MEADFIELD RD
ARNOLD AVE
HALL CL
A227
WROTHAM RD
OAKMEAD
WARWK
BLENHEIM CL
CHEYNE CL
GRNWL CL
Meopham
The Larches
Foxendown
LOMER FARM
MILLERS WAY
CROCKETTS DR
KENT TERR
A227
WELLINGTON COTTS
Meopham Green
STEELE LA
Dunstan Wood
Wood Hill Farm
Brimstone Wood
BRANSCOMBE HILL
DEAN RD
Dene Manor
Rid Ridge
Waares Meadow Farm
Priestwood
ROBIN'S OAK RD
CHANDLER'S HILL
CHANDLER'S HILL RD
PRIESTWOOD RD
Nutfield Farm
Merry Hill
Strawberry Hill
Purvil Wood
Dilmer Wood
Rochester Forest
David Street
Priestwood Green
DEAN LA
PLUG LA
Lenniker Wood
Ham Farm
Coomb Hill Farm
Great Buckland Farm
LOCKYERS HILL
Haddocks Wood
Eastfield Farm
HERON HILL LA
LUXON RD
Luxon Wood
DA13
Dean Mead
Harvel
Lie Wood
Wealdway
WRANGLING LA
FOLLY RD
Beechen Wood
LEAF LA
STRANGES LA
HORNFIELD COTTS
PH
HARVEL ST
Harvel House Farm
Upper Harvel
Harvel Hill Farm
Little Delmar Farm
LOWOOD RD
Boughurst Street Farm
Holly Hill
P
SCHOOL LA
ROSE LA
RHODODENDRON AVE
BEECHWOOD DR
HARPER LA
VALLEY LA
Ridge Wood
WHITE HORSE LA
Poundgate
MEADOW LA
BEECHWOOD LA
HOLLY DR
SOUTHFIELD SQUARE
HARVEL RD
HIGHVIEW
Sparrowhaugh Farm
Swanswood Farm
Wealdway
WHITE HORSE RD
Daniel Chambers
North Downs Way

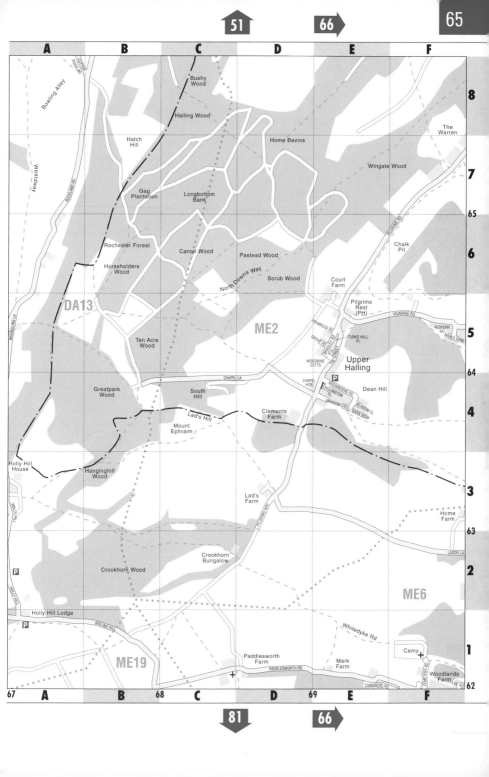

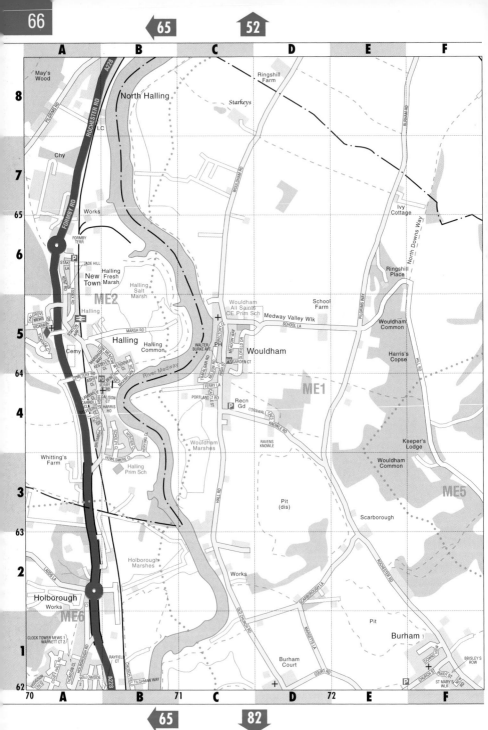

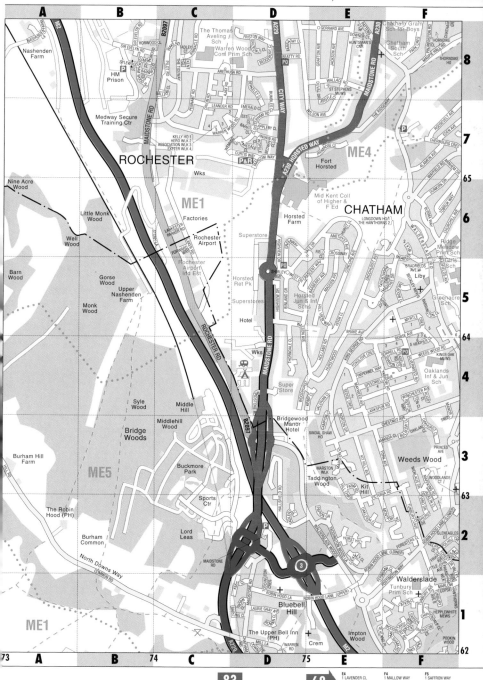

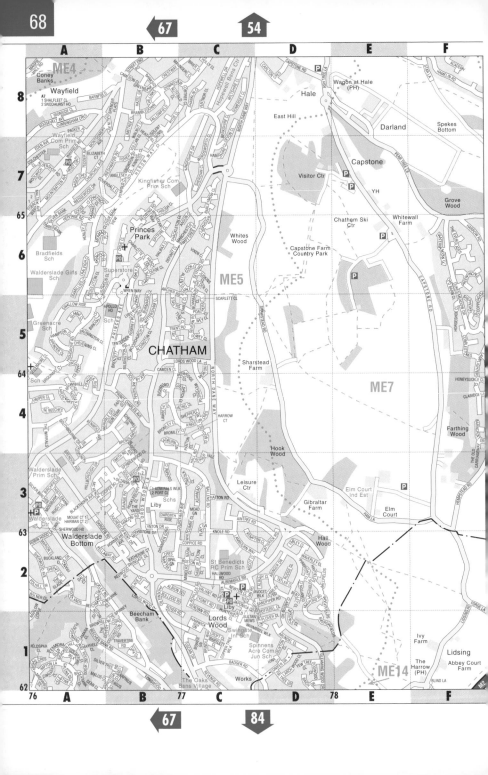

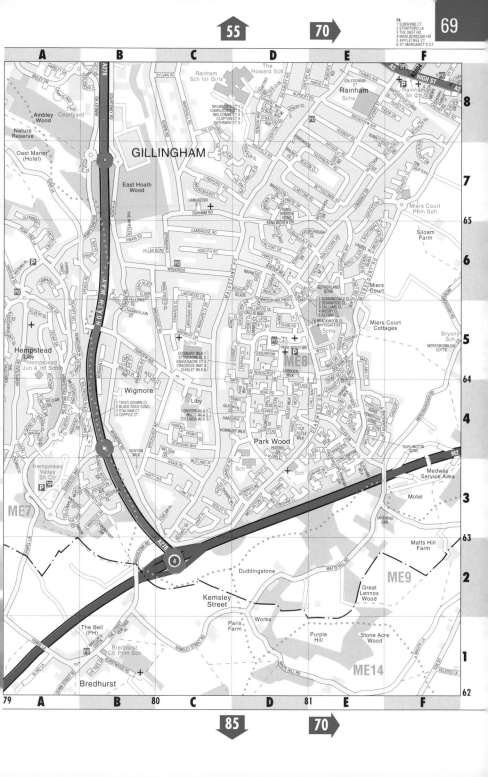

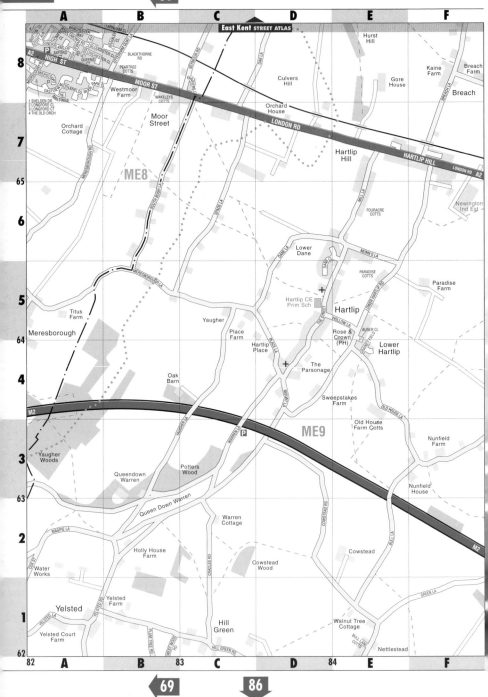

A B C D E F

8

7

65

6

5

64

4

M2

3

63

2

63

1

62

82 A 83 B C 83 D 84 E F

Labels on map:

WINCHESTER
FARNHAM CL
HIGH ST
A2
BLACKTHORNE RD
PEARTREE COTTS
MOOR ST
Westmoor Farm
WAKELEYS COTTS
Moor Street
Orchard Cottage
Orchard House
Culvers Hill
Hurst Hill
Gore House
Kaine Farm
Breach Farm
Breach
LONDON RD
Hartlip Hill
HARTLIP HILL
LONDON RD A2
ME8
Newington Ind Est
FOURACRE COTTS
MILL LA
DANE LA
Lower Dane
DANE CL
MUNN'S LA
PARADISE COTTS
Paradise Farm
Hartlip CE Prim Sch
Hartlip
THE STREET
HOLLOW LA
Rose & Crown (PH)
AUGER CL
LOWER HARTLIP RD
Lower Hartlip
Titus Farm
Meresborough
MERESBOROUGH LA
SOUTH BUSH LA
Yaugher
Place Farm
Hartlip Place
RECK LA
The Parsonage
Oak Barn
Sweepstakes Farm
MOUNT LA
Old House Farm Cotts
OLD HOUSE LA
Nunfield Farm
ME9
M2
Yaugher Woods
Queendown Warren
Potters Wood
WARREN LA
Queen Down Warren
Warren Cottage
Nunfield House
MAGPIE LA
CRADLES RD
Holly House Farm
Cowstead Wood
COWSTEAD RD
Cowstead
BULL LA
GREEN LA
Water Works
Yelsted Farm
YELSTED LA
Yelsted
Hill Green
Walnut Tree Cottage
BULL LANE COTTS
Nettlestead
Yelsted Court Farm
PLUM TREE RD
HILL WOOD
HILL GREEN RD

1 SHELDEN DR
2 LONGFORD CL
3 LONGFORD CT
4 THE OLD ORCH

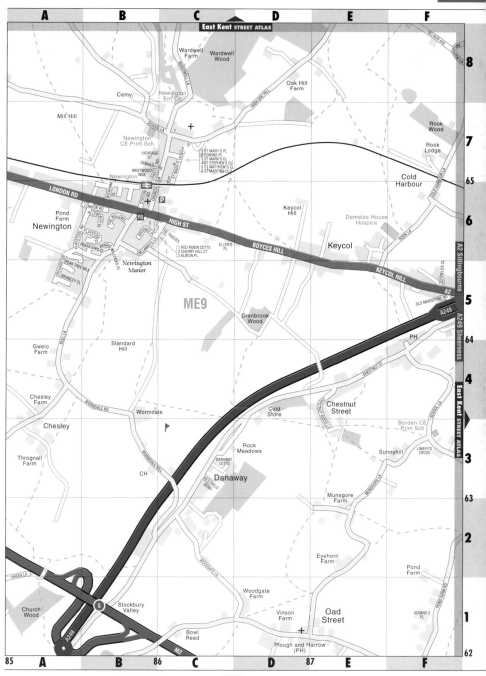

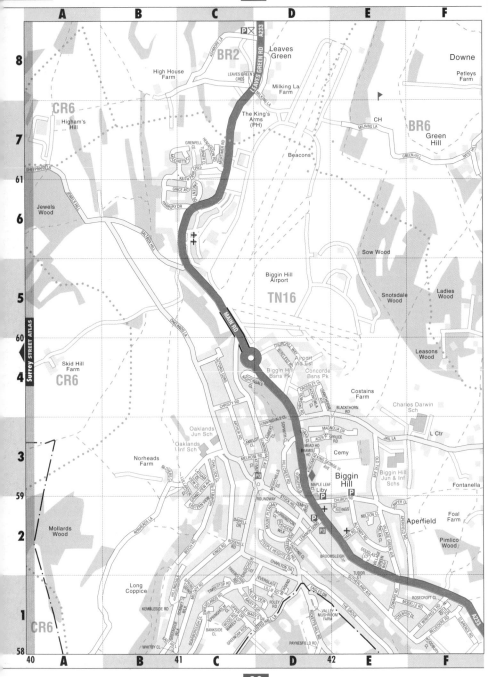

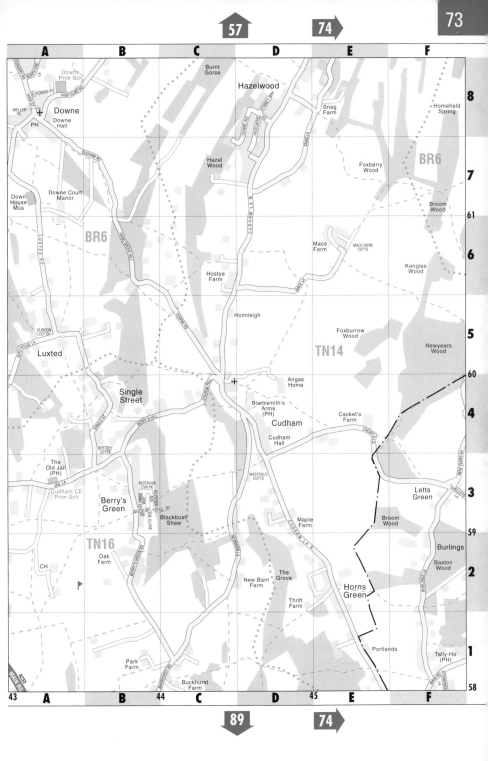

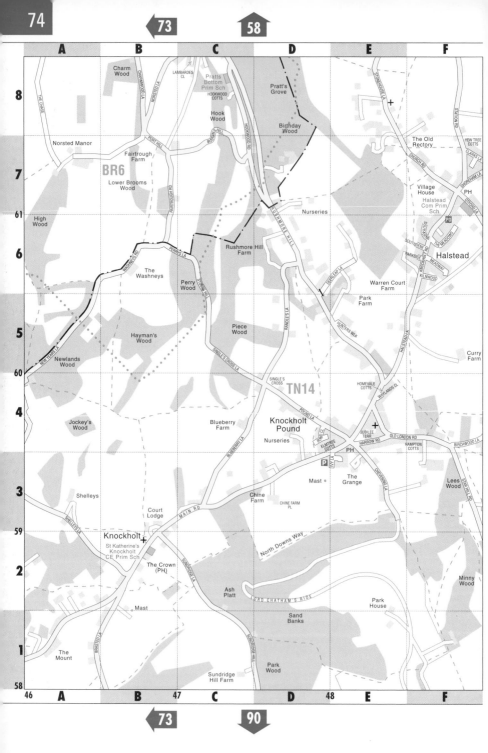

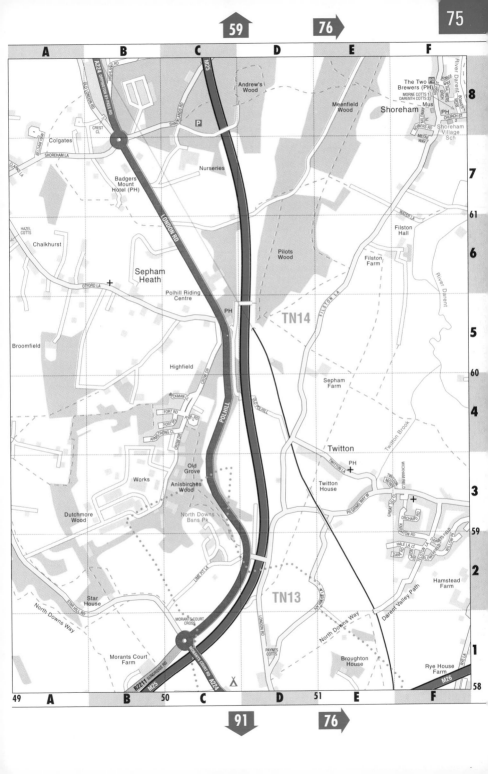

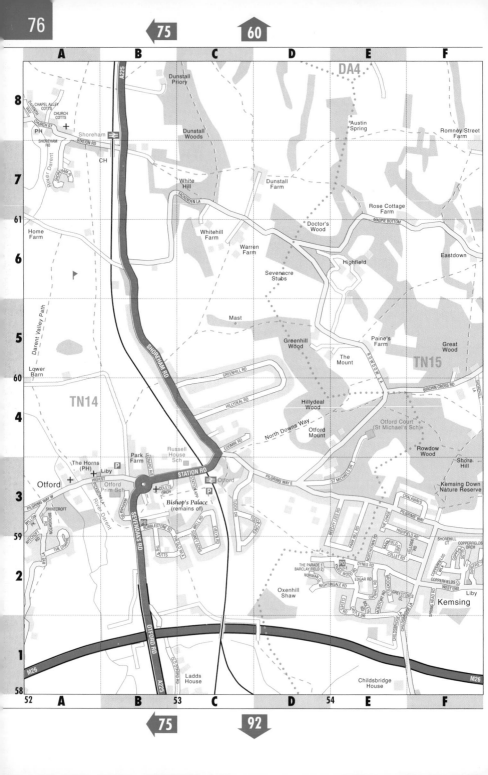

A B C D E F

8

HOLLYWOOD LA

Pells Farm

Garden Ctr

Hollands Farm

TUMBLEFIELD EST

ASH LA

BELSEA

7

ST DEER HILL RD

Gravelpit Wood

Peckham Wood

BENNETT COTT

Plaxdale Green Farm

PLAXDALE GREEN RD

Cox's Wood

Stansted Lodge Farm

TIMBERFIELD RD

61

KNOCK MILL LA

TERRY'S LODGE RD

Terry's Lodge Farm

Thrift Wood

Horse & Groom (PH)

Caravan Park

6

LONDON RD

WROTHAM HILL RD

WT Sta

Mast

Cooper's Wood

Tower Ind Est

LABOUR-IN-VAIN RD

5

Birches Wood

Long Wood

Labour-in-vain

60

OLD TERRY'S LODGE RD

Exedown

TN15

2

P

OLD COACH RD

Butts Hill Wood

A20

4

Chalk Pit Wood

EXEDOWN RD

White Hill

North Downs Way

M20

HOWLANDS CT 1
HOWLANDS 2

PILGRIMS WAY

A20 LONDON RD

BACKLANE

Pilgrims Way

Blacksole Field

Sch

COURT MDW

3

THORNDYKE WAY 1
THOMAS WYATT WAY 2
BLACKSOLE RD 3
NEW WLK 4
RIGGS WAY 5
MOUNTAIN CL 6

CHILDS MED

COURTYARD GDNS

KEMSING RD

New House Farm

WEST ST

BODSWORTH RD

BATTLEFIELDS

WEST GEO...

59

Wrotham

2

Yaldham Manor

FEN POND RD

Martin Spring Wood

M26

Westlands Farm

1

M26

Potters Mede

58

Hook Wood

FEN MDW

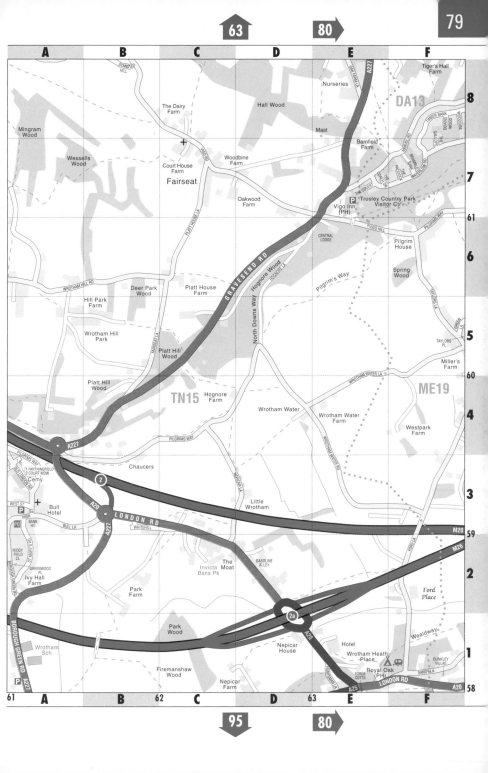

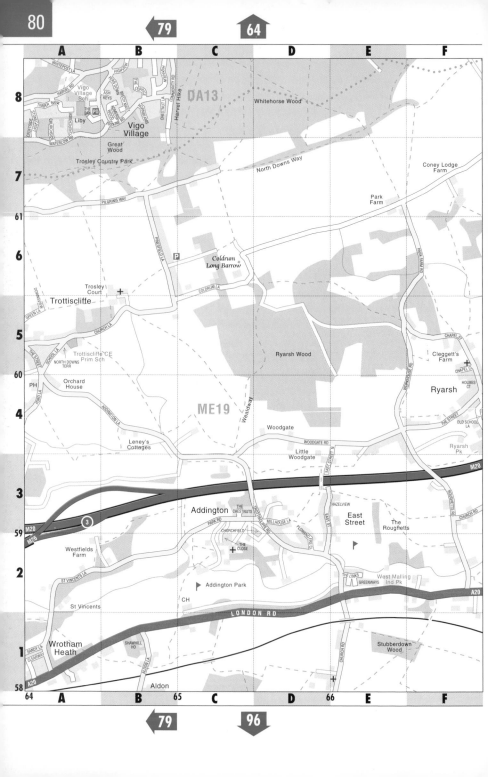

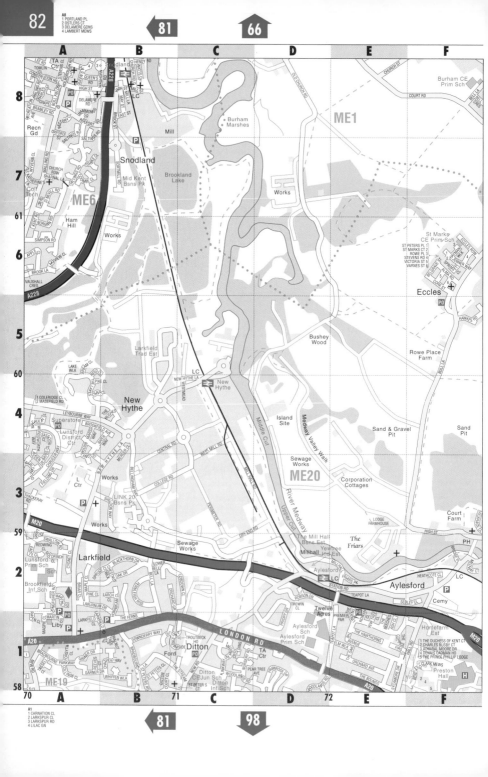

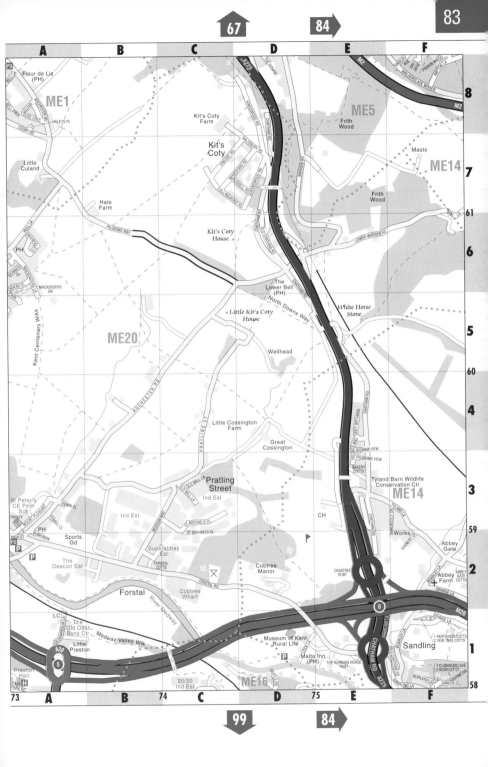

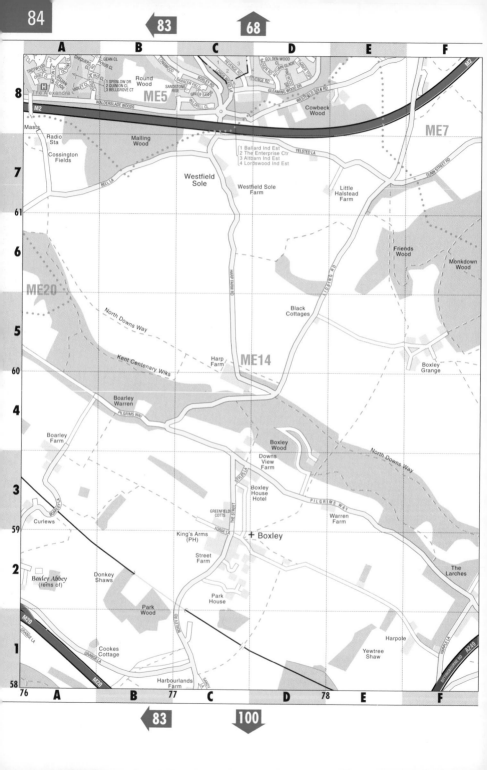

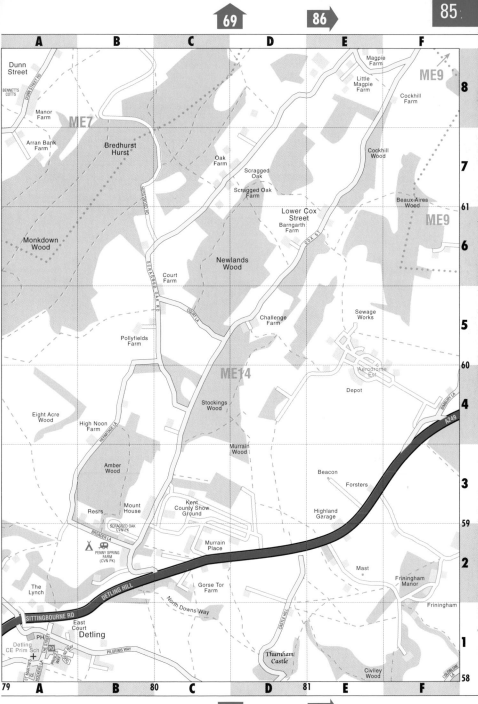

A B C D E F

8

ME9

Dunn
Street

BENNETTS
COTTS

Magpie
Farm

Little
Magpie
Farm

Cockhill
Farm

Manor
Farm

ME7

Arran Bank
Farm

Bredhurst
Hurst

Cockhill
Wood

7

Oak
Farm

Scragged
Oak

Scragged Oak
Farm

Beaux Aires
Wood

61

ME9

Monkdown
Wood

Lower Cox
Street

Barngarth
Farm

Newlands
Wood

Court
Farm

COX ST

6

SCRAGGED OAK RD

HURSTWOOD RD

Challenge
Farm

COURT LA

Sewage
Works

5

Pollyfields
Farm

Aerodrome
Est

60

ME14

Depot

BINBURY LA

Eight Acre
Wood

Stockings
Wood

4

High Noon
Farm

HERMITAGE LA

Murrain
Wood

A249

Amber
Wood

Beacon

Forsters

3

Resrs

Mount
House

Kent
County Show
Ground

Highland
Garage

59

BROADER LA

SCRAGGED OAK
CVN PK

Murrain
Place

Mast

Friningham
Manor

2

PENNY SPRING
FARM
(CVN PK)

The
Lynch

DETLING HILL

Gorse Tor
Farm

Friningham

North Downs Way

CASTLE HILL

COLDBLOW LA

SITTINGBOURNE RD

East
Court

Detling

PH

Thurnham
Castle

1

Detling
CE Prim Sch

ST MARTIN'S CL

THE STREET

PILGRIMS WAY

Civiley
Wood

58

79 A B 80 C D 81 E F

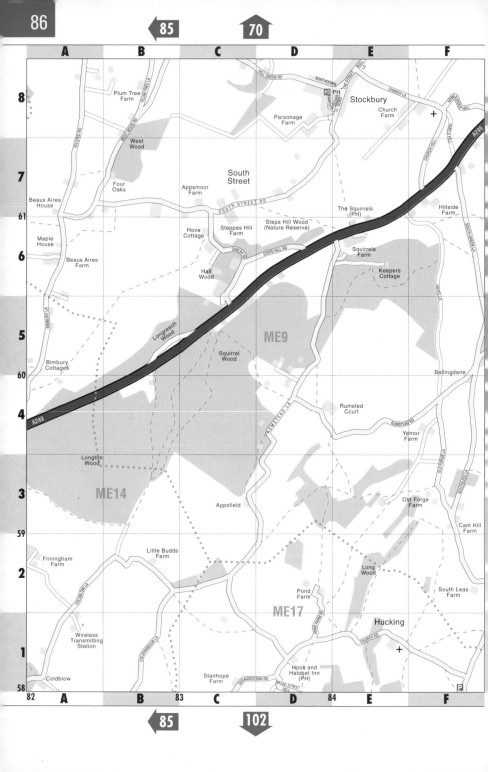

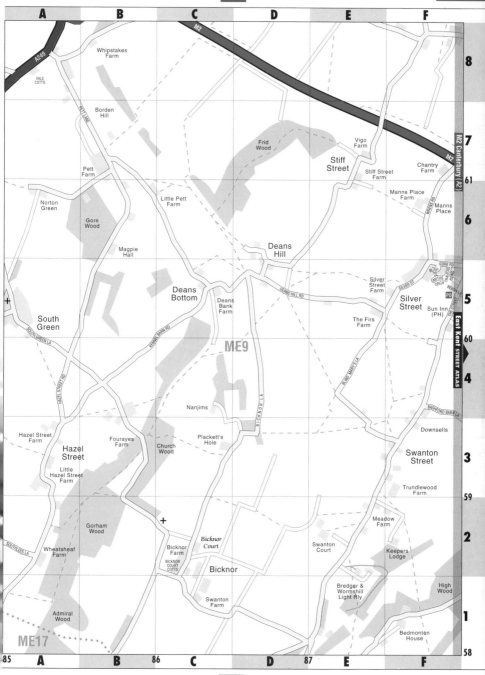

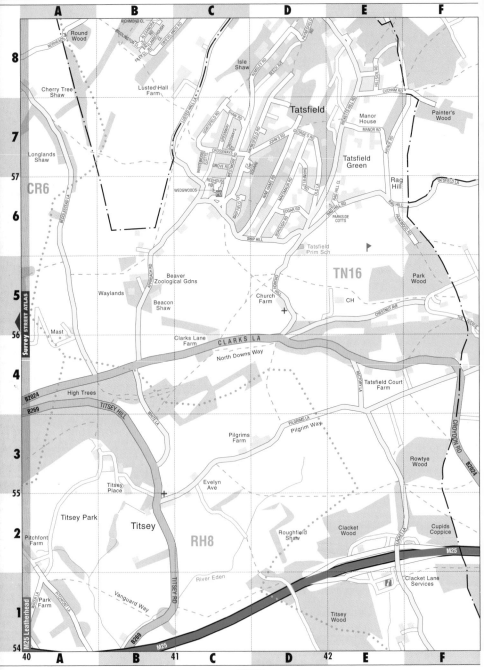

72

A B C D E F

8

Round Wood
Norheads La

Cherry Tree
Shaw

Lusted Hall
Farm

Isle
Shaw

Tatsfield

Manor
House

Painter's
Wood

MANOR RD

CUDHAM RD

7

Longlands
Shaw

CR6

Tatsfield
Green

Rag
Hill

TATSFIELD LA

57

WEDGWOODS

REDHOUSE RD

EDGAR RD

PARKSIDE
COTTS

PARK WOOD RD

6

Beaver
Zoological Gdns

SHIP HILL

Tatsfield
Prim Sch

TN16

Park
Wood

Waylands

Beacon
Shaw

Church
Farm

CHESTNUT AVE

CH

THE AVENUE

5

Mast

Clarks Lane
Farm

CLARKS LA

North Downs Way

56

B2024

B269

High Trees

TITSEY HILL

RECTORY LA

Tatsfield Court
Farm

CROYDON RD

B2024

4

Pilgrims
Farm

PILGRIMS LA

Pilgrim Way

Rowtye
Wood

3

55

Titsey
Place

Evelyn
Ave

Clacket
Wood

CLACKET LA

Cupids
Coppice

Titsey Park

Titsey

RH8

Roughfield
Shaw

M25

Clacket Lane
Services

2

Pitchfont
Farm

TITSEY RD

River Eden

M25 Leatherhead

WATER LA

PITCHFONT LA

Park
Farm

Vanguard Way

B269

M25

Titsey
Wood

1

54

40 A B 41 C D 42 E F

Surrey STREET ATLAS

104

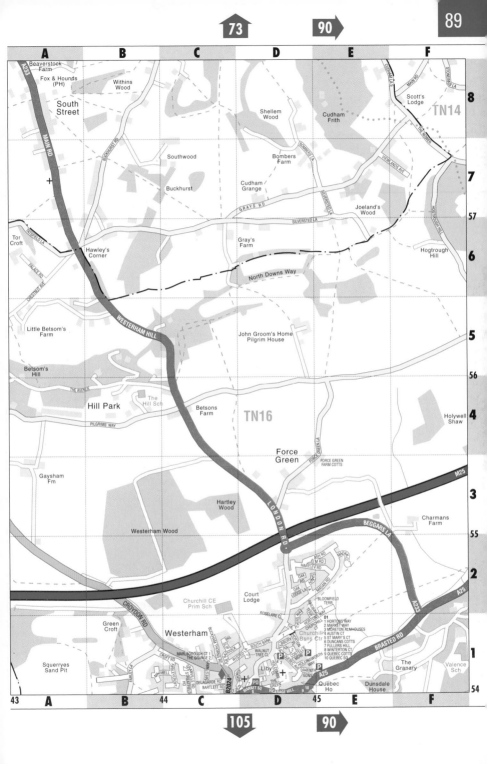

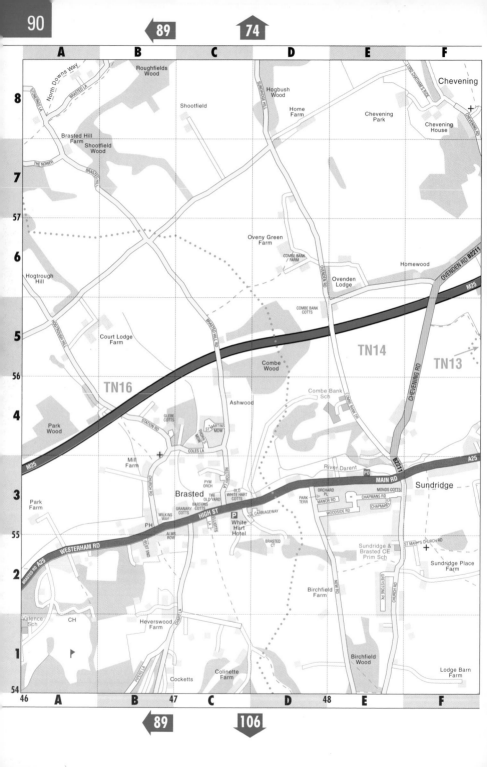

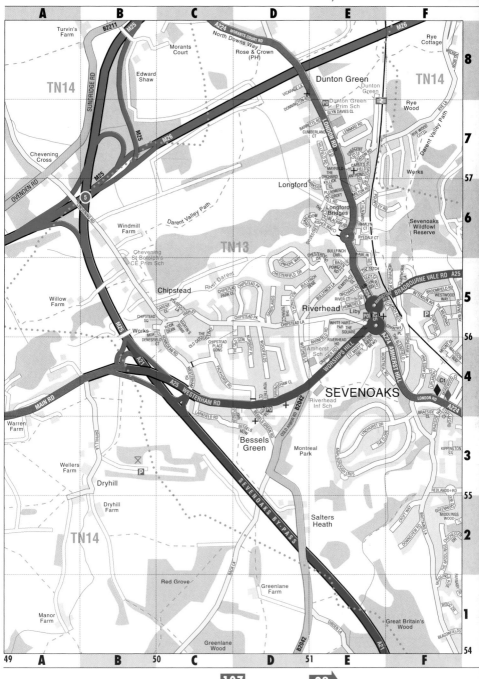

A   B   C   D   E   F

Turvin's Farm
B2211
M25
Morants Court
MORANTS COURT RD
A224
North Downs Way
Rose & Crown (PH)
M26
Rye Cottage
WICKEN

8

TN14
Edward Shaw
VICARAGE LA
DONNINGTON RD
Dunton Green
Dunton Green
Dunton Green Prim Sch
GLYN DAVIES CL
Rye Wood
TN14

Chevening Cross
SUNDRIDGE RD
M25
M26
BARNETTS RD
CUMBERLAND CT
HETFIELD RD
LONDON RD
LENNARD RD
CRESCENT RD
CAREY'S
RYE WOOD COTTS
BRELA
Darent Valley Path

7

57

Willow Farm
OVENDEN RD
M25
Windmill Farm
Darent Valley Path
MAYFIELD
THE ORCHARD
KILLICK CL
PLUMMERS CROFT
HILL RD
MEADSIDE
Longford
Longford Bridges
THE MEADOW
HAMILTON RD
POLHILL RD
Sevenoaks Wildfowl Reserve

6

Chevening St Botolph's CE Prim Sch
TN13
River Darent
SWEETBRIAR
THE BLACKHALL
ASHES WAY
HAMLYN CT
RYEDALE CT
HEATHFIELD RD
Sevenoaks Liby

Chipstead
CHIPSTEAD SQ
FAIRSEAT CL
HIGH ST
MOAT LA
BROOK DEAN
Chipstead Park
CHIPSTEAD PARK CL
CHIPSTEAD RD
CHESTERFIELD DR
BULLFINCH LANE
CHESTERFIELD DR
CHESTERFIELD CT
BULLFINCH CNR
BACK
POUND RD
ORCHARD RD
RIVER CT
BULLFINCH LA
Riverhead
WHITE HART PAR THE SQUARE
A25
BRADBOURNE VALE RD
BROOMFIELD RD
WESTWOOD WAY
A25

5

56

Works
MOAT LA
DENESFIELD
CEDAR RD
THE TERRACE
Chipstead Pk
OLD CARRIAGE
Chipstead Place Gdns
CHIPSTEAD LA
NURSERY RD
WOODFIELDS
BARNES
Riverhead Inf Sch
Amherst Sch
WITCHES LA
HOMEFIELD
GRANGE RD
CHANTRY
WORSHIPS HILL
ST MARY'S DR
MONTREAL RD
SHOREHAM LA
AMHERST HILL
A224
P
A25
CHURCH RD
MONTAGUE
PARK
MOUNT PL

4

M26
A21
WESTERHAM RD
A25
PACKHORSE RD
LARKFIELD RD
YEW TREE
CHEN CL
BESSEL'S MDW
COLD ARBOR RD
B2042
SEVENOAKS BY-PASS
Riverhead
LONDON RD
A225
BRAESIDE CL
LYNHURST DR

SEVENOAKS

Warren Farm
MAIN RD
DRYHILL LA
Bessels Green
Montreal Park
MARLBOROUGH CRES
KIPPINGTON CL
REDLANDS RD

3

55

Wellers Farm
Dryhill
Dryhill Farm
TN14
Red Grove
Greenlane Farm
Salters Heath
B2042
DIBDEN LA
GREENWOOD
MIDDLINGS WOOD
OXFORD RD
DOWNSVIEW DR
CROFT WAY

2

Manor Farm
BLACK LA
Greenlane Wood
Greenlane Farm
Great Britain's Wood
A21
WOOD RD
BEACONFIELDS

1

54

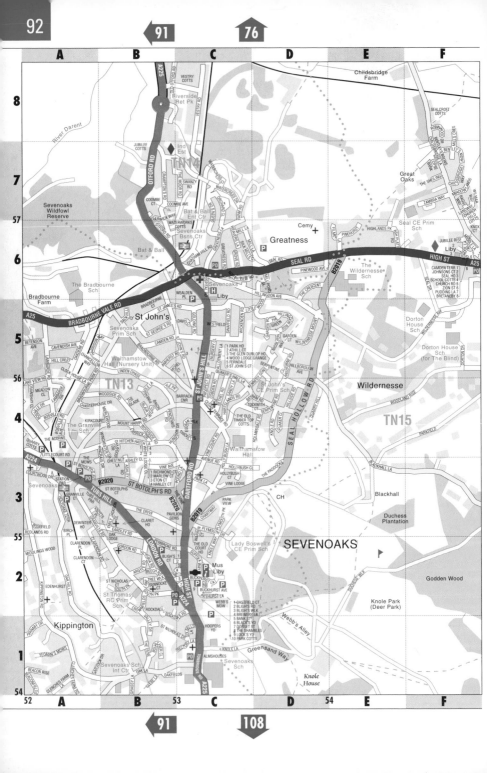

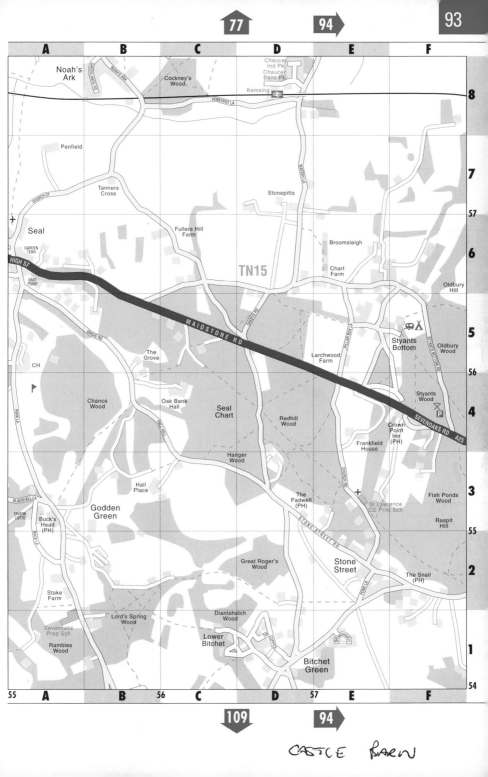

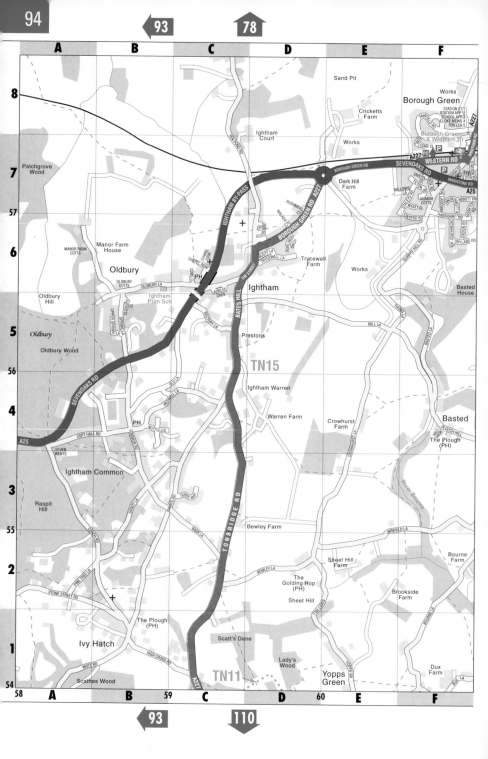

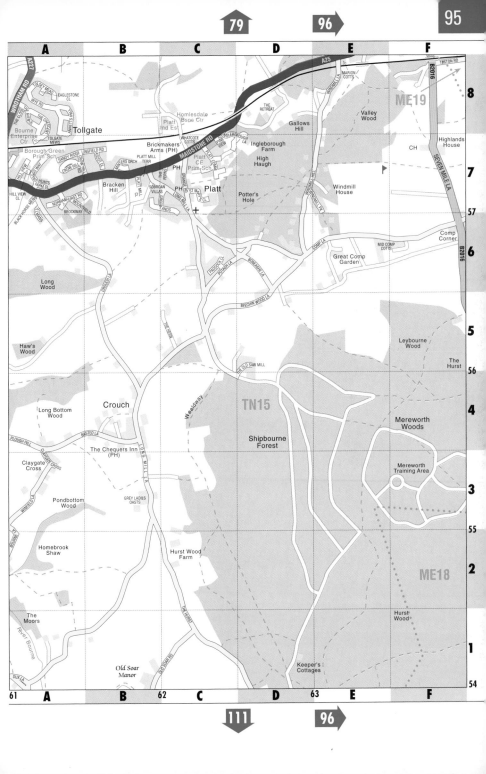

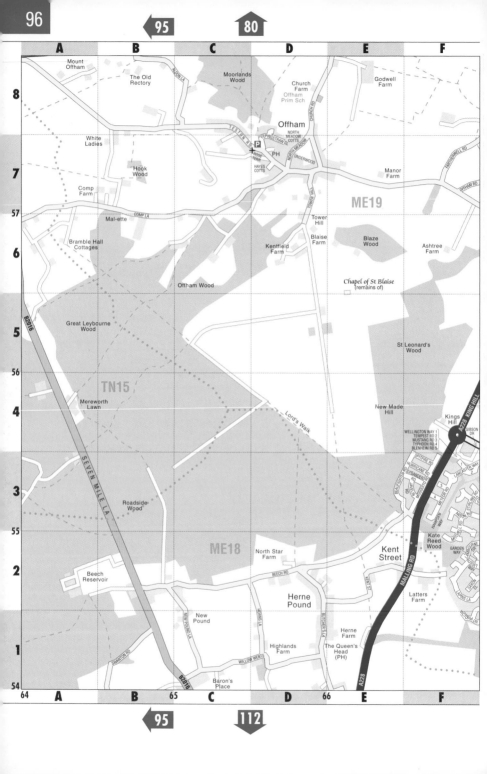

A B C D E F

8

Mount
Offham

The Old
Rectory

Moorlands
Wood

Church
Farm
Offham
Prim Sch

Godwell
Farm

Offham

NORTH MEADOW
COTTS

7

White
Ladies

Hook
Wood

PH

HAYES
COTTS

Manor
Farm

Comp
Farm

COMP LA

57

Mal-ette

Tower
Hill

ME19

Bramble Hall
Cottages

Kentfield
Farm

Blaise
Farm

Blaze
Wood

Ashtree
Farm

6

Offham Wood

Chapel of St Blaise
(remains of)

Great Leybourne
Wood

St Leonard's
Wood

5

56

B2016

TN15

Mereworth
Lawn

Lord's Walk

New Made
Hill

Kings
Hill

A228 KING HILL

GIBSON
DR

4

WELLINGTON WAY 1
TEMPEST RD 2
MUSTANG RD 3
TYPHOON RD 4
BLENHEIM RD 5

SEVEN MILE LA

Roadside
Wood

3

55

ME18

North Star
Farm

Kent
Street

Kate
Reed
Wood

2

Beech
Reservoir

BEECH RD

Herne
Pound

Latters
Farm

MALLING RD

New
Pound

NEW POUND LA

PIPPIN LA

BUTCHER LA

Herne
Farm

1

Highlands
Farm

WILLOW WENTS

The Queen's
Head
(PH)

54

Baron's
Place

B2016

A228

64 A B 65 C D 66 E F

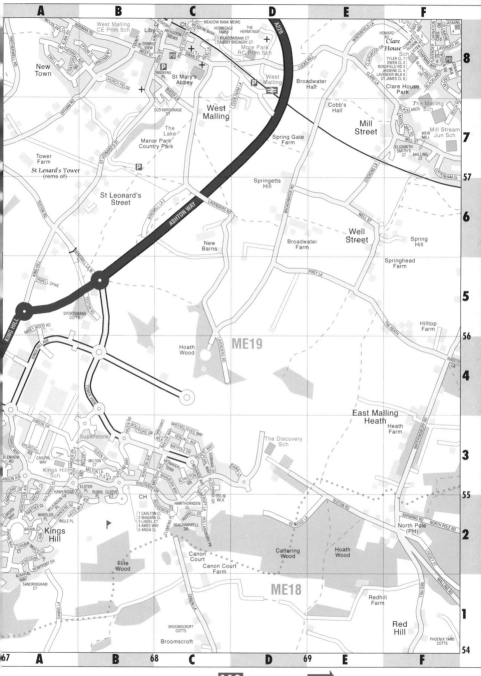

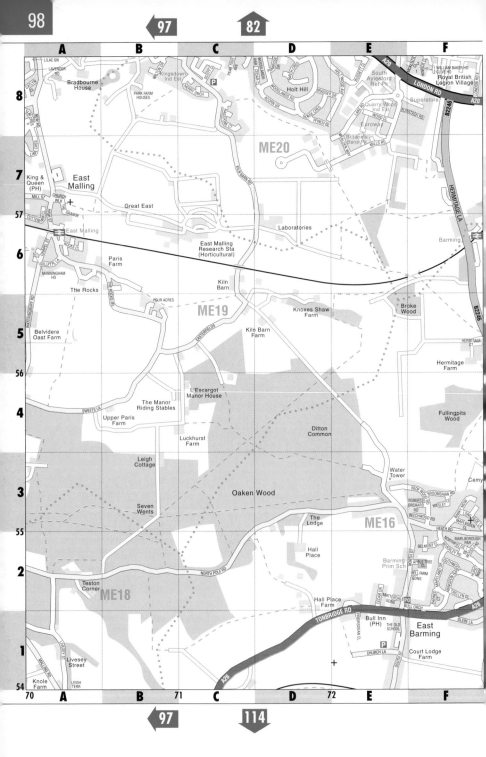

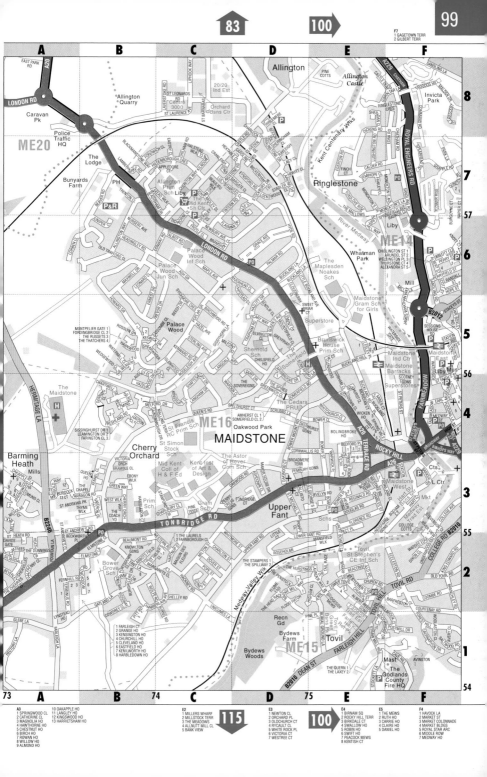

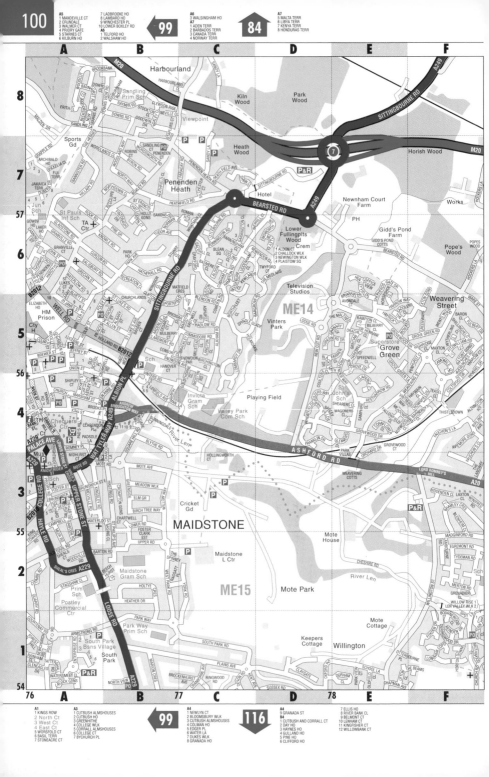

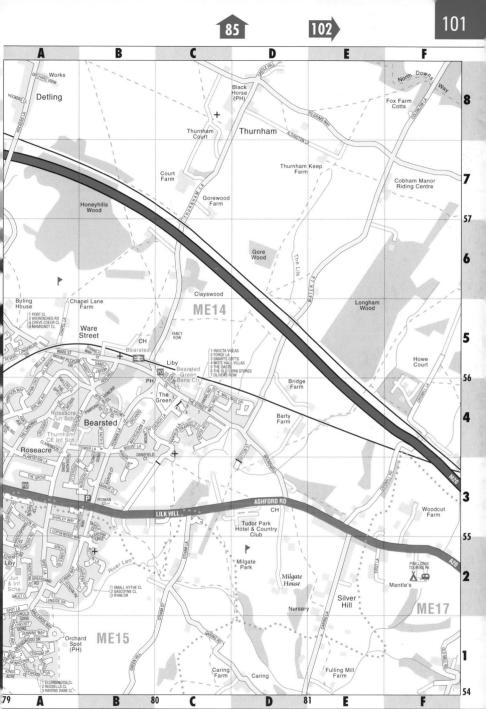

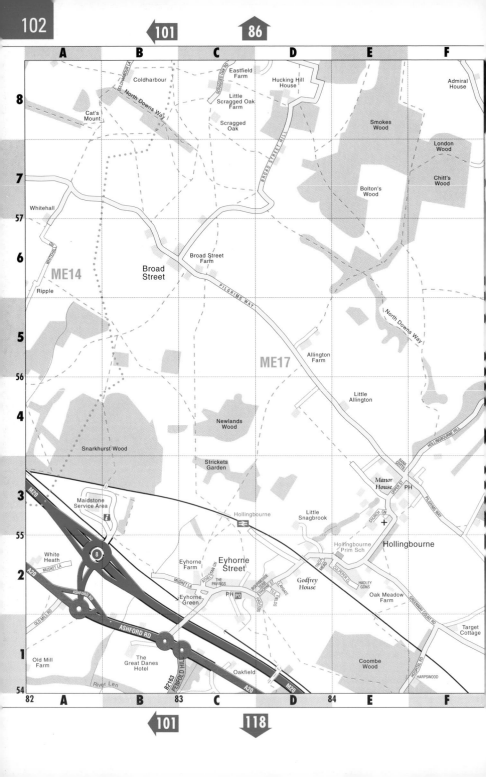

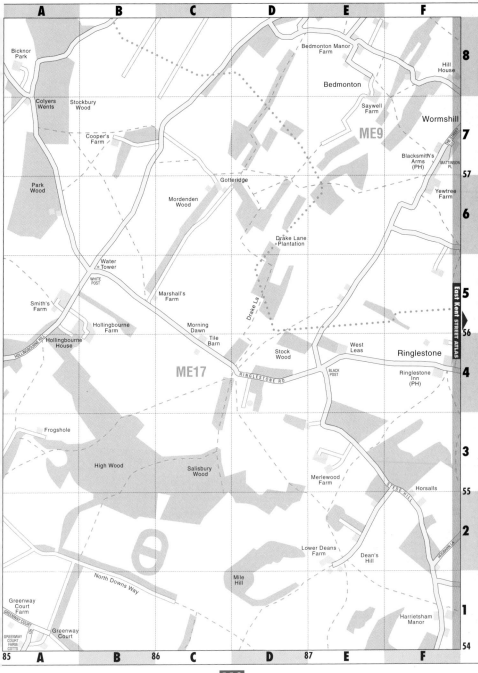

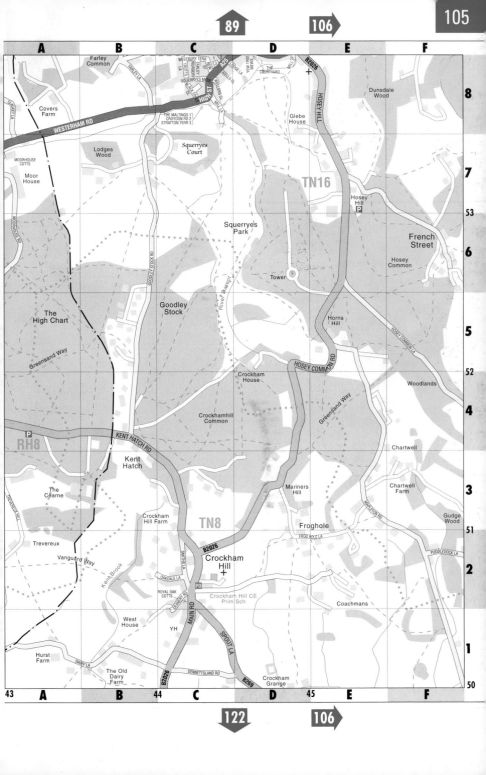

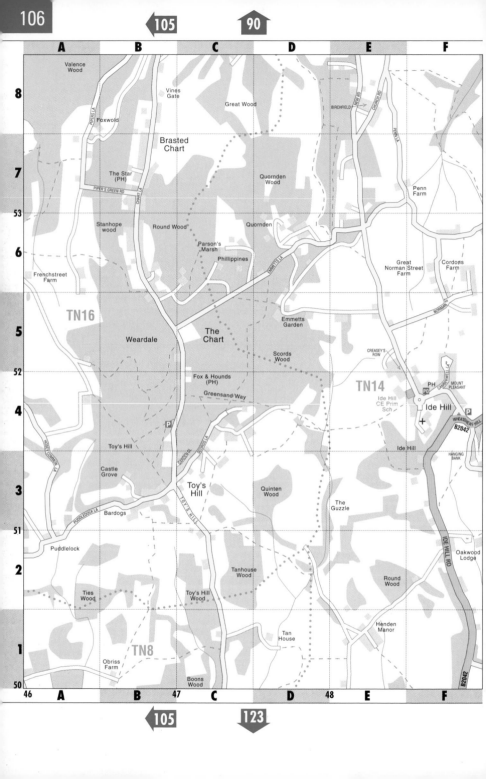

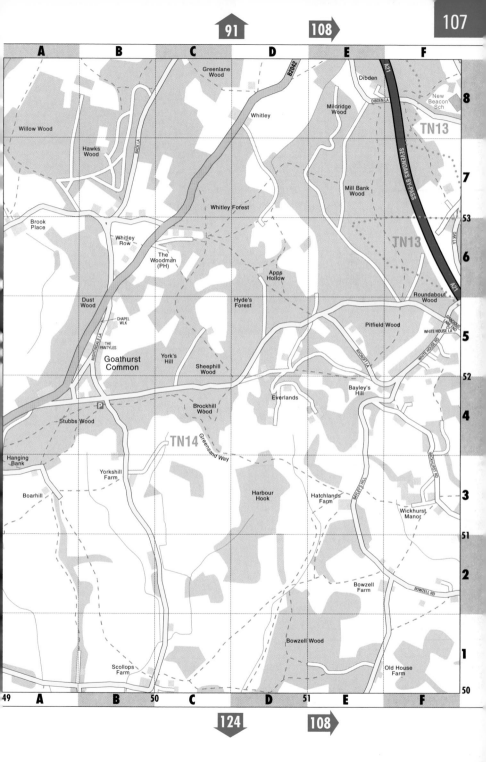

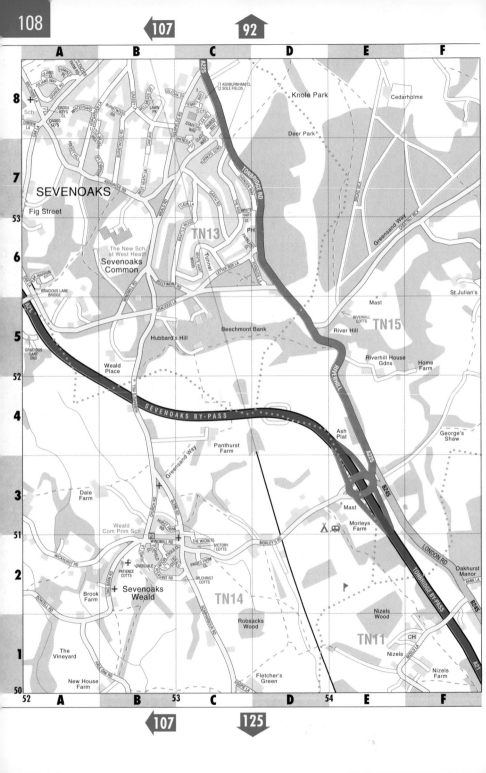

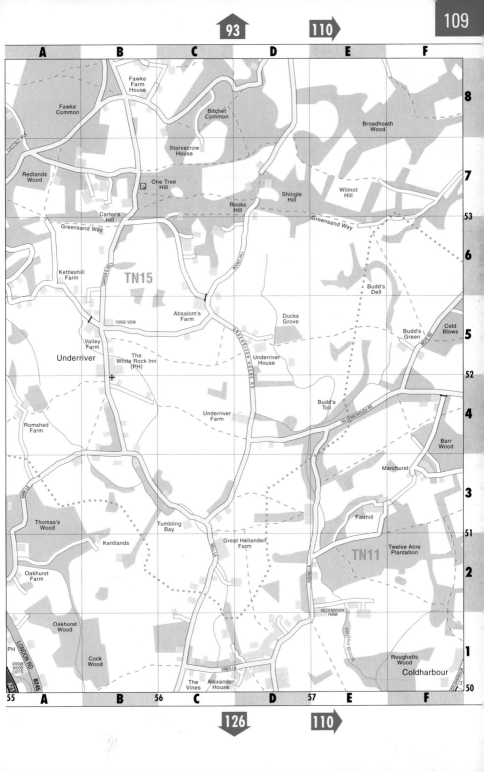

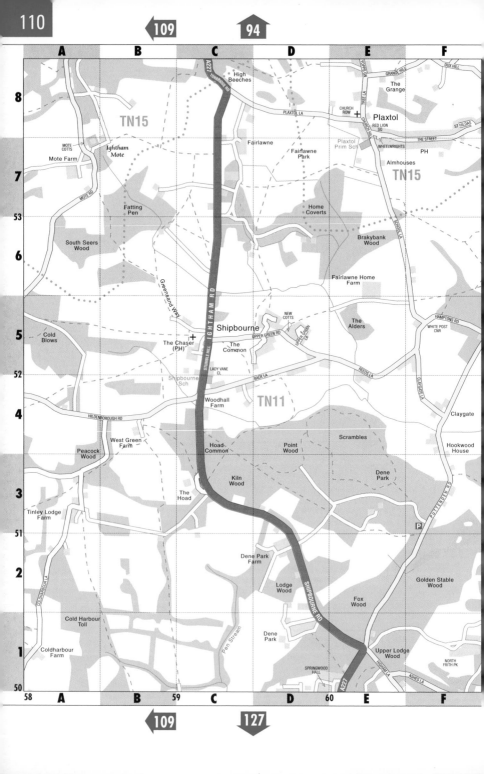

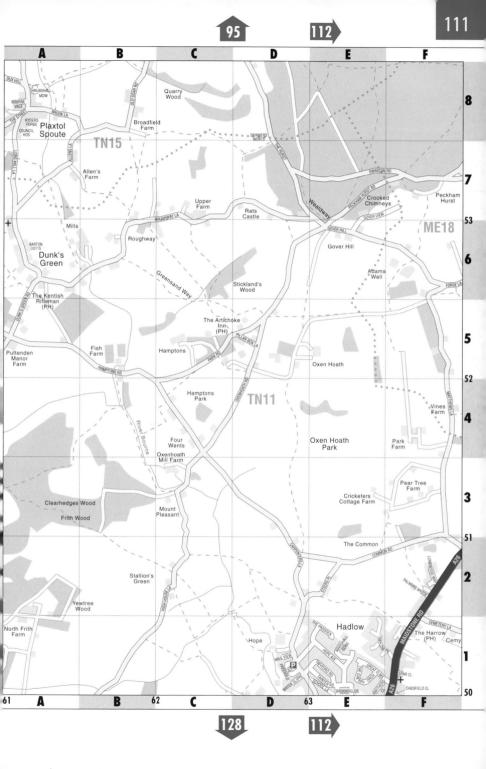

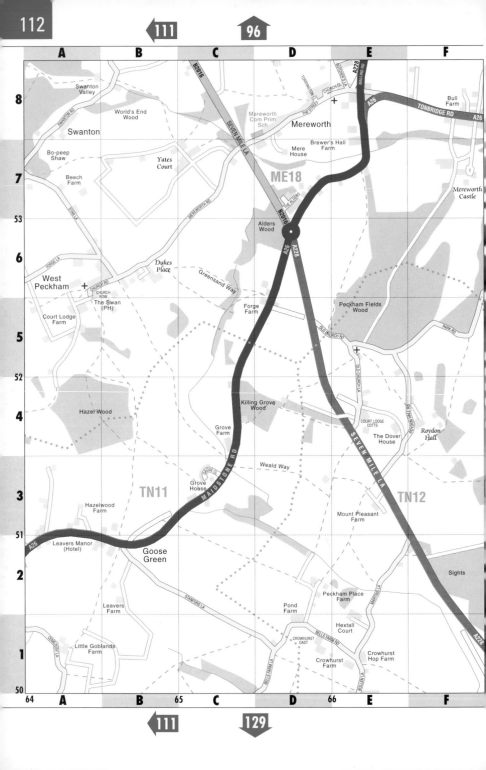

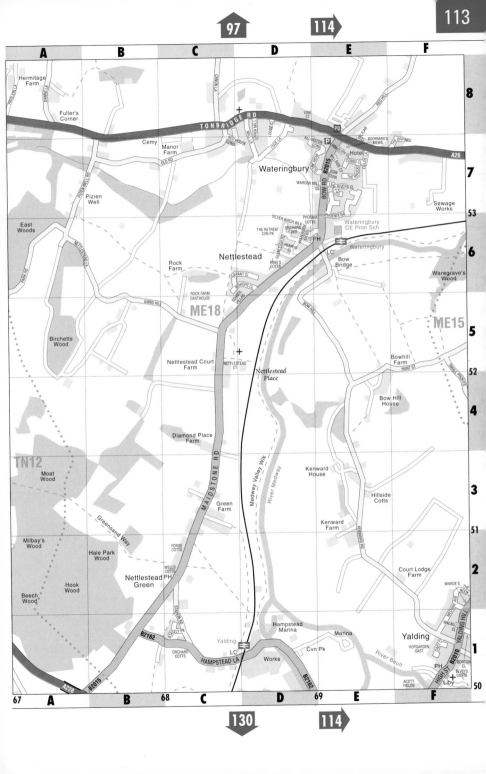

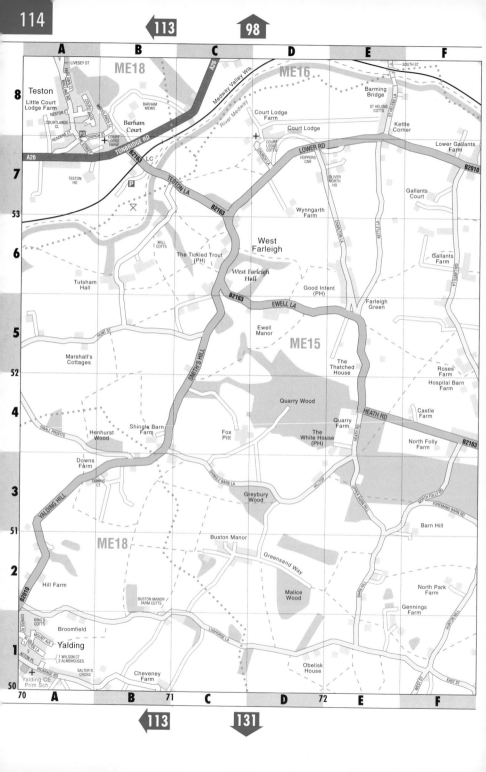

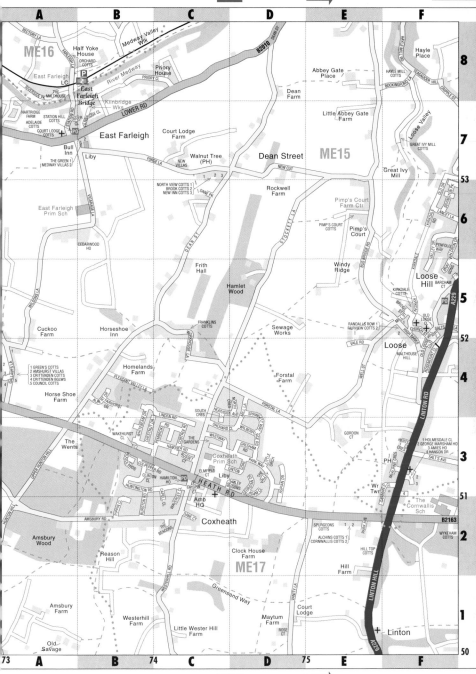

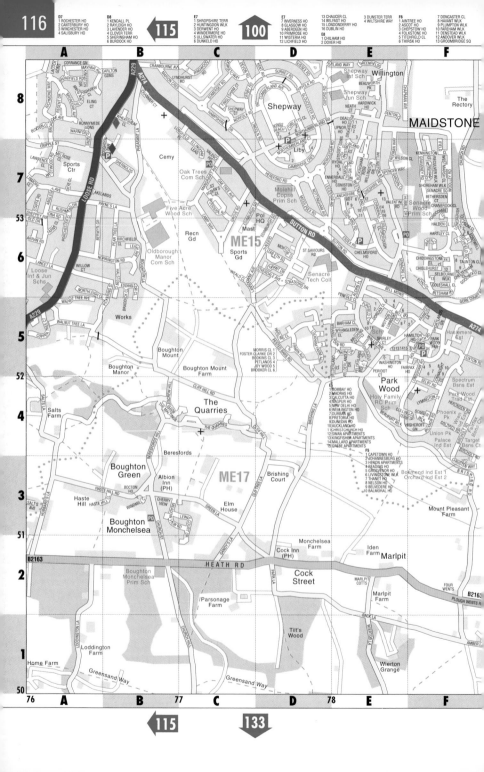

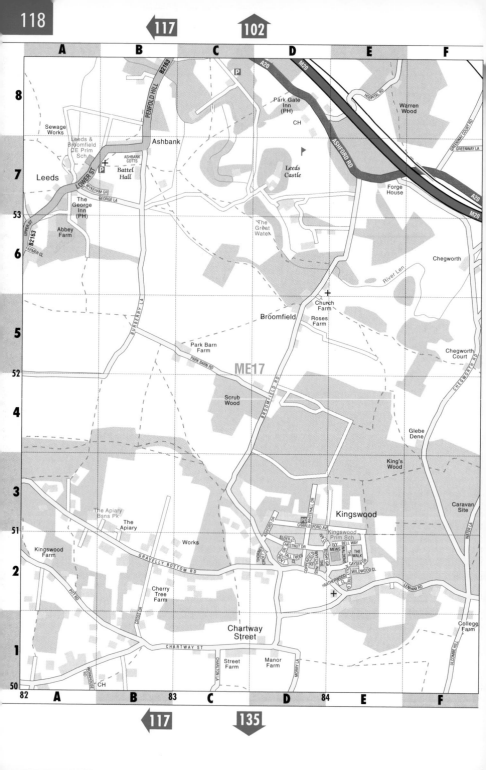

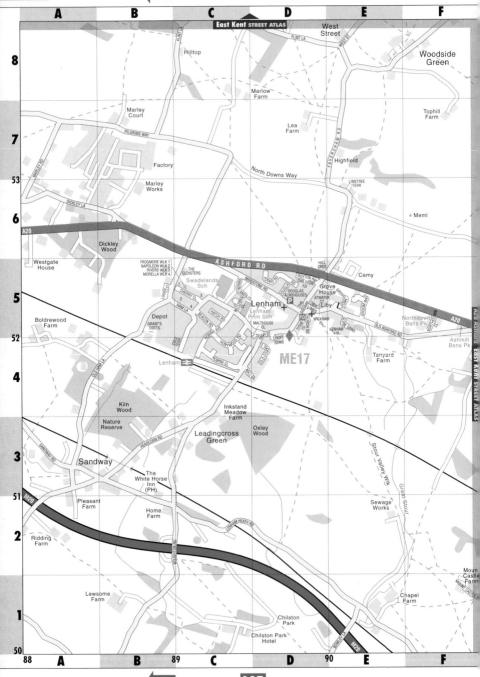

119

East Kent STREET ATLAS

West Street

Woodside Green

Hilltop

Marlow Farm

Tophill Farm

Marley Court

PILGRIMS WAY

Lea Farm

FAVERSHAM RD

Factory

North Downs Way

Highfield

Marley Works

LIMETREE TERR

DICKLEY LA

A20

Meml

Westgate House

Dickley Wood

ASHFORD RD

HILL CRES

Cemy

FROGMORE WLK 1
NAPOLEON WLK 2
RIVERS WLK 3
MORELLA WLK 4

THE CLOISTERS

ROYTON AV
CHILSTON RD

Grove House

Swadelands Sch

CHERRY CL

Douglas Almshouses

ATWATER

Lenham

Lby

Boldrewood Farm

Depot
GRANT'S COTTS

HAM LA

Lenham Prim Sch

MALTHOUSE CL

WICKHAM PL

Northdown Bsns Pk

A20 Ashford Rd

Lenham

CROFT GDNS

OLD ASHFORD RD

Ashmill Bsns Pk

East Kent STREET ATLAS

ME17

Tanyard Farm

Kiln Wood

Inkstand Meadow Farm

Oxley Wood

OLD THROAT LA

Nature Reserve

MAIDSTONE RD

Leadingcross Green

Stour Valley Wlk

Great Stour

Sandway

The White Horse Inn (PH)

SANDWAY RD

Pleasant Farm

Home Farm

Sewage Works

M20

Ridding Farm

LENHAM HEATH RD

Moun Castle Farm

MOUNT CASTLE

Lewsome Farm

Chapel Farm

Chilston Park

A20

Chilston Park Hotel

M20

119   137

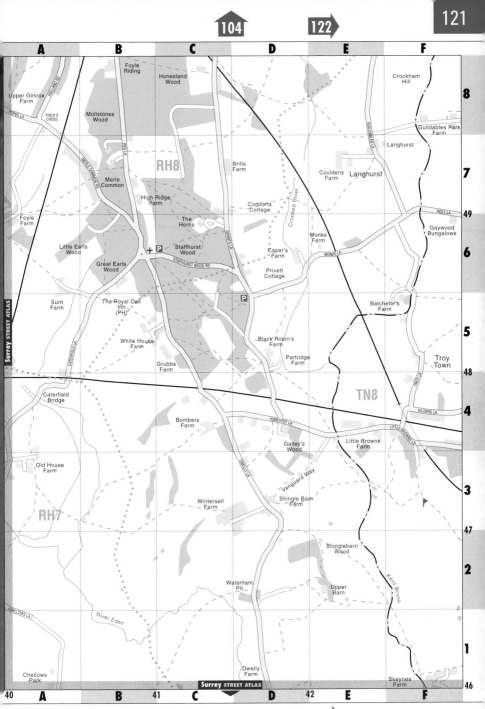

A B C D E F

8

Upper Gincox Farm

Foyle Riding

Honesland Wood

Crockham Hill

POPES LA

FINCH'S CROSS

Mollstones Wood

RED LA

NEW COMMON RD

Guildables Park Farm

Langhurst

GUILDABLES LA

7

RH8

Brills Farm

Couldens Farm

Langhurst

Merle Common

Foyle Farm

High Ridge Farm

Comforts Cottage

Crooked River

HOLE LA

49

Gaywood Bungalows

The Horns

Caper's Farm

Monks Farm

Little Earls Wood

Staffhurst Wood

STAFFHURST WOOD RD

GRANT'S LA

Privett Cottage

MONKS LA

6

Great Earls Wood

Batchelor's Farm

Sunt Farm

The Royal Oak Inn (PH)

White House Farm

Black Robin's Farm

5

Troy Town

FINDE LA

48

CATERFIELD LA

Grubbs Farm

Partridge Farm

Surrey STREET ATLAS

Caterfield Bridge

Bombers Farm

HONEYPOT LA

TN8

HILDERS LA

LITTLE BROWNS LA

4

Galley's Wood

Little Browns Farm

Old House Farm

Vanguard Way

Shingle Barn Farm

3

RH7

Wintersell Farm

Shinglebarn Wood

47

DRELL LA

Waterham Pit

Upper Barn

Kent Brook

2

CHELLOWS LA

River Eden

Dwelly Farm

Skeynes Farm

Chellows Park

Surrey STREET ATLAS

1

46

40 A B 41 C D 42 E F

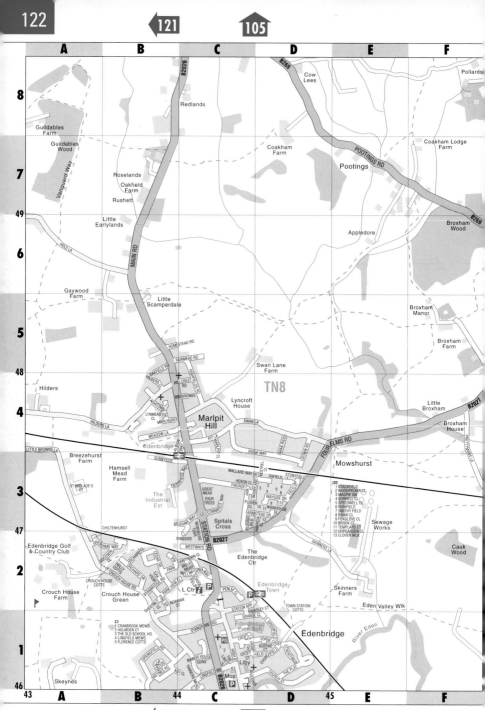

A B C D E F

8

Guildables
Farm

Guildables
Wood

B2026

Redlands

Cow
Lees

B269

Pollards

Coakham
Lodge
Farm

7

Vanguard Way

Roselands

Oakfield
Farm

Rushett

Coakham
Farm

POOTINGS RD

Pootings

49

HOLELA

Little
Earlylands

Appledore

B269

Broxham
Wood

6

MAIN RD

Gaywood
Farm

Little
Scamperdale

Broxham
Manor

5

HOMESTEAD RD

FAIRMEAD RD

Swan Lane
Farm

TN8

Broxham
Farm

48

Hilders

OAKFIELD RD

HILDERS
RD

HILLCREST
RD

BROWNINGS

Little
Broxham

B2027

4

HILDERS LA

ASHCOMBE

LYNMEAD
CL

MEADOW LA

MARLHURST

Marlpit
Hill

SWAN LA

Lyncroft
House

RIDGE WAY

SWAN ROAD

CROWN RD

FOUR ELMS RD

Broxham
House

PRETHANE LA

Mowshurst

LITTLE BROWNS LA

Breezehurst
Farm

Hamsell
Mead
Farm

Edenbridge

SUNNYSIDE

EDENHURST WAY

MALLARD WAY

HERON CL

FIRCROFT

KESTREL

OXFIELD

STONYFIELD

D3
1 STACKFIELD
2 WOODPECKER CL
3 MAGPIE GN
4 SORRELL CL
5 SPEEDWELL CL
6 ROWFIELD
7 SMITHY FIELD
8 BRIAR CL
9 FOXGLOVE CL
10 BROOK CL
11 TEMPLARS CL
12 HOPGARDEN CL
13 CLOVER WLK

3

ST BRELADE'S
CT

The
Industrial
Est

GREAT
MEAD
FOUR
TREES

ST JOHN'S WAY

COMMON WAY

PLOVER
CL

WAINHOUSE

WAYSIDE DR

FAIRMEAD DR

Sewage
Works

47

CHILTENHURST

GRESHAMS WAY

BROOKMEAD

Edenbridge Golf
& Country Club

RINGSIDE

WESTWAYS

Spitals
Cross

STATION RD

B2027

SKINNERS LA

Cauk
Wood

2

Crouch House
Farm

CROUCH HOUSE
COTTS

Crouch House
Green

HOLLY

ORCHARD CL

ORCHARD

PARK

CHESTNUT

MOLES
MEADOW

MARLPIT

HAWTHORN CL

MONIFA AVE

The
Edenbridge
Ctr

Edenbridge
Town

PENS CT

L Ctr

P

C1
1 CRANBROOK MEWS
2 HOLMDEN CT
3 THE OLD SCHOOL HO
4 LINGFIELD MEWS
5 FLORENCE COTTS

P

STATION APP

HEADLEY CT

GRANGE CL

TOWN STATION
COTTS

Skinners
Farm

Eden Valley Wlk

River Eden

Edenbridge

1

Skeynes

SPRINGFIELD

STANGROVE
RD

MANOR HOUSE
GDNS

ASH CL

LINGFIELD RD

CROFT
FIELD

FORGE
CROFT

QUEENS

DELAWARE RD

STREATFIELD

THE PLAT

Edenbridge Prim Sch

Liby

Mus

P

46

43 A 44 B C 45 D E F

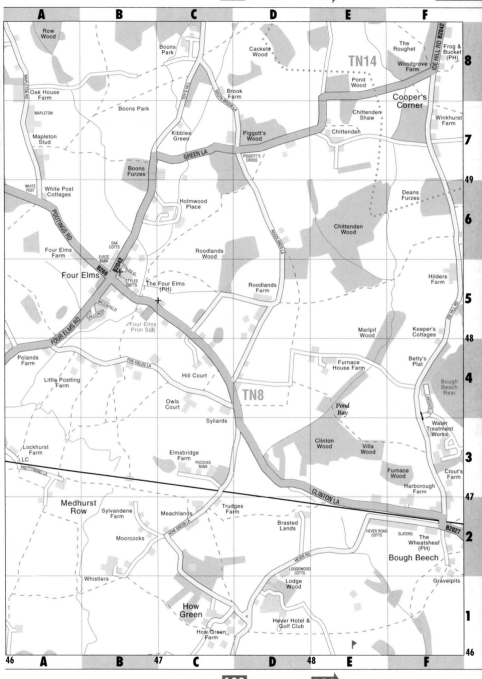

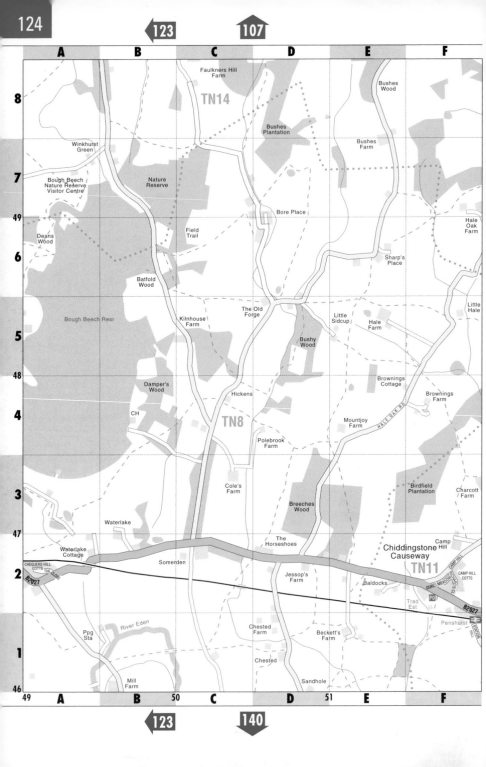

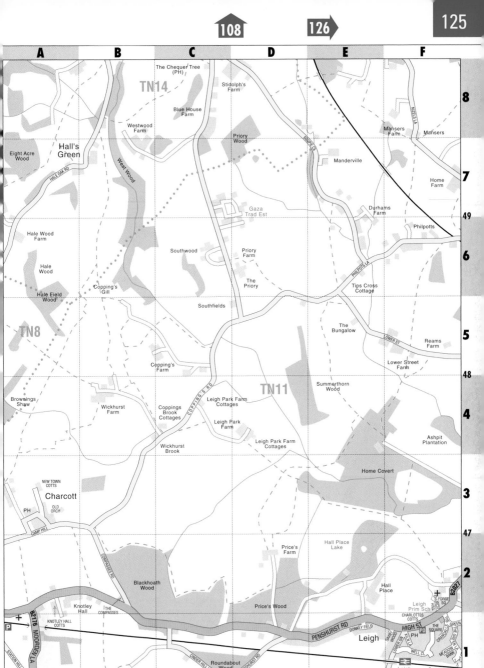

125
109

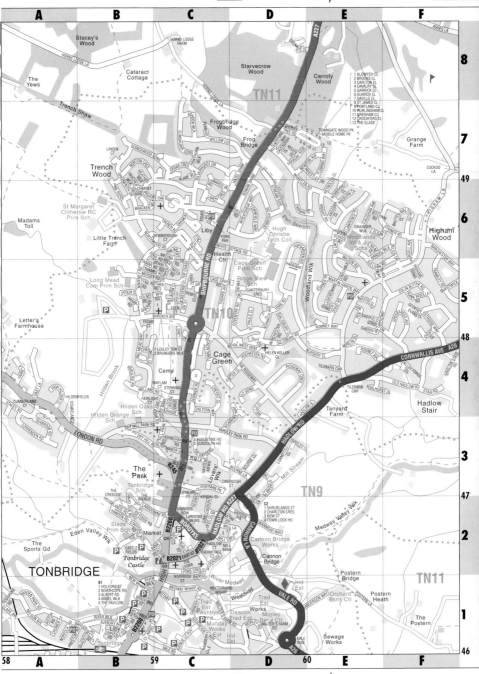

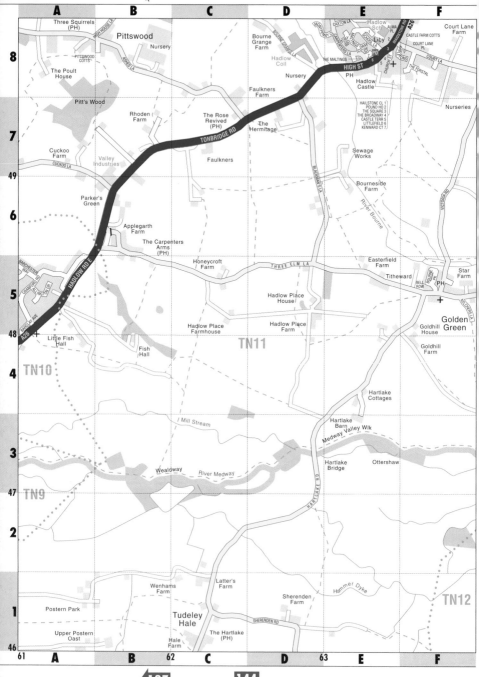

127

111

A B C D E F

8

7

49

6

5

48

4

3

47

2

1

46

Three Squirrels (PH)

Pittswood

PITTSWOOD COTTS

Nursery

The Poult House

Pitt's Wood

Rhoden Farm

Cuckoo Farm

CUCKOO LA

Valley Industries

Parker's Green

Applegarth Farm

The Carpenters Arms (PH)

Honeycroft Farm

HADLOW RD E

MANCHESTER WAY

CRANFORD RD

LINCOLN DR

Little Fish Hall

TN10

Fish Hall

Hadlow Place Farmhouse

Hadlow Place House

Hadlow Place Farm

THREE ELM LA

TN11

Postern Park

Upper Postern Oast

Wealdway

Mill Stream

River Medway

Wenhams Farm

Latter's Farm

Tudeley Hale

Hale Farm

The Hartlake (PH)

SHERENDEN RD

Sherenden Farm

Hammer Dyke

Bourne Grange Farm

RAVENSCROFT LA

MONCKTON

Hadlow Sch

CAXTON LA

ALMA PL

CARPENTERS LA

SCHOOL LA

Liby

Castle Farm Cotts

Court Lane Farm

Court Lane

Court Lane PL

The Forstal

Nurseries

Hadlow Coll

Nursery

THE MALTINGS

HIGH ST

PH

Hadlow Castle

Faulkners Farm

The Rose Revived (PH)

The Hermitage

TONBRIDGE RD

Faulkners

BLACKMANS LA

Sewage Works

Bourneside Farm

River Bourne

HAILSTONE CL 1
POUND HO 2
THE SQUARE 3
THE BROADWAY 4
CASTLE TERR 5
LITTLEFIELD 6
KENWARD CT 7

Easterfield Farm

Titheward

BROADWAY

BELL ROW

PH

KELCHERS LA

VICTORIA RD

Star Farm

Golden Green

Goldhill House

Goldhill Farm

Hartlake Cottages

Hartlake Barn

Medway Valley Wlk

Hartlake Bridge

HARTLAKE RD

Ottershaw

TN12

A26

A26

TN9

127

144

61 A B 62 C D 63 E F

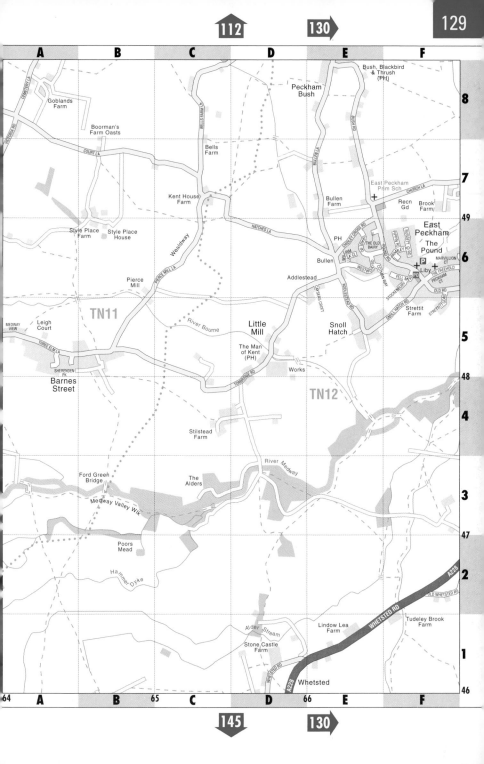

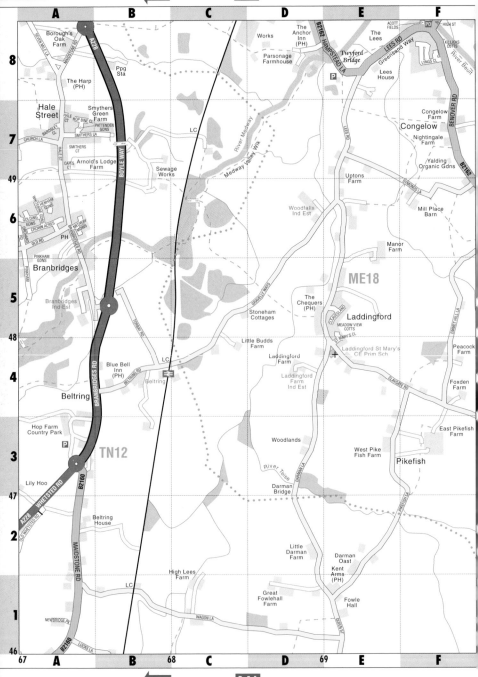

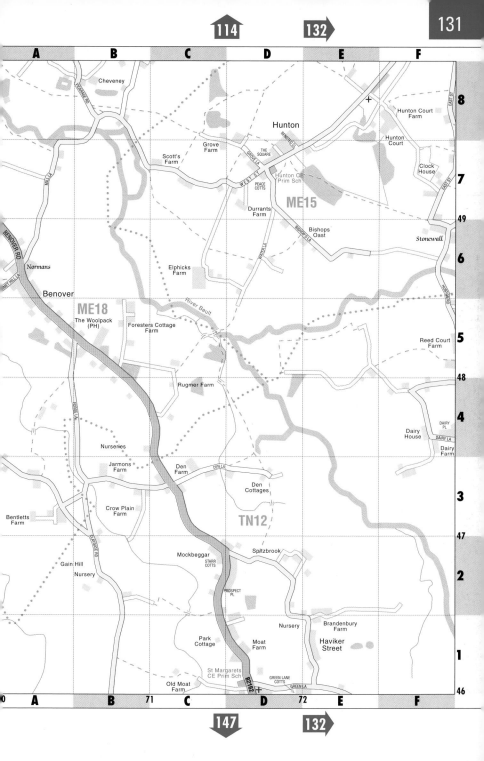

131
115

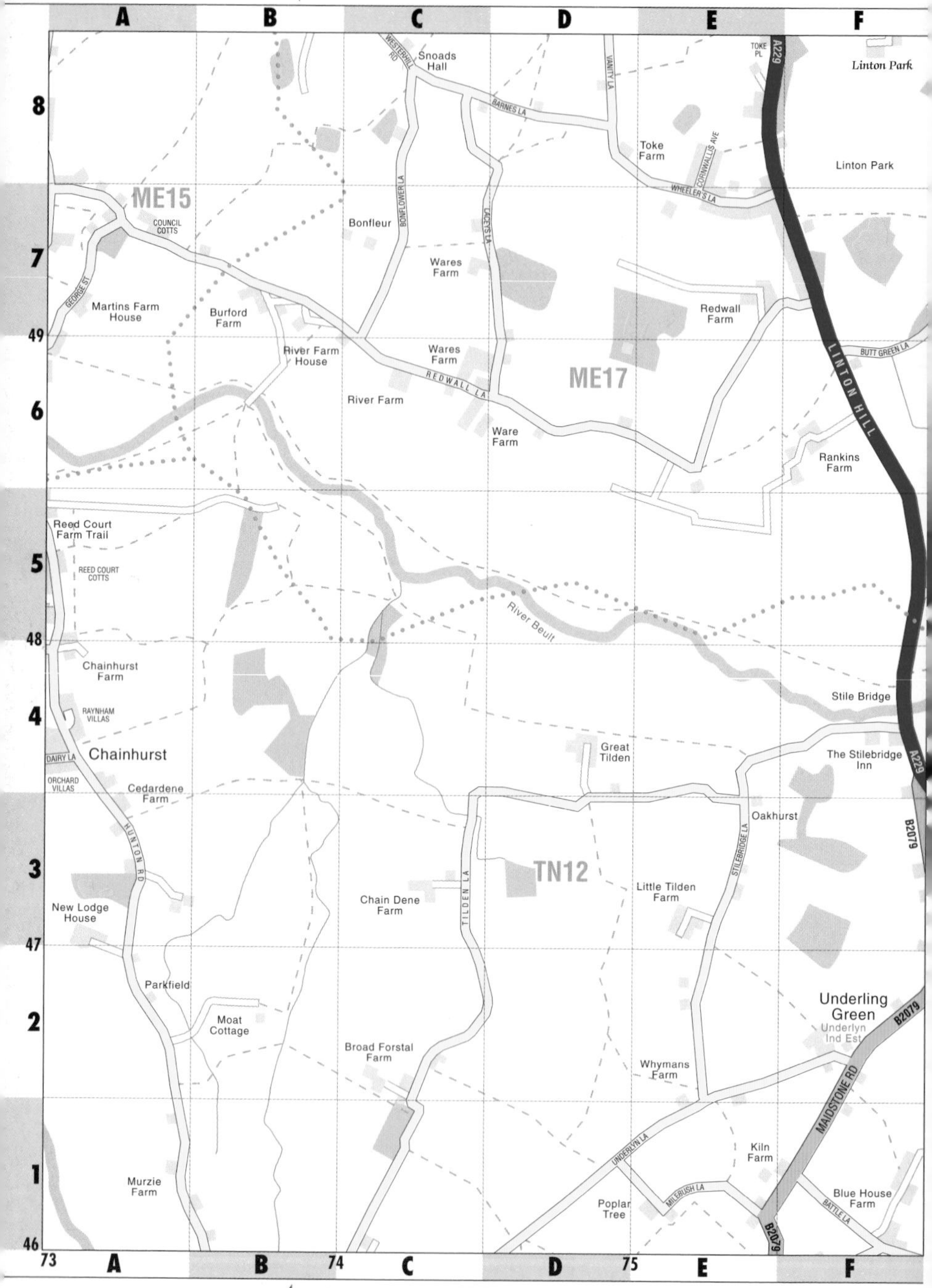
A
B
C
D
E
F
8
7
49
6
5
48
4
3
47
2
1
46
73
74
75
ME15
ME17
TN12
Snoads Hall
WESTERHILL RD
BARNES LA
VANITY LA
TOKE PL
A229
Linton Park
Linton Park
Toke Farm
CORNWALLIS AVE
WHEELER'S LA
COUNCIL COTTS
Bonfleur
BONFLOWER LA
LACEYS LA
Wares Farm
Wares Farm
GEORGE ST
Martins Farm House
Burford Farm
River Farm House
Redwall Farm
REDWALL LA
River Farm
Ware Farm
LINTON HILL
BUTT GREEN LA
Rankins Farm
Reed Court Farm Trail
REED COURT COTTS
River Beult
Chainhurst Farm
RAYNHAM VILLAS
Stile Bridge
Chainhurst
DAIRY LA
ORCHARD VILLAS
Great Tilden
The Stilebridge Inn
A229
Cedardene Farm
Oakhurst
B2079
HUNTON RD
STILEBRIDGE LA
TILDEN LA
Chain Dene Farm
Little Tilden Farm
New Lodge House
Parkfield
Underling Green
Underlyn Ind Est
B2079
Moat Cottage
Broad Forstal Farm
Whymans Farm
MAIDSTONE RD
UNDERLYN LA
Kiln Farm
Murzie Farm
Poplar Tree
MILEBUSH LA
Blue House Farm
BATTLE LA
B2079

131
148

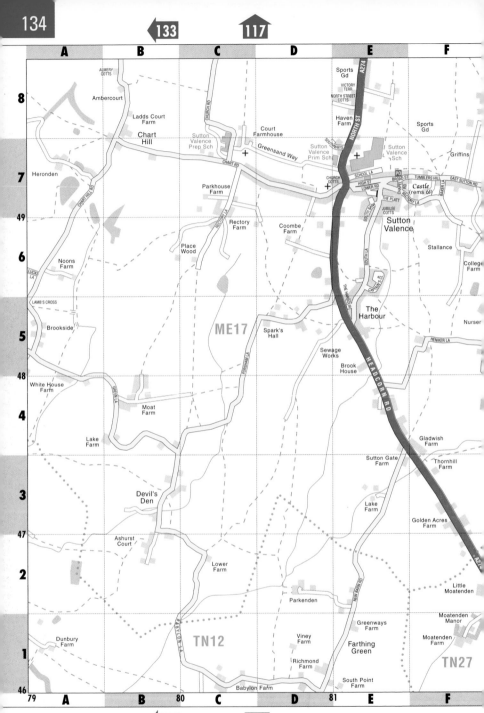

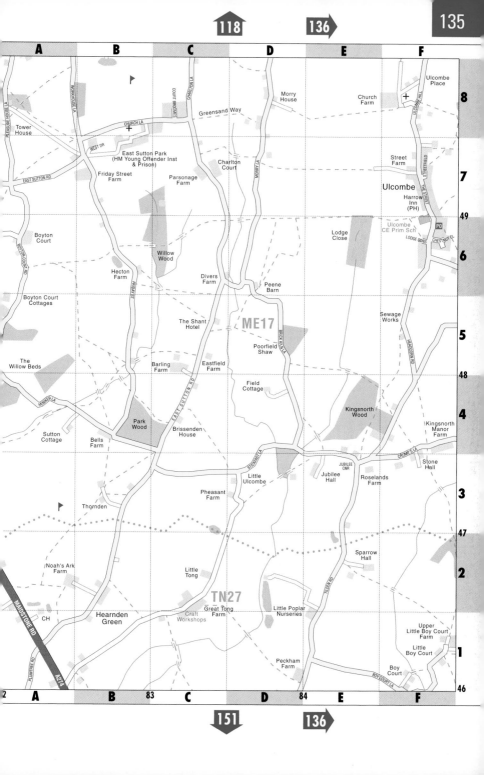

135 119

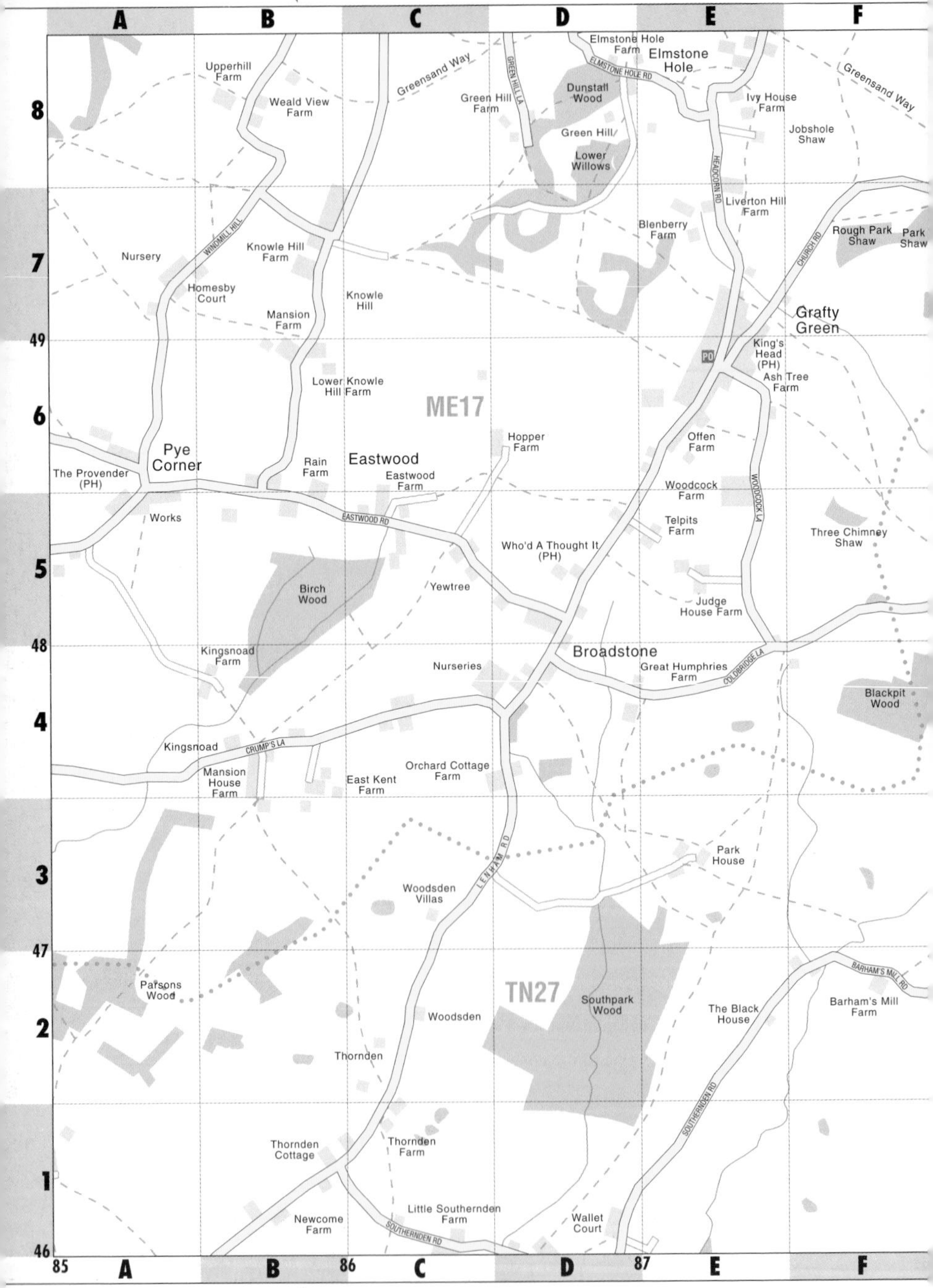

A B C D E F

8

Upperhill Farm
Weald View Farm
Greensand Way
Green Hill Farm
Elmstone Hole Farm
Elmstone Hole
Dunstall Wood
Green Hill
Ivy House Farm
Greensand Way
Jobshole Shaw
Lower Willows
ELMSTONE HOLE RD
GREEN HILL LA
HEADCORN RD

7

Nursery
WINDMILL HILL
Knowle Hill Farm
Homesby Court
Knowle Hill
Mansion Farm
Blenberry Farm
Liverton Hill Farm
Rough Park Shaw
Park Shaw
Grafty Green
CHURCH RD

49

Lower Knowle Hill Farm
ME17
King's Head (PH)
Ash Tree Farm
P0

6

Pye Corner
The Provender (PH)
Rain Farm
Eastwood
Eastwood Farm
Hopper Farm
Offen Farm
Woodcock Farm
WOODCOCK LA

Works
EASTWOOD RD
Who'd A Thought It (PH)
Telpits Farm
Three Chimney Shaw

5

Birch Wood
Yewtree
Judge House Farm

48

Kingsnoad Farm
Nurseries
Broadstone
Great Humphries Farm
Blackpit Wood
OXLEY BRIDGE LA

4

Kingsnoad
Mansion House Farm
CRUMP'S LA
East Kent Farm
Orchard Cottage Farm
Park House

3

Woodsden Villas
LENHAM RD

47

Parsons Wood
TN27
Southpark Wood
The Black House
Barham's Mill Farm
BARHAM'S MILL RD

2

Woodsden
Thornden
SOUTHERNDEN RD

1

Thornden Cottage
Thornden Farm
Little Southernden Farm
Wallet Court

46

Newcome Farm
SOUTHERNDEN RD

85 A B 86 C D 87 E F

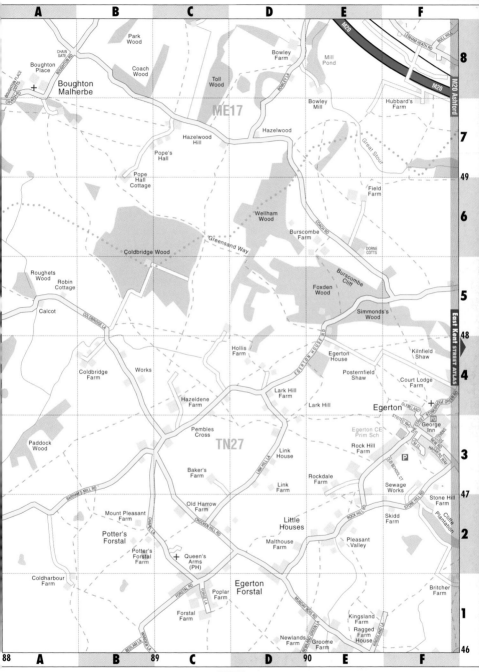

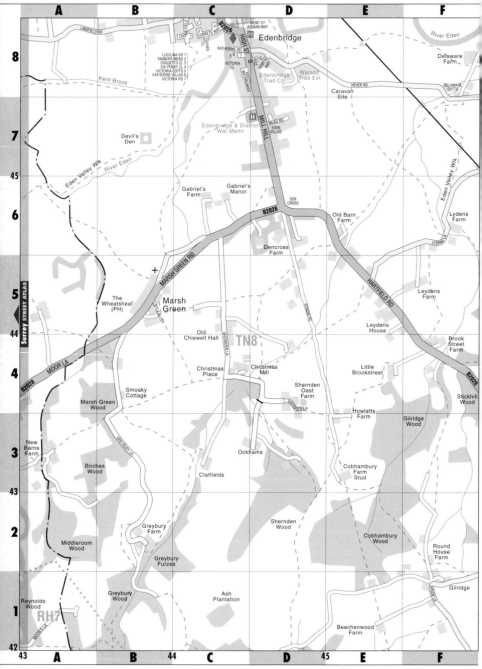

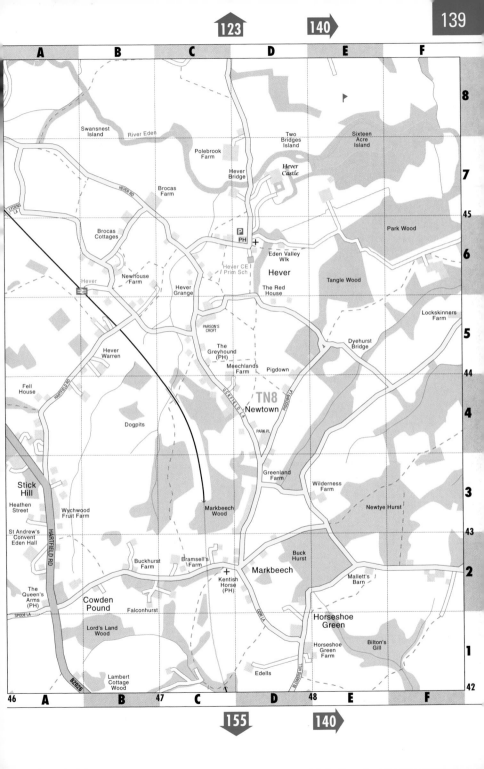

A **B** **C** **D** **E** **F**

8

River Eden

Mill
Shaw

Somerden
Green

The
Grove

River Eden

7

Gilwyns

Chiddingstone

Larkin's
Farm

Vexour
Bridge

Hampkins
Hill

Vexour

Castle Inn
(PH)

PO

Chiddingstone
Castle

Chiddingstone
CE Prim Sch

45

Chantlers

Clappers
Shaw

6

THRESHER
FIELD

Moor
Wood

Hill
Hoath

Hill Hoath
Farm

Eden Valley Wlk

BOURNE
ROW

Weller's
Town

Doubleton
Cottage

Mounters

TN8

SOUTH
ROW

5

The
Slips

Gillridge

44

Sliders

Stock
Wood

Robins
Land

Lew Cross
Farm

Wat
Stock

TN11

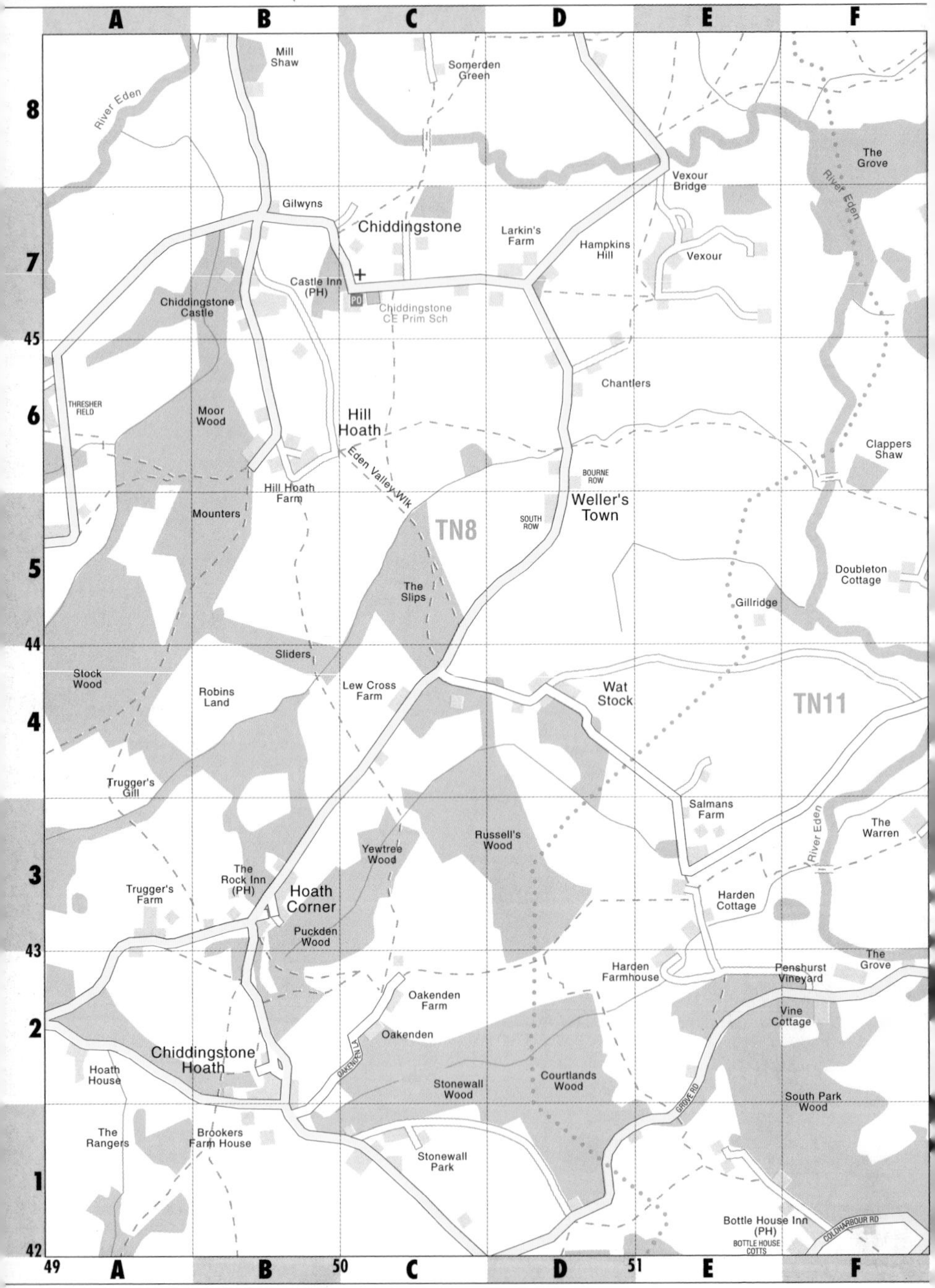

4

Trugger's
Gill

Salmans
Farm

River Eden

The
Warren

3

Trugger's
Farm

The
Rock Inn
(PH)

Hoath
Corner

Yewtree
Wood

Russell's
Wood

Harden
Cottage

Puckden
Wood

43

Harden
Farmhouse

Penshurst
Vineyard

The
Grove

2

Chiddingstone
Hoath

Oakenden
Farm

Oakenden

Vine
Cottage

Hoath
House

Stonewall
Wood

Courtlands
Wood

PRIOR RD

South Park
Wood

The
Rangers

Brookers
Farm House

Stonewall
Park

1

Bottle House Inn
(PH)

COLDHARBOUR RD

BOTTLE HOUSE
COTTS

42

49 **A** **B** **50** **C** **D** **51** **E** **F**

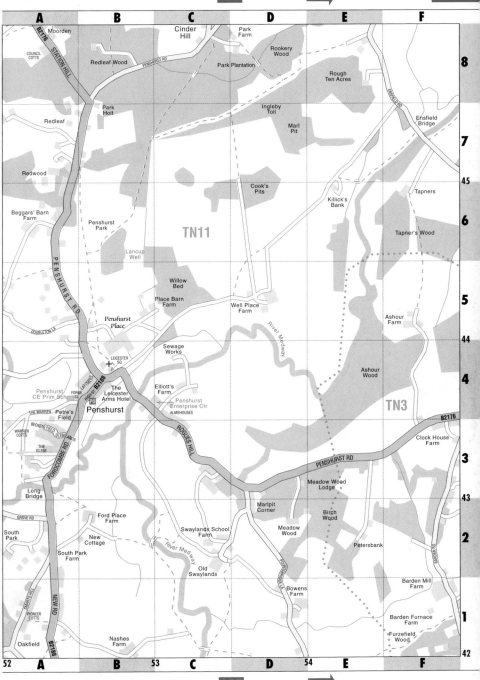

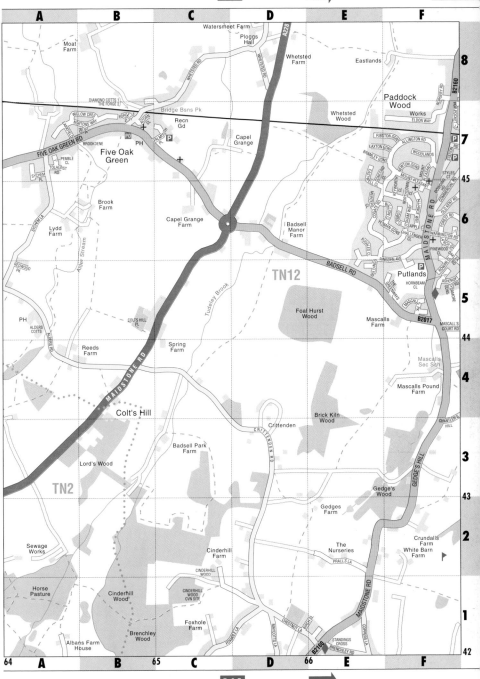

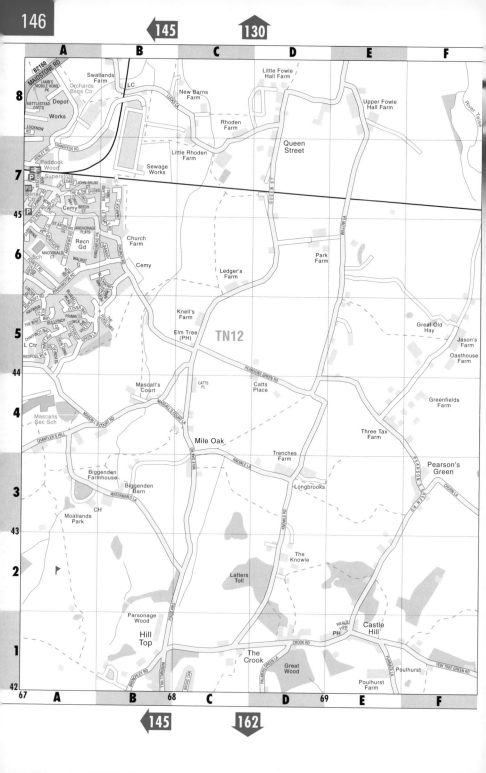

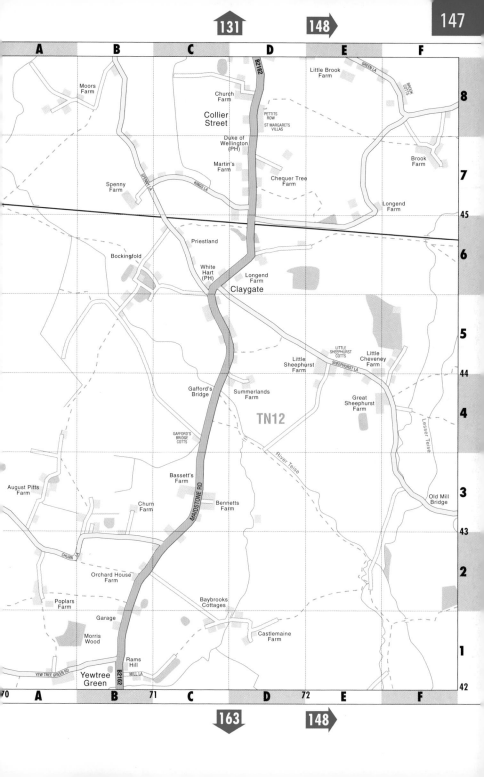

147
132

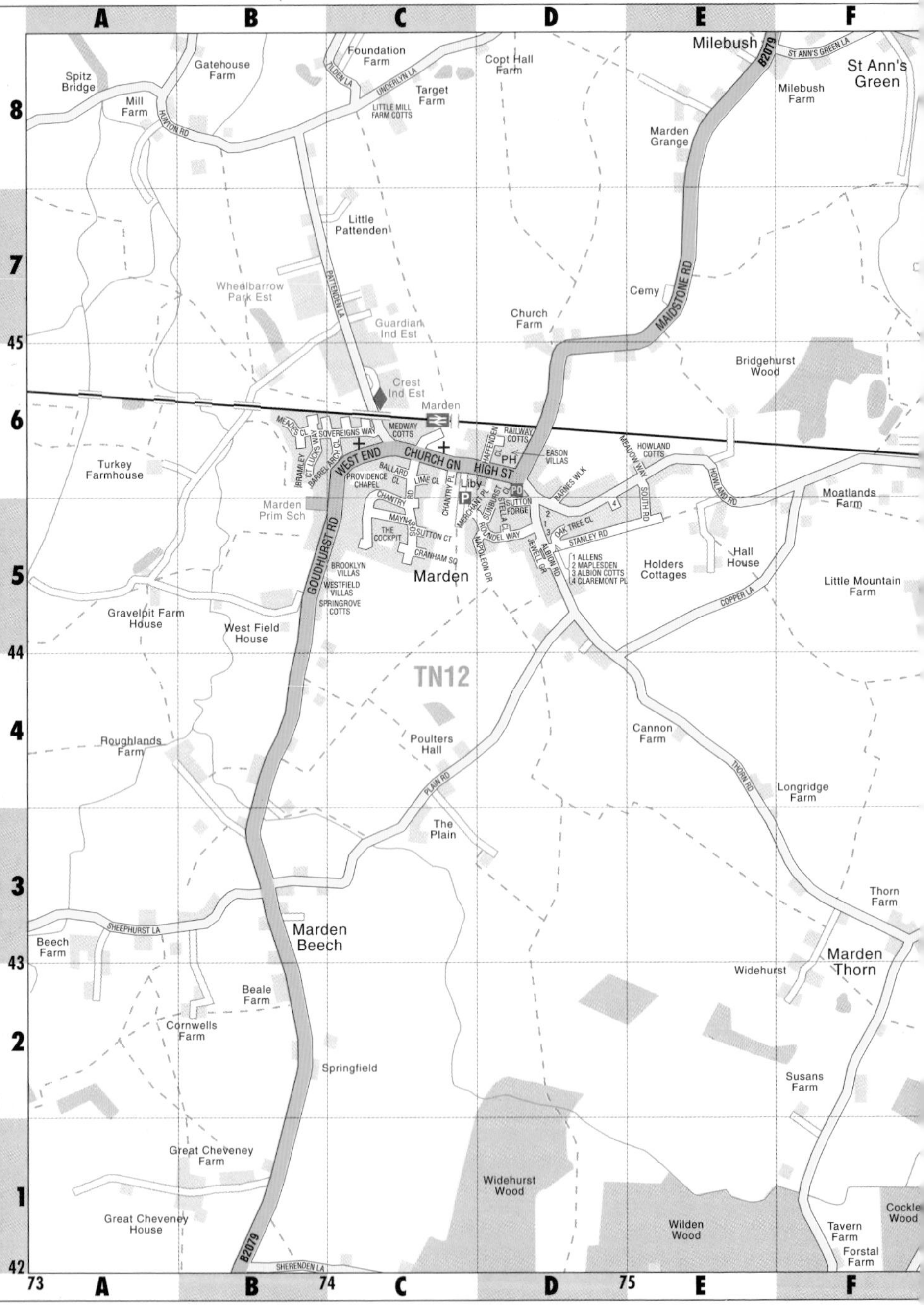

	A	B	C	D	E	F

Milebush
St Ann's Green
St Ann's Green La

8
Spitz Bridge
Mill Farm
Gatehouse Farm
Foundation Farm
Copt Hall Farm
Target Farm
LITTLE MILL FARM COTTS
Milebush Farm

Marden Grange

7
Little Pattenden
Whealbarrow Park Est

Marden Grange

Cemy

45
Guardiark Ind Est
Church Farm
Bridgehurst Wood

6
Crest Ind Est
Marden
Medway Cotts
Railway Cotts
Eason Villas

Turkey Farmhouse
SOVEREIGNS WAY
WEST END
CHURCH GN
HIGH ST
PH
Howland Cotts
Moatlands Farm

PROVIDENCE CHAPEL
Liby
P
SUTTON FORGE
PO
Holders Cottages
Hall House
Little Mountain Farm

5
Marden Prim Sch
THE COCKPIT
MAYM
CRANHAM SQ
Marden
1 ALLENS
2 MAPLESDEN
3 ALBION COTTS
4 CLAREMONT PL

GOUDHURST RD
BROOKLYN VILLAS
WESTFIELD VILLAS
SPRINGROVE COTTS
OAK TREE CL
STANLEY RD
COPPER LA

44
Gravelpit Farm House
West Field House

4
Roughlands Farm
Poulters Hall
Cannon Farm
Longridge Farm

TN12

PLAIN RD
THORN RD

3
The Plain
Thorn Farm

SHEEPHURST LA
Beech Farm

Marden Beech
Widehurst
Marden Thorn

43

2
Cornwells Farm
Beale Farm
Springfield
Susans Farm

1
Great Cheveney Farm
Widehurst Wood
Wilden Wood
Tavern Farm
Cockley Wood

Great Cheveney House
Forstal Farm

42
B2079
SHERENDEN LA

73	A	B	74	C	D	75	E	F

147
164

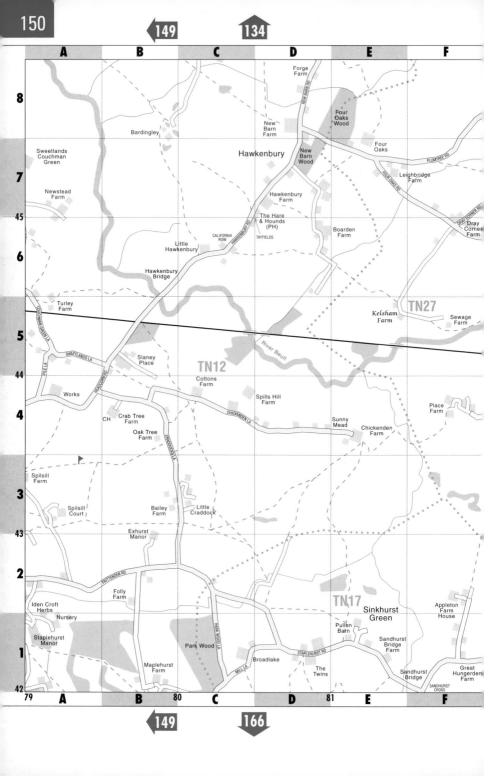

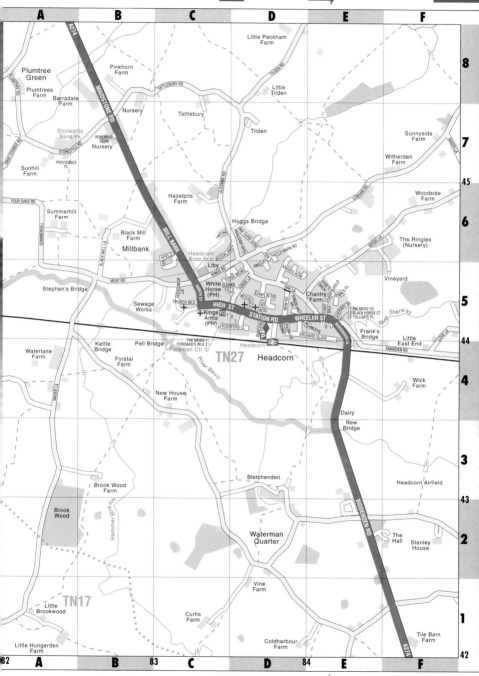

167   152

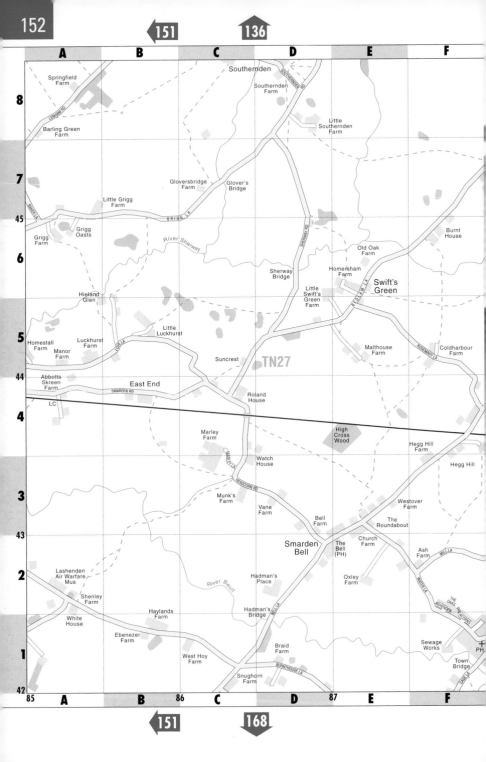

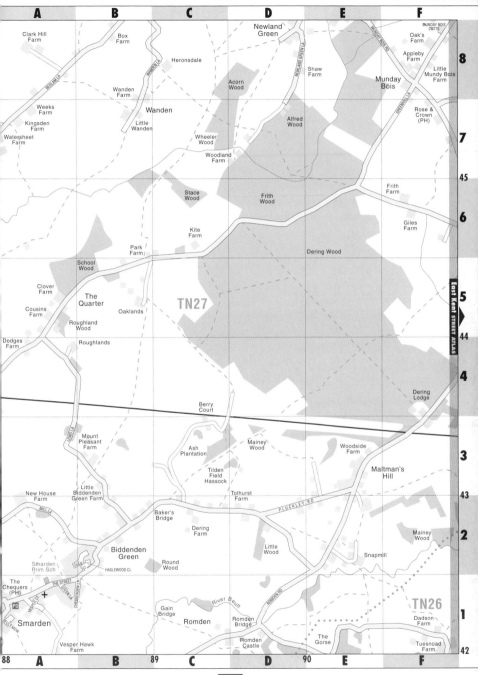

A	B	C	D	E	F

8

Clark Hill Farm

Box Farm

Heronsdale

Newland Green

Oak's Farm

Appleby Farm

Little Mundy Bois Farm

Wanden Farm

Acorn Wood

Shaw Farm

Munday Bois

7

Weeks Farm

Little Wanden

Wanden

Alfred Wood

Rose & Crown (PH)

45

Kingsden Farm

Watersheet Farm

Wheeler Wood

Woodland Farm

Frith Farm

6

Stace Wood

Frith Wood

Giles Farm

Kite Farm

Dering Wood

Park Farm

School Wood

5

Clover Farm

The Quarter

Oaklands

TN27

East Kent STREET ATLAS

Cousins Farm

Roughland Wood

44

Dodges Farm

Roughlands

4

Berry Court

Dering Lodge

Mount Pleasant Farm

Mainey Wood

Woodside Farm

3

Ash Plantation

Maltman's Hill

Little Biddenden Green Farm

Tilden Field Hassock

43

New House Farm

Tolhurst Farm

FLUCKLEY RD

Baker's Bridge

Mainey Wood

2

Dering Farm

Biddenden Green

Round Wood

Little Wood

Snapmill

Smarden Prim Sch

HASLEWOOD CL

1

The Chequers (PH)

Gain Bridge

River Beult

Romden

Romden Bridge

ROMDEN RD

TN26

Dadson Farm

PO

Smarden

The Gorse

Tuesnoad Farm

Vesper Hawk Farm

Romden Castle

42

88	A	B	89	C	D	90	E	F

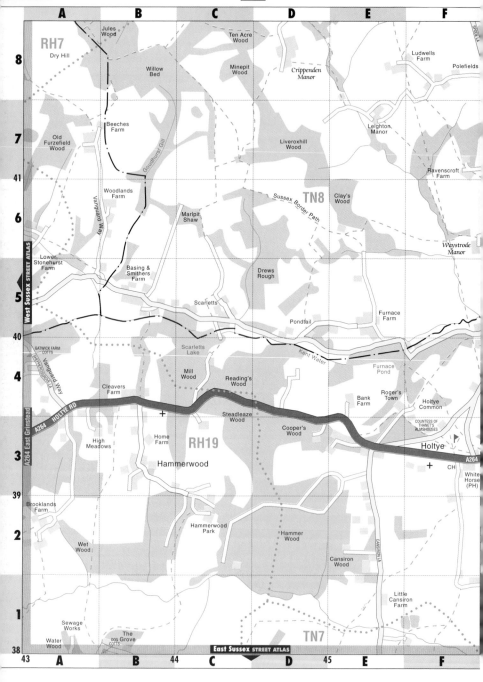

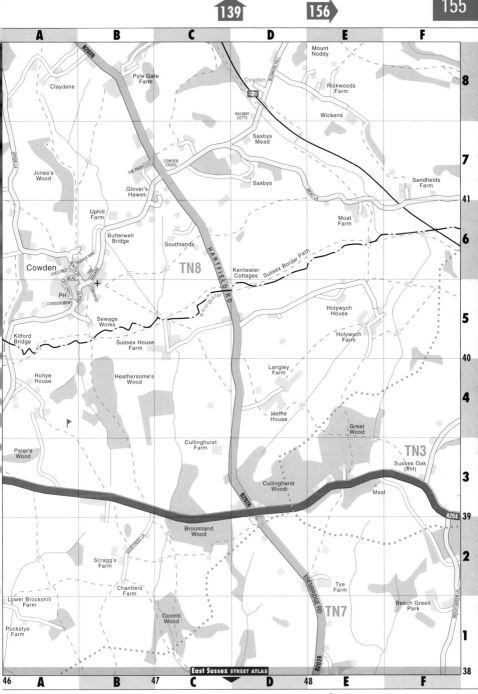

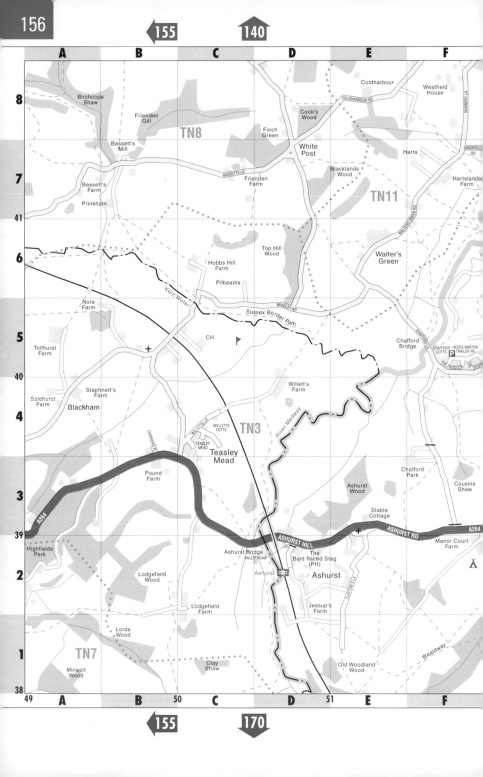

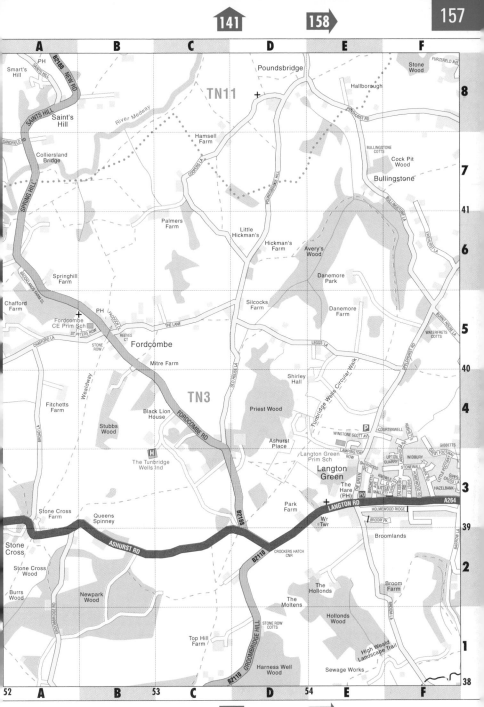

8

Smart's Hill
PH
B2188 NEW RD
Stone Wood
FURZEFIELD AVE
Poundsbridge
TN11
Hallborough
PENSHURST RD

SAINT'S HILL
Saint's Hill
River Medway
Hamsell Farm
Bullingstone COTTS
Cock Pit Wood

7

41

SANDFIELD RD
Colliersland Bridge
SPRING HILL
Bullingstone
BULLINGSTONE LA

Palmers Farm
Little Hickman's
Hickman's Farm
Avery's Wood

6

BROOKLANDS FARM LA
Springhill Farm
POUNDSBRIDGE HILL
Danemore Park
BURNT HOUSE LA

Chafford Farm
PH
PADDOCK
Silcocks Farm
Danemore Farm
ENGLISH LA
WATERFRETS COTTS

Fordcombe CE Prim Sch
ST PETERS ROW
THE LANE
LEGGS LA
PIPELHURST RD

5

CHAFFORD LA
STONE ROW
REEVES CT
Fordcombe
Tunbridge Wells Circular Walk

WEALDWAY
Mitre Farm
TN3
OLD HOUSE LA
Shirley Hall

40

Fitchetts Farm
BROOK LA
Stubbs Wood
Black Lion House
FORDCOMBE RD
Priest Wood

4

Ashurst Place
Langton Green Prim Sch
WINSTONE SCOTT AV
COURTENWELL
P
GIBBETTS
GREAT FOOTWAY

The Tunbridge Wells Ind
H
LAMPINGTON ROW
UPTON QUARRY
WIDBURY
STONE WALL
HAZELBANK

Stone Cross Farm
Queens Spinney
Park Farm
Langton Green
The Hare (PH)
THE GREEN
A264

3

Stone Cross
ASHURST RD
B2188
LANGTON RD
HOLMEWOOD RIDGE
BROOM PK
BARROW LA

39

Stone Cross Wood
B2110
CROCKERS HATCH CNR
Broomlands

2

Burrs Wood
Newpark Wood
The Hollands
Broom Farm

GROOMBRIDGE HILL
Top Hill Farm
STONE ROW COTTS
The Moltens
Hollonds Wood

1

B2110
Harness Well Wood
Sewage Works
High Weald Landscape Trail

38

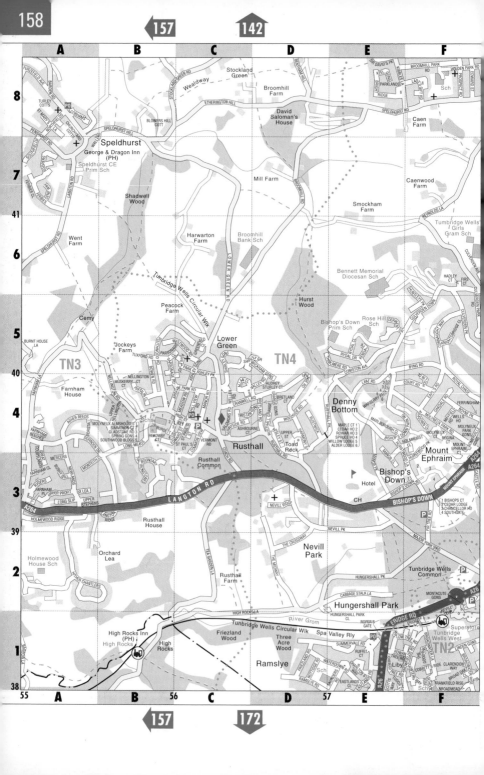

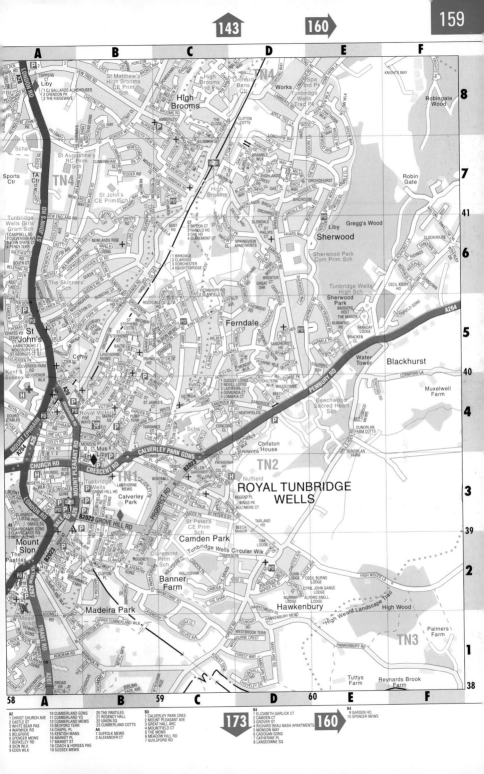

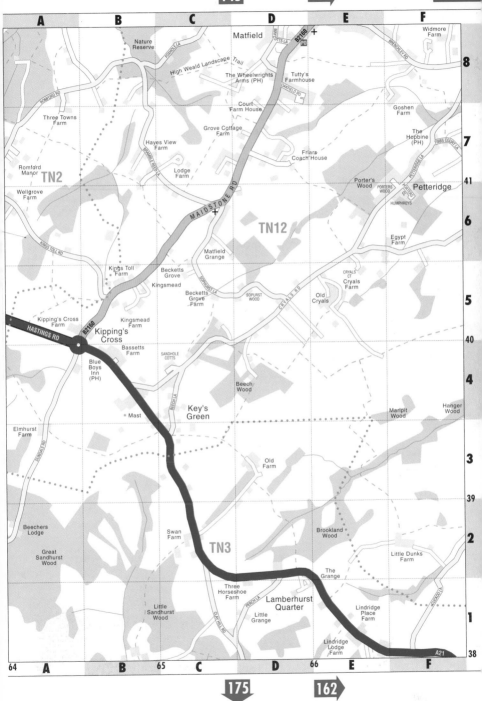

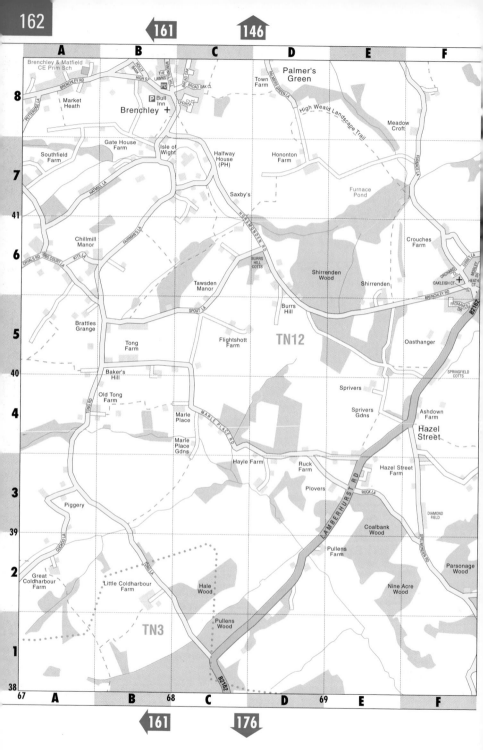

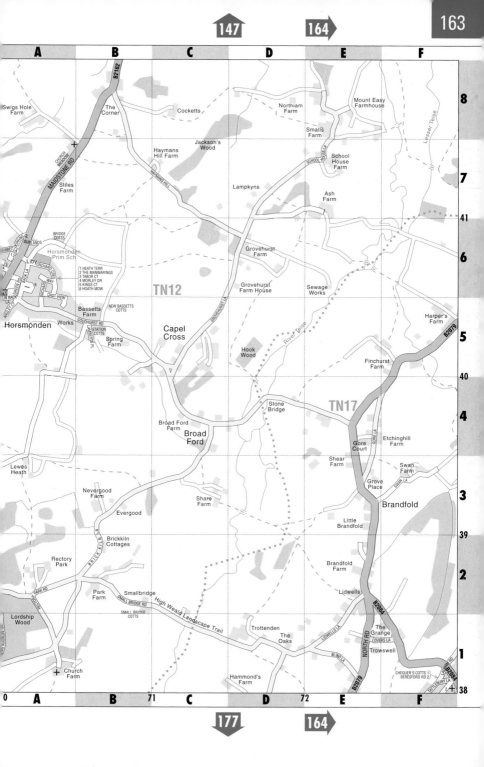

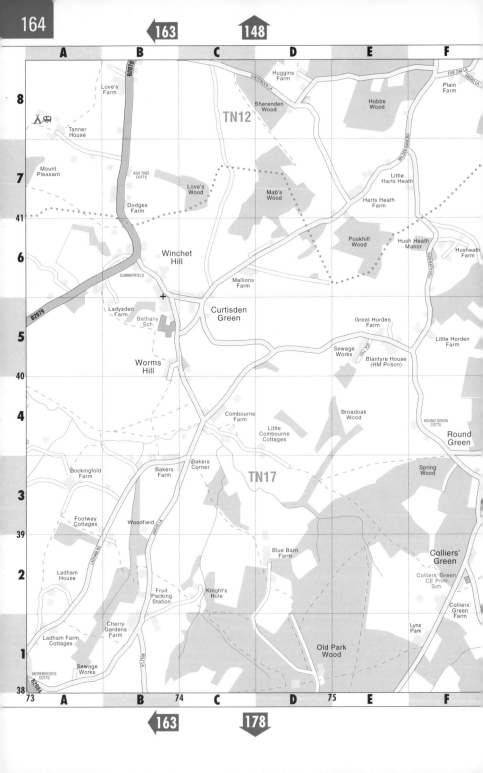

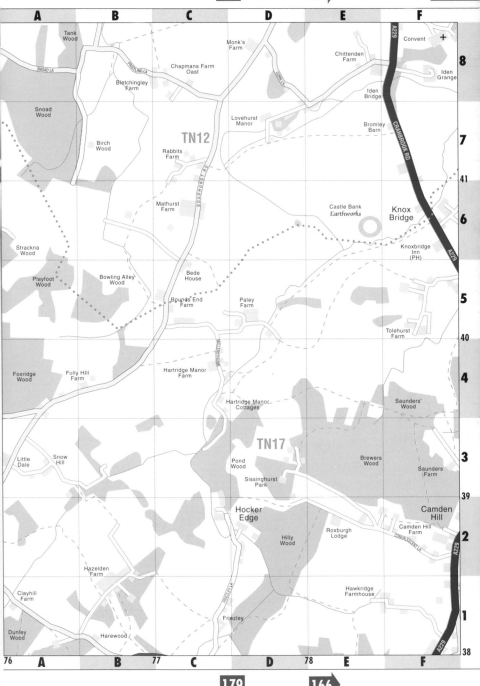

165
150

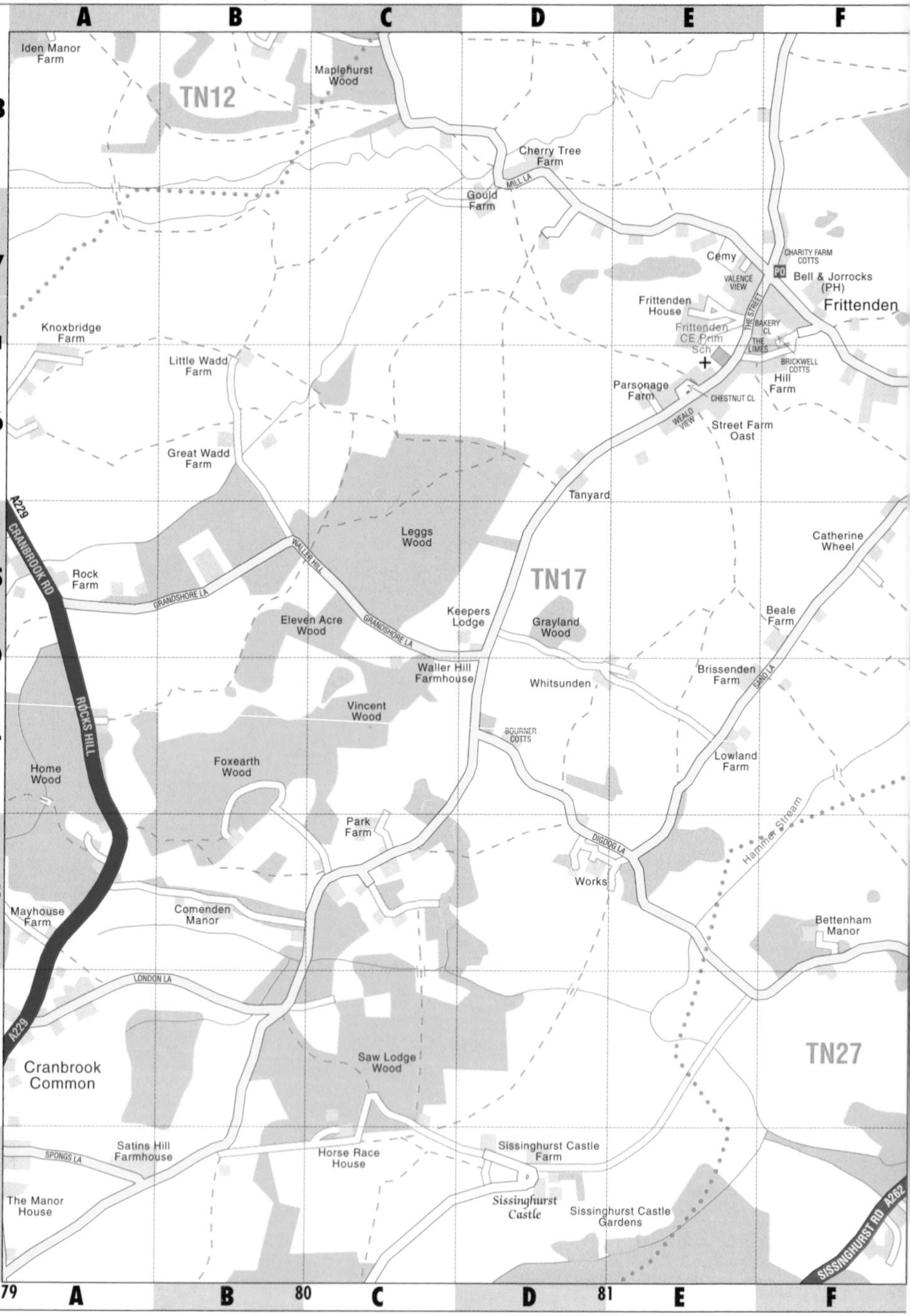

A **B** **C** **D** **E** **F**

Iden Manor Farm

TN12

Maplehurst Wood

8

Cherry Tree Farm

MILL LA

Gould Farm

Cemy

CHARITY FARM COTTS

7

VALENCE VIEW

Bell & Jorrocks (PH)

PO

Frittenden

Frittenden House

Knoxbridge Farm

BAKERY CL

Frittenden CE Prim Sch

THE LIMES

BRICKWELL COTTS

41

Little Wadd Farm

Hill Farm

Parsonage Farm

CHESTNUT CL

WEALD VIEW

6

Great Wadd Farm

Street Farm Oast

Tanyard

WALLER HILL

Rock Farm

A229

CRANBROOK RD

Leggs Wood

TN17

Catherine Wheel

5

GRANDSHORE LA

GRANDSHORE LA

Eleven Acre Wood

Keepers Lodge

Grayland Wood

Beale Farm

40

Waller Hill Farmhouse

Whitsunden

Brissenden Farm

LANE LA

Vincent Wood

4

RICKS HILL

Home Wood

BOURNER COTTS

Lowland Farm

Foxearth Wood

Park Farm

DIGDOG LA

Bettenham Manor

3

Mayhouse Farm

Comenden Manor

Works

Hammer Stream

39

LONDON LA

A229

2

Cranbrook Common

Saw Lodge Wood

TN27

Satins Hill Farmhouse

SPONGS LA

Horse Race House

Sissinghurst Castle Farm

1

The Manor House

Sissinghurst Castle

Sissinghurst Castle Gardens

SISSINGHURST RD A262

38

79   **A**   **B**   80   **C**   **D**   81   **E**   **F**

165
180

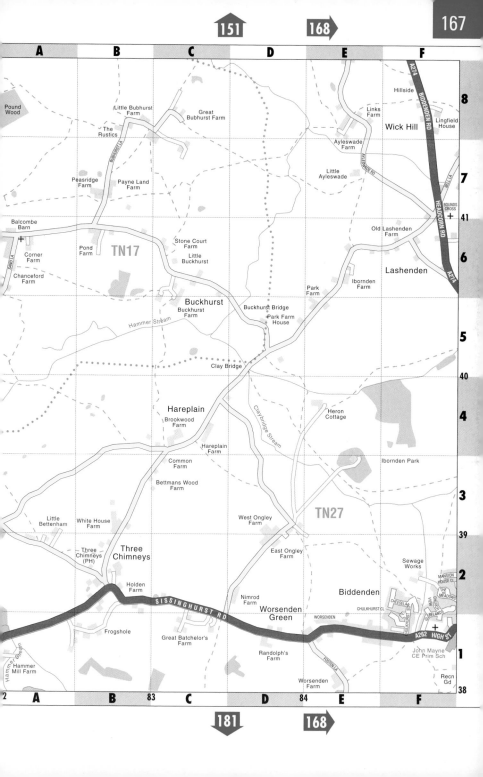

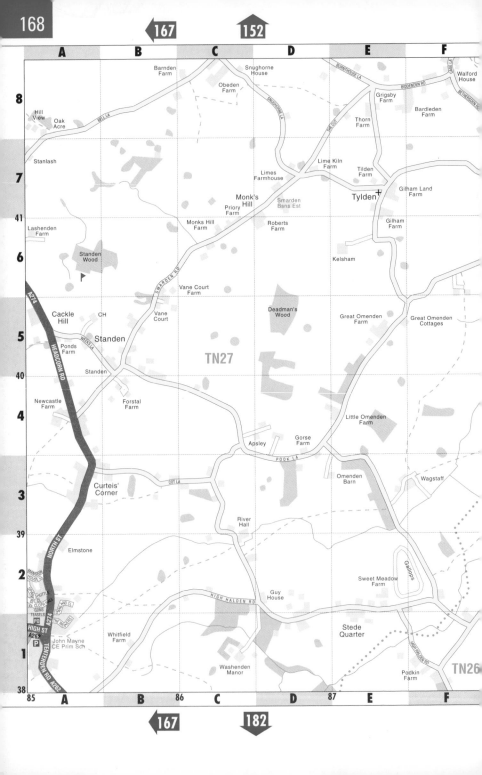

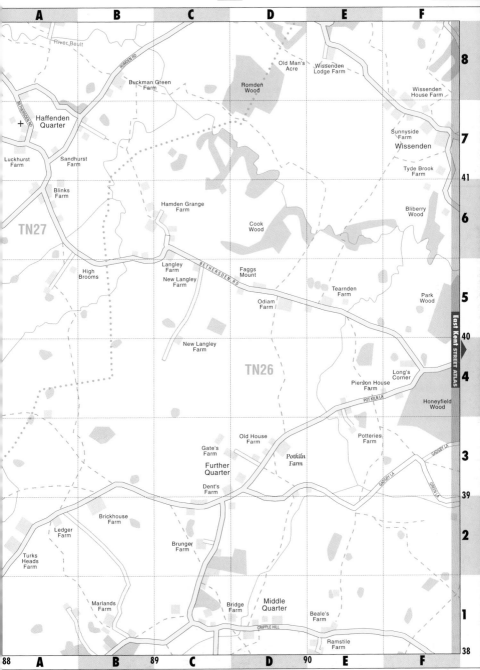

River Beult

BOWDEN RD

Buckman Green Farm

Old Man's Acre

Wissenden Lodge Farm

Romden Wood

Wissenden House Farm

Haffenden Quarter

METHERSDEN RD

Luckhurst Farm

Sandhurst Farm

Sunnyside Farm

Wissenden

Blinks Farm

Tyde Brook Farm

TN27

Hamden Grange Farm

Cook Wood

Bliberry Wood

High Brooms

Langley Farm

BETHERSDEN RD

New Langley Farm

Faggs Mount

Tearnden Farm

Park Wood

Odiam Farm

New Langley Farm

TN26

Long's Corner

Pierson House Farm

Honeyfield Wood

POT KILN LA

Old House Farm

Potteries Farm

Gate's Farm

Potkiln Farm

Further Quarter

GADSBY LA

GREEN LA

Dent's Farm

Brickhouse Farm

Ledger Farm

Brunger Farm

Turks Heads Farm

Marlands Farm

Bridge Farm

Middle Quarter

Beale's Farm

CRIPPLE HILL

Ramstile Farm

East Kent STREET ATLAS

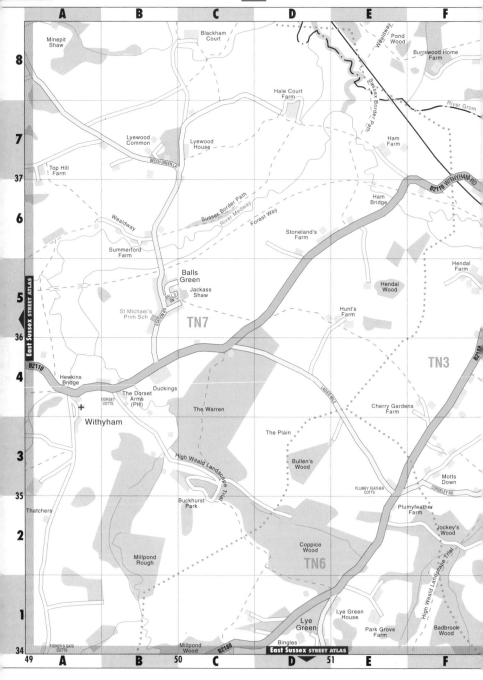

Minepit Shaw

Blackham Court

Pond Wood

Burrswood Home Farm

8

Hale Court Farm

River Grom

7

Lyewood Common

Lyewood House

Ham Farm

Wealdway

Sussex Border Path

BEECH GREEN LA

B2110 WITHYHAM RD

37

Top Hill Farm

Sussex Border Path

Ham Bridge

6

Wealdway

River Medway

Forest Way

Stoneland's Farm

Summerford Farm

Hendal Farm

Balls Green

Jackass Shaw

Hendal Wood

5

St Michael's Prim Sch

BALL'S GN

SHEP'S RD

Hunt's Farm

TN7

TN3

36

B2110

Hewkins Bridge

Duckings

LADIES MILE

B2188

4

Withyham

DORSET COTTS

The Dorset Arms (PH)

The Warren

Cherry Gardens Farm

The Plain

3

High Weald Landscape Trail

Bullen's Wood

Motts Down

CORSELEY RD

35

Thatchers

Buckhurst Park

PLUMEY FEATHER COTTS

Plumyfeather Farm

Jockey's Wood

2

Millpond Rough

Coppice Wood

TN6

High Weald Landscape Trail

1

Lye Green House

Badbrook Wood

Lye Green

Park Grove Farm

Millpond Wood

B2188

Bingles

34

FISHER'S GATE COTTS

49

50

51

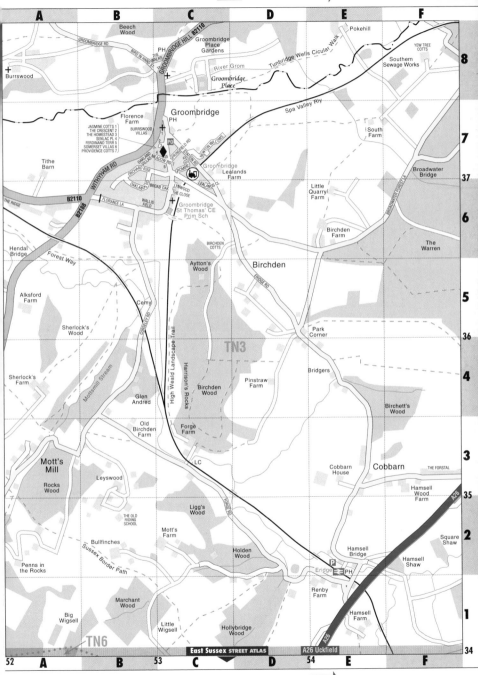

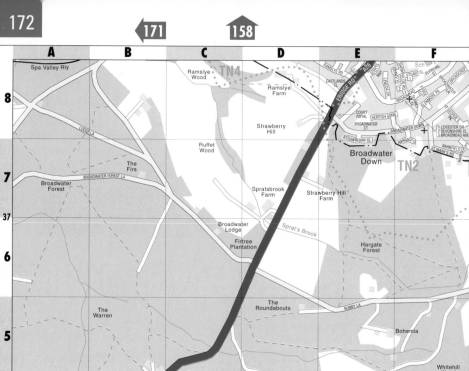

Grid labels (top and bottom)

A B C D E F

Row labels (left side)

8
7
37
6
5
36
4
3
35
2
1
34

Place names

Spa Valley Rly

Ramslye Wood
Ramslye Farm

Eastlands Cl

Court Royal
Broadwater Ct

Strawberry Hill

Broadwater Down

TN2

Lodge La

Ruffet Wood

The Firs

Broadwater Forest La

Broadwater Forest

Sprats brook Farm

Strawberry Hill Farm

Sprat's Brook

Broadwater Lodge

Firtree Plantation

Hargate Forest

The Warren

The Roundabouts

Bunny La

Bohemia

Whitehill Wood

TN3

Eridge Rocks

The Nevill Crest & Gun (PH)

Warren Farm

Warren Farm La

Eridge Park

Eridge Park

Eridge Green

Crown House

Mill Wood

Keepers Cottages

A26

Steel Bridge

High Weald Landscape Trail

Steel Bridge Farm

Forge Wood

Eridge Old Park

Bushy Wood

Great Robbins Shaw

Bushy Shaw

55   56   57

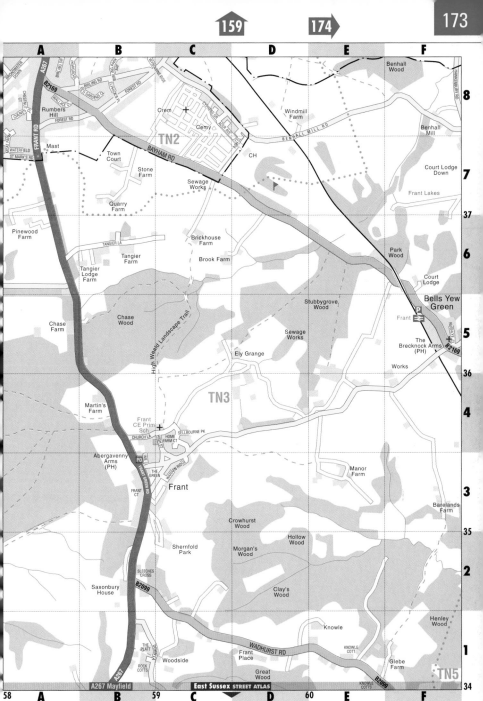

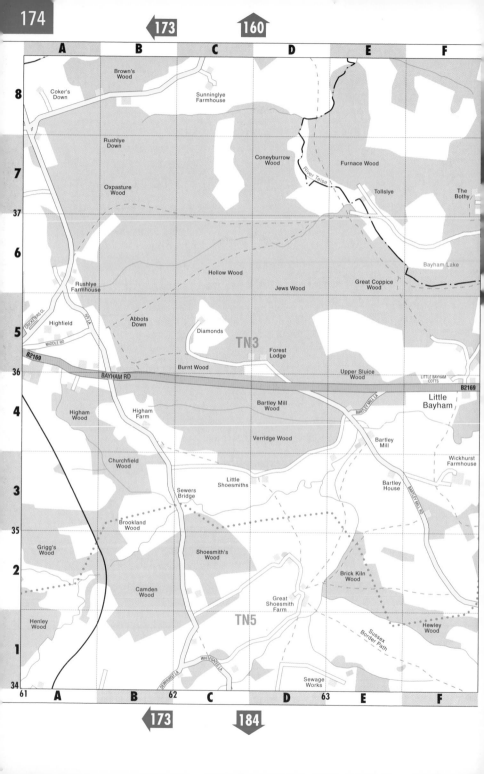

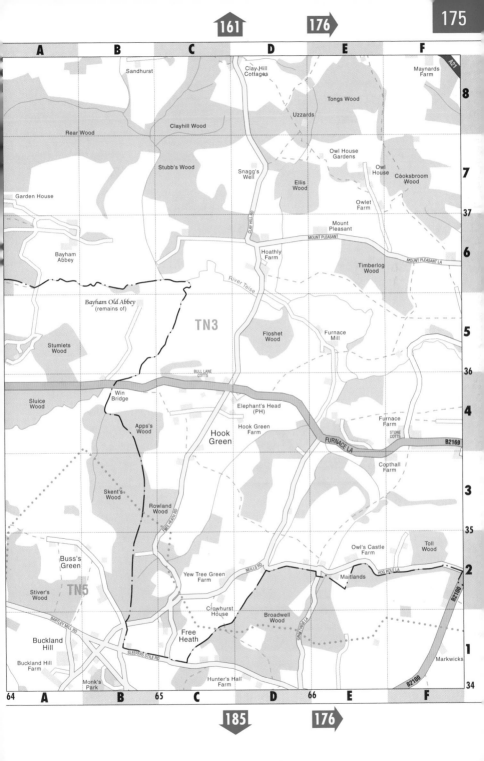

A B C D E F

A21

8

Sandhurst

Clay Hill
Cottages

Maynards
Farm

Tongs Wood

Uzzards

Rear Wood

Clayhill Wood

7

Stubb's Wood

Snagg's
Well

Owl House
Gardens

Owl
House

Cooksbroom
Wood

Ellis
Wood

Owlet
Farm

37

Garden House

CLAY HILL RD

Mount
Pleasant

Bayham
Abbey

Hoathly
Farm

MOUNT PLEASANT

6

MOUNT PLEASANT LA

Timberlog
Wood

River Teise

Bayham Old Abbey
(remains of)

TN3

5

Floshet
Wood

Furnace
Mill

Stumlets
Wood

BULL LANE
COTTS

36

Sluice
Wood

Win
Bridge

Elephant's Head
(PH)

Furnace
Farm

4

Apps's
Wood

Hook Green
Farm

STONE
COTTS

Hook
Green

FURNACE LA

B2169

Copthall
Farm

Skent's
Wood

3

Rowland
Wood

35

NEILS HEATH RD

Buss's
Green

Owl's Castle
Farm

Toll
Wood

TN5

Stiver's
Wood

NEILS RD

Yew Tree Green
Farm

Maitlands

HOG ROLE LA

2

B2100

BARTLEY MILL RD

Crowhurst
House

Broadwell
Wood

SNAPE THORN LA

Buckland
Hill

Free
Heath

1

Buckland Hill
Farm

SLEEPERS STILE RD

B2100

Markwicks

Monk's
Park

Hunter's Hall
Farm

34

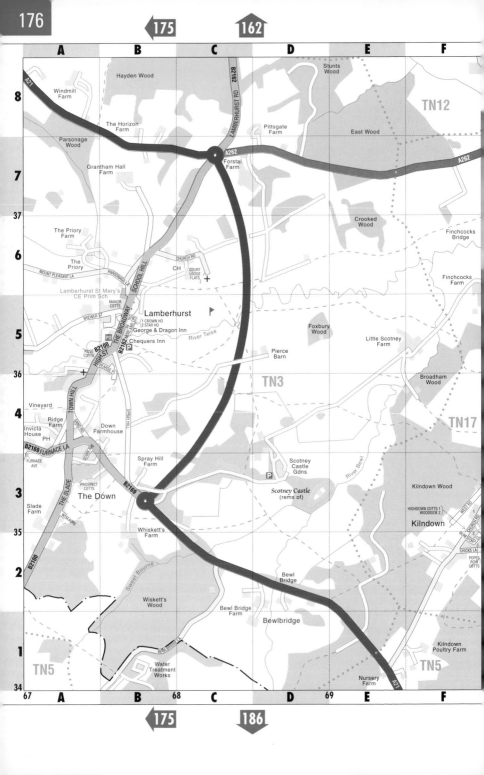

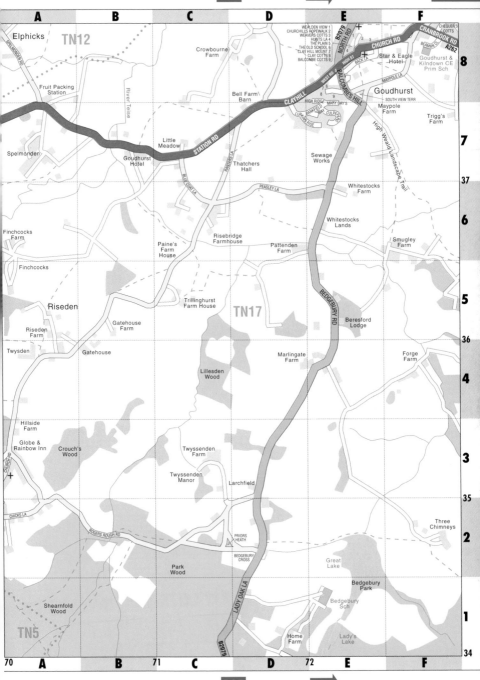

Elphicks

TN12

Fruit Packing Station

River Teise

Crowbourne Farm

Bell Farm Barn

WEALDEN VIEW 1
CHURCHILES ROPEWALK 2
WEAVERS COTTS 3
HINTS LA 4
THE PLAIN 5
THE OLD SCHOOL 6
CLAY HILL MOUNT 7
CLAY COTTS 8
BALCOMBE COTTS 9

Star & Eagle Hotel

Goudhurst & Kilndown CE Prim Sch

CHEQUERS COTTS

CRANBROOK RD

A262

BEAMS

NORTH RD

CHURCH RD

B2079

WEST RD

HIGH ST

BACK LA

BALCOMBES HILL

CLAYHILL

Goudhurst

Spelmonden

Little Meadow

STATION RD

Goudhurst Hotel

PANTERS LA

Thatchers Hall

BLUE COAT LA

HIGH RIDGE
MARY DAY'S
MABLETT'S WAY
CULPEPERS
LILLYS RISE

SOUTH VIEW TERR

Maypole Farm

Trigg's Farm

Sewage Works

PEASLEY LA

Whitestocks Farm

High Weald Landscape Trail

37

7

Finchcocks Farm

Finchcocks

Paine's Farm House

Risebridge Farmhouse

Pattenden Farm

Whitestocks Lands

Smugley Farm

6

Riseden

TN17

Trillinghurst Farm House

BEDGEBURY RD

Beresford Lodge

5

Riseden Farm

Gatehouse Farm

Twysden

Gatehouse

Lillesden Wood

Marlingate Farm

Forge Farm

36

4

Hillside Farm

Globe & Rainbow Inn

ORCHARD RD

Crouch's Wood

Twyssenden Farm

Twyssenden Manor

Larchfield

35

3

CHICKS LA

ROGERS ROUGH RD

Park Wood

PRIORS HEATH

BEDGEBURY CROSS

Great Lake

Three Chimneys

2

Shearnfold Wood

TN5

LADY OAK LA

B2079

Home Farm

Bedgebury Park

Bedgebury Sch

Lady's Lake

Bedgebury Park

1

70   A   B   71   C   D   72   E   F   34

8

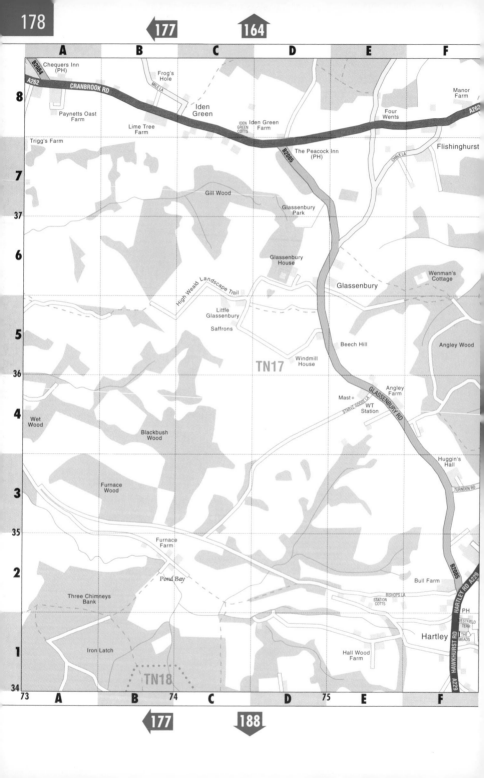

165
180

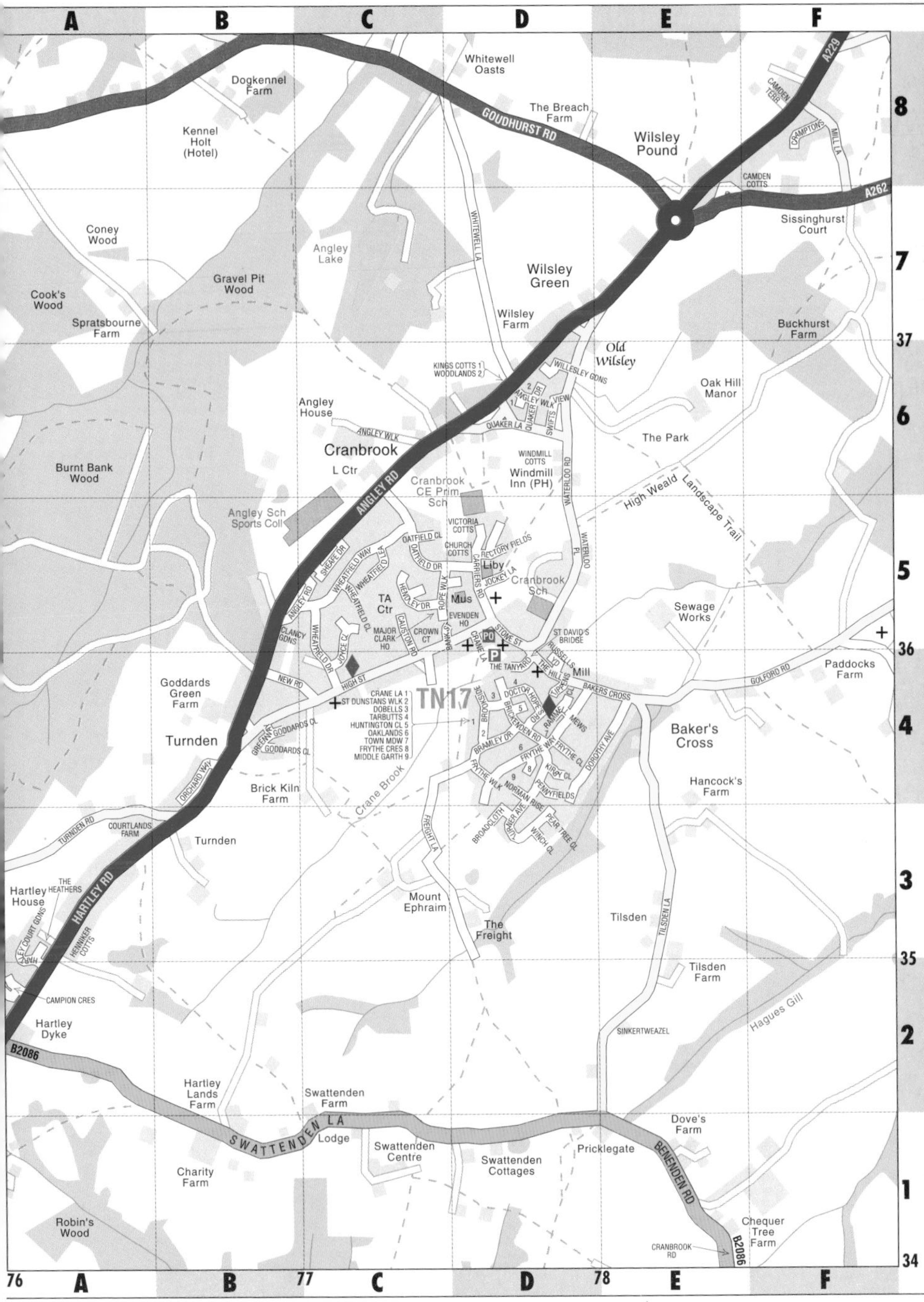

189
180

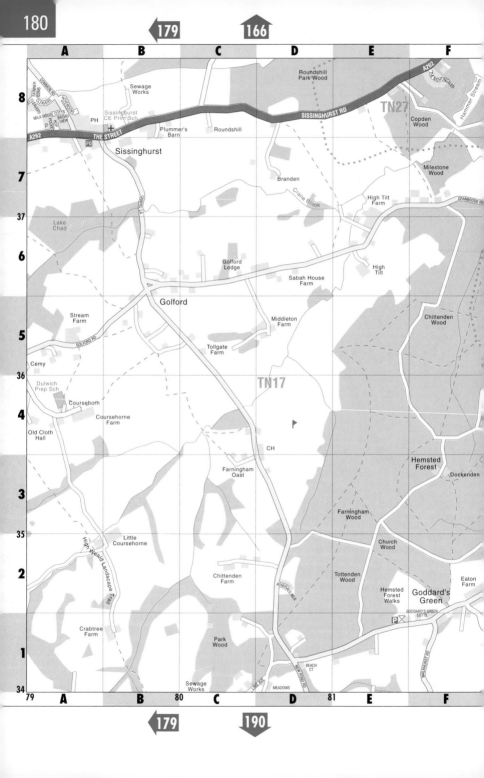

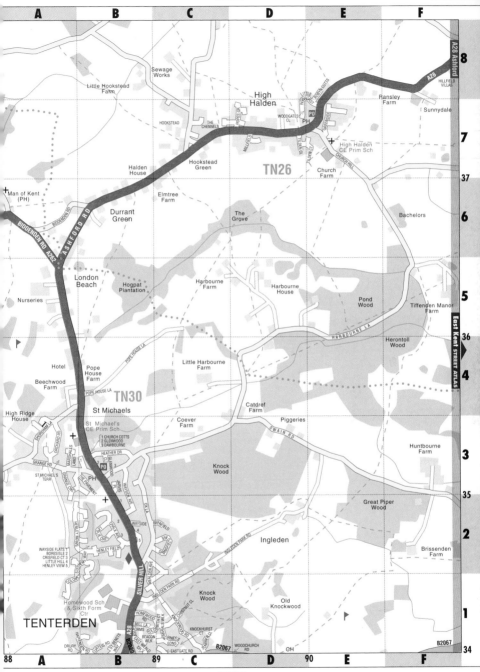

A B C D E F

A28 Ashford

8

HILLFIELD VILLAS

Little Hookstead Farm

Sewage Works

High Halden

Ransley Farm

Sunnydale

7

Hookstead

THE CHENNELS

WOODGATES CL

PH PO

High Halden CE Prim Sch

37

Halden House

Hookstead Green

TN26

Church Farm

Man of Kent (PH)

Elmtree Farm

Durrant Green

The Grove

Bachelors

6

BIDDENDEN RD A262

BIDDENDEN RD

ASHFORD RD

London Beach

Hogpat Plantation

Harbourne Farm

Harbourne House

Pond Wood

Tiffenden Manor Farm

5

Nurseries

HARBOURNE LA

Herontoll Wood

36

East Kent STREET ATLAS

POPE HOUSE LA

Little Harbourne Farm

Hotel

Pope House Farm

TN30

Beechwood Farm

POPE HOUSE LA

St Michaels

Catdref Farm

Piggeries

Huntbourne Farm

4

High Ridge House

St Michael's CE Prim Sch

1 CHURCH COTTS
2 GLENWOOD
3 DAWBOURNE

Coever Farm

SWAIN RD

HEATHER DR

St Michaels Terr

GRANGE RD

PH

Knock Wood

Great Piper Wood

3

35

WAYSIDE

SILVER HILL

INGLEDEN PARK RD

Ingleden

Brissenden Farm

2

WAYSIDE FLATS 1
BORESISLE 2
CRISFIELD CT 3
LITTLE HILL 4
HENLEY VIEW 5

HENLEY FIELDS

Homewood Sch & Sixth Form Ctr

SILVER HILL

INGLEDEN PARK RD

Knock Wood

Old Knockwood

1

TENTERDEN

A28

B2067

DRURY RD

KNOCKHURST CT

WOODCHURCH RD

CH

B2067

EASTGATE RD

B2067

34

A B C D E F

88 89 90

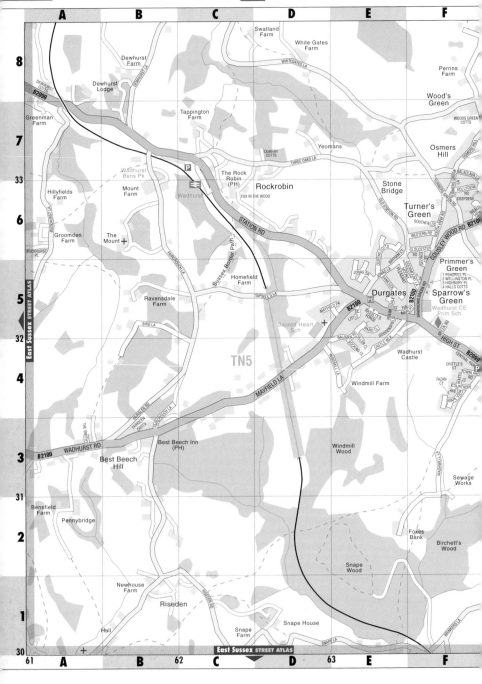

A   B   C   D   E   F

Newbury's

NEWBURY COTTS

NEWBURY LA

WINDMILL LA

The Colleens

B2100

Ladymeads Farm

BEWLBRIDGE LA

8

Lower Cousley Wood

Gate House Farm

MONK'S LA

HILLSIDE COTTS

COUSLEY WOOD RD

PH

Cousley Wood

7

Pell Green

Great Butts

BUTTS LA

Little Butts Farm

33

BALACLAVA LA

1 2
3
4 5

Great Pell Oast

Bewl Water

Bryant's Farm

6

1 FAIR VIEW COTTS
2 DEEPDENE
3 THE LEAS
4 PELL CL
5 BIRCH KILN COTTS

Sussex Border Path

Newbarn

Pell Bridge

Wishdown

5

Vicarage Green

BLACKSMITHS LA

Little Pell Farm

TN5

Southfields

32

CHURCH ST

HIGH ST

Foxhole

Little Whiligh

Chesson's Farm

4

Liby
P

1 THE SQUARE
2 KINGSLEY CT

Wadhurst

FOXHOLE LA

Long Wood

WARD'S LA

Uplands Com Tech Coll

LOWER HIGH ST

PEAR TREE LA

GREAT CROSS RD

Whiligh

BIRCHETTS GREEN LA

Birchett's Green

Birchett's Green Farm

3

Stone Cross

Moseham

31

BRINKERS LA

DARBY'S LA

Darby's Farm

Holbeam Wood

2

HIGH ST

Cattle Breeding Ctr

Wailand Manor

Upper Wallands Farm

STONECRUTS RD

Shover's Green

Normanswood

CHURCHSETTLE LA

Shover's Green House

Bugsey's Farm

B2099

Wallcrouch Farm

Wallcrouch

1

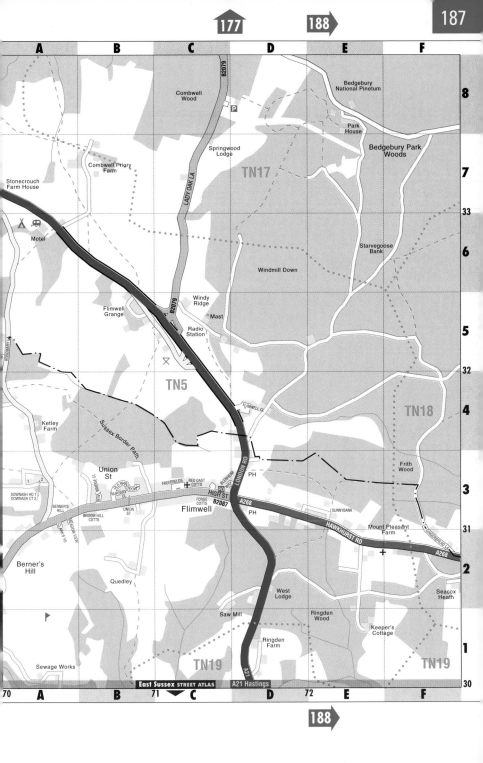

A2
1 HULSONS CT
2 BASDEN COTTS
3 MURTON-NEALE CL
4 CAMERONS
5 BARRETTS GREEN COTTS
6 LAVENDER SQ
7 DUNLOP CT
8 PARK COTTS
9 HAMMONDS

10 KENT HO
11 QUEENS CT
12 QUEEN'S MEWS
13 THOMAS DUNK ALMSHOUSES
14 THE COLONADE

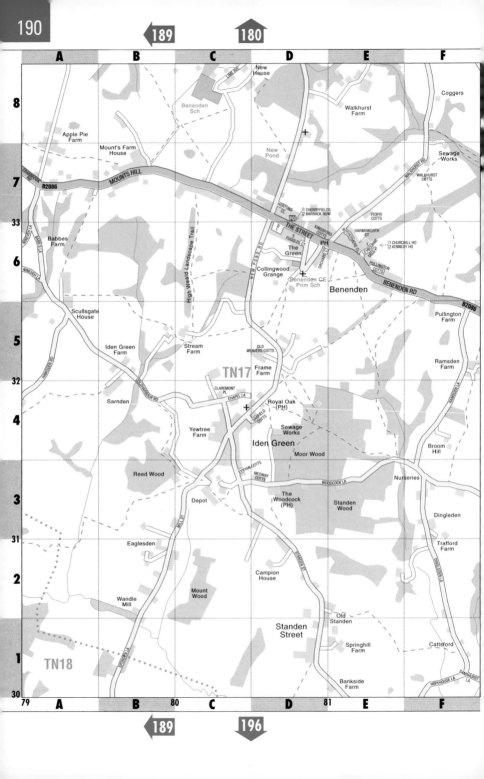

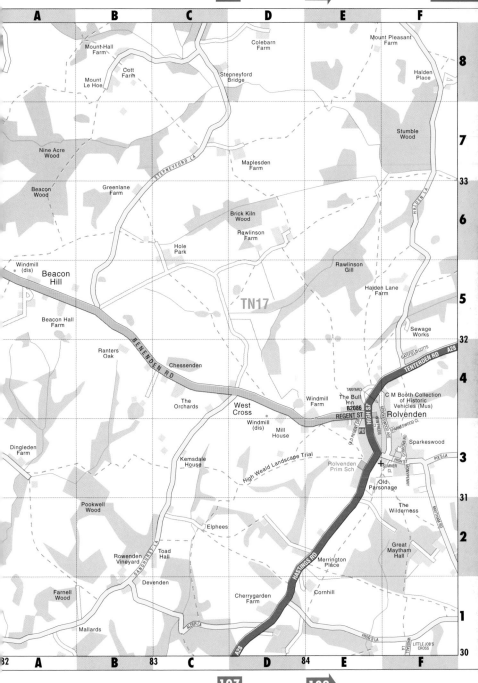

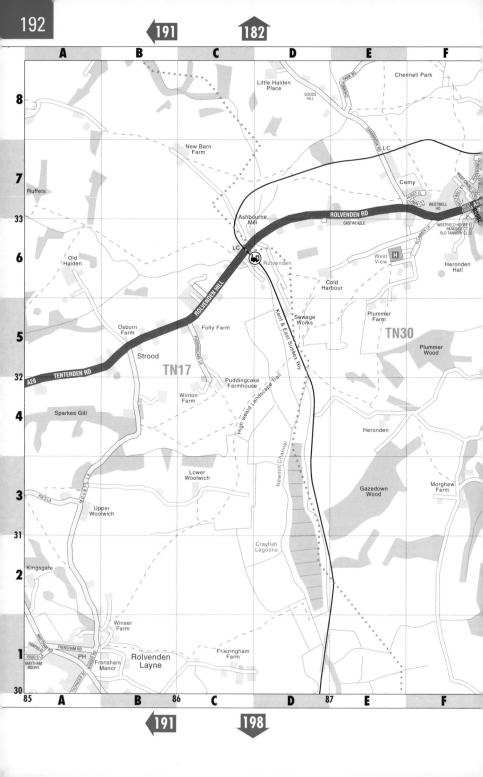

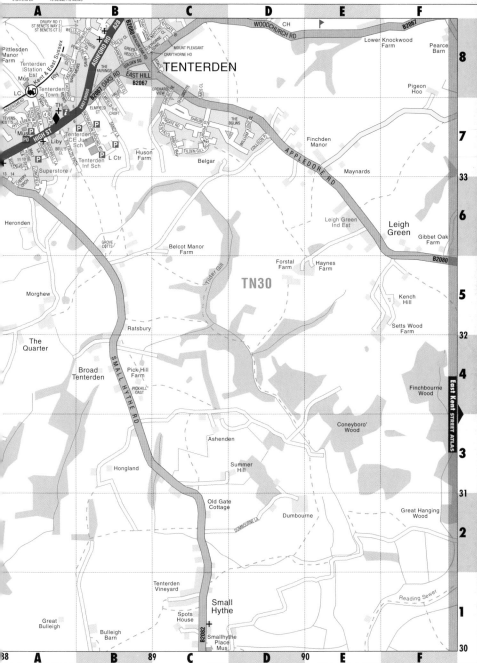

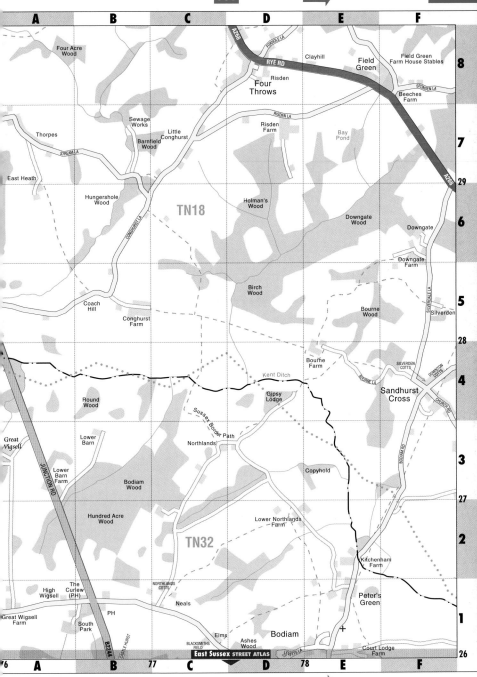

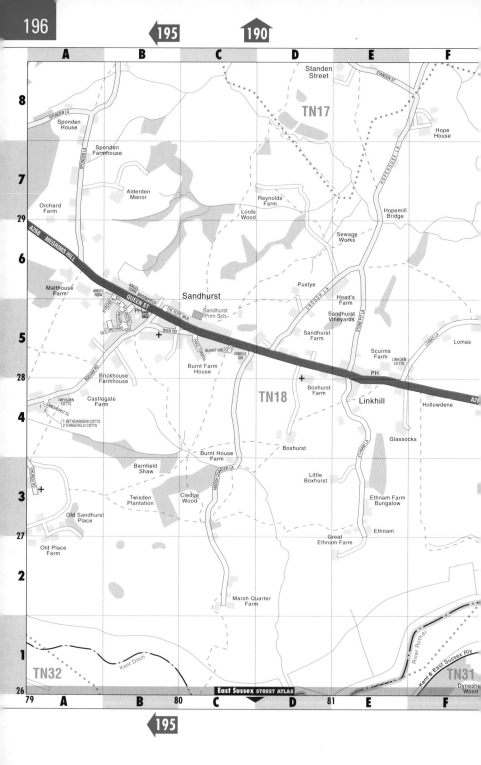

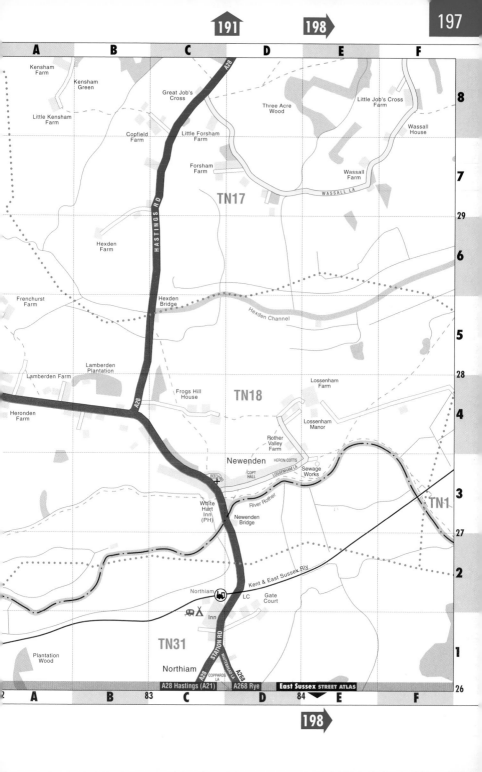

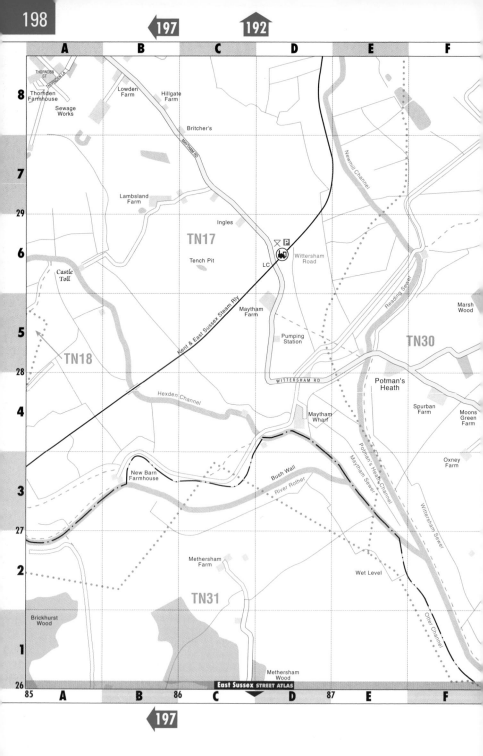

A   B   C   D   E   F

8

7

29

6

5

28

4

3

27

2

1

26

THORNDEN CT
THORNDEN LA
Thornden
Farmhouse
Sewage
Works

Lowden
Farm

Hillgate
Farm

Britcher's

MAYTHAM RD

Lambsland
Farm

Ingles

TN17

Tench Pit

LC

Wittersham
Road

P

Castle
Toll

Maytham
Farm

Kent & East Sussex Steam Rly

TN18

Pumping
Station

WITTERSHAM RD

Hexden Channel

Maytham
Wharf

Bush Wall

River Rother

New Barn
Farmhouse

Newmill Channel

Reading Sewer

Marsh
Wood

TN30

Potman's
Heath

Spurban
Farm

Moons
Green
Farm

Oxney
Farm

Potman's Heath Channel

Maytham Sewer

Wittersham Sewer

Methersham
Farm

Wet Level

TN31

Brickhurst
Wood

Methersham
Wood

Otter Channel

85   A   B   86   C   D   87   E   F

Index

Church Rd **6** Beckenham BR2......... **53** C6

Place name	May be abbreviated on the map
Location number	Present when a number indicates the place's position in a crowded area of mapping
Locality, town or village	Shown when more than one place has the same name
Postcode district	District for the indexed place
Page and grid square	Page number and grid reference for the standard mapping

Public and commercial buildings are highlighted in magenta.   **Places of interest** are highlighted in blue with a star★

Abbreviations used in the index

Acad	**Academy**	Comm	**Common**	Gd	**Ground**	L	**Leisure**	Prom	**Promenade**
App	**Approach**	Cott	**Cottage**	Gdn	**Garden**	La	**Lane**	Rd	**Road**
Arc	**Arcade**	Cres	**Crescent**	Gn	**Green**	Liby	**Library**	Recn	**Recreation**
Ave	**Avenue**	Cswy	**Causeway**	Gr	**Grove**	Mdw	**Meadow**	Ret	**Retail**
Bglw	**Bungalow**	Ct	**Court**	H	**Hall**	Meml	**Memorial**	Sh	**Shopping**
Bldg	**Building**	Ctr	**Centre**	Ho	**House**	Mkt	**Market**	Sq	**Square**
Bsns, Bus	**Business**	Ctry	**Country**	Hospl	**Hospital**	Mus	**Museum**	St	**Street**
Bvd	**Boulevard**	Cty	**County**	HQ	**Headquarters**	Orch	**Orchard**	Sta	**Station**
Cath	**Cathedral**	Dr	**Drive**	Hts	**Heights**	Pal	**Palace**	Terr	**Terrace**
Cir	**Circus**	Dro	**Drove**	Ind	**Industrial**	Par	**Parade**	TH	**Town Hall**
Cl	**Close**	Ed	**Education**	Inst	**Institute**	Pas	**Passage**	Univ	**University**
Cnr	**Corner**	Emb	**Embankment**	Int	**International**	Pk	**Park**	Wk, Wlk	**Walk**
Coll	**College**	Est	**Estate**	Intc	**Interchange**	Pl	**Place**	Wr	**Water**
Com	**Community**	Ex	**Exhibition**	Junc	**Junction**	Prec	**Precinct**	Yd	**Yard**

Index of localities, towns and villages

A

Abbey Wood 3 B3
Addington 80 C3
Aldon 80 B1
Allhallows 9 D1
Allhallows-on-Sea 9 D3
Allington 99 D8
Aperfield 72 F2
Ash 62 E5
Ashurst 118 B7
Ashurst 156 D2
Avery Hill 12 C1
Aylesford 82 E2

B

Badgers Mount 59 B1
Baker's Cross 179 E4
Balls Green 170 C5
Banner Farm 159 C2
Barden Park 126 F1
Barking 3 B8
Barming Heath 99 A3
Barnehurst 14 D4
Barnes Cray 15 B3
Barnes Street 129 A4
Basted 94 F4
Beacon Hill 191 A5
Beal's Green 189 A4
Bean 34 C5
Bearsted 101 B4
Beckton 2 A8
Bedmonton 103 E8
Bells Yew Green 173 F5
Beltring 130 A4
Belvedere 4 B2
Benenden 190 E6
Benover 131 A6
Berry's Green 73 B3
Bessels Green 91 D3
Best Beech Hill 184 B3
Betsham 34 F4
Bewlbridge 176 D1
Bexley 13 C3
Bexleyheath 13 F4
Bickley 42 F7
Bicknor 87 C2
Bidborough 142 D3
Biddenden 167 E2
Biggin Hill 72 E3
Birchden 171 D5
Birchett's Green ...185 F3
Birchwood Corner ...45 C8
Birling 81 C6

C

Cage Green 127 C4
Camden Hill 165 F2
Camden Park 159 C2
Canning Town 1 B8
Capel 144 F5
Capel Cross 163 C5
Capstone 68 E7
Castle Hill 146 E1
Chainhurst 132 A4
Chalk 37 A7

Bishop's Down 158 E3
Bitchet Green 93 D1
Blackfen 13 A1
Blackheath Park 11 A3
Blackhurst 159 F5
Bluewater 34 A8
Bodiam 195 D1
Bogden 133 C2
Borough Green 94 F8
Borstal 53 B2
Bough Beech 123 F2
Boughton Green ...116 B3
Boughton Malherbe ..137 A8
Boughton Monchelsea ..116 B3
Bow Arrow 16 B1
Bowmans 31 F8
Boxley 84 D2
Branbridges 130 A5
Brandfold 163 F3
Brasted 90 C3
Brasted Chart 106 B7
Breach 70 F8
Bredhurst 69 B1
Brenchley 162 B8
Broad Ford 163 C4
Broadstone 136 D4
Broad Street
   Hoo St Werburgh ...40 B5
Broad Street *Maidstone* ..92 A4
Broad Tenterden 193 B4
Broadwater Down ...172 E2
Bromley 42 B6
Bromley Common 42 E3
Brompton 54 A5
Brooklands 32 F7
Brook Street 143 A8
Broomfield 118 D5
Broom Hill 43 F2
Buckhurst 167 C5
Buck's Cross 58 F5
Bullingstone 157 F7
Burham 66 E1

Charcott 125 A3
Charlton 11 D8
Chart Hill 134 B8
Chart Sutton 117 B1
Chartway Street 118 C1
Chatham 53 E5
Chattenden 39 F4
Chelsfield 58 E5
Cherry Orchard 99 B4
Chesley 71 A3
Chestnut Street 71 E4
Chevening 90 F8
Chiddingstone 140 C7
Chiddingstone
   Causeway 124 F2
Chiddingstone Hoath ..140 A2
Chipstead 91 C5
Chislehurst 43 B7
Chislehurst West ...29 A2
Christian Fields 36 C4
Church Street 21 C1
Claygate 147 D6
Clement Street 32 D2
Cliffe 22 B5
Cliffe Woods 39 B7
Cobbarn 171 F3
Cobham 50 F6
Cockshot 188 F1
Cock Street 116 D2
Coldblow 31 D7
Coldharbour 109 F1
Cold Harbour 71 F7
Colliers' Green 164 F2
Collier Street 147 C8
Colt's Hill 145 B4
Congelow 130 F7
Cooling 22 F5
Cooling Street 22 D2
Cooper's Corner ...123 F8
Cousley Wood 185 C7
Cowden 155 A6
Cowden Pound 139 B2
Coxheath 116 A2
Cranbrook 179 C6
Cranbrook Common .166 A2
Crayford 14 D1
Creekmouth 2 F8
Crockenhill 45 D3
Crockham Hill 105 C2
Crockhurst Street ..144 C6
Crofton 57 D8
Cross-at-Hand 133 E1
Crossways 16 D3
Crouch 95 B4
Crowdleham 77 D2

Cudham 73 D4
Culverstone Green ..63 E2
Curteis' Corner 168 A3
Curtisden Green ...164 C5
Custom House 1 C7
Cuxton 52 B2
Cyprus 2 B6

D

Danaway 71 C3
Darenth 33 B4
Darland 68 E8
Dartford 15 E2
Deal Street 64 B5
Deans Bottom 87 C5
Deans Hill 87 D6
Dean Street 115 D7
Denny Bottom 158 E4
Denton 36 E8
Derry Downs 44 D3
Detling 85 B1
Devil's Den 134 B3
Ditton 82 C1
Downe 73 A8
Dryhill 91 B3
Dunk's Green 111 A6
Dunn Street 85 A8
Dunton Green 91 E8
Durgates 184 E5
Durrant Green 183 B6

E

East Barming 98 F1
East End *Benenden* ..181 C3
East End *Headcorn* ..152 B4
East Farleigh 115 B7
East Hill 61 B1
East Malling 98 A2
East Malling Heath ..97 E4
East Peckham 129 F6
East Street 80 E3
East Tilbury 20 C7
East Wickham 13 A7
Eastwood 136 C6
Eccles 82 F6
Edenbridge 122 D1
Egerton 137 F4
Egerton Forstal 137 D1
Elmstead 28 D2
Elmstone Hole 136 E8
Elphicks 177 A8
Eltham 11 E1
Eridge Green 172 B3

Erith 4
Eyhorne Street 102
Eynsford 60

F

Fairbourne Heath ..119
Fairseat 79
Falconwood 12
Farnborough 57
Farningham 46
Farthing Green 134
Farthing Street 56
Fawkham Green 62
Fenn Street 24
Ferndale 159
Field Green 195
Fig Street 108
Fishinghurst 178
Five Oak Green ...117
Five Wents 117
Fleet-Downs 33
Flimwell 187
Foots Cray 30
Force Green 89
Fordcombe 157
Forstal 83
Fosten Green 181
Four Elms 105
Four Throws 195
Four Wents 189
Foxendown 64
Frant 173
French Street 105
Frindsbury 53
Frittenden 154
Froghole 105
Further Quarter ..169

G

Gillingham 54
Gill's Green 188
Glassenbury 178
Goathurst Common ..107
Goddard's Green ...180
Godden Green 94
Goddington 58
Golden Green 128
Gold Street 50
Golford 179
Goose Green *Biddenden* ..181
Goose Green *Hadlow* ..112
Goudhurst 177
Grafty Green 135

ain 27 B6
ange 55 B6
avesend 19 B2
ays 18 A7
eatness 92 D6
eenhithe 17 B2
een Street Green
artley 34 A2
een Street Green
rpington 57 E4
eenwich 1 A3
oombridge 171 C7
ove Green 100 E5
ove Park 28 B5
ubb Street 48 B8
n Green 189 C2

dlow 111 E1
dlow Stair 127 F4
ffenden Quarter 169 A7
le 68 D8
le Street 130 A7
lling 66 B5
ll's Green 125 A7
lstead 74 F6
m Green 199 C1
mmerwood 154 B3
rbourland 100 B8
replain 167 C4
rrietsham 119 D5
rtley Cranbrook 178 F1
rtley New Barn 48 F3
rtley Green 48 E4
rtlip 70 E5
rvel 64 C3
wiker Street 131 E1
wkenbury Headcorn 150 D7
wkenbury
oyal Tunbridge Wells 159 D2
wkhurst 189 A2
wley 32 F3
yes 42 A2
zel Street Bredgar 87 A3
zel Street Horsmonden 162 F4
zelwood 73 D8
adcorn 151 D4
arnden Green 135 B1
ath Side 31 F5
averham 77 E2
mpstead 69 A5
nhurst 50 E8
nley Street 50 F3
nwood Green 160 E6
rne Pound 96 D2
ver 139 D6
xtable 31 E1
gham 38 B4
gham Wood 127 F6
gh Brooms 159 C8
gh Halden 183 D7
gh Halstow 23 F3
gh Street 188 D2
denborough 126 E6
den Park 126 F4
l Green 70 C1
l Hoath 140 C6
l Park 89 B4
l Top 146 B1
ath Corner 140 B3
ckenden 45 B6
cker Edge 165 D2
dsoll Street 63 D2
lborough 66 A2
lland 104 A1
llingbourne 102 E2
ltye 154 F3
ne Sundridge 90 F3
ok Green Lamberhurst 175 C4
ok Green
eopham Station 50 A3
ok Green Northfleet 35 A2
o St Werburgh 40 F5
rns Green 73 E2
rn Street 81 D6
rseshoe Green 139 E1
rsmonden 163 A5
rton Kirby 47 D5
w Green 123 C1
cking 86 E1
ngershall Park 158 E2
nton 131 D8
rst Green Hawkhurst 194 B3
rst Green Oxted 104 B3

e Hill 106 F4
en Green Goudhurst 178 C8
en Green Hawkhurst 190 D4
tham 94 D6
ham Common 94 A3
ead Rise 49 E8
Hatch 94 A1

yden's Wood 31 F4

msing 77 B2
msley Street 69 C2
nt Hatch 105 B3
nt Street 96 E2
ston 56 D6
ston Mark 56 D8

Kevingtown 44 E3
Keycol 71 E6
Key's Green 161 C4
Kidbrooke 11 C5
Kilndown 176 F3
Kings Farm 36 C5
Kings Hill 97 A2
Kingsnorth 41 D5
Kingswood 118 E3
Kipping's Cross 161 B5
Kippington 92 A1
Kit's Coty 83 C7
Knatts Valley 77 D8
Knockhall 17 C1
Knockholt 74 B2
Knockholt Pound 74 D4
Knockmill 77 E7
Knox Bridge 165 F6

L

Labour-in-vain 78 F5
Laddingford 130 E5
Lamberhurst 176 B5
Lamberhurst Quarter 161 D1
Lane End 33 D3
Langhurst 121 E7
Langley 117 C4
Langley Heath 117 F4
Langton Green 157 E3
Larkfield 82 A2
Lashenden 167 F6
Leadingcross Green 120 C3
Leaves Green 72 D8
Leeds 118 A7
Leigh 125 E1
Leigh Green 193 F6
Lenham 120 D5
Lessness Heath 4 B1
Letts Green 73 F3
Lewisham 28 C6
Leybourne 81 D2
Lidsing 68 F1
Limpsfield 104 A6
Linkhill 196 E4
Linton 115 F1
Little Bayham 174 F4
Little Houses 137 D2
Little Mill 129 D5
Liverton Street 119 F1
Locksbottom 57 B7
London Beach 183 B5
Longfield 48 E7
Longfield Hill 49 D5
Longford 91 D6
Longlands 29 D5
Loose 115 F4
Loose Hill 115 F5
Lords Wood 68 C1
Lower Bitchet 93 C1
Lower Bush 51 F3
Lower Cousley Wood 185 E8
Lower Cox Street 85 D6
Lower Green Pembury 160 D8
Lower Green Rusthall 158 C5
Lower Hartlip 70 E4
Lower Haysden 142 D8
Lower Higham 38 D6
Lower Luddesdown 51 A2
Lower Rainham 55 F3
Lower Stoke 25 C5
Lower Twydall 55 C5
Lower Upnor 40 A3
Low Street 19 E8
Luddesdown 50 F1
Lunsford 81 E4
Luton 54 B2
Luxted 73 A5
Lye Green 170 D1

M

Madeira Park 159 B2
Maidstone 100 C3
Maplescombe 61 B5
Marden 148 C5
Marden Beech 148 B3
Marden Thorn 148 F3
Markbeech 139 D2
Marlpit 116 E2
Marlpit Hill 122 C4
Marsh Green 138 B5
Matfield 161 D8
Maypole Dartford 31 E7
Maypole Orpington 58 F4
Medhurst Row 123 A2
Meopham 64 B8
Meopham Green 64 A7
Meopham Station 50 B4
Meresborough 70 A5
Mereworth 112 D8
Middle Quarter 169 D1
Middle Stoke 25 B4
Milebush 148 E8
Mile Oak 146 C4
Millbank 151 B6
Mill Street 97 E7
Milton 19 D1
Modest Corner 142 E1
Monk's Hill 168 C7
Moon's Green 199 A3
Moor Street 70 B7
Mottingham 28 D6
Mott's Hill 171 A3
Mount Ephraim 158 F4
Mount Sion 159 A2
Mowshurst 122 E3
Munday Bois 153 F8

N

Nash 56 A4
Nash Street 50 A7
Nettlestead 113 D6
Nettlestead Green 113 B2
New Ash Green 62 F8
New Barn 49 A7
Newbury's 185 B8
New Charlton 1 C2
New Eltham 29 C6
Newenden 197 D3
Newham 1 C6
New House 35 F6
New Hythe 82 B4
Newington 71 A6
Newland Green 153 D8
New Street 63 D5
Newtown 139 D4
New Town Dartford 16 A1
New Town Halling 66 A6
New Town West Malling 97 A8
Noah's Ark 93 A8
Noke Street 39 B4
North Cray 30 F5
North End 14 F6
Northfleet 18 D1
Northfleet Green 35 C3
North Halling 66 B8
Northiam 197 C1
North Street 24 E1
Northumberland Heath 14 C7
North Woolwich 2 B4

O

Oad Street 71 E1
Ockley 189 A3
Offham 96 D8
Old Bexley 31 B8
Oldbury 94 B6
Orpington 44 C2
Osmers Hill 184 F7
Otford 76 A3
Otham 117 B7
Otham Hole 117 B6

P

Paddock Wood 145 F8
Palmer's Green 162 D8
Parkgate 182 B2
Park Wood Gillingham 69 D4
Park Wood Maidstone 116 E4
Parrock Farm 36 D4
Pearson's Green 146 F3
Peckham Bush 129 E8
Peening Quarter 199 B6
Pell Bridge 185 A5
Pell Green 185 A7
Pembury 160 C6
Penenden Heath 100 B7
Penshurst 141 B4
Pepper Hill 35 C5
Perry Street 35 F8
Petteridge 161 F6
Pettings 63 B3
Petts Wood 43 D5
Pikefish 130 F3
Pinden 48 C7
Pipsden 189 D1
Pittswood 128 B8
Plaistow 28 A2
Platt 95 C7
Platt's Heath 119 E1
Plaxtol 110 E8
Plaxtol Spoute 111 A8
Plumstead 2 E2
Plumtree Green 151 A8
Pootings 122 E7
Potman's Heath 198 E4
Potter's Forstal 137 B2
Poundsbridge 157 D8
Poverest 44 A4
Powder Mills 126 E2
Pratling Street 83 C3
Pratt's Bottom 58 D1
Priestwood 64 B5
Priestwood Green 64 C5
Primmer's Green 184 F5
Princes Park 68 B6
Printstile 142 A3
Puddledock 31 E2
Purfleet 16 A8
Putlands 145 F5
Pye Corner 136 A6

Q

Queen Street 146 D7

R

Rabbit's Cross 133 E3
Rainham Essex 4 F8
Rainham Kent 55 E8
Ramsden 44 C1
Ramslye 158 D1
Red Hill 97 F1
Red Street 35 B2
Ridley 63 B4
Ringlestone Harrietsham 103 F4
Ringlestone Maidstone 99 E7
Riseden Durgates 184 B1
Riseden Kilndown 177 A5
Riverhead 91 E5
Riverview Park 36 E4
Rochester 53 B6
Rockrobin 184 D6
Rolvenden 191 F4
Rolvenden Layne 192 B1
Romden 153 C1
Romford 160 F7
Roseacre 101 A4
Rosherville 18 E1
Round Green 164 F4
Round Street 50 D5
Royal Tunbridge Wells 159 D3
Rusthall 158 C4
Ruxley 30 E1
Ryarsh 80 F4

S

St Ann's Green 148 F8
St John's
Royal Tunbridge Wells 159 A5
St John's Sevenoaks 92 B5
St Leonard's Street 97 B6
St Margarets 33 D1
St Mary Cray 44 B4
St Mary Hoo 24 D6
St Mary's Island 40 C1
St Michaels 183 B4
St Paul's Cray 44 A7
Saint's Hill 157 A8
Sandhurst 196 C6
Sandhurst Cross 195 F4
Sandling 83 F1
Sandway 120 A3
Seal 93 A6
Sepham Heath 75 B6
Sevenoaks 92 D2
Sevenoaks Weald 108 B2
Sheerness 27 B3
Shepway 116 D8
Sherwood 159 E6
Shipbourne 110 C5
Shooters Hill 12 C6
Shoreham 75 F8
Shorne 37 E3
Shorne Ridgeway 37 E2
Shover's Green 185 C1
Sidcup 30 A3
Silver Street 87 F5
Silvertown 1 C4
Single Street 73 B4
Singlewell 36 D2
Sinkhurst Green 150 E2
Sissinghurst 180 B7
Slade Green 15 B6
Small Hythe 193 C1
Smarden 153 A1
Smarden Bell 152 D2
Snodland 82 B7
Snoll Hatch 129 E5
Sole Street 50 C4
Southborough Bromley 42 F3
Southborough
Royal Tunbridge Wells 143 B1
South Darenth 47 D8
Southdowns 47 D7
Southernden 152 C8
Southfleet 35 A3
South Green 87 A5
South Street Biggin Hill 89 A8
South Street Meopham 63 F4
South Street Stockbury 86 C7
Sparrow's Green 184 F5
Speed Gate 61 F8
Speldhurst 158 B7
Standen 168 B5
Standen Street 190 D1
Stansted 62 F1
Staplehurst 149 D4
Stede Quarter 168 E1
Stick Hill 139 A3
Stiff Street 87 E7
Stockbury 86 E8
Stockland Green 142 C1
Stocks Green 126 B4
Stoke 25 A3
Stone 16 F2
Stone Bridge 184 E6
Stone Cross Langton Green 157 A2
Stone Cross Wadhurst 185 A3
Stonecrouch 186 F6
Stone Street 93 E2
Strood Rochester 52 F7
Strood Tenterden 192 B5
Styants Bottom 93 F5
Sundridge 28 C2
Sutton at Hone 33 A1
Sutton Valence 134 E6
Swanley 45 E5
Swanley Village 46 B7
Swanscombe 17 D2
Swanton 112 A8
Swift's Green 152 E6

T

Tatsfield 88 D7
Teasley Mead 156 C4
Temple Hill 16 A3
Tenterden 193 C8
Teston 114 A8
Thamesmead 3 A5
The Chart Limpsfield 104 E5
The Chart Toys Hill 106 C5
The Crook 146 D1
The Down 176 A3
The Harbour 134 E5
The Moor 194 F8
The Quarries 116 C4
The Quarter Headcorn 153 B5
The Quarter Staplehurst 149 E1
The Quarter Tenterden 193 A4
Thong 37 A2
Three Chimneys 167 B2
Three Legged Cross 186 D3
Thurnham 101 D8
Ticehurst 186 E2
Tilbury 19 B4
Timberden Bottom 59 D1
Titsey 88 B2
Tollgate 95 A8
Tonbridge 127 A2
Tovil 99 E1
Toy's Hill 106 C3
Trench Wood 127 B7
Trottiscliffe 80 A5
Troy Town 121 F5
Tudeley 144 B7
Tudeley Hale 128 C1
Turnden 179 B4
Turner's Green 184 F6
Twitton 75 E4
Twydall 55 B2
Tylden 168 E7

U

Ulcombe 135 F7
Underling Green 132 F2
Underriver 109 A5
Union Street 187 B3
Upper Bush 51 F2
Upper Fant 99 D3
Upper Halling 65 E5
Upper Harvel 64 C3
Upper Hayesden 142 C6
Upper Ruxley 31 A1
Upper Tolhurst 186 A2
Upper Upnor 39 F1

V

Vicarage Green 185 A5
Vigo Village 80 B8

W

Wadhurst 185 A4
Wainscott 39 D3
Walderslade 67 F1
Walderslade Bottom 68 A2
Wallcrouch 185 F1
Walter's Green 156 E6
Wanden 153 B7
Wanshurst Green 149 A7
Ware Street 101 B5
Warmlake 117 D1
Wateringbury 113 D7
Waterman Quarter 151 D2
Watts's Cross 126 B7
Wayfield 68 A8
Weardale 106 B5
Weavering Street 100 F5
Weeds Wood 67 F3
Weller's Town 140 D5
Well Hill 59 B4
Welling 13 B4
Well Street 97 E6
Westcourt 36 E6
West Cross 191 D4
Westerham 89 C1
West Farleigh 114 D6
West Heath 13 D8
West Kingsdown 61 F2
West Malling 97 C7
West Peckham 112 A6
West Street 120 E8
West Thurrock 17 B8
West Tilbury 19 E8
Westwood 34 D1
Whetsted 129 E1
Whitehill 48 D7
White Oak 45 F7
White Post 156 D7
Wick Hill 167 F8
Widmore 42 E7
Wierton 133 F8
Wigmore 69 B4
Willington 100 E1
Wilmington 32 C4
Wilsley Green 179 D7
Wilsley Pound 179 E8
Winchet Hill 164 B6
Windmill Hill 36 A7
Wissenden 169 F7
Withyham 170 A3
Wittersham 199 D3
Wombwell Park 35 D6
Woodlands 77 C6
Wood's Green 184 F8
Woodside Green 120 F8
Woolwich 2 B3
Wormshill 103 F7
Worms Hill 164 B5
Worsenden Green 167 D2
Wouldham 66 D5
Wrotham 78 F2
Wrotham Heath 80 A1

Y

Yalding 113 F1
Yelsted 70 A1
Yewtree Green 147 B1
Yopps Green 94 E1

2

20/20 Ind Est ME16 ......99 C8

A

Aaron Hill Rd E6 ......2 A8
Abbess Cl 12 E6 ......1 E8
Abbeville Ho ME1 ......53 C4
Abbey Brewery Ct ME19 ..97 C8
Abbey Court Specl Sch ME2 ......52 E8
Abbey Cres DA17 ......4 A2
Abbey Dr DA2 ......31 E6
Abbey Gate Cotts ME14 ...83 F2
Abbey Gdns BR7 ......43 A8
Abbey Gr SE2 ......3 B2
Abbey Ho SE2 ......3 D1
Abbey Life Ct E13 ......1 B8
Abbey Lodge SE12 ......28 B4
Abbey Mount DA17 ......3 F1
Abbey Pl DA1 ......15 D2
Abbey Rd Bexley DA6,DA7 ..13 E3
Erith DA17 ......3 E3
Gillingham ME8 ......55 A2
Gravesend DA12 ......36 E7
Rochester ME2 ......52 F8
Swanscombe DA9 ......17 C2
Abbey Terr SE2 ......3 C2
Abbey Wood Golden Jubilee Cvn site SE2 ......3 C1
Abbey Wood Rd
Kings Hill ME19 ......97 A5
Woolwich SE2 ......3 C2
Abbey Wood Sch SE2 ......3 A3
Abbey Wood Sta SE2 ......3 C3
Abbeyhill Rd DA15 ......30 C6
Abbots Cl BR5 ......43 C1
Abbots Court Rd ME3 ....40 F4
Abbots Field
Gravesend DA12 ......36 C2
Maidstone ME16 ......99 B2
Abbotswood Cl 7 DA17 ...3 E3
Abbott Rd TN15 ......94 F7
Abbott Way TN30 ......193 C7
Abbott's Wlk DA7 ......13 D7
Abbotts Cl Rochester ME1 ..53 B3
Swanley BR8 ......46 A5
Woolwich SE28 ......3 C6
Aberdeen Ho 9 ME15 ...116 E7
Aberford Gdns SE18 ......11 E6
Abergeldie Rd SE12 ......11 B1
Abery St SE18 ......2 E2
Abigail Cres ME5 ......68 A1
Abingdon Mews ME19 ...97 C8
Abingdon Rd ME16 ......98 F2
Abingdon Way BR6 ......58 B6
Abinger Cl BR1 ......42 E6
Abinger Dr ME5 ......68 D2
Absalom Ct ME8 ......55 C2
Acacia Cl BR5 ......43 D4
Acacia Ct DA11 ......36 A8
Acacia Rd Dartford DA1 ...32 D7
Stone DA9 ......16 E1
Acacia Way DA15 ......29 F7
Acacia Wlk BR8 ......45 D7
Academy Dr ME7 ......54 F1
Academy Pl SE18 ......12 A6
Academy Rd SE18 ......11 F7
Acer Ave TN2 ......173 C8
Acer Rd TN16 ......72 D3
Achilles Rd ME5 ......68 C2
Acland Cl SE18 ......12 D7
Acorn Cl Chislehurst BR7 ...29 C3
Five Oak Green TN12 ......145 B7
Acorn Gr ME20 ......98 D8
Acorn Ind Pk DA1 ......15 A2
Acorn Pl ME15 ......116 E6
Acorn Rd Crayford DA1 ....14 F2
Gillingham ME7 ......54 F4
Acorn Trad Ctr RM20 ......17 E8
Acorn Way
Hurst Green TN19 ......194 A3
Orpington BR6 ......57 B6
Acorn Wharf Rd ME1 ......53 C6
Acorns The
Sevenoaks TN13 ......92 A4
Smarden TN27 ......152 F1
Acott Fields ME18 ......130 F8
Acre Cl ME1 ......53 E1
Acre Gr ME2 ......66 A4
Acres Rise TN5 ......186 E1
Acton La TN30 ......199 F4
Acton Pl ME18 ......114 A1
Acworth Ho 1 SE18 ......12 B8
Acworth Pl DA1 ......15 C1
Adam Cl ME17 ......115 D3
Adams Cl TN30 ......183 B1
Adams Sq DA6 ......13 E4
Adamson Rd E16 ......1 A7
Adbert Dr ME15 ......115 B4
Adcot Wlk 7 BR6 ......57 F6
Adderley Gdns SE9 ......29 A4
Addington La ME19 ......80 B4
Addison Cl Orpington BR5 ..43 C3
West Malling ME19 ......81 F1
Addison Cotts TN30 ......199 D3
Addison Dr SE12 ......11 B2
Addison Rd BR2 ......42 D4
Addlestead Rd TN12 ......129 E6
Adelaide Rd
Chislehurst BR7 ......29 B3
Adelaide Rd *continued*
Gillingham ME7 ......54 C4
Tilbury RM18 ......18 F5
Adelaide The ME3 ......38 C6
Aden Terr 1 ME14 ......100 A7
Adisham Dr ME16 ......99 B7
Admaston Rd SE18 ......12 C8
Admers Wood DA13 ......80 B8
Admiral Cl BR5 ......44 D5
Admiral Ct ME7 ......54 D6
Admiral Moore Dr ME20 ..82 F1
Admiral Seymour Rd SE9 .11 F3
Admiral Way ME19 ......97 A1
Admiral's Wlk ME4 ......53 F7
Admirals Ct E6 ......2 B7
Admirals Wlk
Chatham ME5 ......68 B3
Goddard's Green TN17 ....180 D2
Swanscombe DA9 ......17 B2
Tenterden TN30 ......183 C1
Admiralty Rd ME2 ......39 F1
Admiralty Terr
1 Chatham ME7 ......54 A7
Rochester ME2 ......39 F1
Aerodrome Est ME14 ......85 E4
Afghan Rd ME4 ......53 E4
Agate Cl E16 ......1 D7
Agaton Rd SE9 ......29 C6
Agnes Cl E6 ......2 A6
Ailsa Mews ME1 ......52 F2
Ainsdale Cl BR6 ......43 D1
Aintree Cl DA12 ......36 B5
Aintree Ho 1 ME15 ......116 F6
Aintree Rd ME5 ......68 C3
Airedale Cl DA2 ......33 C7
Airport Ind Est TN16 ......72 D4
Airport Rdbt E16 ......1 D5
Aisher Rd SE28 ......3 C6
Aisher Way TN13 ......91 E6
Ajax Rd ME1 ......67 C8
Akehurst La TN13 ......92 C2
Alabama St SE18 ......12 E7
Alamein Ave ME5 ......67 F7
Alamein Gdns DA2 ......33 D8
Alamein Rd DA10 ......17 D1
Alan Cl DA1 ......15 C3
Alan Marre Ho SE7 ......11 D8
Alanbrooke DA12 ......36 C8
Alanthus Cl SE12 ......11 A1
Alban Cres DA4 ......47 A1
Albany Cl Sidcup DA5 ......30 D8
Tonbridge TN9 ......143 D7
Albany Hill TN2 ......159 C5
Albany Mews BR1 ......28 A2
Albany Park Sta DA14 ......30 D6
Albany Rd Bexley DA17 ......13 F8
Chatham ME4 ......54 B2
Chislehurst BR7 ......29 B3
Gillingham ME7 ......54 D4
Rochester ME1 ......53 C4
Sidcup DA5 ......30 C8
Tilbury RM18 ......19 A6
Albany St ME14 ......100 B5
Albany Terr Chatham ME4 ..53 E4
Gillingham ME7 ......54 D4
Albatross Ave ME2 ......52 C6
Albatross Cl E6 ......1 F8
Albatross St SE18 ......12 E7
Albemarle Rd ME5 ......68 C2
Albert Cotts TN1 ......159 B4
Albert Ho SE28 ......2 C3
Albert Manor ME7 ......54 B5
Albert Murray Cl DA12 ....36 C8
Albert Pl ME2 ......53 B7
Albert Rd
Bromley,Bromley Common BR2 ......42 D4
Bromley,Mottingham SE9 ...28 E5
Chatham ME4 ......54 A3
Dartford DA2 ......32 C5
Erith DA17 ......3 F1
Gillingham ME7 ......54 C4
Newham E16 ......1 F5
Orpington BR5 ......44 B3
Orpington,Green Street Green BR6 ......58 A5
Rochester ME1 ......53 C3
Sidcup DA5 ......31 B8
Swanscombe DA10 ......17 F1
3 Tonbridge TN9 ......127 B1
Albert Reed Gdns ME15 ..99 E2
Albert St Maidstone ME14 ..99 F6
Royal Tunbridge Wells TN1 ......159 B4
Albert Wlk E16 ......2 B4
Alberta Rd DA8 ......14 C6
Albion Cotts TN12 ......148 D5
Albion Ct 2 SE18 ......1 E2
Albion Ho E16 ......2 B5
Albion Mews TN1 ......159 C5
Albion Pl Chattenden ME2 ..40 A3
Maidstone ME14 ......100 B4
Newington ME9 ......71 B6
Albion Rd Bexley DA6 ......14 A3
Chatham ME5 ......68 B2
Gravesend DA12 ......36 C8
Marden TN12 ......148 D5
Royal Tunbridge Wells TN1 ......159 C5
Albion Terr DA12 ......19 D1
Albion Way TN8 ......122 C4
Albright Ind Est RM13 ......4 F8
Albury Ave DA7 ......13 E5
Albury Cl ME5 ......68 D2
Albyfield BR1 ......42 F6
Alchins Cotts ME17 ......115 E2
Alconbury DA6 ......14 B2
Aldeburgh Pl SE10 ......1 A2
Aldeburgh St SE10 ......1 A1
Alder Cl TN4 ......143 D1
Alder La TN17 ......191 C1
Alder Lodge TN4 ......158 E4
Alder Rd DA14 ......29 F5
Alder Way BR8 ......45 D7
Alderman Cl DA1 ......31 E8
Aldermary Rd BR1 ......42 A8
Alderney Rd DA8 ......15 A7
Alders Cotts TN12 ......145 A5
Alders Mdw TN9 ......126 F2
Alders Rd TN11,TN12 ......144 E6
Alders The ME18 ......112 D7
Aldersgrove Ave SE9 ......28 D5
Aldershot Rd ME5 ......68 A7
Alderwick Gr ME18 ......97 C3
Alderwood Prim Sch SE9 .12 E1
Alderwood Rd SE9 ......12 D1
Aldington Cl ME5 ......68 B5
Aldington La ME14 ......101 D8
Aldington Rd
Greenwich SE18 ......1 D3
Maidstone ME14 ......100 F4
Aldon Cl ME14 ......100 C6
Aldon Ct ME14 ......100 C6
Aldon La ME19 ......96 C8
Aldwick Cl SE9 ......29 D5
Aldwych Cl TN10 ......127 D7
Alen Sq TN12 ......149 F4
Alers Rd DA6 ......13 D2
Alestan Beck Rd E16 ......1 D7
Alex Hughes Cl ME6 ......81 F6
Alexander Cl Hayes BR2 ...42 A1
Sidcup DA15 ......12 E1
Alexander Cotts ME2 ......38 C6
Alexander Ct
Greenwich SE3 ......11 B5
1 Rochester ME2 ......53 B8
2 Royal Tunbridge Wells TN1 ......159 A4
Alexander Gr ME18 ......97 A3
Alexander McLeod Prim Sch SE2 ......3 B1
Alexander Rd Bexley DA7 ..13 D5
Chislehurst BR7 ......29 B3
Swanscombe DA9 ......17 C2
Alexandra Ave ME7 ......54 E4
Alexandra Cl BR8 ......45 E7
Alexandra Glen ME5 ......68 A1
Alexandra Hospl The ME5 ......84 A8
Alexandra Rd
Biggin Hill TN16 ......88 B8
Chatham ME4 ......54 B2
Erith DA8 ......14 F8
Gravesend DA12 ......36 E8
Tilbury RM18 ......18 F5
Tonbridge TN9 ......143 B8
Alexandra St
Maidstone ME14 ......99 F6
Newham E16 ......1 A8
Alexandra Wlk DA4 ......47 E7
Alfan La DA2 ......31 D3
Alford Ho 6 SE18 ......12 B8
Alford Rd DA8 ......4 C1
Alford Snell Lodge TN2 .159 D2
Alfred Cl ME4 ......54 B2
Alfred Ho Gravesend DA11 .36 B6
5 Northfleet DA11 ......35 F7
Alfred Pl DA11 ......35 F7
Alfred Rd Erith DA17 ......3 F1
Gravesend DA11 ......36 B6
Hawley DA2 ......32 F4
Alfred St RM17 ......18 C8
Alfriston Cl DA1 ......14 E1
Alfriston Gr ME19 ......97 C3
Alice Thompson Cl SE12 ..28 C6
Alicia Ho DA16 ......13 B6
Alison Cl E6 ......2 A7
Alkerden La DA9,DA10 ....17 C1
Alkham Rd ME14 ......100 C5
Alkham Twr 9 BR5 ......44 C5
All Saints CE Prim Sch ME15 ......100 A3
All Saints Cl DA10 ......17 F2
All Saints Rd
Allhallows ME3 ......9 D2
Hawkhurst TN18 ......189 A1
Royal Tunbridge Wells TN4 ......159 B6
All Saints Rise TN4 ......159 A6
All Saints' CE Prim Sch ME4 ......54 A3
All Saints' Rd DA11 ......35 F7
Allan Cl TN4 ......158 C4
Allandale Pl BR6 ......58 D7
Allandale Rd TN2 ......159 D7
Allard Cl BR5 ......44 C2
Allen Cl ME5 ......68 C6
Allen Gardiner Ho TN2 ..159 C3
Allen St ME14 ......100 B5
Allenby Rd
Biggin Hill TN16 ......72 E2
Woolwich SE28 ......2 C3
Allendale Cl DA2 ......33 D7
Allens TN12 ......148 D5
Allens La TN15,TN11 ......111 A7
Allenswood Rd SE9 ......11 F5
Allhallows Prim Sch ME3 ..9 D2
Allhallows Rd
Lower Stoke ME3 ......25 C5
Newham E6 ......1 E7
Allhallows-on-Sea Est ME3 ......9 E4
Alliance Rd Newham E13 ...1 C8
Woolwich SE18 ......13 A7
Alliance Way TN12 ......145 F6
Allington Cl DA12 ......36 F7
Allington Dr
Rochester ME2 ......52 E8
Tonbridge TN10 ......128 A5
Allington Gdns ME18 ....113 E7
Allington Prim Sch ME16 .99 C7
Allington Rd
Gillingham ME8 ......55 A3
Orpington BR6 ......43 E1
Paddock Wood TN12 ......145 F7
Allington Way ME16 ......99 B6
Allison Ave ME7 ......54 E1
Allnutt Mill Cl 4 ME15 ...99 E2
Allotment La TN13 ......92 C5
Allsworth Cl ME9 ......71 B6
Alma Pl Hadlow TN11 ......128 E8
Rochester ME2 ......53 A7
Alma Rd Eccles ME20 ......82 F6
Orpington BR5 ......58 D8
Sidcup DA14 ......30 A5
Swanscombe DA10 ......17 F2
West Malling ME19 ......97 A8
Alma The DA12 ......36 F4
Almery Cotts ME17 ......134 B8
Almon Pl ME1 ......53 D5
Almond Cl BR2 ......43 A2
Almond Dr BR8 ......45 D7
Almond Gr ME7 ......69 A4
Almond Ho 9 ME16 ......99 A3
Almond Rd DA2 ......33 C8
Almond Way BR2 ......43 A2
Almonds The ME14 ......101 A4
Alms Row TN16 ......90 B3
Almshouses
Crockenhill BR8 ......45 D2
Penshurst TN11 ......141 C4
Sevenoaks TN13 ......92 C1
14 Tonbridge TN9 ......143 B8
Yalding ME18 ......114 A1
Alnwick Ct 8 DA2 ......16 B1
Alnwick Rd Eltham SE12 ...28 B8
Newham E16 ......1 C7
Alonso Ho 4 DA17 ......4 A1
Alpha Cl ME3 ......41 D7
Alpine Bsns Ctr E6 ......2 A8
Alpine Copse 2 BR1 ......43 A7
Alpine Way E6 ......2 A8
Alsike Rd DA18 ......3 E3
Altash Way SE9 ......29 A6
Altbarn Ind Est ME5 ......84 C8
Alton Ave ME19 ......97 A3
Alton Cl DA5 ......30 E7
Alton Cotts DA4 ......60 E8
Alverstone Gdns SE9 ......29 C7
Alwold Cres SE12 ......11 C1
Amanda Cl ME5 ......67 F3
Amar Ct SE18 ......2 F2
Amardeep Ct SE18 ......2 F1
Ambassador Gdns E6 ......1 F8
Amber Ct ME7 ......54 D5
Amber La ME17 ......117 A1
Amber Way ME17 ......117 B1
Amberleaze Dr TN2 ......160 D6
Amberley Cl
2 Orpington BR6 ......57 F5
Tonbridge TN9 ......143 A8
Amberley Ct
Royal Tunbridge Wells TN4 ......159 C8
Sidcup DA14 ......30 C3
Amberley Rd SE2 ......13 D8
Amblecote Cl SE12 ......28 B5
Amblecote Mdw SE12 ......28 B5
Amblecote Rd SE12 ......28 B5
Ambleside Rd DA7 ......14 A5
Ambley Gn ME8 ......69 A8
Ambley Rd ME8 ......69 B8
Ambley Wood Nature Reserve* ME7,ME8 ......69 A8
Ambrook Rd DA17 ......4 A3
Ambrose Cl Crayford DA1 ..15 A3
6 Newham E6 ......1 F8
Orpington BR6 ......57 F7
Ambrose Hill ME5 ......54 C2
Amels Hill ME9 ......86 F8
Ames Ave ME14 ......101 A4
Ames Rd DA10 ......17 E1
Ames Way ME18 ......97 B3
Amesbury Rd BR1 ......42 D6
Amethyst Ave ME5 ......67 E6
Amherst Cl
Maidstone ME16 ......99 D4
Orpington BR5 ......44 A5
Amherst Dr BR5 ......44 A5
Amherst Hill
Chatham ME7 ......54 A6
Sevenoaks TN13 ......91 F4
Amherst Prim Sch TN13 ..91 E4
Amherst Rd
Rochester ME1 ......53 D3
Royal Tunbridge Wells TN4 ......159 A5
Sevenoaks TN13 ......92 B5
Amherst Redoubt ME4 ...54 A5
Amhurst Bank Rd TN2, TN11,TN12 ......144 F4
Amhurst Wlk SE28 ......3 A5
Amies Ho ME15 ......115 F3
Ampleforth Cl BR6 ......58 C6
Ampleforth Rd SE2 ......3 C4
Amsbury Rd ME15,ME17 .115 B2
Amshurst Villas ME15 ...115 A4
Ancaster St SE18 ......12 E7
Anchor & Hope La SE7 ...1 C2
Anchor Bay Ind Est DA8 ..15 A8
Anchor Bvd DA2 ......16 D3
Anchor Ct DA7 ......13 E6
Anchor Ho Newham E16 ....1 C7
Rochester ME1 ......53 B4
Anchor La ME12 ......27 F
Anchor Rd ME1 ......53 C
Anchorage Cl ME3 ......25 C
Anchorage Flats TN12 ..146 A
Anchorage Point Ind Est SE7 ......1 C
Ancona Rd SE18 ......2 D
Andace Pk BR1 ......42 C
Anderson Way DA17 ......4 B
Andorra Ct BR1 ......42 C
Andover Ave E16 ......1 D
Andover Rd BR6 ......43 E
Andover Wlk 12 ME15 ...116 F
Andrew Broughton Way ME14 ......100 B
Andrew Cl DA1 ......14 D
Andrew Manor ME7 ......54 C
Andrew Rd TN4 ......159 C
Andrew Wells Ho 8 BR1 .28 B
Andrewes Gdns E6 ......1 E
Andrews Cl Orpington BR5 .44 D
Royal Tunbridge Wells TN2 ......159 D
Andrews Pl DA2 ......31 E
Andringham Lodge 7 BR1 ......42 B
Andwell Cl SE2 ......3 B
Anerley Cl ME16 ......99 D
Angel La TN9 ......127 B
Angel Row TN18 ......196 B
Angel Terr TN18 ......196 B
Angel Wlk 4 TN9 ......127 B
Angelica Dr E6 ......2 A
Angerstein Bsns Pk SE10 ..1 A
Angle Rd RM20 ......17 D
Anglesea Ave SE18 ......2 B
Anglesea Pl 19 DA11 ......19 B
Anglesea Rd
Orpington BR5 ......44 C
Woolwich SE18 ......2 B
Anglesey Ave ME15 ......116 A
Anglesey Cl ME5 ......68 B
Angley Ct TN12 ......163 A
Angley Rd TN17 ......179 C
Angley Sch Sports Coll TN17 ......179 C
Angley Wlk
Cranbrook TN17 ......179 C
Cranbrook TN17 ......179 D
Anglia Ctr The RM13 ......4 E
Anglian Ind Est IG11 ......3 A
Anglo Saxon Ho DA12 ....36 E
Ankerdine Cres SE18 ......12 B
Ann St SE18 ......2 D
Ann Stroud Ct SE12 ......11 A
Annandale Rd DA15 ......29 F
Anne of Cleves Rd DA1 ...15 D
Annesley Rd SE3 ......11 B
Annetts Hall TN15 ......95 A
Annex The BR8 ......46 B
Annie Rd ME6 ......81 F
Annvera Ho 2 ME7 ......54 C
Ansell Ave ME4 ......54 A
Ansia Cl ME18 ......97 B
Anson Ave M18,ME19 ......96 F
Anson Cl ME5 ......68 C
Anson Pl SE28 ......2 D
Anstridge Rd SE9 ......12 D
Antelope Rd SE18 ......1 F
Anthony Cl TN13 ......91 E
Anthony Rd DA16 ......13 A
Anthony Roper Prim Sch The DA4 ......60 E
Anthonys La BR8 ......46 A
Anthonys Way ME2 ......53 E
Anvil Terr DA2 ......31 E
Aperfield Rd
Biggin Hill TN16 ......72 E
Erith DA8 ......14 F
Apiary Bsns Pk The ME17 ......118 B
Apollo Ave BR1 ......42 B
Apollo Ho ME5 ......68 A
Apollo Way
St Mary's Island ME4 ......40 C
3 Woolwich SE28 ......2 D
Apple Cl ME6 ......82 A
Apple Ct TN12 ......145 F
Apple Orch BR8 ......45 D
Apple Tree Cl ME16 ......98 F
Apple Tree La TN2 ......159 D
Appleby Cl ME1 ......67 D
Appleby Rd E16 ......1 A
Applecross Cl ME1 ......53 B
Appledore Ave DA7 ......14 D
Appledore Cl BR2 ......42 A
Appledore Cres DA14 ......29 F
Appledore Ct ME16 ......99 C
Appledore Rd
Gillingham ME8 ......55 A
Tenterden TN30 ......193 E
Applegarth Dr DA1 ......32 F
Applegarth Ho DA8 ......14 F
Applegarth Rd SE28 ......3 C
Appleshaw Cl DA11 ......36 A
Appleton Cl DA7 ......14 C
Appleton Dr DA2 ......32 B
Appleton Rd SE9 ......11 E
Appletons TN11 ......128 E
Appletree Ct 5 ME8 ......69 F
Appold St DA8 ......14 F
Approach Rd CR6,TN16 ...88 B
Approach The BR6 ......57 F
April Cl BR6 ......57 F
Apsledene DA12 ......36 D
Apsley Ct BR5 ......44 B
Apsley St TN4 ......158 D
Aragon Cl BR2 ......42 F

rborfield DA13 50 A4
rbroath Rd SE9 11 E4
rbrook Cl BR5 44 A6
rbrook Ct BR5 44 A8
rbury Ho BR1 28 E1
rbuthnot La DA5 13 E1
rcade The 2 SE9 12 A1
rcadia Rd DA13 49 F8
rcadian Ave DA5 13 E1
rcadian Cl DA5 13 E1
rcadian Rd DA5 13 E1
rcher Ho ME3 39 F6
rcher Rd Chatham ME5 68 B6
Orpington BR5 44 A4
rcher Way BR8 46 A7
rchery Cl ME3 39 B7
rchery House Hospl
DA2 16 B1
rchery Rd SE9 11 F2
rchibald Ho ME14 100 A7
rchway Ct Dartford DA1 32 D8
4 Rochester ME2 53 B8
rden Bsns Pk ME2 53 E7
rden Cl SE28 3 D7
rden Gr BR6 57 B6
rden Jun Sch ME7 54 D6
rden St ME7 54 C6
rdenlee Dr ME14 100 B5
rethusa Pl DA9 17 B3
rethusa Rd ME1 67 C8
rgali Ho 3 DA18 3 E3
rgent St RM17 18 B7
rgles Cl 4 DA9 17 A2
rgyle Cl ME1 67 E8
Argyle Rd Newham E16 1 B7
Royal Tunbridge Wells
TN4 143 A2
Sevenoaks TN13 92 B2
Argyll Rd SE18 2 C3
Ariel Cl DA12 36 F4
Ariel Ct 5 DA17 4 A1
Arkwright Rd RM18 19 A5
Arlington Cl DA15 29 E8
Arlott Cl ME14 99 F6
Armada Ct ME4 53 E1
Armada Way
Chatham ME4 53 F3
Newham E6 2 C7
Armitage Pl 5 TN18 188 F2
Armoury Dr DA12 36 C8
Armstrong Cl
Badgers Mount TN14 75 B4
Bromley BR1 42 E6
Newham E6 1 F7
Armstrong Rd
Maidstone ME15 100 A1
Woolwich SE18 2 C3
Armytage Cl ME3 40 E4
Arne Cl TN10 127 E6
Arne Gr BR6 57 F7
Arnhem Dr ME5 67 F7
Arnold Ave DA13 64 B8
Arnold Pl RM18 19 C6
Arnold Rd DA12 36 D6
Arnolde Cl ME2 53 E7
Arnolds La DA4 33 A2
Arnott Cl SE28 3 C5
Arnsberg Way DA6,DA7 14 A3
Arnside Rd DA7 14 A6
Arran Cl DA8 14 D8
Arran Gn ME2 52 C6
Arran Rd ME15 116 A6
Arrandene Ho 3 BR5 44 B7
Arras Ho Bexley SE2 13 D8
Erith SE2 3 D1
Arsenal Rd SE9 11 F4
Arsenal Way SE18 2 C3
Artemis Cl DA12 36 E8
Arthur Ct 11 RM17 18 C8
Arthur Gr SE18 2 C2
Arthur Rd Biggin Hill TN16 72 C3
Gillingham ME8 69 E7
Rochester ME1 53 D3
Arthur Ruxley Est DA14 30 D2
Arthur St Erith DA8 14 F7
Gravesend DA11 36 A8
Grays RM17 18 C8
Arthur St W DA11 36 A8
Arthur Toft Ho 6 RM17 18 B8
Artillery Ho SE18 2 A1
Artillery Pl SE18 2 A2
Artillery Row DA12 36 C8
Artington Cl BR6 57 C6
Artisan Cl E6 2 B6
Arun Ct BR5 44 C1
Arundel DA14 30 A3
Arundel Cl Bexley DA5 13 F1
Chatham ME5 68 D1
Tonbridge TN9 143 A8
Arundel Ct 2 DA6 13 E3
Arundel Dr BR6 58 B5
Arundel Ho TN1 159 A3
Arundel Rd Dartford DA1 15 C3
Royal Tunbridge Wells
TN1 159 B2
Arundel St ME14 99 F6
Ascot Cl
Borough Green TN15 95 B7
Chatham ME5 68 C2
Ascot Ct Bromley BR1 42 E7
Sidcup DA5 30 F8
Ascot Ho 2 ME15 116 F6
Ascot Rd Gravesend DA12 36 B5
Orpington BR5 43 F5
Ash Cl Aylesford ME20 82 E1
Chatham ME5 54 C1
Edenbridge TN8 122 B1
Gillingham ME8 55 B3
Ash Cl *continued*
Orpington BR5 43 D4
Royal Tunbridge Wells
TN2 173 D7
Sidcup DA14 30 B5
Swanley BR8 45 D7
Ash Cres Biddenden TN27 182 D7
Higham ME3 38 C3
Ash Croft Ct DA3 62 F7
Ash Ct SE12 28 A8
Ash Gr ME16 99 C6
Ash Ho BR5 44 C5
Ash Keys DA13 80 B8
Ash La TN15 62 D2
Ash Platt Rd TN15 92 E6
Ash Rd Dartford DA1 32 D7
Gravesend DA12 36 C4
Hartley DA3 48 F3
Hawley DA2 32 F4
New Ash Green DA3,TN15 62 E7
Orpington BR6 57 F3
Rochester ME2 52 F6
Westerham TN16 89 E2
Ash Row BR2 43 A3
Ash Tree Cl TN15 61 F2
Ash Tree Cotts TN12 164 B7
Ash Tree Dr TN15 61 F2
Ash Tree La ME5 54 D1
Ashbank Cotts ME17 118 B7
Ashbee Cl ME6 82 A7
Ashbourne Ave DA7 13 E7
Ashbourne Ct TN4 158 D4
Ashbourne Rise BR6 57 E6
Ashburn Ct BR1 28 A1
Ashburn Mews ME7 54 E3
Ashburnham Cl TN13 108 C8
Ashburnham Rd Erith DA17 4 C2
Maidstone ME14 100 B8
Tonbridge TN10 127 C3
Ashburton Rd E16 1 A7
Ashby Cl ME2 66 A4
Ashby's Cl TN8 138 D8
Ashbys Yd TN9 127 C1
Ashcombe Dr TN8 122 B4
Ashcroft Ave DA15 13 A1
Ashcroft Cres DA15 13 A1
Ashcroft Ct Dartford DA1 33 A8
5 Eltham SE9 12 A1
Ashcroft Rd
Paddock Wood TN12 146 A5
Rochester ME2 39 B2
Ashdale Rd SE12 28 B7
Ashden Wlk TN10 127 C7
Ashdown Cl Coldblow DA5 31 C8
Maidstone ME16 99 D3
Royal Tunbridge Wells
TN4 158 F4
Ashen E6 2 A7
Ashen Dr DA1 15 A1
Ashen Grove Mobile Home
Pk TN15 61 B1
Ashen Grove Rd TN15 61 B1
Ashenden TN27 152 F2
Ashenden Cl ME2 39 C2
Ashenden Wlk TN2 159 E8
Asher Reeds TN3 158 A4
Ashes La Plaxtol TN11 110 F1
Tonbridge TN11 128 B8
Ashfield La BR7 29 C1
Ashfield Pl BR7 29 D1
Ashford Dr ME17 118 D3
Ashford Rd
Harrietsham ME17 119 C6
Maidstone ME14 101 D3
Maidstone,Grove Green
ME14 100 D4
Tenterden TN30 193 B8
Tenterden,Durrant Green
TN26,TN30 183 A6
Ashgrove SE12 28 A7
Ashgrove Rd TN13 108 B7
Ashlar Pl 4 SE18 2 B2
Ashleigh Cl DA13 63 F1
Ashleigh Commercial Est
SE18 1 D3
Ashleigh Gdns TN27 151 D6
Ashley Cl TN13 92 B3
Ashley Gdns
Orpington BR6 57 E5
Rusthall TN4 158 C5
Ashley Ho BR5 44 A7
Ashley Park Cl TN4 158 C5
Ashley Pk TN4 158 C5
Ashley Rd Gillingham ME8 55 C2
Sevenoaks TN13 92 B3
Tonbridge TN11 126 E5
Ashly Ct 22 DA14 30 A5
Ashmead Cl ME5 68 C3
Ashmead Gate BR1 42 C8
Ashmill Bsns Pk ME17 120 F6
Ashmore Gdns DA11 35 D5
Ashmore Gr DA16 12 E4
Ashmore La BR2 72 C8
Ashridge Cres SE18 12 C7
Ashridge Ho DA14 29 F4
Ashton Way ME19 97 C6
Ashtree Cl BR6 57 B6
Ashurst Cl DA1 14 F4
Ashurst Hill TN3 156 D2
Ashurst Rd
Maidstone ME14 100 C5
Stone Cross TN3 157 B2
Ashurst Sta TN3 156 D2
Ashwater Rd SE12 28 A7
Ashwell Cl 9 E6 1 E7
Ashwood Cl ME3 39 C7
Ashwood Pl DA2 34 B5
Askern Cl DA6 13 D3
Askews Farm La RM17,
RM20 17 E8
Askham Lodge 10 SE12 28 A8
Aspdin Rd DA11 35 E5
Aspen Cl Orpington BR6 58 A5
Swanley BR8 45 D8
Aspen Copse BR1 42 F7
Aspen Ct DA1 16 A2
Aspen Gn DA18 3 F3
Aspen Ho 2 DA15 30 A5
Aspen Way
2 Chatham ME5 67 E4
Royal Tunbridge Wells
TN4 143 C1
Aspian Dr ME17 115 D3
Asquith Rd ME8 69 C6
Association Wlk ME1 67 C7
Aster Rd ME3 40 E3
Astley RM17 17 F8
Astley St ME14 100 A4
Aston Cl Chatham ME5 68 A2
Sidcup DA14 30 A5
Astor Ct E16 1 C7
Astor of Hever Com Sch The
ME16 99 C3
Astor Rd TN15 61 E4
Astra Dr DA12 36 F3
Atcost Rd IG11 3 A8
Athelstan Gn ME17 102 C2
Athelstan Rd ME4 53 F2
Athelstan Way BR5 44 A8
Athill Ct TN13 92 C5
Athol Rd DA8 4 C1
Atkinson Cl BR6 58 A5
Atkinson Rd E16 1 C8
Atlanta Ct ME4 53 D3
Atlantic Cl DA10 17 E2
Atlas Gdns SE7 1 C2
Atlas Rd DA1 15 F4
Atterbury Cl TN16 89 D1
Attlee Dr DA1 16 A2
Attlee Rd SE28 3 B6
Attwaters La TN18 189 C6
Atwater Ct ME17 120 D5
Auckland Cl RM18 19 A5
Auckland Ho 10 ME15 116 E5
Auckland Rd TN1 159 C5
Auden Rd ME20 82 A3
Audley Ave
Gillingham ME7 54 E1
Tonbridge TN9 126 F2
Audley Cl ME16 99 B5
Audley Dr E16 1 B5
Audley Rise TN9 126 F1
Audley Wlk BR5 44 C3
Audre Lorde Ho E16 1 B8
Audrey Sturley Ct TN4 158 D4
Auger Cl ME9 70 E5
Augusta Cl 1 ME7 54 C7
Augustine Ho TN10 127 C3
Augustine Rd
Gravesend DA12 36 C8
Orpington BR5 44 D6
Aultmore Ct TN2 159 D3
Austell Manor 5 ME7 54 C6
Austen Cl
Swanscombe DA9 17 C1
Tilbury RM18 19 C5
Woolwich SE28 3 B5
Austen Gdns DA1 15 F3
Austen Rd DA8 14 B7
Austen Way ME20 81 F4
Austens Orch 14 TN30 193 A7
Austin Ave BR2 42 E4
Austin Cl ME5 54 E2
Austin Ct 4 TN16 89 D1
Austin Rd Northfleet DA11 35 F7
Orpington BR5 44 A4
Austral Cl DA15 29 F5
Autumn Glade ME5 84 D8
Avalon Cl BR6 58 D7
Avalon Rd BR5,BR6 58 C8
Avard Gdns BR6 57 C6
Avards Cl TN18 194 E8
Avebury Ave TN9 127 B1
Avebury Rd BR6 57 D7
Aveley Cl DA8 14 F8
Aveling Cl ME3 40 D6
Aveling Ct 2 ME2 53 B7
Avenons Rd 3 E16 1 A8
Avenue Le Puy TN9 127 C1
Avenue Rd Bexley DA7,DA6 13 E4
Erith DA8 14 D7
Sevenoaks TN13 92 C3
Tatsfield TN16 88 E7
Avenue The
Aylesford ME20 82 E1
Biggin Hill TN16 88 F5
Borough Green TN15 95 A8
Bromley BR1 42 D6
Gravesend DA11 36 A8
Hill Park TN16 89 A4
Orpington BR6 57 F8
Orpington,Keston Mark BR2 56 D7
Orpington,St Paul's Cray
BR5 30 B1
Sidcup DA5 30 D8
St Mary's Island ME4 40 C2
Swanscombe DA9 17 B2
Tonbridge TN9 127 B2
Averenches Rd ME14 100 F5
Avery Cl Allhallows-on-S ME3 9 E3
Maidstone ME15 99 F1
Avery Ct ME3 9 E3
Avery Hill Rd SE9 29 D7
Avery La ME15, ME17 117 D6
Avery Way Allhallows ME3 9 D2
Dartford DA1 32 F6
Aviemore Gdns ME14 100 F4
Avington Cl ME15 99 F1
Avocet Mews SE28 2 D3
Avocet Wlk ME5 68 D2
Avon Cl Gravesend DA12 36 D6
Tonbridge TN10 127 C5
Avon Ct DA14 30 B5
Avon St TN1 159 C5
Avondale Ct ME14 100 E5
Avondale Pl ME3 25 C4
Avondale Rd Bexley DA16 13 C5
Bromley,Mottingham SE9 28 E6
Bromley,Plaistow BR1 28 A2
Gillingham ME7 54 D5
Avonmouth Rd DA1 15 D2
Avonstowe Cl BR6 57 C7
Awliscombe Rd DA16 12 F5
Axford Ct ME8 70 A8
Axminster Cres DA16 13 C6
Axtaine Rd BR5 44 D2
Axtane DA13 34 F1
Axtane Cl DA4 47 C8
Axton Chase Sch DA3 48 F6
Aycliffe Cl BR1 42 F5
Ayelands DA3 62 E8
Ayelands La DA3 62 E8
Ayers Cotts BR8 32 E2
Aylesbury Rd BR2 42 A6
Aylesford Cres ME8 55 B4
Aylesford Prim Sch
ME20 82 D1
Aylesford Sch ME20 82 D1
Aylesford Sta ME20 82 D2
Aylesham Rd BR6 43 F2
Ayleswade Rd TN27 167 E7
Aynscombe Angle BR6 44 A2
Azalea Dr BR8 45 E5

B

Babb's La TN17 190 A6
Babbacombe Rd BR1 28 B1
Babington House Sch
BR7 28 F2
Babylon La ME17,TN12 134 B1
Back La
Godden Green TN15 93 A2
Goudhurst TN17 177 E8
Horsmonden TN12 163 A6
Ightham TN15 94 C2
Maidstone ME17 116 E1
Sevenoaks TN13,TN14 91 C1
Shipbourne TN11 110 D4
Sidcup DA5 31 A8
Back Rd Sandhurst TN18 196 B5
Sidcup DA14 30 A4
Back St ME17 117 E6
Backfields ME1 53 B4
Baden Powell Ho 11 DA17 4 A3
Baden Powell Rd TN13 91 E5
Baden Rd ME7 54 D7
Bader Cres ME5 68 A7
Bader Wlk DA11 35 F5
Badger Rd ME5 68 C1
Badgers Copse BR6 57 F8
Badgers Croft SE9 29 A5
Badgers Holt TN2 159 E5
Badgers Rd TN14 59 B1
Badgers Rise TN14 59 A1
Badlow Cl DA8 14 E7
Badminton Mews E16 1 A5
Badsell Park Farm
TN12 145 C3
Badsell Rd TN12 145 E5
Baffin Cl ME4 53 F2
Bagshaw Ho 6 BR1 42 A8
Bailey Dr ME7 55 A1
Baird Ho 18 DA17 4 A3
Bakenham Ho 1 ME1 53 C1
Baker Beall Ct DA7 14 B4
Baker Hill Cl DA11 35 F4
Baker La Headcorn TN27 151 F7
Sutton Valence ME17 134 F7
Baker Rd SE18 11 E7
Baker St Burham ME1 66 F1
Rochester ME1 53 C3
Baker's Wlk ME1 53 C6
Bakers Ave TN15 61 E3
Bakers Cross TN17 179 E4
Bakers Mews 9 BR6 57 F4
Bakery Cl TN17 166 E7
Bakery Cotts ME14 83 E3
Balaclava La TN5 185 A6
Balcaskie Rd SE9 11 F2
Balchen Rd SE3 11 D5
Balcombe Cl DA6 13 D3
Balcombe Cotts TN17 177 E8
Balcombes Hill TN17 177 E8
Balder Rise SE12 28 B6
Baldock Rd TN5 184 E4
Baldwyn's Pk DA5 31 D6
Baldwyn's Rd DA5 31 D6
Baldwyns Mans DA2 31 D6
Balfour Inf Sch ME1 53 E1
Balfour Jun Sch ME4 53 E2
Balfour Rd Bromley BR2 42 D4
Chatham ME4 53 E2
Balgowan St SE18 2 F2
Ball's Gn TN7 170 B5
Ballamore Rd BR1 28 A5
Ballard Bsns Pk ME2 52 F5
Ballard Cl TN12 148 C6
Ballard Ct 20 DA14 30 A5
Ballard Ind Est ME5 84 C8
Ballard Way TN12 146 B7
Ballards La RH8 104 C6
Ballens Rd ME5 68 C3
Balliol Rd DA16 13 B5
Balls Cotts ME3 39 F4
Balmer Cl ME8 69 D7
Balmoral Ct SE12 28 B4
Balmoral Gdns DA5 30 F8
Balmoral Ho 10 ME15 116 F5
Balmoral Rd
Gillingham ME7 54 D5
Sutton at H DA4 33 B1
Balmoral Trad Est E6 2 F8
Baltic Ho TN1 159 B5
Baltic Rd TN9 143 B7
Baltic Wharf 1 DA11 19 A1
Baltimore Pl DA16 12 F5
Banbury Villas DA13 34 F1
Banchory Rd SE3 11 B7
Banckside DA3 48 E5
Bancroft Gdns BR6 43 F1
Bancroft La ME18 97 C2
Bancroft Rd TN15 78 F3
Bangor Rd ME2 52 D6
Banister Ho RM20 17 D8
Bank Cotts ME17 102 E3
Bank Ho TN15 79 A3
Bank Hos DA2 33 A3
Bank La TN11,TN15 109 A3
Bank St Chatham ME4 54 B3
Cranbrook TN17 179 C5
Gravesend DA12 19 B1
Maidstone ME14 100 A4
Sevenoaks TN13 92 C2
Tonbridge TN9 127 C2
Bank View 5 ME15 99 E2
Bankfield Way TN17 177 E7
Bankfields TN27 151 C5
Banks La DA6 13 F3
Banks Rd ME2 53 C8
Bankside Chatham ME5 68 B8
Durgates TN5 184 E5
Northfleet DA11 18 C1
Sevenoaks TN13 91 E6
Bankside Cl
Biggin Hill TN16 72 C1
Joyden's Wood DA5 31 D4
Banky Mdw ME16 98 F3
Banner Farm Rd TN2 159 B2
Banning St ME2 53 B8
Bannister Gdns BR5 44 C6
Bannister Rd ME14 100 A7
Bannockburn Prim Sch
SE18 2 F2
Bannockburn Rd SE18 2 F2
Banstead Ct 3 BR1 42 E6
Banwell Rd DA5 13 D1
Bapchild Pl 8 BR5 44 C5
Barbados Terr 2 ME14 100 A7
Barberry Ave ME5 67 E5
Barcham Ct ME15 115 F5
Barchester Way TN10 127 F6
Barclay Ave TN10 128 A5
Barclay Field TN15 76 E2
Barcombe Cl BR5 44 A6
Bardell Terr ME1 53 D5
Barden Ct ME14 100 B5
Barden Park Rd TN9 127 A1
Barden Rd Penshurst TN3 141 F2
Speldhurst TN3 158 A8
Tonbridge TN9 127 B1
Barden St SE18 12 E7
Bardsley Cl TN12 130 A7
Barfield DA4 47 B8
Barfield Rd BR1,BR7 43 A6
Barfleur Manor 3 ME7 54 A6
Barfreston Cl ME15 99 F2
Bargate Cl SE18 2 F1
Bargehouse Rd E16 2 B4
Bargrove Rd ME14 100 C5
Barham Cl Chislehurst BR7 29 B3
Gravesend DA12 36 F7
Maidstone ME15 116 E5
Orpington BR2 42 E1
Barham Ct BR2 42 E1
Barham Mews ME18 114 B8
Barham Rd
Chislehurst BR7 29 B3
Dartford DA1 33 A8
Barham's Mill Rd TN27 137 B3
Baring Cl SE12 28 A6
Baring Prim Sch SE12 28 A8
Baring Rd SE12 28 A6
Bark Hart Rd BR6 44 B1
Barker Rd ME16 99 F3
Barkis Cl ME1 67 D7
Barley Fields ME14 100 D4
Barleycorn ME19 81 E1
Barleycorn Dr ME8 69 E6
Barleymow Cl ME5 68 C7
Barling Cl ME5 67 D1
Barlow Cl ME8 69 E5
Barlow Dr SE18 11 E6
Barlow Way RM13 4 E8
Barlow Way S RM13 4 E7
Barming Prim Sch ME16 98 F2
Barming Rd ME18 97 F2
Barming Sta ME16 98 F6
Barn End Ctr DA2 32 C5
Barn End Dr DA2 32 C5
Barn End La DA2 32 C4
Barn Hill ME15 114 E2
Barn Mdw
Staplehurst TN12 149 E4
Upper Halling ME2 65 E4
Barnaby Terr ME1 53 D2
Barnard Cl
Chislehurst BR7 43 D8

Barnard Cl *continued*
Woolwich SE18 ....2 A3
Barnard Ct Chatham ME4 ..54 A2
21 Dartford DA2 ....16 B1
Barncroft Cl ME14 ....100 F4
Barncroft Dr ME7 ....68 F4
Barndale Ct DA12 ....37 E3
Barned Ct ME16 ....98 F2
Barnehurst Ave DA7,DA8 ..14 C6
Barnehurst Cl DA8 ....14 C6
Barnehurst Inf Sch DA8 ....14 C6
Barnehurst Jun Sch DA8 ..14 C6
Barnehurst Rd DA7 ....14 C5
Barnehurst Sta DA7 ....14 C5
Barnes Cray Prim Sch
DA1 ....15 A3
Barnes Cray Rd DA1 ....15 A3
Barnes Ct E16 ....1 C8
Barnes La ME17 ....132 D8
Barnes Wlk TN12 ....148 D6
Barnesdale Cres BR5 ....44 A4
Barnet Dr BR2 ....56 E8
Barnet Wood Rd BR2 ....56 C8
Barnett Cl DA8 ....14 F5
Barnetts Cl TN4 ....143 C1
Barnetts Rd TN11 ....126 A2
Barnetts Way TN4 ....159 C8
Barney Cl SE7 ....1 C1
Barnfield Chatham ME5 ....68 A8
Gravesend DA11 ....36 A6
Royal Tunbridge Wells
TN2 ....172 F7
Tenterden TN30 ....183 C2
Barnfield Cl
Crockenhill BR8 ....45 C2
New Barn DA3 ....49 D6
Stone DA9 ....16 F1
Barnfield Cres TN15 ....76 E2
Barnfield Gdns SE18 ....12 B8
Barnfield Rd Bexley DA17 ..13 F8
Orpington BR5 ....44 D6
Sevenoaks TN13 ....91 E4
Tatsfield TN16 ....88 D6
Woolwich SE18 ....12 B8
Barnfield Way RH8 ....104 A2
Barnham Dr SE28 ....2 F5
Barnhill Ave BR2 ....42 A4
Barnhurst Rd ME14 ....100 A8
Barnock Cl DA1 ....31 E8
Barnsole Inf Sch ME7 ....54 E4
Barnsole Jun Sch ME7 ....54 E4
Barnsole Rd ME7 ....54 E3
Barnwell Pl ME7 ....54 C5
Barnwell Rd DA1 ....15 F4
Barnwood Cl ME1 ....67 B8
Baron Cl Gillingham ME7 ..54 E7
Maidstone ME14 ....100 F5
Barons Ct TN4 ....159 A5
Barr Rd DA12 ....36 F6
Barrack Cnr TN13 ....92 C4
Barrack Rd ME4 ....54 B8
Barrack Row
Benenden TN17 ....190 D6
17 Gravesend DA11 ....19 B1
Barrel Arch Cl TN12 ....148 C6
Barretts Green Cotts 5
TN18 ....189 A2
Barretts Rd
Hawkhurst TN18 ....189 A2
Sevenoaks TN13 ....91 E7
Barrie Dr 7 ME20 ....81 F4
Barrier Point Rd E16 ....1 C5
Barrier Rd ME4 ....53 F5
Barrington Cl ME5 ....67 F5
Barrington Prim Sch
DA7 ....13 D5
Barrington Rd DA7 ....13 D5
Barrington Villas SE18 ....12 A6
Barrow La TN3 ....157 F2
Barrowfields ME5 ....68 D1
Barry Ave DA7 ....13 E7
Barry Cl BR6 ....57 E7
Barry Rd E6 ....1 E7
Barth Mews SE18 ....2 E2
Barth Rd SE18 ....2 E2
Bartholomew Way BR8 ....45 E6
Bartlett Cl ME5 ....68 C1
Bartlett Rd
Gravesend DA11 ....36 A7
Westerham TN16 ....89 C1
Bartley Mill La TN3 ....174 E4
Bartley Mill Rd TN3 ....174 F3
Barton Cl Bexley DA6 ....13 E2
2 Newham E6 ....1 F7
Barton Cotts TN11 ....111 A6
Barton Rd
Maidstone ME15 ....100 A2
Rochester ME2 ....53 A7
Sidcup DA14 ....30 E2
Sutton at H DA4 ....47 B8
Bartons Cotts TN16 ....90 C3
Bascombe Gr DA1 ....14 E1
Basden Cotts 2 TN18 ....189 A2
Baseing Cl E6 ....2 A6
Bashford Barn La ME9 ....87 F4
Basi Cl ME2 ....39 C1
Basil Terr 6 ME15 ....100 A1
Basildon Rd SE2 ....3 A1
Basilon Rd DA7 ....13 E5
Basing Cl ME15 ....100 B3
Basing Dr DA5 ....13 F1
Basket Gdns SE9 ....11 E2
Basmere Cl ME14 ....100 C6
Bassant Rd SE18 ....12 F8
Bassett's Forge TN5 ....184 E5
Bassetts Cl BR6 ....57 B6
Bassetts La TN8,TN11 ....156 C7
Bassetts Way BR6 ....57 B6
Basted La Basted TN15 ....94 F5
Crouch TN15 ....95 B4
Bastion Rd SE2 ....3 A1
Baston Manor BR2 ....56 B6
Baston Manor Rd BR2,
BR4 ....56 B6
Baston Rd BR2 ....56 B7
Baston Sch BR2 ....56 B8
Bat & Ball Ent Ctr TN14 ..92 C7
Bat & Ball Sta TN14 ....92 C6
Batchelor St ME4 ....54 A4
Batchelors TN2 ....160 E8
Batchwood Gn BR5 ....44 B6
Bates Cl ME20 ....82 A3
Bates Hill TN15 ....94 C5
Bateson St SE18 ....2 E2
Bath Hard ME1 ....53 D5
Bath Rd DA1 ....32 B8
Bath St DA11 ....19 B1
Baths Rd BR2 ....42 D5
Bathurst Cl TN12 ....149 E4
Bathurst Rd TN12 ....149 E3
Bathway 18 SE18 ....2 A2
Batt's Rd DA12 ....51 A4
Batten Cl E6 ....1 F7
Battery Rd SE28 ....2 E4
Battle La TN12 ....149 A8
Battle Rd DA8,DA17 ....4 C2
Battle St DA12 ....50 F6
Battlefields TN15 ....78 F3
Battlesmere Rd ME3 ....39 B8
Baugh Rd DA14 ....30 C3
Baxter Rd E16 ....1 C7
Baxter Way ME18 ....97 C3
Bay Cl ME3 ....40 E3
Bay Manor La RM20 ....16 F8
Bay The DA13 ....80 A8
Bayard Ct DA6 ....14 B3
Bayeux Ho 11 SE7 ....11 C8
Bayfield Rd SE9 ....11 D3
Bayhall Rd TN2 ....159 C3
Bayham Ct TN5 ....184 E6
Bayham Old Abbey*
TN3 ....175 B5
Bayham Rd
Bells Yew Green TN3 ....174 B4
Royal Tunbridge Wells
TN2,TN3 ....173 C7
Sevenoaks TN13 ....92 D4
Bayley Wlk SE2 ....3 E1
Bayley's Hill TN14 ....107 E3
Bayliss Ave SE28 ....3 D6
Bayly Rd DA1 ....16 A1
Bayne Cl E6 ....1 F7
Baynham Cl DA5 ....13 F1
Bays The BR5 ....44 C6
Bayswater Dr ME8 ....69 E4
Baytree Cl Bromley BR1 ..42 D8
Sidcup DA15 ....29 F7
Baywell ME19 ....81 E2
Bazes Shaw DA3 ....62 F8
Beach Ct Eltham SE9 ....11 E1
Goddard's Green TN17 ....180 D1
Beacham Cl SE7 ....11 D8
Beachamwell Dr ME18 ....97 C2
Beacon Cl ME8 ....69 D7
Beacon Dr DA2 ....34 C5
Beacon Hill ME5 ....54 D2
Beacon Hill La ME3 ....39 F4
Beacon Oak Rd TN30 ....193 B8
Beacon Rd Chatham ME5 ..54 C2
Erith DA8 ....15 B7
Lenham ME17 ....120 C5
Beacon Rise TN13 ....92 A1
Beacon Wlk TN30 ....183 B1
Beacon Wood Ctry Pk*
DA2 ....34 B4
Beaconfields TN13 ....92 A1
Beacons Cl 11 E6 ....1 E8
Beacons The ME17 ....115 C2
Beaconsfield Ave ME7 ....54 E5
Beaconsfield Cl SE3 ....11 A8
Beaconsfield Par SE9 ....28 E4
Beaconsfield Rd
Bromley,Mottingham SE9 ..28 E4
Bromley,Widmore BR1 ....42 D6
Chatham ME4 ....53 F3
Greenwich SE3 ....11 A8
Maidstone ME15 ....99 E2
Maypole DA5 ....31 E6
Beadon Rd BR2 ....42 A4
Beagles Cl BR5 ....58 D8
Beagles Wood Rd TN2 ..160 E7
Beal Cl DA16 ....13 A6
Beaman Cl TN17 ....177 F8
Beamish Rd BR5 ....44 C2
Beams The ME15 ....100 F1
Bean Hill Cotts DA2 ....34 C4
Bean La DA2 ....34 B6
Bean Prim Sch DA2 ....34 C4
Bean Rd Bexley DA6 ....13 D3
Swanscombe DA9 ....17 B1
Beane Croft DA12 ....36 F7
Beanshaw SE9 ....29 A4
Bearsted Cl ME8 ....55 B3
Bearsted Green Bsns Ctr
ME14 ....101 C4
Bearsted Rd ME14 ....100 E6
Bearsted Sta ME14 ....101 B5
Beaton Cl DA9 ....17 B2
Beatrice Gdns DA11 ....35 E6
Beatty Ave ME7 ....54 F4
Beatty Cotts ME3 ....9 D1
Beatty Rd ME1 ....67 D8
Beaufighter Rd ME19 ....96 E3
Beaufort E6 ....2 A8
Beaufort Ct ME2 ....53 E6
Beaufort Rd ME2 ....52 E8
Beaufort Wlk ME15 ....116 E4
Beaulieu Ave E16 ....1 B5
Beaulieu Rd TN10 ....127 B4
Beaulieu Rise ME1 ....53 D1
Beaulieu Wlk ME16 ....99 C7
Beaumanor Gdns SE9 ....29 A4
Beaumont Dr DA11 ....35 F8
Beaumont Rd
Maidstone ME16 ....99 B2
Orpington BR5 ....43 D3
Beauworth Pk ME15 ....116 E8
Beaver Rd ME16 ....99 B7
Beaver Zoological Gdns*
TN16 ....88 B5
Beaverbank Rd SE9 ....29 D7
Beavers Lodge DA14 ....29 F3
Beaverwood Rd BR7 ....29 E2
Beaverwood Sch for Girls
BR7 ....29 E2
Bebbington Rd SE18 ....2 E2
Beblets Cl 4 BR6 ....57 F5
Beckenham Dr ME16 ....99 D7
Becket Ct
Headcorn TN27 ....151 D5
2 Tonbridge TN9 ....143 B8
Beckets Field TN11 ....141 A3
Beckett Cl DA17 ....3 F3
Becketts Cl BR6 ....57 F7
Beckford Dr BR5 ....43 D2
Beckley Cl DA12 ....37 B6
Beckley Hill Works ME2 ..38 B8
Beckley Mews ME5 ....67 F5
Beckman Cl TN14 ....75 C4
Becks Rd DA14 ....30 A5
Becksbourne Cl ME14 ....100 A8
Beckton Park Sta E6 ....1 F6
Beckton Rd E16 ....1 A8
Beckton Ret Pk E6 ....2 A8
Beckton Sta E6 ....2 A8
Beckworth Pl ME16 ....99 B2
Becton Pl DA8 ....14 C6
Bedale Wlk DA2 ....33 B7
Beddalls Farm Ct 7 E6 ....1 E8
Beddington Gn BR5 ....43 F8
Beddington Rd BR5 ....43 F8
Beddlestead La CR6 ....88 A6
Beddow Way ME20 ....83 B3
Bedens Rd DA14 ....30 E3
Bedford Ave ME8 ....55 D1
Bedford Pl ME16 ....99 E4
Bedford Rd Dartford DA1 ..33 A8
Northfleet DA11 ....35 F6
Orpington BR6 ....44 B1
Royal Tunbridge Wells
TN4 ....143 A1
Sidcup DA15 ....29 E5
Bedford Sq DA3 ....48 E6
Bedford Terr 18 TN1 ....159 A2
Bedgebury Cl
Maidstone ME14 ....100 C6
Rochester ME1 ....67 D8
Bedgebury Cross TN17 ..177 D2
Bedgebury National
Pinetum* TN17 ....187 E8
Bedgebury Rd Eltham SE9 .11 D3
Goudhurst TN17 ....177 E5
Bedgebury Sch TN17 ....177 E1
Bedivere Rd BR1 ....28 A5
Bedlam La TN27 ....152 E6
Bedonwell Inf Sch DA17 ..13 E8
Bedonwell Jun Sch DA17 .13 E8
Bedonwell Rd
Bexley,Bexleyheath DA7 ....13 F6
Bexley,West Heath DA7,
DA17 ....13 E8
Bedwell Rd DA17 ....4 A1
Bedwin Cl ME1 ....67 D7
Beeby Rd E16 ....1 B8
Beech Ave Sidcup DA15 ....30 A8
Swanley BR8 ....45 F5
Tatsfield TN16 ....88 D8
Beech Copse BR1 ....42 F7
Beech Ct Dartford DA1 ....16 A1
Paddock Wood TN12 ....146 A7
Royal Tunbridge Wells
TN2 ....159 D4
Beech Dell BR2,BR4 ....56 F6
Beech Dr ME16 ....99 C5
Beech Gr ME3 ....38 C4
Beech Green La
Cowden TN7 ....155 F1
Withyham TN7 ....170 B7
Beech Haven Ct DA1 ....14 D2
Beech Ho 7 DA15 ....30 A5
Beech Hurst TN2 ....160 D7
Beech Hurst Cl ME15 ....100 B2
Beech La TN12 ....161 C4
Beech Manor TN2 ....159 D3
Beech Mast DA13 ....80 B8
Beech Rd Biggin Hill TN16 ..72 C2
Dartford DA1 ....32 D7
East Malling ME19 ....97 F7
Herne Pound ME18 ....96 D2
Hoo St Werburgh ME3 ....40 E3
Newenden TN18 ....197 C3
Orpington BR6 ....58 A3
Rochester ME2 ....52 F6
Sevenoaks TN13 ....92 B2
Beech St TN1 ....159 B4
Beech Wlk
Biddenden TN27 ....182 D7
Crayford DA1 ....15 A3
Beecham Rd TN10 ....127 E6
Beechcroft BR7 ....29 A1
Beechcroft Ave DA7 ....14 D5
Beechcroft Cl BR6 ....57 D6
Beechcroft Rd BR6 ....57 D6
Beechen Bank Rd ME5 ....68 A1
Beechenlea La BR8 ....46 B6
Beecher Ct SE12 ....28 B5
Beeches Ct BR1 ....28 A2
Beeches The
Aylesford ME20 ....82 E1
Chatham ME5 ....68 A4
Hextable BR8 ....31 F1
New Barn DA3 ....49 C7
Royal Tunbridge Wells
TN2 ....159 D5
Sole Street DA13 ....50 D5
The Moor TN18 ....194 E7
Tilbury RM18 ....19 B5
Beechfield Cotts 6 BR1 ..42 C7
Beechfield Rd
Bromley BR1 ....42 C7
Erith DA8 ....14 E7
Beechhill Rd SE9 ....12 A2
Beechin Wood La TN15 ....95 D5
Beeching Rd ME5 ....68 B3
Beechings Gn ME8 ....55 C3
Beechings Way ME8 ....55 C3
Beechings Way Ind Ctr
ME8 ....55 B4
Beechlands Cl DA3 ....49 A4
Beechmont Rd TN13 ....108 B6
Beechmont Rise TN10 ....127 B6
Beechmore Dr ME5 ....68 A2
Beechway
Meopham Sta DA13 ....50 B2
Sidcup DA5 ....13 D1
Beechwood Ave
Gillingham ME5 ....54 D2
Orpington BR6 ....57 E4
Beechwood Cres DA7 ....13 E4
Beechwood Dr
Culverstone Green DA13 ..64 A1
Orpington BR2 ....56 D6
Beechwood Gdns DA13 ..64 A1
Beechwood Mews TN2 ..159 E4
Beechwood Rd ME16 ....98 F3
Beechwood Rise BR7 ....29 B4
Beechwood Sacred Heart Sch
TN2 ....159 E4
Beechy Lees Rd TN14 ....76 E3
Beeken Dene BR6 ....57 C6
Beesfield La DA4 ....47 A1
Beeston Ct 4 DA1 ....16 B1
Begbie Rd SE3 ....11 C6
Beggars La TN16 ....89 E3
Begonia Ave ME8 ....55 C2
Beke Rd ME8 ....69 D4
Bekesbourne Twr 12
BR5 ....44 D1
Beldam Haw TN14 ....75 A8
Belfast Ho 14 ME15 ....116 E7
Belfield Rd TN2 ....160 D6
Belford Gr SE18 ....2 A2
Belgrave Cl 5 BR5 ....44 C5
Belgrave Ct SE7 ....11 C7
Belgrave Rd TN1 ....159 B4
Belgrave St ME20 ....82 F6
Belgrove 5 TN1 ....159 A2
Bell Cl DA9 ....16 F2
Bell Cres ME1 ....82 F8
Bell Farm Gdns ME16 ....98 F2
Bell Gdns BR5 ....44 C4
Bell Ho Erith SE2 ....3 D1
Grays RM17 ....17 F8
Bell La Burham ME1 ....82 F8
Chatham ME14 ....84 B7
Larkfield ME20 ....82 B2
Maidstone ME14 ....101 A5
Newham E16 ....1 A5
Standen TN27 ....168 B8
Staplehurst TN12 ....149 E3
Bell Mdw ME15 ....116 E6
Bell Rd ME15 ....116 E5
Bell Row TN11 ....128 F5
Bell St SE18 ....11 E6
Bell Water Gate SE18 ....2 A3
Bell Way ME17 ....118 E2
Bell Wood Prim Sch
ME15 ....116 E5
Bell's Cl TN30 ....193 A7
Bell's La ME3 ....40 E6
Bellarmine Cl SE28 ....2 F4
Belle Vue Rd BR6 ....57 A1
Bellefield Rd BR5 ....44 B4
Bellegrove Cl DA16 ....12 F5
Bellegrove Par DA16 ....12 F4
Bellegrove Rd DA16 ....12 E5
Bellevue Rd DA6 ....13 F2
Bellfield Cl SE3 ....11 B7
Bellflower Cl 2 E6 ....1 E8
Bellgrove Ct ME5 ....84 A8
Bellingham Way ME20 ....82 B3
Bellman Ave DA12 ....36 E7
Bellows La TN15 ....94 F7
Bellring Cl DA17 ....14 A8
Bells Farm La TN11 ....129 C8
Bells Farm Rd TN11,
TN12 ....112 D1
Bells La 9 TN30 ....193 A7
Bellwood Ct ME3 ....24 C3
Belmont Ave DA16 ....12 E4
Belmont Cl ME16 ....98 F2
Belmont Ct 9 ME15 ....100 B4
Belmont La BR7 ....29 C3
Belmont Par BR7 ....29 C3
Belmont Prim Sch DA8 ....14 A7
Belmont Rd
Chislehurst BR7 ....29 B3
Erith DA8 ....14 B6
Gillingham ME7 ....54 C4
Belmont Rd *continued*
Grays RM17 ....17 F
Belnor Ave ME9 ....71 F
Belson Rd SE18 ....1 F
Beltana Dr DA12 ....36 E
Belton Rd DA14 ....30 A
Beltring Rd
Beltring TN12,ME18 ....130 B
Royal Tunbridge Wells
TN4 ....159 A
Beltring Sta TN12 ....130 B
Beltwood Rd DA17 ....4 C
Beluncle Villas ME3 ....41 C
Belvedere Cl DA12 ....36 C
Belvedere Ct DA17 ....3 F
Belvedere Ho 9 ME15 ....116 E
Belvedere Ind Est DA17 ....4 D
Belvedere Inf Sch DA17 ....4 B
Belvedere Jun Sch DA17 ....4 B
Belvedere Link Bsns Pk
DA17 ....4 C
Belvedere Mews SE3 ....11 B
Belvedere Rd Bexley DA7 ..13 F
Biggin Hill TN16 ....72 F
Erith SE28 ....3 D
Belvedere Sta DA17 ....4 B
Belvoir Cl SE9 ....28 E
Ben Tillet Cl E16 ....1 F
Benares Rd SE18 ....2 F
Benden Cl TN12 ....149 F
Bendmore Ave SE2 ....3 A
Bendon Way ME8 ....69 D
Benedict Cl 9 Erith DA17 ..3 E
Halling ME2 ....66 B
Orpington BR6 ....57 E
Benenden CE Prim Sch
TN17 ....190 D
Benenden Gn BR2 ....42 A
Benenden Hospl TN17 ....181 C
Benenden Manor ME8 ....55 B
Benenden Rd
Benenden TN17 ....191 B
Cranbrook TN17 ....179 E
Fosten Green TN27 ....181 F
Rochester ME2 ....39 C
Benenden Sch TN17 ....190 C
Benhall Mill Rd TN2,
TN3 ....173 D
Benjamin Ct 4 DA17 ....13 F
Benn Cl RH8 ....104 A
Benn Ho SE7 ....1 C
Bennett Cl DA16 ....13 A
Bennett Ho DA11 ....35 F
Bennett Meml Diocesan Sch
TN4 ....158 E
Bennett Way DA2 ....33 D
Bennetts Ave TN15 ....78 C
Bennetts Copse BR7 ....28 E
Bennetts Cotts ME7 ....85 A
Bennetts Mews 13 TN30 .193 A
Benover Rd ME18 ....130 F
Benson Rd RM17 ....18 C
Bensted Cl ME15 ....131 D
Bentfield Gdns SE9 ....28 D
Bentham Hill TN3,TN4 ....142 D
Bentham Rd SE28 ....3 B5
Bentley Cl Aylesford ME20 ..82 F1
Chatham ME5 ....68 D2
New Barn DA3 ....49 C7
Bentley St DA12 ....19 C1
Bentley Street Ind Est
DA12 ....19 C1
Bentley's Mdw TN15 ....92 F7
Bentleys Bglws TN15 ....92 F7
Bentlif Cl ME16 ....99 D5
Berber Rd ME2 ....53 B8
Bercta Rd SE9 ....29 C6
Bere Cl DA9 ....17 C2
Berengrave La ME8 ....55 F2
Berens Ct DA14 ....29 F4
Berens Rd BR5 ....44 D4
Berens Way BR5 ....43 F6
Beresford Ave ME1 ....53 E2
Beresford Cl TN17 ....176 F2
Beresford Dr BR1 ....42 E6
Beresford Rd
Gillingham ME7 ....54 D4
Goudhurst TN17 ....163 F1
Kit's Coty ME20 ....83 D7
Northfleet DA11 ....35 E8
Beresford Square Market Pl
SE18 ....2 B2
Beresford St SE18 ....2 B3
Beresfords Hill ME17 ....116 B4
Berger Cl BR5 ....43 E3
Bergland Pk ME2 ....53 D8
Bering Wlk E16 ....1 D7
Berkeley Ave DA7 ....13 D6
Berkeley Cl Orpington BR5 .43 E2
Pembury TN2 ....160 E7
Rochester ME1 ....67 D8
Berkeley Cres DA1 ....32 F7
Berkeley Ct 6 BR8 ....45 E6
Berkeley Mount 8 ME4 ....53 F4
Berkeley Rd 7 TN1 ....159 A2
Berkeley Terr RM18 ....19 A7
Berkhampstead Rd 9
DA17 ....4 A1
Berkley Cres DA12 ....19 C1
Berkley Rd DA12 ....19 B1
Berkshire Cl ME5 ....68 C8
Bermuda Rd RM18 ....19 A5
Bernal Cl SE28 ....3 D6
Bernard Ashley Dr SE7 ....1 B1
Bernard St 24 DA12 ....19 B1
Bernards Ct DA15 ....29 E7
Berner's Hill TN5 ....187 A3
Bernersmede SE3 ....11 A4

erry Rd ME3 .....40 E3
erry's Green Rd TN16 .....73 B2
erry's Hill TN16 .....73 B4
erryfield Cl BR1 .....42 E7
erryhill SE9 .....12 B3
erryhill Gdns SE9 .....12 B3
errylands Hartley DA3 .....49 A3
Orpington BR6 .....58 C7
ert Reilly Ho 1 SE18 .....2 D1
ertha Hollamby Ct
DA14 .....30 C3
ertha James Ct BR2 .....42 B5
ertrand Way SE28 .....3 C6
ertrey Cotts TN16 .....73 B3
erwick Cres DA15 .....12 E1
erwick Ct 12 DA2 .....16 B1
erwick Rd Bexley DA16 .....13 B6
Newham E16 .....1 C7
erwick Way TN14 .....92 B7
erwyn Gr ME15 .....116 A6
eryl Ave E6 .....1 E8
eryl Ho 3 SE18 .....2 F1
esant Ct 15 SE28 .....3 B6
essels Green Rd TN13 .....91 D3
essels Mdw TN13 .....91 D3
essels Way TN13 .....91 D4
essie Lansbury Cl E6 .....2 A7
est St ME4 .....53 F4
eta Rd ME3 .....41 D7
etenson Ave TN13 .....91 F5
ethany Sch TN17 .....164 B5
ethel Rd Bexley DA16 .....13 C4
Sevenoaks TN13 .....92 C4
etherinden Cotts
TN18 .....196 A4
ethersden Ct ME15 .....116 F7
ethersden Rd TN27,
TN26 .....169 C5
eths Gram Sch DA5 .....14 B1
etjeman Cl ME20 .....81 F3
etony Gdns ME14 .....100 F5
etsham Rd
Betsham DA13 .....34 D3
Erith DA8 .....14 F7
Maidstone ME15 .....116 F6
Swanscombe DA10 .....34 E8
etterton Dr DA14 .....30 E6
ettescombe Rd ME8 .....69 E7
etts Rd E16 .....1 B6
eulah Rd TN1 .....159 C4
eult Mdw TN27 .....153 A1
eult Rd DA1 .....15 A3
evan Pl BR8 .....45 F5
evan Rd SE2 .....3 B1
evans Cl DA9 .....17 C1
evercote Wlk 1 DA17 .....13 F8
everidge Ct 1 SE28 .....3 B6
everley Ave DA15 .....29 F8
everley Cl ME8 .....69 F8
everley Cres TN9 .....142 F7
everley Ct 8 DA14 .....30 B4
everley Rd Bexley DA7 .....14 C5
Maidstone ME16 .....98 F2
Orpington BR2 .....56 E8
evile Ho RM17 .....18 B7
evis Cl DA2 .....33 C8
ewl Bridge Cl TN5 .....187 B3
ewl Water Nature Reserve*
TN5 .....186 B7
ewl Water Visitor Ctr*
TN3 .....186 B8
ewlbridge La
Lamberhurst TN3,TN5 .....176 B1
Lower Cousley Wood TN5 .....185 F8
ewley La TN15 .....94 D2
exhill Dr RM17 .....17 F8
exley Cl DA1 .....14 E2
exley Coll Erith DA17 .....4 B1
Erith DA17 .....4 C2
exley Coll (St Joseph's
Campus) SE2 .....13 D8
exley Cotts DA4 .....47 C5
exley Gram Sch DA16 .....13 B3
exley High St DA5 .....31 B7
exley La Crayford DA1 .....14 E2
Sidcup DA14 .....30 C5
exley Rd Eltham SE9 .....12 C2
1 Erith DA8 .....4 E1
Erith DA8 .....4 F1
Erith,Northumberland Heath
DA8 .....14 C8
exley Sta DA5 .....31 A7
exleyheath Sch DA6 .....13 F4
exleyheath Sta DA7 .....13 E5
exon La ME9 .....87 F5
glws The TN30 .....193 D7
ckley Cres BR1 .....42 E5
ckley Ct 2 BR1 .....42 E6
ckley Park Rd BR1 .....42 F6
ckley Park Sch BR1 .....42 E6
ckley Prim Sch BR1 .....42 C7
ckley Rd Bromley BR1 .....42 E7
1 Tonbridge TN9 .....143 B8
ckley Sta BR1 .....42 E6
ckmore Way TN9 .....127 D3
cknor Court Cotts ME9 .....87 C2
cknor La ME9 .....87 D3
cknor Rd
Maidstone ME15 .....116 F4
Orpington BR6 .....43 F2
dborough CE Prim Sch
TN3 .....142 D3
dborough Ct TN3 .....142 B3
dborough Ridge TN4 .....142 E4
ddenden Cl ME15 .....100 F3
ddenden La TN27 .....151 E5
ddenden Rd
Headcorn TN27 .....151 E2

Biddenden Rd *continued*
Tenterden TN30 .....182 E6
Tylden TN27 .....168 F8
Biddenden Vineyards & Cider
Works* TN27 .....182 A5
Biddenden Way
Eltham SE9 .....29 A4
Istead Rise DA13 .....35 E1
Biddulph Ho 17 SE18 .....1 F2
Bideford Rd DA16 .....13 B7
Biggin Hill Airport TN16 .....72 D5
Biggin Hill Bsns Pk TN16 .....72 D4
Biggin Hill Jun & Inf Schs
TN16 .....72 E3
Biggin La RM16 .....19 B8
Bignell Rd SE18 .....2 B1
Bilberry Cl ME14 .....100 E5
Bill Hamling Cl SE9 .....28 F6
Bill Street Rd ME2 .....39 C1
Billet Hill TN15 .....62 C6
Billings DA3 .....48 F3
Bilsby Gr SE9 .....28 D4
Bilsington Cl ME5 .....68 B5
Bilton Rd DA8 .....15 A8
Bimbury La ME14,ME9 .....86 A5
Bines The TN12 .....146 A5
Bingham Point 5 SE18 .....2 B2
Bingham Rd ME2 .....39 C1
Bingley Cl ME6 .....81 F8
Bingley Rd Newham E16 .....1 C7
1 Rochester ME1 .....53 E4
Binland Gr ME5 .....67 D5
Binnacle Rd ME1 .....67 C8
Binney Rd ME3 .....9 D2
Binsey Wlk 1 SE2 .....3 C4
Birbetts Rd SE9 .....28 F6
Birch Cl Eynsford DA4 .....60 D7
Matfield TN12 .....145 D1
New Barn DA3 .....49 C7
Royal Tunbridge Wells
TN2 .....159 D7
Sevenoaks TN13 .....92 B4
Tonbridge TN11 .....126 D4
Birch Cres ME20 .....98 D8
Birch Dr ME5 .....68 D1
Birch Gr Bexley DA16 .....13 A3
Gillingham ME7 .....69 A4
Birch Ho 6 ME16 .....99 A3
Birch Kiln Cotts TN5 .....185 A6
Birch Mead BR6 .....57 A8
Birch Pl Sevenoaks TN13 .....92 A3
Stone DA9 .....16 E1
Birch Rd
Hoo St Werburgh ME3 .....40 E3
Paddock Wood TN12 .....146 A6
Birch Row BR2 .....43 A3
Birch Tree Ho 18 SE7 .....11 C8
Birch Tree Way ME15 .....100 B3
Birch Way TN2 .....159 D7
Birchden Cotts TN3 .....171 C6
Birchdene Dr SE28 .....3 A5
Birches The
Greenwich SE7 .....11 B8
Orpington BR6 .....57 A6
Swanley BR8 .....45 E7
Tonbridge TN9 .....143 B7
Birchetts Ave TN3 .....157 E3
Birchetts Green La TN5 .....186 A2
Birchfield TN14 .....106 E8
Birchfield Cl ME15 .....116 B6
Birchfields ME5 .....68 A3
Birchin Cross Rd TN15 .....77 A5
Birchington Cl Bexley DA7 .....14 B6
Maidstone ME14 .....100 C5
Orpington BR5 .....44 C1
Bircholme TN2 .....159 D7
Bircholt Rd ME15 .....116 F4
Birchway TN15 .....61 F2
Birchwood Ave
Bidborough TN4 .....142 E3
Sidcup DA14 .....30 C5
Birchwood Dr DA2 .....31 E4
Birchwood La TN14 .....74 F4
Birchwood Par DA2 .....31 E4
Birchwood Park Ave BR8 .....45 F6
Birchwood Prim Sch
BR8 .....45 D8
Birchwood Rd
Joyden's Wood DA2,BR8 .....31 D3
Maidstone ME16 .....99 C5
Orpington BR5 .....43 E5
Birchwood Terr BR8 .....45 C8
Bird House La BR6 .....73 A5
Bird in Hand La BR1 .....42 D7
Bird in Hand St TN3 .....171 B8
Bird La TN5 .....184 B5
Birdbrook Rd SE3 .....11 C4
Birdham Cl BR1 .....42 E4
Birkbeck Prim Sch DA14 .....30 B5
Birkbeck Rd DA14 .....30 A5
Birkdale TN1 .....159 B6
Birkdale Cl Erith SE28 .....3 D7
Orpington BR6 .....43 D2
Birkdale Ct 3 ME16 .....99 E4
Birkdale Rd SE2 .....3 A2
Birken Rd TN2 .....159 D6
Birkhall Cl ME5 .....68 A5
Birling Ave Gillingham ME8 .....55 E1
Maidstone ME14 .....101 A4
Birling Cl ME14 .....101 A4
Birling Dr TN2 .....159 A1
Birling Hill DA13,ME19,
ME6 .....65 B1
Birling Park Ave TN2 .....173 B8
Birling Pk ME19 .....81 C5
Birling Rd Bexley DA8 .....14 E6
Leybourne ME19 .....81 C3

Birling Rd *continued*
Royal Tunbridge Wells
TN2 .....173 B8
Ryarsh ME19 .....81 A5
Snodland ME6 .....81 F7
Birnam Sq 1 ME16 .....99 E4
Birtrick Dr DA13 .....49 F4
Bishop Butt Cl BR6 .....57 F7
Bishop John Robinson CE
Prim Sch SE28 .....3 C6
Bishop's Down TN4 .....158 F3
Bishop's Down Park Rd
TN4 .....158 F4
Bishop's Down Prim Sch
TN4 .....158 E5
Bishop's Down Rd TN4 .....158 F3
Bishop's La ME15 .....131 D6
Bishopbourne Gn ME8 .....55 B4
Bishops Ave BR1 .....42 C6
Bishops Cl Eltham SE9 .....29 C6
Nettlestead ME18 .....113 D6
Bishops Ct
Royal Tunbridge Wells
TN4 .....158 F3
Stone DA9 .....16 E2
Bishops Gn BR1 .....42 C8
Bishops La TN17 .....178 E2
Bishops Mews TN9 .....143 C8
Bishops Oak Ride TN10 .....127 C6
Bishops Way ME15 .....99 F4
Bishops Wlk
Chislehurst BR7 .....43 C8
Rochester ME1 .....53 C5
Bishopsbourne Ho 2
BR1 .....28 B1
Black Eagle Cl TN16 .....105 C8
Black Horse Ct TN27 .....151 E5
Black Horse Mews TN15 .....95 A7
Black Horse Rd 14 DA14 .....30 A4
Black Mill La TN27 .....151 B6
Black Post ME17 .....103 E4
Black Rock Gdns ME7 .....69 B4
Black's Yd TN13 .....92 C2
Blackberry Field BR5 .....44 A8
Blackberry Way TN12 .....146 B6
Blackbrook La BR1,BR2 .....43 A5
Blackdale Farm Cotts
DA1 .....33 B6
Blackfen Par DA16 .....13 A1
Blackfen Rd DA15 .....13 B1
Blackfen Sch for Girls
DA15 .....13 B1
Blackhall La TN15 .....92 E3
Blackheath Bluecoat CE Sec
Sch SE3 .....11 B7
Blackheath High Sch
SE3 .....11 A7
Blackheath High Sch GPDST
(Jun Dept) SE3 .....11 A5
Blackheath Pk SE3 .....11 A5
Blackheath Prep Sch
SE3 .....11 A6
Blackhorse Mews TN2 .....160 C6
Blackhurst La TN2 .....159 F6
Blacklands
East Malling ME19 .....97 F7
East Malling ME19 .....97 F8
Blacklands Dr ME19 .....97 F8
Blackman Cl ME3 .....40 D7
Blackman's La TN11 .....128 D6
Blackmans Cl DA1 .....32 C7
Blackmanstone Way
ME16 .....99 B7
Blackmead TN13 .....91 E6
Blackness La BR2 .....56 D2
Blacksmith Dr ME14 .....100 D5
Blacksmith's La TN5 .....185 A5
Blacksmiths Field TN32 .....195 C1
Blacksmiths La BR5 .....44 C4
Blacksole La TN15 .....78 F3
Blacksole Rd TN15 .....78 F3
Blackthorn Ave
Chatham ME5 .....68 A3
Royal Tunbridge Wells
TN4 .....143 C1
Blackthorn Cl TN15 .....61 F2
Blackthorn Dr ME20 .....82 B2
Blackthorn Gr DA7 .....13 E4
Blackthorn Rd TN16 .....72 E3
Blackthorne Rd ME8 .....70 B8
Blackwater Cl RM13 .....4 E8
Bladindon Dr DA5 .....30 D8
Blainey Ho ME3 .....39 F6
Blair Cl DA15 .....12 E2
Blair Dr TN13 .....92 B4
Blake Cl DA16 .....12 E6
Blake Dr 3 ME20 .....81 F4
Blake Gdns DA1 .....15 F3
Blake Way
Royal Tunbridge Wells
TN2 .....159 D7
Tilbury RM18 .....19 C5
Blakemore Way DA17 .....3 E3
Blakeney Cl ME14 .....101 B4
Blaker Ave ME1 .....53 E1
Blaker Ct SE7 .....11 C7
Blanchard Cl SE9 .....28 E5
Blanchard Ho BR7 .....29 C2
Bland St SE9 .....11 D3
Blanmerle Rd SE9 .....29 B7
Blann Cl SE9 .....11 D1
Blatchford Cl ME19 .....81 F1
Blatchington Rd TN1 .....159 B1
Bleak Hill La SE18 .....12 F8
Bleakwood Rd 6 ME5 .....67 F5
Blean Rd ME8 .....55 C2
Blean Sq ME14 .....100 C6
Bledlow Cl SE28 .....3 C6

Blendon Dr DA5 .....13 D1
Blendon Rd
Maidstone ME14 .....100 C5
Sidcup DA5 .....13 D1
Blendon Terr SE18 .....12 C8
Blenheim Ave ME4 .....53 E2
Blenheim Cl Dartford DA1 .....15 C1
Maidstone ME15 .....100 F3
Meopham DA13 .....64 B8
Blenheim Ct Chatham ME4 .....53 E3
Sidcup DA15 .....29 D5
Blenheim Dr DA16 .....12 F6
Blenheim Gr DA12 .....36 C8
Blenheim Ho SE18 .....2 C3
Blenheim Prim Sch BR6 .....58 C8
Blenheim Rd Bromley BR1 .....42 E5
Dartford DA1 .....15 C1
Orpington BR5,BR6 .....58 C8
Sidcup DA15 .....30 C7
Blenheim Way TN5 .....187 C3
Bletchington Ct 3 DA17 .....4 A2
Blewbury Ho 3 SE2 .....3 C4
Bligh Inf Sch ME2 .....52 C7
Bligh Jun Sch ME2 .....52 C7
Bligh Rd DA11 .....19 A1
Bligh Way ME2 .....52 D6
Bligh's Ct TN13 .....92 B2
Bligh's Rd TN13 .....92 B2
Bligh's Wlk TN13 .....92 C2
Blind La Bredhurst ME7 .....69 A1
Gillingham ME7 .....68 F1
Goudhurst TN17 .....163 E1
Blind Mary's La ME9 .....87 E4
Bliss Way TN10 .....127 E5
Blithdale Rd SE2 .....3 A2
Blockhouse Rd 7 RM17 .....18 C8
Blockmakers Ct ME4 .....54 B1
Bloomfield Rd
Bromley BR2 .....42 D4
Woolwich SE18 .....2 B1
Bloomfield Terr TN16 .....89 E2
Bloomsbury Wlk 2
ME15 .....100 A4
Bloors La ME8 .....55 D1
Bloors Wharf Rd ME7 .....55 F4
Blowers Hil Cott TN3 .....158 B8
Blowers Hill TN8 .....155 D8
Blowers Wood Gr ME7 .....69 B3
Bloxam Gdns SE9 .....11 E2
Blue Anchor La RM18 .....19 E8
Blue Boar La ME1 .....53 D5
Blue Chalet Ind Pk TN15 .....61 D4
Blue Coat La TN17 .....177 C6
Bluebell Cl Gillingham ME7 .....54 F6
Orpington BR6 .....57 C8
Bluebell Wlks TN12 .....146 A5
Blueberry La TN14 .....74 C4
Bluebird Way SE28 .....2 D4
Bluehouse Gdns RH8 .....104 A7
Bluehouse La RH8 .....104 A8
Bluett St ME14 .....100 A5
Bluewater DA9 .....33 F8
Bluewater Parkway DA9 .....33 E8
Blunden La ME18 .....114 A1
Blunts Rd SE9 .....12 A2
Blyth Ho 5 DA8 .....4 E1
Blyth Rd SE28 .....3 C6
Blythe Ct SE12 .....28 A8
Blythe Hill BR5 .....44 A8
Blythe Rd ME15 .....100 B4
Boakes Mdw TN14 .....75 F8
Boarders La TN5 .....186 C3
Boarley Ct ME14 .....83 F1
Boarley La ME14 .....83 F2
Boathouse Rd ME12 .....27 F3
Bocking Cl TN5 .....184 E4
Bockingford La ME15 .....115 F8
Bocton Ho ME17 .....116 B3
Bodiam Cl ME8 .....55 C3
Bodiam Ct ME16 .....99 F3
Bodiam Rd TN18,TN32 .....195 F3
Bodkins Cl ME17 .....116 D5
Bodle Ave DA10 .....17 E1
Bodmin Cl BR5 .....44 C1
Bodsham Cres ME15 .....101 B3
Boevey Path
2 Bexley DA17 .....13 F8
Erith DA17 .....3 F1
Bogarde Dr ME2 .....39 B2
Bogey La BR6 .....57 A3
Bognor Rd DA16 .....13 D6
Boley Hill ME1 .....53 C6
Boleyn Rd TN15 .....76 E2
Boleyn Way DA10 .....34 E8
Bolingbroke Ho ME16 .....99 E3
Bollon Ct 9 SE12 .....28 B5
Bolner Cl ME5 .....67 F2
Bombay Ho 1 ME15 .....116 E5
Bombers La TN16 .....89 D7
Bonar Pl BR7 .....28 E1
Bonaventure Ct DA12 .....36 F4
Bonchester Cl BR7 .....29 A1
Bond Cl TN14 .....74 D4
Bond Rd ME8 .....69 E5
Bond St RM17 .....18 C8
Bondfield Cl TN4 .....143 A1
Bondfield Ho SE18 .....12 A7
Bondfield Rd
East Malling ME19 .....97 F8
4 Newham E6 .....1 F8
Bondfield Wlk DA1 .....15 F4
Boneashe La TN15 .....95 D6
Boneta Rd SE18 .....1 F3
Bonflower La ME17 .....132 C7
Bonney Way BR8 .....45 E6
Bonnington Gn ME8 .....55 C3
Bonnington Rd ME14 .....100 C6
Bonnington Twr BR2 .....42 E3

Boorman's Mews
ME18 .....113 E7
Booth Cl SE28 .....3 B6
Booth Rd ME4 .....53 F2
Bootham Cl ME2 .....52 D5
Borden CE Prim Sch ME9 .....71 F3
Bordyke TN9 .....127 C2
Boreham Ave E16 .....1 A7
Boresisle TN30 .....183 B2
Borgard Ho SE18 .....11 E6
Borgard Rd SE18 .....1 F2
Borkwood Ct BR6 .....57 F6
Borkwood Pk BR6 .....57 F6
Borkwood Way BR6 .....57 E6
Borland Cl 5 DA9 .....17 A2
Borough Green & Wrotham
Sta TN15 .....94 F7
Borough Green Prim Sch
TN15 .....95 A7
Borough Green Rd
Borough Green TN15 .....94 E7
Ightham TN15 .....94 D6
Wrotham TN15 .....79 A1
Borough Rd
Gillingham ME7 .....54 D4
Tatsfield TN16 .....88 D6
Borstal HM Prison & Youth
Custody Ctr ME1 .....53 B1
Borstal Manor Com Sch
ME1 .....52 F2
Borstal Mews ME1 .....53 A2
Borstal Rd ME1 .....53 B3
Borstal St ME1 .....53 A2
Borton Cl ME18 .....113 F1
Boscobel Cl BR1 .....42 F7
Bostall Hill SE2 .....3 B1
Bostall La SE2 .....3 B1
Bostall Manorway SE2 .....3 B2
Bostall Park Ave DA7 .....13 E7
Bostall Rd BR5 .....30 B1
Boston Gdns ME8 .....55 C1
Boston Rd ME5 .....68 C2
Bosville Ave TN13 .....92 A4
Bosville Dr TN13 .....92 A4
Bosville Rd TN13 .....92 A4
Boswell Cl BR5 .....44 C3
Boswell Ho BR2 .....42 D4
Bosworth Ho 3 DA8 .....4 E1
Botany TN9 .....127 C1
Botany Bay La BR7 .....43 C7
Botha Rd E13 .....1 C8
Bothwell Cl 7 E16 .....1 A8
Botsom La TN15 .....61 D4
Bott Rd DA2 .....32 F4
Bottle House Cotts
TN11 .....140 F1
Bottlescrew Hill ME17 .....116 B4
Boucher Dr DA11 .....35 F4
Bough Beech Nature Reserve
Visitor Ctr* TN14 .....124 A7
Boughton Cl ME8 .....55 B3
Boughton Ho BR1 .....28 E1
Boughton La ME15 .....116 B6
Boughton Monchelsea Prim
Sch ME17 .....116 B2
Boughton Par ME15 .....116 A7
Boughton Place Cotts
ME17 .....137 A8
Boughton Rd
Sandway ME17 .....120 B2
Woolwich SE28 .....2 E3
Boulevard The DA9 .....17 C3
Boulthurst Way RH8 .....104 B3
Boultwood Rd E6 .....1 F7
Boundary Ho 4 DA11 .....35 F7
Boundary Rd
Chatham ME4 .....53 E3
Royal Tunbridge Wells
TN2 .....159 D1
Sidcup DA15 .....12 E2
Boundary St 2 DA8 .....14 F7
Boundary The TN3 .....158 B3
Bounds Cross TN27 .....167 F7
Bounds Oak Way TN4 .....142 E3
Bounds The ME20 .....82 E1
Bourchier Cl TN13 .....92 B1
Bourdillon Ct SE9 .....28 E6
Bournbrook Rd SE3,SE9 .....11 D4
Bourne Cl TN9 .....127 D3
Bourne Ct ME1 .....53 D5
Bourne Ent Ctr TN15 .....95 A7
Bourne Grange La
TN11 .....128 D8
Bourne Ind Pk DA1 .....14 E2
Bourne La
Cranbrook TN32 .....194 F1
Plaxtol TN15 .....94 F1
Sandhurst Cross TN18 .....195 E4
Tonbridge TN9 .....127 D3
Bourne Mead DA5 .....14 D2
Bourne Par DA5 .....31 B8
Bourne Pk TN11 .....128 F5
Bourne Place Mdws
TN11 .....126 A7
Bourne Rd
Bexley DA1,DA5 .....14 D2
Bromley BR2 .....42 D5
Gravesend DA12 .....36 F6
Sidcup DA5 .....31 B8
Bourne Row TN8 .....140 D6
Bourne Vale Hayes BR2 .....42 A2
Plaxtol Spoute TN15 .....111 A8
Bourne Way Hayes BR2 .....56 A8
Swanley BR8 .....45 C6
Bourner Cotts TN17 .....166 D4

Bourneside Terr ME17 . .102 D2
Bournewood Cl ME15 . . .100 F1
Bournewood Rd
Orpington BR5 . . . . .44 C2
Woolwich SE18,SE2 . . . . .13 A7
Bournville Ave ME4 . . . . . .53 F1
Bovarde Ave ME19 . . . . . . .97 C3
Bow Arrow La
Dartford DA2 . . . . .16 A1
Dartford DA2 . . . . .16 B1
Bow Hill ME18 . . . . .113 D5
Bow Rd ME18 . . . . .113 E7
Bow Terr ME18 . . . . .113 E7
Bowater Pl SE3 . . . . .11 B7
Bowater Rd SE18 . . . . .1 D3
Bowen Rd TN4 . . . . .158 B4
Bower Cl ME16 . . . . .99 E4
Bower Gn ME5 . . . . .68 C1
Bower Grove Sch ME16 . . .99 B2
Bower La Eynsford DA4 . . . .60 F6
Maidstone ME16 . . . . .99 E3
Bower Mount Rd ME16 . . .99 D4
Bower Pl ME16 . . . . .99 E3
Bower Rd BR8 . . . . .32 A2
Bower St ME16 . . . . .99 E4
Bower Terr ME16 . . . . .99 E3
Bower Wlk TN12 . . . . .149 E3
Bowers Ave DA11 . . . . .35 F4
Bowers Ho ME7 . . . . .54 E7
Bowers Rd TN14 . . . . .75 F8
Bowers Wlk 1 E6 . . . . .1 F7
Bowes Cl DA15 . . . . .13 B1
Bowes Ct 24 DA2 . . . . .16 B1
Bowes Rd ME2 . . . . .53 B8
Bowes Wood DA3 . . . . .62 F7
Bowesden La DA12 . . . . . . .37 F1
Bowford Ave DA7 . . . . .13 E6
Bowley La ME17 . . . . .137 D8
Bowling Green Row 1
SE18 . . . . .1 F2
Bowls Pl TN12 . . . . .146 A7
Bowman Ave E16 . . . . .1 A6
Bowman Cl ME5 . . . . .68 C5
Bowmans Rd DA1 . . . . .31 F8
Bowmead SE9 . . . . .28 F6
Bown Cl RM18 . . . . .19 B5
Bowness Rd DA7 . . . . .14 B5
Bowyer Cl E6 . . . . .1 F8
Bowzell Rd TN14 . . . . . . .108 A2
Box Tree Wlk 26 BR5 . . . . .44 D1
Boxgrove Prim Sch SE2 . . . .3 C3
Boxgrove Rd SE2 . . . . .3 C3
Boxley Cl ME14 . . . . .100 B8
Boxley Rd Chatham ME5 . . .68 B2
Maidstone ME14 . . . . .100 B7
Boxley St E16 . . . . .1 B5
Boxmend Ind Est ME15 . .116 F3
Boxshall Ho 7 SE18 . . . . . .12 B8
Boy Court La TN27 . . . . . .135 F1
Boyard Rd SE18 . . . . .2 B1
Boyces Hill ME9 . . . . .71 D6
Boyle Ho 12 DA17 . . . . .4 A3
Boyle Way TN12 . . . . .130 B7
Boyne Pk TN4 . . . . .158 F4
Boyton Court Rd ME17 . .135 A6
Brabourne Ave ME8 . . . . . .55 C3
Brabourne Cres DA7 . . . . .13 F8
Bracken Cl Newham E6 . . . . .1 F8
Royal Tunbridge Wells
TN2 . . . . .159 E5
Bracken Hill ME5 . . . . .68 A1
Bracken Lea ME5 . . . . .54 C1
Bracken Rd TN2 . . . . .159 E5
Bracken Wlk TN10 . . . . . . .127 B6
Brackendene DA2,DA5 . . . .31 E4
Brackens The BR6 . . . . . . .58 A5
Brackley Cl ME14 . . . . . . .100 C5
Brackwood Cl ME8 . . . . . . .69 D5
Bracondale Ave DA13 . . . .49 F8
Bracondale Rd SE2 . . . . .3 A2
Bracton La DA2 . . . . .31 F6
Bradbery Ct 3 DA11 . . . . .35 F7
Bradbourne Ct TN13 . . . . .92 B6
Bradbourne La ME20 . . . . .82 B1
Bradbourne Park Rd
TN13 . . . . .92 A4
Bradbourne Parkway
ME19 . . . . .82 A1
Bradbourne Rd
Grays RM17 . . . . .18 B8
Sevenoaks TN13 . . . . .92 B5
Sidcup DA5 . . . . .31 A8
Bradbourne Sch The
TN13 . . . . .92 A6
Bradbourne Vale Rd
TN13,TN14 . . . . .92 A5
Bradbury Ct 4 SE3 . . . . . . .11 A7
Braddick Cl ME15 . . . . . . .116 B6
Bradenham Ave DA16 . . . . .13 A3
Bradfield Rd E16 . . . . .1 B4
Bradfields Ave ME5 . . . . . .67 F5
Bradfields Ave W ME5 . . . .67 F5
Bradfields Sch ME5 . . . . . .68 A6
Bradford Cl BR2 . . . . .42 F1
Bradford St TN9 . . . . .127 B1
Bradfords Cl ME4 . . . . .40 B2
Bradley Ho ME3 . . . . .25 C4
Bradley Rd Ashurst TN3 . .156 D5
Upper Halling ME2 . . . . .65 E5
Bradley Stone Rd E6 . . . . . .1 F8
Bradymead E6 . . . . .2 B7
Braeburn Way ME19 . . . . .97 C3
Braemar Ave DA7 . . . . .14 C3
Braemar Gdns DA15 . . . . .29 D5
Braes The ME3 . . . . .38 C3
Braeside Ave TN13 . . . . . . .91 F3
Braeside Cl TN13 . . . . .91 F4
Braeside Cres DA7 . . . . . . .14 C3
Braesyde Cl DA17 . . . . .3 F2
Braithwaite Ct ME7 . . . . . .55 A5
Brake Ave ME5 . . . . .67 E5
Brakefield Rd DA13 . . . . . .35 B1
Brakes Pl TN15 . . . . .61 E4
Bramber Ct 9 DA2 . . . . . . .16 B1
Bramble Ave DA2 . . . . .34 C5
Bramble Bank DA13 . . . . . .79 F7
Bramble Cl
Maidstone ME16 . . . . .99 B3
Tonbridge TN11 . . . . .126 F4
Bramble Croft DA8 . . . . .4 C2
Bramble La TN13 . . . . . . .108 B7
Bramble Reed La TN12 . .161 B7
Bramble Wlk TN2 . . . . . . .159 D7
Bramblebury Rd SE18 . . . . .2 C1
Brambledown
Chatham ME5 . . . . .68 B8
Hartley DA3 . . . . .48 F5
Bramblefield Cl DA3 . . . . .48 E6
Brambletree Cotts ME1 . . .52 E2
Brambletree Cres ME1 . . .52 F2
Bramdean Cres SE12 . . . . .28 A7
Bramdean Gdns SE12 . . . .28 A7
Bramhope Ho 16 SE7 . . . . . .11 C8
Bramhope La SE7 . . . . .11 B8
Bramis Ho TN16 . . . . .72 D3
Bramley Cl Gillingham ME8 .70 B8
Istead Rise DA13 . . . . .35 F1
Newington ME9 . . . . .71 A5
Orpington BR6 . . . . .43 B1
Swanley BR8 . . . . .45 E5
Bramley Cres ME15 . . . . .100 F3
Bramley Ct Bexley DA16 . . .13 B6
15 Erith DA17 . . . . .4 A1
Marden TN12 . . . . .148 B6
Bramley Dr TN17 . . . . . . .179 D4
Bramley Gdns
Coxheath ME17 . . . . .115 C3
Paddock Wood TN12 . . . . . .145 E7
Bramley Pl DA1 . . . . .15 A3
Bramley Rd
East Peckham TN12 . . . . . . .129 F6
Snodland ME6 . . . . .82 A8
Bramley Rise ME2 . . . . .52 E8
Bramley Way ME19 . . . . . . .97 A2
Bramleys TN27 . . . . .151 D5
Brampton Prim Sch DA7 . .13 D5
Brampton Rd DA7 . . . . .13 E6
Bramshot Ave SE3,SE7 . . . .11 B8
Bramshott Cl ME16 . . . . . . .99 C6
Branbridges Ind Est
TN12 . . . . .130 A5
Branbridges Rd TN12 . . . .130 B4
Brandon Rd DA1 . . . . .33 A8
Brandon St DA11 . . . . .36 B8
Brandreth Rd E6 . . . . .1 F7
Brands Hatch Circuit*
DA3 .61 E6
Brands Hatch Cotts DA3 . .62 A6
Brands Hatch Rd DA3 . . . .62 A7
Branham Ho 1 SE18 . . . . . . .2 B1
Bransell Cl BR8 . . . . .45 C3
Bransgore Cl ME8 . . . . . . .69 D7
Branston Cres BR5 . . . . . .43 D1
Branstone Ct RM19 . . . . . .16 B8
Brantingham Cl TN9 . . . .142 F7
Branton Rd DA9 . . . . .16 F1
Brantwood Ave DA8 . . . . . .14 C7
Brantwood Rd DA7 . . . . . .14 B4
Brantwood Way BR5 . . . . .44 C6
Brasenose Rd ME7 . . . . . . .54 E4
Brassey Cl RH8 . . . . .104 A6
Brassey Dr ME20 . . . . .98 D8
Brassey Hill RH8 . . . . . . .104 A6
Brassey Rd RH8 . . . . .104 A6
Brasted Cl Bexley DA6 . . . .13 D2
Orpington BR6 . . . . .58 A8
Brasted Ct Brasted TN16 . . .90 D2
Rochester ME2 . . . . .39 A1
Brasted Hill TN14 . . . . . . .90 A7
Brasted Hill Rd TN16 . . . . .90 C5
Brasted La TN14 . . . . .74 A1
Brasted Rd Erith DA8 . . . . . .14 E7
Westerham TN16 . . . . .89 E1
Brattle Farm Mus*
TN12 . . . . .149 D1
Brattle Wood TN13 . . . . .108 C6
Braundton Ave DA15 . . . . .29 F7
Braunstone Dr ME16 . . . . .99 D7
Bray Gdns ME15 . . . . .115 F5
Bray Pas E16 . . . . .1 A6
Braywood Rd SE9 . . . . .12 D3
Breach La ME9 . . . . .70 F8
Breach Rd RM20 . . . . .16 F8
Breakneck Hill DA9 . . . . . .17 B2
Breakspears Dr BR5 . . . . .44 A8
Bream Cl ME20 . . . . .82 A5
Breaside Prep Sch BR1 . . .42 D8
Breckonmead BR1 . . . . . . .42 C7
Brecon Ct 7 SE9 . . . . .12 A1
Bredgar & Wormshill Light
Rly* ME9 . . . . .87 E1
Bredgar Cl ME14 . . . . . . .100 C5
Bredgar Ho 1 BR5 . . . . . . .44 D1
Bredgar Rd ME8 . . . . .55 B4
Bredhurst CE Prim Sch
ME7 .69 B1
Bredhurst Rd ME8 . . . . . . .69 B4
Breedon Ave TN4 . . . . . . .142 F1
Bremner Cl BR8 . . . . .46 A5
Brenchley & Matfield CE
Prim Sch TN12 . . . . .162 A8
Brenchley Ave DA11 . . . . .36 B3
Brenchley Cl
Chislehurst BR7 . . . . .43 A8
Rochester ME1 . . . . .53 D2
Brenchley Rd
Gillingham ME8 . . . . .55 B2
Horsmonden TN12 . . . . . . .162 F6
Maidstone ME15 . . . . .99 F2
Matfield TN12 . . . . .161 F8
St Paul's Cray BR5 . . . . .43 F7
Brenda Ct 4 DA14 . . . . . . .30 A4
Brenda Terr DA10 . . . . .34 E8
Brendon 16 DA14 . . . . .30 A4
Brendon Ave ME5 . . . . .68 A3
Brendon Cl Bexley DA8 . . . .14 E6
Royal Tunbridge Wells
TN2 . . . . .159 D5
Brendon Rd SE9 . . . . .29 D6
Brenley Gdns SE9 . . . . .11 D3
Brennan Ct ME7 . . . . .54 D6
Brennan Rd RM18 . . . . .19 B5
Brent Cl Chatham ME5 . . . . .67 E5
Dartford DA2 . . . . .16 B1
Sidcup DA5 . . . . .30 E7
Brent La DA1 . . . . .33 A7
Brent Prim Sch The DA2 . . .33 C8
Brent Rd Newham E16 . . . . . .1 A8
Woolwich SE18 . . . . .12 B7
Brent The Dartford DA1 . . . .33 B8
Tonbridge TN10 . . . . .127 C6
Brent Way DA2 . . . . .16 B1
Brentfield Rd DA1 . . . . .33 B8
Brentlands Dr DA1 . . . . . . .33 A7
Brentor Ct TN2 . . . . .159 D6
Brentwood Cl SE9 . . . . .29 C7
Brentwood Ho SE18 . . . . . .11 D7
Brenzett Cl ME5 . . . . .68 B5
Brenzett Ho 6 BR5 . . . . . . .44 C4
Bretaneby TN15 . . . . .92 F6
Bretland Ct TN4 . . . . .158 D4
Bretland Rd TN4 . . . . .158 D4
Breton Rd ME1 . . . . .53 C2
Brett Wlk ME8 . . . . .69 D4
Brewer Rd ME3 . . . . .39 B7
Brewer St
Lamberhurst TN3 . . . . .176 A5
Maidstone ME14 . . . . .100 A5
Brewers Field DA2 . . . . . . .32 C4
Brewers Rd DA12 . . . . .51 C8
Brewery La TN13 . . . . .92 C2
Brewery Rd Orpington BR2 .42 E1
Woolwich SE18 . . . . .2 D1
Brewhouse Rd SE18 . . . . . . .1 F2
Brewhouse Yd 15 DA12 . . .19 B1
Brian Cres TN4 . . . . .159 B8
Briar Cl Larkfield ME20 . . . .82 A2
8 Marlpit Hill TN8 . . . . . . .122 D3
Briar Dale ME3 . . . . .38 B4
Briar Fields ME14 . . . . . . .100 E5
Briar Rd DA5 . . . . .31 D5
Briar Wlk TN10 . . . . .127 C6
Briars Cross RH8 . . . . . . .104 D5
Briars The TN15 . . . . .61 D4
Briars Way DA3 . . . . .49 A4
Briarswood Way BR6 . . . . .57 F5
Briary Ct DA14 . . . . .30 B3
Briary Gdns BR1 . . . . .28 B3
Brice Rd ME3 . . . . .38 B3
Brick Ct RM17 . . . . .18 A8
Brick Field View ME2 . . . . .39 C1
Brick Kiln La
Horsmonden TN12 . . . . . . .163 B2
Limpsfield RH8 . . . . .104 C5
Ulcombe ME17 . . . . .135 D5
Brickenden Rd TN17 . . . .179 D4
Brickfield Cotts SE18 . . . . .12 F8
Brickfield Farm DA3 . . . . .49 A6
Brickfield Farm Gdns
BR6 .57 C6
Brickfields Pembury TN2 . .160 E8
West Malling ME19 . . . . .81 B1
Brickwell Cotts TN17 . . . .166 F6
Brickworks Cl TN9 . . . . . .143 B7
Bridewell La TN30 . . . . . .193 A7
Bridge Bsns Pk TN12 . . . .145 C7
Bridge Cl Dartford DA2 . . . .16 D4
Tonbridge TN9 . . . . .143 C8
Bridge Cotts TN12 . . . . . .163 A6
Bridge Ct 28 Dartford DA2 .16 B1
Grays RM17 . . . . .18 B8
Bridge Ho Rochester ME1 . .53 B4
Royal Tunbridge Wells
TN4 . . . . .159 B5
Bridge Mill Way ME15 . . . .99 D2
Bridge Pl ME20 . . . . .82 F2
Bridge Rd Bexley DA7 . . . . .13 E5
Erith DA8 . . . . .14 F6
Gillingham ME7 . . . . .54 C7
Grays RM17 . . . . .18 B8
Orpington BR5 . . . . .44 B3
Rochester ME1 . . . . .53 C2
Bridge St ME15 . . . . .115 F5
Bridge View DA9 . . . . .17 B3
Bridge View Ind Est
RM20 . . . . .16 F8
Bridgeland Rd E16 . . . . .1 A6
Bridgen Rd DA5 . . . . .30 E8
Bridges Dr DA1 . . . . .16 B2
Bridgeside Mews ME15 . . .99 E2
Bridgewater Cl BR7 . . . . . .43 E6
Bridgewater Pl ME19 . . . . .81 E2
Bridle Way BR6 . . . . .57 C6
Bridlington Cl TN16 . . . . . .88 B8
Brier Cl ME5 . . . . .68 C8
Bright Cl DA17 . . . . .3 D2
Bright Ct 8 SE28 . . . . .3 C5
Bright Rd 3 ME4 . . . . .54 B2
Bright Ridge TN4 . . . . . . .158 E8
Brightlands DA11 . . . . .35 E4
Brigstock Rd DA17 . . . . .4 B2
Brimp The ME3 . . . . .9 D3
Brimpsfield Cl SE2 . . . . .3 B3
Brimstone Cl BR6 . . . . .58 C3
Brimstone Hill DA13 . . . . .64 D8
Brindle Gate DA15 . . . . . . .29 E7
Brindle Way ME5 . . . . .68 C1
Brindle's Field TN9 . . . . .143 A7
Brindley Cl DA7 . . . . .14 B4
Brindley Way BR1 . . . . . . .28 A3
Brinkburn Cl SE2 . . . . .3 A2
Brinkers La TN5 . . . . .185 A2
Brinklow Cres SE18 . . . . . .12 B7
Brionne Gdns TN9 . . . . . .143 D8
Brisbane Ho RM18 . . . . . . .18 F6
Brisbane Rd ME4 . . . . .54 A3
Briset Rd SE9 . . . . .11 D3
Brishing Cl ME15 . . . . . . .116 E5
Brishing La ME17 . . . . . . .116 D4
Brishing Rd ME15,ME17 . .116 F3
Brisley's Row ME1 . . . . . . .66 F1
Brissenden Cl ME2 . . . . . . .40 A3
Bristol Cl ME2 . . . . .52 D5
Bristol Rd DA12 . . . . .36 D5
Bristow Rd DA7 . . . . .13 E6
Britannia Bsns Pk ME20 . .98 E7
Britannia Cl Erith DA8 . . . . .14 F8
Halling ME2 . . . . .66 A4
Britannia Dr DA12 . . . . .36 F3
Britannia Gate E16 . . . . .1 A5
Britannia Rd ME3 . . . . .24 A3
Britannia Village Prim Sch
E16 . . . . .1 B5
Brittain Ct SE9 . . . . .28 E7
Brittain Ho SE9 . . . . .28 E7
Brittains La TN13 . . . . .91 F2
Britten Cl TN10 . . . . .127 F6
Brittenden Cl 1 BR6 . . . . .57 F4
Brittenden Par BR6 . . . . . .57 F4
Britton St ME7 . . . . .54 B5
Brixham Rd DA16 . . . . .13 D6
Brixham St E16 . . . . .2 A5
Broad Ditch Rd DA13 . . . . .35 D1
Broad Gr TN2 . . . . .159 A1
Broad La Dartford DA2 . . . .32 B4
Fordcombe TN3 . . . . .157 A4
Broad Lawn SE9 . . . . .29 A7
Broad Oak
Brenchley TN12 . . . . .162 C8
Groombridge TN3 . . . . .171 C6
Broad Oak Cl
Brenchley TN12 . . . . .162 C8
Orpington BR5 . . . . .44 A7
Royal Tunbridge Wells
TN2 . . . . .158 F1
Broad Rd DA10 . . . . .17 E1
Broad St ME17 . . . . .134 E7
Broad Street Hill ME17 . .102 D7
Broad View TN17 . . . . . . .180 A8
Broad Wlk Eltham SE3,SE9 .11 E5
Orpington BR6 . . . . .58 D7
Sevenoaks TN15 . . . . .108 E7
Broadbridge Cl SE3 . . . . . .11 A7
Broadcloth TN17 . . . . . . .179 D3
Broadcroft TN2 . . . . .172 F8
Broadcroft Rd BR5 . . . . . .43 D2
Broader La ME14 . . . . .85 B2
Broadfield Rd ME15 . . . . .116 A8
Broadgate Rd E16 . . . . .1 D7
Broadheath Dr BR7 . . . . . .28 F3
Broadhoath TN15 . . . . .93 E1
Broadlands Dr ME5 . . . . . .68 B4
Broadlands Rd BR1 . . . . . .28 B4
Broadmead TN2 . . . . .172 F8
Broadmead Ave TN2 . . . .172 F8
Broadmere Terr ME16 . . . .99 D3
Broadoak ME19 . . . . .81 E2
Broadoak Ave ME15 . . . . .116 A8
Broadoak Cl DA4 . . . . .33 A2
Broadoak Rd DA8 . . . . .14 D7
Broadview DA13 . . . . .63 F6
Broadview Ave ME8 . . . . . .69 E8
Broadwater Ct TN2 . . . . .172 E8
Broadwater Down TN2 . .172 F8
Broadwater Down Prim Sch
TN2 . . . . .158 F1
Broadwater Forest La
TN3 . . . . .172 B7
Broadwater Gdns BR6 . . . .57 C6
Broadwater Ho DA12 . . . . .19 D1
Broadwater La
Royal Tunbridge Wells
TN2 . . . . .172 F8
Royal Tunbridge Wells
TN2,TN4 . . . . .158 F1
Broadwater Rd
East Malling ME19 . . . . .97 D6
Woolwich SE28 . . . . .2 D3
Broadwater Rise TN2 . . .158 F1
Broadway Bexley DA6 . . . . .13 F3
Bexley DA6 . . . . .14 A3
Crockenhill BR8 . . . . .45 C3
Gillingham ME8 . . . . .55 A3
Grays RM17 . . . . .18 C8
Limpsfield RH8 . . . . .104 B5
Maidstone ME14 . . . . .99 F4
Tilbury RM18 . . . . .18 F5
Broadway Sh Ctr 5 DA6 . .14 A3
Broadway Square Sh Ctr
DA6 .14 A3
Broadway The
Hadlow TN11 . . . . .128 E8
Lamberhurst TN3 . . . . .176 B5
Broadwood DA11 . . . . .36 B3
Broadwood Rd ME3 . . . . . .40 A4
Brock Rd E13 . . . . .1 B8
Brockbank Cl ME5 . . . . . . .68 A1
Brockdene Dr BR2 . . . . . . .56 D6
Brockenhurst Ave ME15 .100 C
Brockenhurst Cl ME8 . . . . .69 C
Brocklebank Ho 7 E16 . . . .2 A
Brocklebank Rd SE7 . . . . . .1 B
Brocklebank Rd Ind Est
SE7 . . . . .1 B
Brockway TN15 . . . . .95 A
Brockwell Cl BR5 . . . . .43 F
Brodrick Gr SE2 . . . . .3 B
Brogden Cres ME17 . . . . .117 F
Broke Farm Dr BR6 . . . . . .58 C
Brokes Way TN4 . . . . .159 B
Brome Ho SE18 . . . . .11 E
Brome Rd SE9 . . . . .11 F
Bromford Cl RH8 . . . . . . .104 A
Bromhedge SE9 . . . . .28 F
Bromholm Rd SE2 . . . . .3 B
Bromley RM17 . . . . .17 F
Bromley Cl ME5 . . . . .68 B
Bromley Coll 9 BR1 . . . . . .42 A
Bromley Coll of F Ed & H Ed
(Old Town Hall) BR1 . . . . .42 A
Bromley Coll of F Ed & H Ed
(Rookery Lane Campus)
BR2 . . . . .42 D
Bromley Comm BR2 . . . . . . .42 D
Bromley High Sch BR1 . . . .43 A
Bromley Ind Ctr BR1 . . . . .42 D
Bromley La BR7 . . . . .29 D
Bromley Manor Mans 3
BR2 . . . . .42 A
Bromley Mus* BR6 . . . . . . .44 E
Bromley North Sta BR1 . . .42 A
Bromley Rd BR7 . . . . .43 E
Bromley South Sta BR1 . . .42 A
Bromley Valley Gymnastics
Ctr BR5 . . . . .44 A
Brompton Dr DA8 . . . . .15 E
Brompton Farm Rd ME2 . .39 A
Brompton Hill ME4 . . . . . . .53 F
Brompton La ME2 . . . . .53 A
Brompton Rd ME7 . . . . .54 E
Brompton-Westbrook Prim
Sch ME7 . . . . .54 A
Bronington Cl ME5 . . . . . . .68 A
Bronte Cl Erith DA8 . . . . . . .14 E
Lunsford ME20 . . . . .81 F
Tilbury RM18 . . . . .19 C
Bronte Gr DA1 15
Bronte Sch DA11 36
Bronte View DA12 . . . . .36 C
Bronze Age Way DA8,DA17 .4 C
Brook Cotts
Collier Street TN12 147
East Farleigh ME15 115
Brook Ct
1 Lewisham SE12 . . . . .28 C
10 Marlpit Hill TN8 . . . . . . .122 D
Brook Hill Cl SE18 . . . . .2 E
Brook La Bexley DA5 . . . . . .13 D
Bromley BR1 28
Greenwich SE3 11
Plaxtol Spoute TN15 111
Snodland ME6 82
Tonbridge TN9 . . . . .127 D
Brook Pk DA1 33
Brook Rd Lunsford ME20 . . .81
Northfleet DA11 35
Royal Tunbridge Wells
TN2 . . . . .159 D
Swanley BR8 . . . . .45 D
Brook Sq SE18 11
Brook St Erith DA8 14
Snodland ME6 82
Tonbridge TN9 143
Brook The ME4 54
Brook Vale DA8 14
Brookbank ME14 100
Brookdale Rd DA5 13
Brookdene TN12 145
Brookdene Rd SE18 2
Brooke Dr DA12 37
Brookend Rd DA15 29
Brooker Cl ME17 116
Brookes Pl ME9 71
Brookfield Four Elms TN8 .123
Kemsing TN15 76
Sandhurst TN18 196
Brookfield Ave ME20 82
Brookfield Ct TN4 143
Brookfield Inf Sch ME20 . .82
Brookfield Jun Sch
ME20 82
Brookfields TN11 111
Brookhill Rd SE18 2
Brookhurst Gdns TN4 142
Brooklands Dartford DA1 . .32
Headcorn TN27 151
Royal Tunbridge Wells
TN2 159
Brooklands Ave DA15 29
Brooklands Farm Cl
TN3 157
Brooklands Pk SE3 11
Brooklands Prim Sch
SE3 .11
Brooklands Rd ME20 82
Brooklyn Paddock ME7 . . .54
Brooklyn Rd BR2 42
Brooklyn Villas TN12 148
Brookmead TN11 126
Brookmead Ave BR1 42
Brookmead Cl BR5 44
Brookmead Rd ME3 39
Brookmead Way BR5 44
Brooks Cl Eltham SE9 29
Staplehurst TN12 149
Tonbridge TN10 127

Brooks Pl ME14 .....100 A4
Brookside
Cranbrook TN17 .....179 D4
Hoo St Werburgh ME3 .....40 E5
Orpington BR6 .....43 F2
Brookside Rd DA13 .....35 F1
Brookvale Workshops
DA11 .....35 C7
Brookway SE3 .....11 A4
Broom Ave BR5 .....44 B7
Broom Cl BR2 .....42 E3
Broom Hill Cotts TN5 .....187 B3
Broom Hill Rd ME2 .....52 F8
Broom La TN3 .....157 F1
Broom Mead DA6 .....14 A2
Broom Pk TN3 .....157 E3
Broomcroft Rd ME8 .....55 F2
Broomfield Ho 4 BR5 .....44 B7
Broomfield Rd
Bexley DA6 .....14 A2
Kingswood ME17 .....118 D4
Sevenoaks TN13 .....91 F5
Swanscombe DA10 .....17 E2
Broomfields DA3 .....48 E4
Broomhill Bank Sch
TN3 .....158 C6
Broomhill Park Rd TN4 .....158 F8
Broomhill Rd
Dartford DA1 .....15 B1
Orpington BR6 .....44 A2
Royal Tunbridge Wells
TN3 .....158 D7
Broomhill Rise DA6 .....14 A2
Broomhills DA13 .....34 E4
Broomlands La RH8 .....104 E8
Broomleigh 3 BR1 .....42 A8
Broomscroft Cotts ME18 .....97 C1
Broomshaw Rd ME16 .....98 F3
Broomsleigh TN16 .....72 E2
Broomwood Cl DA5 .....31 D6
Broomwood Rd BR5 .....44 B7
Brougham Ct 5 DA2 .....16 B1
Broughton Rd
Orpington BR6 .....57 D8
Otford TN14 .....76 A3
Brow Cl BR5 .....44 D2
Brow Cres BR5 .....44 D2
Brown Rd DA12 .....36 E7
Brown St ME8 .....55 F1
Browndens Rd ME2 .....65 E4
Brownelow Copse ME5 .....68 B1
Brownhill Cl ME5 .....68 A4
Browning Cl Bexley DA16 .....12 E6
6 Lunsford ME20 .....81 F4
Browning Rd DA1 .....15 F3
Browning Wlk RM18 .....19 C5
Brownings TN8 .....122 C4
Browns Sch BR6 .....58 F5
Brownspring Dr SE9 .....29 B5
Broxbourne Rd BR6 .....43 F2
Bruce Cl DA16 .....13 B6
Bruce Ct DA15 .....29 F4
Bruce Gr BR6 .....44 A1
Bruces Wharf Rd RM17 .....18 A8
Brucks The ME18 .....113 E7
Brummel Cl DA7 .....14 C4
Brunel Cl RM18 .....19 B4
Brunel Way ME4 .....54 A7
Brungers Wlk TN10 .....127 B5
Brunswick Cl DA6 .....13 D3
Brunswick House Prim Sch
ME16 .....99 E5
Brunswick Rd DA6 .....13 E3
Brunswick St ME15 .....100 A3
Brunswick St E ME15 .....100 A3
Brunswick Terr TN1 .....159 A2
Brunswick Wlk 1 DA12 .....36 D8
Brushwood Lodge 1
DA17 .....4 A2
Bruton Cl BR7 .....28 F1
Bryanston Rd RM18 .....19 C5
Bryant Cl ME18 .....113 D6
Bryant Rd ME2 .....53 A7
Bryant St ME4 .....54 A3
Bryony Sch ME8 .....69 F5
Bubblestone Rd TN14 .....76 B3
Bubhurst La TN17 .....167 B7
Buckden Cl SE12 .....11 A1
Buckham Thorns Rd
TN16 .....89 C1
Buckhole Farm Rd ME23 .....23 C4
Buckhurst Ave TN13 .....92 C2
Buckhurst La
Rockrobin TN5 .....184 A6
Sevenoaks TN13 .....92 C2
Buckhurst Pl TN5 .....184 A6
Buckhurst Rd TN16 .....89 B7
Buckingham Ave DA16 .....12 E3
Buckingham Cl BR5 .....43 E2
Buckingham Dr BR7 .....29 C3
Buckingham Rd
Gillingham ME7 .....54 D5
Northfleet DA11 .....35 D8
Royal Tunbridge Wells
TN1 .....159 B2
Buckingham Row ME15 .....116 E7
Buckland Cl ME5 .....68 A2
Buckland Hill ME16 .....99 E5
Buckland La ME16 .....99 D6
Buckland Pl ME16 .....99 E4
Buckland Rd
Cliffe Woods ME3 .....39 A8
Luddesdown DA13 .....65 A7
Maidstone ME16 .....99 E4
Orpington BR6 .....57 E6
Buckler Gdns SE9 .....28 F5
Bucklers Cl TN2 .....159 C3
Buckles Ct DA17 .....3 D2
Buckley Cl DA1 .....14 F5
Bucks Cross Rd
Chelsfield BR6 .....58 E5
Northfleet DA11 .....35 F5
Buckthorn Ho DA15 .....29 F5
Buckwheat Ct DA18 .....3 D3
Budd Ho 4 SE7 .....1 C1
Budd's Farm Cotts TN30 .....199 E2
Budd's La TN30 .....199 F2
Budgin's Hill BR6 .....74 C8
Budleigh Cres DA16 .....13 C6
Bugglesden Rd TN27,
TN30 .....182 D5
Bugsby's Way SE10,SE7 .....1 B2
Bull Alley DA16 .....13 B4
Bull Fields ME6 .....82 A8
Bull Hill Horton Kirby DA4 .....47 C5
Lenham ME17 .....137 F8
Bull La Chislehurst BR7 .....29 D1
Eccles ME20 .....82 F5
Lower Higham ME3 .....38 D7
Wrotham TN15 .....79 A3
Yelsted ME9 .....70 E2
Bull Lane Cotts
Hook Green TN3 .....175 C4
Yelsted ME9 .....70 E1
Bull Orch ME16 .....98 F2
Bull Rd ME19 .....81 C5
Bull Yd 6 DA11 .....19 B1
Bullace La 3 DA1 .....15 E1
Bullbanks Rd DA17 .....4 C2
Bulldog Rd ME5 .....68 B2
Bullen La TN12 .....129 E7
Buller Rd ME4 .....53 F2
Bullers Cl DA14 .....30 E3
Bullers Wood Dr BR7 .....28 F1
Bullers Wood Sch BR7 .....42 E8
Bullfinch Cl
Paddock Wood TN12 .....146 A5
Sevenoaks TN13 .....91 D5
Bullfinch Cnr TN13 .....91 E5
Bullfinch Dene TN13 .....91 D5
Bullfinch La TN13 .....91 E5
Bullingstone Cotts TN3 .....157 E7
Bullingstone La TN3 .....157 F7
Bullion Cl TN12 .....145 F6
Bullivant Cl 3 DA9 .....17 A2
Bulls Pl TN2 .....160 D6
Bulrush Cl ME5 .....67 F3
Bumbles Cl ME1 .....67 D7
Bunker's Hill Erith DA17 .....4 A2
New Ash Green TN15 .....63 B4
Bunkers Hill DA14 .....30 F5
Bunny La TN3 .....172 E5
Bunters Hill Rd ME3 .....39 B4
Bunton St SE18 .....2 A3
Burberry La ME17 .....118 B5
Burch Rd DA11 .....18 F1
Burcharbro Rd SE2 .....13 D8
Burdens TN27 .....151 D5
Burdett Ave DA12 .....37 F4
Burdett Cl DA14 .....30 E3
Burdett Rd TN4 .....158 B4
Burdock Ct ME16 .....99 A3
Burdock Ho 6 ME15 .....116 D8
Burford Rd BR1 .....42 E5
Burgate Cl DA1 .....14 F4
Burgess Hall Dr ME17 .....117 F6
Burgess Rd ME2 .....53 B7
Burgess Row 10 TN30 .....193 A7
Burghclere Dr ME16 .....99 B2
Burghfield Rd DA13 .....35 F1
Burgoyne Ct ME14 .....99 F7
Burham CE Prim Sch
ME1 .....82 F8
Burham Rd ME1 .....66 E8
Burial Ground La ME15 .....99 E1
Burleigh Ave DA15 .....12 F2
Burleigh Cl ME2 .....52 E8
Burleigh Dr ME14 .....83 F1
Burley Rd E16 .....1 C8
Burlings La TN14 .....73 F2
Burlington Cl
6 Newham E6 .....1 E7
Orpington BR6 .....57 B8
Burlington Gdns ME8 .....69 E4
Burlington Lodge BR7 .....28 F1
Burma Way ME5 .....67 F6
Burman Cl DA2 .....33 C8
Burmarsh Cl ME5 .....68 B5
Burn's Rd ME7 .....54 C7
Burnaby Rd DA11 .....18 E1
Burnell Ave DA16 .....13 A5
Burnett Rd DA8 .....15 D8
Burnham Cres DA1 .....15 C3
Burnham Rd Dartford DA1 .....15 C3
Sidcup DA14 .....30 E6
Burnham Trad Est DA1 .....15 D3
Burnham Wlk ME8 .....69 E3
Burnley Rd RM20 .....17 A6
Burns Ave DA15 .....13 B1
Burns Cl Bexley DA16 .....12 F6
Erith DA8 .....14 F6
Burns Cres TN9 .....143 A7
Burns Ho DA16 .....13 C6
Burns Pl RM18 .....19 B6
Burns Rd ME16 .....99 C2
Burnt Ash Hill SE12 .....28 A7
Burnt Ash Hts BR1 .....28 B3
Burnt Ash La BR1,SE12 .....28 B3
Burnt Ash Prim Sch BR1 .....28 A3
Burnt House Cl
Rochester ME2 .....39 C2
Sandhurst TN18 .....196 C5
Burnt House La
Dartford DA1 .....32 F5
Hawley DA2 .....32 F4
Langton Green TN3 .....158 A5
Burnt Lodge La TN5 .....186 B2
Burnt Oak Jun Sch DA15 .....30 A7
Burnt Oak La DA15 .....13 A1
Burnt Oak Terr ME7 .....54 D6
Burntash Rd ME20 .....98 F8
Burnthouse La TN27 .....152 D1
Burntwood Gr TN13 .....108 B8
Burntwood Rd TN13 .....108 B7
Burr Bank Terr DA2 .....32 C4
Burr Cl DA7 .....13 F4
Burrage Gr SE18 .....2 C2
Burrage Pl SE18 .....2 B1
Burrage Rd SE18 .....2 C1
Burrard Rd E16 .....1 B7
Burrfield Dr BR5 .....44 D4
Burritt Mews ME1 .....53 C3
Burrows La ME3 .....25 C3
Burrs Hill Cotts TN12 .....162 D6
Burrswood Villas TN3 .....171 B7
Bursdon Cl DA15 .....29 F6
Burslem Rd TN2 .....159 E7
Bursted Wood Prim Sch
DA7 .....14 B5
Burston Rd ME17 .....115 B2
Burt Rd E16 .....1 C5
Burton Cl ME3 .....39 C3
Burts Wharf DA17 .....4 C5
Burwash Ct BR5 .....44 C4
Burwash Rd SE18 .....2 D1
Burwood Ave BR2 .....56 B8
Burwood Ho TN2 .....159 E5
Burwood Sch BR6 .....58 D8
Bus Bridge Rd ME15 .....115 E6
Busbridge Rd ME6 .....81 E7
Bush Cl ME9 .....87 F5
Bush Rd Cuxton ME2 .....52 B2
East Peckham TN12 .....129 E8
Bush Row ME20 .....83 A3
Bushell Way BR7 .....29 A3
Bushey Ave BR5 .....43 D2
Bushey Ct DA8 .....15 A6
Bushey Ho SE9 .....28 C5
Bushey Lees DA15 .....12 F1
Bushfield Wlk DA10 .....34 E8
Bushmeadow Rd ME8 .....55 F2
Bushmoor Cres SE18 .....12 B6
Bushy Gill TN3 .....158 A3
Bushy Gr ME17 .....118 D2
Business Acad Bexley Prim
Section The DA18 .....3 E4
Buston Manor Farm Cotts
ME18 .....114 B2
Busty La TN15 .....94 D6
Butcher Cl TN12 .....149 E3
Butcher Wlk DA10 .....34 E8
Butcher's La ME19 .....96 D1
Butchers La TN15 .....62 D8
Butchers Rd E16 .....1 A7
Butchers Yd BR6 .....73 A8
Butler Ho 9 RM17 .....18 B8
Butler's Cotts DA7 .....14 A5
Butler's Pl DA3 .....62 E7
Butt Green La ME17 .....133 A7
Butt Haw Cl ME3 .....40 E5
Buttercup Cl TN12 .....146 A5
Butterfield Sq 10 E6 .....1 F7
Butterfly Ave DA1 .....32 F6
Butterfly La SE9 .....12 B1
Buttermere Cl ME7 .....55 A5
Buttermere Rd BR5 .....44 D5
Buttmarsh Cl SE18 .....2 B1
Button Dr ME3 .....25 C5
Button Ho ME3 .....39 F6
Button La ME15 .....101 B2
Button St BR8,DA4 .....46 C5
Butts La TN5 .....185 C7
Butts The TN14 .....76 B2
Buttway La ME3 .....22 A6
Buxton Cl Chatham ME5 .....68 D1
Loose ME15 .....116 A8
Buxton Rd DA8 .....14 D7
Buzzard Creek Ind Est
IG11 .....3 A8
Bychurch Pl 7 ME15 .....100 A3
Bycliffe Mews 2 DA11 .....35 F8
Bycliffe Terr 3 DA11 .....35 F8
Byland Cl SE2 .....3 B3
Byng Rd TN4 .....158 F5
Bynon Ave DA7 .....13 F4
Byrneside TN11 .....126 E4
Byron Cl SE28 .....3 C5
Byron Dr DA8 .....14 B7
Byron Gdns RM18 .....19 C6
Byron Prim Sch ME7 .....54 C3
Byron Rd Dartford DA1 .....16 B3
Gillingham ME7 .....54 C3
Maidstone ME14 .....100 B7
Bywater Ho SE18 .....1 E3

C

C M Booth Collection of
Historic Vehicles (Mus)*
TN17 .....191 E4
Cabbage Stalk La TN4 .....158 E2
Cables Cl DA8 .....4 C3
Cacket's La TN14 .....73 E4
Cade La TN13 .....108 C7
Cadlocks Hill TN14 .....58 F1
Cadnam Cl ME2 .....52 E8
Cadogan Ave DA2 .....33 D8
Cadogan Gdns 6 TN1 .....159 B4
Cadogan Rd SE18 .....2 C3
Cadwallon Rd SE9 .....29 C6
Caerleon Cl DA14 .....30 C3
Caerleon Terr SE2 .....3 B2
Caernarvon Ct Erith DA8 .....14 D7
Caernarvon Ct *continued*
12 Orpington BR5 .....44 C6
Caernarvon Dr ME15 .....99 F1
Cage Green Prim Sch
TN10 .....127 D5
Cage Green Rd TN10 .....127 C5
Cage La TN27 .....152 F1
Cagney Cl ME3 .....39 C3
Cairns Cl DA1 .....15 D2
Cairns Mews SE18 .....11 E6
Caistor Rd TN9 .....127 A1
Caithness Gdns DA15 .....12 F1
Calais Cotts DA3 .....62 A8
Calcott Wlk SE9 .....28 D4
Calcroft Ave DA9 .....17 C2
Calcutta Ho 3 ME15 .....116 E5
Calcutta Rd RM18 .....19 A5
Calder Rd ME14 .....99 E7
Calderwood DA12 .....36 E2
Calderwood St SE18 .....2 A2
Caldew Ave ME8 .....55 C1
Caldy Rd DA17 .....4 B3
Caledonian Ct ME8 .....69 E8
Calehill Cl ME14 .....100 C6
Caley Rd TN2 .....159 D7
Calfstock La DA4 .....46 F5
California Row TN12 .....150 C6
Caling Croft DA3 .....48 F1
Caliph Cl DA12 .....36 F5
Callams Cl ME8 .....69 D6
Callaways La ME9 .....71 B6
Callis Way ME8 .....69 D5
Callisto Ct ME16 .....99 D3
Calshot Ct 17 DA2 .....16 B1
Calverley Ct TN1 .....159 C3
Calverley Park Cres 1
TN1 .....159 B3
Calverley Park Gdns
TN1 .....159 C4
Calverley Pk TN1 .....159 B3
Calverley Rd
Royal Tunbridge Wells
TN1 .....159 B3
Royal Tunbridge Wells
TN1 .....159 B4
Calverley St TN1 .....159 B4
Calvert Cl Erith DA17 .....4 B2
Sidcup DA14 .....30 E2
Calvert Dr DA2 .....31 D6
Calverton Prim Sch E16 .....1 D7
Calvin Cl BR5 .....44 D6
Calydon Rd SE7 .....1 B1
Cambert Way SE3 .....11 B3
Camberwell La TN14 .....106 F4
Camborne Manor 2
ME7 .....54 C6
Camborne Rd Bexley DA16 .....12 F5
Sidcup DA14 .....30 C5
Cambray Rd BR6 .....43 F2
Cambria Ave ME1 .....52 F2
Cambria Cl DA15 .....29 E7
Cambria Cres DA12 .....36 F4
Cambria Ho 2 DA8 .....14 E7
Cambrian Gr DA11 .....36 A8
Cambrian Rd TN4 .....159 C7
Cambridge Ave DA16 .....12 F3
Cambridge Barracks Rd 5
SE18 .....1 F2
Cambridge Cres ME15 .....116 D7
Cambridge Dr SE12 .....11 A2
Cambridge Gdns TN2 .....159 B2
Cambridge Gn SE9 .....29 B7
Cambridge Ho 7 SE18 .....1 F2
Cambridge Rd
Bromley BR1 .....28 A1
Gillingham ME8 .....69 C6
Rochester ME2 .....53 A8
Sidcup DA14 .....29 E4
Cambridge Row SE18 .....2 B1
Cambridge St TN2 .....159 C3
Cambridge Terr 1 ME4 .....53 F4
Cambus Rd E16 .....1 A8
Camdale Rd SE18 .....12 F7
Camden Ave TN2 .....160 C6
Camden Cl Chatham ME5 .....68 B5
Chislehurst BR7 .....43 C8
Northfleet DA11 .....35 C7
Camden Cotts TN17 .....179 F8
Camden Ct 10 Erith DA17 .....4 A1
Pembury TN2 .....160 D6
2 Royal Tunbridge Wells
TN1 .....159 B4
Camden Gr BR7 .....29 B2
Camden Hill TN2 .....159 B3
Camden Park Rd BR7 .....29 A1
Camden Pk TN2 .....159 C2
Camden Rd
Gillingham ME7 .....54 D7
Royal Tunbridge Wells
TN1 .....159 B4
Sevenoaks TN13 .....92 B5
Sidcup DA5 .....30 F8
Camden St ME14 .....100 A5
Camden Terr Seal TN15 .....92 F6
Sissinghurst TN17 .....179 F8
Camden Way BR7 .....29 A1
Camel Rd E16 .....1 E5
Camellia Cl ME8 .....69 D7
Camelot Cl
Biggin Hill TN16 .....72 C3
Woolwich SE28 .....2 D4
Camer Gdns DA13 .....50 C3
Camer Park Ctry Pk*
DA13 .....50 C2
Camer Park Rd DA13 .....50 C2
Camer Rd DA13 .....50 C3
Camer St DA13 .....50 C3
Cameron Cl Chatham ME5 .....68 B8
Cameron Cl *continued*
Joyden's Wood DA5 .....31 E5
Cameron Rd BR2 .....42 A4
Cameron Terr 10 SE12 .....28 B5
Camerons 4 TN18 .....189 A2
Camomile Dr ME14 .....100 F5
Camp Hill TN11 .....125 A3
Camp Hill Cotts TN11 .....124 F2
Camp Site The DA14 .....31 A1
Camp Way ME15 .....116 C6
Campbell Cl SE18 .....12 A6
Campbell Ho ME3 .....39 F6
Campbell Rd
Maidstone ME15 .....100 A3
Northfleet DA11 .....35 F8
Royal Tunbridge Wells
TN4 .....159 A6
Camperdown Manor 5
ME7 .....54 A6
Campfield Rd SE9 .....28 D8
Campion Cl Chatham ME5 .....67 E3
Newham E6 .....1 F6
Northfleet DA11 .....35 E4
Campion Cres TN17 .....179 A2
Campion Ct 6 RM17 .....18 D8
Campion Pl SE28 .....3 B5
Campleshon Rd ME8 .....69 D5
Campus Way ME8 .....69 A8
Camrose Ave DA8 .....14 B8
Camrose St SE2 .....3 A2
Canada Farm Rd DA4 .....48 A6
Canada Rd DA8 .....15 B7
Canada Terr 3 ME14 .....100 A7
Canadian Ave ME7 .....54 F4
Canal Basin DA12 .....19 D1
Canal Rd Gravesend DA12 .....19 D1
Higham ME3 .....38 C8
Rochester ME2 .....53 C7
Canal Road Ind Pk 2
DA12 .....36 D8
Canberra Rd Bexley DA7 .....13 D8
Greenwich SE7 .....11 D8
Canberra Sq RM18 .....19 A5
Canbury Path BR5 .....44 A5
Canning St ME14 .....100 A6
Cannon Bridge Works
TN9 .....127 D2
Cannon La TN9 .....127 D2
Cannon Pl SE7 .....1 E1
Cannon Rd DA7 .....13 F6
Canon Cl ME1 .....53 B2
Canon La ME18 .....97 C1
Canon Rd BR1 .....42 D6
Cansiron La TN7,TN8 .....154 E2
Canterbury Ave DA15 .....30 C6
Canterbury Cl
Dartford DA1 .....33 A8
7 Newham E6 .....1 F7
Canterbury Cres TN10 .....127 D5
Canterbury Ct 7 SE12 .....28 B5
Canterbury Ho
6 Erith DA8 .....14 F7
2 Maidstone ME15 .....116 D7
Canterbury Rd
Gravesend DA12 .....36 C6
Pembury TN2 .....160 E6
Canterbury St ME7 .....54 C4
Canterbury Way DA1,DA2,
RM20 .....16 D5
Cantwell Ho SE18 .....12 B7
Cantwell Rd SE18 .....12 B7
Capability Way DA9 .....17 C3
Capel Cl Gillingham ME8 .....69 D4
Orpington BR2 .....42 E1
Capel Pl DA2 .....32 C4
Capel Prim Sch TN12 .....144 F7
Capelands DA3 .....63 A8
Capell Cl ME17 .....115 C3
Capella Ho 1 SE7 .....11 B8
Capetown Ho 1 ME15 .....116 F5
Capital Ind Est DA17 .....4 B3
Capstan Ct DA2 .....16 C3
Capstan Ctr RM18 .....18 D7
Capstan Mews 4 DA11 .....35 E8
Capstone Farm Country Pk*
ME7 .....68 D5
Capstone Rd
Chatham ME5 .....54 D1
Gillingham ME7 .....68 F6
Lewisham BR1 .....28 A4
Captain's Cl ME17 .....134 E6
Capulet Mews E16 .....1 A5
Caraway Cl E13 .....1 B8
Cardens Rd ME3 .....39 B8
Cardiff St SE18 .....12 E7
Cardigan Cl ME23 .....23 F3
Cardinal Cl
Chislehurst BR7 .....43 D8
Tonbridge TN9 .....143 D8
Cardinal Wlk ME18 .....97 C3
Cardwell Prim Sch SE18 .....1 F2
Carew Ho 18 SE18 .....1 F2
Carey Ct DA6 .....14 B2
Carey's Field TN13 .....91 E7
Caring La ME14,ME17 .....101 E1
Caring Rd ME15,ME17 .....101 C1
Carisbrooke Ave DA5 .....30 D7
Carisbrooke Ct
23 Dartford DA2 .....16 B1
20 Sidcup DA14 .....30 A4
Carisbrooke Dr ME16 .....99 D4
Carisbrooke Rd
Bromley BR2 .....42 C5
Rochester ME2 .....38 E1
Carl Ekman Ho DA11 .....35 D8

Carleton Pl DA4 .....47 C5
Carleton Rd DA1 .....33 A8
Carlisle Cl ME2 .....52 C6
Carlisle Rd DA1 .....16 A1
Carlton Ave
Gillingham ME7 .....54 E4
Stone DA9 .....16 E1
Carlton Cl Kings Hill ME18 ..97 B3
Tonbridge TN10 .....127 E7
Carlton Cres
Chatham ME5 .....68 D8
Royal Tunbridge Wells TN1 .....159 C4
Carlton Gdns ME15 .....116 B8
Carlton Gn DA14 .....29 F4
Carlton Par BR5 .....44 B2
Carlton Rd Bexley DA16 ...13 B4
Erith DA8 .....14 C8
Royal Tunbridge Wells TN1 .....159 C4
Sidcup DA14 .....29 F3
Carlyle Ave BR1 .....42 D6
Carlyle Rd SE28 .....3 C6
Carman's Cl ME15,ME17 ..115 F3
Carmelite Way DA3 .....48 F4
Carnation Cl 1 ME19 .....82 A1
Carnation Cres ME19 .....81 F1
Carnation Rd ME2 .....52 D7
Carnation St SE2 .....3 B1
Carnbrook Rd SE3 .....11 D4
Carnecke Gdns SE9 .....11 E2
Carnet Cl DA1 .....31 E8
Carnoustie Cl SE28 .....3 D7
Caroline Cres ME16 .....99 D7
Carolyn Dr BR6 .....58 A7
Carp Cl ME20 .....82 A4
Carpeaux Cl ME4 .....54 A4
Carpenters Cl ME1 .....53 E2
Carpenters Ct BR1 .....42 D7
Carpenters La
Hadlow TN11 .....111 D2
Staplehurst TN12 .....149 C8
Carpinus Cl ME5 .....68 B1
Carr Gr SE18 .....1 E2
Carr Ho DA1 .....14 E2
Carrack Ho 1 DA8 .....4 E1
Carriageway The TN16 ...90 D3
Carrick Dr TN13 .....92 B4
Carrie Ho 3 ME16 .....99 E5
Carriers Pl TN3 .....156 B4
Carriers Rd TN17 .....179 D5
Carrill Way DA17 .....3 D3
Carrington DA14 .....30 A3
Carrington Cl ME7 .....54 F6
Carrington Rd DA1 .....16 A1
Carroll Cl ME2 .....66 A4
Carroll Gdns ME20 .....81 F3
Carronade Pl SE28 .....2 D3
Carsington Gdns DA1 ...32 D6
Carson Rd E16 .....1 A8
Carston Cl SE12 .....11 A2
Carter's Hill Bromley SE9 ..28 C7
Underriver TN15 .....109 B6
Carters Hill Cl SE9 .....28 C7
Carters Hill La DA13 .....63 F2
Carters Row DA11 .....35 F6
Cartmel Rd DA7 .....14 A6
Carton Cl ME1 .....53 D2
Carton Rd ME3 .....38 B3
Carville Ave TN4 .....142 F1
Carvoran Way ME8 .....69 C5
Cascade Cl BR5 .....44 C6
Caspian Way DA10 .....17 E2
Caspian Wlk E16 .....1 D7
Cassilda Rd SE2 .....3 A2
Casstine Cl BR8 .....31 F1
Castalia Ct DA1 .....15 F4
Casterbridge Rd SE3 .....11 A4
Castfield Cl ME3 .....22 E1
Castile Rd 12 SE18 .....2 A2
Castilion Prim Sch SE28 ...3 C7
Castle Ave ME1 .....53 C4
Castle Dene ME14 .....99 F8
Castle Dr TN15 .....76 E2
Castle Farm Cotts TN11 .128 F8
Castle Farm Rd TN14 .....60 A3
Castle Fields TN9 .....127 B2
Castle Hill Hartley DA3 ...48 E4
Rochester ME1 .....53 C6
Thurnham ME14 .....85 D1
Tonbridge TN11 .....143 F5
Castle Hill Ct ME1 .....53 C6
Castle Hurst TN32 .....195 B1
Castle La DA12 .....37 B6
Castle Rd Chatham ME4 ....54 B2
Eynsford DA4 .....60 C5
Grays RM17 .....17 F8
Maidstone ME16 .....99 D7
Royal Tunbridge Wells TN4 .....159 A3
Swanscombe DA10 .....17 F1
Castle St Rochester ME2 ...39 E1
2 Royal Tunbridge Wells,Mount Sion TN1 .....159 A2
2 Royal Tunbridge Wells,Southborough TN4 ..142 F2
Stone DA9 .....17 A2
Swanscombe DA10 .....17 F1
Tonbridge TN9 .....127 C2
Wouldham ME1 .....66 C4
Castle Terr Hadlow TN11 ..128 E8
Hawkhurst TN18 .....188 F3
Castle View Bsns Ctr ME1 .....53 C6
Castle View Mews ME1 ...53 C6
Castle View Rd ME2 .....53 A7
Castle Way ME19 .....81 D2
Castle Wlk TN5 .....184 E4
Castlecombe Prim Sch SE9 .....28 E3
Castlecombe Rd SE9 .....28 E4
Castlefields DA13 .....49 F8
Castleford Ave SE9 .....29 B7
Castlemaine Ave ME7 .....54 F6
Castleton Ave DA7 .....14 D5
Castleton Rd SE9 .....28 D4
Castlewood Day Hospl SE18 .....12 A6
Castlewood Dr SE9 .....11 F5
Castweazle TN30 .....192 E6
Caterfield La RH7,RH8 ...121 A5
Cates Ct TN12 .....130 A7
Cathcart Dr BR6 .....43 E1
Catherine Cl 2 ME16 .....99 A3
Catherine of Aragon Ct DA15 .....29 D8
Catherine Pl 7 TN1 .....159 B4
Catherine St ME1 .....53 D3
Catkin Cl ME5 .....67 F1
Catlyn Cl ME19 .....98 A8
Catterick Rd ME5 .....68 D2
Cattistock Rd SE9 .....28 F3
Catts Pl TN12 .....146 C4
Caulkers Ho 7 ME4 .....54 B2
Causton Rd TN17 .....179 C5
Cavalry Cl TN10 .....127 E7
Cave Hill ME15 .....99 F1
Cavell Cres DA1 .....16 A3
Cavendish Ave
Bexley DA16 .....12 F4
Erith DA8 .....14 C8
Gillingham ME7 .....54 E6
Sevenoaks TN13 .....92 A5
Sidcup DA15 .....30 A8
Cavendish Cl TN10 .....127 D7
Cavendish Ct TN9 .....127 D3
Cavendish Dr TN2 .....159 B1
Cavendish Rd ME1 .....53 D3
Cavendish Sq DA3 .....48 D6
Cavendish Way ME15 ...101 B3
Caversham Cl ME8 .....55 F1
Caveside Cl BR7 .....43 A8
Caxton Cl Hartley DA3 .....48 F5
Tenterden TN30 .....192 F7
Caxton Ho RH8 .....104 F3
Caxton La Hadlow TN11 ...128 E8
The Chart RH8 .....104 E4
Cayser Dr ME17 .....118 E2
Caysers Croft TN12 .....129 E6
Cazeneuve St ME1 .....53 C5
Cecil Ave Gillingham ME8 ..55 A2
Rochester ME2 .....53 B8
Cecil Burns Lodge TN2 .159 D2
Cecil Kidby Ho TN2 .....159 F6
Cecil Rd Northfleet DA11 ...35 F7
Rochester ME1 .....53 C3
Cecil Road Prim Sch DA11 .....35 F7
Cecil Way BR2 .....42 A1
Cedar Ave
Gravesend DA12 .....36 C4
Sidcup DA15 .....30 A8
Cedar Cl Ditton ME20 .....98 D8
Meopham Sta DA13 .....50 A3
Orpington BR2 .....56 E7
Swanley BR8 .....45 C7
Cedar Copse BR1 .....42 F7
Cedar Cres Orpington BR2 .56 E7
Tonbridge TN10 .....127 C7
Cedar Ct Eltham SE9 .....11 E1
21 Greenwich SE7 .....11 C8
Maidstone ME14 .....100 B5
Royal Tunbridge Wells TN4 .....159 A5
12 Tenterden TN30 .....193 A7
Cedar Dr Edenbridge TN8 .122 B2
Maidstone ME16 .....98 E2
Sutton at H DA4 .....47 B7
Cedar Gdns ME9 .....86 E8
Cedar Gr Gillingham ME7 ...69 A5
Sidcup DA5 .....13 D1
Cedar Ho TN4 .....158 E4
Cedar La TN27 .....182 D7
Cedar Lodge TN4 .....158 F3
Cedar Mount SE9 .....28 D7
Cedar Pl 3 SE7 .....1 C1
Cedar Rd Bromley BR1 ....42 C7
Dartford DA1 .....32 D7
Erith DA8 .....15 A6
Hoo St Werburgh ME3 .....40 E3
Rochester ME2 .....52 F6
Cedar Ridge TN2 .....159 D5
Cedar Terrace Rd TN13 ...92 C4
Cedarhurst Cotts 5 DA5 .31 A8
Cedarhurst Dr SE9 .....11 C2
Cedarmore Ct BR7 .....43 C8
Cedars PRU The ME16 .....99 D4
Cedars Sch The ME1 .....53 C4
Cedars The TN12 .....146 A7
Cedarwood Ho ME15 .....115 B6
Cedric Rd SE9 .....29 C5
Celandine Dr SE28 .....3 B5
Celestine Cl ME5 .....68 A1
Cement Block Cotts 8 RM17 .....18 C8
Cement Industry Heritage Ctr* DA11 .....18 B2
Cemetery La
Hadlow TN11 .....112 A1
Woolwich SE7 .....11 E8
Cemetery Rd Halling ME2 ..66 A4
Snodland ME6 .....65 F1
Woolwich SE2 .....13 B7
Centenary Ct DA4 .....47 A2
Central Ave Bexley DA16 ..13 A5
Chatham ME4 .....54 B8
Gravesend DA12 .....36 B5
Tilbury RM18 .....19 A6
Central Bsns Pk ME2 .....53 E7
Central Ct 3 SE18 .....2 B2
Central Lodge TN15 .....79 E6
Central Par
Rochester ME1 .....53 D2
Sidcup DA15 .....30 A5
Wadhurst TN5 .....184 F4
Central Par Villas BR5 ....44 C7
Central Park Gdns ME4 ...53 E2
Central Rd Dartford DA1 ...15 E2
New Hythe ME20 .....82 B4
Rochester ME2 .....53 A7
Central Terr ME3 .....39 F6
Central Way SE28 .....3 B6
Centre 2000 ME16 .....99 C8
Centre Common Rd BR7 ..29 C1
Centre Ct ME2 .....53 E7
Centre Rd DA3 .....62 E7
Centurian Way DA18 .....4 A3
Centurion Cl ME8 .....54 F1
Century Ct ME1 .....53 C5
Century Rd ME8 .....69 D8
Ceres Rd SE18 .....2 F2
Cerne Rd DA12 .....36 E5
Cervia Way DA12 .....36 F5
Chada Ave ME7 .....54 E3
Chadd Dr BR1 .....42 E6
Chadfields RM18 .....19 A7
Chadwell Hill RM17 .....19 A8
Chadwick Cl DA11 .....35 E5
Chadwick Ct
2 Dartford DA1 .....15 D1
4 Woolwich SE28 .....3 B5
Chadwick Way SE28 .....3 D6
Chadwin Rd E13 .....1 B8
Chaffey Ho 6 SE7 .....1 C1
Chaffinch Cl ME5 .....68 A7
Chaffinch Way TN12 ....146 A5
Chafford Cotts TN3 .....156 F5
Chafford La TN3 .....156 F5
Chain Gate ME17 .....137 A8
Chalcombe Rd SE2 .....3 B3
Chalet Cl DA5 .....31 D4
Chalfont Ct 3 DA17 .....4 A1
Chalfont Dr ME8 .....69 D6
Chalgrove Mews ME2 ....66 A5
Chalice Way DA9 .....16 F2
Chalk Ave TN30 .....183 B2
Chalk Ct RM17 .....18 A8
Chalk La TN17 .....178 E7
Chalk Pit Ave BR5 .....44 D6
Chalk Pit Hill ME4 .....54 A3
Chalk Rd Chalk DA12 .....37 A6
Lower Higham ME3 .....38 C6
Newham E13 .....1 C8
Chalkenden Ave ME8 .....55 A2
Chalkers Way ME8 .....55 B4
Chalket La TN2 .....160 C5
Chalkstone Cl DA16 .....13 A6
Chalkways TN15 .....76 F3
Chalky Bank DA11 .....36 A3
Chalky Bank Rd ME8 .....55 F2
Chalky Rd ME9 .....86 C6
Challenge Cl DA12 .....36 F4
Challenger Cl TN12 .....145 F6
Challock Cl TN16 .....72 C3
Challock Ho 3 Erith DA8 ..14 F7
3 Orpington BR5 .....44 D1
Challock Wlk ME14 .....100 C6
Chalmers Way ME8 .....55 A4
Chamberlain Ave ME16 ...99 C2
Chamberlain Cl 5 SE28 ...2 D3
Chamberlain Ct ME8 .....69 B5
Chamberlain Rd ME4 .....54 B2
Chambers Cl 2 DA9 .....17 A2
Chancel Cl TN15 .....61 E3
Chancellor Ho TN4 .....158 F3
Chancellor Way TN13 ....92 A5
Chancelot Rd SE2 .....3 B2
Chancery Ct DA1 .....33 A7
Chancery La ME15 .....100 B3
Chancery Rd ME3 .....22 B5
Chanctonbury Cl SE9 .....29 B5
Chandler Ave E16 .....1 A8
Chandler's Hill DA13 .....64 C5
Chandler's Rd DA13 .....64 C5
Chandlers Dr DA8 .....4 E2
Chandlers Mews DA9 .....17 C3
Chandlers Wharf ME1 .....53 B5
Chandos Rd TN1 .....159 C5
Chantler's Hill TN12 .....146 A4
Chantlers Mead TN8 .....155 A5
Chantry Ave DA3 .....48 E3
Chantry Cl DA14 .....30 E3
Chantry Ct DA12 .....19 C1
Chantry Her Ctr* DA12 ...19 C1
Chantry La BR2 .....42 D4
Chantry Pl Marden TN12 ..148 C6
Sevenoaks TN13 .....91 F5
Chantry Prim Sch DA12 ...19 C1
Chantry Rd TN12 .....148 C5
Chapel Alley Cotts TN14 ..76 A8
Chapel Cl Crayford DA1 ....14 E2
Ryarsh ME19 .....80 F5
West Thurrock RM20 .....17 B8
Chapel Cotts ME17 .....117 F5
Chapel Ct DA10 .....17 E1
Chapel Farm Rd SE9 .....28 F6
Chapel Field Cotts DA4 ...47 B8
Chapel Hill DA1 .....14 E2
Chapel Hos ME2 .....65 E4
Chapel La
Egerton Forstal TN27 .....137 B2
Chapel La *continued*
Gillingham ME7 .....69 A2
Gillingham ME7 .....69 A4
Iden Green TN17 .....190 C4
Maidstone ME14 .....101 A5
Sissinghurst TN17 .....180 B7
Staplehurst TN12 .....149 F3
Upper Halling ME2 .....65 C4
Chapel Pl
14 Royal Tunbridge Wells TN1 .....159 A2
Ticehurst TN5 .....186 E1
Chapel Rd Bexley DA7 .....14 A3
Grain ME3 .....27 B5
Limpsfield RH8 .....104 C5
Snodland ME6 .....82 A8
Sutton Valence ME17 .....134 E7
Chapel Row TN15 .....94 C6
Chapel St
East Malling ME19 .....98 A6
Ryarsh ME19 .....80 F5
Chapel The ME16 .....99 B3
Chapel View TN15 .....94 C6
Chapel Wlk
Goathurst Common TN14 ..107 B5
Maypole DA2 .....31 E6
Chapel Wood DA3 .....62 E8
Chapel Wood Rd DA3, TN15 .....62 E8
Chapelsite Ct 6 DA17 .....4 A2
Chaplin Cl ME3 .....39 C3
Chaplin Dr TN27 .....151 D5
Chapman Ave ME15 .....116 E8
Chapman Rd DA17 .....4 B1
Chapman Way
East Malling ME19 .....97 F8
Royal Tunbridge Wells TN2 .....159 C8
Chapman's Hill DA13, TN15 .....63 E4
Chapman's La
Orpington BR5,BR8 .....44 D7
Swanley BR8 .....45 A7
Chapmans Cl TN14 .....90 E3
Chapmans End BR5 .....44 E7
Chapmans Rd TN14 .....90 E3
Chapter Rd ME2 .....52 F8
Chapter Sch ME2 .....52 D7
Chardwell Cl E6 .....1 F7
Charford Rd E16 .....1 A8
Charing Cl BR6 .....57 F6
Charing Ho 5 DA8 .....14 F7
Charing Rd ME8 .....55 B3
Chariot Way ME2 .....52 F4
Charity Farm Cotts TN17 .....166 F7
Charlbury Cl ME16 .....99 C3
Charldane Rd SE9 .....29 B5
Charlecote Ct ME8 .....69 D8
Charles Busby Ct ME20 ...82 F1
Charles Cl Sidcup DA14 ....30 B4
Snodland ME6 .....82 A8
Charles Ct Erith DA8 .....14 E8
Royal Tunbridge Wells TN2 .....159 C3
Charles Darwin Ho 5 BR1 .....28 B1
Charles Darwin Sch TN16 .....72 F3
Charles Dickens Ave ME3 .....38 C2
Charles Dickens Ctr (Mus)* ME1 .....53 C5
Charles Dr ME2 .....52 B2
Charles Flemwell Mews E16 .....1 A5
Charles Garvice Ct SE3 ...11 D4
Charles Grinling Wlk SE18 .2 A2
Charles Rd TN14 .....59 B1
Charles St Chatham ME4 ...53 E3
Grays RM17 .....18 C8
Maidstone ME16 .....99 E3
Newham E16 .....1 C5
Rochester ME2 .....53 A7
Royal Tunbridge Wells TN4 .....159 A8
Stone DA9 .....16 F2
Charles Street Centre PRU The TN4 .....159 A8
Charles Whincup Rd E16 ...1 B5
Charlesfield SE9 .....28 C5
Charlesford Ave ME17 ...118 D3
Charlieville Rd DA8 .....14 C7
Charlock Cl ME16 .....99 D8
Charlotte Cl Bexley DA6 ...13 E2
Chatham ME5 .....68 B6
Charlotte Ct BR7 .....29 B2
Charlotte Dr ME8 .....55 C1
Charlotte Park Ave BR1 ..42 E6
Charlotte Pl RM20 .....17 B8
Charlottes Cotts TN11 ...125 F1
Charlton Church La SE7 ...1 C1
Charlton Cres 2 TN9 .....127 C2
Charlton Dene SE7 .....11 D7
Charlton Dr TN16 .....72 D2
Charlton Gate Bsns Pk SE7 .....1 C2
Charlton La Greenwich SE7 .1 D1
Sutton Valence ME17 .....135 C8
West Farleigh ME15 .....114 E6
Charlton Manor ME7 .....54 B5
Charlton Manor Prim Sch SE7 .....11 D7
Charlton Park La SE7 .....11 E8
Charlton Park Rd SE7 .....11 D8
Charlton Rd SE3,SE7 .....11 B8
Charlton Sch SE7 .....11 E8
Charlton St Grays RM20 ...17 D8
Charlton St *continued*
Maidstone ME16 .....99 C
Charlton Sta SE7 .....1 C
Charlton's Way TN4 .....158 E
Charminster Rd SE9 .....28 C
Charmouth Rd DA16 .....13 C
Charmwood La BR6 .....58 E
Charmwood Villas BR6 ...58 C
Charne The TN14 .....76 A
Charnock BR8 .....45 E
Chart Cnr ME17 .....117 E
Chart Hill Rd ME17 .....134 A
Chart Hills Cl SE28 .....3 E
Chart La TN16 .....106 E
Chart Pl ME8 .....69 C
Chart Rd ME17 .....134 C
Chart View TN15 .....77 E
Charter Dr DA5 .....30 E
Charter St Chatham ME4 ...53 F
Gillingham ME7 .....54 C
Charterhouse Dr TN13 ....92 A
Charterhouse Rd BR6 .....58 A
Charton Cl 5 DA17 .....13 F
Chartway TN13 .....92 C
Chartway St ME17 .....118 C
Chartwell* TN16 .....105 F
Chartwell Bsns Ctr BR1 ...42 D
Chartwell Cl
Rochester ME2 .....39 E
Sidcup SE9 .....29 D
Chartwell Ct Chatham ME4 .53 E
Maidstone ME15 .....100 E
Chartwell Dr
Maidstone ME16 .....99 E
Orpington BR6 .....57 D
Chase Sq 14 DA11 .....19 E
Chase The Bexley DA7 .....14 E
Bromley BR1 .....42 E
Chatham ME4 .....53 D
Gillingham ME8 .....55 A
Kemsing TN15 .....76 E
Pratt's Bottom BR6 .....58 A
Tonbridge TN10 .....127 C
West Thurrock RM20 .....17 D
Chastilian Rd DA1 .....32 A
Chatfield Way ME19 .....82 E
Chatham Ave BR2 .....42 A
Chatham Gr ME4 .....53 F
Chatham Gram Sch for Boys ME4 .....67 F
Chatham Gram Sch for Girls ME5 .....54 C
Chatham Hill ME4 .....54 B
Chatham Hill Rd TN14 ....92 C
Chatham Ho 16 SE18 .....1 F
Chatham Rd
Kit's Coty ME20 .....83 D
Sandling ME14 .....83 E
Sandling ME14 .....83 E
Chatham Ski Ctr ME7 .....68 E
Chatham South Sch ME4 .67 F
Chatham Sta ME4 .....53 E
Chatsworth Ave
Bromley BR1 .....28 B
Sidcup DA15 .....30 A
Chatsworth Dr ME2 .....39 B
Chatsworth Ho 3 BR2 .....42 A
Chatsworth Inf Sch DA15 .30 A
Chatsworth Par BR5 .....43 C
Chatsworth Rd
Dartford DA1 .....15 C
10 Gillingham ME7 .....54 C
Chattenden Barracks Royal Sch of Military Engineering ME3 .....39 F
Chattenden Ct ME14 .....100 B
Chattenden La ME3 .....39 F
Chattenden Prim Sch ME3 .....39 F
Chattenden Terr ME3 .....39 F
Chatterton Rd BR2 .....42 D
Chatwell Ct ME7 .....54 C
Chaucer Bsns Pk TN15 .....93 D
Chaucer Cl
13 Maidstone ME15 .....116 E
Rochester ME2 .....53 E
Tilbury RM18 .....19 C
Chaucer Gdns TN9 .....142 F
Chaucer Ind Pk TN15 .....93 D
Chaucer Pk DA1 .....32 F
Chaucer Rd Bexley DA16 ...12 F
Gillingham ME7 .....54 D
Northfleet DA11 .....35 D
Sidcup DA15 .....30 C
Chaucer Way
Dartford DA1 .....16 A
New Hythe ME20 .....82 A
Chaundrye Cl SE9 .....11 F
Chauntler Cl E16 .....1 B
Chave Rd DA2 .....32 E
Cheeselands TN27 .....167 F
Cheffins Ho ME7 .....54 E
Chegwell Dr ME5 .....68 B
Chegworth La ME17 .....119 A
Chegworth Rd ME17 .....118 F
Cheldoc Rise ME4 .....40 C
Chellows La RH7 .....121 A
Chelmar Rd ME7 .....54 B
Chelmsford Cl E6 .....1 F
Chelmsford Ho ME15 ....116 E
Chelmsford Rd ME2 .....52 D
Chelsea Ct 6 BR1 .....42 E
Chelsfield Hill BR6 .....58 C
Chelsfield Ho ME16 .....99 D
Chelsfield La
Badgers Mount BR6,TN14 ...59 B
Chelsfield BR5,BR6 .....58 D
Orpington BR5 .....44 D

helsfield Park Hospl
BR6 58 F5
helsfield Prim Sch BR6 58 E5
helsfield Rd BR5 44 C3
helsfield Sta BR6 58 B5
helsiter Ct DA14 29 F4
helsworth Dr SE18 12 D8
heltenham Cl
Gravesend DA12 36 C3
Maidstone ME15 116 F6
heltenham Rd BR6 58 A7
heney Cl ME8 69 D5
henies Cl TN2 173 A8
henies The
Joyden's Wood DA2 31 E4
Orpington BR6 43 E3
hennell Park Rd TN30 182 E1
hennels The TN26 183 C7
hepstow Ho 3 ME15 116 F6
hequer's Cotts TN17 177 F8
hequers Cl Chatham ME5 84 A8
Istead Rise DA13 49 F7
Orpington BR5 43 F5
hequers Ct ME2 39 A1
hequers Ctr ME15 100 A4
hequers Hill Cotts
TN8 124 A2
hequers La RM9 3 F8
herbourg Cres ME5 67 F7
herbury Cl SE28 3 D7
heriton Ave BR2 42 A4
heriton Ct 12 SE12 28 A8
heriton Dr SE18 12 D8
heriton Rd ME8 69 D8
heriton Way ME16 99 C7
herries The ME16 99 A2
herry Amber Cl ME8 69 F8
herry Ave BR8 45 D5
herry Cl ME17 120 C5
herry Ct DA14 30 B5
herry Gr TN10 127 E5
herry Hill Ct ME9 71 B6
herry Orch Ditton ME20 98 C8
Greenwich SE7 11 C8
Tenterden TN30 193 A6
herry Orch The TN11 111 E1
herry Orchard Cl BR5 44 C4
herry Orchard Prim Sch
SE7 11 C7
herry Orchard Rd BR2 56 E8
herry Orchard Way
ME16 99 B3
herry Rd ME3 40 E3
herry Tree Cl RM17 18 C8
herry Tree Ct 19 SE7 11 C8
herry Tree Gr TN15 61 B1
herry Tree La DA2 31 F5
herry Tree Rd
Gillingham ME8 69 F8
Royal Tunbridge Wells
TN2 158 E1
Tonbridge TN10 127 D7
herry Trees DA3 48 F4
herry View ME17 116 B3
herry Wlk BR2 42 A1
herrycot Hill BR6 57 D6
herrycot Rise BR6 57 C6
herrydown Rd DA14 30 D6
herryfields TN17 190 D6
herrywood Dr DA11 35 E5
hervil Mews SE28 3 B5
hervilles ME16 99 A2
herwell Cl TN10 127 B4
hesfield Cl TN11 111 F1
hesham Ave BR5 43 B3
hesham Dr ME8 69 E6
heshire Rd
Maidstone ME15 116 E7
Maidstone,Willington
ME15 100 E2
heshunt Cl DA13 50 A3
heshunt Rd DA17 4 A1
hesil Ho 1 BR7 43 D8
hessenden La TN27 153 A1
hessington Ave DA7 13 E7
hester Ave TN2 159 D2
hester Cl ME2 52 D6
hester Rd
Gillingham ME7 54 D2
Sidcup DA15 12 E2
hesterfield Cl BR5 44 D5
hesterfield Dr
Dartford DA1 15 B2
Sevenoaks TN13 91 D5
hesterford Ho SE18 11 D7
hesterton Rd Cliffe ME3 22 B5
5 Lunsford ME20 81 F4
hesterton Way RM18 19 C5
hestfield Cl ME8 55 E2
hestnut Ave
Chatham ME5 67 F3
Hill Park TN16 89 A6
Royal Tunbridge Wells
TN4 159 B8
Staplehurst TN12 149 F4
Stone DA9 33 F8
Tatsfield TN16 88 E5
hestnut Cl
Edenbridge TN8 122 B2
Frittenden TN17 166 E6
Kings Hill ME19 97 A2
Northfleet DA11 18 F1
Orpington BR6 58 A5
Royal Tunbridge Wells
TN4 159 B8
Sidcup DA15 30 A6
Tenterden TN30 183 C1
Ulcombe ME17 135 F6

Chestnut Copse RH8 104 B2
Chestnut Ct TN2 173 A8
Chestnut Dr Bexley DA7 13 E4
Coxheath ME17 115 B3
Kingswood ME17 118 D2
Chestnut Gr DA2 31 E4
Chestnut Ho 5 ME16 99 A3
Chestnut La
Matfield TN12 145 D1
Sevenoaks TN13 92 B3
Vigo Village DA13 80 B8
Chestnut Pl TN8 155 A6
Chestnut Rd Dartford DA1 32 D7
Rochester ME2 52 E6
Chestnut Rise SE18 2 E1
Chestnut St ME9 71 E4
Chestnut Wlk
Larkfield ME20 82 B2
Sevenoaks TN15 108 F6
Tonbridge TN9 126 F2
Chestnut Wood La ME9 71 E3
Chestnuts Royal BR7 29 D1
Chestnuts The
Addington ME19 80 C3
Chislehurst BR7 29 D1
7 Erith DA17 3 F1
The Moor TN18 194 F8
Woolwich SE18 12 B6
Cheswick Cl DA1 14 F3
Chesworth Cl DA8 14 E5
Chetney Cl ME2 52 C7
Chetwood Wlk 15 E6 1 E8
Chevender BR7 29 B1
Cheveney Wlk 2 BR2 42 A6
Chevening CE Prim Sch
TN13 91 B5
Chevening Cl ME5 68 A5
Chevening Ct BR6 58 A8
Chevening Ho BR5 44 A8
Chevening La TN14 74 E3
Chevening Rd
3 Greenwich SE10 1 A1
Sevenoaks TN13,TN14 91 B6
Sundridge TN14 90 F4
Chevenings The DA14 30 C5
Cheviot Cl Bexley DA7 14 E5
Tonbridge TN9 127 C4
Cheviot Gdns ME15 101 A1
Cheviot Ho DA11 18 D1
Chevron Cl E16 1 A7
Chevron Ho RM17 18 B7
Cheyne Cl BR2 56 E7
Cheyne Wlk Longfield DA3 48 D6
Meopham DA13 64 A8
Chicago Ave ME7 54 F5
Chichester Cl
Gillingham ME8 70 A8
Greenwich SE3 11 C6
Newham E6 1 E7
Chichester Ct 3 DA5 31 A8
Chichester Dr TN13 91 F2
Chichester Rd Stone DA9 16 F1
Tonbridge TN9 143 A8
Chichester Rise DA12 36 D4
Chichester Wharf 14 DA8 4 E1
Chickenden La NT17 150 C4
Chickfield Gdns 4 ME5 54 C2
Chicks La TN17 176 F2
Chiddingstone Ave DA7 13 F7
Chiddingstone Castle*
TN8 140 B7
Chiddingstone CE Prim Sch
TN8 140 C7
Chiddingstone Cl ME15 116 F6
Chidley Cross Rd TN12 129 E6
Chieftain Cl ME7 55 B1
Chieveley Dr TN2 159 D1
Chieveley Par DA7 14 B4
Chieveley Rd DA7 14 B3
Chiffinch Gdns DA11 35 E5
Childs Cres DA10 17 D1
Childs Way TN15 78 F3
Childsbridge La TN15 92 F7
Childsbridge Way TN15 92 F7
Childscroft Rd ME8 55 F2
Chilham Cl Chatham ME4 53 E3
Sidcup DA5 30 F8
Chilham Ho
1 Maidstone ME15 116 E8
Rochester ME2 39 C1
Chilham Rd Bromley SE9 28 E4
Gillingham ME8 55 A3
Maidstone ME16 99 C7
Chilham Way BR2 42 A2
Chillington Cl ME2 65 E4
Chillington St ME14 99 F6
Chilliwack Rd ME3 39 F5
Chilston Cl TN4 159 A5
Chilston Rd
Lenham ME17 120 D5
Royal Tunbridge Wells
TN4 159 A5
Chiltenhurst TN8 122 A2
Chiltern Cl Bexley DA7 14 E6
Maidstone ME15 100 F1
Chiltern Ct 11 SE9 12 A1
Chiltern Rd DA11 35 E5
Chiltern Way TN9 127 C4
Chiltern Wlk TN2 159 D4
Chilterns DA14 30 A3
Chilterns, The BR1 42 B7
Chilton Ct ME8 55 E1
Chilton Dr ME3 38 B3
Chimes The ME1 53 C5
Chinbrook Cres 8 SE12 28 B5
Chinbrook Rd SE12 28 B5
Chine Farm Pl TN14 74 D3
Chinnery Ct DA13 50 A2

Chippendale Cl ME5 67 F1
Chippendayle Dr ME17 119 D6
Chipperfield Rd
Orpington BR5 44 A7
Orpington BR5 44 B5
Chipstead Cl ME16 99 D6
Chipstead La TN13 91 D5
Chipstead Park Cl TN13 91 C5
Chipstead Pk TN13 91 D5
Chipstead Place Gdns
TN13 91 D5
Chipstead Rd Erith DA8 14 E7
Gillingham ME8 69 D4
Chipstead Sq TN13 91 C5
Chislehurst & Sidcup Gram
Sch DA15 30 B6
Chislehurst (St Nicholas) CE
Prim Sch BR7 29 C1
Chislehurst Caves* BR7 43 A8
Chislehurst Cl ME15 116 F6
Chislehurst High St BR7 29 B2
Chislehurst Rd
Bromley BR1,BR2 42 E8
Orpington BR6 44 A2
Orpington,Broom Hill BR6 43 F2
Orpington,Petts Wood BR5,
BR6 43 E4
Sidcup DA14 30 A3
Chislehurst Sta BR7 43 A7
Chislet Wlk ME8 69 D5
Chiswell Sq SE3 11 B5
Chorleywood Cres BR5 44 A7
Christ Church Ave 1
TN1 159 A2
Christ Church CE Sch
SE18 12 A6
Christ Church Cres 2
DA12 36 C8
Christ Church Erith CE Prim
Sch DA8 14 D8
Christ Church Rd 3
DA12 36 C8
Christchurch Ave DA8 14 E8
Christchurch Ct 3 ME5 54 C2
Christchurch Ho 11
ME15 116 E5
Christchurch Rd
Dartford DA1 15 C1
Sidcup DA15 29 F5
Tilbury RM18 19 A6
Christen Way ME15,
ME17 116 F3
Christian Ct 3 ME2 53 C8
Christian Fields Ave
DA12 36 C4
Christie Cl ME5 68 B6
Christie Dr 8 ME20 81 F4
Christie Ho DA6 14 B2
Christies Ave TN14 59 B1
Christmas La ME23 23 F3
Christmas St ME7 54 E7
Christopher Cl DA15 12 F2
Christy Rd TN16 72 C4
Chudleigh 7 DA14 30 B4
Chulkhurst TN27 167 F1
Chulkhurst Cl TN27 167 F1
Church Alley 11 DA11 19 B1
Church Ave DA14 30 B3
Church Cl
Brenchley TN12 162 C8
Cliffe ME3 22 B6
Mereworth ME18 112 D8
Church Cotts
Cranbrook TN17 179 D5
Crockenhill BR8 45 D2
Shoreham TN14 76 A8
Sutton Valence ME17 134 E7
Tenterden TN30 183 B3
Church Cres ME17 119 F6
Church Ct DA2 32 D5
Church Farm Cl
Crockenhill BR8 45 D3
Hoo St Werburgh ME3 40 E4
Church Field
Dartford DA2 32 D6
Sevenoaks TN13 91 F5
Snodland ME6 66 B1
Church Field Cotts TN15 92 F7
Church Fields ME19 97 B8
Church Gn
Hollingbourne ME17 102 E3
Marden TN12 148 C6
Rochester ME2 53 C8
Staplehurst TN12 149 E2
Church Hill Chatham ME5 54 C2
Crayford DA1 14 E3
Cudham TN14,TN16 73 C4
Dartford DA2 32 D6
High Halden TN26 183 E7
Leigh TN11 125 F2
Linton ME17 133 B7
Orpington BR6 44 A2
Plaxtol TN15 110 E8
Stockbury ME9 86 F7
Stone DA9 16 E2
Tatsfield TN16 88 D5
Woolwich SE18 1 F3
Church Hill Wood BR5 43 F4
Church Hyde SE18 12 E8
Church La Capel TN12 144 F6
Chalk DA12 37 C6
Chatham ME4 53 F6
Chislehurst BR7 43 C8
East Peckham TN12 129 F7
Frant TN3 173 B4
Harrietsham ME17 119 E6
Kemsing TN15 77 B2
Maidstone ME16 98 E1

Church La *continued*
Maidstone,Bearsted ME14 101 C4
Newington ME9 71 B6
Orpington BR2 42 E1
Stockbury ME9 86 E8
Sutton Valence ME17 135 B8
Tonbridge TN9 127 C2
Trottiscliffe ME19 80 B5
West Farleigh ME15 114 D7
Church Manor Way SE18,
SE2 3 A2
Church Manorway DA8 4 D3
Church Mdw TN12 163 A7
Church Mews ME8 69 F8
Church Path
Gillingham ME7 54 E6
Northfleet DA11 18 C1
Stone DA9 16 F1
Church Rd Bexley DA7,DA6 13 F4
Bexley,Welling DA16 13 B5
Biggin Hill TN16 72 E2
Bitchet Green TN15 93 E3
Brasted TN16 90 B3
Bromley BR1,BR2 42 A7
Chelsfield BR6 58 D4
Crockenhill BR8 45 D2
Erith DA8 4 D1
Goudhurst TN17 177 F8
Grafty Green ME17 136 F7
Gravesend DA12,DA13 36 D1
Halstead TN14 74 F7
Harrietsham ME17 119 E6
Hartley DA3 49 A2
Hawley DA4 32 F1
Henhurst DA13 50 C8
Hucking ME17 86 E1
Kilndown TN17 176 F3
Lamberhurst TN3 176 C6
Maidstone ME15 116 F7
Maidstone,Tovil ME15 99 E2
Offham ME18 96 D8
Orpington BR6 57 D5
Orpington, Keston BR2 56 D3
Paddock Wood TN12 146 B6
Pembury TN2 160 D8
Royal Tunbridge Wells
TN1 159 A3
Royal Tunbridge
Wells,Southborough TN4 142 F2
Ryarsh ME19 81 A3
Sandhurst Cross TN18 195 F4
Seal TN15 92 F6
Sevenoaks Weald TN14 108 B3
Sidcup DA14 30 A4
Stone DA9 16 F2
Sundridge TN14 90 E2
Sutton at H DA4 33 A2
Sutton Valence ME17 134 C8
Swanley Village BR8 46 D8
Swanscombe DA10 17 F1
Tenterden TN30 193 A7
Tilbury RM18 18 F6
Tonbridge TN11 126 D6
West Kingsdown TN15 61 E3
West Peckham ME18 112 A6
West Tilbury RM18 19 E8
Pembury TN2 144 D1
Church Row
Chislehurst BR7 43 C8
Plaxtol TN15 110 E8
Snodland ME6 82 A7
West Peckham ME18 112 B6
Church Row Mews BR7 29 C1
Church Sq ME17 120 D5
Church St Burham ME1 66 F1
Chatham ME4 54 A4
Cliffe ME3 22 B5
Cowden TN8 155 B5
Edenbridge TN8 122 D1
Gillingham ME7 54 E6
Gravesend DA11 19 B1
Grays RM17 18 C8
Hadlow TN11 128 E8
Hoo St Werburgh ME3 40 E5
Loose ME15 115 F5
Lower Higham ME3 38 D7
Maidstone ME14 100 A4
Maidstone, Boughton Monchelsea
ME17 116 B2
Maidstone,Tovil ME15 99 E2
Newham E16 2 B5
Northfleet DA13 35 A3
Rochester ME1 53 D4
Seal TN15 93 A7
Shoreham TN14 76 A8
Teston ME18 114 A8
Ticehurst TN5 186 D1
Tonbridge TN9 127 C2
Wadhurst TN5 185 A4
Church Terr ME5 54 C2
Church Trad Est DA8 15 A7
Church View
Biddenden TN27 167 F2
4 Dartford DA1 15 E1
Swanley BR8 45 D6
Church Wlk Dartford DA2 32 D5
East Malling ME19 98 A7
Eynsford DA4 60 E7
Gravesend DA12 36 D7
Gravesend DA12 36 D8
Hawkhurst TN18 189 A1
Headcorn TN27 151 C5
Churchbury Rd SE9 28 D8
Churchfield
Addington ME19 80 D3
Edenbridge TN8 122 D1
Churchfield Rd DA16 13 A4
Churchfield Sch SE2 3 A2

Churchfields Terr ME1 53 B4
Churchill Ave ME5 68 A7
Churchill Bsns Ctr TN16 89 D1
Churchill CE Prim Sch
TN16 89 C2
Churchill Cl DA1 33 B7
Churchill Cotts ME17 117 F6
Churchill Ct
4 Orpington BR6 57 C5
Westerham TN16 89 D1
Churchill Ho
Benenden TN17 190 E6
Maidstone ME16 99 B2
1 Woolwich SE18 2 B2
Churchill Pk DA1 16 A2
Churchill Rd Grays RM17 18 D8
Horton Kirby DA4 47 C5
Newham E16 1 C7
Northfleet DA11 35 F7
Churchill Sq ME19 97 A3
Churchill Way
Biggin Hill TN16 72 D4
Bromley BR1 42 A7
Churchills Ropewalk
TN17 177 E8
Churchlands ME14 100 B5
Churchsettle La TN5 185 C1
Churchside DA13 80 A8
Churchside Cl TN16 72 C2
Churchyard Cotts TN3 158 A8
Churn La TN12 147 A2
Chute Cl ME8 69 D4
Chyngton Cl DA15 29 F5
Cimba Wood DA12 36 E4
Cinder Hill La TN11 125 C1
Cinderhill Wood TN12 145 C2
Cinderhill Wood Cvn Site
TN12 145 C1
Cinnabar Cl ME5 68 A1
Circle The RM18 19 A6
Circuit Rd SE28 3 A4
Circular Way SE18 12 A8
Cirrus Cres DA12 36 E3
City Way ME1 53 D2
Civic Sq RM18 19 A5
Civic Way TN1 159 A3
CJ Gallards Almshouses
TN4 159 A8
Clacket La Tatsfield TN16 88 E2
Westerham TN16 105 A8
Clacketts Farm ME19 81 B5
Claire Ho 4 ME16 99 E5
Clancy Gdns TN17 179 B5
Clandon Ct BR1 28 A2
Clandon Rd ME5 68 D2
Clanricarde Gdns 1
TN1 159 A3
Clanricarde Rd 2 TN1 159 A3
Claphatch La TN5 186 A5
Clapper La TN12 149 D6
Clara Pl SE18 2 A2
Clare Ave TN9 126 F1
Clare Cnr SE9 29 B8
Clare Cswy DA9 16 F3
Clare Ct BR7 42 F8
Clare La ME19 97 E8
Clare Way Bexley DA7 13 E6
Sevenoaks TN13 108 C8
Claremont Cl Newham E16 2 A5
Orpington BR6 57 A6
Claremont Cres DA1 14 E3
Claremont Ct 4 TN2 159 C7
Claremont Gdns TN2 159 B2
Claremont Pl
1 Gravesend DA11 36 B8
Iden Green TN17 190 C4
Marden TN12 148 D4
Claremont Prim Sch
TN2 159 B2
Claremont Rd
Bromley BR1 42 F5
Hextable BR8 31 E1
Maidstone ME14 100 B5
Royal Tunbridge Wells
TN1 159 B2
Claremont St E16 2 A4
Claremont Way 2 ME4 53 F3
Clarence Ave Bromley BR1 42 E5
Rochester ME1 53 C4
Clarence Cres DA14 30 B5
Clarence Ct
2 Grays RM17 18 B8
Maidstone ME14 100 E4
Pratt's Bottom BR6 58 C2
Clarence Lodge TN1 159 A3
Clarence Pl DA12 36 B7
Clarence Rd Bexley DA6 13 E3
Biggin Hill TN16 72 F1
Bromley,Mottingham SE9 28 E6
Bromley,Widmore BR1 42 E6
Chatham ME4 54 B2
Grays RM17 18 B8
Royal Tunbridge Wells
TN1 159 A3
Sidcup DA14 30 B5
Clarence Row
Gravesend DA12 36 B8
Royal Tunbridge Wells
TN1 159 A3
Clarendon Cl
Maidstone ME14 101 A4
Orpington BR5 44 A6
Clarendon Ct TN13 92 A2
Clarendon Dr ME2 39 A1

Clarendon Gdns
Dartford DA2 33 D8
Royal Tunbridge Wells TN2 159 A1
Clarendon Gn BR5 44 A5
Clarendon Gr BR5 44 A5
Clarendon Mews DA5 31 B7
Clarendon Path BR5 44 A6
Clarendon Pl
Joyden's Wood DA2 31 E3
Maidstone ME14 100 A4
Sevenoaks TN13 92 A2
Clarendon Rd
Gravesend DA12 19 C1
Sevenoaks TN13 92 A2
Clarendon Way
Royal Tunbridge Wells TN2 159 A1
St Paul's Cray BR5,BR7 43 F6
Claret Ho TN13 92 B3
Clareville Rd BR5 57 C8
Clarewood Dr ME19 97 E8
Claridge TN1 159 B6
Claridge Ct ME7 68 F4
Clark Cl DA8 15 A6
Clark Mews ME20 82 F1
Clark's Yd TN5 187 A3
Clarkbourne Dr RM17 18 D8
Clarkes Green Rd TN15 77 B5
Clarks La Halstead TN14 74 F7
Titsey CR6,RH8,TN16 88 C4
Claston Cl DA1 14 E3
Clavadal Rd TN12 146 A7
Clavell Cl ME8 69 E4
Clay Cotts TN17 177 E8
Clay Hill Mount TN17 177 E8
Clay Hill Rd TN3 175 D6
Clay Wood Cl BR6 43 E2
Claybridge Rd SE12 28 C4
Claydown Mews SE18 2 A1
Clayfarm Rd SE9 29 C6
Claygate
Eyhorne Street ME17 102 D2
Maidstone ME15 100 D1
Claygate Cross TN15 95 A3
Claygate La TN11 110 F4
Claygate Rd TN12 131 B2
Clayhill TN17 177 D8
Clayhill Cres SE9 28 D4
Claymill Ho 2 SE18 2 C1
Clayton Cl 3 E6 1 F7
Clayton Croft Rd DA2 32 A6
Clayton's La TN3 156 E2
Claytonville Terr DA17 4 C4
Claywood La DA2 34 D5
Clayworth Cl DA15 13 B1
Cleanthus Cl SE18 12 B6
Cleanthus Rd SE18 12 B6
Clearway ME19 80 A1
Clearways Bsns Est TN15 61 E3
Clearways Mobile Home Pk
TN15 61 D3
Cleave Ave BR6 57 E4
Cleave Rd ME7 54 E3
Cleavers TN17 180 A8
Cleavers Cl TN17 180 A8
Cleavesland ME18 130 E5
Cleeve Ave TN2 159 D2
Cleeve Ct ME19 97 B3
Cleeve Park Gdns DA14 30 B6
Cleeve Park Sch DA14 30 C5
Clegg Ho SE3 11 B3
Clematis Ave ME8 69 B5
Clemens Pl ME18 97 C2
Clement Ct ME16 99 D5
Clement St BR8,DA4 32 E2
Clements Ave E16 1 A6
Cleminson Ct DA14 30 D2
Clenches Farm La TN13 92 A1
Clenches Farm Rd TN13 92 A1
Clendon Way SE18 2 D2
Clerks Field TN27 151 D5
Clermont Cl ME7 69 A4
Cleve Rd DA14 30 D5
Clevedon Ho BR1 28 E1
Cleveland TN2 159 D4
Cleveland Ho
Maidstone ME16 99 B2
Northfleet DA11 18 D1
Cleveland Rd Bexley DA16 12 F5
Gillingham ME7 54 D6
Clevely Cl SE7 1 D2
Cleves Rd TN15 76 E2
Cleves View 4 DA1 15 D1
Clewer Ho 8 SE2 3 D4
Clewson Rise ME14 100 B8
Cliff Hill ME17 116 D4
Cliff Hill Rd ME17 116 C4
Cliff Reach DA9 16 F1
Cliffe Ct ME3 22 B5
Cliffe Pools Nature Reserve*
ME3 5 E1
Cliffe Rd ME2 39 A1
Cliffe Woods Prim Sch
ME3 39 C8
Clifford Ave BR7 28 F2
Clifford Ho 6 ME14 100 B4
Clifton Cl
Maidstone ME14 100 B5
8 Orpington BR6 57 C5
Rochester ME2 52 F7
Clifton Cotts TN2 159 D8
Clifton Gr DA11 36 B8
Clifton Marine Par DA11 18 F1
Clifton Pl TN1 159 B2
Clifton Rd Bexley DA16 13 C4
Gillingham ME7 54 C7
Gravesend DA11 19 A1
Royal Tunbridge Wells
TN2 159 C7
Sidcup DA14 29 E4
Cliftonville Ct SE12 28 A7
Clinch Ct 15 E16 1 A8
Clinch St ME3 24 A4
Clinton Ave Bexley DA16 13 A3
Clinton Bsns Ctr TN12 149 E5
Clinton Cl ME17 115 B3
Clinton La TN8 123 E3
Clipper Bvd DA9 16 E3
Clipper Bvd W DA2 16 D4
Clipper Cl ME2 53 E7
Clipper Cres DA12 36 F4
Clipper Ct ME2 53 E7
Clive Ave DA1 14 F1
Clive Ho ME20 98 F8
Clive Rd Erith DA17 4 A2
Gravesend DA11 19 B1
Rochester ME1 53 C3
Cliveden Cl ME16 99 D7
Clock Ho The DA15 30 A7
Clock House La TN13 92 A4
Clock Tower Mews
Snodland ME6 66 A1
Woolwich SE28 3 B6
Clockhouse TN2 159 F6
Cloisterham Rd ME1 67 D7
Cloisters Ave BR2 42 F4
Cloisters Ct DA7 14 B4
Cloisters The
1 Dartford DA1 15 E1
Lenham ME17 120 C5
Cloke Mews TN15 94 F7
Cloonmore Ave BR6 57 F6
Clopton Ct ME8 69 D8
Close The Addington ME19 80 C2
Birling ME19 81 B5
Borough Green TN15 95 A8
Bough Beech TN8 124 A2
Cudham TN16 73 B3
Dartford DA2 32 D5
Groombridge TN3 171 C6
Ightham TN15 94 D6
New Barn DA3 49 B7
Orpington BR5 43 E3
Rochester ME1 53 C4
Royal Tunbridge Wells
TN2 159 C8
Sevenoaks TN13 91 E3
Sidcup DA14 30 B3
1 Sidcup,Old Bexley DA5 31 A8
Cloth Hall Gdns TN27 168 A2
Clothier Ho SE7 1 E1
Clothworkers Rd SE18 12 D7
Cloudberry Cl ME16 99 D6
Cloudesley Cl ME1 53 B1
Cloudesley Rd Bexley DA7 13 F6
Erith DA8 14 F6
Clovelly Rd DA7 13 E8
Clovelly Way BR6 43 F3
Clover Bank View ME5 68 B6
Clover Ct 12 RM17 18 D8
Clover Rd ME3 40 E3
Clover St 3 ME4 53 F4
Clover Terr 4 ME15 116 D8
Clover Way TN12 146 A5
Clover Wlk 13 TN8 122 D3
Cloverdale Gdns DA15 12 F1
Clovers The DA11 35 E4
Club Cotts TN11 126 D8
Club Gardens Rd BR2 42 A2
Clyde Rd TN10 127 C6
Clydesdale Ho DA18 3 E4
Clydon Cl DA8 14 E8
Coach & Horses Pas 18
TN2 159 A2
Coach Dr The DA13 79 E7
Coach House Mews 8
BR1 42 A6
Coach Rd
Egerton ME17,TN27 137 E6
Ightham TN15 94 B2
Rusthall TN4 158 C3
Coach Yd The ME16 99 B3
Coal Ct RM17 18 A8
Coalhouse Fort* RM18 20 E6
Coastguard Cotts ME3 27 B5
Coates Hill Rd BR1 43 A7
Cob Dr DA12 37 E3
Cobb Cl ME2 52 D8
Cobbets Way TN8 138 C8
Cobbett Cl ME19 97 F8
Cobbett Rd SE9 11 E4
Cobbett's Ride TN2 158 F1
Cobblestones ME7 68 F5
Cobbs Cl
Paddock Wood TN12 145 F6
Wateringbury ME18 113 E7
Cobden Ct Bromley BR2 42 C5
9 Woolwich SE28 3 C5
Cobden Rd
4 Chatham ME4 54 B2
Orpington BR6 57 D6
Sevenoaks TN13 92 C4
Cobdown Cl ME20 82 C2
Cobfield ME17 117 A1
Cobham Cl Bromley BR2 42 E2
Maidstone ME16 99 E4
Rochester ME2 52 E7
2 Sidcup DA15 13 B1
Swanscombe DA9 17 B1
Cobham Dr ME18 97 C3
Cobham Hall Sch DA12 51 C6
Cobham Ho 4 DA8 14 F7
Cobham Pl DA6 13 D2
Cobham Prim Sch DA12 51 A5
Cobham Rise ME7 54 F5
Cobham St DA11 36 B8
Cobham Terr DA9 17 B1
Cobhambury Rd DA12 51 B4
Cobhams TN3 158 A8
Cobland Rd SE12 28 C4
Cobs Cl TN15 94 C6
Cobsdene DA12 36 D2
Cobtree Cl ME5 68 C8
Cobtree Rd ME17 115 C3
Cobtree Wharf ME20 83 C2
Cockerhurst Rd TN14 59 E2
Cockmannings La BR5 44 E1
Cockmannings Rd BR5 44 D2
Cockmount La TN5 184 F5
Cockpit The TN12 148 C5
Cocksett Ave BR6 57 E4
Cocksure La DA14 31 A4
Codrington Cres DA12 36 D3
Codrington Gdns DA12 36 D3
Cogate Rd TN12 145 E6
Cokers Yd TN4 143 A1
Colchester Cl ME5 68 A7
Cold Arbor Rd TN13 91 D3
Cold Blow Cres DA5 31 D7
Cold Harbour La ME9 71 F6
Coldblow La ME14 86 A2
Coldbridge La TN27 137 B5
Coldharbour Crest SE9 29 A5
Coldharbour La
Aylesford ME20 83 A1
Hucking ME14,ME9 86 B1
Rainham RM13 4 F6
Shipbourne TN11 110 A2
Tonbridge TN11 126 E7
Coldharbour Rd
Ashurst TN8,TN11 156 E8
Gravesend DA11 36 A4
Iden Green TN17 190 B4
Northfleet DA11 35 F5
Coldharbour Sports Ctr
SE9 29 A6
Coldred Rd ME15 116 F4
Coldrum La ME19 80 C6
Coldshott RH8 104 A2
Cole Cl SE28 3 B5
Cole Terr ME17 120 C4
Colebrook Ind Est TN2 143 E1
Colebrook Rd TN4 159 C8
Colebrook St 1 DA8 14 F8
Colebrooke Ct DA14 30 B4
Colegate Dr ME14 101 C4
Coleman Rd DA17 4 A2
Colemans Heath SE9 29 B5
Colepits Wood Rd SE9 12 D2
Coleraine Rd 1 SE3 11 A8
Coleridge Cl 4 ME20 81 F4
Coleridge Rd
Dartford DA1 16 B3
Tilbury RM18 19 C5
Coleridge Way BR6 44 A3
Coles Ct TN2 159 C3
Coles La TN16 90 C4
Colesdane ME17 119 E8
Coleshall Cl ME15 116 F6
Colets Orch TN14 76 B3
Colewood Dr ME2 52 B8
Colfe's Prep Sch SE12 11 B1
Colin Blythe Rd TN10 127 F5
Colin Chapman Way DA3 61 E6
Colin Cl DA2 16 B1
College Ave
Gillingham ME7 54 B4
Maidstone ME15 99 F3
Tonbridge TN9 143 A7
College Cotts ME16 99 F3
College Ct 6 ME15 100 A3
College Dr TN2 159 D4
College Gn 10 BR1 42 A8
College Pl DA9 17 C3
College Rd Bromley BR1 28 A1
Chatham ME4 54 A7
Hextable BR8 31 F1
Maidstone ME15 99 F2
New Hythe ME20 82 B3
Northfleet DA11 18 B2
College View SE9 28 D7
College Wlk 4 ME15 100 A3
College Yd ME1 53 C6
Coller Cres DA2 33 E3
Collet Rd TN15 76 E2
Collet Wlk ME8 69 D4
Collier Cl E6 2 B6
Colliers Shaw BR2 56 D5
Colliers' Green CE Prim Sch
TN17 164 F2
Collindale Ave Erith DA8 14 B8
Sidcup DA15 30 A7
Collinge Cl ME19 82 A1
Collings Wlk ME8 69 D4
Collington Cl DA11 35 E8
Collington Ho 3 SE7 11 B8
Collington Terr ME15 116 E4
Collingwood Ho DA9 17 D2
Collingwood Ind Ctr
ME17 117 E2
Collingwood Rd ME20 83 C7
Collis St ME2 53 A8
Collison Pl TN30 193 D7
Colman Ho 4 ME14 100 A4
Colman Rd E16 1 C8
Colne Rd TN10 127 B5
Colney Rd DA1 15 F1
Colonade The 14 TN18 189 A2
Colonel Stephens Way
TN30 183 B2
Colonel's Way TN4 143 A2
Coltness Cres SE2 3 B1
Colts Hill Pl TN12 145 B5
Coltsfoot Ct RM17 18 D8
Coltsfoot Dr ME14 100 F4
Coltsfoot Ho E16 1 B8
Coltsfoot La RH8 104 A1
Coltstead DA3 62 E7
Columbia Wharf Rd
RM17 18 A8
Columbine Ave E6 1 E8
Columbine Cl
Rochester ME2 52 E7
West Malling ME19 81 F1
Columbine Rd
East Malling ME19 97 F8
Rochester ME2 52 E7
Columbus Sq DA8 14 F8
Colveiw Ct SE9 28 D7
Colyer Cl SE9 29 B6
Colyer Ho SE2 3 D1
Colyer Rd DA11 35 D6
Colyers Cl DA8 14 D6
Colyers La DA8 14 D6
Colyers Prim Sch DA8 14 D6
Colyers Wlk DA8 14 E6
Colyton Cl DA16 13 D6
Combe Bank Cotts TN14 90 D5
Combe Bank Dr TN14 90 E4
Combe Bank Farm TN14 90 D6
Combe Bank Sch TN14 90 E4
Combedale Rd SE10 1 A1
Combeside SE18 12 F7
Combwell Cres SE2 3 A3
Comforts Farm Ave
RH8 104 A3
Comfrey Ct RM17 18 D8
Command Rd ME14 99 F8
Commerce Way TN8 122 C3
Commercial Pl DA12 19 C1
Commercial Rd
Paddock Wood TN12 145 F6
Rochester ME2 53 B7
Royal Tunbridge Wells
TN1 159 B5
Tonbridge TN9 143 C8
Commissioner's Rd ME2 53 C8
Commissioners Ct ME4 53 F6
Commodore Rd ME14 100 C5
Common La Cliffe ME3 22 C6
Dartford DA2 32 B5
Common Rd Burham ME5 67 B1
Cliffe Woods ME3 39 B5
Hadlow TN11 111 E2
Ightham TN15 94 B4
Sissinghurst TN17 180 A8
Common The ME1 53 C6
Common View TN4 158 C4
Common Wall ME3 22 D6
Commonside BR2 56 C6
Commonwealth Ho 5
RM18 19 A5
Commonwealth Way SE2 3 C1
Commority Rd DA13 80 B8
Comp La TN15 95 E6
Compass Cl ME1 53 C1
Compass Ct DA11 18 E1
Compass Ctr ME4 54 B8
Compasses Rd TN11 125 B2
Compasses The TN11 125 B2
Compton Cl ME5 68 D2
Compton Pl DA8 14 F8
Concord Ave ME5 67 E5
Concord Cl
Paddock Wood TN12 145 E7
Royal Tunbridge Wells
TN2 159 C4
Concorde Bsns Pk TN16 72 D4
Concorde Dr E6 1 F8
Concrete Cotts ME3 21 E4
Condover Cres SE18 12 B7
Condovers Cotts RM18 19 F8
Conduit Rd SE18 2 B1
Coney Mews ME4 54 A1
Coneyburrow Rd TN2 159 E5
Conference Rd SE2 3 C2
Conghurst La TN18 195 B6
Congleton Gr SE18 2 C1
Congo Rd SE18 2 D1
Congress Rd SE2 3 C2
Congreve Rd SE9 11 F4
Congreve Wlk 6 E16 1 D8
Conifer Ave DA3 48 E3
Conifer Cl BR6 57 D6
Conifer Dr Chatham ME5 68 D1
Culverstone Green DA13 63 F2
Conifer Way BR8 45 C8
Conisborough Ct 13 DA2 16 B1
Coniscliffe Cl BR7 43 A8
Coniston Ave Bexley DA16 12 E4
Purfleet RM19 16 C8
Royal Tunbridge Wells
TN4 158 E5
Coniston Cl Bexley DA7 14 C6
Dartford DA1 32 B7
Erith DA8 14 E7
Gillingham ME7 55 A6
Coniston Ho ME15 116 E7
Coniston Rd DA7 14 C6
Connaught Bridge E16 1 D6
Connaught Cl ME15 116 F4
Connaught Mews
2 Chatham ME4 54 C2
Woolwich SE18 2 A1
Connaught Rd
Chatham ME4 54 C2
Connaught Rd *continued*
Gillingham ME7 54
Newham,Silvertown E16 1
Woolwich SE18 2
Connaught Way TN4 158
Conquest Ind Est ME2 53
Conrad Cl ME8 69
Consort Cl ME14 100
Constable Ave E16 1
Constable Rd
Northfleet DA11 35
Tonbridge TN10 127
Constance St E16 1
Constitution Cres DA12 36
Constitution Hill
8 Chatham ME5 54
Gravesend DA12 36
Snodland ME6 82
Constitution Rd ME5 54
Constitution Rise SE18 12
Constitutional Hill Rd
TN4 142
Consul Gdns BR8 32
Contessa Cl BR6 57
Convalescent La TN17 165
Conway Cl ME2 38
Conway Ct BR5 44
Conway Gdns RM17 18
Conway Hall 16 ME7 54
Conway Mews ME7 54
Conway Prim Sch SE18 2
Conway Rd
Maidstone ME16 99
Woolwich SE18 2
Conyerd Rd TN15 94
Conyers Wlk ME8 69
Cooden Cl BR1 28
Cook Cl ME5 68
Cook Sq DA8 14
Cookham Dene Cl BR7 43
Cookham Hill ME1 53
Cookham Rd DA14,BR8 45
Cookham Wood Rd ME1 67
Cookhill Rd SE2 3
Cooks Wharf ME1 53
Cookson Gr DA8 14
Coolfin Rd E16 1
Cooling Castle* ME3 22
Cooling Cl ME14 100
Cooling Comm ME3 39
Cooling Rd Cliffe ME3 22
High Halstow ME23 23
Rochester ME2 39
Cooling St ME3 22
Coomb Field TN8 138
Coombe Ave TN14 92
Coombe Cl Chatham ME5 68
Snodland ME6 82
Coombe Ct TN14 92
Coombe Farm La ME3 24
Coombe La TN30 193
Coombe Lands TN30 199
Coombe Lea BR1 42
Coombe Lodge SE7 11
Coombe Rd
Gravesend DA12 36
Hoo St Werburgh ME3 40
Maidstone ME15 99
Otford TN14 76
Coombfield Dr DA2 33
Cooper Cl DA9 16
Cooper Ct SE18 12
Cooper Rd Chatham ME5 68
Snodland ME6 81
Cooper Shaw Rd RM18 19
Cooper's Rd DA11 35
Coopers Cl DA4 47
Coopers Cotts DA2 33
Coopers Dr DA2 31
Coopers La
Lewisham SE12 28
Poundsbridge TN11,TN3 157
Coopers Tech Coll BR7 43
Coopers' Lane Prim Sch
SE12 28
Coote Rd DA7 13
Copenhagen Rd ME7 54
Copley Dene BR1 42
Coppards La TN31 197
Copper Beech Cl
Gravesend DA12 36
7 Orpington BR5 44
Copper Beech View
TN9 143
Copper La TN12 148
Copper Tree Ct ME15 116
Copper Tree Wlk ME5 68
Copperfield Cl
Chalk DA12 37
Kingswood ME17 118
Copperfield Cres ME3 38
Copperfield Ct DA1 14
Copperfield Dr ME17 117
Copperfield Ho 6 ME4 53
Copperfield Rd Erith SE28 3
Rochester ME1 53
Copperfield Way BR7 29
Copperfields
2 Dartford DA1 15
Kemsing TN15 76
Copperfields Cl TN15 76
Copperfields Orch TN15 76
Copperfields The ME1 53
Copperfields Wlk TN15 76
Coppergate ME7 68
Coppergate Cl BR1 42
Copperhouse La ME7 55
Copperhouse Rd ME2 52

opperpenny Dr ME7 ....69 B3
oppers Ct TN4 ....159 A8
oppers La TN12 ....145 E1
oppice Ct ME7 ....69 B4
oppice Rd ME5 ....68 C2
oppice The
Aylesford ME20 ....82 E1
Bitchet Green TN15 ....93 D1
Joyden's Wood DA5 ....31 D5
Pembury TN2 ....160 D7
Vigo Village DA13 ....80 B8
oppice View ME14 .....100 E6
opping's Rd TN11 .....125 C4
opse Bank TN15 ....92 F7
opse Cl Greenwich SE7 ...11 B8
Rochester ME1 ....53 E1
opse Rd TN11 ....126 E4
opse Side DA3 ....48 E6
opse The ME3 ....40 E3
opsehill ME19 ....81 E2
opsewood Cl DA15 ....12 E1
opsewood Way ME15 ..101 A3
opt Hall TN18 ....197 D3
opt Hall Rd
Ightham TN15 ....94 A4
Sole Street DA13 ....50 B5
optefield Dr DA17 ....3 E3
opthall Ave TN18 ......189 A1
opthorne Ave BR2 ....56 F8
oralline Wlk 4 SE2 ......3 C4
orben Cl ME16 ....99 B6
orbridge Ho SE2 ....3 C3
orbylands Rd DA15 .....29 E7
ordelia Cres ME1 ....52 F2
orelli Rd SE18,SE3 ....11 E6
orhaven Ho 3 DA8 .....14 E7
orinthian Ct ME3 ....27 B5
orinthian Manorway
DA8 ....4 D2
orinthian Rd DA8 ....4 D2
ork Ho BR5 ....44 B6
ork La TN12 ....165 D8
ork St ME20 ....82 F6
orkwell St ME4 ....53 E3
ormorant Cl ME2 ....52 C7
orn Mill Dr BR6 ....44 A2
ornel Ho 4 DA15 ....30 A5
ornelia Pl DA8 ....14 E8
ornell Cl DA14 ....30 E2
orner Farm Rd TN12 ...149 E4
orner Gn SE3 ....11 A5
ornfield Way TN10 ....127 D6
ornflower Cl ME14 .....100 E4
ornford Cl Hayes BR2 ....42 A4
Pembury TN2 ....160 B6
Cornford La TN2 ....160 B5
Cornford Pk TN2 ....160 C6
Cornforth Cl TN12 ......149 F4
Cornwall Ave DA16 ....12 F4
Cornwall Cl ME15 ....116 E7
Cornwall Cres ME1 ....66 D4
Cornwall Dr BR5 ....30 C1
Cornwall Rd Dartford DA1 .15 F4
Gillingham ME7 ....54 D6
Rochester ME1 ....53 C3
Cornwallis Ave
Chatham ME4 ....53 E1
Gillingham ME8 ....55 A4
Linton ME17 ....132 E8
Sidcup SE9 ....29 D6
Tonbridge TN10 ....127 F4
Cornwallis Cl DA8 ....14 F8
Cornwallis Cotts ME17 ..115 E2
Cornwallis Rd
Maidstone ME16 ....99 D4
Woolwich SE18 ....2 B3
Woolwich SE18 ....2 C3
Cornwallis Rdbt ME8 .....55 A4
Cornwallis Sch The
ME15 ....115 F2
Cornwallis Wlk SE9 ......11 F4
Cornwell Ave DA12 ....36 C5
Corona Rd SE12 ....28 A8
Corona Terr ME6 ....81 F6
Coronation Cl DA5 ....13 D1
Coronation Cotts
Stoke ME3 ....25 A3
Ticehurst TN5 ....186 F2
Coronation Ct DA8 ....14 D7
Coronation Flats 5 ME4 ..53 F3
Coronation Rd
Chatham ME5 ....54 C2
Grain ME3 ....27 B5
Corporation Rd ME7 ......54 D7
Corporation St ME1 ......53 C6
Corral Cl ME5 ....54 D2
Corral Hts 13 DA8 ....4 E1
Corrall Almshouses 5
ME15 ....100 A3
Corrance Gn ME15 ......116 A8
Correnden Rd TN10 .....127 A3
Corseley Rd TN3 ....171 B5
Cortland Cl DA1 ....14 E1
Cory's Rd ME1 ....53 D6
Cossack St ME1 ....53 D3
Cossington Rd ME5 ......68 B1
Costells Mdw TN16 ....89 D1
Cot La TN27 ....168 B3
Cotleigh Ave DA5 ....30 D6
Cotman Way TN12 ......129 E6
Cotman's Ash La TN15 ...77 D4
Cotmandene Cres BR5 ....44 A7
Coton Rd DA16 ....13 A4
Cotswold Cl DA7 ....14 E5
Cotswold Gdns ME15 ...101 A2
Cotswold Rd DA11 ....35 E5
Cotswold Rise BR6 ....43 F3
Cottage Ave BR2 ....42 E1
Cottage Field Cl DA14 ....30 C7
Cottage Rd ME4 ....53 F6
Cottall Ave ME4 ....53 F2
Cottenham Cl ME19 ......97 F7
Cotton La DA2,DA9 ....16 C2
Couchman Green La
TN12 ....149 F7
Coulman St ME7 ....54 D5
Coulter Ho DA9 ....17 C2
Coulters Cl ME14 ....100 D5
Coulton Ave DA11 ....35 E7
Council Ave DA11 ....18 C1
Council Cotts
Chainhurst ME15 ....132 A7
Chiddingstone Causeway
TN11 ....141 A8
Coxheath ME15 ....115 A4
Council Hos TN15 ....111 A8
Countess of Thanet's
Almshouses TN8 ....154 F3
County Gate SE9 ....29 C5
County Gr ME19 ....97 B8
County Ho SE18 ....12 A8
County Rd
Maidstone ME14 ....100 A5
Newham E6 ....2 B8
Coupland Pl SE18 ....2 C1
Courier Rd RM13 ....4 D8
Course The SE9 ....29 A5
Court Ave DA17 ....3 F1
Court Broomes ME17 ...135 C8
Court Cres BR8 ....45 E5
Court Dr ME16 ....99 D4
Court Farm Rd SE9 ....28 E5
Court La Detling ME14 ....85 C5
Hadlow TN11 ....129 B7
Court Lane Pl TN11 .....128 F8
Court Lodge Erith DA17 ....4 A1
Shorne DA12 ....37 E2
Court Lodge Cotts
East Farleigh ME15 ....115 A7
Horton Kirby DA4 ....47 C6
Mereworth TN12 ....112 E4
West Farleigh ME15 ......114 D7
Court Lodge Farm
ME18 ....114 B7
Court Lodge Flats TN3 ..176 C6
Court Lodge Rd ME7 .....54 F6
Court Mdw Gillingham ME8 .55 B2
Wrotham TN15 ....78 F3
Court Mews DA11 ....18 B1
Court Rd Burham ME1 .....82 F8
Dartford DA2 ....33 E3
Eltham SE9 ....28 F7
Royal Tunbridge Wells
TN4 ....158 F4
Court Road (Orpington
By-Pass)
Chelsfield BR6,TN14 ....58 D5
Orpington BR6 ....44 B2
Court Royal TN2 ....172 E8
Court St BR1 ....42 A7
Court Yd SE9 ....11 F1
Courtaulds Cl SE28 ....3 A5
Courtenay Rd ME15 ......99 F2
Courteney Rd ME8 ....69 B8
Courtenwell TN3 ....157 F4
Courtfield Ave ME5 ......68 B3
Courthope TN12 ....146 A6
Courthope Ave TN5 .....184 F4
Courtland Gr SE28 ....3 D6
Courtlands
Chislehurst BR7 ....29 B2
Teston ME18 ....114 A8
Tonbridge TN10 ....127 A3
Courtlands Ave SE12 .....11 B2
Courtlands Cl ME18 .....114 A8
Courtlands Farm TN17 ..179 A3
Courtleet Dr DA8 ....14 B6
Courtwood Dr TN13 ......92 A3
Courtyard Gdns TN15 .....78 F3
Courtyard The
Gillingham ME8 ....69 A8
Watts's Cross TN11 ......126 A7
Westerham TN16 ....105 D8
Cousley Wood Rd TN5 ..185 C7
Couthurst Rd SE3 ....11 B7
Coutts Ave DA12 ....37 E4
Covelees Wall E6 ....2 A7
Coventry Cl 9 Newham E6 ..1 F7
Rochester ME2 ....52 D6
Coventry Rd TN10 ......127 D5
Coverdale Ave ME15 ....116 D6
Coverdale Cl ME5 ....68 B7
Covert The Chatham ME5 ..68 B1
Orpington BR6 ....43 E3
Vigo Village DA13 ....79 E7
Covesfield DA11 ....35 F8
Covet Wood Cl BR5 ......43 F3
Covey Hall Rd ME6 ....66 A1
Cow La TN8 ....139 D1
Cow Leaze E6 ....2 A7
Cowan Cl E6 ....1 E8
Cowbeck Cl ME8 ....69 D6
Cowden Cl TN18 ....194 E8
Cowden Cross TN8 ......155 C7
Cowden La TN18 ....194 E7
Cowden Mews TN8 .....155 A5
Cowden Rd
Maidstone ME14 ....100 C5
Orpington BR6 ....43 F2
Cowden Sta TN8 ....155 D8
Cowdrey Cl
Maidstone ME16 ....99 B2
Rochester ME1 ....53 B2
Cowdrey Ct DA1 ....32 B8
Cowdreys TN9 ....143 C8
Cowen Ho 4 SE18 ....12 B8
Cowley Ave DA9 ....17 A2
Cowper Ave RM18 ....19 B6
Cowper Cl Bexley DA16 ....13 A2
Bromley BR2 ....42 D5
Cowper Rd Bromley BR2 ...42 D5
Erith DA17 ....4 A2
Gillingham ME7 ....54 D3
Cowstead Rd ME9 ....70 D2
Cox Gdns ME8 ....55 A2
Cox St ME14 ....85 E6
Cox's Cl ME6 ....81 F8
Coxheath Prim Sch
ME17 ....115 C3
Coxmount Rd SE7 ....1 D1
Coxwell Rd SE18 ....2 D1
Cozenton Cl ME8 ....55 E1
Crabbs Croft Cl 7 BR6 ...57 C5
Crabtree Cl ME19 ....97 A2
Crabtree Manorway N
DA17 ....4 C5
Crabtree Manorway S
DA17 ....4 C3
Crabtree Rd ME8 ....69 D8
Crabtree Rdbt ME14 .....83 E2
Craddock Way ME8 ......69 D5
Cradducks La TN12 .....150 B4
Cradles Rd ME9 ....70 C2
Cradley Rd SE9 ....29 D7
Craft Workshops TN27 ..135 C1
Cragie Wlk ME8 ....69 E4
Craig Ho Greenwich SE3 ...11 B7
Rochester ME1 ....53 E1
Craigerne Rd SE3 ....11 B7
Craigholm SE18 ....12 A6
Craigie Ct DA1 ....33 A8
Craigton Rd SE9 ....11 F3
Crales Ho SE18 ....1 E3
Cramonde Pl DA16 ....13 A5
Crampton's Rd TN14 .....92 B7
Cramptons TN17 ....179 F8
Cranborne Ave ME15 ...100 C1
Cranbourne Ave ME15 ..116 B8
Cranbrook CE Prim Sch
TN17 ....179 D5
Cranbrook Cl
Gillingham ME8 ....55 C3
Hayes BR2 ....42 A3
Maidstone ME15 ....116 F7
Cranbrook Ho 1 DA8 ....14 F7
Cranbrook Mews 1
TN8 ....122 C1
Cranbrook Mus* TN17 ..179 D5
Cranbrook Rd
Benenden TN17 ....189 F8
Bexley DA7 ....13 F6
Fosten Green TN27 ....181 C6
Goudhurst TN17 ....178 A8
Hawkhurst TN18 ....188 F4
Knox Bridge TN12,TN17 ...165 F7
Parkgate TN30 ....182 C1
Tenterden TN30 ....192 E7
Cranbrook Sch TN17 ....179 D5
Cranbrook Union Mill*
TN17 ....179 D4
Crandalls TN11 ....125 F1
Cranden Wlk DA4 ....47 E7
Crane Ho 11 TN18 ......188 F2
Crane House Gdns 10
TN18 ....188 F2
Crane La TN17 ....179 D5
Cranford Cl ME8 ....55 D1
Cranford Ho DA1 ....15 A2
Cranford Rd Dartford DA1 .32 E7
Tonbridge TN10 ....128 A5
Cranham Sq TN12 ......148 C5
Cranleigh Cl
Orpington BR6 ....58 A7
Sidcup DA5 ....14 B1
Cranleigh Dr BR8 ....45 E5
Cranleigh Gdns
Chatham ME4 ....53 D3
Maidstone ME16 ....99 C7
Cranley Par SE9 ....28 E4
Cranley Rd E13 ....1 B8
Cranmer Ct ME15 ....116 B8
Cranmer Rd TN13 ....91 E4
Cranmere Ct ME2 ....53 C8
Cranmore Rd BR7 ....28 F3
Cranstone Ct 12 DA14 ...30 B4
Cranwell Rd TN4 ....158 C4
Crates Yd TN4 ....159 A5
Crathie Rd SE12 ....11 B1
Craven Rd BR6 ....58 D7
Crawford Ct SE18 ....13 A8
Crawfords BR8 ....31 E1
Crawley Ct 1 DA11 ......19 B1
Crawshay Cl TN13 ....92 A4
Cray Ave BR5 ....44 B4
Cray Bldgs DA14 ....30 C2
Cray Cl DA1 ....15 A3
Cray Rd Crockenhill BR8 ...45 C3
Erith DA17 ....14 A8
Sidcup DA14 ....30 C2
Cray Valley Rd BR5 ......44 B4
Craybrooke Rd DA14 .....30 B4
Crayburne DA13 ....34 F4
Craybury End SE9 ....29 C6
Craydene Rd DA8 ....14 F6
Crayfields Bsns Pk BR5 ..44 C8
Crayfields Ind Pk BR5 ....44 C7
Crayford Cl
Maidstone ME14 ....100 C6
Newham E6 ....1 E7
Crayford Commercial Ctr
DA1 ....14 E1
Crayford High St DA1 ....14 E2
Crayford Ind Est DA1 ....14 F2
Crayford Rd DA1 ....14 F2
Crayford Sta DA1 ....14 E1
Crayford Way DA1 ....15 A3
Craylands BR5 ....44 C6
Craylands La DA10 ....17 D2
Craylands Sq DA10 ....17 D2
Crayleigh Terr DA14 .....30 C2
Craymill Sq DA1 ....14 F5
Crays Par The BR5 ....44 C7
Crayside Ind Est DA1 ....15 B3
Craythorne TN30 ....193 B8
Craythorne Ho TN30 ....193 B8
Creasey's Row TN14 ....106 E5
Credenhall Dr BR2 ....42 F1
Crediton Rd E16 ....1 A7
Credo Way RM20 ....17 B8
Creek La ME3 ....25 B2
Creek The DA11 ....18 B2
Creek Way RM13 ....4 E8
Cremorne Rd 1 DA11 .....35 F8
Crendon Pk TN4 ....159 A8
Crescent Ave RM17 ......18 D8
Crescent Cotts TN13 .....91 E7
Crescent Ct
1 Grays RM17 ....18 D8
Sidcup DA15 ....30 A5
Crescent Dr BR5 ....43 C3
Crescent Gdns BR8 ......45 A5
Crescent Ho ME2 ....53 C7
Crescent Rd Bromley BR1 ..28 A1
Erith DA8 ....14 F8
Royal Tunbridge Wells
TN1 ....159 B3
Sidcup DA15 ....29 F5
Woolwich SE18 ....2 B2
Crescent The
Bidborough TN4 ....142 E4
Borough Green TN15 ......95 A8
Groombridge TN3 ....171 C7
Longfield DA3 ....48 E6
Maidstone ME14 ....99 F8
Northfleet DA11 ....35 F6
Sevenoaks TN13 ....92 D6
Sidcup DA14 ....29 F4
Sidcup DA5 ....30 C8
St Mary's Island ME4 ......40 B1
Swanscombe DA9 ....17 C2
Tonbridge TN9 ....127 B2
Crescent Way
Chatham ME5 ....67 D5
Orpington BR6 ....57 E5
Cressey Ct 7 ME4 ....53 E4
Cressingham Ct 1 DA17 ...4 A3
Crest Ave RM17 ....18 B7
Crest Cl TN14 ....75 B8
Crest Ind Est TN12 .....148 C6
Crest Rd ME1 ....53 C1
Crest View DA9 ....17 A3
Crest View Dr BR5 ....43 C4
Crestway ME5 ....68 B8
Crete Hall Rd DA11 ......18 E1
Creton St SE18 ....2 A3
Creve Coeur Cl ME14 ...101 A5
Crevequer Chambers 1
ME8 ....55 F1
Cricket Ground Rd BR7 ...43 B8
Cricketers Cl
Bells Yew Green TN3 .....174 A5
Erith DA8 ....4 E1
Harrietsham ME17 ....119 D6
Cricketers Dr DA13 ....64 A7
Cripple Hill TN26 ....169 D1
Cripple St ME15 ....116 A7
Crisfield Ct TN30 ....183 B2
Crismill La ME14 ....101 F4
Crismill Rd ME14,ME17 ..101 F3
Crispe Cl ME8 ....69 D4
Crispin Ct ME17 ....115 C3
Crispin Rd ME2 ....52 E8
Crispin Way ME19 ....97 A3
Crittall's Cnr DA14 ....30 C1
Crittenden Bglws ME15 ..115 A4
Crittenden Cotts ME15 ..115 A4
Crittenden Rd TN12 .....145 D3
Crittle's Ct TN5 ....184 F4
Crocken Hill Rd TN27 ...137 C2
Crockenhall Way DA13 ...35 E1
Crockenhill Hill BR5 .....44 D4
Crockenhill La BR8,DA4 ...46 C2
Crockenhill Prim Sch
BR8 ....45 C3
Crockenhill Rd BR5,BR8 ...44 E4
Crockers Hatch Cnr
TN3 ....157 D2
Crockford Cl TN10 ......127 E7
Crockham Hill CE Prim Sch
TN8 ....105 C2
Crockham Way SE9 ......29 A4
Croft Cl Bromley BR7 .....28 F3
Chatham ME5 ....68 C1
Erith DA17 ....3 F1
Tonbridge TN10 ....127 F5
Croft Ct TN8 ....122 C1
Croft Gdns ME17 ....120 D4
Croft La TN8 ....122 C1
Croft Rd Bromley BR1 .....28 A2
Westerham TN16 ....89 C1
Croft The Leybourne ME19 ..81 E2
Swanley BR8 ....45 C6
Tenterden TN30 ....193 B7
Croft Way Sevenoaks TN13 .91 F2
Sidcup DA15 ....29 E5
Crofters The ME8 ....69 F7
Crofton Ave
Orpington BR5,BR6 ....57 C8
Sidcup DA5 ....30 D8
Crofton Inf Sch BR5 .....43 D2
Crofton Jun Sch BR5 ....43 D2
Crofton La BR5,BR6 .....43 D2
Crofton Rd BR6 ....57 B8
Croftside DA13 ....80 A8
Cromarty Ct 8 BR1 ......42 C7
Crombie Rd DA15 ....29 D7
Cromer Pl 5 BR6 ....43 D1
Cromer Rd ME2 ....53 B8
Cromer St TN9 ....127 A1
Cromford Cl BR6 ....57 E7
Cromlix Cl BR7 ....43 B7
Crompton Gdns ME15 ..100 B3
Cromwell Ave BR2 ....42 B5
Cromwell Cl BR2 ....42 B5
Cromwell Mews BR7 .....43 A8
Cromwell Rd
Maidstone ME14 ....100 B5
Royal Tunbridge Wells
TN2 ....159 C3
Cromwell Terr ME4 ....54 A3
Cronin Cl 2 ME20 ....81 F4
Crook Log DA6 ....13 D3
Crook Log Prim Sch DA6 .13 D3
Crook Rd TN12 ....146 D1
Crooked La DA11,DA12 ....19 B1
Crookston Rd SE9 ....12 A4
Croombs Rd E16 ....1 C8
Crosby Ho DA1 ....15 A1
Crosier Cl SE3 ....11 E6
Crosley Rd ME7 ....54 D3
Cross Ct 11 SE28 ....3 B6
Cross Dr ME17 ....118 B1
Cross Keys
Maidstone ME14 ....101 C4
Sevenoaks TN13 ....108 A8
Cross Keys Cl TN13 .....108 A8
Cross La Sidcup DA5 ......30 F8
Ticehurst TN5 ....186 D2
Cross Lane E DA12 ....36 B6
Cross Lane Gdns TN5 ...186 D1
Cross Lane W DA11 ......36 B6
Cross Rd Dartford DA1 ....15 C1
Hawley DA2 ....32 F4
Northfleet DA11 ....18 F1
Orpington,Keston Mark BR2 .56 E8
Orpington,St Mary Cray BR5 .44 B4
Sidcup DA14 ....30 B4
Cross St Chatham ME4 ....54 A4
Erith DA8 ....14 E8
Gillingham ME7 ....54 C6
27 Gravesend DA12 ....19 B1
Maidstone ME14 ....100 A6
Rochester ME2 ....53 B8
Cross Way ME1 ....53 C3
Cross-at-Hand Cotts
TN12 ....133 E2
Crossbrook Rd SE3 ......11 E4
Crossley Cl TN16 ....72 D4
Crossmead SE9 ....28 F7
Crossway Chatham ME5 ...67 E6
Erith SE28 ....3 D7
Orpington BR5 ....43 D4
Crossway The
Bromley SE9 ....28 D6
Royal Tunbridge Wells
TN4 ....158 D2
Crossways
Chart Sutton ME17 ....117 B1
Hextable BR8 ....31 F1
Tatsfield TN16 ....88 C7
Crossways Bvd DA2,DA9 ..16 E3
Crossways Ct TN16 ......88 C7
Crouch Croft SE9 ....29 A5
Crouch House Cotts
TN8 ....122 B2
Crouch House Rd TN8 ..122 B2
Crouch La Crouch TN15 ....95 B6
Linkhill TN18 ....196 D6
Crow Cnr ME1 ....53 C5
Crow Dr TN14 ....75 C4
Crow Hill TN15 ....95 A7
Crow Hill Rd TN15 ....95 A7
Crow La ME1 ....53 C5
Crowden Way SE28 ....3 C6
Crowfoot Cl SE28 ....2 E5
Crowhurst La
Basted TN15 ....94 E4
West Kingsdown TN15 ......62 B4
Crowhurst Oast TN12 ...112 D1
Crowhurst Rd TN15 ......94 F6
Crowhurst Way BR5 .....44 C4
Crown Acres TN12 ......130 A6
Crown Cl BR6 ....58 A6
Crown Ct Bromley BR2 ....42 E4
Cranbrook TN17 ....179 C5
Eltham SE12 ....11 B1
Tilbury RM18 ....19 A5
Crown Gn DA12 ....37 E3
Crown Ho
Lamberhurst TN3 ....176 B5
Rochester ME1 ....53 B4
Crown La Bromley BR2 ....42 D4
Chislehurst BR7 ....43 C8
Shorne DA12 ....37 E4
Crown Lane Spur BR2 ....42 D3
Crown Rd Grays RM17 ....18 A8
Marlpit Hill TN8 ....122 D4
Orpington BR6 ....58 A5
Shoreham TN14 ....59 F1
Crown St ME7 ....54 D6
Crown Woods Sch SE9 ....12 C2
Crown Woods Way SE9 ...12 D2
Crownfields
Maidstone ME14 ....100 F4
Sevenoaks TN13 ....92 B2
Crowther Cl TN12 ....149 E4
Croxley Cl BR5 ....44 B7

Croxley Gn BR5 .....44 B8
Croyde Cl DA15 .....29 D8
Croydon Cl ME5 .....68 C4
Croydon Rd
Hayes BR2,BR4,BR6 .....56 C7
Tatsfield TN16 .....88 F3
Westerham TN16 .....89 B2
Crozier Ho SE3 .....11 B4
Cruden Rd DA12 .....36 F6
Crump's La ME17 .....136 B4
Crumpsall St SE2 .....3 C2
Crundale 2 ME14 .....100 A5
Crundale Rd ME8 .....55 C3
Crundale Twr BR5 .....44 C1
Crundwell Rd TN4 .....142 F1
Crusader Cl ME8 .....69 B8
Crusader Ct DA1 .....15 F3
Crusoe Rd DA8 .....4 D1
Crutches La ME3,ME2 .....38 B1
Cryals Ct TN12 .....161 E5
Cryals Rd TN12 .....161 D5
Crystal Ho 2 SE18 .....2 F1
Cuckmere Ct 18 BR5 .....44 D1
Cuckold's Cnr ME3 .....38 C6
Cuckold's Cnr TN12 .....149 F4
Cuckolds Cnr DA3 .....63 B7
Cuckolds Green Rd ME3 .....25 B5
Cuckoo La
Lamberhurst TN12 .....162 A2
Tonbridge TN11 .....128 A7
Cuckoowood Ave ME14 .....83 F1
Cudham CE Prim Sch TN16 .....73 A3
Cudham Cl ME14 .....100 C6
Cudham La N TN14 .....73 D7
Cudham La S TN14 .....73 D2
Cudham Park Rd TN14 .....57 E1
Cudham Rd Downe BR6 .....73 B7
Tatsfield TN16 .....88 E8
Cuff Cres SE9 .....11 D1
Cugley Rd DA2 .....33 C8
Culcroft DA3 .....48 F6
Culpeper Cl
Hollingbourne ME17 .....102 E2
Rochester ME2 .....53 E6
Culpepers TN17 .....177 E7
Culpepper Rd
Coxheath ME17 .....115 B3
Gillingham ME8 .....69 D4
Culverden Ave TN4 .....159 A6
Culverden Down TN4 .....158 F5
Culverden Park Rd TN4 .....158 F5
Culverden Pk TN4 .....158 F5
Culverden Sq TN4 .....159 A5
Culverden St TN1 .....159 A4
Culverstone Green Prim Sch DA13 .....63 F3
Culverstone Ho BR5 .....44 B6
Culverton Ct 19 DA14 .....30 A4
Culvey Cl DA3 .....48 E4
Cumberland Ave
Bexley DA16 .....12 F3
Gravesend DA12 .....36 C8
Maidstone ME15 .....116 D8
Cumberland Cotts 23 TN1 .....159 A2
Cumberland Ct
Sevenoaks TN13 .....91 E7
Tonbridge TN10 .....127 A4
Cumberland Dr
Dartford DA1 .....32 F8
Erith DA7 .....13 E7
Cumberland Gdns 10 TN1 .....159 A2
Cumberland Ho SE28 .....2 D4
Cumberland Mews 12 TN1 .....159 A2
Cumberland Rd
Chatham ME4,ME7 .....54 B7
Gillingham ME7 .....54 C7
Newham E13 .....1 B8
Cumberland Sch E16 .....1 A8
Cumberland Villas 5 DA12 .....36 C8
Cumberland Wlk TN1 .....159 A2
Cumberland Yd 11 TN1 .....159 A2
Cumbrian Ave DA7 .....14 E5
Cundy Rd E16 .....1 C7
Cunningham Cl TN4 .....159 B7
Cunningham Cres ME5 .....68 A8
Cunningham Ho ME1 .....53 B4
Cunningham Rd TN4 .....159 B7
Cupola Cl BR1 .....28 B3
Curates Wlk DA2 .....32 D5
Curlew Cl SE28 .....3 D6
Curlew Cres ME2 .....52 C6
Curlews The DA12 .....36 D6
Curran Ave DA15 .....12 F2
Currie Rd TN4 .....159 A5
Curteis Rd TN30 .....183 B1
Curtis Ct BR6 .....44 A2
Curtis Way Rochester ME1 .....67 D7
7 Woolwich SE28 .....3 B6
Curtismill Cl BR5 .....44 B6
Curtismill Way BR5 .....44 B6
Curzon Cl BR6 .....57 D6
Curzon Ct SE9 .....29 C5
Curzon Dr RM17 .....18 C7
Curzon Rd Chatham ME4 .....53 F3
Maidstone ME14 .....100 A6
Custom House for Excel Sta E16 .....1 B6
Cut The TN27 .....168 E8
Cutbush & Corrall Ct 1 ME14 .....100 B4
Cutbush Almshouses
3 Maidstone ME14 .....100 A4
1 Maidstone ME15 .....100 A3
Cutbush Cl ME17 .....119 D6
Cutbush Ho 2 ME15 .....100 A3
Cutmore St DA11 .....36 B8
Cutter Cl ME2 .....39 F3
Cutter Ho 6 DA8 .....4 E1
Cutter Ridge Rd DA13 .....51 A1
Cutty Sark Ct 6 DA9 .....17 A2
Cuxton BR5 .....43 C4
Cuxton Cl DA6 .....13 E2
Cuxton Com Inf Sch ME2 .....52 B2
Cuxton Com Jun Sch ME2 .....52 B2
Cuxton Ind Est ME2 .....52 C2
Cuxton Rd
Maidstone ME15 .....116 F5
Rochester ME2 .....52 F5
Cuxton Sta ME2 .....52 C2
Cyclamen Rd BR8 .....45 D5
Cygnet Cl ME20 .....82 A2
Cygnet Gdns DA11 .....35 F6
Cygnet L Ctr DA11 .....35 E6
Cygnet Rd ME5 .....68 C2
Cypress Ave ME3 .....40 E3
Cypress Ct ME7 .....54 F6
Cypress Gr TN2 .....173 C8
Cypress Rd ME2 .....39 C1
Cypress Tree Cl DA15 .....29 F7
Cyprus Pl E6 .....2 A6
Cyprus Sta E6 .....2 A6
Cyril Hall Ct DA11 .....18 F1
Cyril John Gange Lodge TN2 .....159 D2
Cyril Lodge 6 DA14 .....30 A4
Cyril Rd Bexley DA7 .....13 E5
Orpington BR6 .....44 A2

D

D'arcy Pl BR2 .....42 A5
Dabbling Cl DA8 .....15 B7
Daerwood Cl BR2 .....42 F1
Daffodil Rd ME2 .....52 E7
Dagmar Rd ME4 .....54 B2
Dagonet Gdns BR1 .....28 A5
Dagonet Rd BR1 .....28 A5
Dahlia Dr BR8 .....45 F7
Dahlia Rd SE2 .....3 B2
Dainton Cl 2 BR1 .....42 B8
Daintons Cotts 2 TN18 .....188 F2
Dairsie Ct 4 BR1 .....42 C7
Dairsie Rd SE9 .....12 A4
Dairy Cl 3 Bromley BR1 .....28 B1
Sutton at H DA4 .....33 B1
Dairy La Chainhurst TN12 .....131 F4
Crockham Hill TN8 .....105 B1
Woolwich SE18 .....1 F2
Dairy Pl TN12 .....131 F4
Daisy Munns Ho SE9 .....29 C7
Dajen Bsns Pk ME4 .....54 C1
Dalberg Way SE2 .....3 D3
Dale Cl Crayford DA1 .....14 F1
Greenwich SE3 .....11 A4
Dale Ct Bromley BR1 .....42 D6
Chatham ME5 .....68 A2
Dale End DA1 .....14 F1
Dale Rd Crayford DA1 .....14 F1
Northfleet DA13 .....35 A4
Rochester ME1 .....53 C3
Swanley BR8 .....45 C6
Dale St Chatham ME4 .....53 E2
Royal Tunbridge Wells TN1 .....159 B4
Dale The BR2 .....56 D6
Dale View DA8 .....14 F5
Dale Wlk DA2 .....33 C7
Dale Wood Rd BR6 .....43 E1
Dalemain Mews E16 .....1 A5
Daleside BR6 .....58 A5
Daleside Cl BR6 .....58 A4
Dalison Ct ME2 .....66 B4
Dallin Rd Bexley DA6 .....13 D3
Woolwich SE18 .....12 B7
Dalmeny Rd DA8 .....14 B6
Dalton Cl BR6 .....57 E7
Dalton St ME7 .....54 C6
Daltons Rd BR6,BR8 .....59 C7
Damiem Cl ME4 .....54 A2
Damigos Rd DA12 .....36 F7
Damon Cl DA14 .....30 B5
Damon Ct DA14 .....30 B5
Damson Ct BR8 .....45 D5
Damson Dr ME3 .....40 E3
Danaway Cotts ME9 .....71 C3
Dando Cres SE3 .....11 B4
Dane Cl Chatham ME5 .....68 C2
Hartlip ME9 .....70 D6
Orpington BR6 .....57 D5
Sidcup DA5 .....31 A8
Dane Ct ME17 .....115 C2
Dane La ME9 .....70 D6
Dane Pk ME15 .....115 C6
Dane Rd TN14 .....75 F2
Danecourt Com Sch ME8 .....55 A2
Danefield Ct ME14 .....101 B4
Danehill Wlk DA14 .....30 A5
Danemore TN30 .....193 B8
Danes Cl DA11 .....35 C5
Danes Hill ME7 .....55 A6
Danescombe SE12 .....28 A7
Daniel Ho 5 ME16 .....99 E5
Danns La ME18,ME19 .....97 A1
Dansington Rd DA16 .....13 A3
Danson Cres DA16 .....13 B4
Danson Ho* DA6 .....13 C3
Danson La DA16 .....13 B3
Danson Mead DA16 .....13 C4
Danson Prim Sch DA16 .....13 A3
Danson Rd Bexley DA5 .....13 D1
Bexley DA5,DA6 .....13 D2
Danson Underpass DA5 .....13 C1
Danson Way ME8 .....55 D2
Danvers Rd TN9 .....127 B1
Darby Gdns ME3 .....38 B3
Darby's La TN5 .....185 B2
Darent Cl TN13 .....91 C5
Darent Ind Pk DA8 .....15 D8
Darent Mead DA4 .....47 B8
Darent Valley Hospl DA2 .....33 E7
Darenth Ave TN10 .....127 C5
Darenth Cotts TN14 .....75 F8
Darenth Ct 19 BR5 .....44 D1
Darenth Dr DA12 .....37 B7
Darenth Gdns TN16 .....89 D1
Darenth Hill DA2 .....33 C3
Darenth La TN13 .....91 E6
Darenth Park Ave DA2 .....33 D6
Darenth Prim Sch DA2 .....33 E2
Darenth Rd Bexley DA16 .....13 A6
Dartford DA1 .....32 F7
Darenth Rd S DA2 .....33 B4
Darenth Rise ME5 .....68 B3
Darenth Way TN14 .....76 A8
Darenth Wood Rd DA2 .....33 E6
Dargate Cl ME16 .....99 D7
Dargets Rd ME5 .....68 A3
Darland Ave ME7 .....54 E1
Darland Ho SE9 .....12 D1
Darlton Cl DA1 .....14 F4
Darman La TN12,ME18 .....130 D3
Darnets Field TN14 .....75 F2
Darnley Cl ME2 .....52 D6
Darnley Ct DA11 .....36 A8
Darnley Dr TN4 .....142 E4
Darnley Rd
Gravesend DA11 .....36 A8
1 Grays RM17 .....18 B8
Rochester ME2 .....52 E6
Darnley St DA11 .....36 B8
Darns Hill BR8 .....45 C2
Darrick Wood Ho BR6 .....57 C7
Darrick Wood Inf & Jun Schs BR6 .....57 B6
Darrick Wood Rd BR6 .....57 D8
Darrick Wood Sch BR6 .....57 B7
Darrick Wood Sports Ctr BR6 .....57 B7
Dart Cl ME2 .....52 F7
Dartford Borough Mus* DA1 .....32 E8
Dartford Gram Sch DA1 .....15 C1
Dartford Gram Sch for Girls DA1 .....32 C8
Dartford Hospl Specl Sch DA3 .....49 A6
Dartford Rd Coldblow DA5 .....31 C7
Dartford DA1 .....15 B1
Farningham DA4 .....47 A5
Sevenoaks TN13 .....92 C3
Dartford Sta DA1 .....15 E1
Dartford Technology Coll DA1 .....32 D8
Dartford Trad Pk DA1 .....32 F6
Dartford West Technology Coll for Girls DA1 .....32 C8
Dartmouth Rd BR2 .....42 A2
Darwin Cl BR6 .....57 D5
Darwin Ct Eltham SE9 .....12 A1
Rochester ME1 .....53 D5
Darwin Dr TN10 .....127 D6
Darwin Rd Bexley DA16 .....12 F4
Tilbury RM18 .....18 F6
Dashmonden Cl ME2 .....39 C2
Dashwood Cl DA6 .....14 A2
Dashwood Rd DA11 .....36 A6
Davall Ho 10 RM17 .....18 B8
Davema Cl BR7 .....43 A8
Davenport Ave ME7 .....54 E7
Davenport Rd DA14 .....30 E6
Davey Ct ME1 .....53 C5
David Coffer Ct DA17 .....4 B2
David Ho 23 DA14 .....30 A5
David Ramsey Ho SE18 .....2 D2
David Saloman's Ho* TN3 .....158 D8
Davidson Ho DA9 .....17 C2
Davis Ave DA11 .....35 E7
Davis Cl TN13 .....92 C5
Davy's Pl DA12 .....36 E2
Dawbourne TN30 .....183 B3
Dawell Dr TN16 .....72 C2
Dawes Cl DA9 .....16 F2
Dawes St ME7 .....54 C5
Dawn La ME18 .....97 D3
Dawson Ave BR5 .....44 B7
Dawson Cl SE18 .....2 C2
Dawson Ct 7 ME7 .....54 A6
Dawson Dr BR8 .....31 E1
Day Ho 2 ME14 .....100 B4
Days La DA15 .....29 E8
Days Lane Prim Sch DA15 .....12 F1
Dayton Dr DA8 .....15 D8
De Lapre Cl BR5 .....44 D2
De Luci Rd DA8 .....4 C1
De Lucy Prim Sch SE2 .....3 B4
De Lucy St SE2 .....3 B2
De Mere Cl ME8 .....69 D6
De Quincey Mews E16 .....1 A5
De Warren Ho DA11 .....18 D1
Deacon Cl ME2 .....52 E8
Deacon Est The ME20 .....83 A2
Deacon Trad Ctr ME2 .....53 A6
Deacon Trad Est TN9 .....127 D1
Deacons Leas BR6 .....57 D6
Deakin Leas TN9 .....143 B7
Deakins Terr BR6 .....44 A2
Deal Ho ME15 .....116 E8
Dean & Chapter Cotts DA13 .....35 B2
Dean La DA13 .....64 C5
Dean Rd Luddesdown DA13 .....64 E8
Rochester ME2 .....52 F8
Woolwich SE28 .....3 A6
Dean St ME15 .....115 C6
Deane Ct 8 ME7 .....54 C6
Deanery Rd TN8 .....105 C2
Deans Ct 7 TN9 .....143 B8
Deans Hill Rd ME9 .....87 D5
Deansfield Prim Sch SE9 .....12 A4
Deanwood Cl ME8 .....69 D6
Deanwood Dr ME8 .....69 E4
Deanwood Prim Education Tech Sch ME8 .....69 D3
Debrabant Cl DA8 .....14 D8
Decimus Pl TN1 .....159 B4
Decoy Hill Rd ME23 .....23 F6
Deepdene TN5 .....185 A6
Deepdene Rd DA16 .....13 A4
Deerhurst Cl DA3 .....49 C6
Deerhurst Gdns ME16 .....99 D4
Deering Cl ME4 .....40 B2
Deerleap La TN14 .....74 E6
Defiance Wlk SE18 .....1 F3
Defiant Cl ME5 .....68 B6
Defoe Cl Chatham ME5 .....68 B6
Erith DA8 .....14 F6
Degema Rd BR7 .....29 B3
Deidre Chapman Ho DA10 .....17 E1
Delacourt Rd SE3 .....11 B7
Delafield Rd SE7 .....1 C1
Delagarde Rd TN16 .....89 C1
Delamere Gdns 3 ME6 .....82 A8
Delamere Rd ME6 .....82 A8
Delarue Cl TN11 .....127 D8
Delaware Cotts TN8 .....138 F8
Delce Jun & Inf Schs ME1 .....53 D2
Delce Rd ME1 .....53 D4
Delisle Rd SE28 .....2 E4
Delius Dr TN10 .....127 F6
Dell Dr TN2 .....159 D4
Dell The Maypole DA5 .....31 E7
Swanscombe DA9 .....17 B2
Woolwich SE2 .....3 A1
Delme Cres SE3 .....11 B5
Delmonden La TN18 .....194 C8
Delmonden Rd TN18 .....188 B1
Delvan Cl SE18 .....12 A7
Delves Ave TN2 .....159 C1
Demelza Cl ME2 .....52 A2
Demelza House Hospice ME9 .....71 F6
Den Cross TN8 .....138 D6
Den La TN12 .....131 C3
Denbeigh Dr TN10 .....127 D6
Denberry Dr DA14 .....30 B5
Denbigh Ave ME8 .....55 D1
Denbigh Cl BR7 .....28 F2
Denbigh Rd TN4 .....159 C7
Denbridge Rd BR1 .....42 F7
Dene Ave DA15 .....30 B8
Dene Cl DA2 .....31 E4
Dene Dr New Barn DA3 .....49 B7
Orpington BR6 .....58 B7
Dene Holm Rd DA11 .....35 E5
Dene Lodge Cl TN15 .....94 F7
Dene Rd DA1 .....32 F8
Dene The TN13 .....92 B1
Dene Way TN3 .....158 A7
Dene Wlk DA3 .....48 E6
Denecourt BR5 .....44 C1
Denesfield Ct TN13 .....91 C4
Denesway DA13 .....50 B3
Denham Cl DA16 .....13 C4
Denham Rd ME9 .....71 B7
Denham St 2 SE10 .....1 A1
Denison Mews ME3 .....25 C4
Deniston Ave DA5 .....30 E7
Denmark Ho 10 SE18 .....1 E2
Denmark Rd BR1 .....42 B8
Denmark St E13 .....1 B8
Dennard Way BR6 .....57 A6
Dennettsland Rd TN8 .....105 C1
Denning Cl ME16 .....99 B4
Dennington Ct TN4 .....143 A2
Dennis Cadman Ho ME20 .....82 F1
Dennis Rd DA11 .....36 B5
Dennis Wilcocks Cl ME9 .....71 B6
Denny Cl 13 E6 .....1 E8
Denny Ct 3 DA2 .....16 B1
Denstead Wlk 11 ME15 .....116 F6
Denton Cl ME15 .....116 E8
Denton Court Rd DA12 .....36 E8
Denton Ct BR2 .....43 A2
Denton Gn ME8 .....55 B4
Denton Rd Bexley DA16 .....13 C7
Dartford DA1 .....31 E8
Maypole DA5 .....31 E7
Denton St DA12 .....36 E8
Denton Terr DA5 .....31 E6
Denver Cl BR6 .....43 E3
Denver Ind Est RM13 .....4 F8
Denver Rd DA1 .....32 A8
Derby Cl TN11 .....126 E6
Derby Rd Gillingham ME5 .....54 E2
Grays RM17 .....18 B8
Maidstone ME15 .....116 C8
Derby Road Bridge RM17 .....18 B8
Derifall Cl E6 .....1 F8
Dering Way DA12 36
Deringwood Dr ME15 100
Dernier Rd TN10,TN9 .....127 C
Derrick Gdns SE7 .....1 C
Derry Downs BR5 .....44 C
Derwent Cl DA1 .....32 E
Derwent Cres DA7 .....14 A
Derwent Dr Orpington BR5 .....43 D
Royal Tunbridge Wells TN4 .....158 F
Derwent Ho 3 ME15 .....116 E
Derwent Rd TN10 .....127 C
Derwent Way ME8 .....69 D
Detillens La RH8 .....104 A
Detling CE Prim Sch ME14 .....85 A
Detling Cl ME8 .....55 C
Detling Hill ME14 .....85 E
Detling Rd Bromley BR1 .....28 A
Erith DA8 .....14 D
Northfleet DA11 .....35 D
Devalls Cl E6 .....2 A
Devenish Rd SE2 .....3 A
Devon Cl Chatham ME5 .....68 C
Rainham ME8 .....55 F
Devon Ct DA4 .....47 B
Devon Rd
Maidstone ME15 .....116 C
Sutton at H DA4 .....47 C
Devonshire Ave DA1 .....15 B
Devonshire Cl TN2 .....172 F
Devonshire Rd
Bexley DA6 .....13 E
Bromley SE9 .....28 E
Gillingham ME7 .....54 D
Gravesend DA12 .....36 B
Newham E16 .....1 B
Orpington BR6 .....44 A
West Thurrock RM20 .....17 E
Devonshire Sq BR2 .....42 B
Dewberry Cl ME4 .....40 B
Dewberry Gdns E6 .....1 E
Dewhurst Cotts TN5 .....184 A
Dewhurst La TN5 .....184 B
DeWinter Ho TN13 .....92 A
Dewlands Ave DA2 .....33 B
Dexter Ho 2 DA18 .....3 E
Dhekelia Cl ME14 .....100 A
Dial Cl Gillingham ME7 .....54 F
Swanscombe DA9 .....17 D
Dial Rd ME7 .....54 F
Diameter Rd BR5 .....43 C
Diamond Cotts TN12 .....145 B7
Diamond Field TN12 .....162 F3
Diana Ct DA8 .....14 E8
Diana Rd ME4 .....54 A2
Dianne Ct SE12 .....28 A7
Dianthus Cl SE2 .....3 B1
Dibden La TN13,TN14 .....107 E8
Dickens Ave Dartford DA1 .....16 A3
Tilbury RM18 .....19 B6
Dickens Cl Erith DA8 .....14 B7
Hartley DA3 .....48 F4
Langley Heath ME17 .....117 E4
Dickens Ct Higham ME3 .....38 C4
Rochester ME2 .....53 D8
Staplehurst TN12 .....149 F5
Dickens Dr
Chislehurst BR7 .....29 C2
West Malling ME19 .....81 F1
Dickens Ho 3 DA17 .....3 F1
Dickens Rd
Gravesend DA12 .....36 E7
Maidstone ME14 .....99 E8
Rochester ME1 .....53 C2
Dickens Way TN18 .....189 A2
Dickensian Cl ME3 .....25 A2
Dickley La ME17 .....120 A6
Dickson Ho SE18 .....11 E6
Dickson Rd SE9 .....11 E4
Digdog La TN12,TN17 .....166 D3
Diggerland* ME2 .....52 F4
Dignals Cl ME8 .....55 F2
Dilhorne Cl SE12 .....28 B5
Dillon Way TN2 .....159 D7
Dilly Wood Fields ME3 .....39 A3
Dillywood Cotts ME3 .....38 F2
Dillywood La ME3 .....38 F2
Dimmock Cl TN12 .....146 B7
Dingleden La TN17 .....190 F2
Dippers Cl TN15 .....76 F2
Discovery Dr ME19 .....97 B3
Discovery Rd ME15 .....101 B2
Discovery Sch The ME18 .....97 D3
Dislingbury Rd TN11 .....144 C4
Disraeli Cl
Maidstone ME15 .....116 E5
Woolwich SE28 .....3 C5
Dittisham Rd SE9 .....28 E4
Ditton CE Jun Sch ME20 .....82 C1
Ditton Court Cl ME20 .....82 B1
Ditton Inf Sch ME20 .....82 C1
Ditton Pl ME20 .....82 B1
Ditton Rd DA6 .....13 E2
Dixon Cl Maidstone ME15 .....99 F2
4 Newham E6 .....1 F7
Dixon Ho SE2 .....3 C1
Dixwell Cl ME8 .....69 D5
Dobell Rd SE9 .....11 F2
Dobells TN17 .....179 D4
Dobson Rd DA12 .....36 E3
Dock Approach Rd RM17 .....18 E8
Dock Head Rd
Chatham ME4 .....54 A8
St Mary's Island ME4 .....40 A1
Dock Rd Chatham ME4 .....53 F6
Chatham ME4 .....54 A7
Grays RM17 .....18 D8

ck Rd *continued*
rays RM17 18 E7
ilbury RM18 18 E5
ckland St E16 2 A5
ckside Outlet Ctr ME4 54 A8
ckside Rd E16 1 D6
ctor Hope's Rd TN17 179 D4
dd Rd TN10 127 E5
ddington Ct ME16 99 E5
ddington Rd ME8 55 D3
ebury Wlk SE18 13 A8
g Cotts RH19 154 B1
ggetts Cl TN8 138 C8
ggetts Row ME3 27 B6
gwood Cl Chatham ME5 68 D1
orthfleet DA11 35 F4
lphin Cl SE28 3 D7
lphin Dr ME8 69 E5
lphin Ho ME1 53 E5
mbey Cl Higham ME3 38 C3
ochester ME1 53 C3
monic Dr SE9 29 B5
nald Biggs Dr DA12 36 D8
nald Troup Ho ME1 53 C4
naldson Rd SE18 12 A6
ncaster Cl 7 ME15 116 F6
net Cl ME8 69 C5
ngola Rd ME2 39 B1
nkey Field TN11 125 E1
nkey La DA4 61 B8
nnington Ct 1 DA2 16 B1
nnington Rd TN13 91 D7
on Brae TN4 143 A2
rado Gdns BR6 58 D7
ran Gr SE18 12 E7
rchester TN1 159 B6
rchester Ave DA5 30 D8
rchester Cl
iffe Woods ME3 39 B7
artford DA1 32 F7
rpington BR5 30 B1
rchester Rd DA12 36 D5
rcis Ave DA7 13 E5
reen Bird Coll (Birbeck
tr) DA15 30 A5
reen Bird Coll (Studio Ho)
A15 30 A5
ria Dr DA12 36 F5
ric Ave TN4 142 F1
ric Cl TN4 142 F1
rin Ct TN2 159 C3
ris Ave DA8 14 C6
rking Rd TN1 159 C6
rmers Dr DA13 50 B2
rnberg Cl SE3 11 A7
rnberg Rd SE3 11 B7
rnden Dr TN3 158 A4
rnden Gdns ME5 68 B2
rne Cotts TN27 137 E6
rney Rise BR5 43 F5
rothy Ave TN17 179 E4
rothy Evans Cl DA7 14 B3
rrit Way
hislehurst BR7 29 C2
chester ME1 53 D2
rset Ave DA16 12 F3
rset Cotts TN7 170 B4
rset Cres DA12 36 E4
rset Rd Bromley SE9 28 E6
yal Tunbridge Wells
2 159 D2
rset Road Inf Sch SE9 28 E6
rset Sq ME8 55 D1
rset St TN13 92 C2
rset Way ME15 116 C8
rton Dr TN15 92 F5
rton House (Royal London
ociety Sch for the Blind)
15 92 F5
rton House Sch TN15 92 F5
rville Rd SE12 11 A2
thill Rd SE18 12 C7
tterel Cl ME5 68 D2
ubleton La TN11 141 A5
ug Siddons Ct 12
17 18 C8
uglas Almshouses
17 120 D5
uglas Bldgs TN12 149 E5
uglas Ct TN16 72 E2
uglas Rd Bexley DA16 13 B6
nham ME17 120 D5
aidstone ME16 99 E3
Newham E16 1 A8
nbridge TN9 143 A8
uro Stables TN4 159 A4
ust Way ME1 53 D5
ve App E6 1 E8
ve Cl ME5 68 B6
ve Rd TN10 127 C6
vedale Cl DA16 13 A5
vedale Rd DA2 33 C7
veney Cl BR5 44 D6
ver Ho
Maidstone ME15 116 E8
chester ME2 39 C1
ver Patrol SE3 11 B5
ver Rd Northfleet DA11 35 D8
olwich DA16 12 C5
ver Rd E DA11 35 F7
ver Road Com Prim Sch
11 35 E7
ver St ME16 99 C2
ves Cl BR2 56 E8
wding Ho TN12 145 F6
wding Rd TN16 72 D4
wding Way TN2 143 E1
wding Wlk 3 DA11 35 E5

Dower Ho The DA14 30 F5
Dower House Cres TN4 142 E3
Dowgate Cl TN9 143 D7
Dowlerville Rd BR6 57 F4
Dowling Cl ME6 81 E7
Dowling Ho DA17 3 F3
Down Ave TN3 176 A4
Down House Mus* BR6 73 A7
Down La TN3 173 B1
Down's Cl TN27 151 E5
Downage The DA11 36 A6
Downash Ct TN5 187 A3
Downash Ho TN5 187 A3
Downbank Ave DA7 14 D5
Downderry Way ME20 82 B1
Downe Ave TN14 73 D8
Downe Cl DA16 13 C7
Downe Ho 10 SE7 11 C8
Downe Prim Sch BR6 73 A8
Downe Rd
Cudham BR6,TN14 73 C5
Farthing Street BR2 56 E2
Downend SE18 12 B7
Downer Ct ME1 67 E8
Downham Way BR1 28 A4
Downings E6 2 A7
Downlands ME17 119 F6
Downleys Cl SE9 28 F6
Downman Rd SE9 11 E4
Downs Ave Bromley BR7 28 F3
Dartford DA1 33 A8
Downs Cl ME14 100 B8
Downs Ct ME18 114 B3
Downs Rd
Istead Rise DA13 35 D3
Maidstone ME14 100 B8
Yalding ME18 114 A1
Downs The ME5 67 D1
Downs Valley DA3 48 E5
Downs View Burham ME1 66 F1
West Malling ME19 97 B8
Downs View Cl BR6 58 C1
Downs View Rd ME14 100 B8
Downs Wood DA13 79 F8
Downside ME2 53 A7
Downsland Ho ME2 52 C2
Downsview Chatham ME5 68 C8
Trottiscliffe ME19 80 A5
Downsview Cl BR8 45 F6
Downsview Prim Sch
BR8 46 A6
Downsview Rd TN13 91 F2
Downsway BR6 57 E5
Downton Cotts TN18 195 F4
Doyle Cl DA8 14 E6
Doyle Way RM18 19 C5
Drage Rd TN12 129 E6
Drake Cres SE28 3 C7
Drake Ct BR5 44 B3
Drake Hall E16 1 B5
Drake Mews BR2 42 C5
Drake Point 12 DA8 4 E1
Drake's Ave ME2 52 F8
Draper Cl DA17 3 F2
Draper Ct BR1 42 E5
Draper St 3 TN4 142 F2
Drawbridge Cl ME15 116 E8
Drawell Cl SE18 2 E1
Dray Corner Rd TN27 150 F7
Dray Ct TN11 128 E8
Drays Cotts DA4 47 B5
Drayton Ave BR6 43 B1
Drayton Cl ME23 23 E4
Drayton Rd TN9 143 C8
Drew Prim Sch E16 1 E5
Drew Rd E16 1 E5
Drewery Dr ME8 69 C5
Driffield Gdns TN9 142 F7
Drift The BR2 56 D7
Drive The Ashurst TN3 156 F5
Bexley DA5 30 D8
Chislehurst BR7 43 E8
Erith DA8 14 B8
Gravesend DA12 36 E4
New Barn DA3 49 B6
Orpington BR6 57 F8
Royal Tunbridge Wells
TN2 159 B1
Sevenoaks TN13 92 B3
Sidcup DA14 30 B4
St Paul's Cray BR7 43 F6
Tonbridge TN9 143 B7
Drove Way The DA13 35 E1
Drudgeon Way DA2 34 B5
Drummond Cl DA8 14 E6
Drury Rd TN30 183 B1
Dry Bank Ct TN10 127 C4
Dry Bank Rd TN10 127 C4
Dry End Rd ME20 82 C3
Dry Hill Park Cres TN10 127 C3
Dry Hill Park Rd TN10 127 B3
Dry Hill Rd TN9 127 B3
Dryden Ho BR2 42 D4
Dryden Pl RM18 19 B6
Dryden Rd DA16 12 F6
Dryden Way BR6 44 A1
Dryhill La TN14 91 B3
Dryhill Rd DA17 13 F8
Dryland Ave 6 BR6 57 F6
Dryland Rd
Borough Green TN15 94 F6
Snodland ME6 81 F8
Dublin Ho 18 ME15 116 E7
Duchess Cl ME2 52 E8
Duchess of Kent Ct The
ME20 82 F1
Duchess Of Kent Dr ME5 68 B3
Duchess' Wlk TN15 92 E2

Ducie Ho 9 SE7 11 C8
Ducketts Rd DA1 14 F2
Duddington Cl SE9 28 D4
Dudely Rd DA11 35 E8
Dudley Keen Ct TN9 143 E8
Dudley Lodge TN2 159 C4
Dudley Rd TN1 159 A4
Dudsbury Rd Dartford DA1 15 B2
Sidcup DA14 30 B2
Duggan Dr BR7 28 E2
Duke Of Wellington Ave
SE18,SE28 2 C3
Dukes Mdw TN11 124 F2
Dukes Meadow Dr ME7 68 F6
Dukes Orch DA5 31 C7
Dukes Rd TN1 159 C5
Dukes Wlk 7 ME15 100 A4
Dulverton Prim Sch SE9 29 D6
Dulverton Rd SE9 29 D6
Dulwich Prep Sch TN17 180 A4
Dumbourne La TN30 193 D2
Dumbreck Rd SE9 12 A4
Dunbar Ct BR2 42 A5
Dunblane Rd SE9 11 E5
Duncan Ho 2 SE7 11 B8
Duncan Rd ME7 54 D5
Duncans Cotts 6 TN16 89 D1
Duncroft SE18 12 E7
Dundale Rd TN12,TN3 161 A3
Dundonald Cl 7 E6 1 E7
Dunedin Ho
9 Maidstone ME15 116 E5
Newham E16 1 F5
2 Tilbury RM18 19 A5
Dunera Dr ME14 100 A7
Dunk's Green Rd TN11 111 A5
Dunkeld Ho 6 ME15 116 E7
Dunkery Rd SE9 28 E5
Dunkin Rd DA1 16 A3
Dunkirk Cl DA12 36 C3
Dunkirk Dr ME5 67 F6
Dunkley Villas TN15 79 F1
Dunlin Dr ME4 40 C2
Dunlop Ct 7 TN18 189 A2
Dunlop Rd RM18 18 F6
Dunn Lodge TN2 159 D2
Dunn Street Rd ME7 85 A8
Dunning's La ME1 53 C4
Dunnings The ME16 99 A2
Dunnock Rd E6 1 E7
Dunnose Ct RM19 16 B8
Dunoon Cotts BR6 73 A5
Dunorlan Farm TN2 159 E4
Dunorlan Farm Cotts
TN2 159 E4
Dunstable Ct 5 SE3 11 A7
Dunstall Welling Est
DA16 13 B5
Dunstan Glade BR5 43 D3
Dunstan Gr TN4 159 B6
Dunstan Rd TN4 159 B6
Dunster Ct 16 DA2 16 B1
Dunster Terr 3 ME15 116 E8
Dunton Green Prim Sch
TN13 91 E7
Dunton Green Sta TN13 91 E7
Dunvegan Rd SE9 11 F3
Dunwich Rd DA7 13 F6
Dupree Rd SE7 1 B1
Durant Rd BR8 32 A2
Durban Ho 7 ME15 116 E5
Durham Cl ME15 100 E1
Durham Rd Bromley BR2 42 A5
Gillingham ME8 69 C7
Sidcup DA14 30 B3
Durham Rise SE18 2 D1
Duriun Way DA8 15 B7
Durley Gdns BR6 58 B7
Durlings Orch TN15 94 D6
Durndale La
Northfleet DA11 35 E4
Northfleet DA11 35 F5
Durrant Way
Orpington BR6 57 D5
Swanscombe DA10 34 E8
Durrell Gdns ME5 54 C1
Dursley Cl SE3 11 C5
Dursley Gdns SE3 11 D6
Dursley Rd SE3 11 C5
Duval Dr ME1 67 E8
Duvard's Pl ME9 71 F1
Dux Court Rd ME23 23 D2
Dux Hill TN15 110 F8
Dux La TN15 94 F1
Duxberry Cl BR2 42 E4
Duxford Ho 12 SE2 3 D4
Dwelly La TN8 121 D3
Dyke Dr BR5 44 C2
Dykewood Cl DA5 31 E5
Dylan Rd DA17 4 A3
Dymchurch Cl BR6 57 E6
Dyneley Rd SE12 28 C5
Dynes Rd TN15 76 E2
Dynevor Rd TN4 159 C7

E

Eagle Cl ME20 82 A2
Eagle Heights Bird of Prey
Ctr* DA4 60 B8
Eagle Ho RM17 17 F8
Eagle Way DA11 18 A2
Eagles Dr TN16 72 D1
Eagles Rd DA9 17 B2
Eaglesfield Rd SE18 12 B6
Eaglesfield Sch SE18 12 A6
Eaglestone Cl TN15 95 A8

Ealdham Prim Sch SE9 11 C3
Ealdham Sq SE9 11 C3
Ealing Cl ME5 68 C4
Eardemont Cl DA1 14 F3
Eardley Point 7 SE18 2 B2
Eardley Rd Erith DA17 4 A1
Sevenoaks TN13 92 B3
Earl Cl ME5 68 B4
Earl Rd DA11 35 E6
Earl Rise SE18 2 D2
Earl St ME14 99 F4
Earl's Rd TN4 158 F4
Earlshall Rd SE9 12 A3
Eason Villas TN12 148 D6
East Beckton District Ctr
E6 1 F8
East Borough Prim Sch
ME14 100 B5
East Cliff Rd TN4 159 A6
East Crescent Rd DA12 19 C1
East Cross TN30 193 B7
East Ct 4 ME15 100 A1
East Dr BR5 44 B3
East End Rd ME4,ME7 54 D8
East Farleigh Prim Sch
ME15 115 B6
East Farleigh Sta ME16 115 B8
East Hall Hill ME17 133 E7
East Hall Rd BR5 44 F2
East Ham Ind Est E6 1 E8
East Ham Manor Way E6 2 A7
East Hill Biggin Hill TN16 72 B1
Dartford DA1 32 F8
Sutton at H DA4 47 D7
Tenterden TN30 193 B8
East Hill Dr DA1 32 F8
East Hill Farm Cvn Pk
TN15 61 C1
East Hill Farm Pk TN15 61 B1
East Hill Rd TN15 77 B7
East Ho DA1 15 F4
East Holme DA8 14 D6
East Kent Ave DA11 18 C1
East La DA4 47 D7
East Malling Research Sta
(Horticultural) ME19 98 C6
East Malling Sta ME19 98 A6
East Mascalls 17 SE7 11 C8
East Mill DA11 18 F1
East Milton Rd DA12 36 D8
East Park Rd ME20 99 A8
East Peckham Prim Sch
TN12 129 E7
East Point TN15 93 A6
East Rd Bexley DA16 13 B5
Chatham ME4 54 A7
East Rochester Way
Coldblow DA1 31 D8
Sidcup DA5,DA15 13 C1
East Row ME1 53 C5
East St Addington ME19 80 D3
Bexley DA7 14 A3
Bromley BR1 42 A7
Chatham ME4 54 A3
Gillingham ME7 54 D6
Grays RM20 17 E8
Harrietsham ME17 119 E5
Hunton ME15 131 F7
Snodland ME6 82 B8
Tonbridge TN9 127 C2
East Street N ME19 80 D3
East Sutton Park (HM Young
Offender Inst & Prison)
ME17 135 B7
East Sutton Rd
Sutton Valence ME17 135 A7
Sutton Valence ME17,
TN27 135 C4
East Terr Gravesend DA12 19 C1
Sidcup DA15 29 E7
East Thamesmead Bsns Pk
DA18 3 F4
East Thurrock Rd RM17 18 C8
East Weald Dr TN30 183 B1
East Wickham Inf Sch
DA16 12 F6
East Wickham Jun Sch
DA16 13 A6
East Woodside DA5 30 E7
Eastbrook Rd SE3 11 B6
Eastbury Rd Newham E6 2 A8
Orpington BR5 43 D3
Eastcombe Ave SE7 11 B8
Eastcote BR6 43 F1
Eastcote Prim Sch DA16 12 D4
Eastcote Rd DA16 12 D5
Eastcourt Gn ME8 55 B4
Eastcourt La
Gillingham ME7,ME8 55 B4
Gillingham ME8 55 B3
Easterfields ME19 98 C5
Eastern Ave RM20 16 F8
Eastern Rd ME7 54 F6
Eastern View TN16 72 C2
Eastern Way Erith SE28 3 D5
1 Grays RM17 18 A8
Eastfield Gdns TN10 127 E5
Eastfield Ho ME16 99 B2
Eastgate ME1 53 C5
Eastgate Cl SE28 3 D7
Eastgate Ct ME1 53 C5
Eastgate Rd TN30 193 C8
Eastgate Terr ME1 53 C5
Eastland Ct 3 BR1 42 C7
Eastlands Cl TN4 172 E8
Eastlands Rd TN4 158 E1
Eastleigh Rd DA7 14 C4
Eastling Cl ME8 55 D3

Eastling Ho 8 BR5 44 D1
Eastmead Cl BR1 42 E7
Eastmoor Pl SE7 1 D3
Eastmoor St SE7 1 D3
Eastnor Rd SE9 29 C7
Eastry Cl ME16 99 C7
Eastry Rd DA8 14 A7
Eastview Ave SE18 12 E7
Eastway BR2 42 A2
Eastwell 5 TN30 193 A7
Eastwell Barn Mews
TN30 193 A8
Eastwell Cl
Maidstone ME14 100 C5
Paddock Wood TN12 145 E6
Eastwell Mdws TN30 193 A8
Eastwood Rd ME17 136 C5
Eaton Ct BR7 29 C2
Eaton Rd DA14 30 D6
Eaton Sq DA3 48 D6
Ebbsfleet Ind Est DA11 18 A2
Ebbsfleet Wlk DA11 18 B1
Ebdon Way SE3 11 B4
Ebony Wlk ME16 99 B3
Ebury Cl BR2 56 E7
Eccles Row ME20 82 F6
Eccleston Cl BR6 43 D1
Eccleston Rd ME15 99 F2
Echo Cl ME15 116 F6
Echo Ct DA12 36 C6
Echo Sq DA12 36 C6
Eclipse Rd E13 1 B8
Edam Ct 11 DA14 30 A5
Eddington Cl ME15 116 B6
Eden Ave ME5 68 A7
Eden Cl DA5 31 D4
Eden Ct
1 Hawkhurst TN18 188 F2
17 Orpington BR5 44 D1
Tonbridge TN10 127 C5
Eden Farm La ME19 97 D8
Eden Pl DA12 36 B8
Eden Rd
High Halstow ME23 23 E4
Joyden's Wood DA5 31 D4
Royal Tunbridge Wells
TN1 159 A2
Eden Valley Mus* TN8 122 C1
Eden Villas TN8 138 D7
Eden Wlk 9 TN1 159 A2
Edenbridge & District War
Meml Hospl TN8 138 D7
Edenbridge Cl BR5 44 D5
Edenbridge Prim Sch
TN8 122 D1
Edenbridge Rd TN7 155 E1
Edenbridge Sta TN8 122 C3
Edenbridge Town Sta
TN8 122 D2
Edenbridge Trad Ctr
TN8 138 D8
Edendale Rd DA7 14 D5
Edenhurst TN13 92 A2
Edensmuir Ct SE3 11 A7
Edgar Cl BR8 45 F6
Edgar Rd Kemsing TN15 76 E2
Tatsfield TN16 88 D6
Edge Hill SE18 12 B8
Edge Hill Ct DA14 29 F4
Edgeborough Way BR1 42 D8
Edgebury BR7,SE9 29 B4
Edgebury Prim Sch BR7 29 C4
Edgebury Wlk BR7 29 C5
Edgefield Cl DA1 33 B7
Edgehill Gdns DA13 49 F8
Edgehill Rd BR7 29 C4
Edgeler Ct ME6 81 F7
Edger Pl 5 ME15 100 A4
Edgeway ME4 40 B2
Edgewood Dr BR6 58 A5
Edgeworth Rd SE9 11 D3
Edgington Way DA14 30 D1
Edinburgh Ct DA8 14 D7
Edinburgh Mews RM18 19 B5
Edinburgh Rd
Chatham ME4 54 C2
Gillingham ME7 54 D5
Grain ME3 27 B5
Edinburgh Sq ME15 116 C7
Edington Rd SE2 3 B3
Edisbury Wlk ME8 69 D5
Edison Gr SE18 12 F7
Edison Rd Bexley DA16 12 F6
2 Bromley BR2 42 A7
Edith Cavell Way SE18 11 E6
Edith Ct BR1 42 D6
Edith Pond Ct SE9 29 B6
Edith Rd BR6 58 A5
Ediva Rd DA13 50 A4
Edmund Cl
Maidstone ME16 99 A3
Meopham Sta DA13 50 A4
Edmund Hurst Dr E6 2 B8
Edmund Rd Bexley DA16 13 A4
Orpington BR5 44 C3
Edmunds Ave BR5 44 D6
Edna Rd ME14 99 F8
Edward Ct Chatham ME5 54 C1
2 Newham E16 1 A8
Edward Harvey Ct DA17 3 F1
Edward Rd
Biggin Hill TN16 72 E1
Bromley BR1 28 C1
Chislehurst BR7 29 B3
Edward St Chatham ME4 54 A3

Edward St *continued*
Rochester ME2 .....53 B7
Royal Tunbridge Wells TN4 .....158 F8
Rusthall TN4 .....158 C4
Edward Tyler Rd SE12 .....28 C6
Edward Wlk ME19 .....97 F8
Edwards Cl ME8 .....69 C5
Edwards Ct DA4 .....60 E7
Edwards Gdns BR8 .....45 D5
Edwards Rd DA17 .....4 A2
Edwin Arnold Ct DA15 .....29 F4
Edwin Cl DA7 .....13 F8
Edwin Petty Pl DA2 .....33 C8
Edwin Rd Dartford DA2 .....32 C5
Gillingham ME8 .....69 C8
Edwin St Gravesend DA12 .....36 B8
Newham E16 .....1 A8
Edwins Pl ME9 .....71 C7
Egdean Wlk TN13 .....92 C4
Egerton Ave BR8 .....45 F8
Egerton CE Prim Sch TN27 .....137 F3
Egerton Cl DA1 .....32 B7
Egerton House Rd TN27 .....137 E4
Egerton Rd ME14 .....99 E7
Eggpie La TN11,TN14 .....125 E7
Egham Rd E13 .....1 B8
Eglantine La DA4 .....47 B3
Eglinton Hill SE18 .....12 B7
Eglinton Prim Sch SE18 .....12 A8
Eglinton Rd
Swanscombe DA10 .....17 F1
Woolwich SE18 .....12 B8
Egremont Rd ME15 .....100 F2
Egret Cl ME4 .....40 B2
Eileen Ct BR7 .....29 A3
Eisenhower Dr E6 .....1 E8
Elaine Ave ME2 .....52 E7
Elaine Ct ME2 .....52 E6
Elaine Prim Sch ME2 .....52 E6
Elbourne Trad Est DA17 .....4 B3
Elbury Dr E16 .....1 A7
Elder Cl Kingswood ME17 .....118 D2
Sidcup DA15 .....29 F7
Elder Ct ME8 .....69 B6
Elderslie Rd SE9 .....12 A2
Eldon St ME4 .....54 A4
Eldon Way TN12 .....145 F7
Eldred Dr BR5 .....58 D8
Eleanor Smith Sch E16 .....1 C8
Eleanor Wlk 19 SE18 .....1 F2
Elford Cl SE3 .....11 C3
Elford Rd ME3 .....22 B5
Elgal Cl BR6 .....57 B5
Elgar Cl TN10 .....127 E6
Elgar Gdns RM18 .....19 B6
Elgin Gdns ME2 .....52 D5
Elham Cl Bromley BR1 .....28 D1
Gillingham ME8 .....55 B3
Elibank Rd SE9 .....12 A3
Eling Ct ME15 .....116 A8
Eliot Rd DA1 .....16 B2
Eliza Cook Cl DA9 .....17 B3
Elizabeth Cl RM18 .....19 B5
Elizabeth Cotts DA4 .....60 E8
Elizabeth Ct Chatham ME5 .....68 A7
Dartford DA2 .....33 D3
Erith DA8 .....14 D7
Gillingham ME8 .....55 C1
6 Gravesend DA11 .....19 A1
Elizabeth Fry Pl SE18 .....11 E6
Elizabeth Garlick Ct 1 TN1 .....159 B4
Elizabeth Garrett Anderson Ho 9 DA17 .....4 A3
Elizabeth Ho
Maidstone ME14 .....100 A6
Rochester ME1 .....53 C4
Elizabeth Huggins Cotts DA11 .....36 B6
Elizabeth Pl DA4 .....46 E3
Elizabeth Smith's Ct ME19 .....97 F7
Elizabeth St DA9 .....16 E2
Elizabeth Terr SE9 .....11 F1
Elizabeth Way BR5 .....44 C4
Ellard Ct DA16 .....13 C4
Ellen Cl BR1 .....42 D6
Ellen Wilkinson Prim Sch E6 .....1 E8
Ellen's Pl ME9 .....71 C6
Ellenborough Rd DA14 .....30 E3
Ellenswood Cl ME15 .....101 A1
Ellerman Rd RM18 .....18 F5
Ellerslie DA12 .....36 D8
Ellerslie Ct 3 DA12 .....36 D8
Ellesmere Ct SE12 .....28 A8
Ellingham Leas ME15 .....116 C7
Elliott Rd BR2 .....42 D5
Elliott St DA12 .....36 D8
Elliotts La TN16 .....90 C3
Ellis Cl Eltham SE9 .....29 C6
Swanley BR8 .....45 D5
Ellis Ct DA1 .....33 B7
Ellis Ho 7 ME14 .....100 B4
Ellis Way DA1 .....32 F6
Elliscombe Mount SE7 .....11 C8
Elliscombe Rd SE7 .....11 C8
Ellison Rd DA15 .....29 D7
Elliston Ho 8 SE18 .....2 A2
Elm Ave Chatham ME4 .....53 E1
Chattenden ME3 .....40 A4
Elm Cl Dartford DA1 .....32 C7
Egerton TN27 .....137 F3
Elm Cl *continued*
Higham ME3 .....38 C3
Elm Cotts BR8 .....46 B8
Elm Court Ind Est ME7 .....68 E3
Elm Cres ME19 .....97 F8
Elm Dr BR8 .....45 D7
Elm Gr Erith DA8 .....14 D7
Maidstone ME15 .....100 B3
Orpington BR6 .....43 F1
Tonbridge TN11 .....126 F5
Elm La TN10 .....127 C3
Elm Par 10 DA14 .....30 A4
Elm Rd Dartford DA1 .....32 D7
Erith DA8 .....15 A6
Gillingham ME7 .....54 E6
Gravesend DA12 .....36 C5
Grays RM17 .....18 C8
Hoo St Werburgh ME3 .....40 E3
Orpington BR6 .....58 A3
Royal Tunbridge Wells TN4 .....142 F1
Sidcup DA14 .....30 A4
Stone DA9 .....16 E1
Westerham TN16 .....89 E2
Elm Terr 3 Eltham SE9 .....12 A1
West Thurrock RM20 .....17 B8
Elm Tree Cotts ME3 .....25 A3
Elm Tree Ct 20 SE7 .....11 C8
Elm Tree Dr ME1 .....53 A2
Elm Wlk Aylesford ME20 .....82 E1
Orpington BR6 .....56 F7
Elmbank Dr BR1 .....42 D7
Elmbourne Dr DA17 .....4 B2
Elmbrook Gdns SE9 .....11 E3
Elmcroft Ave DA15 .....13 A1
Elmcroft Rd BR6 .....44 A2
Elmdene Rd SE18 .....2 B1
Elmfield Gillingham ME8 .....55 A3
Tenterden TN30 .....193 B8
Elmfield Cl
Gravesend DA11 .....36 B7
Sevenoaks Weald TN14 .....108 B2
Elmfield Ct Bexley DA16 .....13 B6
Coxheath ME17 .....115 C3
Tenterden TN30 .....193 B8
Elmfield Pk BR1 .....42 A6
Elmfield Rd BR1 .....42 A6
Elmhurst Bexley DA17 .....13 E8
Swanscombe DA9 .....17 B1
Elmhurst Ave TN2 .....160 D8
Elmhurst Gdns ME4 .....53 E3
Elmhurst Rd SE9 .....28 E5
Elmington Cl DA5 .....14 B1
Elmlee Cl BR7 .....28 F2
Elmley Cl 16 E6 .....1 E8
Elmley St SE18 .....2 D2
Elmshurst Gdns TN10 .....127 C7
Elmslie Ct SE9 .....12 A1
Elmstead Ave BR7 .....28 F3
Elmstead Cl TN13 .....91 E5
Elmstead Glade BR7 .....28 F2
Elmstead La BR7 .....28 F3
Elmstead Rd DA8 .....14 E6
Elmstead Woods Sta BR7 .....28 E2
Elmsted Cres DA16 .....13 C8
Elmstone Cl ME16 .....99 B2
Elmstone Hole Rd ME17 .....136 D8
Elmstone La ME16 .....99 B2
Elmstone Rd ME8 .....69 D7
Elmstone Terr 3 BR5 .....44 C5
Elmtree Cotts TN14 .....74 D4
Elmwood Dr DA5 .....30 E8
Elmwood Rd ME3 .....39 F6
Elphick's Pl TN2 .....173 B8
Elrick Cl DA8 .....14 E8
Elsa Rd DA16 .....13 C5
Elsinore Ho 8 SE18 .....1 E2
Elster Pl ME19 .....97 B3
Elstow Cl Eltham SE9 .....11 F2
Eltham SE9 .....12 A2
Elstree Gdns DA17 .....3 E2
Elswyn Ho 14 DA14 .....30 A5
Eltham CE Prim Sch SE9 .....11 F2
Eltham Coll SE9 .....28 D6
Eltham Green Rd SE9 .....11 C3
Eltham Green Sch SE9 .....11 D1
Eltham High St SE9 .....11 F1
Eltham Hill SE9 .....11 E2
Eltham Hill Tech Coll for Girls SE9 .....11 E1
Eltham Pal* SE9 .....11 E1
Eltham Palace Rd SE9 .....11 D1
Eltham Park Gdns SE9 .....12 A3
Eltham Rd SE12,SE9 .....11 B2
Eltham Sta SE9 .....11 F2
Elveys Cotts ME18 .....113 F1
Elvington Cl ME16 .....99 D5
Elwick Ct DA1 .....15 A3
Elwill Way DA13 .....49 F8
Elwyn Gdns SE12 .....28 A8
Ely Cl Erith DA8 .....14 F5
Gillingham ME8 .....55 E2
Ely Ct TN1 .....159 B4
Ely Gdns TN10 .....127 D4
Elysian Ave BR5 .....43 F3
Embassy Cl ME7 .....54 F1
Embassy Ct Bexley DA16 .....13 B4
Sidcup DA14 .....30 B5
Ember Cl BR5 .....43 C2
Emblin Ct 2 DA14 .....30 A4
Emerald Cl Newham E16 .....1 E7
Rochester ME1 .....67 D7
Emersons Ave BR8 .....31 F1
Emerton Cl DA6 .....13 E3
Emes Rd DA8 .....14 C7
Emily Jackson Cl TN13 .....92 B3
Emily Jackson Ho TN13 .....92 B3
Emily Rd ME5 .....68 B6
Emmanuel Ho 2 SE18 .....2 D1
Emmet Hill La ME18 .....130 F5
Emmetts Garden* TN14 .....106 D5
Emmetts La TN14,TN16 .....106 D6
Empress Dr BR7 .....29 B2
Empress Rd DA12 .....36 E8
Emsworth Gr ME14 .....100 D6
Endeavour Foyer The 8 ME4 .....54 B2
Enderfield Ct BR7 .....43 A8
Engineer Cl SE18 .....12 A8
Englefield Cl BR5 .....43 F5
Englefield Cres
Cliffe Woods ME3 .....39 B7
Orpington BR5 .....44 A5
Englefield Path BR5 .....44 A5
English Martyrs' RC Prim Sch ME2 .....53 B8
Ennerdale Ho ME15 .....116 E7
Ennerdale Rd DA7 .....14 A6
Ennis Rd SE18 .....12 C8
Ensfield Rd Leigh TN11 .....125 E1
Tonbridge TN11 .....142 A6
Ensign Ho RM17 .....17 F8
Enslin Rd SE9 .....29 A8
Enterprise Bsns Est ME2 .....53 E7
Enterprise Cl ME2 .....53 D8
Enterprise Ctr The ME5 .....84 C8
Enterprise Rd ME15 .....100 A1
Enterprise Way TN8 .....122 C3
Epaul La ME1 .....53 C6
Eppe Cl 2 ME2 .....53 B8
Epsom Cl Bexley DA7 .....14 B4
Maidstone ME15 .....116 F6
West Malling ME19 .....97 B8
Epstein Rd SE28 .....3 B5
Erebus Dr SE28 .....2 C4
Erica Ct BR8 .....45 E5
Eridge Ct TN2 .....158 F1
Eridge Green Cl BR5 .....44 C1
Eridge Rd
Groombridge TN3 .....171 D5
Royal Tunbridge Wells TN2,TN4 .....158 E1
Eridge Sta TN3 .....171 E2
Erindale SE18 .....12 D8
Erindale Terr SE18 .....12 D8
Erith & District Hospl DA8 .....14 D8
Erith Cl ME14 .....100 A8
Erith High St DA8 .....4 E1
Erith Mus* DA8 .....4 E1
Erith Rd Bexley DA7 .....14 B4
Erith DA8,DA17 .....4 B1
Erith Sch DA8 .....14 D7
Erith Small Bsns Ctr 2 DA8 .....14 F8
Erith Sta DA8 .....4 E1
Ermington Rd SE9 .....29 C6
Ernest Dr ME16 .....99 B5
Ernest Rd ME4 .....54 A3
Erskine Ho 8 SE7 .....11 C8
Erskine Park Rd TN4 .....158 C4
Erskine Rd DA13 .....80 B8
Erwood Rd SE7 .....1 E1
Escott Gdns SE9 .....28 E4
Escreet Gr SE18 .....2 A2
Eshcol Rd ME3 .....41 C6
Esher Cl DA5 .....30 E7
Eskdale Cl DA2 .....33 C7
Eskdale Rd DA7 .....14 A6
Esmonde Ho 15 ME7 .....54 A6
Esplanade ME1 .....53 B5
Essenden Rd DA17 .....4 A1
Essex Cl TN2 .....172 F8
Essex Rd 1 Dartford DA1 .....15 D1
Gravesend DA11 .....36 A7
Halling ME2 .....66 A6
Longfield DA3 .....48 D7
Maidstone ME15 .....116 E6
West Thurrock RM20 .....17 A8
Estelle Cl ME1 .....67 D7
Estridge Way TN10 .....127 F5
Estuary Cotts RM18 .....20 D7
Etfield Gr DA14 .....30 B3
Ethel Brooks Ho SE18 .....12 B8
Ethel Rd E16 .....1 B7
Ethel Terr BR6 .....58 C2
Ethel-Maud Ct ME7 .....54 D7
Ethelbert Rd Bromley BR1 .....42 A6
Erith DA8 .....14 C7
Hawley DA2 .....32 E3
Orpington BR5 .....44 D6
Rochester ME1 .....53 C4
Etherington Hill TN3 .....158 C8
Ethnam La TN18 .....196 E4
Ethronvi Rd DA7 .....13 E4
Eton Cl ME5 .....67 F4
Eton Ct TN13 .....92 B4
Eton Rd BR6 .....58 B6
Eton Way DA1 .....15 C3
Eugenie Mews BR7 .....43 B8
Europa Pk RM20 .....17 C8
Europa Trad Est DA8 .....4 D1
Europe Rd SE18 .....1 F3
Euroway ME20 .....98 E8
Eustace Pl 2 SE18 .....1 F2
Eva Rd ME7 .....54 D3
Evanlode Ho 5 SE2 .....3 C4
Evans Cl DA9 .....17 A2
Evans Ct SE9 .....28 E6
Evelyn Cl ME2 .....53 C8
Evelyn Denington Rd E6 .....1 F8
Evelyn Ho 5 ME2 .....53 C8
Evelyn Rd Maidstone ME16 .....99 E3
Newham E16 .....1 B5
Evelyn Rd *continued*
Otford TN14 .....76 C2
Evenden Ho TN17 .....179 D5
Evenden Rd DA13 .....50 A2
Everard Ave BR2 .....42 A1
Everest Cl 1 DA11 .....35 E5
Everest Ct SE9 .....28 E6
Everest Dr ME3 .....40 E4
Everest La ME2 .....39 B1
Everest Mews ME3 .....40 E4
Everest Pl BR8 .....45 D5
Everest Rd SE9 .....11 F2
Everett Wlk DA17 .....3 F1
Everglade TN16 .....72 D1
Everglade Cl DA3 .....48 F5
Everglades The ME7 .....68 F6
Evergreen Cl
Gillingham ME7 .....69 A5
Higham ME3 .....38 B3
Leybourne ME19 .....81 E2
Eversfield Ct SE12 .....28 B6
Eversley Ave DA7,DA8 .....14 E5
Eversley Cl ME16 .....99 C6
Eversley Cross DA7 .....14 E5
Eversley Rd SE7 .....11 B8
Evesham Rd DA12 .....36 D6
Evorg Ho 6 ME4 .....54 B2
Evry Rd DA14 .....30 C2
Ewart Rd ME4 .....53 E1
Ewehurst La TN3 .....157 F6
Ewell Ave ME19 .....97 A8
Ewell La ME15 .....114 D5
Ewins Cl TN12 .....146 A6
Excel Waterfront E16 .....1 B6
Exedown Rd TN15 .....78 C4
Exeter Cl Newham E6 .....1 F7
Tonbridge TN10 .....127 D4
Exeter Rd Bexley DA16 .....12 F5
Gravesend DA12 .....36 D5
Newham E16 .....1 A8
Exeter Wlk ME1 .....67 C7
Exford Gdns SE12 .....28 B7
Exford Rd SE12 .....28 B7
Exmouth Rd Bexley DA16 .....13 C7
Gillingham ME7 .....54 C7
Grays RM17 .....18 B8
Exton Cl ME5 .....68 C2
Exton Gdns ME14 .....100 F5
Eye The ME4 .....53 F5
Eyhorne St ME17 .....102 D2
Eynsford Castle* DA4 .....60 E8
Eynsford Cl BR5 .....43 C3
Eynsford Cres DA5 .....30 D7
Eynsford Rd
Crockenhill BR8 .....45 E3
Eynsford DA4 .....46 F1
Maidstone ME16 .....99 D7
Swanscombe DA9 .....17 C2
Eynsford Rise DA4 .....60 D6
Eynsford Sta DA4 .....60 D6
Eynsham Dr SE2 .....3 B3
Eynswood Dr DA14 .....30 C3

F

F Ave SE18 .....2 B3
Fackenden La TN14 .....76 C7
Factory Rd Newham E16 .....1 E5
Northfleet DA11 .....18 C1
Faesten Way DA5 .....31 E5
Fagus Cl ME5 .....68 B1
Fair Acres BR2 .....42 A4
Fair View Com Inf Sch ME8 .....69 C5
Fair View Com Jun Sch ME8 .....69 C5
Fair View Cotts TN5 .....185 A6
Fairacre Pl DA3 .....48 E6
Fairbank Ave BR6 .....57 B8
Fairbourne Heath Cotts ME17 .....119 B1
Fairbourne La ME17 .....119 C4
Fairby La DA3 .....48 E3
Fairby Rd SE12 .....11 B2
Faircrouch La TN5 .....184 B5
Fairfax Bsns Ctr ME15 .....116 F4
Fairfax Cl ME8 .....69 D5
Fairfax Gdns SE3 .....11 C6
Fairfax Ho ME15 .....116 F5
Fairfax Mews E16 .....1 B5
Fairfax Rd RM18 .....18 F6
Fairfield Ave TN2 .....159 C5
Fairfield Cl Kemsing TN15 .....77 A1
Sidcup DA15 .....12 F1
Fairfield Cres TN9 .....143 C8
Fairfield Gr SE7 .....11 D8
Fairfield Rd Bexley DA7 .....13 F5
Borough Green TN15 .....94 F8
Bromley BR1 .....28 A1
Orpington BR5 .....43 D3
Fairfield Way TN11 .....126 F5
Fairfields DA12 .....36 E3
Fairford Ave DA7 .....14 D6
Fairglen Cotts TN5 .....184 B3
Fairglen Rd TN5 .....184 B4
Fairhurst Dr ME15 .....115 B4
Fairings The TN30 .....193 B8
Fairland Ho BR2 .....42 B5
Fairlands Ct 6 SE9 .....12 A1
Fairlawn SE7 .....11 C8
Fairlawn Ave DA7 .....13 D5
Fairlawn Cl ME18 .....114 A8
Fairlawn Ct SE7 .....11 C7
Fairlead Rd ME1 .....53 D1
Fairlight Cl TN4 .....143 A2
Fairlight Cross DA3 .....49 C6
Fairlight Ct TN10 .....127 B4
Fairman's La TN12 162
Fairmead BR1 42
Fairmead Cl BR1 42
Fairmead Rd TN8 122
Fairmeadow ME14 99
Fairmile Ho BR5 44
Fairmile Rd TN2 159
Fairmont Cl DA17 3
Fairoak Cl BR5 43
Fairoak Dr SE9 12
Fairseat La Fairseat TN15 79
Stansted TN15 63
Fairthorn Rd SE7 1
Fairtrough Rd BR6 74
Fairview Erith DA8 14
Hawkhurst TN18 188
New Ash Green DA3 62
Fairview Ave ME8 69
Fairview Cl TN9 143
Fairview Cotts ME15 115
Fairview Dr Higham ME3 38
Orpington BR6 57
Fairview Gdns DA13 50
Fairview Ind PK RM13 4
Fairview Rd DA13 35
Fairview Trad Est RH8 104
Fairwater Ave DA16 13
Fairway Bexley DA6 13
Orpington BR5 .....43 C
Fairway Cl ME1 .....53 C
Fairway Ct 12 SE9 12
Fairway Dr Dartford DA2 33
Erith SE28 3
Fairway The
Bromley,Southborough BR1 42
9 Bromley,Sundridge BR1 28
Gravesend DA11 36
Rochester ME1 .....53 C
Fairways Ct 11 DA11 36
Fairways The TN4 159
Falcon Ave Bromley BR1 42
Grays RM17 .....18 C
Falcon Cl DA1 15
Falcon Gn ME20 81
Falcon Mews DA11 35
Falcons Cl TN16 .....72 D
Falconwood Ave DA16 12
Falconwood Par DA16 12
Falconwood Sta SE9 .....12 D
Falkland Pl ME5 67
Fallowfield Bean DA2 34
Chatham ME5 68
Fallowfield Cl ME14 100
Falmouth Pl TN12 .....145 C
Falstaff Cl DA1 31
Fanconi Rd ME5 .....68 B
Fancy Row ME14 .....101 C
Fane Way ME8 .....69 C
Fant La ME16 99
Fantail Cl SE28 .....3 C
Faraday Ave DA14 30
Faraday Ho Erith DA17 .....4 A
Rochester ME1 .....53 D
Faraday Lodge TN2 159
Faraday Rd Bexley DA16 13
Maidstone ME14 .....100 C
Faraday Ride TN10 .....127 D
Faraday Way
Greenwich SE18 .....1 D
Orpington BR5 44
Fareham Wlk 10 ME15 116
Faringdon Ave BR2 43
Farington Cl ME16 99
Farjeon Rd SE18,SE3 .....11 C
Farleigh Ave BR2 .....42 A
Farleigh Ct ME16 .....99 A
Farleigh Hill ME15 99
Farleigh Hill Ret Pk ME15 99
Farleigh La ME16 .....99 A
Farleigh Trad Est ME15 99
Farley Cl ME5 .....68 D
Farley La TN16 .....105 B
Farley Nursery TN16 .....105 C
Farley Rd DA12 36
Farleycroft TN16 .....89 C
Farlow Cl DA11 35
Farm Ave BR8 .....45 C
Farm Ground Cl TN9 143
Farm Hill Ave ME2 38
Farm Holt DA3 48
Farm La TN10 .....127 A
Farm Pl DA1 .....15 A
Farm Rd Chatham ME5 67
Sevenoaks TN14 .....92 C
Farm Vale DA5 .....14 B
Farmcombe Cl TN2 .....159 B
Farmcombe La TN2 .....159 B
Farmcombe Rd TN2 .....159 C
Farmcote Rd SE12 .....28 A
Farmcroft DA11 .....36 A
Farmdale Ave ME1 52
Farmdale Rd SE10 .....1 A
Farmer Cl ME17 .....118 A
Farmland Wlk BR7 .....29 B
Farmstead Dr TN8 .....122 D
Farnaby Dr TN13 .....92 A
Farnaby Rd SE9 .....11 C
Farnborough Cl ME16 .....99 C
Farnborough Comm BR6 .....57 A
Farnborough Ct 2 BR6 .....57 C
Farnborough Hill BR6 .....57 E
Farnborough Prim Sch BR6 .....57 C
Farnborough Way BR6 .....57 D
Farne Cl ME15 .....116 A
Farnham Beeches TN3 .....158 A

arnham Cl
illingham ME8 .... 70 A8
angton Green TN3 .... 158 A3
arnham La TN3 .... 158 A4
arnham Pl TN3 .... 158 A3
arnham Rd DA16 .... 13 C5
arningham Cl ME14 .... 100 C6
arningham Hill Rd DA4 .. 46 D4
arningham Road Sta
A4 .... 47 B7
arningham Wood (Nature
Reserve)* BR8,DA4 .... 46 D5
arnol Rd DA1 .... 16 A3
aro Cl BR1 .... 43 A7
arraday Cl ME1 .... 67 D8
arrance Ct TN1 .... 159 B4
arrant Cl BR6 .... 58 A3
arrants Ct BR1 .... 42 F7
arrell Ct DA2 .... 32 C5
arrier Cl Bromley BR1 .... 42 D6
Maidstone ME14 .... 100 E5
arriers Cl DA12 .... 36 F7
arriers Ct ME8 .... 70 C8
arrington Ave BR5 .... 44 B6
arrington Pl BR7 .... 29 D1
arringtons & Stratford Ho
Sch BR7 .... 29 D1
artherwell Ave ME19 .... 97 A8
artherwell Rd ME19 .... 97 A8
arthing Cl DA1 .... 15 F3
arthing Cnr ME9 .... 69 E3
arthing Hill TN5 .... 186 E1
arthing St BR6 .... 56 F2
arthingfield TN15 .... 79 A3
arthings Cotts ME14 .... 83 F1
arwell Rd DA14 .... 30 C4
arwig La BR1 .... 42 A8
ashoda Rd BR2 .... 42 D5
auchon's Cl ME14 .... 100 F3
auchon's La ME14 .... 100 F4
aversham Rd ME17 .... 120 E7
awkes Ave DA1 .... 32 F6
awkham Ave DA3 .... 49 C6
awkham CE Prim Sch
DA3 .... 48 B1
awkham Green Rd DA3 .. 62 B7
awkham Ho 10 BR5 .... 44 D1
awkham Manor Hospl
DA3 .... 48 C1
awkham Rd
Longfield DA3 .... 48 D6
West Kingsdown TN15 .... 62 A4
awley Cl ME14 .... 99 E7
ay Cl ME1 .... 53 B3
aygate Cres DA6 .... 14 A2
azan Ct TN5 .... 184 F4
earon St SE10 .... 1 A1
eatherby Cotts ME7 .... 54 F6
eatherby Inf Sch ME8 .... 55 A3
eatherby Jun Sch ME8 .... 55 A3
eatherby Rd
Gillingham,Grange ME7 .... 55 A5
Gillingham,Twydall ME8 .... 55 A3
ederation Rd SE2 .... 3 C2
eenan Highway RM18 .... 19 B6
elderland Cl ME17 .... 116 E5
elderland Dr ME17 .... 116 E5
elderland Rd ME17 .... 116 E5
eldspar Cl ME5 .... 68 A1
elhampton Rd SE9 .... 29 B5
elix Manor BR7 .... 29 E2
elixstowe Ct E16 .... 2 B5
elixstowe Rd SE2 .... 3 B3
ell Mead TN12 .... 129 F6
ellowes Way TN11 .... 126 E5
ellows Cl ME8 .... 69 B6
elltram Way SE7 .... 1 A1
elma Ho 12 SE7 .... 11 C8
elspar Cl SE18 .... 2 F1
elstead Rd BR6 .... 58 B8
elsted Rd E16 .... 1 D7
elton Cl BR5 .... 43 B3
elton Ho SE3 .... 11 C3
elton Lea DA14 .... 29 F3
en Gr DA15 .... 12 F1
en Mdw TN15 .... 78 C1
en Pond Rd TN15 .... 94 C7
endyke Rd DA17 .... 3 D3
enn Cl BR1 .... 28 A2
enn St ME3 .... 24 B4
ennel Cl ME16 .... 99 B3
ennell Cl ME1 .... 53 B3
ennell St SE18 .... 12 A8
ens Way BR8 .... 32 A2
enton Cl BR7 .... 28 F3
enwick Cl 16 SE18 .... 12 A8
eoffe Cotts TN17 .... 190 E7
erbies TN3 .... 158 A7
erbies Cl TN3 .... 158 A7
erby Ct DA15 .... 29 F4
erdinand Terr TN3 .... 171 C7
erguson Ave DA12 .... 36 C4
ern Bank DA4 .... 60 E8
ern Cl DA8 .... 15 B6
ern Ct DA7 .... 14 A3
ern Down DA13 .... 80 B8
ern Hill Pl 3 BR6 .... 57 C5
ernbank Cl ME5 .... 67 F2
erndale Bromley BR1 .... 42 C7
Royal Tunbridge Wells
TN2 .... 159 D5
Sevenoaks TN13 .... 92 C5
erndale Cl Bexley DA7 .... 13 E6
Royal Tunbridge Wells
TN2 .... 159 C4
erndale Point TN2 .... 159 C4
erndale Rd
Gillingham ME7 .... 54 E5

Ferndale Rd *continued*
Gravesend DA12 .... 36 B6
Ferndale St E6 .... 2 B7
Ferndale Way BR6 .... 57 D5
Ferndell Ave DA5 .... 31 D5
Ferndene DA3 .... 49 D6
Ferndown Ave BR6 .... 43 D1
Ferndown Cl ME7 .... 69 A5
Ferndown Rd SE9 .... 28 D8
Fernheath Way DA2 .... 31 D3
Fernhill Rd ME16 .... 99 A2
Fernhill St E16 .... 1 F5
Fernholt TN10 .... 127 C7
Fernhurst Cres TN4 .... 143 A2
Fernleigh Rise ME20 .... 82 B2
Ferns The Larkfield ME20 .. 82 B1
Platt TN15 .... 95 C7
Royal Tunbridge Wells
TN1 .... 159 C4
Fernside La TN13 .... 108 D6
Fernwood Cl BR1 .... 42 C7
Ferranti Cl SE18 .... 1 D3
Ferrier Cl ME8 .... 69 E4
Ferrier Point 8 E16 .... 1 A8
Ferringham TN4 .... 158 F4
Ferry La Rainham RM13 .... 4 E7
Wouldham ME1 .... 66 C4
Ferry La Ind Est RM13 .... 4 F8
Ferry Pl SE18 .... 2 A3
Ferry Rd Halling ME2 .... 66 B4
Tilbury RM18 .... 19 A4
Festival Ave DA3 .... 49 D6
Festival Cl Erith DA8 .... 14 F7
Sidcup DA5 .... 30 D7
Festoon Way E16 .... 1 D6
Ffinch Cl ME20 .... 98 D8
Fiddlers Cl DA9 .... 17 B3
Field Cl Bromley BR1 .... 42 C7
Chatham ME5 .... 67 E6
Field Dr TN8 .... 122 D3
Field Rd DA13,TN15 .... 63 E6
Fieldfare Rd SE28 .... 3 C6
Fielding Ave RM18 .... 19 B6
Fielding Dr ME20 .... 82 A3
Fields La ME18 .... 113 E7
Fieldside Cl BR6 .... 57 C6
Fieldway BR5 .... 43 D3
Fieldways TN18 .... 189 A1
Fieldworks Rd ME7 .... 54 A7
Fiennes Way TN13 .... 108 C8
Fiesta Dr RM9 .... 4 C8
Fife Rd E16 .... 1 A8
Fifteenpenny Fields SE9 . 12 A2
Fifth Ave RM20 .... 17 A8
Fiji Terr ME14 .... 100 A7
Filborough Way DA12 .... 37 B6
Filey Cl TN16 .... 88 B8
Filmer La TN14 .... 92 E6
Filston La TN14 .... 75 E5
Filston Rd DA8 .... 4 C1
Finch Ct Maidstone ME14 .. 99 E7
Sidcup DA14 .... 30 B5
Finch's Cross RH8 .... 121 A8
Finchale Rd SE2 .... 3 A3
Finchcocks* TN17 .... 177 A5
Finchley Cl DA1 .... 16 A1
Finchley Rd RM17 .... 18 B8
Findlay Cl ME8 .... 69 D6
Finglesham Cl BR5 .... 44 D1
Finglesham Ct ME15 .... 116 C8
Finsbury Way DA5 .... 13 F1
Fintonagh Dr ME14 .... 100 B6
Finucane Dr BR5 .... 44 C2
Fir Dene BR6 .... 57 A7
Fir Tree Cl Grays RM17 .... 18 D8
5 Orpington BR6 .... 57 F5
Staplehurst TN12 .... 149 F3
Tonbridge TN11 .... 126 E5
Fir Tree Gr Bredhurst ME7 .. 69 B1
Chatham ME5 .... 68 D1
Fir Tree Rd TN4 .... 158 F3
Firbank Cl E16 .... 1 D8
Fircroft Way TN8 .... 122 C3
Firecrest Cl DA3 .... 49 B6
Firepower (Mus)* SE18 .... 2 B3
Firethorn Cl ME7 .... 54 E6
Firmin Ave ME17 .... 116 D5
Firmin Rd DA1 .... 15 C2
Firmingers Rd BR6 .... 59 C5
Firs Cl ME20 .... 82 E1
Firs Ct TN4 .... 158 F6
Firs The Coldblow DA5 .... 31 D7
Sidcup DA15 .... 29 F5
Firside Gr DA15 .... 29 F7
First Ave Bexley DA7 .... 13 C7
Chatham ME4 .... 54 C2
Gillingham ME7 .... 54 E3
Northfleet DA11 .... 35 E7
West Thurrock RM20 .... 17 A8
First La ME17 .... 101 E2
First St TN3 .... 157 F3
Fisher Rd ME5 .... 68 B7
Fisher St
Maidstone ME14 .... 100 A6
Newham E16 .... 1 A8
Fisher's Gate Cotts TN7 . 170 A1
Fisher's Way DA17 .... 4 C5
Fishermans Wlk SE28 .... 2 E4
Fishermen's Hill DA11 .... 18 B2
Fishers Cl TN12 .... 149 F5
Fishers Rd TN12 .... 149 F5
Fishguard Way E16 .... 2 B5
Fishponds Rd BR2 .... 56 D5
Fitzroy Ct DA1 .... 33 B7
Fitzthorold Ho ME7 .... 54 E7
Fitzwilliam Mews E16 .... 1 A5
Fitzwilliam Rd ME14 .... 100 F5

Five Acre Wood Sch
ME15 .... 116 B7
Five Arches Bsns Est
DA14 .... 30 D3
Five Bells La 5 ME1 .... 53 D4
Five Elms Rd BR2 .... 56 C7
Five Fields La TN8 .... 123 B4
Five Oak Green Rd
Capel TN11,TN12 .... 144 D6
Tonbridge TN11 .... 143 F7
Five Oak La TN12 .... 149 B1
Five Oaks Mews BR1 .... 28 A5
Five Ways TN1 .... 159 B4
Five Ways Ct ME4 .... 54 A4
Five Wents BR8 .... 46 A7
Fiveash Rd DA11 .... 35 F8
Fiveways L Ctr ME4 .... 54 A4
Flack Gdns ME3 .... 40 E5
Flamborough Cl TN16 .... 88 B8
Flamingo Cl ME5 .... 68 A7
Flamsteed Rd SE7 .... 1 E1
Flats The Gravesend DA12 .. 36 E8
Swanscombe DA9 .... 17 C2
Flaxman Ct
13 Chatham ME7 .... 54 A6
Erith DA17 .... 4 A1
Flaxman Dr ME16 .... 99 C6
Flaxmore Ct DA7 .... 14 B4
Flaxmore Pl TN4 .... 143 A2
Flaxton Rd SE18 .... 12 E7
Fleet Ave DA2 .... 33 C7
Fleet Dale Par DA2 .... 33 C7
Fleet Ho DA13 .... 35 B2
Fleet Rd Dartford DA2 .... 33 C7
Northfleet DA11 .... 35 C6
Rochester ME1 .... 53 D1
Fleet Terr DA11 .... 35 D7
Fleetdown Inf Sch DA2 .. 33 C6
Fleetdown Jun Sch DA2 .. 33 C6
Fleetwood Cl E16 .... 1 D8
Fleetwood Ct
1 Newham E6 .... 1 F8
Orpington BR6 .... 57 A6
Fleming Gdns RM18 .... 19 C6
Fleming Ho SE2 .... 3 C1
Fleming Way Erith SE28 .... 3 D6
Tonbridge TN10 .... 127 E7
Fletcher Cl E6 .... 2 B6
Fletcher Rd TN12 .... 149 E3
Fletchers Cl BR2 .... 42 B5
Fletching Rd SE7 .... 11 D8
Flimwell Cl TN5 .... 187 D4
Flint Cl 8 BR6 .... 57 F4
Flint Down Cl BR5 .... 44 A8
Flint Gn ME5 .... 68 C3
Flint La
Woodside Green ME17 .... 120 C8
Woodside Green ME17 .... 120 D8
Flint St RM20 .... 17 B8
Flintmill Cres SE3,SE9 .... 11 E5
Floathaven Cl SE28 .... 3 A5
Floats The TN13 .... 91 E6
Flood Hatch ME15 .... 99 D2
Flora St DA17 .... 3 F1
Florance La TN3 .... 171 B6
Florence Cl RM17,RM20 .... 17 E8
Florence Cotts 5 TN8 .. 122 C1
Florence Farm Mobile Home
Pk TN15 .... 61 D4
Florence Ho SE18 .... 11 F6
Florence Rd
4 Bromley BR1 .... 42 A8
Erith DA17,SE2 .... 3 C2
Maidstone ME16 .... 99 E3
Florence St 3 ME2 .... 53 B8
Florin Dr ME1 .... 53 B4
Flower Rise ME14 .... 99 F7
Flowerfield TN14 .... 75 F2
Flowerhill Way DA13 .... 35 E1
Floyd Cl TN4 .... 159 A7
Floyd Rd SE7 .... 1 C1
Flume End ME15 .... 99 D2
Flyers Way The TN16 .... 89 D1
Foalhurst Cl TN10 .... 127 E4
Foley Ct DA1 .... 33 B7
Foley Rd TN16 .... 72 D1
Foley St ME14 .... 100 A5
Folkstone Ho 4 ME15 .... 116 F6
Fontwell Cl ME15 .... 116 F6
Fontwell Dr BR2 .... 43 A4
Foord Almshouses ME1 .. 53 B3
Foord Cl DA2 .... 33 E6
Foord Rd ME17 .... 120 D5
Foord St ME1 .... 53 D4
Footbury Hill Rd BR6 .... 44 A2
Foots Cray High St DA14 . 30 D2
Foots Cray La DA14 .... 30 C7
Footscray Rd SE9 .... 29 C7
Force Green Farm Cotts
TN16 .... 89 E3
Force Green La TN16 .... 89 E4
Ford Ho 2 SE18 .... 2 B1
Ford La Trottiscliffe ME19 .. 80 A4
Wrotham Heath TN15,ME19 . 79 F2
Ford Rd DA11 .... 18 B2
Fordcombe CE Prim Sch
TN3 .... 157 B5
Fordcombe Cl ME15 .... 116 F7
Fordcombe Rd
Fordcombe TN3 .... 157 C4
Penshurst TN11 .... 141 A3
Fordcroft Rd BR5 .... 44 B4
Forde Ave BR1 .... 42 C6
Fordgate Bsns Pk DA17 .... 4 C4
Fordingbridge Cl ME16 .... 99 B5
Fords Park Rd E16 .... 1 A7
Fordwich Cl
Maidstone ME16 .... 99 B7

Fordwich Cl *continued*
Orpington BR6 .... 43 F2
Fordwich Dr ME2 .... 39 A2
Fordwich Gn ME8 .... 55 C3
Foreland St SE18 .... 2 D2
Foreman Ctr TN27 .... 151 D5
Foreman's Wlk TN27 .... 151 D5
Foremans Barn Rd
ME15 .... 114 F3
Forest Cl BR7 .... 43 A8
Forest Dene TN2 .... 159 C1
Forest Dr Chatham ME5 .... 67 F2
Orpington BR2 .... 56 E6
Forest Gr TN10 .... 127 C5
Forest Hill ME15 .... 99 F1
Forest Lawns BR1 .... 42 C8
Forest Rd Erith DA8 .... 15 A6
Paddock Wood TN12 .... 146 A6
Royal Tunbridge Wells
TN2 .... 159 C1
Forest Ridge BR2 .... 56 F6
Forest Way Eltham DA15 .. 29 D8
Kings Hill ME19 .... 97 A3
Orpington BR5 .... 43 F4
Pembury TN2 .... 160 D8
Royal Tunbridge Wells
TN2 .... 159 D1
Forestdale Rd ME5 .... 84 A8
Foresters Cl ME5 .... 67 F2
Foresters Cres DA7 .... 14 B3
Foresters Homes The
DA7 .... 14 B3
Forge Cl
Five Oak Green TN12 .... 145 B7
Hayes BR2 .... 42 A1
Penshurst TN11 .... 141 B4
Forge Cotts Flimwell TN5 . 187 C3
Nettlestead Green ME18 .. 113 C2
Wrotham Heath TN15 .... 79 E1
Forge Croft TN8 .... 122 D1
Forge La Benover ME18 .. 131 B4
Boxley ME14 .... 84 C2
Bredhurst ME7 .... 69 A1
East Farleigh ME15 .... 115 C7
Egerton Forstal TN27 .... 137 C1
Gillingham ME7 .... 54 E7
Gravesend DA12 .... 36 F6
Headcorn TN27 .... 151 D5
High Halstow ME23 .... 23 E3
Higham ME3 .... 38 C3
Horton Kirby DA4 .... 47 C5
Leeds ME17 .... 117 F7
Maidstone ME14 .... 101 C4
Rabbit's Cross ME17,
TN12 .... 133 F3
Shorne DA12 .... 37 E3
West Kingsdown TN15 .... 62 A1
West Peckham ME18 .... 112 A6
Forge Mdw ME17 .... 119 D6
Forge Mdws TN27 .... 151 D5
Forge Meads TN30 .... 199 E3
Forge Pl DA12 .... 36 F7
Forge Rd Cobbarn TN3 .... 171 C2
Royal Tunbridge Wells
TN4 .... 143 A1
Forge Sq TN11 .... 125 F2
Forge The TN12 .... 145 B7
Forge View TN15 .... 109 B5
Forge Way
Paddock Wood TN12 .... 146 A7
Shoreham TN14 .... 75 F8
Forgefield TN16 .... 72 D3
Forgefield Cotts TN18 .... 196 A4
Forgefield Ct BR5 .... 44 C4
Formation The E16 .... 2 B4
Formby Rd ME2 .... 66 A7
Formby Terr ME2 .... 66 A6
Forsham La ME17 .... 134 C5
Forson Cl TN30 .... 193 B8
Forstal Cl BR2 .... 42 A6
Forstal Cotts ME20 .... 83 B2
Forstal La ME17 .... 115 D4
Forstal Rd
Egerton Forstal TN27 .... 137 C1
Forstal ME20 .... 83 C2
Forstal The Cobbarn TN3 .. 171 F3
Hadlow TN11 .... 128 F8
Pembury TN2 .... 160 E8
Forstall TN3 .... 158 A4
Forstall The TN11 .... 126 A2
Forsters ME17 .... 117 E4
Forsyth Cl ME19 .... 82 A1
Forsyth Ct 7 ME7 .... 54 C7
Fort Amherst Heritage Pk &
Caverns* ME4 .... 53 F5
Fort Luton (Mus)* ME4 .. 54 A1
Fort Pitt Gram Sch ME4 .. 53 E4
Fort Pitt Hill ME1,ME4 .... 53 E4
Fort Pitt St ME4 .... 53 E3
Fort Rd
Badgers Mount TN14 .... 75 C4
Tilbury RM18 .... 19 C5
Fort St Newham E16 .... 1 B5
Rochester ME1 .... 53 D4
Fortis Cl E16 .... 1 C7
Fortrye Cl DA11 .... 35 E6
Fortuna Cl DA3 .... 48 F5
Fortune Way ME18 .... 97 B3
Fortune Wlk 7 SE28 .... 2 D3
Forty Acre La E16 .... 1 A8
Forward Way ME1 .... 67 C6
Fossdene Prim Sch SE7 .. 1 B1
Fossdene Rd SE7 .... 1 B1
Fosse Bank Cl TN9 .... 143 A7
Fosse Bank New Sch
TN11 .... 126 E7
Fosse Rd TN9 .... 127 B2
Fossett Lodge DA7 .... 14 C6

Fossington Rd DA17 .... 3 D2
Fosten La TN27 .... 181 E7
Foster Clark Est ME15 .. 100 B2
Foster Clarke Dr ME17 .. 116 D5
Foster St ME15 .... 100 A3
Fosters Cl BR7 .... 28 F3
Fosters Mews DA3 .... 48 E7
Fosters Old Sch DA16 .... 13 B5
Fosters Prim Sch DA16 .. 13 C4
Fostington Way ME5 .... 67 F1
Foulds Cl ME8 .... 69 B5
Founder Cl E6 .... 2 B7
Foundry Wharf ME1 .... 53 E4
Fountain Ct Eynsford DA4 .. 60 E8
Sidcup DA15 .... 13 B1
Fountain La ME16 .... 99 A2
Fountain Rd ME2 .... 38 E1
Fountain Wlk DA11 .... 18 F1
Four Acres ME19 .... 98 B5
Four Elms Hill ME3 .... 39 E4
Four Elms Prim Sch
TN8 .... 123 B5
Four Elms Rd TN8 .... 122 D4
Four Elms Rdbt ME3 .... 39 E3
Four Oaks Rd TN12,TN27 . 150 E7
Four Trees TN8 .... 122 C3
Four Wents
Langley Heath ME17 .... 117 E3
Maidstone ME17 .... 116 F2
Fouracre Cotts ME9 .... 70 E6
Fourth Ave Gillingham ME7 . 54 E4
West Thurrock RM20 .... 17 A8
Fourwents Rd ME3 .... 40 D7
Fowey Cl ME5 .... 68 C5
Fowler Cl Gillingham ME8 .. 69 C3
Sidcup DA14 .... 30 E3
Fox Cl Newham E16 .... 1 A8
Orpington BR6 .... 58 A5
Fox Hill BR2 .... 56 C5
Fox Hollow Cl 2 SE18 .... 2 E1
Fox Hollow Dr DA7 .... 13 D4
Fox House Rd DA17 .... 4 B1
Fox in the Wood TN5 .... 184 C6
Fox La BR2 .... 56 C5
Fox Lea TN15 .... 94 F7
Fox Manor Way RM20 .... 17 B8
Fox St ME7 .... 54 C6
Foxburrow Cl ME8 .... 69 D5
Foxbury DA3 .... 62 E7
Foxbury Ave BR7 .... 29 D2
Foxbury Cl Bromley BR1 .. 28 B2
Orpington BR6 .... 58 A5
Foxbury Dr BR6 .... 58 A4
Foxbury Rd BR1 .... 28 B2
Foxbury Wlk DA11 .... 35 D4
Foxbush TN11 .... 126 C6
Foxcroft Rd SE18 .... 12 B6
Foxden Dr ME15 .... 100 F1
Foxearth Cl TN16 .... 72 E1
Foxendown La DA13 .... 50 B1
Foxes Dale SE3 .... 11 A4
Foxfield Prim Sch SE18 .... 2 C1
Foxfield Rd BR6 .... 57 D8
Foxglove Cl
9 Marlpit Hill TN8 .... 122 D3
Sidcup DA15 .... 13 A1
Foxglove Cres ME5 .... 67 E4
Foxglove Rise ME14 .... 99 E7
Foxgloves The TN12 .... 146 B5
Foxgrove Path SE28 .... 2 E5
Foxhole La
Four Throws TN18 .... 195 D8
Hawkhurst TN18 .... 189 E1
Matfield TN12 .... 161 C8
Wadhurst TN5 .... 185 B4
Foxhole Rd SE9 .... 11 E2
Foxhome Cl BR7 .... 29 A2
Foxtail Cl ME4 .... 40 B2
Foxton Ho E16 .... 2 A4
Foxton Rd RM20 .... 17 D8
Foxwood Gr
Northfleet DA11 .... 35 E7
Pratt's Bottom BR6 .... 58 C1
Foxwood Rd DA2 .... 34 B5
Foxwood Way DA3 .... 49 D7
Framley Rd TN10 .... 127 F5
Framlingham Cres SE9 .... 28 F4
Frances St SE18 .... 1 F2
Francis Ave DA7 .... 14 A5
Francis Ct 7 DA8 .... 4 E1
Francis Dr ME5 .... 68 A2
Francis La ME15 .... 116 F5
Francis Rd Dartford DA1 .. 15 D2
Orpington BR5 .... 44 D6
Tonbridge TN11 .... 126 D6
Frank Burton Cl 5 SE7 .... 1 B1
Frank Godley Ct DA14 .... 30 B3
Frank Woolley Rd TN10 . 127 F5
Frank's Hollow Rd TN3 .. 142 C2
Frankapps Cl ME9 .... 71 B6
Frankfield Rise TN2 .... 159 A1
Franklin Dr ME14 .... 100 D4
Franklin Pas SE9 .... 11 E4
Franklin Rd Bexley DA7 .... 13 E6
Gillingham ME7 .... 54 D5
Gravesend DA12 .... 36 D3
Maypole DA2 .... 31 E6
Franklins Cotts ME15 .... 115 C5
Franks Ct ME8 .... 55 B2
Franks La DA4 .... 47 B4
Frankswood Ave BR5 .... 43 C4
Frant CE Prim Sch TN3 .. 173 B4
Frant Cotts TN5 .... 186 E1
Frant Ct TN3 .... 173 B3
Frant Field TN8 .... 122 C1

Frant Green Rd TN3 ... 173 B3
Frant Rd TN2,TN3 ... 173 A7
Frant Sta TN3 ... 173 F5
Fraser Cl Coldblow DA5 ... 31 C7
4 Newham E6 ... 1 E7
Fraser Ho 3 SE18 ... 2 B2
Fraser Rd DA8 ... 4 D1
Frederick Andrews Ct
RM17 ... 18 D8
Frederick Ho 4 SE18 ... 1 E3
Frederick Pl SE18 ... 2 B1
Frederick Rd ME7 ... 54 C4
Free Heath Rd TN3,TN5 ... 175 C3
Freehold The
East Peckham TN12 ... 129 F6
Hadlow TN11 ... 111 D1
Freeland Ct 24 DA14 ... 30 A5
Freeland Way DA8 ... 15 A6
Freelands Gr BR1 ... 42 B8
Freelands Rd Bromley BR1 ... 42 B8
Snodland ME6 ... 81 F8
Freeman Gdns ME4 ... 53 F2
Freeman Rd DA12 ... 36 E5
Freeman Way ME15 ... 116 E7
Freemasons Rd E16 ... 1 B7
Freesia Cl Gillingham ME7 ... 54 F6
Orpington BR6 ... 57 F5
Freight La TN17 ... 179 C3
Fremantle Ho RM18 ... 18 F6
Fremantle Rd DA17 ... 4 A2
Fremlin Cl TN4 ... 158 B4
Fremlins Rd ME14 ... 101 C4
Frensham Rd
Rolvenden TN17 ... 192 A1
Sidcup SE9 ... 29 D6
Frensham Wlk ME5 ... 67 F1
Freshland Rd ME16 ... 99 B4
Freshwater Rd ME5 ... 68 B7
Freta Rd DA6 ... 13 F2
Frewing Cl BR7 ... 29 A3
Friar Rd BR5 ... 44 A4
Friars Ave ME5 ... 67 F2
Friars Mews SE9 ... 12 A2
Friars Pk ME20 ... 82 E2
Friars The* ME20 ... 82 E2
Friars Way TN2 ... 159 D6
Friars Wlk SE2 ... 3 D1
Friary Pl 3 ME2 ... 53 B7
Friary Prec ME2 ... 53 B7
Friday Rd DA8 ... 4 D1
Friday St ME17 ... 135 B6
Friezland Rd TN4 ... 158 D1
Friezley La TN17 ... 165 C1
Frimley Ct DA14 ... 30 C3
Frindsbury Hill ME2 ... 39 C1
Frindsbury Rd ME2 ... 53 B8
Frinstead Gr BR5 ... 44 D5
Frinstead Wlk ME16 ... 99 B7
Frinsted Cl ME8 ... 55 C3
Frinsted Rd DA8 ... 14 D7
Frinton Rd DA14 ... 30 E6
Friston Way ME1 ... 67 D8
Friswell Pl 1 DA6 ... 14 A3
Frithwood Cl ME15 ... 100 F1
Frittenden CE Prim Sch
TN17 ... 166 E6
Frittenden Rd
Rochester ME2 ... 39 D2
Staplehurst TN12 ... 150 B2
Frobisher Ct 3 DA1 ... 15 D1
Frobisher Gdns ME1 ... 53 C2
Frobisher Rd Erith DA8 ... 15 A7
Newham E6 ... 2 A7
Frobisher Way
Gravesend DA12 ... 36 E3
Swanscombe DA9 ... 17 B3
Frog Hole La TN8,TN16 ... 105 D2
Frog La Rainham RM13 ... 4 D8
Royal Tunbridge Wells
TN1 ... 159 A2
West Malling ME19 ... 97 C8
Frog's La TN17 ... 191 E1
Frogmore Wlk ME17 ... 120 C5
Frognal Ave DA14 ... 30 A2
Frognal Cnr BR7 ... 29 F2
Frognal Pl DA14 ... 30 A3
Frogs Hole La TN17,
TN27 ... 181 E3
Froissart Rd SE9 ... 11 E2
Fromandez Dr TN12 ... 162 F5
Frome Ct TN10 ... 127 B5
Frost Cres ME5 ... 68 A7
Froyle Cl ME16 ... 99 C6
Fruitfields TN5 ... 187 C3
Fry Cl ME3 ... 27 A6
Fry's Cotts ME3 ... 25 C4
Frythe Cl TN17 ... 179 D4
Frythe Cres TN17 ... 179 D4
Frythe Way TN17 ... 179 D4
Frythe Wlk TN17 ... 179 D4
Fuchsia St SE2 ... 3 B1
Fuggles Cl TN12 ... 145 E6
Fuggles Ct TN17 ... 190 D6
Fulbert Dr ME14 ... 100 F5
Fuller Cl Durgates TN5 ... 184 E5
Orpington BR6 ... 57 F5
Fullers Cl ME14 ... 101 A4
Fullers Hill 7 TN16 ... 89 D1
Fulmar Rd ME2 ... 52 D6
Fulmer Rd E16 ... 1 D8
Fulthorp Rd SE3 ... 11 A5
Fulwich Rd DA1 ... 15 F1
Furfield Cl ME17 ... 116 E5
Furnace Ave TN3 ... 176 A3
Furnace La
Hook Green TN3 ... 175 E4
Horsmonden TN12 ... 162 F7
Furner Cl DA1 ... 14 F4
Furness Sch BR8 ... 31 F2
Furnival Ct TN2 ... 172 F8
Furrell's Rd ME1 ... 53 D5
Further Field TN12 ... 149 E5
Furze Bank TN8 ... 123 B5
Furzefield Ave TN3 ... 158 A8
Furzefield Cl BR7 ... 29 B2
Furzefield Rd SE3 ... 11 B7
Furzehill Sq BR5 ... 44 B5
Fyfe Way BR1 ... 42 A7

G

Gable Cl DA1 ... 15 A2
Gables Cl SE12 ... 28 A7
Gables The
11 Bromley BR1 ... 28 B1
New Barn DA3 ... 49 C6
Gabriel Gdns DA12 ... 36 E3
Gabriel Spring Road (East)
DA3 ... 61 F8
Gabriel's Hill ME15 ... 100 A4
Gabrielspring Rd DA3 ... 61 D8
Gads Hill ME7 ... 54 F6
Gads Hill Sch ME3 ... 38 C2
Gadsby La TN26 ... 169 F3
Gadwall Cl E16 ... 1 B7
Gadwall Way SE28 ... 2 D4
Gafford's Bridge Cotts
TN12 ... 147 C4
Gagetown Terr 1 ME14 ... 99 F7
Gainsborough Ave
Dartford DA1 ... 15 C2
Tilbury RM18 ... 19 B6
Gainsborough Cl ME8 ... 69 D6
Gainsborough Ct 3 BR2 ... 42 C5
Gainsborough Dr
Maidstone ME16 ... 99 B4
Northfleet DA11 ... 35 D5
Gainsborough Gdns
TN10 ... 127 E5
Gainsborough Ho ME1 ... 53 D5
Gainsborough Sq DA7 ... 13 D4
Gaitskell Rd SE9 ... 29 C7
Galahad Ave ME2 ... 52 E6
Galahad Rd BR1 ... 28 A4
Galena Cl ME5 ... 68 A1
Galena Ho 4 SE18 ... 2 F1
Gallants La ME15 ... 114 F6
Galleon Bvd DA2 ... 16 D3
Galleon Cl Erith DA8 ... 4 D2
Rochester ME1 ... 67 C8
Galleon Mews 3 DA11 ... 35 E8
Galleon Way ME2 ... 39 F3
Galley Hill Rd DA11,DA10 ... 17 F2
Galley Hill Trad Est DA10 ... 17 E2
Gallions Mount Prim Sch
SE18 ... 2 F1
Gallions Prim Sch E6 ... 2 B7
Gallions Rd SE7 ... 1 B2
Gallions Reach Sh Pk E6 ... 2 C8
Gallions Reach Sta E6 ... 2 B6
Gallions View Rd SE28 ... 2 E4
Gallon Cl SE7 ... 1 C2
Gallops The DA13 ... 79 F7
Gallosson Rd SE18 ... 2 E2
Galloway Dr DA1 ... 31 E8
Gallows Wood DA3 ... 62 A6
Gallus Sq SE3 ... 11 B4
Galsworthy Cl SE28 ... 3 B5
Galsworthy Cres SE3 ... 11 C6
Galsworthy Rd RM18 ... 19 C6
Galton Ho SE18 ... 11 F6
Games Ho 7 SE7 ... 11 C8
Gamma Rd ME3 ... 41 D7
Gandy's La ME17 ... 116 C2
Garden Ave DA7 ... 14 A4
Garden Cl Lewisham SE12 ... 28 B5
Maidstone ME15 ... 116 E7
Staplehurst TN12 ... 149 F1
Toy's Hill TN16 ... 106 C3
Garden Cotts Leigh TN11 ... 126 A2
Orpington BR5 ... 44 C7
Garden Ct 10 Eltham SE9 ... 12 A1
Sevenoaks TN13 ... 92 D5
Wouldham ME1 ... 66 C5
Garden Ho 9 TN1 ... 159 B4
Garden La BR1 ... 28 B2
Garden of England Pk
(Mobile Home Pk)
ME17 ... 119 B7
Garden Pl DA2 ... 32 D5
Garden Rd Bromley BR1 ... 28 B2
Royal Tunbridge Wells
TN1 ... 159 B4
Sevenoaks TN13 ... 92 D5
Tonbridge TN9 ... 127 D2
Garden Row DA11 ... 35 F5
Garden St Chatham ME7 ... 54 A6
Royal Tunbridge Wells
TN1 ... 159 B4
Garden Terr TN15 ... 93 A6
Garden Way ME19 ... 96 F2
Gardeners Cl SE9 ... 28 E5
Gardenia Cl ME2 ... 39 B2
Gardens The ME17 ... 115 C3
Gardiner Cl BR5 ... 44 C7
Gardiner Ho SE18 ... 11 E7
Gardiner St ME7 ... 54 C6
Gardyne Mews 12 TN9 ... 143 B8
Gareth Gr BR1 ... 28 A4
Garfield Rd ME7 ... 54 D6
Garganey Wlk SE28 ... 3 D6
Gargery Cl DA12 ... 36 F7
Garibaldi St SE18 ... 2 E2
Garland Rd SE18 ... 12 D7
Garlands TN11 ... 126 D8
Garlinge Rd TN4 ... 143 A1
Garner Ct RM18 ... 18 F5
Garner Dr ME19 ... 82 A1
Garnet Wlk 9 E6 ... 1 E8
Garnett Cl SE9 ... 11 F4
Garrard Cl Bexley DA7 ... 14 A4
Chislehurst BR7 ... 29 B3
Garrick Cl TN10 ... 127 E7
Garrick Dr SE28 ... 2 D3
Garrick St 18 DA11 ... 19 B1
Garrington Cl ME14 ... 100 C6
Garrison Cl SE18 ... 12 A7
Garrison Rd ME12 ... 27 F3
Garrolds Cl BR8 ... 45 D7
Garrow DA3 ... 49 B6
Garside Cl SE28 ... 2 D3
Garth Rd TN13 ... 108 C7
Gartly Cotts DA1 ... 15 C1
Garvary Rd E16 ... 1 B7
Garvock Dr TN13 ... 92 A1
Gas House Rd ME1 ... 53 C6
Gascoyne Cl ME15 ... 101 B2
Gascoyne Dr DA1 ... 14 F4
Gasoline Alley TN15 ... 79 D2
Gasson Rd DA10 ... 17 E1
Gassons Rd ME6 ... 81 E8
Gatcombe Cl
Chatham ME5 ... 68 A5
Maidstone ME16 ... 99 B5
Gatcombe Rd E16 ... 1 A5
Gate Farm Rd TN3,TN11 ... 142 C4
Gate House Cotts SE12 ... 28 B6
Gateacre Ct 14 DA14 ... 30 B4
Gatefield Cotts TN17 ... 191 F4
Gatehouse Farm Cotts
TN3 ... 142 C4
Gatekeeper Chase ME8 ... 69 F8
Gates Green Rd BR2,BR4 ... 56 A6
Gateway Par DA12 ... 36 F4
Gateway Prim Sch The
DA2 ... 16 B1
Gatland La ME16 ... 99 B2
Gatling Rd SE2 ... 3 A1
Gattons Way DA14 ... 30 F4
Gatwick Farm Cotts
RH19 ... 154 A4
Gatwick Rd DA12 ... 36 B6
Gault Cl ME15 ... 101 A2
Gautrey Sq 5 E6 ... 1 F7
Gavestone Cres SE12 ... 28 B8
Gavestone Rd SE12 ... 28 B8
Gavestone Terr SE12 ... 28 B8
Gavin Ho SE18 ... 2 E2
Gayhurst Cl ME8 ... 69 D6
Gaylor Rd RM18 ... 18 F6
Gayton Rd SE2 ... 3 C3
Gaza Trad Est TN11 ... 125 D7
Gazelle Glade DA12 ... 36 F3
Gean Cl ME5 ... 84 A8
Geddes Pl 3 DA6 ... 14 A3
Gedge's Hill TN12 ... 145 F3
Geffery's Ct SE9 ... 28 E5
General Gordon Pl 2
SE18 ... 2 B2
Genesta Glade DA12 ... 37 A3
Genesta Rd SE18 ... 12 C8
Geneva Ave ME8 ... 55 A2
Gentian Cl
4 Chatham ME5 ... 67 E4
Maidstone ME14 ... 100 E5
George Akass Ho 3 SE18 ... 2 C1
George Crooks Ho 7
RM17 ... 18 B8
George La Hayes BR2 ... 42 B1
Leeds ME17 ... 118 B7
Rochester ME1 ... 53 C6
George Marsham Ho
ME15 ... 115 F3
George St
Chainhurst ME15 ... 132 A7
Grays RM17 ... 18 A8
Maidstone ME15 ... 100 A3
Royal Tunbridge Wells
TN2 ... 159 C3
Sparrow's Green TN5 ... 184 F5
Staplehurst TN12 ... 149 E6
Tonbridge TN9 ... 143 B8
George Summers Cl ME2 ... 53 E8
George's Rd TN16 ... 88 D7
Georges Cl BR5 ... 44 C6
Georgia Pl TN2 ... 159 C4
Georgian Cl BR2 ... 42 B1
Georgian Dr ME17 ... 115 D3
Georgian Way ME8 ... 69 C4
Geraint Rd BR1 ... 28 A4
Gerald Ave ME4 ... 53 F2
Gerald Rd DA12 ... 36 E8
Gerda Rd SE9 ... 29 C6
Gerdview Dr DA2 ... 32 C4
Gerrard Ave ME1 ... 67 E8
Gerrard Ho 4 BR2 ... 42 C5
Gertrude Rd DA17 ... 4 A2
Gibbet La TN12 ... 162 F6
Gibbetts TN3 ... 157 F3
Gibbs Hill Headcorn TN27 ... 151 E5
Nettlestead ME18 ... 113 B5
Gibraltar Ave ME7 ... 54 B7
Gibraltar Hill ME4 ... 53 F4
Gibraltar La ME14 ... 99 F8
Gibson Cl DA11 ... 35 F5
Gibson Dr ME19 ... 96 F4
Gibson Ho ME3 ... 39 F6
Gidd's Pond Cotts ME14 ... 100 E6
Giddyhorn La ME16 ... 99 C5
Gideon Cl DA17 ... 4 B2
Gifford Cl ME8 ... 55 C3
Giggs Hill BR5 ... 44 A8
Gighill Rd ME20 ... 81 F4
Gilbert Cl Gillingham ME7 ... 69 A5
Swanscombe DA10 ... 17 D1
Woolwich SE18 ... 11 F6
Gilbert Rd Bromley BR1 ... 28 A1
Erith DA17 ... 4 A3
Gilbert Terr 2 ME14 ... 99 F7
Gilbourne Rd SE18 ... 12 F8
Gilchrist Cotts TN14 ... 108 C2
Gildenhill Rd BR8 ... 32 C1
Gildersome St SE18 ... 12 A8
Giles Field DA12 ... 36 F7
Gill Ave Newham E16 ... 1 A7
Rochester ME2 ... 39 D2
Gill Cres DA11 ... 35 F5
Gill Ct SE18 ... 2 C2
Gill The TN2 ... 160 E8
Gill's Rd
Green Street Green DA2 ... 34 B1
Sutton at H DA4 ... 47 F8
Gillan Ct 1 SE12 ... 28 B5
Gilletts La ME19 ... 98 A6
Gillies Ct DA14 ... 29 E4
Gillies Rd TN15 ... 61 E5
Gillingham Coll The ME7 ... 54 F4
Gillingham Gate ME7 ... 54 C8
Gillingham Gate Rd ME7 ... 54 C8
Gillingham Gn ME7 ... 54 E6
Gillingham Rd ME7 ... 54 D5
Gillingham Sta ME7 ... 54 D5
Gillmans Rd BR5 ... 44 B1
Gilroy Way BR5 ... 44 B2
Gimble Way TN2 ... 144 D1
Gingerbread La TN18 ... 187 F2
Ginsbury Cl ME2 ... 53 E6
Gipps Cross La TN3 ... 157 F3
Gipsy La RM17 ... 18 C8
Gipsy Rd DA16 ... 13 D5
Giralda Cl E16 ... 1 D8
Glade Bsns Ctr The RM20 ... 16 F8
Glade The Bromley BR1 ... 42 D7
Chatham ME5 ... 68 A2
Greenwich SE7 ... 11 C7
Sevenoaks TN13 ... 92 B4
Tonbridge TN10 ... 127 E7
Glades Sh Ctr The BR1 ... 42 A7
Glades The DA12 ... 36 D2
Gladeswood Rd DA17 ... 4 B2
Gladstone Rd
Chatham ME4 ... 53 E2
Dartford DA1 ... 15 F1
Maidstone ME14 ... 100 A6
Orpington BR6 ... 57 C5
Rusthall TN4 ... 158 B4
Tonbridge TN9 ... 127 B1
Gladwell Rd BR1 ... 28 A2
Gladwyn Cl ME8 ... 69 D4
Glamford Rd ME2 ... 52 D5
Glamis Cl ME5 ... 68 A5
Glanfield Ct TN1 ... 159 C5
Glanville Rd Bromley BR2 ... 42 B6
Gillingham ME7 ... 54 D5
Rochester ME2 ... 53 A8
Glasbrook Rd SE9 ... 28 D8
Glasgow Ho 8 ME15 ... 116 E7
Glass Yd SE18 ... 2 A3
Glassenbury Rd TN17 ... 178 E4
Glassmill La BR2 ... 42 A7
Glastonbury Cl BR5 ... 44 C1
Gleaming Wood Dr ME5 ... 84 D8
Gleaners Cl ME14 ... 100 E4
Gleanings Mews ME1 ... 53 C5
Glebe Cl TN27 ... 153 B2
Glebe Cotts TN16 ... 90 B4
Glebe Gdns ME17 ... 120 E5
Glebe Ho 7 SE18 ... 2 A2
Glebe House Dr BR2 ... 42 B1
Glebe La Maidstone ME16 ... 99 A1
Sevenoaks TN13 ... 92 B1
Glebe Mdw ME18 ... 113 E7
Glebe Pl DA4 ... 47 C5
Glebe Rd Bromley BR1 ... 42 A8
Gillingham ME7 ... 54 E3
Northfleet DA11 ... 35 F7
Sevenoaks Weald TN14 ... 108 B3
Glebe The
Bidborough TN3 ... 142 D3
Chislehurst BR7 ... 43 C8
Cuxton ME2 ... 52 C2
Pembury TN2 ... 160 D8
Penshurst TN11 ... 141 A3
Glebe Way DA8 ... 14 E8
Glebefield The TN13 ... 91 F4
Glebeland TN27 ... 137 F4
Glebelands
Bidborough TN3 ... 142 C3
Biddenden TN27 ... 167 F1
Crayford DA1 ... 14 F3
Penshurst TN11 ... 141 A3
Gleeson Dr BR6 ... 57 F6
Glen Ct Lewisham SE12 ... 28 A8
Sidcup DA14 ... 30 A4
Glen Dunlop Ho The
TN13 ... 92 C5
Glen Ho 6 E16 ... 2 A5
Glen The BR6 ... 57 A7
Glen View DA12 ... 36 C7
Glen View Rd BR1 ... 42 D7
Glenalvon Way 7 SE18 ... 1 E2
Glenbarr Cl SE9 ... 12 B4
Glencairne Cl E16 ... 1 D8
Glencoe Jun Sch ME4 ... 54 A2
Glencoe Rd ME4 ... 54 A2
Glendale BR8 ... 45 F4
Glendale Cl SE9 ... 12 A4
Glendale Ct TN2 ... 159 D
Glendale Rd Erith DA8 ... 4 C
Northfleet DA11 ... 35 E
Glendale Way SE28 ... 3
Glendower Cres BR6 ... 44 A
Glendown Rd SE2 ... 3 A
Gleneagles Cl BR6 ... 43 D
Gleneagles Ct ME5 ... 67 F
Gleneagles Dr ME15 ... 100 A
Gleneagles Gn 1 BR6 ... 43 D
Glenesk Rd SE9 ... 12 E
Glengall Rd DA7 ... 13 E
Glenhead Cl SE9 ... 12 E
Glenhouse Rd SE9 ... 12 A
Glenhurst Ave DA5 ... 30
Glenister St E16 ... 2 A
Glenlea Rd SE9 ... 12 A
Glenleigh Rd ME18 ... 113 D
Glenluce Rd SE3 ... 11 A
Glenlyon Rd SE9 ... 12 A
Glenmore Pk TN2 ... 172 F
Glenmore Rd DA16 ... 12 F
Glenmount Path 1 SE18 ... 2 C
Glenrose Ct DA14 ... 30 B
Glenshiel Rd SE9 ... 12 A
Glentrammon Ave BR6 ... 57 F
Glentrammon Cl BR6 ... 57 F
Glentrammon Gdns BR6 ... 57 F
Glentrammon Rd
Orpington BR6 ... 58 A
Orpington BR6 ... 57 F
Glenure Rd SE9 ... 12 A
Glenview SE2 ... 13 D
Glenwood TN30 ... 183 B
Glenwood Cl
Chatham ME5 ... 54 C
Gillingham ME7 ... 69 A
Maidstone ME16 ... 99 C
Tenterden TN30 ... 183 B
Glenwood Ct 18 DA14 ... 30 A
Glimpsing Gn DA18 ... 3 E
Glistening Glade ME8 ... 69 E
Gload Cres BR5 ... 58 D
Globe Ct SE18 ... 12 C
Globe La ME4 ... 53 F
Globe Yd 13 DA11 ... 19 B
Gloucester Ave
Bexley DA16 ... 12 F
Sidcup DA15 ... 29 E
Gloucester Cl ME8 ... 70 A
Gloucester Ct RM18 ... 18 F
Gloucester Par DA15 ... 13 A
Gloucester Rd
Dartford DA1 ... 32 B
Erith DA17 ... 3 F
Gravesend DA12 ... 36 C
Maidstone ME15 ... 116 D
Turner's Green TN5 ... 184 F
Glover Cl SE2 ... 3 C
Glovers Cl TN16 ... 72 B
Glovers Mill ME4 ... 53 D
Gloxinia Rd DA13 ... 35 E
Glyn Davies Cl TN13 ... 91 E
Glyn Dr DA14 ... 30 B
Glynde Rd DA7 ... 13 E
Glyndebourne Pk BR6 ... 57 B
Glyndon Rd SE18 ... 2 D
Glynne Cl ME8 ... 69 D
Goad Ave ME5 ... 68 B
Goatsfield Rd TN16 ... 88 C
Goddard's Green Cotts
TN17 ... 180 F
Goddards Cl TN17 ... 179 B
Godden Rd ME6 ... 81 F
Godden Way ME8 ... 55 A
Goddings Dr ME1 ... 53 A
Goddington Chase BR6 ... 58 B
Goddington Ho BR6 ... 58 C
Goddington La
Harrietsham ME17 ... 119 B
Orpington BR6 ... 58 A
Goddington Rd ME2 ... 53 B
Godfrey Cl ME2 ... 38 F
Godfrey Evans Cl TN10 ... 127 F
Godfrey Hill SE18 ... 1 E
Godfrey Rd SE18 ... 1 F
Godstow Rd SE2 ... 3 C
Godwin Ho SE18 ... 11 F
Godwin Rd BR2 ... 42 C
Gold St DA12,DA13 ... 50 E
Goldace RM17 ... 17 F
Goldcrest Cl Newham E16 ... 1 D
Woolwich SE28 ... 3 C
Goldcrest Dr ME4 ... 40 C
Golden Plover Cl E16 ... 1 A
Golden Sq TN30 ... 193 B
Golden Wood Cl ME5 ... 84 D
Goldfinch Cl
Larkfield ME20 ... 82 A
Orpington BR6 ... 58 A
Paddock Wood TN12 ... 146 A
Goldfinch Rd SE28 ... 2 D
Goldie Leigh Hospl SE2 ... 13 C
Golding Cl Ditton ME20 ... 82 C
Rochester ME1 ... 53 E
Golding Gdns TN12 ... 130 A
Golding Rd TN13 ... 92 C
Goldings TN12 ... 145 E
Goldings Cl ME19 ... 97 A
Goldings The ME8 ... 69 C
Goldmark Ho SE3 ... 11 B
Goldsel Rd BR8 ... 45 E
Goldsmid Rd TN9 ... 143 C
Goldsmid St 3 SE18 ... 2 E
Goldsmith RM17 ... 17 F
Goldsmith Ct TN30 ... 183 B
Goldsmith Rd ME8 ... 69 E
Goldstone Wlk ME5 ... 68 A

Gol – Gro 217

oldsworth Dr ME2 39 A1
oldthorne Cl ME14 100 C5
oldwing Cl E16 1 A7
olf Links Ave DA11 36 B3
olf Rd BR1 43 A6
olford Rd TN17 179 F4
ollogly Terr 8 SE7 1 C1
ooch Cl ME16 99 D8
oodall Cl ME8 69 E5
oodbury Rd TN15 77 B6
oodensfield TN5 184 E5
ooding Ho SE7 1 C1
oodley Stock Rd TN8, TN16 105 B6
oodmead Rd BR6 44 A2
oods Hill TN30 192 D8
oods Station Rd TN1 159 B4
oodtrees La TN8 155 B2
oodwin Cl TN8 122 B2
oodwin Dr
Maidstone ME14 100 B8
Sidcup DA14 30 D6
oodwin Rd ME3 39 B7
oodwins The TN2 158 F1
oodwood Cl
High Halstow ME23 23 E4
Maidstone ME15 116 F6
oodwood Cres DA12 36 C2
oodworth Rd TN15 78 F3
oosander Way SE28 2 D3
oose Cl ME5 68 A7
oose Green Cl BR5 44 A7
oose Sq 8 E6 1 F7
ooseneck La TN27 151 C5
ordon Cl RM18 20 D7
ordon Ct ME17 115 E3
ordon Ho SE12 28 A8
ordon Inf Sch ME2 53 A8
ordon Jun Sch ME2 53 A8
ordon Pl DA12 19 C1
ordon Prim Sch SE9 11 F3
ordon Promenade E DA12 19 D1
ordon Rd Chatham ME4 54 A7
Chatham,Luton ME4 54 B2
Dartford DA1 32 D8
Erith DA17 4 C2
Gillingham ME7 54 E5
Hoo St Werburgh ME3 40 D5
Northfleet DA11 35 E8
Rochester ME2 53 A8
Royal Tunbridge Wells TN4 159 C7
Sevenoaks TN13 92 B2
Sidcup DA15 12 E2
ordon Terr ME1 53 C4
ordon Way BR1 42 A8
ore Cotts DA2 33 C4
ore Court Rd ME15 116 F5
ore Farm Cotts DA2 33 C5
ore Green Rd ME3 38 E7
ore La TN17 163 E4
ore Rd Dartford DA2 33 C6
Silver Street ME9 87 F5
orham Cl ME6 81 F7
orham Dr
Maidstone ME15 101 A1
Tonbridge TN9 143 E8
orman Rd SE18 1 F2
orringe Ave DA4 47 D7
orse Ave ME5 67 F5
orse Cl E16 1 A7
orse Cres ME20 98 D8
orse Rd Orpington BR5 59 A8
Rochester ME2 52 F8
Royal Tunbridge Wells TN2 159 E5
orse Way DA3 49 A4
orse Wood Rd
Hartley DA3 49 A5
New Barn DA3 49 A6
orst St ME7 54 C5
oss Hill BR8,DA2 32 C2
ossage Rd SE18 2 D1
osshill Rd BR7 43 A7
ossington Cl BR7 29 B4
othic Cl DA1 32 D5
oudhurst & Kilndown CE Prim Sch TN17 177 F8
oudhurst Cl ME16 99 E4
oudhurst Rd
Cranbrook TN17 179 D8
Gillingham ME8 55 B3
Horsmonden TN12 163 B5
Knox Bridge TN12,TN17 165 C6
Marden TN12 148 B5
ouge Ave DA11 35 E7
ould Rd ME5 68 B3
ourock Rd SE9 12 A2
over Hill TN11,ME18 111 E6
over View TN11 111 E7
ower Ho ME14 100 A6
race Ave Bexley DA7 13 F5
Maidstone ME16 99 D6
race Cl SE9 28 D5
racious La TN13 108 B5
racious Lane Bridge TN13 108 A6
racious Lane End TN14 107 F5
rafton Ave ME1 67 E8
raham Cl ME4 53 F6
raham Ct 12 BR1 28 B1
raham Ho SE18 12 B7
raham Rd DA7 14 A3
rain Rd Gillingham ME8 69 C3
Grain ME3 26 D3
rainey Field ME9 70 E4
Grainger Wlk TN10 127 E6
Gram Sch for Girls Wilmington The DA2 32 B5
Grampian Cl
Orpington BR6 43 F3
Royal Tunbridge Wells TN2 159 D5
Grampian Way ME15 101 A1
Granada Ho 8 ME15 100 A4
Granada St 9 ME15 100 A4
Granary TN12 146 B6
Granary Cl
Maidstone ME14 100 E5
Rainham ME8 55 F1
Granary Cotts TN16 90 C3
Granby Ho 8 SE18 1 F2
Granby Rd Eltham SE9 11 F4
Northfleet DA11 18 D1
Woolwich SE18 2 B3
Grand Ct 7 ME7 54 C6
Grand Depot Rd SE18 2 A1
Grand View Ave TN16 72 C3
Grandshore La TN17 166 B5
Grandsire Gdns ME3 40 E6
Grange Cl
Edenbridge TN8 122 C1
Leybourne ME19 81 C2
Sidcup DA15 30 A5
Westerham TN16 89 C1
Grange Cres
6 Dartford DA2 16 B1
Erith SE28 3 C7
Tenterden TN30 183 A3
Grange Dr Bromley BR7 28 F2
Pratt's Bottom BR6 58 C2
Grange Gdns TN4 158 D4
Grange Hill Chatham ME5 54 B3
Plaxtol TN15 110 E8
Grange Ho Erith DA8 15 A5
Gravesend DA11 36 A8
Maidstone ME16 99 A2
Grange La Boxley ME14 84 A1
Hartley DA3 49 B2
Grange Park Sch ME19 81 B3
Grange Rd Gillingham ME7 55 A6
Gravesend DA11 36 A8
Grays RM17 18 B8
Orpington BR6 57 C8
Platt TN15 95 C7
Rochester ME2 53 B7
Rusthall TN4 158 D4
Sevenoaks TN13 108 A8
Tenterden TN30 182 F3
Grange Rdbt ME7 55 A6
Grange The
East Malling ME19 98 A7
Sutton at H DA4 47 D8
West Kingsdown TN15 61 F2
Westerham TN16 89 C1
Grange Way Erith DA8 15 B7
Hartley DA3 48 F3
Rochester ME1 53 C3
Grangehill Pl SE9 11 F4
Grangehill Rd SE9 11 F3
Grangeways Cl DA11 35 F4
Grangewood DA5 30 F7
Granite St SE18 2 F1
Grant Cl ME7 55 B1
Grant Dr ME15 116 D6
Grant Rd ME3 39 C3
Grant's Cotts ME17 120 B5
Granton Rd DA14 30 C2
Grants La TN8,RH8 121 C6
Granville Ct Erith SE2 3 D1
Maidstone ME14 100 A6
Sevenoaks TN13 92 A3
Granville Mews DA14 30 A4
Granville Rd Bexley DA16 13 C4
Gillingham ME7 54 E5
Limpsfield RH8 104 A7
Maidstone ME14 100 A6
Northfleet DA11 35 F7
Royal Tunbridge Wells TN1 159 C5
Sevenoaks TN13 92 A3
Sidcup DA14 30 B4
Westerham TN16 89 C1
Granville Sch The TN13 92 A4
Grapple Rd ME14 100 A7
Grasdene Rd SE18 13 A7
Grasmere Ave BR6 57 B7
Grasmere Gdns BR6 57 B7
Grasmere Gr ME2 39 C2
Grasmere Rd Bexley DA7 14 C5
Orpington BR6 57 B7
Grasshaven Way SE28 2 F5
Grassington Rd 11 DA14 30 A4
Grasslands ME17 117 E4
Grassmere ME19 81 F2
Grassy Glade ME7 69 B6
Grassy La TN13 108 B8
Gravel Hill DA6 14 B2
Gravel Hill Cl DA6 14 B1
Gravel Hill Prim Sch DA6 14 B3
Gravel Pit Way BR6 44 A1
Gravel Rd Orpington BR2 56 E8
Sutton at H DA4 33 B1
Gravel Wlk ME1 53 D5
Gravelly Bottom Rd ME17 118 B2
Gravelly Ways TN12 130 D5
Gravelwood Cl BR7 29 C5
Graveney Cl ME3 39 C7
Graveney Rd ME15 116 F7
Graves Est DA16 13 B5
Gravesend & North Kent Hospl DA11 19 A1
Gravesend Gram Sch DA12 36 D8
Gravesend Gram Sch for Girls DA11 36 A7
Gravesend Rd
Higham ME2,ME3,DA12 38 C2
Rochester ME2 52 F8
Shorne DA12 37 D5
Vigo Village TN15 79 D6
Gravesend Sta DA11 19 B1
Gravesham Ct 8 DA12 36 B8
Gravesham Mus* DA11 19 B1
Gray Ho SE2 3 D1
Grayland Cl BR1 42 D8
Graylands RM17 17 E8
Graylings The ME1 53 B3
Grayne Ave ME3 27 B5
Grays Farm Prim Sch BR5 44 B8
Grays Farm Production Village BR5 44 B8
Grays Farm Rd BR5 44 B8
Grays Rd TN16 89 D7
Grays Sh Ctr RM17 18 A8
Grays Sta RM17 18 A8
Grazeley Cl DA6 14 C2
Great Ash BR7 29 A1
Great Basin Rd ME12 27 F2
Great Bounds Dr TN4 142 E3
Great Brooms Rd TN4 159 C8
Great Courtlands TN3 158 A3
Great Elms TN11 111 E1
Great Elms Rd BR2 42 C5
Great Footway TN3 157 F3
Great Hall Arc 3 TN1 159 B3
Great Harry Dr SE9 29 A5
Great Ivy Mill Cotts ME15 115 F7
Great Lines ME7 54 B5
Great Lodge Ret Pk TN2 143 E1
Great Maytham Hall* TN17 191 F2
Great Mead TN8 122 C3
Great Oak
Hurst Green TN19 194 A3
Royal Tunbridge Wells TN2 159 D6
Great Queen St DA1 15 F1
Great South Ave ME4 54 A1
Great Thrift BR5 43 C5
Great Till Cl TN14 75 E3
Greatness La TN14 92 C6
Greatness Rd TN14 92 C6
Greatwood BR7 29 A1
Grebe Apartments 15 ME15 116 E5
Grebe Cl ME3 25 C4
Grebe Ct ME20 81 F1
Grecian Rd TN1 159 B2
Grecian St ME14 100 A6
Green Acres DA14 29 F4
Green Bank Cl ME7 69 A5
Green Cl ME1 53 D2
Green Court Rd BR8 45 D3
Green Farm Cl BR6 57 F5
Green Farm La DA12 37 E5
Green Gdns BR6 57 C5
Green Hedges TN30 193 B8
Green Hill Biggin Hill BR6 72 F7
Maidstone ME15 101 B1
Woolwich SE18 1 F1
Green Hill La ME17 119 D1
Green La Cliffe ME3 22 B6
Collier Street TN12 147 E8
East End TN17 181 C2
Eltham BR7,SE9 29 B5
Four Elms TN8 123 C7
Grain ME3 27 B5
High Halden TN26 169 F3
Langley Heath ME17 117 E3
Maidstone ME17 116 C3
Meopham Sta DA13 50 B2
Paddock Wood TN12 146 A5
Platt's Heath ME17 119 F2
Smarden TN27 153 A1
Sutton Valence ME17 134 B4
Trottiscliffe ME19 80 A5
Yelsted ME9 70 F1
Green La The TN11 125 F1
Green Lane Bsns Pk SE9 29 A6
Green Lane Cotts
Collier Street TN12 131 D1
Langley Heath ME17 117 E3
Green Lawns 10 SE18 2 B2
Green Pl DA1 14 E2
Green Rd TN12 163 A6
Green Sands ME5 84 C8
Green Sq TN5 184 F5
Green St ME7 54 C5
Green Street Green Prim Sch BR6 57 F4
Green Street Green Rd DA1,DA2 33 D4
Green The
Bexley,Bexleyheath DA7 14 A6
Bexley,Falconwood DA16 12 E3
Biddenden TN27 182 D6
Dartford DA2 33 D6
East Farleigh ME15 115 B7
Frant TN3 173 B3
Hayes BR2 42 A2
Langton Green TN3 157 E3
Leigh TN11 125 F1
Lewisham BR1 28 A5
Orpington BR5 30 B1
Sevenoaks TN13 92 D5
Sidcup DA14 30 A4
Green The *continued*
West Tilbury RM18 19 E8
Westerham TN16 89 D1
Green Vale DA6 13 D2
Green View Ave TN11 126 A1
Green Way Bromley BR2 42 E3
Eltham SE9 11 D2
Hartley DA3 48 E4
Maidstone ME16 99 B3
Royal Tunbridge Wells TN2 159 E8
Green Wlk DA1 14 F3
Green's Cotts ME15 115 A4
Greenacre DA1 32 D6
Greenacre Cl
Chatham ME5 68 A5
Swanley BR8 45 E5
Greenacre Sch ME5 67 F5
Greenacres SE9 12 A1
Greenacres Cl BR6 57 C6
Greenacres Prim Sch & Language Impairment Unit SE9 29 A6
Greenbank ME5 68 B8
Greenbank Lodge 2 BR7 43 A8
Greenbanks DA1 32 E6
Greenbay Rd SE7 11 D7
Greenborough Cl ME15 116 E6
Greencourt Rd BR5 43 E4
Greencroft Cl E6 1 D8
Greendale Wlk 4 DA11 35 E5
Greenfield TN8 122 D1
Greenfield Cl Eccles ME20 83 A6
Rusthall TN4 158 C5
Greenfield Cotts ME14 84 C3
Greenfield Ct SE9 28 E5
Greenfield Dr BR1 42 C7
Greenfield Gdns BR5 43 D2
Greenfield Rd
Gillingham ME7 54 D6
Joyden's Wood DA2 31 D3
Greenfields ME15 116 E8
Greenfields Cl ME3 39 D3
Greenfinches
Gillingham ME7 68 F6
New Barn DA3 49 B6
Greenfrith Dr TN10 127 B6
Greenhaven Dr SE28 3 B7
Greenhill TN12 149 E5
Greenhill Cts SE18 1 F1
Greenhill La TN27 153 F7
Greenhill Rd
Northfleet DA11 35 F6
Otford TN14 76 C5
Greenhill Terr SE18 1 F1
Greenhithe 3 ME15 100 A3
Greenhithe Cl DA15 29 E8
Greenhithe for Bluewater Sta DA9 17 A2
Greenholm Rd SE9 12 B2
Greenhurst La
Limpsfield RH8 104 A4
Oxted RH8 104 A3
Greening St SE2 3 C2
Greenlands Platt TN15 95 C7
Sole Street DA12 50 D4
Greenlands Rd TN15 93 B8
Greenlaw St SE18 2 A3
Greenleas TN2 160 C6
Greenleigh Ave BR5 44 B5
Greenoak Rise TN16 72 C1
Greens End SE18 2 B2
Greensand Rd ME15 101 A2
Greenshields Ind Est E16 1 A4
Greenside
High Halden TN26 183 E7
Maidstone ME15 100 B3
Sidcup DA5 30 E7
Swanley BR8 45 D7
Greenside Wlk TN16 72 B1
Greenslade Prim Sch SE18 12 D8
Greensleeves Way ME18 97 C3
Greentrees Ave TN10 127 F5
Greenvale Gdns ME8 55 B2
Greenvale Inf Sch ME4 54 A2
Greenvale Rd SE9 12 A3
Greenview Cres TN11 126 E4
Greenview Wlk ME8 55 A4
Greenway Chatham ME5 67 D6
Chislehurst BR7 29 B3
Cranbrook TN17 179 B4
Tatsfield TN16 88 C7
Greenway Court Farm Cotts ME17 103 A1
Greenway Court Rd ME17 103 A1
Greenway La ME17 119 A7
Greenway The
Orpington BR5 44 B3
Oxted RH8 104 B2
Greenways
Addington ME19 80 E2
Maidstone ME14 100 F5
New Barn DA3 49 D6
Greenways The TN12 145 F5
Greenwich Cl
Chatham ME5 68 B4
Maidstone ME16 99 D4
Greenwich Com Coll SE18 2 C2
Greenwich Cres E6 1 E8
Greenwich Hts SE18 11 E7
Greenwich Sh Pk SE7 1 B2
Greenwood Cl
Orpington BR5 43 E3
Sidcup DA15 30 A6
Greenwood Gdns RH8 104 A1
Greenwood Ho 8 RM17 18 B8
Greenwood Pl TN15 79 A2
Greenwood Rd DA5 31 D4
Greenwood Way TN13 91 F2
Greggs Wood Rd TN2 159 E7
Gregor Mews SE3 11 A7
Gregory Cl ME8 69 E4
Gregory Cres SE9 28 D8
Gregory Ho SE3 11 B5
Grenada Rd SE7 11 C7
Grenadier Cl ME15 100 F2
Grenadier St E16 2 A5
Grenfell Cl TN16 72 C7
Grenville Cl DA13 64 A8
Gresham Ave DA3 48 F4
Gresham Cl
3 Rainham ME8 55 F1
Sidcup DA5 13 F1
Tonbridge TN10 127 E7
Gresham Rd
Coxheath ME17 115 D3
Newham E16 1 B7
Greshams Way TN8 122 A2
Gresswell Cl DA14 30 A5
Grey Ladies Oasts TN15 95 B3
Grey Wethers ME14 83 E4
Greybury La TN8 138 B3
Greyfriars Cl ME16 99 D5
Greyhound Way DA1 14 E1
Greys Park Cl BR2 56 D5
Greystone Pk TN14 90 E2
Greystones Cl TN15 76 E2
Greystones Rd ME15 101 A2
Gribble Bridge La TN27 182 B5
Grice Ave TN16 72 C6
Grieves Rd DA11 35 F5
Grieveson Ho ME4 54 A4
Griffin Manor Way SE28 2 D3
Griffin Rd SE18 2 D2
Griffin Way SE28 2 E3
Griffin Wlk DA9 16 F2
Griffiths Ho 2 SE18 12 B8
Grigg La TN27 152 C7
Grigg's Cross BR5 44 D3
Griggs Way TN15 95 A7
Grimsby Gr E16 2 B4
Grinling Ho 6 SE18 2 A2
Grizedale Cl ME1 67 D8
Gromenfield TN3 171 C7
Groom Cl BR2 42 B5
Groom Way ME17 120 E6
Groombridge Cl DA16 13 A2
Groombridge Hill TN3 157 D1
Groombridge Pl* TN3 171 C8
Groombridge Place Gdns* TN3 171 C8
Groombridge Rd TN3 157 A1
Groombridge Sq 13 ME15 116 F6
Groombridge St Thomas' CE Prim Sch TN3 171 C6
Groombridge Sta* TN3 171 C7
Grosmont Rd SE18 2 F1
Grosvenor Ave ME4 53 E3
Grosvenor Bridge TN1 159 B5
Grosvenor Cres DA1 15 D2
Grosvenor Ho 5 ME15 116 F5
Grosvenor Manor DA5 31 D6
Grosvenor Pk TN1 159 A4
Grosvenor Rd Bexley DA6 13 E2
Erith DA17 14 A8
Gillingham ME7 55 A1
Orpington BR5 43 E3
Royal Tunbridge Wells TN1 159 A4
Grosvenor Sq DA3 48 E6
Grosvenor Wlk TN1 159 A4
Grove Ave TN1 159 A2
Grove Cl
Goose Green TN11 112 C3
Hayes BR2 56 A8
Grove Cotts TN30 193 B6
Grove Ct Greenwich SE3 11 A6
4 Rochester ME2 53 B7
Grove Green La ME14 100 E5
Grove Green Rd ME14 100 F5
Grove Hill Gdns TN1 159 B2
Grove Hill Ho TN1 159 B3
Grove Hill Rd TN1 159 B3
Grove La ME15 131 D7
Grove Market Pl SE9 11 F1
Grove Park Rd SE9 28 D6
Grove Park Sta SE12 28 B5
Grove Rd
Bexley,Bexleyheath DA7 14 C3
8 Bexley,West Heath DA17 13 F8
Chatham ME4 54 B2
Gillingham ME7 55 A6
Grays RM17 18 C8
Maidstone ME15 116 C7
Northfleet DA11 18 B2
Penshurst TN11,TN8 140 E2
Rochester ME2 53 B8
Seal TN15 93 B5
Sevenoaks TN14 92 C6
Tatsfield TN16 88 C7
Upper Halling ME2 65 E5
Grove The Bexley DA6 13 D3
Biggin Hill TN16 72 E1
Fawkham Green DA3 48 A2
Gravesend DA12 36 B8
Maidstone ME14 101 A3
Pembury TN2 160 D8
Sidcup DA14 30 E4
Swanley BR8 45 F6

Grove The *continued*
Swanscombe DA10 17 F2
West Kingsdown TN15 61 F1
Grove Vale BR7 29 A2
Grove Wood Cotts TN11 109 A1
Grovebury Cl DA8 14 D8
Grovebury Ct DA6 14 B2
Grovebury Rd SE2 3 B4
Groveherst Rd DA1 15 F4
Grovehurst La TN12 163 C5
Grovelands ME17 120 E5
Grovelands Rd BR5 30 A1
Grovelands Way RM17 17 F8
Grover St 3 TN1 159 B4
Groves The ME6 81 F7
Grovewood Ct ME14 100 E4
Grovewood Dr ME14 100 E4
Grub St RH8 104 C6
Guardian Ct ME8 55 C1
Guardian Ind Est TN12 148 C7
Guards Cl TN10 127 E7
Guestwick TN10 127 F5
Guibal Rd SE12 28 B7
Guild Rd Erith DA8 14 F7
Greenwich SE7 11 D8
Guildables La RH8,TN8 121 E7
Guildford Gdns ME2 52 C6
Guildford Rd Newham E6 1 F7
7 Royal Tunbridge Wells TN1 159 B3
Guildhall Mus The* ME1 53 C6
Guiness Dr ME2 39 B2
Gulland Ho 4 ME14 100 B4
Gullands ME17 117 E4
Gulliver Rd DA15 29 E6
Gumley Rd RM20 17 E8
Gumping Rd BR5,BR6 57 C8
Gun Back La TN12 163 A5
Gun Hill RM18 19 D8
Gun La ME2 53 B7
Gun Tower Mews ME1 53 B4
Gundulph Ho TN10 127 C3
Gundulph Rd Bromley BR2 42 C6
Rochester ME1 53 E4
Gundulph Sq ME1 53 C6
Gunfleet Cl DA12 36 E8
Gunlands TN12 163 A6
Gunn Rd DA10 17 E1
Gunner La SE18 2 A1
Gunnery Terr SE18 2 C3
Gunning St SE18 2 E2
Gunnis Cl ME8 69 D4
Gurdon Rd SE7 1 B1
Guston Rd ME14 100 C6
Guy Barnett Gr SE3 11 A4
Gwillim Cl DA15 13 A2
Gwynn Rd DA11 35 C6
Gybbon Rise TN12 149 E3
Gybbons Rd TN17 191 F3
Gypsy Way ME23 23 E3

H

Ha-Ha Rd SE18 11 F8
Hackney Rd ME16 99 C2
Hadden Rd SE28 2 E3
Haddon Gr DA15 30 A8
Haddon Rd BR5 44 C4
Hadleigh Ct ME7 69 A3
Hadleigh Wlk 1 E6 1 E7
Hadley Cl DA13 64 B8
Hadley Ct TN4 158 F6
Hadley Gdns ME17 102 E2
Hadley House BR5 43 F7
Hadley Rd DA17 3 F2
Hadlow Coll TN11 128 D8
Hadlow Coll Mottingham Ctr SE12 28 C7
Hadlow Coll Nature Reserve* SE12 28 C7
Hadlow Ct TN9 127 C2
Hadlow Pk TN11 111 E1
Hadlow Rd Bexley DA16 13 C7
Maidstone ME14 100 C5
Sidcup DA14 30 A4
Tonbridge TN9 127 D3
Hadlow Rd E TN10,TN11 128 A5
Hadlow Sch TN11 128 E8
Hadlow Stair Rd TN10 127 F4
Hadlow Way DA13 35 E1
Haffenden Cl TN12 148 D6
Haffenden Rd TN30 183 B1
Haig Ave Chatham ME1 53 D1
Chatham ME4 54 A2
Gillingham ME7 54 E4
Haig Ct BR7 29 B3
Haig Gdns DA12 36 C8
Haig Rd TN16 72 E2
Haig Villas ME3 40 A5
Hailey Rd DA18 4 A4
Hailey Rd Bsns Pk DA18 4 A4
Haileybury Rd BR6 58 A6
Hailing Mews BR2 42 B6
Hailstone Cl TN11 128 E8
Haimo Prim Sch SE9 11 D2
Haimo Rd SE9 11 D2
Hainault St SE9 29 B7
Halcot Ave DA6 14 C2
Haldane Gdns DA11 35 C7
Haldane Rd SE28 3 D6
Halden Cl ME15 116 F6
Halden La TN17 191 F6
Hale Cl BR6 57 C6
Hale Cotts DA9 17 C2
Hale Ct TN12 130 A7
Hale La TN14 75 F2
Hale Oak Rd
Hall's Green TN8,TN14 124 E4
Sevenoaks Weald TN14 108 B1
Hale Rd ME3 39 C7
Hale St TN12 130 A7
Hales Cl TN30 193 B8
Hales Ct TN30 193 B8
Haleys Pl ME1 83 A8
Half Moon La TN11 126 D6
Half Moon Way ME23 23 E3
Halfpence La DA12 51 B7
Halfpenny Cl ME16 99 A2
Halfway St DA15 29 E7
Halifax Cl ME5 68 B6
Halifield Dr DA17 3 E3
Hall Hill TN15 93 C4
Hall Pl* DA5 14 C1
Hall Place Cres DA1,DA5 14 D2
Hall Rd Aylesford ME20 82 F1
Chatham ME5 68 C3
Dartford DA1 15 F3
High Halstow ME3 24 C6
Northfleet,Pepper Hill DA11 35 C5
Northfleet,Wombwell Park DA11 35 D6
Wouldham ME1 66 C3
Hall The SE3 11 A4
Hall View SE9 28 D6
Hall's Hole Rd TN2 159 E4
Hallam Cl BR7 28 F3
Hallford Way DA1 15 C2
Hallgate SE3 11 A4
Halling Prim Sch ME2 66 B3
Halling Sta ME2 66 A5
Halls Cotts TN5 184 F5
Hallsfield Rd ME5 67 D2
Hallsville Prim Sch E16 1 A7
Hallwards TN12 149 E2
Hallwood Cl ME8 69 D5
Hallwood Ho ME5 68 C2
Hallywell Cres E6 1 F8
Halons Rd SE9 29 A8
Halsbrook Rd SE3 11 D4
Halstead Com Prim Sch TN14 74 F7
Halstead La TN14 74 E5
Halstead Rd DA8 14 E6
Halstead Wlk ME16 99 C7
Halstow Cl ME15 116 B6
Halstow Prim Sch SE10 1 A1
Halstow Rd SE10,SE3 1 A1
Halt Cvn Pk The TN15 61 E1
Halt Robin La DA17 4 B2
Halt Robin Rd DA17 4 B2
Ham La Gillingham ME7 68 E3
Lenham ME17 120 C5
Ham River Hill ME3 39 A6
Ham Shades Cl 1 DA15 30 A5
Hamble Rd TN10 127 B5
Hambledon Ct ME16 99 B3
Hambledown Rd DA15 29 E8
Hambro Ave BR2 42 A1
Hamelin Rd ME7 68 F8
Hamerton Rd DA11 18 B2
Hamilton Ct Chatham ME5 54 C1
Rochester ME1 53 B4
Royal Tunbridge Wells TN4 159 A5
Hamilton Ho
Coxheath ME17 115 C3
Maidstone ME15 116 F5
Royal Tunbridge Wells TN4 159 A5
Hamilton Rd Bexley DA7 13 E5
Gillingham ME7 54 D7
Sidcup DA15 30 A4
Hamilton Wlk DA8 14 F7
Hamlea Cl SE12 11 A2
Hamlet Est DA8 4 D1
Hamlet Ho Eltham SE9 12 A2
5 Erith DA8 14 E7
Hamlin Rd TN13 91 E6
Hamlyn Ct TN13 91 E6
Hammelton Rd 2 BR1 42 A8
Hammerwood Pk* RH19 154 C2
Hammond Way 2 SE28 3 B6
Hammonds 9 TN18 189 A2
Hammonds Sq ME6 82 A8
Hamond Hill 6 ME4 53 E4
Hampden Way ME19 96 F3
Hampshire Cl ME5 68 C7
Hampshire Dr ME15 116 C8
Hampshires The ME17 119 C6
Hampson Way ME14 101 A4
Hampstead Cl SE28 3 B5
Hampstead La ME18 113 C1
Hampton Cl ME5 68 A5
Hampton Cotts TN14 74 F4
Hampton Cres DA12 36 E6
Hampton Ct DA8 14 D7
Hampton Ho DA7 14 B5
Hampton Rd ME14 100 C6
Hamptons Rd TN11 111 B5
Hamwick Gn ME5 68 C1
Hanameel St E16 1 B5
Hanbury Cl ME18 113 E7
Hanbury Dr TN16 72 B6
Hanbury Wlk DA5 31 E5
Hancock Cl ME3 39 B1
Handel Cres RM18 19 A7
Handel Wlk TN10 127 E6
Hands Wlk E16 1 A7
Hanes Dene ME2 65 F5
Hang Grove Hill BR6 73 B6
Hanging Bank TN14 106 F3
Hangmans Cnr BR7 43 B8
Hanley Ct TN13 92 B4
Hanmer Way TN12 149 E2
Hanover Ave E16 1 A5
Hanover Ct
10 Bromley BR2 42 A6
Maidstone ME14 100 B5
Hanover Dr
Chislehurst BR7 29 C4
Gillingham ME8 69 C4
Hanover Gn ME20 81 F3
Hanover Pl DA3 62 F8
Hanover Rd
Coxheath ME17 115 C3
Royal Tunbridge Wells TN1 159 A4
Hanover Way DA7 13 D4
Hansol Rd DA6 13 E2
Hansom Terr 1 BR1 42 B8
Hanson Dr ME15 115 F3
Hanway ME8 55 A2
Harbex Cl DA5 31 B8
Harbledown Ho ME16 99 B2
Harbledown Manor ME8 55 B3
Harbledown Pl 7 BR5 44 C5
Harborough Ave DA15 29 F8
Harbour The ME17 134 E5
Harbourland Cl ME14 100 B8
Harbourne La TN26, TN30 183 E5
Harcourt Ave DA15 30 C8
Harcourt Gdns ME8 69 E4
Harcourt Rd DA6 13 E3
Harden Ct 1 SE18 1 E2
Harden Rd DA11 35 F6
Hardie Cl ME19 81 F1
Harding Ho 9 SE18 1 F2
Harding Rd DA7 13 F5
Hardinge Ave TN4 142 E3
Hardinge Cl ME8 69 D4
Hardinge Cres SE18 2 C3
Hardinge St SE18 2 B3
Hardman Rd SE7 1 B1
Hardres Terr BR5 58 D8
Hards Town ME4 54 A4
Hardwick Cres 2 DA2 16 B1
Hardwick Ct DA8 14 D8
Hardwick Ho ME15 116 E8
Hardwick Rd TN11 126 E6
Hardy Ave Newham E16 1 A5
Northfleet DA11 35 E6
Hardy Cl ME5 68 B6
Hardy Gr DA1 16 A3
Hardy Lodge ME1 53 B4
Hardy Rd 2 SE3 11 A8
Hardy St ME14 100 A6
Hare St 2 Chatham ME4 54 B3
Woolwich SE18 2 A3
Harebell Cl
3 Chatham ME5 67 F4
Maidstone ME14 100 E5
Harebell Dr E6 2 A8
Haredale Cl ME1 67 D7
Harefield Rd DA14 30 D5
Harenc Sch DA14 30 C3
Harescroft TN2 172 F7
Harewood Lincoln Ho DA11 18 D1
Harfst Way BR8 45 C8
Hargate Cl TN2 172 F8
Hargood Rd SE3 11 C6
Harland Ave DA15 29 E6
Harland Rd SE12 28 A7
Harland Way TN4 142 F4
Harlands Gr BR6 57 B6
Harlech Cl ME2 38 F1
Harlequin Ho 1 DA18 3 E3
Harley 5 BR7 43 D8
Harley Gdns BR6 57 E6
Harleyford BR1 42 C8
Harling Cl ME17 116 D5
Harlinger St SE18 1 E3
Harlington Rd DA7 13 E4
Harman Ave DA11 36 B3
Harman Ct ME5 68 B3
Harman Dr DA15 12 F1
Harmer Ct
Royal Tunbridge Wells TN4 143 A2
Swanscombe DA10 17 F1
Harmer Rd DA10 17 F1
Harmer St DA12 19 C1
Harmers Way TN27 137 F3
Harmony St TN4 158 D4
Harmony Way 1 BR1, BR2 42 A7
Harmsworth Ct TN17 190 E6
Harness Rd SE28 3 A4
Harnetts Cl BR8 45 D2
Harold Ave Erith DA17 3 F1
Gillingham ME7 54 E4
Harold Campbell Ct DA1 32 D8
Harold Gibbons Ct SE7 11 C8
Harold Ho 2 TN2 159 C7
Harold Rd Cuxton ME2 52 C3
Hawley DA2 32 F4
Harp Farm Rd ME14 84 C6
Harper Rd E6 1 F7
Harple La ME14 84 F1
Harpswood ME17 102 F1
Harptree Dr ME5 67 F5
Harraden Rd SE3 11 C6
Harrier Mews SE28 2 D4
Harrier Way E6 1 F8
Harries Rd TN2 159 E7
Harrietsham Sta ME17 119 D6
Harriet Dr ME1 53 B3
Harrietsham Ho 13 ME16 99 A3
Harrietsham Prim Sch ME17 119 E6
Harrington Ho 7 BR1 42 A8
Harrington Way SE18 1 D3
Harris Cl DA11 35 F5
Harris Ho ME2 66 B4
Harris Rd DA7 13 F6
Harrison Ct 4 ME8 55 F1
Harrison Dr
Harrietsham ME17 119 E6
High Halstow ME23 23 E4
Harrison Rd TN15 94 F7
Harrison Way TN13 92 A5
Harrogate Ct 6 SE12 28 A8
Harrow Cl TN8 122 D3
Harrow Ct Chatham ME5 68 C4
Stockbury ME9 86 D8
Harrow Gdns BR6 58 B6
Harrow Manor Way SE2 3 C3
Harrow Rd Gillingham ME7 68 F6
Halstead TN14 74 E4
Harrow Way ME14 100 E5
Harrowby Gdns DA11 35 E6
Hart Dyke Cres BR8 45 D6
Hart Dyke Rd
Orpington BR5 44 C1
Swanley BR8 45 D6
Hart Ho BR6 44 A2
Hart Shaw DA3 49 B7
Hart St ME16 99 F3
Hart Street Bsns Ctr ME16 99 F3
Hartfield Cl TN10 127 E5
Hartfield Cres BR4 56 A7
Hartfield Pl DA11 35 D8
Hartfield Rd
Cowden TN8 155 C6
Hayes BR4 56 A6
Hever TN8 139 A4
Hartford Rd DA5 14 A1
Hartford Wlk 13 DA17 4 A1
Harting Rd SE9 28 E5
Hartington Cl BR6 57 C5
Hartington Rd E16 1 B7
Hartington St ME4 54 A3
Hartlake Rd TN11 128 D3
Hartlands Cl DA5 13 F1
Hartlepool Ct E16 2 B4
Hartley Bottom Rd DA3 49 C2
Hartley Cl Bromley BR1 42 F7
Maidstone ME15 116 F6
Hartley Court Gdns TN17 179 A3
Hartley Hill DA3 49 A1
Hartley Mews ME8 55 B3
Hartley Prim Sch DA3 48 E3
Hartley Rd Bexley DA16 13 C7
Hartley TN17 179 A3
Longfield DA3 48 E7
Westerham TN16 89 D2
Hartlip CE Prim Sch ME9 70 D5
Hartlip Hill ME9 70 F7
Hartmann Rd E16 1 E5
Hartnokes TN18 189 A2
Hartnup St ME16 99 C2
Harton Cl BR1 42 D8
Hartpiece Cl ME8 55 F2
Hartridge Farm ME15 115 A7
Hartshill Rd DA11 35 F6
Hartslands Rd TN13 92 C4
Hartslock Dr DA18,SE2 3 D4
Hartsmead Rd SE9 28 F6
Hartville Rd SE18 2 E2
Hartwell Ho 2 SE7 1 B1
Harty Ave ME8 69 B3
Harvard Ct 9 SE9 12 A1
Harvel Ave ME2 52 F7
Harvel Cl BR5,BR7 44 A6
Harvel Cres SE2 3 D1
Harvel La DA13 64 B2
Harvel Rd DA13 80 A8
Harvel St DA13 64 C3
Harvest Bank Rd BR4 56 A7
Harvest Rd TN10 127 D6
Harvest Ridge ME19 81 D2
Harvest Way BR8 45 D2
Harvesters Cl ME8 69 E7
Harvesters Way ME14 100 D4
Harvey Gdns SE7 1 C1
Harvey Point 9 E16 1 A8
Harvey Rd ME8 69 E8
Harvill Rd DA14 30 E3
Harwood Ave BR1 42 B7
Harwood Ct 3 RM17 18 C8
Haslemere Est ME15 116 F5
Haslemere Rd DA7 14 A5
Hasler Cl SE28 3 C6
Hasletts Cl TN1 159 B6
Haslewood Cl TN27 153 B2
Hassendean Rd SE3 11 B7
Hassock Wood BR2 56 E6
Hassop Wlk SE9 28 E4
Hast Hill Ho BR2 56 B6
Haste Hill Cl ME17 116 B3
Haste Hill Rd ME17 116 B3
Hasted Cl DA9 17 C1
Hasted Rd Greenwich SE7 1 D1
Newington ME9 71 B7
Hasteds ME17 102 D2
Hastings Cl RM17 17 E8
Hastings Ho SE18 1 F2
Hastings Rd
Maidstone ME15 100 B3
Newenden TN17,TN18 197 C6
Orpington BR2 56 E8
Pembury TN2 160 D6
Pembury,Kipping's Cross TN2 160 F5
Hastings Rd *continued*
The Moor TN18 194 F
Hastings St SE18 2 C
Hatch Rd ME17 120 C
Hatches La TN11,TN12 129 D
Hatfield Ct SE3 11 A
Hatfield Rd ME2 53 A
Hatham Green La TN15 62 D
Hathaway Cl BR2 42 F
Hathaway Ct
Gillingham ME8 69 D
Rochester ME1 53 B
Hatherall Rd ME14 100 B
Hatherley Cres DA14 30 A
Hatherley Rd DA14 30 A
Hathern Gdns SE9 29 A
Hatmill La TN12 162 A
Hattersfield Cl DA17 3 F
Hatton Cl Northfleet DA11 35 E
Woolwich SE18 12 D
Hatton Ct BR7 28 F
Hatton Rd ME5 68 C
Havant Wlk 8 ME15 116 F
Havelock Rd Bromley BR2 42 C
Dartford DA1 15 B
Erith DA17 3 F
Northfleet DA11 35 F
Tonbridge TN9 127 B
Haven Cl Eltham SE9 28 F
Istead Rise DA13 49 F
Rochester ME1 53 C
Sidcup DA14 30 C
Swanley BR8 45 F
Haven Hill TN15 63 A
Haven Lodge 9 SE18 2 B
Haven St ME3 39 C
Haven Way ME4 40 B
Havengore Ave DA12 36 E
Havering Cl TN2 159 F
Haverstock Ct 2 BR5 44 B
Haverthwaite Rd BR6 57 D
Havisham Cl ME1 53 D
Havisham Rd DA12 37 A
Havock La 1 ME14 99 F
Hawbeck Rd ME8 69 C
Hawden Cl TN11 126 F
Hawden La TN11 126 F
Hawden Rd TN9 127 B
Hawes Rd BR1 42 B
Hawfield Bank BR6 58 D
Hawkenbury Cl TN2 159 D
Hawkenbury Mead TN2 159 D
Hawkenbury Rd
Hawkenbury TN12 150 C
Royal Tunbridge Wells TN2, TN3 159 E
Hawkenbury Rise ME2 39 B
Hawkes Cl RM17 18 B
Hawkes Pl TN13 108 A
Hawkes Rd ME20 82 F
Hawkhurst CE Prim Sch TN18 189 B
Hawkhurst Cottage Hospl TN18 188 D
Hawkhurst Rd
Flimwell TN5,TN18 187 E
Gill's Green TN17,TN18 188 F
Gillingham ME8 55 B
Hawkinge Wlk BR5 44 B
Hawkins Ave DA12 36 C
Hawkins Cl ME7 54 A
Hawkridge Gr ME18 97 A
Hawksmoor Cl
3 Newham E6 1 E
Woolwich SE18 2 E
Hawksmoor Sch SE28 3 B
Hawkwell Bsns Ctr TN2 144 F
Hawkwell Cotts TN2 144 F
Hawkwood ME16 99 B
Hawkwood Cl ME1 53 D
Hawkwood La BR7 43 C
Hawley Ct ME16 99 E
Hawley Rd DA1,DA2,DA4 33 A
Hawley Terr DA2 33 A
Hawley Vale DA2 33 A
Hawser Rd ME1 53 C
Hawstead La BR6 58 F
Hawthorn Cl
Edenbridge TN8 122 C
Gravesend DA12 36 C
Orpington BR5 43 D
Hawthorn Cotts 6 DA16 13 A
Hawthorn Ho 5 ME5 67 F
Hawthorn La TN13 91 F
Hawthorn Pl DA8 4 C
Hawthorn Rd Bexley DA6 13 F
Dartford DA1 32 D
Rochester ME2 52 E
Hawthorn Terr DA15 12 F
Hawthorn Wlk
Royal Tunbridge Wells TN2 159 E
Tonbridge TN10 127 C
Hawthornden Cl ME18 97 C
Hawthorndene Cl BR2 56 A
Hawthorndene Rd BR2 56 A
Hawthorne Ave
Biggin Hill TN16 72 D
Gillingham ME8 55 C
Hawthorne Cl BR1 42 F
Hawthorne Ho 4 ME16 99 A
Hawthorne Rd BR1 42 F
Hawthorns Chatham ME5 67 F
Hartley DA3 48 F
Hawthorns The
Aylesford ME20 82 E
Chatham ME5 67 F
Oxted RH8 104 A

awthorns The *continued*
he Moor TN18 194 F8
xted Rd BR1 42 B8
ay's Mead DA13 50 F3
ayday Rd E16 1 A8
aydens Cl BR5 44 C3
aydens Mews TN9 127 C3
aydens The TN9 127 C3
aydon Cl ME16 99 B4
ayes Cl Hayes BR2 56 A8
igham ME3 38 C3
Vest Thurrock RM20 17 C8
ayes Cotts ME19 96 D7
ayes Gdn BR2 42 A1
ayes La Hayes BR2 42 A4
tockbury ME9 86 F6
ayes Prim Sch BR2 42 B1
ayes Rd Bromley BR2 42 A5
Stone DA9 33 E8
ayes Sch BR2 56 B8
ayes St BR2 42 B1
ayes Sta BR2 42 A1
ayes Terr DA12 37 E3
ayes Wlk ME19 97 A2
ayes Wood Ave BR2 42 B1
ayesbrook Sch TN9 143 A8
ayesden La TN11,TN3 142 B5
ayesford Park Dr BR2 42 A4
ayfield ME19 81 E2
ayfield Rd BR5 44 A4
ayfields ME5 68 D2
aygate Ho ME1 53 C4
ayle Mill Cotts ME15 115 F8
ayle Mill Rd ME15 115 F8
ayle Rd ME15 100 A3
ayley Cl ME2 52 C2
ayley Ho DA17 14 A8
ayman Wlk ME20 82 F6
aymans Hill TN12 163 C7
aymen St ME4 53 E3
aynes Ho 3 ME14 100 B4
aynes Rd
Gravesend DA11 36 A6
Northfleet DA11 35 F5
ayrick Cl ME14 100 E5
ays Rd ME6 81 F6
aysden Ctry Pk*
TN11 142 D8
aywain Cl
Maidstone ME14 100 F4
Paddock Wood TN12 146 A5
ayward Ave ME2 53 B8
ayward Cl DA1 14 D2
ayward Dr DA1 32 F6
ayward's Ho ME1 53 C6
aywood Rd BR2 42 D5
aywood Rise BR6 57 E5
azard Ho 4 DA11 19 A1
azel Ave
Hoo St Werburgh ME3 40 E3
Maidstone ME16 99 C5
azel Cotts TN14 75 A6
azel Dr DA8 15 B6
azel End BR8 45 E4
azel Gr Chatham ME5 68 B8
Orpington BR6 57 B8
azel Rd Dartford DA1 32 D6
Erith DA8 15 A6
azel Shaw TN10 127 D7
azel Street Rd ME9 87 A4
azel Wlk BR2 43 A3
azelbank TN3 157 F3
azelden Cl TN15 62 A2
azelden Cotts ME2 38 C6
azeldene Rd DA16 13 C5
azelmere 8 DA14 30 A4
azelmere Rd BR5 43 D5
azelmere Way BR2 42 A3
azels The ME8 69 B5
azelview ME19 80 E3
azelwood Cl TN2 159 D8
azelwood Cotts TN5 186 D1
azelwood Dr ME16 99 B4
azelwood Hts RH8 104 A4
azelwood Rd
Downe TN14 73 D8
Oxted RH8 104 B3
azelwood Sch RH8 104 A4
azen Rd ME18 97 B3
azlemere Dr ME7 55 A5
azlitt Ct 4 SE28 3 C5
azlitt Dr ME16 99 D5
ead Race The ME15 99 D2
eadcorn Prim Sch
TN27 151 C5
eadcorn Rd Bromley BR1 28 A3
Gillingham ME8 55 B4
Lashenden TN27 168 A5
Platt's Heath ME17 119 F1
Smarden Bell TN27 152 C3
Staplehurst TN12 150 B4
Sutton Valence ME17 134 E4
Ulcombe ME17 135 F5
eadcorn Sta TN27 151 D4
eadingley Rd ME16 99 B6
eadley Ct TN8 122 C2
eadley Ho 5 BR5 44 B7
eadway Ct TN4 158 B4
ealy Dr 1 BR6 57 F6
eansill La TN18 194 E8
earns Rd BR5 44 C5
eartenoak Rd TN18 189 B3
eath Ave DA7 13 D8
eath Cl Orpington BR5 44 C3
Swanley BR8 45 E7
eath Ct TN12 162 F6
eath Gdns DA1 32 C7
eath Gr ME16 99 A2
Heath Ho DA15 29 F4
Heath La Dartford DA1 32 C7
Dartford DA1,DA2 32 B7
Heath Park Dr BR1 42 E6
Heath Rd Coldblow DA5 31 C7
Coxheath ME17 115 C3
Crayford DA1 14 F1
East Farleigh ME15 114 E4
Langley Heath ME17 117 E4
Maidstone,Cock Street
ME17 116 C2
Maidstone,East Barming
ME16 98 F3
Heath Rise BR2 42 A3
Heath Side BR5 43 C2
Heath St DA1 32 D8
Heath Terr TN12 163 A6
Heath The ME19 97 F5
Heath View Dr SE2 13 D8
Heath Villas SE18 2 F1
Heath Way DA7,DA8 14 D6
Heathclose Ave DA1 32 B8
Heathclose Rd DA1 32 B7
Heathcote Cl ME20 82 F2
Heathdene Dr DA17 4 B2
Heathend Rd DA5 31 E7
Heather Bank TN12 146 B6
Heather Cl Chatham ME5 67 F4
Newham E6 2 A7
Heather Dr Dartford DA1 32 A8
Maidstone ME15 100 B2
Tenterden TN30 183 B3
Heather End BR8 45 D5
Heather Rd SE12 28 A7
Heather Wlk TN10 127 B6
Heatherbank
Chislehurst BR7 43 A7
Eltham SE9 11 F5
Heatherbank Cl DA1 14 E1
Heathers The TN17 179 A3
Heatherside Rd DA14 30 C5
Heatherwood Cl ME17 118 E2
Heathfield Chislehurst BR7 29 C2
Langley Heath ME17 117 E4
Heathfield Ave ME14 100 C7
Heathfield Cl
Chatham ME5 68 B7
Maidstone ME14 100 B7
Newham E16 1 D8
Orpington BR2 56 C5
Heathfield Ct DA14 30 B3
Heathfield La BR7 29 C2
Heathfield Rd Bexley DA6 13 F3
Maidstone ME14 100 C7
Orpington BR2 56 D5
Sevenoaks TN13 91 F5
Heathfield Terr
Bexley SE18 12 F8
Swanley BR8 45 D7
Heathfields TN2 159 D4
Heathlands Rise DA1 15 B1
Heathlee Rd DA1 14 E1
Heathley End BR7 29 C2
Heathorn St ME14 100 B5
Heathside Ave Bexley DA7 13 E5
Coxheath ME17 115 C4
Heathview TN4 142 F2
Heathview Ave DA1 14 E1
Heathview Cres DA1 32 B7
Heathway SE3 11 A7
Heathwood Gdns
Swanley BR8 45 C7
Woolwich SE7 1 E1
Heathwood Wlk DA5 31 E7
Heaverham Rd TN15 77 C2
Heavitree Cl 3 SE18 2 D1
Heavitree Rd SE18 2 D1
Hector St SE18 2 E2
Hectorage Rd TN9 143 D8
Hedge Barton Trailer Pk
TN3 156 F5
Hedge Place Rd DA9 17 A1
Hedgerow The ME14 100 E5
Hedgerows The DA11 35 E6
Hedges The ME14 100 A7
Hedley Ave RM20 17 C8
Hedley St ME14 100 A5
Heights The SE7 1 C1
Helegan Cl BR6 57 F6
Helen Allison Sch DA13 50 A2
Helen Cl DA1 32 B8
Helen Ct 9 DA14 30 B4
Helen Keller Cl TN10 127 D4
Helen St SE18 2 B2
Hellyar Ct ME1 53 C4
Hemmings Cl DA14 30 B6
Hempstead Inf Sch ME7 69 A5
Hempstead Jun Sch ME7 69 A5
Hempstead Rd
Gillingham ME7 69 A5
Gillingham ME7,ME8 69 B6
Hempstead Valley Dr
ME7 69 A4
Hempstead Valley Sh Ctr
ME7 69 A3
Hemstead Forest Walks*
Fosten Green TN27 181 A7
* Fosten Green TN27 181 C5
Hemsted Forest Walks*
TN17 180 E2
Hemsted Rd DA8 14 E7
Henbane Cl ME14 100 E5
Henderson Dr DA1 16 A3
Henderson Rd TN16 72 C7
Hendley Dr TN17 179 C5
Hendry Ho ME3 39 F6
Hendy Rd ME6 82 B8
Henfield Cl DA5 14 A1
Hengist Rd Eltham SE12 28 B8
Erith DA8 14 C7
Hengrove Ct DA5 30 E7
Henham Gdns TN12 130 A6
Henhurst Hill DA12 50 D8
Henhurst Rd
Gravesend DA13 36 E1
Henhurst DA12 50 E8
Heniker La ME17 135 A4
Henley Bsns Pk ME2 53 D7
Henley Cl Chatham ME5 68 A6
Gillingham ME8 69 D8
Royal Tunbridge Wells
TN2 159 C4
Henley Ct DA5 30 F8
Henley Deane DA11 35 E4
Henley Fields
Maidstone ME14 100 E6
Tenterden TN30 183 B2
Henley Mdws TN30 183 A2
Henley Rd Newham E16 1 F4
Paddock Wood TN12 146 A7
Henley St DA13 50 F3
Henley View TN30 183 B2
Henniker Cotts TN17 179 A3
Henry Addlington Cl E6 2 B8
Henry Cooper Way SE9 28 D4
Henry St Bromley BR1 42 B8
Chatham ME4 54 B3
14 Grays RM17 18 C8
Henrys Cl ME18 113 D6
Henson Cl BR6 57 B8
Henville Rd BR1 42 B8
Henwick Prim Sch SE9 11 E4
Henwick Rd SE9 11 E4
Henwood Green Rd
TN2 160 E6
Henwoods Cres TN2 160 D6
Henwoods Mount TN2 160 E6
Herald Wlk DA1 15 F2
Herbert Pl SE18 12 B8
Herbert Rd Bexley DA7 13 E5
Bromley BR2 42 E4
Chatham ME4 54 A3
Gillingham ME8 69 E8
Hextable BR8 32 B2
Swanscombe DA10 17 F1
Woolwich SE18 12 B8
Herdsdown ME3 40 D5
Hereford Cl ME8 55 D2
Hereford Rd ME15 116 D7
Heritage Dr ME7 54 F1
Heritage Hill BR2 56 C5
Heritage Quay DA12 19 C1
Heritage Rd ME5 68 A6
Heritage The BR6 44 A2
Herman Terr ME4 54 A3
Hermitage Cl SE2 3 C3
Hermitage Cnr ME17 133 F6
Hermitage Ct
Maidstone ME16 98 F5
Tonbridge TN9 127 C2
Hermitage Farm ME19 97 C8
Hermitage La
Detling ME14 85 B4
Maidstone ME16,ME20 98 F6
Rabbit's Cross ME17 133 E6
Hermitage Rd ME3 38 E4
Hermitage The ME19 97 D8
Hern The TN15 95 C5
Herne Rd ME8 55 C2
Hero Wlk ME1 67 C7
Heron Apartments 3
ME15 116 F5
Heron Cl TN8 122 C3
Heron Cotts TN18 197 D3
Heron Cres DA14 29 E4
Heron Ct BR2 42 C5
Heron Hill DA17 3 F2
Heron Hill La DA13 64 A4
Heron Ho DA14 30 B5
Heron Rd ME20 81 F1
Heron Way Chatham ME5 68 B7
Lower Stoke ME3 25 C4
Heronden Rd ME15 116 F4
Herongate Rd BR8 31 E2
Herons Way TN2 160 E8
Heronsgate Prim Sch
SE28 2 D3
Herringham Rd SE7 1 C3
Herts Cres ME15 115 F3
Hertsfield Ave ME2 39 A2
Hertsfield Farm Cotts
TN12 133 B4
Hervey Rd SE3 11 B6
Herying Cl ME2 66 B4
Hesketh Ave DA2 33 B7
Heskett Pk TN2 160 E6
Hever Ave TN15 61 E4
Hever Castle* TN8 139 D7
Hever CE Prim Sch TN8 139 D6
Hever Cl ME15 116 F6
Hever Court Rd DA12 36 D2
Hever Croft Eltham SE9 29 A4
Rochester ME2 52 F5
Hever Gdns Bromley BR1 43 A7
Maidstone ME16 99 E3
Hever Ho ME2 39 C1
Hever Rd
Bough Beech TN8 123 D2
Hever TN8 139 B7
West Kingsdown TN15 61 E4
Hever Road Cotts TN8 123 E2
Hever Sta TN8 139 B6
Hever Wood Rd TN15 61 E4
Heverham Rd SE18 2 E2
Heversham Rd DA7 14 A6
Heverswood TN14 59 A2
Hewett Ho 7 SE18 2 B1
Hewett Pl BR8 45 D5
Hewitt Cl Gillingham ME7 54 F6
Maidstone ME16 99 D7
Hewitts Rd BR6,TN14 58 F3
Hextable Cl ME16 99 D7
Hextable Inf Sch BR8 31 F2
Hextable Jun Sch BR8 31 F2
Hextable Sch BR8 45 F8
Hibbs Cl BR8 45 D7
Hibernia Dr DA12 36 F5
Hibernia Point 11 SE2 3 D4
Hickin Cl SE7 1 D2
Hickman Cl E16 1 D8
Hickory Dell ME7 69 A5
Hide E6 2 A7
Higgins' La ME4 53 F5
High Bank ME1 53 D2
High Banks ME15 115 F5
High Beeches
Orpington BR6 58 A4
Royal Tunbridge Wells
TN2 159 D6
Sidcup DA14 30 E3
High Brooms Ind Pk
TN2 159 C8
High Brooms Rd TN4 159 C7
High Brooms Sta TN4 159 C7
High Croft Cotts BR8 46 A5
High Cross Rd TN15 94 B1
High Dewar Rd ME8 70 A8
High Elms ME8 55 E1
High Elms Ctry Pk* BR6 57 D3
High Elms Rd BR6 57 C2
High Firs BR8 45 E5
High Firs Prim Sch BR8 45 F5
High Gr Bromley BR1 42 D8
Woolwich SE18 12 D6
High Halden CE Prim Sch
TN26 183 E7
High Halden Rd TN26,
TN27 168 C2
High Halstow Prim Sch
ME23 23 E3
High Hilden Cl TN10 127 A4
High House La TN11 111 C2
High Meads Rd E16 1 D7
High Oak Hill ME9 71 D8
High Point SE9 29 B5
High Rd DA2 32 C5
High Ridge TN17 177 E8
High Rocks* TN3 158 B1
High Rocks La TN3,TN4 158 C1
High Rocks Sta* TN3 158 B1
High St Aylesford ME20 82 F3
Bean DA2 34 B5
Bidborough TN3 142 C3
Biddenden TN27 167 F1
Borough Green TN15 94 F7
Brasted TN14,TN16 90 C3
Brenchley TN12 162 B8
Bromley BR1 42 A6
Bromley BR1 42 A7
Chatham ME4 54 A4
Chatham ME7 54 A6
Cowden TN8 155 B5
Cranbrook TN17 179 C4
Dartford DA1 15 E1
Downe BR6 73 A8
East Malling ME19 98 A6
Edenbridge TN8 122 C1
Eynsford DA4 60 E8
Farningham DA4 46 F2
Flimwell TN5 187 C3
Frant TN3 173 C4
Gillingham ME7 54 C5
Gillingham,Rainham ME8 69 F8
Goudhurst TN17 177 E8
Grain ME3 27 B6
Gravesend DA11 19 B1
2 Grays RM17 18 A8
Hadlow TN11 128 E8
Halling ME2 66 A4
Hawkhurst TN18 188 E2
Headcorn TN27 151 C5
Kemsing TN15 77 B2
Lamberhurst TN3 176 B5
Leigh TN11 125 F1
Lenham ME17 120 D5
Limpsfield RH8 104 B7
Lower Stoke ME3 25 C4
Maidstone ME14 99 F4
Marden TN12 148 D6
Newington ME9 71 C6
Northfleet DA11 18 C1
Orpington,Broom Hill BR6 44 A1
Orpington,Farnborough BR6 57 C5
Orpington,Green Street Green
BR6 57 F4
Orpington,St Mary Cray BR5 44 C4
Otford TN14 76 A3
Pembury TN2 160 C6
Penshurst TN11 141 B4
Rochester ME1 53 C6
Rochester,Strood ME2 53 B7
Rochester,Upper Upnor
ME2 39 F1
Rolvenden TN17 191 E4
Royal Tunbridge Wells
TN1 159 A2
Rusthall TN4 158 C4
Seal TN15 92 F6
Sevenoaks TN13 92 C2
Sevenoaks,Chipstead TN13 91 C5
Shoreham TN14 59 F1
Sidcup DA14 30 A4
Snodland ME6 82 A8
Staplehurst TN12 149 F3
High St *continued*
Sutton Valence ME17 134 E7
Swanley BR8 45 F5
Swanscombe DA10 17 F2
Swanscombe,Greenhithe
DA9 17 B3
Tenterden TN30 193 A7
Ticehurst TN5 186 C1
Tonbridge TN9 127 C2
Wadhurst TN5 184 F4
West Malling ME19 97 C8
Westerham TN16 105 C8
Wouldham ME1 66 C5
Wrotham TN15 79 A3
Yalding ME18 113 F1
High Tor Cl BR1 28 B1
High Tor View SE28 2 E5
High Trees DA2 16 B1
High View ME3 38 C4
High Woods La TN3 160 B3
Higham Cl ME15 99 E2
Higham Gdns TN10 127 F5
Higham La TN10,TN11 127 F6
Higham Prim Sch ME3 38 C5
Higham Rd Cliffe ME3 22 A4
Rochester ME3 39 C3
Higham School Rd
TN10 127 E6
Higham Sta ME3 38 D6
Higham View ME14 83 E4
Highbanks Cl DA16 13 B7
Highberry ME19 81 E2
Highbrook Rd SE3 11 D4
Highbury La TN30 193 A7
Highbury Pl TN5 184 F5
Highcombe SE7 11 B8
Highcombe Cl SE9 28 E7
Highcroft Gn ME15 116 F4
Highcroft Hall BR8 45 D1
Highcross Rd DA13 34 D2
Highdown Cotts TN17 176 F3
Highfield Ave Erith DA8 14 B8
Orpington BR6 57 F5
Highfield Cl
Gillingham ME8 69 D7
Hawkhurst TN18 189 A1
Pembury TN2 160 D6
Highfield Cotts DA2 32 B2
Highfield Ct DA1 32 D8
Highfield Rd Bexley DA6 13 F2
Biggin Hill TN16 72 C3
Bromley BR1 42 F5
Dartford DA1 32 D8
Gillingham ME8 69 D7
Kemsing TN15 76 F3
Royal Tunbridge Wells
TN4 159 C7
St Paul's Cray BR7 43 F6
Highfield Rd N DA1 15 D1
Highfield Rd S DA1 32 D7
Highfields Rd TN8 122 C4
Highgate Ct 8 TN18 188 F2
Highgate Hill TN18 188 F1
Highgrove TN2 173 A8
Highgrove Cl BR7 42 E8
Highgrove Rd ME5 68 A5
Highland Rd
Badgers Mount TN14 75 B8
Bexley DA6 14 A3
Maidstone ME15 116 E6
Highlands Dartford DA1 32 C8
Royal Tunbridge Wells
TN2 159 D7
Highlands Cl ME2 52 D5
Highlands Hill BR8 46 A8
Highlands Pk TN15 92 E6
Highlands Rd BR5 44 C2
Highmead SE18 12 F7
Highridge ME7 54 F1
Highridge Cl ME14 100 F5
Highstead Cres DA8 14 E7
Highview Vigo Village DA13 80 B8
Woolwich SE18 12 B7
Highview Cl ME15 116 A8
Highview Dr ME5 67 D5
Highview Rd DA14 30 B4
Highway Prim Sch The
BR6 58 C5
Highway The BR6 58 C5
Highwood Cl BR6 57 C8
Highwood Dr BR6 57 C8
Highwoods Cl ME3 38 C4
Hilary Cl DA8 14 C6
Hilary Gdns ME1 52 F1
Hilbert Cl TN2 159 C5
Hilbert Rd TN2 159 C5
Hilborough Way BR6 57 D5
Hilda May Ave BR8 45 E7
Hilda Rd ME4 54 A3
Hilda Vale Cl BR6 57 A6
Hilda Vale Rd BR6 57 B6
Hilden Ave TN11 126 F4
Hilden Dr DA8 15 B7
Hilden Grange Sch
TN10 127 B3
Hilden Oaks Sch TN10 127 B3
Hilden Park Rd TN11 126 F4
Hildenborough CE Prim Sch
TN11 126 D6
Hildenborough Cres
ME16 99 C7
Hildenborough Rd
Leigh TN11 126 A3
Shipbourne TN11,TN15 109 E4

Hildenborough Sta
TN11 126 B6
Hildenbrook Farm TN11 109 E2
Hildenfields TN10 127 A4
Hilders Cl TN8 122 B4
Hilders La TN8 122 A4
Hill Brow Bromley BR1 42 D8
Crayford DA1 14 F1
Maidstone ME14 101 A5
Hill Chase ME5 67 E3
Hill Cl Chislehurst BR7 29 B3
Istead Rise DA13 35 E1
Hill Cres Coldblow DA5 31 C7
Lenham ME17 120 D5
Hill Crest
Royal Tunbridge Wells
TN4 159 B8
Sevenoaks TN13 92 A5
Sidcup DA15 30 B8
Hill Ct ME3 39 F4
Hill End Orpington BR6 57 F8
Woolwich SE18 12 A6
Hill Farm Cl ME23 23 E3
Hill Green Rd ME9 86 D8
Hill House Rd DA2 33 C8
Hill Rd Dartford DA2 32 E6
Rochester ME1 53 A2
Wouldham ME1 66 F5
Hill Rise DA2 33 E3
Hill Sch The TN16 89 B4
Hill Shaw DA3 48 F3
Hill St TN1 159 B5
Hill The Cranbrook TN17 179 D4
Northfleet DA11 18 C1
Hill Top TN17 164 E5
Hill Top Cotts ME17 115 E2
Hill View Basted TN15 94 F4
Borough Green TN15 95 A7
Hill View Cl TN15 95 A7
Hill View Dr Bexley DA16 12 E5
Woolwich SE28 2 E5
Hill View Rd
New Barn DA3 49 B6
Orpington BR6 57 F8
Rusthall TN4 158 C4
Tonbridge TN11 126 F5
Hill View Way ME5 67 E5
Hill's Terr ME4 53 F3
Hillary Ave DA11 35 E5
Hillary Ct SE9 28 E6
Hillary Rd ME14 100 A7
Hillborough Ave TN13 92 D5
Hillborough Gr ME5 68 A3
Hillbrow Cl DA5 31 D4
Hillbury Gdns TN5 186 D1
Hillcrest TN8 123 B5
Hillcrest Ave RM20 17 A8
Hillcrest Dr Cuxton ME2 52 C2
Royal Tunbridge Wells
TN2 159 D7
Stone DA9 17 A2
Hillcrest Rd
Biggin Hill TN16 72 D3
Bromley BR1 28 A4
Chatham ME4 53 F2
Dartford DA1 31 F8
Marlpit Hill TN8 122 C4
Orpington BR6 58 A8
Hillcroft DA4 60 D7
Hillcroft Rd E6 2 B8
Hillden Shaw ME15 116 A8
Hilldown Lodge BR6 58 B8
Hilldrop Rd BR1 28 B2
Hillfield Rd TN13 91 E7
Hillfield Villas TN26 183 F8
Hillgarth TN4 159 A8
Hillingdale TN16 72 B1
Hillingdon Ave TN13 92 D6
Hillingdon Rd Bexley DA7 14 C4
Gravesend DA11 36 B6
Hillingdon Rise TN13 92 D5
Hillreach SE18 1 F1
Hills La TN15 77 C7
Hillsgrove Cl DA16 13 C7
Hillsgrove Prim Sch
DA16 13 C7
Hillshaw Cres ME2 52 D5
Hillside Dartford DA2 33 E3
Erith DA17 4 C2
Farningham DA4 46 F2
Rochester ME1 53 A2
Tonbridge TN9 143 A7
Hillside Ave
Gravesend DA12 36 D6
Rochester ME2 53 B8
Hillside Cotts TN5 185 B8
Hillside Ct
2 Rochester ME2 53 A7
Swanley BR8 46 A5
Wateringbury ME18 113 E7
Hillside Dr DA12 36 D6
Hillside La BR2 56 A8
Hillside Prim Sch BR5 44 C2
Hillside Rd Chatham ME4 54 A4
Dartford DA1 15 A1
Kemsing TN15 76 F2
Sevenoaks TN13 92 D4
Tatsfield TN16 88 E8
Hillside Terr DA12 36 B7
Hillside The BR6 58 B2
Hillsley Ct 13 DA14 30 A4
Hilltop Tonbridge TN9 143 B7
West Farleigh ME15 114 D3
Hilltop Gdns Dartford DA1 15 F2
Orpington BR6 57 E8
Hilltop Prim Sch ME2 39 C1
Hilltop Rd Rochester ME2 39 C1
West Thurrock RM20 17 B8
Hillview Cres BR6 43 F1
Hillview Ho DA12 36 C7
Hillview Rd BR7 29 A4
Hillview Sch for Girls
TN9 143 D8
Hillydeal Rd TN14 76 C4
Hillyfield Cl ME2 38 F1
Hilton Rd ME3 39 B7
Hind Cres DA8 14 D7
Hines Terr ME5 54 C1
Hinksden Rd TN17,TN18 189 F3
Hinksey Path SE2 3 D3
Hinstock Rd SE18 12 C7
Hinton Cl SE9 28 E7
Hinton Cres ME7 69 A6
Historic Dockyard The*
ME4 54 A8
Hitchen Hatch La TN13 92 B4
Hither Chantlers TN3 158 A2
Hither Farm Rd SE3 11 C4
Hive La DA11 18 B2
Hive The DA11 18 B1
Hoath Cl ME8 69 B7
Hoath La ME8 69 B7
Hoath Mdw TN12 163 A6
Hoath Way ME7,ME8 69 B5
Hobart Rd RM18 19 A6
Hoblands End BR7 29 E2
Hockenden La BR8 45 B7
Hockers Cl ME14 101 A8
Hockers La ME14 101 A8
Hoddesdon Rd DA17 4 A1
Hodgkins Cl SE28 3 D6
Hodgson Cres ME6 66 A1
Hodsoll Ct BR5 44 D4
Hodsoll St TN15 63 D1
Hodson Cres BR5 44 D3
Hog Hill ME14 101 B5
Hog Hole La TN3 175 F2
Hog La DA11 35 D5
Hogarth Cl E16 1 D8
Hogbarn La ME17 103 F2
Hognore La TN15 79 D6
Hogs Orch BR8 46 B8
Hogtrough Hill TN16 90 A5
Holbeach Gdns DA15 12 F1
Holborn La ME4 53 F5
Holborn Rd E13 1 B8
Holborough Rd ME6 66 A1
Holbrook Ho BR7 43 D8
Holbrook La BR7 29 D1
Holbrook Way BR2 42 F4
Holburne Cl SE3 11 C6
Holburne Gdns SE3 11 D6
Holburne Rd SE3 11 D6
Holcombe Cl TN16 89 D1
Holcombe Rd
Chatham ME4 53 F2
Rochester ME1 53 C3
Holcote Cl DA17 3 E3
Holden Cnr TN4 142 F1
Holden Park Rd TN4 159 A8
Holden Rd TN4 142 F1
Holder Cl ME5 68 C6
Holding St ME8 55 F1
Hole La TN8 122 A6
Holford St 1 TN9 127 B1
Holgate St SE7 1 D3
Holland Cres RH8 104 A2
Holland Ho ME1 53 D5
Holland Jun Sch RH8 104 A1
Holland La RH8 104 A2
Holland Rd Chatham ME5 67 E4
Maidstone ME14 100 B5
Oxted RH8 104 A1
Hollandbury Pk ME18 97 C2
Hollands Cl DA12 37 E3
Hollies Ave DA15 29 F7
Hollies The
Gravesend DA12 36 D2
New Barn DA3 49 C6
Sidcup DA15 30 A8
Holligrave Rd BR1 42 A8
Hollin Cl TN4 158 F4
Hollingbourne Ave DA7 13 F6
Hollingbourne Hill
ME17 102 F4
Hollingbourne Prim Sch
ME17 102 E2
Hollingbourne Rd ME8 55 C2
Hollingbourne Sta
ME17 102 C3
Hollingbourne Twr 4
BR5 44 D1
Hollington Ct BR7 29 B2
Hollingworth Ct ME14 100 C3
Hollingworth Rd
Maidstone ME15 116 F5
Orpington BR2,BR5 43 B2
Hollingworth Way TN16 89 D1
Hollow La Hartlip ME9 70 E5
Snodland ME6 81 F6
Hollow Trees Dr TN11 126 A1
Holly Bank TN12 162 B8
Holly Bush La TN13 92 C3
Holly Cl Chatham ME5 68 C8
Gillingham ME7 54 E6
Holly Cotts TN8 122 B2
Holly Ct 1 DA14 30 B4
Holly Farm Rd ME15 117 C6
Holly Gdns Bexley DA7 14 C3
Maidstone ME14 100 B7
Holly Hill DA13 64 F3
Holly Hill Rd DA8,DA17 4 B1
Holly Rd Dartford DA1 32 D7
Holly Rd *continued*
Orpington BR6 58 A3
Rochester ME2 39 D2
Rochester,Strood ME2 52 E5
Holly Tree Cl ME17 118 E2
Hollybrake Cl BR7 29 D1
Hollybush Cl TN13 92 C3
Hollybush Ct TN13 92 C3
Hollybush La BR6 59 A4
Hollybush Rd DA12 36 C6
Hollycroft ME2 52 C2
Hollydale Dr BR2 56 F7
Hollydene Rd TN5 184 F6
Hollyshaw TN2 159 C2
Hollyshaw Cl TN2 159 C2
Hollytree Ave BR8 45 E7
Hollytree Dr ME3 38 B3
Hollytree Par DA14 30 C2
Hollywood La
Knockmill TN15 77 F8
Rochester ME2 39 C2
Hollywood Way DA8 15 B6
Holm Ct 5 SE12 28 B5
Holm Mill La ME17 119 B6
Holm Wlk SE3 11 A5
Holmbury Manor 21
DA14 30 A4
Holmbury Pk BR7 28 E1
Holmcroft Way BR2 42 F4
Holmdale Rd BR7 29 C3
Holmden Ct 2 TN8 122 C1
Holmdene Ct 5 BR1 42 E6
Holmes Cl ME23 23 E3
Holmes Ct ME19 80 F4
Holmesdale Cl
Durgates TN5 184 E5
Maidstone ME15 115 F3
Holmesdale Hill DA4 47 D8
Holmesdale Rd
Bexley DA7 13 D5
Sevenoaks TN13 92 D4
Sutton at H DA4 47 C8
Holmesdale Tech Coll
ME6 81 F7
Holmewood House Sch
TN3 158 A2
Holmewood Rd TN4 159 C7
Holmewood Ridge TN3 157 F3
Holmhurst Cl TN4 158 F4
Holmhurst Rd DA17 4 B1
Holmleigh Ave DA1 15 C2
Holmoaks Gillingham ME8 55 E2
Maidstone ME14 100 C5
Holmsdale Gr DA1,DA7 14 E4
Holmside ME7 54 E3
Holmwood Cotts BR6 58 C1
Holmwood Ct DA14 29 F3
Holstein Way 6 DA18 3 E3
Holt Cl SE28 3 C6
Holt Rd E16 1 E5
Holt Wood Ave ME20 98 E8
Holtwood Cl ME8 69 D6
Holtye Cres ME15 100 B2
Holtye Rd RH19 154 A4
Holwood Park Ave BR2,
BR4 56 F6
Holy Family RC Prim Sch
Eltham SE3 11 C3
Maidstone ME15 116 F4
Holy Innocents RC Prim Sch
BR6 57 F7
Holy Trinity CE Prim Sch
Dartford DA1 15 C2
Gravesend DA12 36 C8
Holy Trinity Coll Prep Sch
BR1 42 C8
Holy Trinity Lamorbey CE
Prim Sch DA15 30 A7
Holyhead Cl 3 E6 1 F8
Holyoake Terr TN13 92 A3
Holyrood Mews E16 1 A5
Holywell Cl Greenwich SE3 11 A8
Orpington BR6 58 A6
Home Farm BR6 59 A5
Home Farm Cl TN11 126 A3
Home Farm Cotts BR5 44 D8
Home Farm Ct TN3 173 C4
Home Farm La TN2 159 E8
Home Gdns DA1 15 E1
Home Hill BR8 31 F1
Home Lea BR6 57 F5
Home Mead Cl 6 DA12 36 B8
Home Pk RH8 104 A4
Homedean Rd TN13 91 C4
Homefarm Est ME20 82 F1
Homefield Cl
Orpington BR5 44 B5
Swanley BR8 45 F6
Homefield Rd
Bromley BR1 42 C8
Sevenoaks TN13 91 E5
Homefield Rise BR6 44 A1
Homemead
7 Gravesend DA12 36 B8
Swanscombe DA9 17 B1
Homemead Rd BR2 42 F4
Homer Cl DA7 14 C6
Homesdale Bsns Ctr BR1 42 D6
Homesdale Rd
Bromley BR1,BR2 42 C6
Orpington BR5 43 E2
Homestead Rd
Marlpit Hill TN8 122 B5
Orpington BR6 58 B4
Homestead The
Crayford DA1 14 E2
Dartford DA1 15 C1
Groombridge TN3 171 C7
Homevale Cotts TN14 74 E4
Homewards Rd ME3 9 B2
Homewood Cotts DA12 37 E1
Homewood Cres BR7 29 E2
Homewood Rd
Langton Green TN3 157 F3
Tenterden TN30 183 B1
Homewood Sch & Sixth Form
Ctr TN30 183 B1
Homlesdale Bsns Ctr
TN15 95 C8
Homoepathic Hospl
TN1 159 A3
Honduras Terr 8 ME14 100 A7
Hone St ME2 53 B8
Honey Bee Glade ME8 69 E6
Honey Cl ME7 69 A5
Honey La ME15 117 B6
Honeybourne Way BR5 43 D1
Honeycombe Lodge
DA11 18 D1
Honeycrest Ind Pk
TN12 149 E5
Honeycrock Hill ME9 86 F8
Honeyden Rd DA14 30 E2
Honeypot Cl ME2 53 B8
Honeypot La
Hodsoll Street TN15 63 D2
Kemsing TN15 93 C8
Limpsfield TN8 121 D4
Honeysuckle Cl
3 Chatham ME5 67 E4
Gillingham ME7 68 F4
Honeysuckle Ct 4 SE12 28 A8
Honiton Rd DA16 12 F5
Honywood Rd ME17 120 C4
Hoo Comm ME3 40 A4
Hoo Rd ME2,ME3 39 D3
Hoo St Werburgh Prim Sch
ME3 40 D5
Hood Ave BR5 44 B4
Hook Cl ME5 67 E5
Hook Farm Rd BR2 42 D4
Hook Green Ct DA13 50 A4
Hook Green La DA2 31 F5
Hook Green Rd DA13 34 F1
Hook Hill TN5 186 A6
Hook La Bexley DA16 13 A4
Harrietsham ME17 119 C6
Hook Lane Prim Sch
DA16 13 A4
Hook Place Cotts DA13 35 A2
Hook Rd ME6 81 F8
Hookfields DA11 35 E5
Hookstead TN26 183 C7
Hookwood Bglws RH8 104 B7
Hookwood Cnr RH8 104 B7
Hookwood Cotts TN14 74 C8
Hookwood Rd BR6,TN14 74 C7
Hooper Rd E16 1 A7
Hooper's Pl ME1 53 C4
Hooper's Rd ME1 53 C4
Hoopers La ME3 24 F5
Hoopers Yd TN13 92 C1
Hop Bine Cl TN12 130 A7
Hop Farm Country Pk*
TN12 130 A3
Hop Pocket Cl TN17 180 A8
Hop Pocket La TN12 145 F7
Hope Ave TN11 111 E1
Hope Cl SE12 28 B5
Hope Cotts DA2 34 B6
Hope Rd DA10 17 F1
Hope St Chatham ME4 54 A3
Maidstone ME14 99 F6
Hope Terr ME3 38 D7
Hopedale Rd SE7 11 B8
Hopehouse La TN17,
TN18 196 E7
Hopes Gr TN26 183 D7
Hopewell Bsns Ctr ME5 68 C8
Hopewell Dr
Chatham ME5 68 C8
Gravesend DA12 36 F3
Hopgarden Cl 12 TN8 122 D3
Hopgarden La TN13 108 A8
Hopgarden Oast ME18 113 F1
Hopgarden Rd TN10 127 D6
Hoppers Cnr ME15 114 D7
Hopton Ct BR2 42 A1
Hopton Rd SE18 2 B3
Hopwood Gdns TN4 159 A6
Horatio Pl ME1 53 B4
Horizon Cl TN4 159 B8
Horley Cl DA6 14 A2
Horley Rd SE9 28 E4
Horn La SE10 1 A2
Horn Link Way SE10 1 A2
Horn Park Cl SE12 11 B2
Horn Park La SE12 11 B1
Horn Park Prim Sch
SE12 28 B8
Horn Yd 7 DA11 19 B1
Horn's Oak Rd DA13 64 B6
Hornbeam Ave
Chatham ME5 68 B2
Royal Tunbridge Wells
TN4 143 D1
Hornbeam Cl
Larkfield ME20 82 B2
Paddock Wood TN12 145 F5
Hornbeam Ho 6 DA15 30 A5
Hornbeam La DA7 14 C5
Hornbeam Way BR2 43 A3
Hornbeams DA13 80 B8
Horncastle Cl SE12 28 A8
Horncastle Rd SE12 28 A8
Horne Ho SE18 11 E6
Hornfair Rd SE7 11 D
Hornfield Cotts DA13 64 C
Horning Cl SE9 28 E
Horns La ME18 96 D
Horns Lodge Farm
TN11 127 C
Horns Lodge La TN11 127 A
Horns Rd The Moor TN18 194 B
The Moor TN18 194 D
The Moor TN18 194 F
Horsa Rd Eltham SE12 28 C
Erith DA8 14 C
Horse Leaze E6 2 A
Horse Wash La ME1 53 C
Horsecroft Cl BR6 44 B
Horsegrove Ave TN5 186 F
Horsell Rd BR5 44 B
Horseshoe Cl
Gillingham ME7 68 F
Maidstone ME14 100 E
Horseshoes La ME17 117 E
Horsfeld Gdns SE9 11 E
Horsfeld Rd SE9 11 D
Horsfield Cl DA2 33 C
Horsham Rd DA6 14 A
Horsley Ho SE18 12 A
Horsley Rd Bromley BR1 42 B
Rochester ME1 53 B
Horsmonden Cl BR6 43 F
Horsmonden Prim Sch
TN12 163 A
Horsmonden Rd TN12 162 D
Horsted Ave ME4 53 E
Horsted Inf Sch ME4 67 D
Horsted Jun Sch ME5 67 D
Horsted Ret Pk ME5 67 D
Horsted Way ME1 67 D
Horton Downs ME15 100 F
Horton Kirby CE Prim Sch
DA4 47 C
Horton Pl TN16 89 D
Horton Rd DA4 47 C
Horton Twr 2 BR5 44 C
Horton Way DA4 46 F
Hortons Cl TN17 190 D
Hortons Way 1 TN16 89 D
Horwood Cl ME1 67 B
Hoselands View DA3 48 E
Hoser Ave SE12 28 A
Hosey Common La
TN16 105 F
Hosey Common Rd TN8,
TN16 105 D
Hosey Hill TN16 105 E
Hoskin's Cl E16 1 C
Hospital La 3 ME1 53 E
Hospital Rd
Hollingbourne ME17 118 E
Sevenoaks TN13 92 C
Hostier Cl ME2 66 B
Hotel Rd ME8 55 A
Hotham Cl Sutton at H DA4 33 B
Swanley Village BR8 46 B
Hothfield Rd ME8 55 F
Hottsfield DA3 48 E
Hougham Ho 11 BR5 44 D
Houghton Ave ME7 69 B
Houselands Rd TN9 127 B
Hove Cl RM17 18 A
Hovendens TN17 180 A
Hoveton Rd SE28 3 C
How Green La TN8 123 C
Howard Ave
Rochester ME1 53 D
Sidcup DA5 30 C
Howard Dr ME16 99 B
Howard Gdns TN2 159 A
Howard Rd Bromley BR1 28 A
Dartford DA1 16 A
East Malling ME19 97 F
Howard Sch The ME8 69 D
Howarth Rd SE2 3 A
Howbury Ctr PRU The
DA8 15 A
Howbury La DA8 15 A
Howbury Wlk ME8 69 D
Howden Cl SE28 3 D
Howells Cl TN15 61 E
Howerd Way SE18 11 E
Howes Cotts TN18 194 F
Howick Cl ME20 98 F
Howick Mans SE18 1 E
Howland Cotts TN12 148 E
Howland Rd TN12 148 E
Howlands TN15 78 F
Howlands Ct TN15 78 F
Howlsmere Cl ME2 66 B
Hubbard's Hill TN13,
TN14 108 B
Hubbard's La ME15 116 A
Hubble Dr ME15 116 E
Huckleberry Cl ME5 68 B
Hudson Cl ME8 55 C
Hudson Ho DA4 47 D
Hudson Pl SE18 2 C
Hudson Rd DA7 13 F
Huggen's College
Almshouses DA11 18 B
Hugh Christie Tech Coll
TN10 127 D
Hughes Dr ME2 39 D
Hulberry Farm DA4 60 B
Hulkes La ME1 53 E
Hull Pl E16 2 C
Hulsewood Cl DA2 32 B
Hulsons Ct 1 TN18 189 A
Humber Cres ME2 52 F
Humber Rd Dartford DA1 15 D

Humber Rd *continued*
Greenwich SE3 11 A8
Humboldt Ct TN2 159 D5
Hume Ave RM18 19 B5
Hume Cl RM18 19 A4
Hume Terr E16 1 B7
Humphreys TN12 161 F6
Hundred of Hoo Comp Sch The ME3 40 C5
Hungershall Park Cl TN4 158 E1
Hungershall Pk TN4 158 E2
Hunsdon Dr TN13 92 B4
Hunstanton Cl ME8 69 E3
Hunt Rd Northfleet DA11 35 F5
Tonbridge TN10 127 E6
Hunt St
Nettlestead ME15,ME18 113 F5
West Farleigh ME15 114 B5
Hunter Seal TN11 126 E2
Hunter's Gr BR6 57 C6
Hunters Cl DA5 31 E5
Hunters Ct 5 ME7 54 C7
Hunters Lodge 10 DA15 30 A5
Hunters Way
Gillingham ME7 54 E1
Royal Tunbridge Wells TN2 158 F1
Hunters Way W ME5 54 E1
Hunters Wlk TN14 74 E5
Huntersfield Cl ME5 68 C1
Huntingdon Wlk 2 ME15 116 E7
Huntingfield Rd DA13 50 A2
Huntington Cl TN17 179 D4
Huntington Rd ME17 115 B3
Huntley Ave DA11 18 C1
Huntley Mill Rd TN5 186 E3
Huntleys Pk TN4 158 F5
Hunton CE Prim Sch ME15 131 D7
Hunton Hill ME15 114 F1
Hunton Ho 4 BR5 44 C4
Hunton Rd TN12 132 A3
Hunts Farm Cl TN15 95 A7
Hunts La TN17 177 E8
Hunts Mede Cl BR7 28 F1
Huntsman Ho 2 DA11 35 F8
Huntsman La
Maidstone ME14 100 B4
Wrotham Heath TN15 79 E1
Huntsman's Cnr ME4 67 E8
Huntsmans Cl ME1 53 E1
Huntsmoor Ho BR5 44 B5
Hurlfield DA2 32 C5
Hurlingham Cl TN10 127 E7
Hurlingham Rd DA7 13 F7
Huron Cl 5 BR6 57 F4
Hurricane Rd ME19 96 F3
Hurst Cl Chatham ME5 67 E6
Staplehurst TN12 149 F4
Tenterden TN30 192 F7
Hurst Ct Newham E6 1 D8
Sidcup DA15 30 A6
Hurst Farm Rd TN14 108 B3
Hurst Green CE Prim Sch TN19 194 A2
Hurst Green Cl RH8 104 A3
Hurst Green Inf Sch RH8 104 A3
Hurst Green Rd RH8 104 A3
Hurst Hill ME5 67 E2
Hurst Ho SE2 3 D1
Hurst La Erith SE2 3 D1
Sevenoaks Weald TN14 108 B2
Hurst Pl Gillingham ME8 69 F8
Woolwich SE2 3 C1
Hurst Prim Sch DA5 30 D7
Hurst Rd Erith DA8 14 C7
Sidcup DA5 30 D7
Hurst Springs DA5 30 E7
Hurst The Crouch TN11 111 D7
Plaxtol Spoute TN15 95 C1
Royal Tunbridge Wells TN2 159 E7
Hurst Way
Maidstone ME16 98 F2
Sevenoaks TN13 108 C8
Hurstbourne Cotts DA5 31 B8
Hurstfield BR2 42 A4
Hurstings The ME15 99 D2
Hurstlands RH8 104 A3
Hurstmere Foundation Sch for Boys DA15 30 C7
Hurstwood ME5 67 E4
Hurstwood Ave
Bexley DA7,DA8 14 E6
Sidcup DA5 30 E7
Hurstwood Dr BR1 42 F6
Hurstwood La TN4 158 F3
Hurstwood Pk TN4 158 F3
Hurstwood Rd
Bredhurst ME7 69 B1
Bredhurst,Bredhurst Hurst ME14 85 B7
Husheath Hill TN17 164 F6
Hussar Ho ME1 53 C3
Husseywell Cres BR2 42 A1
Hutchins Rd SE28 3 A5
Hutsford Cl ME8 69 D5
Hutson Terr RM19 16 D8
Huxley Ct 3 ME1 53 D4
Huxley Ho SE2 3 D1
Huxley Rd DA16 12 F4
Hyacinth Rd ME2 52 E6
Hybrid Cl ME1 53 D1
Hyde Dr BR5 44 B5
Hyde Rd Bexley DA7 13 F5
Hyde Rd *continued*
Maidstone ME16 99 D6
Hyde's Orch TN27 151 E5
Hyders Forge TN15 111 A8
Hylton St SE18 2 F2
Hyndford Cres DA9 17 C2
Hyperion Dr ME2 38 F1
Hythe Ave DA7 13 F7
Hythe Cl Orpington BR5 44 C5
Royal Tunbridge Wells TN4 143 A1
Hythe St Dartford DA1 15 E1
Dartford DA1 15 E2

I

Ice Bowl The* ME8 55 A1
Ickleton Rd SE9 28 E4
Icough Ct SE3 11 B7
Iddenden Cotts TN18 188 D2
Ide Hill CE Prim Sch TN14 106 F4
Ide Hill Rd
Bough Beech TN8,TN14 123 F5
Ide Hill TN14 106 F2
Iden Cres TN12 149 F2
Iden Croft Herbs* TN12 150 A1
Iden Green Cotts TN17 178 C8
Iden Rd ME2 39 C1
Idenwood Cl ME8 69 D6
Idleigh Court Rd DA3, DA13 63 C8
Ifield Cl ME15 116 F7
Ifield Sch The DA12 36 C3
Ifield Way DA12 36 D2
Ightham By-Pass TN15 94 C7
Ightham Cotts DA2 34 B6
Ightham Mote* TN15 110 A7
Ightham Prim Sch TN15 94 B6
Ightham Rd Bexley DA8 14 A7
Shipbourne TN11,TN15 110 C5
Ilkley Rd E16 1 C8
Illustrious Cl ME5 68 A6
Imber Ct 4 SE9 12 A1
Impala Gdns TN4 159 B6
Imperial Bsns Pk DA11 18 F1
Imperial Ct BR7 29 B2
Imperial Dr DA12 36 F3
Imperial Pl BR7 43 A8
Imperial Rd ME7 54 C3
Imperial Ret Pk DA11 19 A1
Imperial Way BR7 29 C5
Impton La ME5 68 A1
Inca Dr SE9 29 B8
Indus Rd SE7 11 C7
Industrial Est The TN8 122 B3
Ingle Pl ME18 97 A2
Ingle Rd ME4 53 F2
Ingleborough La TN15 95 C8
Ingleby Way BR7 29 A3
Ingleden Park Rd TN30 183 C1
Ingledew Rd SE18 2 D1
Ingleside Gr 3 SE3 11 A8
Ingleton Ave DA16 13 A2
Inglewood Chislehurst BR7 29 D2
Swanley BR8 45 E7
Inglewood Copse BR1 42 F7
Inglewood Rd DA7 14 D3
Ingoldsby Rd DA12 36 F7
Ingram Rd Dartford DA1 32 E7
Gillingham ME7 54 E6
Ingress Gdns DA9 17 D2
Ingress Park Ave DA9 17 C3
Ingress Terr DA13 34 E4
Inigo Jones Rd SE7 11 E7
Inner Lines ME7 54 A6
Institute Rd ME4 54 A4
Instone Rd DA1 32 D8
Inverary Pl SE18 12 D8
Inverine Rd SE7 1 B1
Invermore Pl SE18 2 C2
Inverness Ho 7 ME15 116 E7
Inverness Mews E16 2 C5
Invicta Bsns Pk TN15 79 C2
Invicta Cl BR7 29 A3
Invicta Gram Sch ME14 100 C4
Invicta Par 3 DA14 30 B4
Invicta Prim Sch SE3 11 A7
Invicta Rd Dartford DA2 16 B1
Greenwich SE3 11 A8
Invicta Villas ME14 101 C4
Io Ctr SE18 2 C3
Iona Cl ME5 68 D1
Iona Rd ME15 116 A7
Ionia Wlk DA12 36 F5
Ireland Cl E6 1 F8
Irene Rd BR6 43 F2
Iris Ave DA5 13 E1
Iris Cl ME5 84 A8
Iris Cres DA7 13 F8
Iron Mill La DA1 14 F3
Iron Mill Pl DA1 14 F3
Ironside Cl ME5 68 A8
Ironstones TN3 158 B3
Irvine Rd ME3 38 B3
Irvine Way BR6 43 F2
Irving Ho TN1 159 B5
Irving Way BR8 45 D7
Irving Wlk DA10 34 E8
Irwin Ave SE18 12 E7
Isabella Dr BR6 57 C6
Isla Rd SE18 12 C8
Island Way E ME4 40 C1
Island Way W ME4 40 B2
Islehurst Cl BR7 43 A8
Islingham Farm Rd ME3 39 D4
Ismays Rd TN15 94 C3
Istead Rise DA13 35 F1
Istead Rise Prim Sch DA13 49 E8
Itchingwood Common Rd RH8 104 E2
Ito Way ME8 55 A3
Ivedon Rd DA16 13 C5
Ivens Way ME17 119 D6
Iverhurst Cl DA6 13 D2
Iversgate Cl ME8 55 F2
Ives Rd TN9 126 F1
Ivor Gr SE9 29 B7
Ivor Ho DA14 30 C3
Ivorydown BR1 28 A4
Ivy Bower Cl DA9 17 B2
Ivy Cl Dartford DA1 33 A8
Gravesend DA12 36 D5
Kingswood ME17 118 D2
Ivy House La TN13,TN14 75 E2
Ivy La
Bells Yew Green TN3 174 A5
Knockholt TN14 74 E3
Ivy Mews ME17 118 E2
Ivy Pl ME1 53 A2
Ivy Rd E16 1 A7
Ivy St ME8 69 F8
Ivy Villas DA9 17 A2
Ivybridge Ct 1 BR7 43 A8
Izane Rd DA6 13 F3

J

Jackass La BR2 56 C4
Jacklin Cl ME5 67 F2
Jackson Ave ME1 67 E8
Jackson Cl Rainham ME8 55 C1
1 Stone DA9 17 A2
Jackson Ho 4 SE7 11 B8
Jackson Rd BR2 56 F8
Jackson St SE18 12 A8
Jackson Way TN17 181 C3
Jackson's Cnr ME3 24 A3
Jacksons La 8 TN30 193 A7
Jacob Ho 5 DA18 3 D4
Jacob's La ME3 41 B6
Jade Cl E16 1 D7
Jade Hill ME2 66 A6
Jaffray Rd BR2 42 D5
Jaggard Way TN12 149 E3
Jagger Cl DA2 33 C8
Jago Cl SE18 12 C8
Jail La Biggin Hill TN16 72 E3
Cudham TN16 73 A3
Jamaica Terr ME14 100 A7
James Newman Ct SE9 29 A5
James Rd Cuxton ME2 52 C2
Dartford DA1 15 A1
James St 5 Chatham ME4 53 F4
Gillingham ME7 54 C6
Maidstone ME14 100 A5
Rochester ME1 53 C4
James Watt Way DA8 14 F8
James Whatman Way ME14 99 F5
Jane Seymour Ct DA15 29 D8
Janet Ct 4 DA7 14 A3
Janson Ct 11 DA14 30 B4
Japonica Cl ME5 68 C2
Jaquets Ct DA5 31 A6
Jarrah Cotts RM19 16 D8
Jarrett Ave ME2 39 C2
Jarvis La TN17 164 B3
Jarvis Pl TN30 183 B3
Jasmine Cl
2 Chatham ME5 67 F4
East Malling ME19 97 F8
Orpington BR6 57 B8
Jasmine Cotts
Borough Green TN15 94 F7
Groombridge TN3 171 C7
Jasmine Ct SE12 11 A1
Jasmine Rd ME19 97 F8
Jason Wlk SE9 29 A4
Jasper Ave ME1 53 D2
Jasper Rd E16 1 D7
Javelin Rd ME19 96 F3
Jay Gdns BR7 28 F4
Jefferson Dr ME8 55 C1
Jefferson Wlk 13 SE18 12 A8
Jeffery St ME7 54 C6
Jeffrey Cl TN12 149 E4
Jeffrey Ct DA8 14 C7
Jeffrey Row SE12 11 B2
Jeffrey St ME14 100 A5
Jeken Rd SE9 11 C3
Jellicoe Ave DA12 36 C5
Jellicoe Ave W DA12 36 C5
Jenkins Dr ME15 116 E5
Jenkins' Dale ME4 53 F3
Jenner Cl DA14 30 A4
Jenner Ho 4 DA17 4 A3
Jenner Rd ME1 53 C4
Jenner Way ME20 82 F6
Jennifer Ct ME3 40 F5
Jenningtree Rd DA8 15 B7
Jenningtree Way DA17 4 C4
Jenton Ave DA7 13 E5
Jerome Rd ME20 81 F4
Jersey Dr BR5 43 D3
Jersey Rd Newham E16 1 C8
Rochester ME2 53 A8
Jeskyns Rd DA12 50 E6
Jessamine Pl DA2 33 C8
Jessamine Terr BR8 45 C8
Jessett Cl DA8 4 D2
Jessup Cl SE18 2 C2
Jetty Rd Kingsnorth ME3 41 D7
Sheerness ME12 27 F3
Jetty Wlk 3 RM17 18 A8
Jevington Way SE12 28 B7
Jewell Gr TN12 148 D5
Jewels Hill TN16 72 A6
Jeyes Rd ME7 54 C4
Jezreels Rd ME7 54 D3
Jim Bradley Cl 10 SE18 2 A2
Jiniwin Rd ME1 67 D7
Joan Cres SE9 28 D8
Jockey La TN17 179 D5
Johannesburg Ho 2 ME15 116 F5
John Brunt Ct TN12 146 A7
John Burns Cotts RH8 104 E5
John Coopper Ho ME3 25 C5
John Hunt Ct SE9 28 E6
John Mayne CE Prim Sch TN27 167 F1
John Newton Ct DA16 13 B4
John Spare Ct TN4 159 A6
John St Grays RM17 18 C8
Maidstone ME14 100 A6
Rochester ME1 53 C4
Royal Tunbridge Wells TN4 159 A5
John Wesley Ct SE9 12 A3
John Wilson St SE18 2 A2
John's Rd
Meopham Sta DA13 49 F4
Tatsfield TN16 88 D7
Johns Cl DA3 48 F4
Johns Rd TN16 73 B3
Johnson Ave ME7 54 C7
Johnson Cl DA11 35 D5
Johnson Rd BR2 42 D4
Johnsons Ave TN14 59 B1
Johnsons Ct TN15 92 F6
Johnsons Way DA9 17 C1
Joiners Ct ME4 54 B2
Jonas Dr TN5 184 E5
Jonas La TN5 184 E5
Jordan Cl ME15 116 E5
Josling Cl RM17 17 F8
Joy Rd DA12 36 C7
Joy Wood ME17 116 D5
Joyce Cl TN17 179 C5
Joyce Dawson Way SE28 3 A6
Joyce Green Ho DA1 15 F4
Joyce Green Hspl DA1 15 E4
Joyce Green La
Dartford DA1 15 E6
Dartford,Temple Hill DA1 15 F4
Joyce Green Wlk DA1 15 F3
Joyce Page Cl SE7 11 D8
Joyden's Wood Rd DA5 31 E5
Joydens Wood Inf Sch DA5 31 E4
Joydens Wood Jun Sch DA2 31 E4
Jubilee Cl DA9 17 C1
Jubilee Cnr ME17 135 E3
Jubilee Cotts
Sevenoaks TN14 92 B7
Sutton Valence ME17 134 E7
Jubilee Cres
Gravesend DA12 36 E6
Ightham TN15 94 C6
Jubilee Ct DA1 32 D8
Jubilee Field TN30 199 E4
Jubilee Park Ctry Pk* BR1,BR5 43 B5
Jubilee Prim Sch SE28 3 C6
Jubilee Rd Chelsfield BR6 59 A4
West Thurrock RM20 17 B8
Jubilee Rise TN15 92 F6
Jubilee Terr
Gillingham ME7 54 C6
Knockholt TN14 74 E4
Jubilee Way DA14 30 A6
Judd Rd TN9 143 B7
Judd Sch The TN9 143 A8
Judeth Gdns DA12 36 E3
Judkins Cl ME5 68 C6
Juglans Rd BR6 44 A1
Julia Garfield Mews E16 1 B5
Julian Ct 3 DA14 30 A4
Julian Rd BR6 58 A4
Julians Cl TN13 108 A8
Julians Way TN13 108 A8
Junction Rd
Bodiam TN18,TN32 195 A3
Dartford DA1 15 D1
Gillingham ME7 54 D4
Juniper Cl Biggin Hill TN16 72 E2
Chatham ME5 68 A4
Maidstone ME16 99 B6
Royal Tunbridge Wells TN4 143 D1
Juniper La E6 1 E8
Juniper Wlk BR8 45 D7
Jury St 12 DA11 19 B1
Jutland Cl ME3 9 D1
Jutland Ho SE18 1 E2

K

K9 Est RM13 4 E7
Kale Rd DA18 3 E4
Karloff Way ME2 39 B2
Kashgar Rd SE18 2 F2
Kashmir Rd SE7 11 D7
Katherine Ct ME5 68 B2
Katherine Gdns SE9 11 D3
Katherine Rd TN8 138 C8
Katherine Villas TN8 138 C8
Kay St DA16 13 B6
Keary Rd DA10 34 F8
Keating Cl ME1 53 A3
Keats Ave E16 1 B5
Keats Gdns RM18 19 B5
Keats Ho DA1 14 E2
Keats Rd Bexley DA16 12 F6
Erith DA17 4 C3
Lunsford ME20 81 F3
Kechill Gdns BR2 42 A2
Kedleston Dr BR5 43 F4
Keeble Cl SE18 12 B8
Keedonwood Rd BR1 28 A3
Keefe Cl ME5 67 D1
Keel Gdns TN4 158 E8
Keeley Mews ME7 54 E3
Keeling Rd SE9 11 D2
Keemor Cl SE18 12 A7
Keep The SE3 11 A5
Keightley Dr SE9 29 C7
Keir Hardie Prim Sch E16 1 A8
Keir Hardy Ho 7 DA17 4 A3
Keith Ave DA4 33 B2
Keith Park Cres TN16 72 C7
Keith Sutton Ho SE9 29 C6
Kelbrook Rd SE3 11 E4
Kelchers La TN11 128 F5
Kelham Ho 10 SE18 12 B8
Kellaway Rd Chatham ME5 68 A2
Greenwich SE3 11 D5
Kellner Rd SE28 2 F3
Kelly Dr ME7 54 C7
Kelly Ho 15 Greenwich SE7 11 C8
Rochester ME1 67 C7
Kelsall Cl SE3 11 B5
Kelsey Rd BR5 44 B7
Kelso Dr DA12 36 F4
Kelvin Cl TN10 127 D7
Kelvin Ho 3 DA17 4 A3
Kelvin Par BR6 43 E1
Kelvin Rd Bexley DA16 13 A4
Tilbury RM18 19 A5
Kemble Cl TN2 159 E7
Kemble Dr BR2 56 E7
Kembleside Rd TN16 72 C1
Kemnal Rd BR7 29 D3
Kemnal Tech Coll BR5 30 B1
Kemnal Warren BR7 29 D2
Kemp Cl ME5 67 E4
Kempley Ct 2 RM17 18 D8
Kempt St SE18 12 A8
Kempton Cl Chatham ME5 68 C2
Erith DA8 14 C8
Kemsing Cl DA5 30 E8
Kemsing Prim Sch TN15 77 A2
Kemsing Rd
Greenwich SE10 1 A1
Wrotham TN15 78 C3
Kemsing Sta TN15 93 D8
Kemsley Cl
Northfleet DA11 35 F4
Swanscombe DA9 17 B1
Kemsley Ct BR5 44 B8
Kemsley Rd TN16 88 D8
Kemsley Street Rd ME7 69 C1
Kencot Cl DA18 3 F4
Kendal Cl TN9 127 C2
Kendal Dr TN9 127 C2
Kendal Pk TN4 158 E5
Kendal Way ME8 69 D8
Kendall Ave ME18 97 C3
Kendall Ct DA15 30 A5
Kendall Gdns DA11 35 F8
Kendall Lodge 5 BR1 42 B8
Kendall Pl 1 ME15 116 D8
Kendall Rd SE18 11 E6
Kendon Bsns Pk ME2 53 D8
Kenia Wlk DA12 36 F5
Kenilworth Ct 10 DA2 16 B1
Kenilworth Dr ME8 69 D6
Kenilworth Gdns
Gillingham ME8 69 D7
Woolwich SE18 12 B5
Kenilworth Ho ME16 99 B2
Kenilworth Rd BR5 43 C3
Kenley Cl Sidcup DA5 31 A8
St Paul's Cray BR7 43 E6
Kenley Ho 6 BR5 44 B7
Kenmere Rd DA16 13 C5
Kennacraig Cl E16 1 A5
Kennard Cl ME1 52 F2
Kennard St E16 1 F5
Kennedy Cl BR5 43 D1
Kennedy Gdns TN13 92 D5
Kennedy Ho
Benenden TN17 190 E6
Northfleet DA11 35 D5
Kennel Barn Rd ME9 87 C5
Kennet Ct 2 BR8 45 E6
Kennet Rd Crayford DA1 15 A4
Tonbridge TN10 127 C5
Kennett Ct 16 BR5 44 D1
Kennington Cl
Gillingham ME8 55 B4
Maidstone ME15 116 F7
Kensington Ct 5 RM17 18 C8
Kensington Ho ME16 99 A2
Kent & East Sussex Rly* TN17 192 D5
Kent & East Sussex Rly Mus* TN30 193 A8
Kent & East Sussex Steam Rly* TN17 198 C5
Kent & Sussex Hospl TN4 159 A4

Kent Ave Bexley DA16 ... 12 F2
Maidstone ME15 ... 100 C1
Kent Cl Orpington BR6 ... 57 E4
Paddock Wood TN12 ... 146 A6
Rochester ME1 ... 67 C8
Kent Coll TN2 ... 144 D3
Kent County Optholmic & Aural Hospl ME14 ... 100 A4
Kent County Show Gd ME14 ... 85 C3
Kent Hatch Rd
Crockham Hill RH8,TN8 ... 105 B4
The Chart RH8,TN8 ... 104 D4
Kent Ho
10 Hawkhurst TN18 ... 189 A2
Royal Tunbridge Wells TN1 ... 159 C6
Sutton at H DA4 ... 47 D7
Kent Inst of Art & Design
Maidstone ME16 ... 99 C3
Rochester ME1 ... 53 E4
Kent Kraft Ind Est DA11 ... 17 F2
Kent Rd Dartford DA1 ... 15 E1
Gravesend DA11 ... 36 A7
4 Grays RM17 ... 18 C8
Halling ME2 ... 66 A6
Longfield DA3 ... 48 D7
Orpington BR5 ... 44 B3
Royal Tunbridge Wells TN4 ... 159 A6
Snodland ME6 ... 82 A6
Kent St ME18 ... 96 E2
Kent Terr
Lower Higham ME3 ... 38 D7
Meopham DA13 ... 64 A7
Kentish Ct 8 ME16 ... 99 E4
Kentish Gdns TN2 ... 172 E8
Kentish Mans 15 TN1 ... 159 A2
Kentish Rd DA17 ... 4 A2
Kentish Way BR1,BR2 ... 42 B6
Kentlea Rd SE28 ... 2 E4
Kentmere Rd SE18 ... 2 E2
Kentstone Ct ME4 ... 54 A4
Kenward Ct TN11 ... 128 E8
Kenward Rd Eltham SE9 ... 11 D2
Maidstone ME16 ... 99 C5
Yalding ME18 ... 113 E2
Kenwood Ave
Chatham ME5 ... 68 A4
New Barn DA3 ... 49 C6
Kenwyn Rd DA1 ... 15 D2
Kenya Rd SE7 ... 11 D7
Kenya Terr 7 ME14 ... 100 A7
Kenyon Wlk ME8 ... 69 B3
Kerry Cl E16 ... 1 B7
Kerry Hill Way ME14 ... 99 E6
Kersey Gdns SE9 ... 28 E4
Kesteven Cl ME2 ... 66 B5
Kestlake Rd DA5 ... 13 C1
Keston Ave BR2 ... 56 C5
Keston CE Prim Sch BR2 ... 56 D5
Keston Cl DA16 ... 13 C7
Keston Ct Gillingham ME8 ... 55 A2
Sidcup DA5 ... 30 F8
Keston Gdns BR2 ... 56 C6
Keston Park Cl BR2 ... 56 F7
Kestrel Ave E6 ... 1 E8
Kestrel Cl TN8 ... 122 D3
Kestrel Ho ME7 ... 54 B6
Kestrel Rd ME5 ... 68 C2
Keswick Cl TN9 ... 127 C2
Keswick Ct ME7 ... 55 A5
Keswick Dr ME16 ... 99 B5
Keswick Gdns RM19 ... 16 C8
Keswick Rd Bexley DA7 ... 14 A6
Orpington BR6 ... 44 A2
Ketridge La ME18 ... 97 D2
Kettle La ME15 ... 114 E6
Kettlewell Ct BR8 ... 45 F7
Kevington Cl BR5 ... 43 F5
Kevington Dr BR7 ... 43 F5
Kewlands ME14 ... 100 C6
Keycol Hill ME9 ... 71 F5
Keyes Ave ME4 ... 53 F2
Keyes Gdns TN9 ... 142 F7
Keyes Rd DA1 ... 16 A3
Keymer Cl TN16 ... 72 D3
Keynes Ct 9 SE28 ... 3 B6
Keynsham Gdns SE9 ... 11 E2
Keynsham Rd SE9 ... 11 E2
Keyworth Cl TN12 ... 145 F6
Khalsa Ave DA12 ... 36 C8
Khartoum Pl DA12 ... 19 C1
Khartoum Rd ME4 ... 53 F6
Khyber Rd ME4,ME7 ... 54 B7
Kibbles La TN4 ... 158 E8
Kidbrooke Gdns SE3 ... 11 A6
Kidbrooke Gr SE3 ... 11 B6
Kidbrooke La SE9 ... 11 E3
Kidbrooke Park Cl SE3 ... 11 B6
Kidbrooke Park Prim Sch SE3 ... 11 C6
Kidbrooke Park Rd SE12, SE3 ... 11 B4
Kidbrooke Sch SE3 ... 11 D5
Kidbrooke Sta SE3 ... 11 B4
Kidbrooke Way SE3 ... 11 B5
Kidd Pl SE7 ... 1 E1
Kiddens BR8 ... 45 B7
Kidds Cotts BR8 ... 45 D3
Kierbeck Bsns Complex E16 ... 1 B4
Kilburn Ho 6 ME14 ... 100 A5
Kildare Rd E16 ... 1 A8
Killewarren Way BR5 ... 44 C3
Killick Cl TN13 ... 91 E6
Killick Rd ME3 ... 40 D5
Killicks Cotts ME18 ... 130 F8
Killigarth Ct 22 DA14 ... 30 A4
Kiln Barn Rd ME19,ME20 ... 98 C7
Kiln Field TN30 ... 193 C7
Kiln La TN11 ... 125 F1
Kiln Way TN12 ... 146 A5
Kilnbank TN2 ... 159 C7
Kilnbridge Cl ME15 ... 115 B7
Kilnbridge Wks ME15 ... 115 B7
Kilndown DA12 ... 36 D2
Kilndown Cl ME16 ... 99 C7
Kilnfields BR6 ... 59 A4
Kilnwood TN14 ... 74 F6
Kimbell Pl SE3 ... 11 C3
Kimber Ho 11 SE18 ... 12 B8
Kimberley Dr DA14 ... 30 D6
Kimberley Rd ME7 ... 54 D3
Kimberly Ct DA17 ... 3 F2
Kimmeridge Gdns SE9 ... 28 E4
Kimmeridge Rd SE9 ... 28 E4
Kincraig BR7 ... 43 A8
Kincraig Dr TN13 ... 92 B4
Kinder Cl SE28 ... 3 D6
King & Queen Cl SE9 ... 28 E4
King Arthur's Dr ME2 ... 39 A1
King Edward Ave DA1 ... 15 D1
King Edward Rd
Chatham ME4 ... 53 F2
Gillingham ME7 ... 54 F6
Maidstone ME15 ... 99 F2
Rochester ME1 ... 53 C5
Stone DA9 ... 17 A2
King George Ave E16 ... 1 D7
King George Rd ME5 ... 67 E4
King George V Hill TN1 ... 159 C5
King George V Meml Houses ME8 ... 55 C2
King George VI Ave TN16 ... 72 D3
King Harolds Way DA7 ... 13 E7
King Henry Mews 7 BR6 ... 57 F5
King Hill ME19 ... 97 A5
King John's Wlk SE9 ... 11 E1
King St Chatham ME4 ... 54 A4
Gillingham ME7 ... 54 C6
Gravesend DA12 ... 19 B1
Maidstone ME14 ... 100 A4
Rochester ME1 ... 53 C4
West Malling ME19 ... 97 C8
King William Rd 6 ME7 ... 54 C7
King's Ave ME1 ... 53 C3
King's Bastion ME7 ... 54 A5
King's Cotts
Wateringbury ME18 ... 113 D6
Yalding ME18 ... 114 A1
King's Highway SE18,SE2 ... 12 F8
King's Orch Eltham SE9 ... 11 E1
Rochester ME1 ... 53 C5
King's Rd Chatham ME5 ... 54 D1
Tonbridge TN9 ... 143 D7
King's Sch ME1 ... 53 C5
King's Standing Ind Est TN2 ... 143 F2
Kingfisher Apartments 13 ME15 ... 116 E5
Kingfisher Cl Erith SE28 ... 3 C6
Orpington BR5 ... 44 D5
Kingfisher Com Prim Sch ME5 ... 68 B7
Kingfisher Ct
11 Maidstone ME15 ... 100 B4
West Kingsdown TN15 ... 61 E3
Kingfisher Dr
Chatham ME5 ... 68 C7
Swanscombe DA9 ... 17 A1
Kingfisher Ho BR5 ... 44 C8
Kingfisher Pl DA4 ... 47 C7
Kingfisher Rd ME20 ... 82 A2
Kingfisher St E6 ... 1 E8
Kings Acre ME15 ... 101 A1
Kings Ave BR1 ... 28 A2
Kings Cl DA1 ... 14 E3
Kings Cotts
Cranbrook TN17 ... 179 D6
Leeds ME17 ... 117 F6
Kings Ct
Horsmonden TN12 ... 163 A6
21 Sidcup DA14 ... 30 A5
Kings Dr DA12 ... 36 B5
Kings Farm Prim Sch DA11 ... 36 C3
Kings Hill Ave ME19 ... 97 A4
Kings Hill Sch ME19 ... 97 A3
Kings La TN12 ... 147 C7
Kings Oak Mews ME5 ... 67 F4
Kings Pk TN2 ... 159 D3
Kings Rd Biggin Hill TN16 ... 72 C2
Headcorn TN27 ... 151 C5
Orpington BR6 ... 57 F6
Kings Reach ME15 ... 116 D8
Kings Row
1 Maidstone ME15 ... 100 A1
Rochester ME1 ... 53 B4
Kings Standing Way TN2 ... 143 F1
Kings Toll Rd TN2 ... 161 A6
Kings Wlk Grays RM17 ... 18 A8
Maidstone ME14 ... 100 B5
Kingsand Rd SE12 ... 28 A6
Kingsdale Ct
Chatham ME5 ... 54 C1
Swanscombe DA10 ... 17 E1
Kingsdale Rd SE18 ... 12 F8
Kingsdown Cl
Gillingham ME7 ... 69 B4
Gravesend DA12 ... 36 F7
Kingsdown Cl *continued*
Maidstone ME16 ... 99 E4
Kingsdown Ind Est ME20 ... 98 B8
Kingsdown Way BR2 ... 42 A3
Kingsfield Ho SE9 ... 28 D5
Kingsford Com Sch E6 ... 1 F7
Kingsford Cotts TN17 ... 190 D6
Kingsford Way E6 ... 1 F8
Kingsgate Cl Bexley DA7 ... 13 E6
Maidstone ME16 ... 99 C4
Orpington BR5 ... 44 C6
Kingsgate La TN30 ... 199 C5
Kingsground SE9 ... 11 E1
Kingshill Dr ME3 ... 40 D6
Kingsholm Gdns SE9 ... 11 E3
Kingshurst Rd SE12 ... 28 A8
Kingsingfield Cl TN15 ... 61 E3
Kingsingfield Rd TN15 ... 61 E2
Kingsland Gr TN27 ... 151 D5
Kingsland La TN27 ... 137 E1
Kingsley Ave DA1 ... 16 A2
Kingsley Ct Bexley DA6 ... 14 A3
Wadhurst TN5 ... 185 A4
1 Woolwich SE28 ... 3 C5
Kingsley Mews BR7 ... 29 B2
Kingsley Rd
Maidstone ME15 ... 100 A3
Orpington BR6 ... 57 F3
Kingsley Wood Dr SE9 ... 28 F5
Kingsman Par SE18 ... 1 F3
Kingsman St SE18 ... 1 F2
Kingsmead TN16 ... 72 D3
Kingsmead Cl DA15 ... 30 A6
Kingsmead Cotts BR2 ... 42 E1
Kingsmead Pk
Allhallows-on-S ME3 ... 9 E3
Paddock Wood TN12 ... 146 A6
Kingsmere BR7 ... 42 E8
Kingsnorth Cl ME3 ... 40 E6
Kingsnorth Ct BR8 ... 45 C3
Kingsnorth Ind Est ME3 ... 41 D7
Kingsnorth Rd ME8 ... 55 C4
Kingsridge Gdns DA1 ... 15 D1
Kingston Cres ME5 ... 68 C4
Kingston Ct DA11 ... 18 B1
Kingston Dr ME15 ... 116 A8
Kingsway Chatham ME5 ... 54 D1
Gillingham ME7 ... 54 E1
Orpington BR5 ... 43 D4
Kingswear Gdns ME2 ... 53 C7
Kingswood Ave
Chatham ME4 ... 53 F2
Erith DA17 ... 3 F2
Swanley BR8 ... 45 F6
Kingswood Cl
Dartford DA1 ... 15 C1
Orpington BR6 ... 43 D2
Royal Tunbridge Wells TN2 ... 159 C3
Kingswood Ho
12 Maidstone ME16 ... 99 A3
16 Sidcup DA14 ... 30 B4
Kingswood Prim Sch ME17 ... 118 E2
Kingswood Rd
Gillingham ME7 ... 54 D6
Kit's Coty ME20 ... 83 D8
Royal Tunbridge Wells TN2 ... 159 C3
Sevenoaks TN13 ... 91 E7
Kinlet Rd SE18 ... 12 C6
Kinnell Ct 13 DA14 ... 30 B4
Kinnings Row TN9 ... 127 C2
Kinross Cl ME5 ... 68 B7
Kinveachy Gdns SE7 ... 1 E1
Kipling Ave RM18 ... 19 C6
Kipling Dr ME20 ... 81 F4
Kipling Rd Bexley DA7 ... 13 E6
Dartford DA1 ... 16 B2
Kippington Cl TN13 ... 91 F3
Kippington Dr SE9 ... 28 D7
Kippington Rd TN13 ... 92 A2
Kirby Cl TN17 ... 179 D4
Kirby Rd Chattenden ME3 ... 39 F5
Dartford DA2 ... 33 D8
Kirk La SE18 ... 12 C8
Kirkcourt TN13 ... 92 A4
Kirkdale ME15 ... 115 F5
Kirkdale Cl ME5 ... 68 D1
Kirkdale Cotts ME15 ... 115 F5
Kirkdale Rd
Maidstone ME15 ... 115 F6
Royal Tunbridge Wells TN1 ... 159 B4
Kirkham Rd E6 ... 1 E7
Kirkham St SE18 ... 12 E8
Kirkins Cl TN12 ... 163 A6
Kirkland Cl DA15 ... 12 E1
Kirkman Ct TN12 ... 149 E3
Kirkside Rd SE3 ... 11 A8
Kit Hill Ave ME5 ... 67 E3
Kit's Coty Ho* ME20 ... 83 C6
Kitchener Ave
Chatham ME4 ... 54 A1
Gravesend DA12 ... 36 C5
Kitchener Cotts ME3 ... 25 C4
Kitchener Rd
Chattenden ME3 ... 39 F4
Rochester ME2 ... 53 A8
Kite La TN12 ... 162 A6
Knatts La TN15 ... 77 E8
Knatts Valley Rd TN15 ... 61 D2
Knave Wood Rd TN15 ... 76 E2
Knaves Acre TN27 ... 151 D5
Knavesacre Ct ME8 ... 69 D5
Knee Hill SE2 ... 3 C1
Knee Hill Cres SE2 ... 3 C2
Knight Ave ME7 ... 54 D7
Knight Rd Rochester ME2 ... 53 A6
Tonbridge TN10 ... 127 E6
Knight's Ct 7 DA8 ... 14 F7
Knight's Ridge TN2 ... 160 D7
Knight's Way TN27 ... 151 D6
Knighton Rd TN14 ... 75 F2
Knightrider Ct ME15 ... 100 A3
Knightrider St ME15 ... 100 A3
Knights Cl
Hoo St Werburgh ME3 ... 40 E5
Pembury TN2 ... 160 D7
Knights Croft DA3 ... 62 F7
Knights Field DA4 ... 60 E7
Knights Manor Way DA1 ... 15 F1
Knights Pk Rochester ME2 ... 53 A6
Royal Tunbridge Wells TN11 ... 143 F1
Knights Rd
Hoo St Werburgh ME3 ... 40 D5
Newham E16 ... 1 A4
Knights Ridge BR6 ... 58 B5
Knights Way TN2,TN11 ... 143 F1
Knightsbridge Cl TN4 ... 158 F5
Knightsbridge Ct TN1 ... 159 B6
Knightsbridge Mews BR7 ... 28 F1
Knock Mill La TN15 ... 78 A5
Knockhall Chase DA9 ... 17 C2
Knockhall Com Prim Sch DA9 ... 17 C2
Knockhall Rd DA9 ... 17 C2
Knockholt Rd Eltham SE9 ... 11 D2
Halstead TN14 ... 74 F6
Knockholt Sta TN14 ... 58 E2
Knockhurst Ct TN30 ... 183 C1
Knockwood Rd TN30 ... 183 C1
Knole Cl TN14 ... 108 B2
Knole Gate DA15 ... 29 E5
Knole Ho* TN15 ... 92 D1
Knole La TN13,TN15 ... 92 C1
Knole Rd Chatham ME5 ... 68 C3
Dartford DA1 ... 32 B8
Sevenoaks TN13 ... 92 D4
Knole The Eltham SE9 ... 29 A4
Istead Rise DA13 ... 35 E1
Knole Way TN13 ... 92 C2
Knoll Ct BR6 ... 57 F8
Knoll Rd Sidcup DA14 ... 30 B4
Sidcup,Old Bexley DA5 ... 14 A1
Knoll Rise BR6 ... 43 F1
Knoll The BR2 ... 42 A1
Knotley Hall Cotts TN11 ... 125 A2
Knott Ct ME14 ... 99 F6
Knotts Pl TN13 ... 92 A3
Knowle Ave DA7 ... 13 F7
Knowle Cl TN3 ... 157 F3
Knowle Cott TN3 ... 173 E1
Knowle Cotts TN3 ... 173 E1
Knowle La TN12 ... 146 C3
Knowle Lodge BR7 ... 28 F2
Knowle Rd
Maidstone ME14 ... 100 B6
Orpington BR2 ... 56 E8
Paddock Wood TN12 ... 146 D3
Wouldham ME1 ... 66 D4
Knowles Gdns TN27 ... 151 D5
Knowles Wlk TN12 ... 149 F4
Knowlton Gdns ME16 ... 99 B2
Knowlton Gn BR2 ... 42 A4
Knowsley Way TN11 ... 126 D6
Knox Ct TN15 ... 92 F6
Koonowla Cl TN16 ... 72 D4
Kydbrook Cl BR5 ... 43 C2
Kyetop Wlk ME8 ... 69 D6
Kynaston Rd Bromley BR1 ... 28 A3
Orpington BR5 ... 44 B2

L

La Providence ME1 ... 53 C5
La Tourne Gdns BR6 ... 57 C7
Labour-in-vain Rd TN15 ... 78 E5
Laburnham Pl SE9 ... 12 A2
Laburnum Ave
Dartford DA1 ... 32 D7
Swanley BR8 ... 45 D6
Laburnum Ct TN2 ... 159 C7
Laburnum Dr ME20 ... 82 A2
Laburnum Gr DA11 ... 35 D8
Laburnum Rd ME2 ... 52 E5
Laburnum Way BR2 ... 43 B2
Lacebark Cl DA15 ... 29 F8
Lacey Cl ME17 ... 117 E4
Laceys La ME17 ... 132 C7
Lacknut Cotts DA13 ... 63 E2
Lacock Gdns
Loose ME15 ... 116 A8
Maidstone ME15 ... 100 A1
Lacy Cl ME16 ... 99 D7
Ladbrooke Cres DA14 ... 30 D5
Ladbrooke Ho 7 ME14 ... 100 A5
Laddingford Farm Ind Est ME18 ... 130 D4
Laddingford St Mary's CE Prim Sch ME18 ... 130 E4
Ladds Cnr ME7 ... 55 B5
Ladds La ME6 ... 66 A2
Ladds Way BR8 ... 45 D5
Ladham Rd TN17 ... 164 A2
Ladies Mile TN6,TN7 ... 170 D4
Lady Boswell's CE Prim Sch TN13 ... 92 C2
Lady Oak La TN5,TN17 ... 187 C7
Lady Vane Cl TN11 ... 110 C5
Lady's Gift Rd TN4 ... 158 F8
Ladyclose Ave ME3 ... 39 A7
Ladycroft Gdns 6 BR6 ... 57 C5
Ladycroft Way BR6 ... 57 C5
Ladyfern Ct TN2 ... 159
Ladyfields Chatham ME5 ... 68
Northfleet DA11 ... 35
Ladyfields Cl ME9 ... 71
Ladysmith Rd SE9 ... 12
Ladywell Ho 7 BR5 ... 44
Ladywood Ave BR5 ... 43
Ladywood Rd Cuxton ME2 ... 52
Dartford DA2 ... 33
Lagonda Way DA1 ... 15
Lagoon Rd BR5 ... 44
Lake Ave BR1 ... 28
Lake Dr ME3 ... 38
Lake Rd Ditton ME20 ... 98
Royal Tunbridge Wells TN4 ... 158
Lake View Rd TN13 ... 92
Lake Wlk ME20 ... 82
Lakedale Rd SE18 ... 2
Lakelands
Harrietsham ME17 ... 119
Loose ME15 ... 116
Lakeman Way TN4 ... 159
Laker Ho ME14 ... 100
Laker Rd ME1 ... 67
Lakes Rd BR2 ... 56
Lakes The ME20 ... 82
Lakeside
Royal Tunbridge Wells TN2 ... 159
Snodland ME6 ... 81
Lakeside Ave SE28 ... 3
Lakeside Cl
Bexley DA5,DA15 ... 13
Bough Beech TN8 ... 123
Lakeside Dr BR2 ... 56
Lakeside Pk ME2 ... 53
Lakeswood Rd BR5 ... 43
Lakeview Cl ME6 ... 82
Lakeview Rd DA16 ... 13
Lakewood Dr ME8 ... 69
Lamb Cl RM18 ... 19
Lamb's Cross ME17 ... 134
Lamb's Mobile Home Pk TN12 ... 146
Lambard Ho 8 ME14 ... 100
Lambarde Ave SE9 ... 29
Lambarde Cl ME2 ... 66
Lambarde Dr TN13 ... 92
Lambarde Rd TN13 ... 92
Lambardes DA3 ... 62
Lambardes Cl TN14 ... 74
Lamberhurst Cl 14 BR5 ... 44
Lamberhurst Gn ME8 ... 55
Lamberhurst Rd
Horsmonden TN12,TN3 ... 162
Lamberhurst TN3,TN12 ... 176
Maidstone ME16 ... 99
Lamberhurst St Mary's CE Prim Sch TN3 ... 176
Lamberhurst Vineyard* TN3 ... 176
Lambersart Cl TN4 ... 143
Lambert Cl TN16 ... 72
Lambert Ct DA8 ... 14
Lambert Mews 4 ME6 ... 82
Lambert Rd E16 ... 1
Lambert's Yd TN9 ... 127
Lamberts Pl TN12 ... 163
Lamberts Rd TN2 ... 159
Lambes Ct ME8 ... 69
Lambeth Cl ME5 ... 68
Lambourn Dr ME19 ... 97
Lambourn Ho BR1 ... 28
Lambourn Way
Chatham ME5 ... 68
Royal Tunbridge Wells TN2 ... 159
Lambourne Pl SE3 ... 11
Lambourne Rd ME15 ... 100
Lambs Bank TN9 ... 143
Lambscroft Ave SE9 ... 28
Lambsfrith Gr ME7 ... 69
Lamorbey Cl DA15 ... 29
Lamorna Ave DA12 ... 36
Lamorna Cl BR6 ... 44
Lampington Row TN3 ... 157
Lamplighters Cl
2 Dartford DA1 ... 15
Gillingham ME7 ... 68
Lamport Cl SE18 ... 1
Lamson Rd RM13 ... 4
Lancashire Rd ME15 ... 116
Lancaster Ct
Gillingham ME8 ... 69
Gravesend DA12 ... 36
Lancaster Gdns BR1 ... 42
Lancaster Way ME19 ... 96
Lance Croft DA3 ... 62
Lancelot Ave ME2 ... 52
Lancelot Cl ME2 ... 52
Lancelot Ct BR6 ... 58
Lancelot Rd DA16 ... 13
Lancer Ho ME1 ... 53
Lances Cl DA13 ... 50
Lancet La ME15 ... 116
Lancey Cl SE7 ... 1
Lancing Rd BR6 ... 58 B8
Land Way ME3 ... 38 D5
Landale Gdns DA1 ... 32 C8
Landor Ct ME7 ... 69 A3
Landseer Ave DA11 ... 35 D5
Landseer Cl TN10 ... 127 E6
Landstead Rd SE18 ... 12 D7
Landway TN15 ... 92 F7
Landway The
Borough Green TN15 ... 94 F7
Kemsing TN15 ... 77 A2

andway The *continued*
Maidstone ME14 ...101 A4
Orpington BR5 ...44 C6
ane Ave DA9 ...17 C1
ane End DA7 ...14 B4
ane The Fordcombe TN3 .157 C5
Greenwich SE3 ...11 A4
anes Ave DA11 ...36 A5
aneside BR7 ...29 C3
angafel CE Prim Sch
DA3 ...49 A6
angafel Cl DA3 ...48 E7
angbrook Rd SE3 ...11 D5
angdale Cl
Gillingham ME8 ...55 D1
Orpington BR6 ...57 B7
angdale Cres DA7 ...14 A6
angdale Rise ME16 ...99 C5
angdale Wlk 5 DA11 ...35 E5
angdon Rd Bromley BR2 ..42 B6
Rochester ME1 ...53 C4
angdon Shaw DA14 ...29 F3
angford Pl DA14 ...30 A5
angham Gr ME16 ...99 C4
angholm Rd TN3 ...157 F3
anghorne Ho 6 SE7 ...11 C8
anglands Dr DA2 ...33 E3
angley Ct 13 SE9 ...12 A1
angley Gdns
2 Bromley BR2 ...42 C5
Orpington BR5 ...43 B3
angley Ho
6 Bromley BR1 ...28 B1
11 Maidstone ME16 ...99 A3
angley Rd DA16 ...13 C8
angmore Ct DA7 ...13 D4
angton Cl ME14 ...100 C5
angton Green Prim Sch
TN3 ...157 E4
angton Rd
Rusthall TN3,TN4 ...158 C3
Speldhurst TN3 ...158 A7
angton Ridge TN3 ...158 B3
angton Way SE3 ...11 B7
angworth Cl DA2 ...32 D5
ankester Parker Rd
ME1 ...67 C6
annoy Rd SE9 ...29 C7
anridge Rd SE2 ...3 D3
ansbury Cres DA1 ...16 A2
ansbury Ct 4 SE28 ...3 B6
ansbury Gdns RM18 ...19 A6
ansbury Ho 5 DA17 ...3 F1
ansdown Pl DA11 ...35 F7
ansdown Rd Sidcup DA14 .30 B5
Tilbury RM18 ...18 F5
ansdowne Ave
Bexley DA7 ...13 D7
Maidstone ME15 ...116 C6
Orpington BR6 ...43 B1
ansdowne Ct 9 ME4 ...53 F4
ansdowne La SE7 ...1 D1
ansdowne Mews SE7 ...1 D1
ansdowne Prim Sch
RM18 ...18 F5
ansdowne Rd
Bromley BR1 ...28 B1
Chatham ME4 ...53 E2
Royal Tunbridge Wells
TN1 ...159 B4
Sevenoaks TN13 ...92 D5
Tonbridge TN9 ...127 B2
ansdowne Sq
Northfleet DA11 ...18 F1
8 Royal Tunbridge Wells
TN1 ...159 B4
antern Ho SE18 ...2 A1
anthorne Mews
Royal Tunbridge Wells
TN1 ...159 B5
Royal Tunbridge
Wells,Calverley Park TN1 ..159 B3
apins La ME19 ...96 F2
apis Cl DA12 ...37 B7
apwing Cl DA8 ...15 B7
apwing Rd ME3 ...27 B5
apwings DA3 ...49 B6
apwings The DA12 ...36 D6
apworth Cl BR6 ...58 C8
arch Cl ME20 ...82 B2
arch Cres
Hoo St Werburgh ME3 ...40 E3
Tonbridge TN10 ...127 C6
arch Dene BR6 ...57 A8
arch Gr
Paddock Wood TN12 ...145 F6
Sidcup DA15 ...29 F7
arch Rd DA1 ...32 D7
arch Way BR2 ...43 A2
arch Wlk BR8 ...45 D7
arch Wood Cl ME5 ...68 D1
archcroft ME5 ...68 A4
arches The ME3 ...38 C3
archwood Rd SE9 ...29 B6
argo Wlk DA8 ...14 E6
arkfield TN12 ...145 A7
arkfield Ave ME7 ...54 E4
arkfield Cl Hayes BR2 ...56 A8
Larkfield ME20 ...82 A1
arkfield Rd
Larkfield ME20 ...82 B1
Sevenoaks TN13 ...91 C4
Sidcup DA14 ...29 F5
arkfield Trad Est ME20 ..82 B5
arkfields DA11 ...35 E5
arkin Cl ME2 ...39 B2
arking Dr ME16 ...99 D7
arks Field DA3 ...48 F5
Larkspur Cl
2 East Malling ME19 ...82 A1
4 Newham E6 ...1 E8
Orpington BR6 ...58 C7
Larkspur Lodge DA14 ...30 B5
Larkspur Rd Chatham ME5 .67 E4
West Malling ME19 ...81 F1
Larkstore Pk TN12 ...149 E5
Larkswood Cl DA8 ...15 A6
Larkwell La DA3 ...48 F5
Larner Rd DA8 ...14 E7
Laser Quay ME2 ...53 D6
Lashenden Air Warfare Mus*
TN27 ...152 A2
Lassa Rd SE9 ...11 F2
Latham Cl Biggin Hill TN16 .72 C3
Dartford DA2 ...33 E6
Newham E6 ...1 E7
Latham Rd DA6 ...14 A2
Latimer Pl 4 ME7 ...54 C7
Latona Dr DA12 ...36 F3
Latymers TN11 ...141 B4
Launcelot Prim Sch BR1 .28 A4
Launcelot Rd BR1 ...28 A4
Launder Way ME15 ...99 E2
Launton Dr DA6 ...13 D3
Laura Dr BR8 ...32 A1
Laura Pl ME1 ...53 A2
Laurel Ave DA12 ...36 C6
Laurel Bank
Royal Tunbridge Wells
TN4 ...159 B8
Wadhurst TN5 ...185 A4
Laurel Cl Dartford DA1 ...32 C7
Sidcup DA14 ...30 A5
Laurel Gdns BR1 ...42 E5
Laurel Gr ME17 ...118 D2
Laurel Ho SE7 ...11 C8
Laurel Rd Gillingham ME7 ..54 C7
Royal Tunbridge Wells
TN2 ...159 D7
Laurel Way TN2 ...159 D7
Laurel Wlk ME8 ...69 E6
Laurels The
12 Bromley BR1 ...42 B8
Bromley BR2 ...42 A5
Dartford DA2 ...32 C5
18 Erith DA17 ...4 A1
Maidstone ME16 ...99 C2
New Barn DA3 ...49 D6
Laurie Gray Ave ME5 ...67 D1
Lavenda Cl ME7 ...69 A4
Lavender Cl Bromley BR2 ..42 E3
1 Chatham ME5 ...67 E4
East Malling ME19 ...97 F8
Lavender Gdns TN5 ...186 E1
Lavender Hill
Swanley BR8 ...45 D6
Tonbridge TN9 ...143 C8
Lavender Ho 3 ME15 ...116 D8
Lavender Rd ME19 ...97 F8
Lavender Sq 6 TN18 ...189 A2
Lavender Wlk ME19 ...97 F8
Lavenders Rd ME19 ...97 C6
Lavernock Rd DA7 ...14 A5
Laverstoke Rd ME16 ...99 C8
Lavidge Rd SE9 ...28 F6
Lavinia Rd 1 DA1 ...15 F1
Lavisham Ho BR1 ...28 B3
Lawford Gdns DA1 ...15 C2
Lawn Cl Bromley BR1 ...28 B1
Chatham ME4 ...54 B2
Swanley BR8 ...45 C7
Tenterden TN30 ...192 F7
Lawn Pk TN13 ...108 B8
Lawn Prim Sch DA11 ...18 C1
Lawn Rd Northfleet DA11 ..18 C1
Tonbridge TN9 ...143 B8
Lawns Cres RM17 ...18 D8
Lawns The
Brenchley TN12 ...162 B8
Sidcup DA14 ...30 B4
Lawrance Sq DA11 ...35 F5
Lawrence Cl ME15 ...116 A7
Lawrence Dr DA12 ...51 A5
Lawrence Gdns RM18 ...19 B7
Lawrence Hill Gdns DA1 ..15 C1
Lawrence Hill Rd DA1 ...15 C1
Lawrence Rd Erith DA8 ...14 B7
Hayes BR4 ...56 A6
Tonbridge TN10 ...127 E6
Lawrence St ME7 ...54 C5
Lawson Cl E16 ...1 C8
Lawson Gdns DA1 ...15 D3
Lawson Ho 1 SE18 ...12 A8
Lawson Rd DA1 ...15 D3
Lawsons Mews TN9 ...127 C2
Laxey Rd BR6 ...57 F4
Laxey The ME15 ...99 E1
Laxton Cl ME15 ...100 F3
Laxton Dr ME17 ...117 A1
Laxton Gdns TN12 ...145 E7
Laxton Wk ME18 ...97 B3
Layfield Ho 4 SE10 ...1 A1
Layfield Rd ME7 ...54 F7
Layhams Rd BR2 ...56 A3
Laymarsh Cl DA17 ...3 F3
Layzell Wlk SE9 ...28 D7
Le May Ave SE12 ...28 B5
Le Temple Rd TN12 ...146 B6
Lea Ct ME4 ...53 E1
Lea Rd TN13 ...108 C8
Lea Vale DA1 ...14 D3
Leafield La DA14 ...30 F5
Leafy Glade ME8 ...69 B6
Leafy Gr BR2 ...56 C5
Leafy La DA13 ...64 A3
Leafy Oak Rd SE12 ...28 C5
Leake Ho 2 ME1 ...53 C1
Lealands Ave TN11 ...126 A1
Lealands Cl TN3 ...171 C6
Leaman Cl ME23 ...23 E4
Leamington Ave
Bromley BR1 ...28 C3
Orpington BR6 ...57 E6
Leamington Cl BR1 ...28 C3
Leamington Dr ME16 ...99 B4
Leamouth Rd E6 ...1 E8
Leander Dr DA12 ...36 F4
Leander Rd ME1 ...67 C7
Learoyd Gdns E6 ...2 A6
Leas Dale SE9 ...29 A5
Leas Gn BR7 ...29 F2
Leas The
Turner's Green TN5 ...185 A6
Woolwich SE18 ...12 B6
Leather Cl TN8 ...138 C8
Leatherbottle Gn DA18 ...3 F3
Leaves Gn BR2 ...72 D8
Leaves Green Cres BR2 ..72 C8
Leaves Green Rd
Biggin Hill BR2 ...72 D8
Keston BR2 ...56 D1
Lebanon Gdns TN16 ...72 D2
Lebrun Sq SE3 ...11 B4
Leckwith Ave DA7 ...13 E8
Leclair Ho SE3 ...11 B4
Leconfield Cl TN9 ...142 F7
Leda Rd SE18 ...1 F3
Lee Gn BR5 ...44 A4
Lee Green Rd ME3 ...39 B6
Lee Rd ME6 ...82 A8
Lee Sta SE12 ...11 A1
Leech Ct ME1 ...53 D5
Leechcroft Ave
Sidcup DA15 ...12 F2
Swanley BR8 ...45 F6
Leeds & Broomfield CE Prim
Sch ME17 ...118 A7
Leeds Castle* ME17 ...118 D7
Leeds Cl BR6 ...58 D8
Leeds Ho ME2 ...39 C1
Leeds Rd ME17 ...117 E3
Leeds Sq ME8 ...55 B3
Lees Rd ME18 ...130 E7
Leesons Hill BR5,BR7 ...44 A6
Leesons Prim Sch BR5 ...44 B6
Leesons Way BR5 ...43 F7
Leet Cl ME7 ...54 E6
Leeward Rd ME1 ...53 C1
Leewood Cl SE12 ...11 A1
Leewood Pl BR8 ...45 D5
Legatt Rd SE9 ...11 D2
Legge La ME19 ...81 D6
Leggs' La TN3 ...157 E5
Leghorn Rd SE18 ...2 D1
Leicester Dr TN2 ...172 F8
Leicester Rd
Maidstone ME15 ...116 D7
Tilbury RM18 ...18 F6
Leicester Sq TN11 ...141 B4
Leigh Ave ME15 ...116 B6
Leigh City Tech Coll The
DA1 ...33 A7
Leigh Green Ind Est
TN30 ...193 E6
Leigh Halt TN11 ...125 F1
Leigh Pl DA16 ...13 A5
Leigh Prim Sch TN11 ...125 F1
Leigh Rd Gravesend DA11 ..36 B6
Rochester ME3 ...39 C3
Tonbridge TN11 ...126 D3
Leigh Terr
2 Orpington BR5 ...44 B6
Teston ME18 ...98 A1
Leighton Cl TN4 ...159 A7
Leighton Gdns RM18 ...19 A7
Leila Parnell Pl 22 SE7 ...11 C8
Leitch Row ME7 ...54 A7
Leith Hill BR5 ...44 A8
Leith Hill Gn BR5 ...44 A8
Leith Park Rd DA12 ...36 B7
Lemonwell Ct SE9 ...12 C2
Lemonwell Dr SE9 ...12 C2
Len Clifton Ho 6 SE18 ...1 F2
Len Valley Wlk ME15 ...100 F1
Lenderyou Ct DA1 ...32 E8
Lendon Rd TN15 ...94 F6
Lendrim Cl 11 ME7 ...54 A6
Leneda Dr TN2 ...172 E8
Leney Rd ME18 ...113 E7
Lenfield Ave ME14 ...100 B4
Lenham Ct 10 ME15 ...100 B4
Lenham Heath Rd ME17 .120 C2
Lenham Ho
Lenham ME17 ...120 E5
13 Orpington BR5 ...44 D1
Lenham Prim Sch ME17 .120 C5
Lenham Rd Bexley DA7 ...13 F8
Broadstone TN27,ME17 ...136 D3
Fairbourne Heath ME17 ...119 C1
Headcorn TN27 ...151 E6
Lenham Sta ME17 ...120 C4
Lenham Way ME8 ...55 A3
Lennard Rd Orpington BR2 .42 F1
Sevenoaks TN13 ...91 E7
Lennox Ave DA11 ...19 A1
Lennox Ho 6 DA17 ...4 A3
Lennox Rd Northfleet DA11 .35 F8
Gravesend DA11 ...36 A8
Lennox Rd E DA11 ...36 A8
Lenor Cl DA6 ...13 E3
Lensbury Way SE2 ...3 D3
Lenside Dr ME15 ...101 A2
Lenton St SE18 ...2 D2
Leonard Ave Otford TN14 ..76 B3
Leonard Ave *continued*
Swanscombe DA10 ...34 E8
Leonard Cl ME16 ...99 B6
Leonard Ct DA14 ...30 B5
Leonard Judge Ho DA2 ...33 E3
Leonard Pl BR2 ...56 E7
Leonard Rd 7 ME4 ...54 B3
Leonard Robbins Path 3
SE28 ...3 B6
Leonard St E16 ...1 E5
Leopold Rd 2 ME4 ...54 A3
Lesley Cl Istead Rise DA13 .49 F8
Sidcup DA5 ...31 B8
Swanley BR8 ...45 D6
Lesley Pl ME16 ...99 E5
Lesley Tew Ct TN10 ...127 C5
Leslie Cres TN30 ...183 B2
Leslie Rd Gillingham ME7 ..54 D7
Newham E16 ...1 B7
Leslie Smith Sq 7 SE18 ..12 A8
Lesnes Abbey (remains of)*
SE2 ...3 D2
Lesney Park Rd DA8 ...14 D8
Lesney Pk DA8 ...14 D8
Lessness Ave DA7 ...13 D7
Lessness Heath Prim Sch
DA17 ...4 A1
Lessness Pk DA17 ...4 A1
Lessness Rd 12 DA17 ...4 A1
Lested La ME17 ...117 B1
Lester Rd ME4 ...54 A3
Lestock Ho SE3 ...11 D6
Letchworth Ave ME4 ...53 F1
Letchworth Cl BR2 ...42 A4
Letchworth Dr BR2 ...42 A4
Letter Box La TN13 ...108 C6
Leverholme Gdns SE9 ...29 A4
Levett Cl ME3 ...27 B6
Levetts La TN32 ...195 D1
Leviathan Way ME4 ...40 A1
Lewd La TN27 ...153 A3
Lewes Cl RM17 ...18 A8
Lewes Rd BR1 ...42 D7
Lewin Ct SE18 ...2 E2
Lewin Rd DA6 ...13 E3
Lewing Cl BR6 ...43 E1
Lewis Ave ME8 ...55 B2
Lewis Court Dr ME17 ...116 C3
Lewis Ct DA11 ...35 F6
Lewis King Ho 7 BR1 ...28 B1
Lewis Mews ME6 ...81 F6
Lewis Rd Bexley DA16 ...13 C4
Istead Rise DA13 ...49 F8
Sidcup DA14 ...30 C5
Swanscombe DA10 ...17 E1
Lewis Row ME17 ...133 E6
Leybank TN11 ...126 F4
Leybourne Cl
Chatham ME5 ...68 A2
Hayes BR2 ...42 A3
Leybourne Dell TN17 ...190 E6
Leybourne Rd ME2 ...52 F8
Leybourne Way ME20 ...81 F4
Leybourne, St Peter & St
Paul CE Prim Sch ME19 .81 E2
Leybridge Ct SE12 ...11 A2
Leyburn Ct TN9 ...127 C3
Leyburn Ho SE18 ...11 E7
Leycroft Gdns DA8 ...15 B6
Leydenhatch La BR8 ...45 D8
Leyes Rd E16 ...1 D7
Leyhill Cl BR8 ...45 E4
Leyland Rd SE12 ...11 A2
Leysdown Ave DA7 ...14 C3
Leysdown Rd SE9 ...28 F6
Leyton Ave ME7 ...54 E1
Leyton Cross DA2 ...32 A6
Leyton Cross Rd DA2 ...31 F5
Leywood Rd DA13 ...64 D3
Lezayre Rd BR6 ...57 F4
Liberty Mews BR6 ...57 F8
Libya Terr 6 ME14 ...100 A7
Lichdale Cl 8 BR6 ...57 F6
Lichfield Cl ME8 ...55 D2
Lichfield Ho 12 ME15 ...116 E7
Liddon Rd BR1 ...42 D6
Lidsing Rd ME14 ...84 E6
Lidwells La TN17 ...163 E1
Lieth Park Rd DA12 ...36 C7
Liffler Rd SE18 ...2 E1
Lighterman's Mews 2
DA11 ...35 E8
Lightermans Way DA9 ...17 C3
Lightfoot Gn TN18 ...188 E3
Lila Pl BR8 ...45 E5
Lilac Cres ME2 ...52 E6
Lilac Gdns BR8 ...45 D6
Lilac Gn 4 ME19 ...82 A1
Lilac Pl DA13 ...50 B2
Lilac Rd ME2 ...52 E5
Lilburne Gdns SE9 ...11 E2
Lilburne Rd SE9 ...11 E2
Lilian Barker Cl SE12 ...11 A2
Lilk Hill ME14 ...101 C3
Lillechurch Rd ME3 ...38 F7
Lillie Rd TN16 ...72 D1
Lillieburn ME19 ...81 D2
Lily Nichols Ho E16 ...1 E5
Limavady Ho SE18 ...2 A2
Lime Ave Benenden TN17 .190 C8
Northfleet DA11 ...35 D8
Lime Cl Bromley BR1 ...42 E5
Frant TN3 ...173 B3
Marden TN12 ...148 C6
Lime Cotts TN12 ...149 F3
Lime Cres ME19 ...98 A7
Lime Ct Eltham SE9 ...29 B6
Gillingham ME8 ...69 C3
Lime Gr Biddenden TN27 ..182 D7
Orpington BR6 ...57 B8
Sidcup DA15 ...12 F1
Lime Hill Rd TN1 ...159 A4
Lime Kiln Dr SE7 ...11 B8
Lime Pit La TN13,TN14 ...75 C2
Lime Rd BR8 ...45 D6
Lime Row DA18 ...3 F3
Lime Tree Ave DA9 ...34 A7
Lime Tree Cl TN9 ...127 C2
Lime Tree Wlk TN13 ...92 B2
Lime Trees TN12 ...149 E4
Limepits Cross ME9 ...71 F3
Limes Cl TN30 ...193 C8
Limes Gr TN18 ...188 F5
Limes Row BR6 ...57 B5
Limes The
Edenbridge TN8 ...122 C1
Frittenden TN17 ...166 E6
Lenham ME17 ...120 D5
Orpington BR2 ...56 E8
Limetree Cl ME5 ...68 B8
Limetree Terr
5 Bexley DA16 ...13 A4
Lenham ME17 ...120 E6
Limewood Rd DA8 ...14 C7
Limpsfield CE Inf Sch
RH8 ...104 C6
Limpsfield Grange Sch
RH8 ...104 A8
Linchmere Rd 7 SE12 ...28 A8
Lincol n Rd ME7 ...54 D7
Lincoln Cl Erith DA8 ...14 F5
Rochester ME2 ...52 D6
Lincoln Ct 3 SE12 ...28 C5
Lincoln Green Rd BR5 ...43 F4
Lincoln Rd Erith DA8 ...14 F5
Maidstone ME15 ...116 D8
Sidcup DA14 ...30 B3
Lincolnshire Terr DA2 ...33 D4
Lincolnshott DA13 ...35 B3
Lindel Ct ME18 ...97 B3
Linden Ave DA1 ...32 C7
Linden Chase TN13 ...92 B5
Linden Cl Orpington BR6 ...58 A5
Paddock Wood TN12 ...146 A6
Purfleet RM19 ...16 C8
Royal Tunbridge Wells
TN4 ...159 A2
Linden Ct Sidcup DA14 ...29 E4
Tonbridge TN10 ...127 B7
Linden Gdns TN2 ...158 F1
Linden Ho 4 Bromley BR1 .28 B1
5 Chatham ME5 ...67 F4
Linden Park Rd TN2 ...159 A2
Linden Rd
Coxheath ME17 ...115 C4
Gillingham ME7 ...54 E5
Linden Sq TN13 ...91 E5
Lindenfield BR7 ...43 B7
Lindens The ME20 ...82 E1
Lindisfarne Cl DA12 ...36 E6
Lindisfarne Gdns ME16 ...99 E3
Lindridge La TN12 ...149 C5
Lindsay Ho 2 SE18 ...2 A2
Lindsey Cl BR1 ...42 E6
Lindwood Cl 8 E6 ...1 F8
Lineacre Cl ME8 ...69 D6
Lines Terr ME4 ...54 A4
Ling Rd Erith DA8 ...14 C8
Newham E16 ...1 A8
Lingey Cl DA15 ...29 F6
Lingfield Ave DA2 ...33 B8
Lingfield Cres SE9 ...12 D3
Lingfield Mews 4 TN8 ..122 C1
Lingfield Rd
Borough Green TN15 ...95 B7
Edenbridge TN8 ...138 A8
Gravesend DA12 ...36 B6
Lingley Dr ME2 ...39 C2
Lingwood DA7 ...14 B5
LINK 20 Bsns Pk ME20 ...82 B3
Link Field BR2 ...42 A3
Link Hill La TN27 ...137 D3
Link The Eltham SE9 ...29 A5
New Ash Green DA3 ...62 F8
Link Way Bromley BR2 ...42 E2
Royal Tunbridge Wells
TN2 ...159 E8
Linkden Cotts TN18 ...196 E5
Links Ct SE9 ...29 B7
Links The Addington ME19 ..80 E2
Chatham ME5 ...68 B8
Links View Dartford DA1 ...32 C7
Woolwich SE18 ...12 B6
Linkway ME20 ...82 C1
Linley Cl RM18 ...20 D7
Linnet Ave TN12 ...146 A5
Linnet Cl SE28 ...3 C6
Linslade Rd BR6 ...58 A4
Linsted Ct SE9 ...12 E1
Linton Cl Bexley DA16 ...13 B6
2 Greenwich SE7 ...1 C1
Linton Dann Cl ME3 ...40 D6
Linton Gdns E6 ...1 E7
Linton Gore ME17 ...115 D3
Linton Hill TN12 ...132 F6
Linton Mead Prim Sch
SE28 ...3 B6
Linton Rd ME15 ...115 F4
Lintorn Symonds Rd ME3 .39 F5
Linwood Ave ME2 ...52 E8
Lion Rd Bexley DA6 ...13 F3
Newham E6 ...1 F8
Lionel Gdns SE9 ...11 D2

Lionel Oxley Ho 5 RM17 .18 B8
Lionel Rd Eltham SE9 .....11 D2
Tonbridge TN9 ....143 A8
Lions Cl SE9 ....28 D5
Liphook Way ME16 ....99 C8
Lipscombe Rd TN2 .....159 D6
Lipton Cl SE28 ....3 C6
Liptraps La TN2 ....159 D7
Lipwell Hill ME23 ....23 B4
Liskeard Cl BR7 ....29 C2
Liskeard Gdns SE3 ....11 A6
Lisle Cl DA12 ....37 B6
Lismore Cl ME15 ....116 A7
Lister Cl ME19 ....97 F8
Lister Ho SE2 ....3 D1
Lister Rd RM18 ....19 A5
Lister Wlk SE28 ....3 D6
Listmas Rd ME4 ....54 B3
Little Alley TN8 ....138 B5
Little Bayham Cotts
TN3 ....174 F4
Little Birches DA15 ....29 E6
Little Boundes Cl TN4 ...142 F3
Little Brook Hospl DA2 ...16 C1
Little Browns La TN8 ....121 F4
Little Buckland Ave
ME16 ....99 D6
Little Ct ME16 ....99 D2
Little Field TN12 ....149 E5
Little Footway TN3 ......157 F3
Little Heath SE7 ....1 E1
Little Heath Rd DA7 ......13 F7
Little Hill TN30 ....183 B2
Little Job's Cross TN17 ..191 F1
Little John Ave ME5 ......67 F2
Little Julians Hill TN13 ..108 A8
Little Kit's Coty Ho*
ME20 ....83 C5
Little Mallett TN3 ....157 F3
Little Market Row ME19 ..81 E2
Little Mill Farm Cotts
TN12 ....148 C8
Little Mount Sion TN1 ..159 A2
Little Oakham Ct ME3 ....25 C4
Little Orch ME17 ....115 D3
Little Oxley ME19 ....81 E2
Little Pk TN5 ....184 E5
Little Queen St DA1 ......32 F8
Little Redlands BR1 ......42 E7
Little Robhurst TN26 ....183 D8
Little Sheephurst Cotts
TN12 ....147 E5
Little Thrift BR5 ....43 C5
Little Wood TN13 ....92 D5
Little Wood Cl BR5 ....44 A8
Little York Mdws ME7 ....55 C4
Littlebourne Ave ME8 ....55 B4
Littlebourne Rd ME14 ...100 C6
Littlebrook Manor Way
DA1 ....16 A2
Littlecombe SE7 ....11 B8
Littlecourt Rd TN13 ......92 A3
Littlecroft Eltham SE9 .....12 A4
Istead Rise DA13 ....35 E1
Littledale Dartford DA2 ...33 C5
Woolwich SE2 ....13 A8
Littlefield TN11 ....128 E8
Littlejohn Rd BR5 ....44 B4
Littlemede SE9 ....28 F5
Littlemore Rd SE2 ....3 A4
Liveryman Wlk DA9 ......17 C3
Livesey Cl SE28 ....2 C3
Livesey St ME18 ....98 A1
Livingstone Bldgs ME7 ...54 D5
Livingstone Circ ME7 ....54 D5
Livingstone Gdns DA12 ...36 D3
Livingstone Hospl DA1 ...32 F8
Livingstone Rd
Gillingham ME7 ....54 E5
Gravesend DA12 ....36 D3
Livingstone Wlk 6
ME15 ....116 F5
Lizban St SE3 ....11 B7
Llanover Rd SE18 ....12 A7
Lloyd Ho BR1 ....28 B3
Lloyds Gn TN30 ....199 D4
Loaland Bsns Ctr ME2 ....53 D8
Loam Ct DA1 ....32 E7
Loampits Cl TN9 ....127 D3
Lobelia Cl Gillingham ME7 ..54 E6
5 Newham E6 ....1 E8
Locarno Ave ME8 ....55 A2
Lochat Rd ME3 ....39 E6
Lochmere Cl DA8 ....14 B8
Lock La ME14 ....83 D1
Lock St ME7 ....54 C5
Lock's Yd TN13 ....92 C2
Lockesley Dr BR5 ....44 A3
Lockham Farm Ave
ME17 ....116 D5
Lockington Cl TN9 ......142 F7
Lockington Gr ME1 ....53 C5
Lockside TN9 ....127 C2
Locksley Cl ME5 ....67 E2
Lockswood ME16 ....99 D7
Lockyer Rd RM19 ....16 C8
Lockyers Hill DA13 ....64 F5
Lodden Ct 15 BR5 ....44 D1
Loddington La ME17 ....133 A8
Loder Cl ME17 ....120 B5
Lodge Ave DA1 ....15 C1
Lodge Cl Orpington BR6 ....44 B1
Wateringbury ME18 .....113 D8
Lodge Cres BR6 ....44 B1
Lodge Farmhouse ME20 ..82 E3
Lodge Gdns ME17 ....135 F6
Lodge Hill DA16 ....13 B7
Lodge Hill La ME3 ....39 F7
Lodge La Cobham DA12 ....51 B5
Royal Tunbridge Wells
TN3 ....172 A8
Sidcup DA5 ....13 D1
Westerham TN16 ....105 C8
Lodge Oak La TN9 ......143 D8
Lodge Rd Bromley BR1 ....28 C1
Maidstone ME14 ....100 D5
Staplehurst TN12 ....149 E5
Tonbridge TN9 ....127 B2
Lodgewood Cotts TN8 ..123 D2
Logs Hill BR1,BR2 ....42 E8
Logs Hill Cl BR7 ....42 E8
Lolland Ho 9 SE18 ....1 E2
Lomaria Ct TN2 ....159 C4
Lomas La TN18 ....196 F5
Lombard St DA4 ....47 C5
Lombard Trad Est SE7 .....1 B2
Lombard Wall SE7 ....1 B2
Lombardy Cl ME7 ....69 A6
Lombardy Dr ME14 ......100 C5
Lomer Farm DA13 ....64 A8
London City Airport E16 ...1 E5
London Ind Pk E6 ....2 B8
London La Bromley BR1 ...28 A1
Sissinghurst TN17 ....166 A2
London Rd
Addington ME19 ....80 D2
Badgers Mount TN14 ......75 C6
Bidborough TN4 ....142 F3
Bromley BR1 ....42 A8
Chelsfield TN14 ....58 F2
Crayford DA1 ....14 D2
Ditton ME20 ....82 C1
Farningham BR8,DA4 .....46 D3
Flimwell TN5 ....187 D3
Gillingham ME8 ....55 C1
Grays RM17,RM20 ....17 E8
Hartlip ME8,ME9 ....70 D7
Hildenborough TN11,TN13,
TN15 ....126 B7
Hurst Green TN19 ....194 A3
Maidstone ME16 ....99 C6
Newington ME9 ....71 A6
Northfleet DA11 ....18 E1
Otford TN13 ....75 D1
Rochester ME2 ....53 A7
Royal Tunbridge Wells
TN4 ....159 A8
Royal Tunbridge Wells,Mount Sion
TN1 ....159 A3
Sevenoaks TN13 ....92 B2
Sevenoaks,Dunton Green
TN13 ....91 E7
Stone DA2,DA9 ....16 E1
Swanley BR8 ....45 D7
Swanley BR8 ....45 E6
Swanscombe DA9 ....17 C2
Tilbury RM18 ....19 B5
Tonbridge TN10,TN11 .....127 B3
West Kingsdown TN15 .....62 A1
Wrotham TN15 ....79 B3
Wrotham Heath TN15,ME19 .79 F1
London Rd E ME20 ....98 F8
London Road Purfleet
RM19 ....16 C8
London Road West Thurrock
RM20 ....17 A8
Londonderry Ho 15
ME15 ....116 E7
Londonderry Par DA8 ....14 D7
Lonewood Way TN11 ....111 F2
Long Acre BR6 ....58 D8
Long Barn Rd TN14 .....108 B2
Long Catlis Rd ME8 ....69 D4
Long La Bexley DA7 ....13 E6
Rabbit's Cross ME17 .....133 D5
Long Mark Rd 5 E16 ....1 D8
Long Mead Com Prim Sch
TN10 ....127 B5
Long Mead Way TN10 ...127 B4
Long Meads TN3 ....158 B4
Long Mill La Crouch TN15 ..95 B3
Platt TN15 ....95 C7
Long Rede La ME16 ......98 F3
Long Slip TN3 ....158 A3
Long Wlk SE18 ....12 B8
Longbury Cl BR5 ....44 B6
Longbury Dr BR5 ....44 B7
Longcroft SE9 ....29 A5
Longdon Wood BR2 ....56 E6
Longdown Ho ME5 ....67 F6
Longfellow Rd ME7 ....54 C3
Longfield TN30 ....193 A6
Longfield Ave
High Halstow ME23 ....23 E4
New Barn DA3,DA13 ......49 D7
Longfield Pl ME15 ....116 C8
Longfield Rd
Meopham Sta DA3,DA13 ....49 E3
Royal Tunbridge Wells
TN1,TN2,TN11 ....143 E1
Longfield Sta DA3 ....48 E6
Longfields Dr ME14 .....101 A5
Longford Cl ME8 ....70 A8
Longford Ct ME8 ....70 A8
Longham Copse ME15 ...100 F1
Longhill Ave ME5 ....54 B3
Longhurst Dr ME5 ....67 F2
Longlands Ct DA15 ....29 F5
Longlands Park Cres
DA15 ....29 E6
Longlands Prim Sch
DA15 ....29 E5
Longlands Rd DA15 ......29 F5
Longleat Ct 3 DA6 ....13 E3
Longleigh La SE2,DA7 ....13 C8
Longley Rd Rainham ME8 ..55 F1
Rochester ME1 ....53 C4
Longmarsh La SE28 ....2 E5
Longmarsh View DA4 .....47 B8
Longmead BR7 ....43 A7
Longmead Dr DA14 ....30 D6
Longmeade DA12 ....36 F7
Longmeadow TN13 ....91 D6
Longmeadow Rd DA15 ....29 E7
Longparish Cl ME15 .....116 F6
Longreach Rd DA8 ....15 B7
Longshaw Rd ME15 ......116 F5
Longten's Cotts DA12 ....37 E6
Longtown Ct 10 DA2 ......16 B1
Longview Way TN2 .....159 D7
Longwalk DA13 ....49 E8
Longwood ME5 ....68 B1
Longworth Cl SE28 ....3 D7
Lonsdale Cl SE9 ....28 D5
Lonsdale Cres DA2 ....33 C7
Lonsdale Dr ME8 ....69 E7
Lonsdale Gdns TN1 .....159 A3
Lonsdale Rd DA7 ....13 F5
Loop Rd BR7 ....29 C2
Loose Inf & Jun Schs
ME15 ....116 A6
Loose Rd ME15 ....116 A7
Loraine Ct BR7 ....29 B3
Lord Chatham's Ride
TN14 ....74 D2
Lord Roberts Terr SE18 ....2 A1
Lord Romney's Hill
ME14 ....100 F3
Lord St Gravesend DA12 ...36 B8
Newham E16 ....1 E5
Lord Warwick St SE18 .....1 F3
Lords Wood Cl ME5 ......68 B2
Lords Wood La ME5 ......68 B3
Lordswood Cl DA2 ....33 E4
Lordswood Ind Est ME5 ..84 C8
Lordswood Inf & Jun Sch
ME5 ....68 B3
Lorenden Pk TN18 ......188 F1
Lorimar Bsns Ctr RM13 ....4 E8
Lorraine Ct DA9 ....17 B1
Lorton Cl DA12 ....36 E6
Lossenham La TN18 ....197 D3
Lotus Rd TN16 ....72 F1
Louis Gdns BR7 ....28 F4
Louise Ct 8 DA6 ....13 E3
Louisville Ave ME7 ....54 D4
Louvain Rd DA9 ....33 E8
Lovage App E6 ....1 E8
Love La East Tilbury RM18 ..20 C8
Rochester ME1 ....53 C5
Sidcup DA5 ....14 A1
Swift's Green TN27 ......152 B5
Wateringbury ME18 ......113 D7
Woolwich SE18 ....2 B2
Lovel Ave DA16 ....13 A5
Lovelace Ave BR2 ....43 A3
Lovelace Cl
Gillingham ME8 ....69 D4
West Kingsdown TN15 .....61 E4
Lovelace Gn SE9 ....11 F4
Lover's La DA9,DA10 .....17 D3
Lovers La TN17 ....163 F1
Lovibonds Ave BR6 ......57 B7
Low Cl DA9 ....17 A2
Low Mdw ME2 ....66 B5
Low Street La RM18 ......19 F8
Lowe Ave E16 ....1 A8
Lower Bell La ME20 ......82 B2
Lower Bloors La ME8 .....55 E3
Lower Boxley Rd 10
ME14 ....100 A5
Lower Camden BR7 ......42 F8
Lower Church Hill DA9 ...16 E2
Lower Croft BR8 ....45 F5
Lower Fant Rd ME16 .....99 D2
Lower Farm Rd ME17 ...133 D5
Lower Gn TN11 ....125 F1
Lower Gravel Rd BR2 .....42 F1
Lower Green Rd
Pembury TN2 ....160 D7
Rusthall TN3,TN4 ....158 C6
Lower Hartlip Rd ME9 ....70 E5
Lower Haysden La
TN11,TN9 ....142 D8
Lower Hazelhurst
Ticehurst TN5 ....186 A4
Ticehurst TN5 ....186 B4
Lower High St TN5 .....185 A4
Lower Higham Rd DA12 ..37 B7
Lower Park Rd DA17 ....4 A2
Lower Platts TN5 ....186 F1
Lower Rainham Rd ME7 ..55 D5
Lower Range Rd DA12 ....36 E8
Lower Rd
East Farleigh ME15 ......115 B7
Erith DA17 ....4 B3
Erith DA8 ....4 D2
Hextable BR8 ....32 B1
Higham DA12,ME3 ....38 B6
Maidstone ME15 ....100 B3
Northfleet DA11 ....18 A3
Orpington BR5 ....44 B3
Shorne DA12 ....37 E6
Sutton Valence ME17 ....134 E7
West Farleigh ME15 .....114 D7
Lower Rochester Rd ME3 .38 E6
Lower St Leeds ME17 ....118 A7
Tonbridge TN11 ....125 F5
Lower Station Rd DA1 ....14 E1
Lower Stone St ME15 ...100 A3
Lower Tovil ME15 ....99 E2
Lower Twydall La ME7,
ME8 ....55 C4
Lower Warren Rd ME20 ..83 E6
Lower Woodlands Rd
ME7 ....55 A6
Lowestoft Mews E16 ......2 B4
Lowfield St DA1 ....32 E8
Lownds Ct BR1 ....42 A7
Lowry Cl DA8 ....4 D2
Lowry The 4 TN9 ....143 B8
Loxwood Cl BR5,BR6 .....58 D8
Lubbock Cl ME15 ....116 E5
Lubbock Ct BR7 ....28 F1
Lubbock Ho BR6 ....57 E8
Lubbock Rd BR7 ....28 F1
Lubbock Wlk ME8 ....69 D5
Lucas Cres DA9 ....17 C3
Lucas Rd ME6 ....81 E7
Lucerne Ct 5 DA18 ....3 E3
Lucerne Rd BR6 ....43 F1
Lucerne St ME14 ....100 A5
Lucilina Dr TN8 ....138 C8
Lucknow Rd TN12 ......146 A8
Lucknow St SE18 ....12 E7
Lucks Hill ME19 ....97 D8
Lucks La
Paddock Wood TN12 ......146 B8
Rabbit's Cross ME17 .....133 F6
Lucks Way TN12 ....148 B6
Luddenham Cl ME14 ....100 C6
Luddesdon Rd DA8 ....14 A7
Luddesdown Ho 5 BR5 ..44 C4
Luddesdown Rd DA13 ....51 A2
Ludham Cl SE28 ....3 C7
Ludlow Cl BR2 ....42 A6
Luffield Rd SE2 ....3 B3
Luffman Rd SE12 ....28 B5
Lughorse La ME15,ME18 .114 C1
Lullarook Cl TN16 ....72 C3
Lullingstone Ave BR8 ....45 F6
Lullingstone Castle*
DA4 ....60 B5
Lullingstone Cl
Gillingham ME7 ....69 B3
Orpington BR5 ....30 B1
Lullingstone Cres BR5 ....30 B1
Lullingstone La DA4 .....60 C8
Lullingstone Pk* DA4 ....59 F6
Lullingstone Pk Visitor Ctr*
DA4 ....60 B4
Lullingstone Rd
3 Bexley DA17 ....13 F8
Maidstone ME16 ....99 C7
Lullingstone Roman Villa
(rems of)* DA4 ....60 B7
Lulworth Rd Bexley DA16 ..12 F5
Bromley SE9 ....28 E6
Lumley Cl DA17 ....4 A1
Lumsden Terr 8 ME4 .....53 E4
Lunar Cl TN16 ....72 D3
Lunedale Rd DA2 ....33 C7
Lunsford District Ctr
ME20 ....82 A4
Lunsford La ME20 ....81 F2
Lunsford Prim Sch ME20 .82 A2
Lupton Cl SE12 ....28 B4
Lurkins Rise TN17 ......177 D7
Lushington Rd ME14 .....99 E7
Lusted Hall La TN16 ......88 C7
Lusted Rd TN13 ....91 E7
Luton High St ME5 ....54 C2
Luton Inf Sch ME5 ....54 C2
Luton Jun Sch ME4 ....54 C2
Luton Rd
Chatham ME4,ME5 ....54 B2
Sidcup DA14 ....30 C5
Luxfield Rd SE9 ....28 E7
Luxon Rd DA13 ....64 E4
Luxted Rd BR6 ....73 A6
Lyall Way ME8 ....69 E4
Lych Gate Rd BR6 ....44 A1
Lychfield Dr ME2 ....53 A8
Lydd Cl DA14 ....29 E5
Lydd Rd Bexley DA7 ....13 F7
Chatham ME5 ....68 B5
Lydden Ct SE9 ....12 E1
Lydens La TN8 ....138 F6
Lydford Ct 18 DA2 ....16 B1
Lydia Cotts 2 DA11 ....36 B8
Lydia Rd DA8 ....14 F8
Lydstep Rd BR7 ....29 A4
Lyford St SE18 ....1 E2
Lyle Cl ME2 ....53 B8
Lyle Ct ME16 ....99 C5
Lyle Pk TN13 ....92 B4
Lyme Farm Rd SE12 ......11 B3
Lyme Rd DA16 ....13 B6
Lyminge Cl
Gillingham ME8 ....55 C2
Sidcup DA14 ....29 F4
Lymington Cl 2 E6 ....1 F8
Lymington Ct ME15 .....116 F4
Lyndale Est RM20 ....17 B8
Lyndean Ind Est SE2 ......3 C3
Lynden Way BR8 ....45 D6
Lyndhurst BR7 ....29 B2
Lyndhurst Ave ME8 ......69 C7
Lyndhurst Cl Bexley DA7 ...14 B4
Orpington BR6 ....57 B6
Lyndhurst Dr TN13 ......91 E3
Lyndhurst Rd Bexley DA7 ..14 B4
Maidstone ME15 ....116 C8
Lyndhurst Way DA13 .....49 F8
Lyndon Ave DA15 ....12 F2
Lyndon Rd DA17 ....4 A2
Lynette Ave ME2 ....39 A1
Lyngs Cl ME18 ....130 F8
Lynmead Cl TN8 ....122 B4
Lynmere Rd DA16 13
Lynmouth Rise BR5 44
Lynne Cl 7 BR6 57
Lynors Ave ME2 39
Lynstead Cl BR1 42
Lynstead Ho ME16 99
Lynsted Cl DA6 14
Lynsted Gdns SE9 11
Lynsted Rd ME8 55
Lynton Ave BR5 44
Lynton Dr ME5 68
Lynton Rd DA11 36
Lynton Rd S DA11 36
Lynwood TN3 171
Lynwood Gr BR6 43
Lynx Way E16 1
Lyons Cres TN9 127
Lyons The TN9 127
Lyoth Rd BR5 57
Lysander Rd ME19 96
Lysander Way BR6 57
Lytchet Rd BR1 28
Lytham Cl SE28 3
Lytton Strachey Path 8
SE28 3
Lyveden Rd SE3 11

M

Mabbett Ho 2 SE18 12
Mabel Cotts DA3 49
Mabel Rd BR8 32
Mabledon Rd TN9 143
Macallister Ho 8 SE18 ...12
Macaulay Cl ME20 82
Macaulay Way 2 SE28 3
Macbean St SE18 2
Macdonald Ct TN12 146
Macdonald Rd ME7 54
Mace Ct RM17 18
Mace Farm Cotts TN14 ..73
Mace La TN14 73
Macgregor Rd E16 1
Mackenders Cl ME20 83
Mackenders Gn ME20 83
Mackenders La ME20 83
Mackenzie Way DA12 36
Mackintosh Cl ME23 23
Macleod Ho SE18 11
Macmillan Gdns 2 DA1 ..16
Macoma Rd SE18 12
Macoma Terr SE18 12
Mada Rd BR6 57
Madan Cl TN16 89
Madan Rd TN16 89
Madden Ave ME5 67
Madden Cl DA10 17
Maddocks Cl DA14 30
Madeira Pk TN2 159
Madginford Cl ME15 101
Madginford Park Inf Sch
ME15 101
Madginford Park Jun Sch
ME15 101
Madginford Rd ME15 100
Madison Cres DA7 13
Madison Gdns DA7 13
Madison Way TN13 91
Madras Ho 2 ME15 116
Maesmaur Rd TN16 88
Mafeking Rd ME5 67
Magdalen Cl ME7 69
Magdelan Gr BR6 58
Magnet Rd RM20 17
Magnolia Ave ME8 69
Magnolia Cl TN9 143
Magnolia Dr TN16 72
Magnolia Ho 3 ME16 99
Magpie Bottom TN15 76
Magpie Cl ME20 82
Magpie Gn 3 TN8 122
Magpie Hall Cl BR2 42
Magpie Hall La BR2 42
Magpie Hall Rd ME4 54
Magpie La ME9,ME14 69
Magwitch Cl ME1 53
Maida Rd Chatham ME4 ...54
Erith DA17 4
Maida Vale Rd DA1 15
Maiden Erlegh Ave DA5 ..30
Maiden La DA1 15
Maidstone Barracks Sta
ME16 99
Maidstone East Sta ME14 .99
Maidstone Gram Sch
ME15 100
Maidstone Gram Sch for Girls
ME16 99
Maidstone Hospl The
ME16 99
Maidstone Ind Ctr ME14 ..99
Maidstone L Ctr ME15 ...100
Maidstone Mus & Bentlif Art
Gallery* ME14 99
Maidstone Rd
Bredhurst ME7,ME8 69
Chatham ME4 53
Chatham ME5 67
Colt's Hill TN12,TN2 145
Danaway ME9 71
Five Wents ME17 117
Gillingham ME8 69
Goose Green ME18,TN11 .112
Grays RM17 18
Headcorn TN27 151
Horsmonden TN12 163

Maidstone Rd continued
Horsmonden,Claygate TN12 147 C3
Lenham ME17 120 D5
Matfield TN12 161 C6
Nettlestead Green ME18 113 C3
Pembury TN2 144 E1
Platt TN15 95 C7
Rochester ME1 53 C3
Seal TN15 93 C5
Sevenoaks TN13 91 E5
Sidcup DA14 30 F1
Staplehurst TN12 149 E7
Swanley DA14,BR8 45 B8
Underling Green TN12 132 F2
Maidstone St Michaels CE Jun Sch ME16 99 E3
Maidstone West Sta ME16 99 F3
Mailyns The ME8 69 D7
Main Gate Rd ME4 53 F7
Main Rd Biggin Hill TN16 72 C5
Chattenden ME3 39 F4
Cooling ME3 22 F4
Crockenhill BR8 45 D3
Crockham Hill TN8 105 C1
Cudham TN16 89 A7
Farningham DA4 46 F3
Halstead TN14 74 C3
Hoo St Werburgh ME3 40 C5
Kingsnorth ME3 41 D7
Longfield DA3 48 E7
Marlpit Hill TN8 122 B6
Orpington BR5 44 C7
Sidcup DA14,DA15 29 E5
Sundridge TN14 90 E3
Sutton at H DA4 33 B1
Swanley BR8 45 F8
Main Road Gorse Hill DA4 61 D7
Main St ME4 40 B2
Mainridge Rd BR7 29 A4
Maison Des Fleurs ME16 99 C2
Majendie Rd SE18 2 D1
Major Clark Ho TN17 179 C5
Major York's Rd TN4 158 F2
Malan Cl TN16 72 E2
Malden Dr ME14 100 A8
Mall The 6 Bexley DA6 14 A3
4 Bromley BR1 42 A6
Mallard Apartments 14 ME15 116 E5
Mallard Cl DA1 15 F2
Mallard Path 6 SE28 2 D3
Mallard Way
Lower Stoke ME3 25 C4
Marlpit Hill TN8 122 C3
Mallard Wlk
Larkfield ME20 81 F2
Sidcup DA14 30 C2
Mallards Way ME15 101 A1
Malling Ct ME19 97 F7
Malling Rd
Kings Hill M18,ME19 96 F2
Lunsford ME6,ME20 81 F5
Snodland ME6 82 A7
Teston ME18 98 A1
Malling Sch The ME19 97 F7
Malling Terr ME16 99 C4
Mallingdene Cl ME3 39 B8
Mallings Dr ME14 101 C4
Mallings La ME14 101 C4
Mallow Cl DA11 35 E4
Mallow Ct RM17 18 D8
Mallow Way 1 ME5 67 F4
Mallows The ME14 99 E7
Mallys Pl DA4 47 C8
Malmaynes Hall Rd ME3 24 D3
Malory Sch BR1 28 A4
Malt House La TN30 193 A7
Malt Mews ME1 53 C5
Malt Shovel Cotts DA4 60 D7
Malta Ave ME5 68 A7
Malta Rd RM18 18 F5
Malta Terr 5 ME14 100 A7
Maltby Cl BR6 44 A1
Malthouse Cl ME17 120 D5
Malthouse Hill ME15 115 F4
Malthouse La DA12 37 E3
Malthouse Rd TN15 62 F2
Malthouse The ME16 115 A8
Malthus Path 7 SE28 3 C5
Maltings Cl TN11 128 E8
Maltings Ent Ctr The DA12 36 F7
Maltings The
Gillingham ME8 70 A8
3 Gravesend DA11 19 A1
Hadlow TN11 128 E8
Loose ME17 116 B4
Maidstone, Grove Green ME14 100 E5
Orpington BR6 43 F1
Westerham TN16 105 C8
Malton Mews SE18 12 E8
Malton St SE18 12 E8
Malton Way TN2 159 F7
Malus Cl ME5 68 B1
Malvern Ave DA7 13 E7
Malvern Ho DA11 18 D1
Malvern Rd
Gillingham ME7 54 E3
Orpington BR6 58 B6
Malvina Ave DA12 36 C6
Malyons Rd BR8 31 F1
Mamignot Cl ME14 101 A5
Manchester Cl ME5 68 C6
Manchester Ct E16 1 B7
Mandela Ho SE18 12 D8
Mandela Rd E16 1 A7
Mandeville Cl 1 SE3 11 A7
Mandeville Ct 1 ME14 100 A5
Manford Ind Est DA8 15 B8
Mangold Way 4 DA18 3 E3
Mangravet Ave ME15 116 C7
Manister Rd SE2 3 A3
Manitoba Gdns 6 BR6 57 F4
Mann Sq TN9 143 D7
Manning Ct 3 SE28 3 B5
Manning Rd BR5 44 D4
Manningham Ho ME19 98 A6
Mannock Rd DA1 15 F4
Manor Cl Chalk DA12 37 B6
Crayford DA1 14 E3
Dartford DA2 32 A5
Erith SE28 3 C7
Maidstone ME14 101 B3
Royal Tunbridge Wells TN4 158 E3
Manor Cotts
Lamberhurst TN3 176 B5
Langley ME17 117 C5
Manor Ct Gillingham ME7 55 C4
Maidstone ME14 101 B3
Sole Street DA13 50 D4
Manor Dr DA3 49 A3
Manor Farm Cotts TN15 94 A6
Manor Field DA12 37 E3
Manor Forstal DA3 62 F7
Manor Gdns ME5 67 F4
Manor Gr TN10 127 C3
Manor Ho
14 Chatham ME7 54 A6
Chislehurst BR7 43 D8
Manor Ho The
Limpsfield RH8 104 B7
Sidcup DA15 30 A7
Sidcup,Old Bexley DA5 31 B7
Manor House Dr ME16 99 D3
Manor House Gdns TN8 122 C1
Manor La
Fawkham Green DA3 48 C2
Hartley DA3 49 A3
Rochester ME1 52 F3
Manor Oak Prim Sch BR5 44 D4
Manor Park Ctry Pk* ME19 97 B7
Manor Park Rd BR7 43 D8
Manor Pk Chislehurst BR7 43 D8
Erith DA8 15 A8
Royal Tunbridge Wells TN4 158 E3
Manor Pl Bromley BR1 42 E8
Chislehurst BR7 43 D7
Manor Rd Chatham ME4 53 F4
Crayford DA1 14 E3
Edenbridge TN8 122 B1
Erith DA8 15 B8
22 Gravesend DA12 19 B1
Grays RM17 18 C8
Knockmill TN15 77 F8
New Barn DA3 49 C4
Royal Tunbridge Wells TN4 142 E1
Rusthall TN4 158 C4
Sidcup DA15 30 A5
Sidcup,Old Bexley DA5 31 B7
Sole Street DA13 50 D4
Sundridge TN14 90 D3
Swanscombe DA10 34 E8
Tatsfield TN16 88 E7
Tilbury RM18 19 A5
West Thurrock RM20 17 C8
Manor Rise ME14 101 B3
Manor St ME7 54 A6
Manor The TN2 159 E5
Manor Way Bexley DA7 14 D4
Bromley BR2 42 E3
Eltham SE3 11 A3
Grays RM17 18 B7
Grays RM17 18 D7
Northfleet DA11 18 A3
Orpington BR5 43 C5
Sidcup DA5 31 A7
Swanscombe DA10 17 E3
Manor Way Bsns Ctr RM13 4 D8
Manorbrook SE3 11 A3
Manordene Rd SE28 3 D7
Manorfields Cl BR7 43 F6
Manorside Cl SE2 3 D2
Manse Ct DA14 30 C3
Manse Par BR8 46 A5
Manse Way BR8 46 A5
Mansel Dr ME1 53 A2
Mansergh Cl SE18 11 E7
Mansfield Cl BR5 44 D2
Mansfield Rd BR8 31 F2
Mansfield Wlk ME16 99 E2
Mansion House Cl TN27 168 A2
Mansion Row ME7 54 A6
Manthorpe Rd SE18 2 C1
Manton Rd SE2 3 A2
Manwarings The TN12 163 A6
Manwood St E16 1 F5
Maple Ave Gillingham ME7 54 E6
Maidstone ME16 99 C6
Maple Cl Larkfield ME20 82 A2
Orpington BR5 43 D4
Royal Tunbridge Wells TN2 159 A1
Swanley BR8 45 E7
Maple Cres DA15 13 A1
Maple Ct Erith DA8 14 F7
Newham E6 2 A8
Maple Ct continued
Royal Tunbridge Wells TN4 158 E4
Sidcup DA14 30 B3
Stone DA9 33 E8
Maple Leaf Cl TN16 72 D3
Maple Leaf Dr DA15 29 F7
Maple Rd Dartford DA1 32 C7
Gravesend DA12 36 C4
Grays RM17 18 C8
Hoo St Werburgh ME3 40 E3
Rochester ME2 52 F6
Maple Tree Pl SE3 11 E6
Maplecroft Cl E6 1 E7
Mapledene BR7 29 C3
Maplehurst Cl DA2 31 E6
Maples The DA3 49 B6
Maplescombe Farm Cotts DA4 61 B5
Maplescombe La DA4 61 B6
Maplesden TN12 148 D5
Maplesden Cl ME16 98 F3
Maplesden Noakes Sch The ME16 99 E6
Mapleton TN8 123 A7
Mapleton Cl BR2 42 A3
Mapleton Rd
Four Elms TN8 123 A8
Westerham TN8,TN16 105 E3
Maplin Ho 9 SE2 3 D4
Maplin Rd E16 1 B7
Maplins Cl 5 ME8 55 F1
Mar Ho 5 SE7 11 C8
Mara Ct ME4 53 F1
Maran Way DA18 3 D3
Marathon Paddock ME7 54 D4
Marathon Way SE28 2 F4
Marble Ho 1 SE18 2 F1
Marbrook Ct SE12 28 C5
Marc Brunel Way ME4 54 A7
Marcellina Way BR6 57 F7
Marcet Rd DA1 15 C2
Marconi Ho SE2 3 C1
Marconi Rd DA11 35 D5
Marconi Way ME1 67 D7
Marcus Rd DA1 32 A8
Marden Ave BR2 42 A3
Marden Cres DA5 14 C2
Marden Prim Sch TN12 148 B5
Marden Rd Rochester ME2 39 C1
Staplehurst TN12 149 C5
Marden Sta TN12 148 C6
Marechal Niel Ave DA15 29 D5
Marechal Niel Par DA15 29 D5
Margaret Barr Row DA10 34 E8
Margaret Gardner Dr SE9 28 F6
Margaret Rd DA5 13 D1
Margate Cl ME7 54 E6
Margetts La ME1 66 D1
Margetts Pl ME2 40 A3
Marian Sq TN12 149 F4
Marigold Way ME16 99 A3
Marina Cl 1 BR2 42 A6
Marina Dr Bexley DA16 12 E5
Dartford DA1 33 A7
Northfleet DA11 18 F1
Marine Dr
Hoo St Werburgh ME3 40 E3
Woolwich SE18 1 F2
Marine View ME4 40 B1
Mariners Ct DA9 17 B3
Mariners The ME1 53 B4
Mariners View ME7 54 F7
Mariners Way 5 DA11 35 E8
Mariners Wlk DA8 14 F8
Marion Cl ME5 68 A2
Marion Cotts TN15 95 E8
Marion Cres
Maidstone ME15 116 B8
Orpington BR5 44 B4
Maritime Cl
Rochester ME2 53 D8
Swanscombe DA9 17 B2
Maritime Est ME2 53 D8
Maritime Gate DA11 35 E8
Maritime Ind Est SE7 1 B2
Maritime Way ME4 54 A8
Marjorie McClure Sch BR7 43 C8
Marjory Pease Cotts RH8 104 E5
Mark Cl Bexley DA7 13 E6
Orpington BR2 56 E6
Mark La DA12 19 E1
Mark St ME4 54 A2
Mark Way BR8 46 A4
Markers Lodge DA12 36 E8
Market Alley 9 DA11 19 B1
Market Bldgs 4 ME14 99 F4
Market Colonnade 3 ME14 99 F4
Market Mdw BR5 44 C5
Market Par Bromley BR1 42 A8
5 Sidcup DA14 30 B4
Market Pl 2 Bexley DA6 14 A3
Dartford DA1 32 E8
16 Royal Tunbridge Wells TN2 159 A2
1 Tilbury RM18 19 A5
Market Sq Bromley BR1 42 A7
Royal Tunbridge Wells TN1 159 B4
Westerham TN16 89 D1
Market St Dartford DA1 32 E8
2 Maidstone ME14 99 F4
17 Royal Tunbridge Wells TN2 159 A2
Market St continued
Staplehurst TN12 149 F5
Woolwich SE18 2 A2
Market Way 2 TN16 89 D1
Marks Sq DA11 35 F4
Marlborough Cl
Orpington BR6 43 F3
Royal Tunbridge Wells TN4 158 E4
Marlborough Cres TN13 91 E3
Marlborough Ct TN16 89 C1
Marlborough Ho 4 ME8 69 F8
Marlborough House Sch TN18 188 E2
Marlborough La SE7 11 C7
Marlborough Par ME16 98 F2
Marlborough Park Ave DA15 30 A7
Marlborough Rd
Bexley DA7 13 D4
Bromley BR2 42 C5
Dartford DA1 15 C1
Gillingham ME7 54 B5
Woolwich SE18 2 C3
Marlborough Sch DA15 30 A8
Marle Place Gdns* TN12 162 C4
Marle Place Rd TN12 162 C4
Marler Ho DA8 14 F5
Marley Ave DA7 13 D8
Marley La TN27 152 C3
Marley Rd
Harrietsham ME17 119 F6
Hoo St Werburgh ME3 40 D6
Marley Way ME1 53 C2
Marlfield TN12 149 E4
Marlhurst TN8 122 B4
Marlin Ct 12 DA14 30 A4
Marling Cross DA12 36 E1
Marling Way DA12 36 E3
Marlings Cl BR7 43 E5
Marlings Park Ave BR7 43 E6
Marlow Copse ME5 67 F1
Marlow Ct TN13 92 B4
Marlowe Cl BR7 29 D2
Marlowe Gdns SE9 12 A1
Marlowe Rd ME20 82 A3
Marlowes The DA1 14 D3
Marlpit Cl TN8 122 C4
Marlpit Cotts ME17 116 E2
Marlpit Gdns TN5 186 E1
Marlpit The TN5 184 E5
Marlwood Cl DA15 29 E6
Marmadon Rd SE18 2 F2
Marne Ave DA16 13 A4
Marquis Dr ME7 69 B3
Marrabon Cl DA15 30 A7
Marram Ct RM17 18 E8
Marrians View 1 ME5 54 C2
Marriott Rd DA1 33 A8
Marriotts Wharf 2 DA11 19 B1
Marsden Way 2 BR6 57 F6
Marsh Cres ME23 23 E4
Marsh Green Rd TN8 138 C5
Marsh La ME3 22 B6
Marsh Quarter La TN18 196 C3
Marsh Rd ME2 66 B5
Marsh St Dartford DA1 16 A3
Dartford DA1 16 A5
Rochester ME2 53 B7
Marsh View DA12 36 F7
Marsh Way
New Hythe ME20 82 A4
Rainham RM13 4 D8
Marshall Gdns TN11 111 E1
Marshall Path 10 SE28 3 B6
Marshall Rd ME8 69 C8
Marshalls Gr SE18 1 E2
Marshalls Land TN30 183 A3
Marsham Cl BR7 29 B3
Marsham Cres ME17 117 B1
Marsham St ME14 100 A4
Marsham Way ME2 66 A5
Marshbrook Cl SE3 11 D4
Marshland View ME3 25 C5
Marston Cl ME5 67 E3
Marston Ct DA14 29 F4
Marston Dr ME14 100 C5
Marston Ho RM17 18 A8
Marston Wlk ME5 67 E3
Martens Ave DA7 14 C3
Martens Cl DA7 14 C3
Martham Cl SE28 3 D6
Martin Bowes Rd SE9 11 F4
Martin Ct ME7 69 A3
Martin Dene DA6 13 F2
Martin Dr DA2 16 C1
Martin Hardie Way TN10 127 E5
Martin Ho Dartford DA2 33 C8
Gravesend DA11 36 A5
Northfleet DA11 35 F6
Martin Rd Dartford DA2 32 C5
Rochester ME2 53 B8
Martin Rise DA6 13 F2
Martin Sq ME20 82 A2
Martin St SE28 2 E5
Martin's Shaw TN13 91 C5
Martindale Ave
Newham E16 1 A6
Orpington BR6 58 A5
Martins Cl
Lower Higham ME3 38 D6
Orpington BR5 44 D6
Tenterden TN30 193 C8
Martins La TN12 112 E2
Martins Pl SE28 2 E5
Martins Wlk SE28 2 E5
Martyn Ho SE2 13 D8
Marvels Cl SE12 28 B6
Marvels La SE12 28 C5
Marvels Lane Prim Sch SE12 28 C4
Marvillion Ct TN12 129 F6
Marvin Ho 9 SE18 12 B8
Marwell TN16 89 B1
Marwood Cl DA16 13 B4
Mary Burrows Gdns TN15 77 B2
Mary Ct ME4 54 A2
Mary Day's TN17 177 E7
Mary Last Cl ME6 81 E7
Mary Lawrenson Pl 2 SE3 11 A7
Mary Macarthur Ho 5 DA17 4 A3
Mary Magdalene Ho 8 TN9 143 B8
Mary Rose Mall E6 1 F8
Mary Slessor Ho 14 DA17 4 A3
Marybank SE18 1 F2
Maryfield Cl DA5 31 E5
Maryland Ct ME8 69 E5
Maryland Dr ME16 98 F2
Maryland Rd TN2 159 D1
Maryon Ct BR5 44 B5
Maryon Gr SE7 1 E2
Maryon Rd SE7,SE18 1 E2
Maryville DA16 12 F5
Mascall's Court La TN12 146 B4
Mascall's Court Rd TN12 146 A4
Mascalls Ct 23 SE7 11 C8
Mascalls Pk TN12 145 F5
Mascalls Rd SE7 11 C8
Mascalls Sec Sch TN12 146 A4
Masefield Cl DA8 14 F6
Masefield Dr ME3 39 B8
Masefield Rd
Dartford DA1 16 B2
Lunsford ME20 81 F4
Northfleet DA11 35 D5
Masefield View BR6 57 C7
Masefield Way TN9 142 F7
Masham Ho 6 DA18 3 D4
Mason Cl Bexley DA7 14 B4
Newham E16 1 A6
Mason Way ME2 39 B2
Masons Hill Bromley BR2 42 B5
Woolwich SE18 2 B2
Master Gunner Pl SE18 11 E6
Masters La ME19 81 B5
Masterson Ho DA4 47 D7
Masthead Cl DA2 16 C3
Matchless Dr SE18 12 A7
Matfield Cl BR2 42 A4
Matfield Cres ME14 100 C5
Matfield Rd DA17 14 A8
Matilda Cl ME8 69 B8
Matrix Bsns Ctr DA1 15 E2
Matterdale Gdns ME16 98 E2
Matthews Ho 13 SE7 11 C8
Matthews La TN11,ME18 111 F4
Mattinson Pl ME9 103 F7
Matts Hill Rd ME9 69 E2
Maud Cashmore Way SE18 1 F3
Maude Rd BR8 32 A2
Maudslay Rd SE9 11 F4
Maundene Sch ME5 68 B5
Maunders Cl ME5 68 C8
Mavelstone Cl BR1 42 E8
Mavelstone Rd BR1 42 E8
Mavis Wlk 10 E6 1 E8
Maxey Rd SE18 2 C2
Maxim Rd Crayford DA1 14 E2
Erith DA8 4 E2
Maximfeldt Rd DA8 4 E1
Maximilian Dr ME2 66 B4
Maxton Cl ME14 100 F5
Maxwell Dr ME16 99 B6
Maxwell Gdns BR6 57 F7
Maxwell Ho
Chislehurst BR7 29 B1
12 Woolwich SE18 12 B8
Maxwell Rd Bexley DA16 13 A4
Chatham ME7 54 A6
May Ave Northfleet DA11 35 F7
Orpington BR5 44 B4
May Avenue Est 1 DA11 35 F7
May Ct RM17 18 E8
May Pl DA12 50 D4
May Rd Gillingham ME7 54 C4
Hawley DA2 32 F4
Rochester ME1 53 C3
May St Cuxton ME2 52 B2
Snodland ME6 82 B8
May Terr 2 ME7 54 A7
May Wynne Ho E16 1 B7
Maybury Ave DA2 33 C7
Maybury Cl BR5 43 B4
Maycotts La TN12 145 D1
Mayday Gdns SE3 11 E5
Mayerne Rd SE9 11 D2
Mayes Cl BR8 46 A5
Mayeswood Rd SE12 28 C4
Mayfair 2 ME2 53 C8
Mayfair Ave Bexley DA7 13 D6
Loose ME15 116 A8
Mayfair Rd DA1 15 D2
Mayfield Bexley DA7 13 F4
Sevenoaks TN13 91 E7
Swanscombe DA10 17 E1

Mayfield Ave BR6 43 F2
Mayfield Cl Chatham ME5 68 A1
Gillingham ME8 55 E2
Mayfield Ct DA14 30 B3
Mayfield La TN5 184 D4
Mayfield Pk TN5 184 E5
Mayfield Rd Bromley BR1 42 E4
Erith DA17 4 C2
Northfleet DA11 35 F8
Royal Tunbridge Wells TN4 158 F4
Mayfield Villas DA14 30 C2
Mayflower Ho ME1 53 B4
Mayfly Cl BR5 44 D5
Mayford Rd ME5 68 D2
Mayhill Rd SE7 11 B8
Maylam Ct TN10 127 C4
Maylands Dr DA14 30 D5
Maynard Cl DA8 14 F7
Maynard Ho SE18 2 C2
Maynard Pl ME5 54 D2
Maynards TN12 148 C5
Mayor's La DA2 32 C3
Mayor's Pl 11 TN30 193 A7
Mayplace Ave DA1 15 A3
Mayplace Cl DA7 14 B4
Mayplace La
Woolwich SE18 12 B7
Woolwich SE18 12 B5
Mayplace Prim Sch DA7 14 D3
Mayplace Rd E DA7 14 C4
Mayplace Rd W DA7 14 A3
Maypole Cotts BR6 59 A4
Maypole Cres DA8 15 D8
Maypole Dr ME18 97 C3
Maypole La TN17 177 F8
Maypole Prim Sch DA5 31 E5
Maypole Rd Chelsfield BR6 58 F4
Gravesend DA12 36 F7
Mayston Mews 6 SE10 1 A1
Maytham Bglws TN17 192 A1
Maytham Rd TN17 198 C7
Mayview DA1 32 E7
Mayweed Ave ME5 67 E4
Mc Call Cres SE7 1 E1
Mc Kenzie Rd ME5 68 A3
Mc Kinlay Ct DA16 13 C4
McAlpine Cres ME15 115 F3
McAuley Cl SE9 12 A2
McCabe Cl TN12 149 E2
McCudden Rd DA1 15 F4
McCudden Row 8 ME7 54 A6
McDermott Rd TN15 94 F7
McDowall Cl 11 E16 1 A8
McIntyre Ct 6 SE18 1 E2
McKenzie Cl ME20 98 F8
McKillop Way DA14 30 C1
McLeod Rd SE2 3 B2
McMichaels Way TN19 194 A3
McMillan Cl DA12 36 C4
Mead Cl BR8 46 A4
Mead Cres DA1 32 D7
Mead Gn ME5 68 C3
Mead Ho TN16 72 D3
Mead Rd Chislehurst BR7 29 C2
Dartford DA1 32 D7
Edenbridge TN8 138 D7
Gravesend DA11 36 B6
Mead Road Inf Sch BR7 29 C2
Mead Sch The TN2 159 A1
Mead The Leybourne ME19 81 E2
New Ash Green DA3 62 E8
Mead Wall ME3 5 F2
Mead Way BR2 42 A3
Meades Cl TN12 148 B6
Meadfield Rd DA13 64 A8
Meadow Bank
Leigh TN11 125 F1
West Malling ME19 97 C8
Meadow Bank Cl TN15 61 F2
Meadow Bank Mews ME19 97 C8
Meadow Cl Bexley DA6 13 F2
Chatham ME5 67 F5
Chislehurst BR7 29 B3
Sevenoaks TN13 92 A4
Upper Halling ME2 65 E4
Meadow Cres ME2 65 E4
Meadow Croft BR1 42 F6
Meadow Hill Rd 6 TN1 159 B3
Meadow La
Culverstone Green DA13 64 A1
Lewisham SE12 28 B5
Marlpit Hill TN8 122 B4
Meadow Rd
Gravesend DA11 36 A6
Groombridge TN3 171 C7
Northfleet DA11 35 C7
Royal Tunbridge Wells TN1 159 A4
Royal Tunbridge Wells,Southborough TN4 142 F1
Rusthall TN4 158 C4
Tonbridge TN9 143 B8
Meadow The
Chislehurst BR7 29 C2
Pembury TN2 160 E8
Meadow View
Flimwell TN5 187 A3
Sidcup DA15 30 B8
Meadow View Cotts
Hurst Green TN19 194 A3
Laddingford ME18 130 E5
Meadow View Rd ME17 116 B3
Meadow Way
Dartford DA2 33 C8
Marden TN12 148 E6
Orpington BR6 57 A7
Wouldham ME1 66 C5
Meadow Wlk
Dartford DA2 32 C4
Maidstone ME15 100 B3
Snodland ME6 81 F7
Meadowbank Ct ME19 97 C8
Meadowbank Rd ME4 54 A4
Meadowdown ME14 100 E4
Meadowdown Cl ME7 69 A4
Meadowford Cl SE28 3 A6
Meadowlands
Oxted RH8 104 A1
Seal TN15 92 F7
Meadows TN17 180 D1
Meadows Ct DA14 30 B2
Meadows Sch TN4 142 F2
Meadows The
Biddenden TN27 167 F2
Halstead TN14 74 F6
3 Maidstone ME15 99 E2
Orpington BR6 58 C4
Wittersham TN30 199 D4
Meadowside Dartford DA1 32 E7
Eltham SE3,SE9 11 C3
Meadowside Cotts TN5 186 F1
Meadowsweet Cl 3 E16 1 D8
Meadowsweet View ME4 40 B2
Meadowview BR5 44 C6
Meadowview Rd DA5 13 F1
Meads The Hartley TN17 178 F1
Royal Tunbridge Wells TN2 159 C2
Meadside Wlk ME5 67 F6
Meadway Halstead TN14 74 F6
Tonbridge TN11 126 E5
Meadway The
Orpington BR6 58 B4
Sevenoaks TN13 91 F5
Meath Cl BR5 44 B4
Medbury Rd DA12 36 F7
Mede Ho BR1 28 B3
Medebourne Cl SE3 11 A4
Medhurst Cres DA12 36 F6
Medhurst Gdns DA12 36 F5
Medick Ct RM17 18 E8
Medina Ho 6 DA8 14 E7
Medina Rd Ditton ME20 82 C1
Tonbridge TN10 127 C6
Medlar Gr ME7 69 A4
Medlar Ho 3 DA15 30 A5
Medlar Rd RM17 18 E8
Medlars The
Maidstone ME14 100 D6
Meopham Sta DA13 50 A3
Medway Ave
High Halstow ME23 23 E4
Yalding ME18 113 F1
Medway City Est ME2 53 D7
Medway Com Coll ME4 54 A1
Medway Cotts
Iden Green TN17 190 D3
Marden TN12 148 C6
Medway Ct Aylesford ME20 82 F2
20 Orpington BR5 44 D1
Medway Ent Ctr ME2 53 D8
Medway Gdns ME4 53 F7
Medway Heritage Ctr* ME4 53 F5
Medway Ho 7 ME14 99 F4
Medway Hts 5 ME4 53 E4
Medway Maritime Hospl ME7 54 B4
Medway Mdws TN12 130 A6
Medway Rd Crayford DA1 15 A4
Gillingham ME7 54 C7
Royal Tunbridge Wells TN1 159 B5
Medway St Chatham ME4 53 F5
Maidstone ME14 99 F4
Medway Trad Est ME16 99 F3
Medway View
Barnes Street TN11 129 A5
Middle Stoke ME3 25 C3
Medway Villas ME15 115 B7
Medway Wharf Rd TN9 127 C1
Meerbrook Rd SE3 11 C4
Meeson's La RM17 17 F8
Meeting House La 2 ME4 53 F4
Megby Cl ME8 69 D6
Megrims Hill TN18 196 A6
Meirs Court Rd ME8 69 E6
Melanda Cl BR7 28 F3
Melanie Cl DA7 13 E6
Melba Gdns RM18 19 A7
Melbourne Cl BR6 43 E2
Melbourne Ct RM18 18 E6
Melbourne Quay 4 DA11 19 B1
Melbourne Rd
Chatham ME4 54 A3
Tilbury RM18 18 E6
Melbury Cl BR7 28 F2
Melbury Grange BR1 42 E8
Meldrum Cl Orpington BR5 44 C3
Oxted RH8 104 A3
Melford Dr ME16 99 C4
Melliker La DA13 50 A3
Melling St SE18 12 E8
Mellish Ind Est SE18 1 D3
Mells Cres SE9 28 F4
Melody Cl ME8 69 C4
Melody Rd TN16 72 C1
Melrose Ave Dartford DA1 31 E8
Kings Hill ME19 97 C3
Melrose Cl Lewisham SE12 28 B7
Loose ME15 116 A7
Melrose Cres BR6 57 D5
Melrose Rd TN16 72 C3
Melthorpe Gdns SE3 11 E6
Melville Ct ME4 53 F6
Melville Rd
Maidstone ME15 100 A3
Sidcup DA14 30 C6
Memess Path 4 SE18 12 A8
Memorial Hospl SE18 12 A5
Mendip Ho DA11 18 D1
Mendip Rd DA7 14 E6
Mendip Wlk TN2 159 D5
Mennie Ho SE18 11 F6
Meon Ct 21 BR5 44 D1
Meopham Com Prim Sch
Meopham DA13 64 A8
Meopham Sta DA13 50 A2
Meopham Sta DA13 50 A4
Mera Dr DA7 14 A3
Merbury Rd SE28 2 E4
Mercer Cl ME20 82 B4
Mercer Dr ME17 119 F6
Mercer St TN1 159 B5
Mercer Way ME17 117 B1
Mercers Hawkhurst TN18 189 A1
Langton Green TN3 158 A3
Mercers Cl TN12 145 E6
Mercers Pl ME19 97 A2
Merchant Pl TN12 148 C5
Merchland Rd SE9 29 C7
Mercury Cl ME1 53 A3
Mere Cl BR6 57 B8
Meredith Cl ME17 117 F7
Meresborough Cotts ME8 69 F5
Meresborough La ME8, ME9 70 B5
Meresborough Rd ME8 70 A7
Mereside BR6 57 A8
Merevale Ho 3 TN1 159 A3
Merewood Cl 1 BR1 43 A7
Merewood Rd DA7 14 C5
Mereworth Cl ME8 55 A3
Mereworth Com Prim Sch ME18 112 D8
Mereworth Dr SE18 12 C7
Mereworth Ho ME2 39 C1
Mereworth Rd
Royal Tunbridge Wells TN4 159 A6
West Peckham ME18 112 C7
Merganser Gdns SE28 2 D3
Meriden Cl BR1 28 D1
Meridian Ct ME16 99 E4
Meridian Pk ME2 53 E6
Meridian Rd SE7 11 D7
Meridian Trad Est SE7 1 B2
Meriel Wk DA9 17 B3
Merifield Rd SE9 11 C3
Merileys Cl DA3 49 C6
Merino Pl DA15 13 A2
Merivale Gr ME5 68 B4
Merle Common Rd RH8 121 B7
Merlewood TN13 92 B4
Merlewood Dr BR7 42 F8
Merlin Ave ME20 81 F2
Merlin Cl TN10 127 E4
Merlin Gdns BR1 28 A5
Merlin Ho ME4 54 B8
Merlin Prim Sch BR1 28 A5
Merlin Rd DA16 13 A3
Merlin Rd N DA16 13 A3
Mermaid Cl Chatham ME5 68 A6
Northfleet DA11 35 D8
Mermerus Gdns DA12 36 F4
Merrals Wood Rd ME2 52 D5
Merrilees Rd DA15 29 E8
Merriman Ho ME3 39 F6
Merriman Rd SE3 11 C6
Merriments Gdns* TN19 194 B5
Merriments La
Hurst Green TN18, TN19 194 D5
Hurst Green TN19 194 B5
Merrion Cl TN4 159 B7
Merrion Way TN4 159 B7
Merry Boys Rd ME3 39 B8
Merrydown Way BR7 42 F8
Merryfield SE3 11 A5
Merryfield Ct 9 TN9 143 B8
Merryfield Ho 4 SE9 28 C5
Merryfields ME2 39 A1
Merryfields Cl DA3 48 F5
Merryhills Cl TN16 72 D3
Merryweather Cl DA1 15 F1
Mersey Rd TN10 127 B5
Merston Ct ME3 38 C4
Merton Ave DA3 48 F5
Merton Cl ME5 68 C5
Merton Court Sch DA14 30 C4
Merton Ct DA16 13 B5
Merton Gdns BR5 43 B4
Merton Rd ME15 100 F2
Mervyn Ave SE9 29 C6
Mervyn Stockwood Ho SE9 29 C6
Mesne Way TN14 75 F7
Messent Rd SE9 11 D2
Messeter Pl SE9 12 A1
Meteor Rd ME19 96 F3
Methuen Rd Bexley DA6 13 F3
Erith DA17 4 B2
Metro Ctr The BR5 44 B3
Mews The
Headcorn TN27 151 C5
Longfield DA3 48 E6
Mews The continued
1 Maidstone ME16 99 E5
Pembury TN2 160 C6
Rochester ME2 52 F7
5 Royal Tunbridge Wells TN1 159 B3
Sevenoaks TN13 92 A3
7 Sidcup DA14 30 A4
Mewsend TN16 72 D1
Meyer Rd DA8 14 D8
Micawber Cl ME5 68 A1
Michael Gdns DA12 36 E3
Michael Marshall Ho SE9 29 C6
Michaels La DA3,TN15 62 C8
Michele Cotts ME3 38 C6
Mickleham Cl BR5 44 A7
Mickleham Rd BR5 44 A7
Mid Comp Cotts TN15 95 E6
Mid Kent Bsns Pk ME6 82 B7
Mid Kent Coll (City Way Ctr) ME1 53 D4
Mid Kent Coll of H & F Ed ME16 99 C3
Mid Kent Coll of Higher & F Ed ME5 67 E6
Mid Kent Sh Ctr The ME16 99 C7
Middle Field TN2 160 E8
Middle Garth TN17 179 D4
Middle La TN15 92 F6
Middle Mill Rd ME19 97 F7
Middle Park Ave SE9 28 E8
Middle Park Prim Sch SE9 28 D8
Middle Rd TN3 174 A5
Middle Row 6 ME14 99 F4
Middle St 4 ME7 54 A6
Middle Wlk TN2 159 E8
Middlefields ME8 70 A8
Middleham Ct 26 DA2 16 B1
Middlesex Rd ME15 116 D7
Middleton Ave DA14 30 C3
Middleton Cl ME8 69 E4
Middleton Ct 13 BR1 28 B1
Middlings Rise TN13 91 F1
Middlings The TN13 91 F2
Middlings Wood TN13 92 A2
Midfield Ave Bexley DA7 14 C4
Hextable BR8 32 B2
Midfield Prim Sch BR5 30 A1
Midfield Way BR5 44 B8
Midhurst Ct ME15 100 A3
Midhurst Hill DA6 14 A2
Midley Cl ME16 99 C7
Midsummer Ct SE12 11 A3
Midsummer Rd ME6 81 E8
Midway The TN4 158 D2
Midwinter Cl 3 DA16 13 A4
Miers Court Prim Sch ME8 69 F7
Mierscourt Cl ME8 70 A8
Mierscourt Rd ME8 69 E6
Mike Spring Ct DA12 36 D4
Milburn Rd ME7 54 C7
Mildmay Pl TN14 75 F8
Mildred Cl DA1 16 A1
Mildred Rd DA8 4 E1
Mile End Green Cotts DA3 48 D7
Mile La TN17 178 B8
Mile Oak Rd TN12 146 C3
Mile Stone Rd DA2 16 B1
Milebush La TN12 132 E1
Miles Dr SE28 2 E5
Miles Pl ME1 53 D3
Milestone Bldgs TN12 149 F3
Milford Cl Bexley SE2 13 E8
Maidstone ME16 99 D5
Military Rd ME4 53 F5
Milk House Cotts TN17 180 A8
Milk St Bromley BR1 28 B2
Newham E16 2 B5
Milking La
Biggin Hill,Downe BR6 72 E7
Biggin Hill,Leaves Green BR2 72 D8
Mill Bank Headcorn TN27 151 C6
Tonbridge TN9 127 C2
Mill Brook Rd BR5 44 C5
Mill Cl Lenham ME17 120 C4
Rochester ME2 39 B1
Mill Cotts ME15 114 B6
Mill Cres TN9 127 C2
Mill Ct Sutton at H DA4 47 C7
14 Woolwich SE28 3 B6
Mill Hall Bsns Est The ME20 82 D2
Mill Hall Rd ME20 82 C3
Mill Hill TN8 138 D7
Mill Hill La DA12 37 D3
Mill House Cl DA4 46 E1
Mill La Benover ME18 131 A7
Chatham,Bluebell Hill ME5 67 D1
Chatham,Luton ME5 54 C1
Coxheath ME17 115 D4
Eynsford DA4 46 E1
Farthing Street BR6 57 B1
Frittenden TN17 166 D8
Hartlip ME9 70 E6
Hildenborough TN11,TN15 109 C2
Horsmonden TN12 147 B1
Ightham TN15 94 E5
Maidstone ME14 99 F6
Oxted RH8 104 A1
Sevenoaks TN14 92 D6
Shoreham TN14 59 F1
Sissinghurst TN17 179 F8
Mill La continued
Smarden TN27 153 A
Snodland ME6 82 B
Tenterden TN30 183 B
The Chart RH8 104 F
Tonbridge TN9 127 C
Wateringbury ME18 113 D
West Thurrock RM20 17 D
Westerham TN16 105 C
Woolwich SE18 2 A
Mill Pl Chislehurst BR7 43 B
Crayford DA1 15 A
Mill Pond Cl TN14 92 D
Mill Pond Rd DA1 15 E
Mill Rd Erith DA8 14 C
Gillingham ME7 54 C
Hawley DA2 32 F
Newham E16 1 B
Northfleet DA11 35 E
Rochester ME2 53 B
Sevenoaks TN13 91 E
Mill Row DA5 31 B
Mill St East Malling ME19 97 F
Iden Green TN17,TN18 190 C
Loose ME15 115 F
Maidstone ME15 99 F
Snodland ME6 82 B
Westerham TN16 105 D
Mill Stone Cl DA4 47 C
Mill Stream Jun Sch ME19 97 F
Mill Stream Pl TN9 127 D
Mill Vale BR2 42 A
Mill View TN11 111 D
Mill Wlk ME16 99 A
Millais Pl RM18 19 A
Millars Mdw SE12 11 A
Millbank Way SE12 11 A
Millbro BR8 46 A
Millbrook ME19 81 D
Millbrook Ave DA16 12 D
Millbrook Cl ME15 99 F
Millcroft Rd ME3 22 B
Millen Ct DA4 47 C
Millennium Cl E16 1 B
Miller Cl BR1 28 B
Miller Ct DA7 14 B
Miller Rd DA12 37 A
Miller Way ME2 39 D
Millers Cotts TN11 144 C
Millers Wharf 1 ME15 99 E
Millers Wlk DA13 64 A
Millersthumb TN17 165 C
Millfield
High Halden TN26 183 D
New Ash Green DA3 62 E
Millfield Dr DA11 35 E
Millfield La DA3 62 E
Millfield Rd TN15 61 D
Millfields ME5 68 D
Millfields Cl BR5 44 B
Millfields Cotts BR5 44 B
Millfordhope Rd ME2 52 C
Millhall ME20 82 E
Millhouse La ME19 80 D
Millman Ct SE3 11 B
Millpond Cl ME2 53 B
Millpond La TN30 182 D
Mills Cres TN15 92 F
Mills Rd ME20 98 E
Mills Terr ME4 54 A
Millside Ind Est DA1 15 D
Millstock Terr 2 ME15 99 E
Millstone Mews DA4 47 C
Millstream Cl TN3 156 D
Millwood Ct 4 ME4 53 F
Millwood Ho 1 SE28 2 D
Millwood Rd BR5 44 C
Milne Gdns SE9 11 E
Milne Ho 11 SE18 1 F
Milner Rd ME7 54 D
Milner Wlk SE9 29 D
Milners ME17 117 F
Milroy Ave DA11 35 E
Milstead Cl ME14 100 C
Milsted Rd ME8 55 C
Milton Ave
Badgers Mount TN14 59 B
Cliffe Woods ME3 39 B
Gravesend DA12 36 C
Milton Ct Gravesend DA12 36 C
Kings Hill ME18 97 A
Milton Dr TN2 159 D
Milton Gdns Tilbury RM18 19 B
Tonbridge TN9 142 F
Milton Hall Rd DA12 36 D
Milton Ho DA1 14 E
Milton La ME18 97 B
Milton Lodge 9 DA14 30 A
Milton Pl DA12 19 C
Milton Rd Bexley DA16 12 F
Erith DA17 4 A
Gillingham ME7 54 C
Gravesend DA12 36 C
Sevenoaks TN13 91 E
Swanscombe DA10 17 E
Milton Rd Bsns Pk 4 DA12 36 C
Milton St Maidstone ME16 99 C
Swanscombe DA10 17 D
Milverton Way SE9 29 A
Milward Wlk 14 SE18 12 A
Mimosa Cl BR6 58 C
Mincers Cl ME5 68 C
Mineral St SE18 2 E
Minerva Cl DA14 29 E
Minerva Rd ME2 53 A
Ministry Way SE9 28 F

Minshaw Ct DA14 ....29 F4
Minster Rd Bromley BR1 ...28 B1
Gillingham ME8 ....55 C3
Mint Bsns Pk E16 ....1 A8
Minters Orch TN15 ....95 B7
Miranda Ho 6 DA17 ....4 A1
Mirfield St SE7 ....1 D3
Miriam Ct DA14 ....30 B4
Miriam Rd SE18 ....2 E1
Mirror Path SE9 ....28 C5
Miskin Cotts ME3 ....22 B6
Miskin Rd Dartford DA1 ...32 D8
Hoo St Werburgh ME3 ......40 E5
Miskin Way DA12 ....36 D2
Mitchell Ave Chatham ME4 .53 F2
Northfleet DA11 ....35 D6
Mitchell Cl Dartford DA1 ...32 E6
Erith DA17 ....4 C3
Lenham ME17 ....120 C5
Woolwich SE2 ....3 C2
Mitchell Rd
Kings Hill ME19 ....96 F2
Orpington BR6 ....57 F6
Mitchell Way 5 BR1 .....42 A8
Mitchell Wlk Newham E6 ...1 F8
Swanscombe DA10 ....34 E8
Mitchem Cl TN15 ....61 E3
Mitre Ct 5 Erith DA17 ......4 A2
Tonbridge TN9 ....127 C2
Mitre Rd ME1 ....53 B4
Moat Cl Orpington BR6 .....57 F4
Sevenoaks TN13 ....91 D5
Moat Croft DA16 ....13 C4
Moat Ct Eltham SE9 ....11 F1
Sidcup DA15 ....29 F5
Moat Farm TN2 ....173 A7
Moat Farm Rd ME3 ....24 D6
Moat La Cowden TN8 .....155 E7
Erith DA8 ....15 A6
Moat Rd TN27 ....151 B5
Moatbridge Sch SE9 .....11 D1
Mockbeggar La TN17,
TN27 ....181 C4
Model Farm Cl SE9 ......28 E5
Modest Cnr TN4 ....142 E1
Moira Rd SE9 ....11 F3
Molash Rd BR5 ....44 D5
Molehill Copse Prim Sch
ME15 ....116 D7
Moles Mead TN8 ....122 C2
Molescroft SE9 ....29 C5
Molescroft Way TN9 .....142 F7
Mollison Rise DA12 ......36 E3
Molyneux Almshouses
TN4 ....158 B4
Molyneux Ct TN4 ....158 F4
Molyneux Park Gdns
TN4 ....158 F4
Molyneux Park Rd TN4 ..158 F4
Monarch Cl Chatham ME5 ..68 A6
Tilbury RM18 ....19 B5
Monarch Dr E16 ....1 D8
Monarch Rd 8 DA17 ......4 A3
Monarch Terr ME18 ......97 C3
Monckton's Ave ME14 ....99 F7
Monckton's Dr ME14 .....99 E7
Monckton's La ME14 .....99 F7
Moncrieff Cl 5 E6 ....1 E7
Moncrif Cl ME14 ....101 B4
Monds Cotts TN14 ....90 E3
Monica James Ho 12
DA14 ....30 A5
Monk Dr E16 ....1 A6
Monk St SE18 ....2 A2
Monk's Well DA9 ....17 C3
Monkdown ME15 ....101 A1
Monkreed Villas DA3 .....49 D4
Monks Cl SE2 ....3 D2
Monks La Limpsfield TN8 ..121 E6
Newbury's TN5 ....185 B8
Monks Orch DA1 ....32 D6
Monks Way BR5 ....43 D1
Monks Wlk
Northfleet DA13 ....35 A2
6 Tonbridge TN9 ....143 B8
Monkton Rd Bexley DA16 ..12 F5
Borough Green TN15 ....94 F7
Monkwood Cl ME1 ....67 B8
Monmouth Cl
Bexley DA16 ....13 A3
Gillingham ME8 ....55 D2
Mons Way BR2 ....42 E3
Monson Rd TN1 ....159 B4
Monson Way 5 TN1 ....159 B4
Mont St Aignan Way
TN8 ....138 C8
Montacute Gdns TN2 ....158 F2
Montacute Rd TN2 ......159 A1
Montague Ct 15 DA15 ....30 A5
Montague Pl BR8 ....45 F5
Montague Terr 1 BR2 ....42 A5
Montbelle Prim Sch SE9 ..29 B5
Montbelle Rd SE9 ....29 B5
Montbretia Cl BR5 ....44 C5
Montcalm Cl BR2 ....42 A3
Montcalm Rd SE7 ....11 D7
Monteith Cl TN3 ....158 A3
Monterey Cl DA5 ....31 C6
Montfort Dr ME19 ....97 A2
Montfort Rd Chatham ME5 .67 F2
Kemsing TN15 ....76 E2
Rochester ME2 ....53 A8
Montgomery Ave ME5 ....68 A7
Montgomery Cl DA15 .....12 F1
Montgomery Rd
Gillingham ME7 ....54 C3
Royal Tunbridge Wells
TN4 ....159 B7
Montgomery Rd continued
Sutton at H DA4 ....47 D8
Montpelier Ave DA5 .....30 D8
Montpelier Gate ME16 ....99 B5
Montreal Rd
Sevenoaks TN13 ....91 E4
Tilbury RM18 ....19 A5
Montrose Ave
Bexley DA16 ....12 E4
Gillingham ME5 ....54 E2
Sidcup DA15 ....30 A8
Montrose Cl DA16 ....12 F4
Monypenny TN17 ....191 F3
Monypenny Cl TN11 ....128 D8
Moon Ct SE12 ....11 A3
Moon's La
Edenbridge RH7 ....138 A1
Edenbridge RH7 ....138 A1
Moonstone Dr ME5 ......68 B2
Moor Hill TN18 ....194 F8
Moor La TN8 ....138 A4
Moor Park Cl ME8 ....70 A8
Moor Rd The TN14 ....92 C7
Moor St ME8 ....70 B8
Moor The TN18 ....194 F8
Moorcroft Gdns BR2 .....42 E4
Moorden La TN11 ....125 A1
Moordown SE18 ....12 B6
Moore Ave Grays RM20 ....17 E8
Tilbury RM18 ....19 B5
Moore Cl DA2 ....33 D6
Moore Rd DA10 ....17 E1
Moore St ME2 ....53 A8
Mooreland Rd 1 BR1 ....42 A8
Moorfield Rd BR6 ....44 A2
Moorhead Way SE3 ......11 B4
Moorhen Cl DA8 ....15 B7
Moorhouse Cotts TN16 ..105 A7
Moorhouse Rd RH8,
TN16 ....105 A6
Mooring Rd ME1 ....53 D1
Moorings The E16 ....1 C8
Moorlands BR7 ....29 B1
Moorside Rd BR1 ....28 A4
Morants Court Cross
TN14 ....75 C1
Morants Court Rd TN13 ..91 C8
Morden Rd SE3 ....11 A5
Morden Road Mews SE3 .11 A5
Morden St ME1 ....53 C4
More Park RC Prim Sch
ME19 ....97 D8
Morebreddis Cotts
TN17 ....164 A1
Morel Ct TN13 ....92 B5
Morella Wlk ME17 ......120 C5
Morello Cl BR8 ....45 D5
Morement Rd ME3 ....40 D6
Moreton DA14 ....30 A3
Moreton Almshouses 3
TN16 ....89 D1
Moreton Ct DA1 ....14 E4
Moreton Ind Est BR8 .....46 A4
Morewood Cl TN13 ......91 F4
Morgan Dr DA9 ....33 E8
Morgan Rd Bromley BR1 ...28 A1
Rochester ME2 ....53 A8
Morgan St E16 ....1 A8
Morhen Cl ME6 ....81 E7
Morland Ave DA1 ....15 B2
Morland Dr
Lamberhurst TN3 ....176 B5
Rochester ME2 ....39 A1
Morland Ho 4 BR7 ......43 A8
Morley Bsns Ctr TN9 ....127 D1
Morley Cl BR6 ....57 B8
Morley Dr TN12 ....163 A6
Morley Rd Chislehurst BR7 .43 C8
Tonbridge TN9 ....127 D1
Morley's Rd TN14 ......108 D2
Morne Cotts TN14 ....75 F8
Morning Cross Cotts
ME3 ....22 B4
Mornington Ave BR1 .....42 C6
Mornington Cl TN16 .....72 D2
Mornington Ct DA5 ......31 D7
Morris Cl
Maidstone ME17 ....116 D5
Orpington BR6 ....57 E7
West Malling ME19 ....81 F1
Morris Gdns DA1 ....16 A2
Morry La ME17 ....135 D7
Morston Gdns SE9 ....28 F4
Mortgramit Sq SE18 ....2 A3
Mortimer Rd
Biggin Hill TN16 ....72 C7
Erith DA8 ....14 D8
Orpington BR6 ....44 A1
Mortimers Ave ME3 ......39 A8
Mortlake Rd E16 ....1 B7
Mortley Cl TN9 ....127 C2
Morton Cl
Maidstone ME15 ....116 D6
Swanley BR8 ....45 E7
Morvale Cl DA17 ....3 F2
Moselle Rd TN16 ....72 F1
Mosquito Rd ME19 ....96 F3
Moss Way DA2 ....33 D4
Mossbank ME5 ....68 A3
Mossdown Cl DA17 ....4 A2
Mosslea Rd Bromley BR2 ..42 D4
Orpington BR6 ....57 C7
Mossy Glade ME8 ....69 E6
Mostyn Rd ME14 ....100 C4
Mosul Way BR2 ....42 E3
Mosyer Dr BR5 ....58 D8
Mote Ave ME15 ....100 B3
Mote Cotts TN15 ....110 A7
Mote Hall Villas ME14 ...101 C4
Mote Pk ME15 ....100 D2
Mote Rd Maidstone ME15 .100 A3
Shipbourne TN15,TN11 ....110 A7
Mote The DA3 ....62 F8
Motherwell Way RM20 ...17 A8
Mottingham Ct SE9 ......28 F7
Mottingham Gdns SE9 ...28 D7
Mottingham La
Bromley SE12,SE9 ....28 C7
Eltham SE12 ....28 C8
Mottingham Prim Sch
SE9 ....28 F5
Mottingham Rd SE9 ......28 F5
Mottingham Sta SE9 .....28 F7
Mottisfont Rd SE2 ....3 B2
Mouat Ct ME5 ....68 A3
Mouchotte Cl TN16 ......72 C7
Moultain Hill BR8 ....46 A5
Mound The SE9 ....29 A5
Mount Ave ME18 ....114 A1
Mount Castle La ME17 ..120 F1
Mount Cl Bromley BR1 .....42 E8
Sevenoaks TN13 ....91 F4
Mount Culver Ave DA14 ..30 D2
Mount Dr Bexley DA6 ......13 E2
Maidstone ME14 ....101 B4
Mount Edgcumbe Rd
TN4 ....159 A3
Mount Ephraim TN4 ....159 A4
Mount Ephraim Ct TN4 ..158 F4
Mount Ephraim Rd TN1 .159 A4
Mount Harry Rd TN13 ....92 B4
Mount La Hartlip ME9 .....70 D4
Maidstone ME14 ....101 B4
Mount Lodge ME1 ....53 B2
Mount Pleasant
Aylesford ME20 ....83 A3
Biggin Hill TN16 ....72 D2
Chatham ME5 ....54 B3
Durgates TN5 ....184 E5
Ide Hill TN14 ....106 F4
Lamberhurst TN3 ....175 E6
Paddock Wood TN12 ......145 F7
Tenterden TN30 ....193 C8
The Moor TN18 ....194 F8
Tonbridge TN11 ....126 D6
Mount Pleasant Ave 2
TN1 ....159 B3
Mount Pleasant Ct
TN11 ....126 D6
Mount Pleasant Dr
ME14 ....101 A5
Mount Pleasant La TN3 .176 A6
Mount Pleasant Pl SE18 ...2 D2
Mount Pleasant Rd
Dartford DA1 ....15 F1
Royal Tunbridge Wells
TN1 ....159 A3
Sevenoaks Weald TN14 ...108 B2
Mount Pleasant Terr
ME17 ....119 E2
Mount Pleasant Wlk DA5 .14 C2
Mount Rd Bexley DA6 .....13 E2
Chatham ME4 ....53 F3
Crayford DA1 ....14 F1
Rochester ME1 ....53 B2
Mount Sion TN1 ....159 A2
Mount The Bexley DA6 ....14 B2
3 Chislehurst BR7 ....43 A8
Mount View Ct 3 ME4 ....53 F3
Mountain Cl TN15 ....78 F3
Mountbatten Ave
Chatham ME5 ....68 A7
Higham ME3 ....38 C4
Mountbatten Cl SE18 .....12 E8
Mountfield TN15 ....95 A7
Mountfield Cl DA13 ......63 F2
Mountfield Ct 4 TN1 ...159 B3
Mountfield Gdns TN1 ...159 B3
Mountfield Pk TN9 .....143 C8
Mountfield Rd TN1 .....159 B3
Mountfield Way 1 BR5 ...44 C5
Mounthurst Rd BR2 ......42 A2
Mountjoy Cl SE2 ....3 B4
Mounts Hill TN17 ....190 B7
Mounts La TN17 ....192 A3
Mounts Rd DA9 ....17 B1
Mountsfield Cl ME16 .....99 D5
Mountview Rd BR6 ......44 A2
Moyle Cl ME8 ....69 D4
Mozart Ct ME4 ....53 E3
Muir Rd ME15 ....100 A2
Muir St E16 ....1 E5
Mulbarton Ct BR7 ....29 D2
Mulberry Cl
Gillingham ME7 ....69 A4
Greenwich SE7 ....11 D8
Meopham Sta DA13 ....50 B3
Royal Tunbridge Wells
TN4 ....143 D1
Mulberry Ct Bexley DA16 ..12 F5
Maidstone ME14 ....100 B5
Mulberry Rd DA11 ....35 E4
Mulberry Way DA17 ....4 C4
Mulgrave Ho 18 SE18 ......1 F2
Mulgrave Prim Sch SE18 ..2 B3
Mulgrave Rd SE18 ....2 A2
Mullein Ct 7 RM17 ......18 D8
Mullender Ct DA12 ....37 A7
Muller Ho SE18 ....2 A1
Multon Rd TN15 ....61 E4
Munday Bois Cotts
TN27 ....153 F8
Munday Bois Rd TN27 ...137 E1
Munday Rd E16 ....1 A7
Munday Works Est TN9 .127 C1
Munford Dr DA10 ....34 E8
Mungeam Ho ME1 ....53 C4
Mungo Park Rd DA12 .....36 D3
Mungo Park Way BR5 ....44 D2
Munn's La ME9 ....70 E6
Munnery Way BR6 ....57 B8
Munnings Ho E16 ....1 B5
Munsgore La ME9 ....71 E3
Murchison Ave DA5 ......30 E7
Murrain Dr ME15 ....101 A1
Murray Ave BR1 ....42 B7
Murray Bsns Ctr BR5 .....44 B6
Murray Ho 15 SE18 ....1 F2
Murray Lodge TN2 ......159 D2
Murray Rd Orpington BR5 ..44 B6
Rochester ME2 ....53 C8
Murray Sq E16 ....1 B6
Murton-Neale Cl 3
TN18 ....189 A2
Mus of Artillery in the
Rotunda* SE18 ....1 F1
Muscovy Ho DA18 ....3 E4
Museum of Kent Rural Life*
ME14 ....83 D1
Museum St ME14 ....99 F4
Muskerry Ct TN4 ....158 B4
Musket La
Eyhorne Street ME17 .....102 C2
Leeds ME17 ....102 A2
Mussenden La DA3,DA4 ...47 E3
Mustang Rd ME19 ....96 F3
Mycenae Rd SE3 ....11 A8
Mynn Cres ME14 ....101 A4
Myra St SE2 ....3 A2
Myrtle Alley SE18 ....2 A3
Myrtle Cl DA8 ....14 E6
Myrtle Cres ME5 ....67 F5
Myrtle Pl DA2 ....33 D8
Myrtle Rd DA1 ....32 D6
Myrtledene Rd SE2 ....3 A1

N

Nadine St SE7 ....1 C1
Nag's Head La
Bexley DA16 ....13 B4
Rochester ME1 ....53 D4
Nagpur Ho 4 ME15 .....116 E5
Nairn Ct RM18 ....18 F5
Nansen Rd DA12 ....36 D4
Napier Com Sch ME7 ....54 D4
Napier Ct
2 Lewisham SE12 ....28 B5
Maidstone ME14 ....99 F7
Napier Rd Bromley BR2 ....42 B5
Erith DA17 ....3 F2
Gillingham ME7 ....54 D4
Northfleet DA11 ....35 F7
Royal Tunbridge Wells
TN2 ....159 D2
Napoleon Dr TN12 ......148 D5
Napoleon Wlk ME17 ....120 C5
Napwood Cl ME8 ....69 D6
Nares Rd ME8 ....69 D4
Narrow Boat Cl SE28 ......2 D4
Narrow Way BR2 ....42 E3
Naseby Ct DA14 ....29 F4
Nash Bank DA13 ....49 F7
Nash Cl ME5 ....68 C2
Nash Cotts 16 DA14 .....30 A5
Nash Croft DA11 ....35 E4
Nash Gn BR1 ....28 A2
Nash La BR2 ....56 A4
Nash St DA13 ....50 A7
Nashenden Farm La ME1 .67 A8
Nashenden La ME1 ....52 F1
Nassau Path 6 SE28 ......3 C5
Natal Rd ME4 ....54 A3
Nathan Way SE28,SE18 .....2 E3
Naylor's Cotts ME7 ....69 B1
Neal Rd TN15 ....61 E5
Neale St ME4 ....53 F2
Neatscourt Rd E6 ....1 D8
Neills Rd TN3 ....175 D2
Nellington Ct TN4 ......158 B4
Nellington Rd TN3,TN4 ..158 B4
Nelson Ave TN9 ....127 A1
Nelson Cl TN16 ....72 E2
Nelson Ct ME5 ....54 C1
Nelson Ho
8 Maidstone ME15 ......116 F5
Swanscombe DA9 ....17 D2
Nelson Mandela Rd SE3 ..11 C4
Nelson Rd Bromley BR2 ...42 C5
Dartford DA1 ....15 C1
Erith DA17 ....3 F1
Gillingham ME7 ....54 D4
Northfleet DA11 ....35 F6
Royal Tunbridge Wells
TN2 ....159 D2
Sidcup DA14 ....30 A4
Wouldham ME1 ....66 C5
Nelson Terr ME5 ....54 C1
Nepicar Farm* TN15 .....79 D1
Nepicar La TN15 ....79 D3
Neptune Bsns Pk ME2 ....53 E7
Neptune Cl ME2 ....53 E7
Neptune Way ME2 ....53 E6
Neptune Wlk DA8 ....4 D2
Nesbit Rd SE9 ....11 D3
Nesbitt Ho DA6 ....14 B2
Ness Rd DA8 ....15 D8
Nestor Ct ME18 ....114 A8
Nethercombe Ho 4 SE3 ..11 A8
Nethewode Ct DA17 ....4 B3
Netley Cl ME14 ....100 D6
Nettlestead Cotts TN12 .146 A7
Nettlestead Ct ME18 ....113 C5
Nettlestead La ME18 ....113 A6
Nevill Ct ME19 ....81 C1
Nevill Gate TN2 ....159 B1
Nevill Lodge TN2 ......159 C4
Nevill Pk TN4 ....158 E3
Nevill Pl ME6 ....82 A7
Nevill Rd ME6 ....82 A7
Nevill Ridge TN4 ....158 D3
Nevill St TN2 ....159 A2
Nevill Terr TN2 ....158 F2
Neville Cl
Maidstone ME14 ....100 B8
Sidcup DA15 ....29 F4
Neville Rd ME4 ....53 E2
New Acres Rd SE28 ....2 E4
New Ash Green Prim Sch
DA3 ....62 F8
New Barn Pk BR8 ....45 E8
New Barn Rd
Northfleet DA13 ....35 C3
Sutton Valence ME17,
TN12 ....134 E2
Swanley BR8 ....45 F8
New Barn St E13 ....1 B8
New Barns Rd ME14 ....100 A8
New Bassetts Cotts
TN12 ....163 B5
New Beacon Sch TN14 ..107 F8
New College of Cobham
DA12 ....51 A5
New Cotts Bean DA2 ......34 B5
Shipbourne TN11 ....110 D5
The Moor TN18 ....194 B7
Tilbury RM16 ....19 B8
New Covenant Pl 4 ME1 .53 D4
New Ct 3 TN9 ....127 C2
New Cut Chatham ME4 ....53 F4
East Farleigh ME15 ......115 D7
New Cut Rd ME14 ......100 D5
New Delhi Ho 5 ME15 ..116 E5
New Eltham Sta SE9 .....29 C7
New England Rd TN4 ...159 A7
New Farm Ave BR2 ......42 A5
New Ferry App SE18 ......2 A3
New Hall Farm La ME3 ...25 B6
New House La DA11 .....36 A6
New Hythe La ME20 ......82 B3
New Hythe Sta ME20 .....82 C4
New Inn Cotts ME15 ....115 C7
New Lydenburg Commercial
Est SE7 ....1 C3
New Lydenburg St SE7 ....1 C3
New Mill Rd BR5 ....44 C8
New Pond Rd TN17 .....190 D6
New Pound La ME18 .....96 C1
New Rd Bexley DA16 .....13 B5
Burham ME1 ....66 F1
Chatham ME4 ....53 F4
Cliffe ME3 ....22 A4
Cranbrook TN17 ....179 B4
Ditton ME20 ....82 C1
East Malling ME19 ....98 A8
Egerton TN27 ....137 F3
Erith SE2 ....3 D1
Fordcombe TN11 ....141 A1
Gravesend DA11 ....19 B1
Grays RM17 ....18 B8
Headcorn TN27 ....151 D5
Hextable BR8 ....31 F1
Langley ME17 ....117 C5
Limpsfield RH8 ....104 B5
Meopham Sta DA13 ....49 F4
Orpington BR6 ....44 A2
Paddock Wood TN12 .....146 A6
Rochester ME1 ....53 D4
Sundridge TN14 ....90 E2
Sutton at H DA4 ....47 D7
Swanley BR8 ....45 F6
New Road Ave ME4 ......53 E4
New Road Hill BR2,BR4 ...56 F2
New Road Sch ME4 ......54 A3
New Sch at West Heath The
TN13 ....108 B6
New St Chatham ME4 .....53 E3
New Street TN15 ....63 D4
Westerham TN16 ....105 C8
New Street Hill BR1 ......28 C3
New Street Rd DA13,TN15 .63 C6
New Strs ME4 ....53 F6
New Swan Yd 8 DA12 ...19 B1
New Tavern Fort* DA12 ..19 C1
New Town Cotts TN11 ..125 A3
New Villas ME15 ....115 C7
New Wharf Rd TN9 .....127 B1
New Wlk TN15 ....78 F3
New Years La BR6,TN14 ...74 A5
Newark Ct 1 ME2 ....53 B7
Newark Knok E6 ....2 A7
Newark Yd ME2 ....53 B7
Newbarn La TN14,TN16 ...73 C2
Newbery Rd DA8 ....14 F6
Newborough Ct TN10 ...127 C6
Newbridge Pk TN12 .....130 A1
Newbury Ave ME16 ......99 C6
Newbury Cl
Cliffe Woods ME3 ....39 B8
Dartford DA1 ....33 B8
Newbury Cotts TN5 .....185 B8
Newbury Ct DA14 ....29 F4
Newbury La TN5 ....185 C8
Newbury Rd BR2 ....42 A6
Newchurch Rd ME15 ....100 A1
Newcomen Rd TN4 ......159 A5
Newenden Cl ME14 .....100 D6
Newenden Rd ME2 ....39 C2

Newham Coll of FE (Royal Docks Campus) E16 2 C5
Newham Way E13 1 B8
Newhaven Gdns SE9 11 D3
Newhaven La 4 E16 1 A8
Newhouse Terr TN8 122 C3
Newick Cl DA5 14 B1
Newing Gn BR1 28 D1
Newington CE Prim Sch ME9 71 B7
Newington Ct TN5 186 E1
Newington Ent Ctr ME9 71 C8
Newington Ho 9 BR5 44 D1
Newington Ind Est ME9 70 F6
Newington Sta ME9 71 B6
Newington Wlk ME14 100 C6
Newitt Rd ME3 40 E5
Newland Green La TN27 153 D8
Newland St E16 1 F5
Newlands TN3 158 A3
Newlands Ct 8 SE9 12 A1
Newlands Farm Rd ME3 24 B4
Newlands La DA13 63 F1
Newlands Lodge DA8 14 D8
Newlands Rd TN4 159 B7
Newlands Rise TN4 159 A6
Newlands Way TN4 159 B7
Newling Cl E6 1 F7
Newlyn Cl BR6 58 A6
Newlyn Ct 1 ME14 100 A4
Newlyn Dr TN12 149 F5
Newlyn Rd DA16 12 F5
Newman Ct 11 BR1 42 A8
Newman Ho SE18 12 A7
Newman Rd BR1 42 A8
Newman's Rd DA11 35 F6
Newmarket Gn SE9 28 D8
Newmarsh Rd SE28 2 F5
Newnham Cl ME8 55 C2
Newnham Lodge DA17 4 A1
Newnham St ME4 54 B3
Newnhams Cl BR1 42 F6
Newports BR8 45 D2
Newstead Ave BR6 57 E8
Newstead Wood Sch for Girls BR6 57 D7
Newton Abbot Rd DA11 35 F6
Newton Ave TN10 127 E7
Newton Cl Chatham ME5 68 C2
1 Maidstone ME16 99 E3
Newton Ct 4 BR1 42 E6
Newton Gdns TN12 145 F7
Newton Ho
Swanscombe DA9 17 D2
Woolwich SE2 3 C1
Newton Rd Bexley DA16 13 A4
Royal Tunbridge Wells TN1 159 B4
Tilbury RM18 19 A5
Newton Terr BR2 42 D3
Newton Willows TN3 171 C7
Newton's Ct DA9 16 D3
Newtown Cotts TN12 149 E6
Niagara Cl ME18 97 B3
Nichol La BR1 28 A1
Nicholas Cl ME16 99 A3
Nicholas Ct SE12 28 A7
Nicholas Stacey Ho 4 SE7 1 B1
Nicholson Ho SE18 11 E7
Nickelby Cl SE28 3 C7
Nicklaus Dr ME5 67 F3
Nickleby Cl ME1 53 C2
Nickleby Rd DA12 37 A7
Nicola Terr DA7 13 E6
Nicolson Rd BR5 44 D2
Nicolson Way TN13 92 D5
Nigeria Rd SE7 11 D7
Nightingale Cl
Biggin Hill TN16 72 C4
Gillingham ME8 69 E6
Larkfield ME20 81 F2
Northfleet DA11 35 E4
Nightingale Cnr BR5 44 D5
Nightingale Ct ME2 52 C6
Nightingale Gr 3 DA1 16 A3
Nightingale Ho SE18 2 A1
Nightingale La
Bromley BR1 42 D7
Goathurst Common TN14 107 B5
Nightingale Pl SE18 12 B8
Nightingale Prim Sch SE18 2 B1
Nightingale Rd
Kemsing TN15 76 E2
Orpington BR5 43 C3
Nightingale Vale SE18 12 A8
Nightingale Way
Newham E6 1 E8
Swanley BR8 45 E6
Nightingales The
Royal Tunbridge Wells TN4 159 A5
Sissinghurst TN27 180 F8
Nile Path 6 SE18 12 A8
Nile Rd ME7 54 C4
Nimrod Ho E16 1 B8
Nine Acres Rd ME2 52 B3
Nine Elms Gr DA11 36 A8
Nine Hams Rd TN16 88 D6
Nineveh La TN17,TN18 189 E6
Ninhams Wood BR6 57 A6
Nita Ct SE12 28 A7
Nithdale Rd SE18 12 C7
Niven Cl ME3 39 C3
Nizels La TN11 125 F8
No 1 St SE18 2 B3
Noah's Ark TN15 77 B1
Noble Tree Cross TN11 126 B6
Noble Tree Rd TN11 126 B6
Noel Terr 15 DA14 30 B4
Nook The ME18 113 F2
Norah La ME3 38 B3
Nordenfeldt Rd DA8 4 D1
Nore Cl ME7 54 E1
Norfield Rd DA2 31 D3
Norfolk Cl Chatham ME5 68 C3
Dartford DA1 16 A2
Gillingham ME8 55 D2
Norfolk Cres DA15 29 E8
Norfolk Gdns DA7 13 F6
Norfolk Pl DA16 13 A5
Norfolk Rd
Gravesend DA12 36 D8
Maidstone ME15 116 C8
Royal Tunbridge Wells TN1 159 B2
Tonbridge TN9 127 A1
Norham Ct 25 DA2 16 B1
Norheads La TN16 72 B2
Norlands Cres BR7 43 B8
Norman Cl Gillingham ME8 69 B5
Kemsing TN15 76 D2
Maidstone ME14 100 B6
Orpington BR6 57 C7
Rochester ME2 52 F4
Norman Ct TN8 122 B2
Norman Par DA14 30 D6
Norman Rd Dartford DA1 32 E7
Erith DA17 4 B3
Erith DA17 4 B5
Royal Tunbridge Wells TN1 159 B5
Snodland ME6 82 A6
West Malling ME19 97 B8
Norman Rise TN17 179 D4
Norman St TN14 106 F5
Norman Villas 4 TN18 188 F2
Normandy Prim Sch DA7 14 D6
Normandy Terr E16 1 B7
Normandy Way DA8 14 E6
Normanhurst Ave DA7, DA16 13 D6
Normanhurst Rd
Borough Green TN15 95 A7
Orpington BR5 44 B7
Normans Cl DA11 36 A8
Norreys Rd ME8 69 E7
Norrington Rd ME15 116 B6
Norris Ho 14 SE7 11 C8
Norris Way DA1 14 F4
Norstead Gdns TN4 159 B8
Norsted La BR6 74 B8
North Ash Rd DA3 62 F7
North Bank Cl ME2 52 F5
North Beckton Prim Sch E6 1 F8
North Borough Jun Sch ME14 100 A6
North Cl DA6 13 D3
North Cray Rd DA14 30 E4
North Cres ME17 115 D4
North Ct 4 Bromley BR1 42 B8
2 Maidstone ME15 100 A1
North Dane Way ME5 68 C4
North Down TN12 149 E4
North Down View ME17 119 F6
North Downs Bsns Pk TN13 75 C3
North Downs Terr ME19 80 A5
North Dr BR6 57 E6
North End Farm DA13 34 F4
North End La BR6 57 B2
North End Trad Est DA8 14 E6
North Farm La TN2 143 E2
North Farm Rd TN2 159 C8
North Folly Rd ME15 114 F3
North Frith Pk TN11 110 F1
North Glade The DA5 30 F7
North Hill Rd TN18 188 C1
North Kent Ave DA11 18 C1
North Lockside Rd ME4 54 D8
North Mdw ME19 96 D7
North Meadow Cotts ME19 96 D7
North Pk SE9 12 A1
North Pole La BR2 56 A4
North Pole Rd ME16, ME18 98 C2
North Pondside Rd ME4 54 A8
North Rd Bromley BR1 42 B8
Chatham ME4 54 B8
Chatham ME4,ME7 54 A7
Cliffe ME3 22 B6
Dartford DA1 15 A1
Erith DA17 4 B4
Goudhurst TN17 163 E1
Woolwich SE18 2 E2
North Riding DA3 49 D6
North Side Three Rd ME4 54 C8
North St Bexley DA7 14 A3
Biddenden TN27 168 A2
Bromley BR1 42 A8
Cowden TN8 155 A6
Dartford DA1 32 D8
Gravesend DA12 36 B8
Headcorn TN27 151 C5
Maidstone ME16 98 F2
Rochester ME2 53 B7
Royal Tunbridge Wells TN2 159 C3
North St *continued*
Sutton Valence ME17 134 E8
North Street Cotts ME17 134 E8
North Terr ME3 39 F6
North View ME15 100 B1
North View Cotts ME15 115 C7
North View Rd TN13,TN14 92 C6
North Way ME14 100 B7
North West Kent Coll DA12 36 F7
North West Kent College (Dartford Campus) DA1 32 C6
North Woolwich Old Sta Mus* E16 2 A4
North Woolwich Rd E16 1 A5
North Woolwich Rdbt E16 1 D5
North Woolwich Sta E16 2 A4
Northall Rd DA7 14 C5
Northbourne BR2 42 A2
Northbourne Rd ME8 55 B4
Northcote Rd
Northfleet DA11 35 F7
Rochester ME2 53 A7
Sidcup DA14 29 E4
2 Tonbridge TN9 127 B1
Northcourt Prim Sch DA12 36 E7
Northdown ME9 86 D8
Northdown Bsns Pk ME17 120 F6
Northdown Cl
Lenham ME17 120 F6
Maidstone ME14 100 B7
Paddock Wood TN12 145 F6
Northdown Rd
Bexley DA16 13 C5
Kemsing TN15 76 E2
Longfield DA3 48 E7
Northend Prim Sch DA8 14 F6
Northend Rd DA8 14 F6
Northfield DA3 48 F6
Northfield Ave BR5 44 C3
Northfield Cl BR1 42 E8
Northfields
Maidstone ME16 98 F2
Speldhurst TN3 158 A8
Northfleet Cl ME14 100 C5
Northfleet Ind Est DA11 17 F3
Northfleet Sch for Girls DA11 35 D6
Northfleet Sta DA11 18 B1
Northfleet Tech Coll DA11 35 D7
Northgate ME1 53 C6
Northgrove Rd 9 TN18 188 F2
Northiam Sta* TN31 197 C2
Northlands 5 BR1 42 C7
Northlands Ave BR6 57 E6
Northlands Cotts TN32 195 C1
Northleigh Cl ME15 116 A6
Northolme Rise BR6 57 E8
Northover BR1 28 A4
Northpoint 12 BR1 42 A8
Northpoint Bsns Est ME2 53 D8
Northridge Rd DA12 36 C5
Northside Rd BR1 42 A8
Northumberland Ave
Bexley DA16 12 E4
Gillingham ME8 55 E1
Northumberland Cl DA8 14 C7
Northumberland Ct
Bexley DA8 14 C6
Maidstone ME15 116 D7
Northumberland Gdns BR1 43 A5
Northumberland Heath Prim Sch DA8 14 B7
Northumberland Pk DA8 14 C7
Northumberland Rd
Istead Rise DA13 35 F1
Maidstone ME15 116 D8
Newham E6 1 E7
Northumberland Way DA8 14 D6
Northview BR8 45 E7
Northview Ave RM18 19 A6
Northward Hill Nature Reserve* ME23 23 E5
Northwood Ave ME23 23 E4
Northwood Pl DA18 3 F3
Northwood Prim Sch DA18 3 F3
Northwood Rd TN10 127 C6
Norton Cres TN10 127 B7
Norton Gr ME5 67 E3
Norton Rd
Five Wents ME17 117 D1
Royal Tunbridge Wells TN4 143 A1
Nortons La TN30 182 E5
Nortons Way TN12 145 B7
Norvic Ho DA8 14 F7
Norway Terr 4 ME14 100 A7
Norwich Ave TN10 127 D5
Norwich Cl ME2 52 D6
Norwich Pl 7 DA6 14 A3
Norwood Cl ME3 22 B4
Norwood Ct 5 DA1 16 A3
Norwood La DA13 50 B3
Notre Dame RC Prim Sch SE18 12 B8
Nottidge Rd TN4 158 D1
Nottingham Ave
Maidstone ME15 116 D7
Newham E16 1 C7
Nottingham Wlk ME2 52 D6
Novar Cl BR6 43 F2
Novar Rd SE9 29 C7
Nower The TN14,TN16 89 F8
Nuffield Hospl TN2 159 C3
Nuffield Rd BR8 32 A2
Nugent Ind Pk BR5 44 C5
Nunappleton Way RH8 104 A3
Nunnery La TN11 156 F8
Nunnington Cl SE9 28 E5
Nursery Ave Bexley DA7 13 F4
Maidstone ME16 99 B6
Maidstone,Bearsted ME14 101 B3
Nursery Cl Dartford DA2 33 C8
Flimwell TN5 187 B3
Orpington BR6 44 A2
Sevenoaks TN13 92 C5
Swanley BR8 45 C7
Tonbridge TN10 127 E4
Nursery Gdns
Chislehurst BR7 29 B2
Hoo St Werburgh ME3 40 E5
Nursery Ho DA4 47 C5
Nursery Pl TN13 91 D4
Nursery Rd Ditton ME20 82 C1
Gillingham ME8 69 D8
Meopham Sta DA13 50 A4
Paddock Wood TN12 145 F8
Royal Tunbridge Wells TN4 159 B8
Nursery The DA8 14 F7
Nurstead Ave DA3 49 D6
Nurstead Church La DA13 50 A5
Nurstead La DA3,DA13 49 D5
Nurstead Rd DA8 14 A7
Nut Tree Cl BR6 58 D7
Nutfield Cl ME5 68 B8
Nutfield Ct 7 BR1 42 A6
Nutfield Way BR6 57 B8
Nutfields TN15 94 B4
Nuthatch DA3 49 B7
Nuthatch Gdns SE28 2 D4
Nutley Cl BR8 45 F8
Nutmead Cl DA5 31 C7
Nuttall Ct BR5 44 B6
Nutwood Cl ME14 100 E4
Nuxley Rd DA17 4 A1
Nyanza St SE18 12 D8

O

O'Neill Path 11 SE18 12 A8
Oak Apple Ct SE12 28 A7
Oak Ave Biddenden TN27 182 D7
Gillingham ME7 54 E6
Sevenoaks TN13 108 B7
Oak Cl Crayford DA1 14 F3
Hoo St Werburgh ME3 40 E3
Oak Cotts TN8 123 B6
Oak Ct BR1 42 F7
Oak Dr Higham ME3 38 B4
Larkfield ME20 82 B2
Oak End Cl TN4 143 A2
Oak Farm Gdns TN27 151 D6
Oak Farm La TN15 63 E1
Oak Hill Rd TN13 92 A2
Oak Ho 6 Chatham ME5 67 F4
3 Royal Tunbridge Wells TN2 159 C7
18 Sidcup DA15 30 A5
Oak La Gillingham ME8 70 D8
Headcorn TN27 151 D5
Sevenoaks TN13 108 A8
Oak Lodge
Royal Tunbridge Wells TN2 159 D2
Sevenoaks TN13 92 A3
Oak Lodge La TN16 89 D2
Oak Rd Erith DA8 15 A5
Erith,Northumberland Heath DA8 14 C7
Five Oak Green TN12 145 B7
Gravesend DA12 36 C4
Grays RM17 18 C8
Hoo St Werburgh ME3 40 E3
Orpington BR6 58 A3
Rochester ME2 52 E6
Royal Tunbridge Wells TN2 159 D7
Stone DA9 16 E1
Westerham TN16 89 D2
Oak Terr 3 TN18 188 F2
Oak Tree Ave
Maidstone ME15 116 C7
Stone DA9 33 F8
Oak Tree Cl
Marden TN12 148 D5
Royal Tunbridge Wells TN2 159 A1
Oak Tree Gdns BR1 28 B3
Oak Trees Com Sch ME15 116 C7
Oak View TN8 122 B2
Oak Warren TN13 108 A6
Oakapple Ho 10 ME16 99 A3
Oakapple La ME16 99 A3
Oakbrook Cl BR1 28 B4
Oakcroft 3 SE12 28 B5
Oakdale La TN8 105 C2
Oakdale Rd TN4 158 F4
Oakdene Ave
Chislehurst BR7 29 A3
Erith DA8 14 C8
Oakdene Rd
Orpington BR5 44 A3
Sevenoaks TN13 92 A5
Oakenden La TN8 140 C2
Oakenden Rd DA13 50 E1
Oakenholt Ho 1 SE2 3 D
Oakes Cl E6 1 F
Oakfield Hawkhurst TN18 188 F
Rolvenden TN17 192 A
Oakfield Cotts TN17 190 D
Oakfield Court Rd TN2 159 C
Oakfield Inf Sch DA1 32 D
Oakfield Jun Sch DA1 32 D
Oakfield La
Dartford DA1,DA2 32 B
Orpington BR2 56 D
Oakfield Park Rd DA1 32 D
Oakfield Pl DA1 32 D
Oakfield Rd
Marlpit Hill TN8 122 B
Matfield TN12 161 D
Oakfields TN13 92 B
Oakham Dr BR2 42 A
Oakhill Ho BR5 44 A
Oakhill Rd BR6 57 F
Oakhouse Rd DA6 14 A
Oakhurst Ave DA7 13 E
Oakhurst Cl Bromley BR7 42 F
Chatham ME5 67 F
Oakhurst Gdns DA7 13 E
Oakland Cl ME5 67 F
Oakland Villas TN3 171 B
Oaklands Chislehurst BR7 29 D
Cranbrook TN17 179 D
Oaklands Ave DA15 29 F
Oaklands Cl Bexley DA6 13 F
Orpington BR5 43 E
West Kingsdown TN15 61 E
Oaklands Ct BR6 57 C
Oaklands Inf & Jun Sch ME5 67 F
Oaklands Inf Sch TN16 72 C
Oaklands Jun Sch TN16 72 C
Oaklands La TN16 72 C
Oaklands Rd Bexley DA6 13 F
Dartford DA2 33 C
Groombridge TN3 171 B
Hawkhurst TN18 189 A
Northfleet DA11 35 F
Oaklands Way TN11 126 F
Oaklea Rd TN12 145 F
Oakleigh Cl Chatham ME5 67 E
Swanley BR8 45 E
Oakleigh Ct TN12 162 F
Oakleigh Gdns BR6 57 E
Oakleigh Park Ave BR7 43 A
Oakley Cl 8 Newham E6 1 E
West Thurrock RM20 17 C
Oakley Ct DA1 33 B
Oakley Dr Orpington BR2 56 E
Sidcup SE9 29 D
Oakley Lodge SE12 28 A
Oakley Pk DA5 30 C
Oakley Rd BR2 56 E
Oakmead Meopham DA13 64 A
Tonbridge TN10 127 C
Oakmead Ave BR2 42 A
Oakmere Rd SE2 13 A
Oakmont Pl 6 BR6 43 D
Oaks Bsns Village The ME5 68 C
Oaks Dene ME5 67 F
Oaks Forstal TN18 196 C
Oaks Rd TN30 193 B
Oaks The Aylesford ME20 82 E
Dartford DA2 16 B
Smarden TN27 152 F
Swanley BR8 45 E
Woolwich SE18 2 C
Oakum Ct ME4 54 B
Oakway Cl DA5 13 E
Oakways SE9 12 B
Oakwood Ave BR2 42 B
Oakwood Cl
Chislehurst BR7 29 A
Dartford DA1 33 B
Oakwood Ct
Maidstone ME16 99 D
Swanley BR8 45 C
Oakwood Dr Bexley DA7 14 C
Sevenoaks TN13 92 B
Oakwood Gdns BR6 57 C
Oakwood Ind Est DA11 18 A
Oakwood Park Gram Sch ME16 99 C
Oakwood Rd
Maidstone ME16 99 D
Orpington BR6 57 C
Oakwood Rise
Longfield DA3 48 E
Royal Tunbridge Wells TN2 159 E
Oakwood Sch DA7 14 D
Oasis The 7 BR1 42 C
Oast Cl TN2 159 D
Oast Ct ME18 113 F
Oast Ho The 3 ME8 69 F
Oast House Way BR5 44 B
Oast La TN10 127 A
Oast View TN12 163 A
Oast Way DA3 48 E
Oastfield Ct TN15 92 C
Oasts The ME14 101 C
Oastview ME8 70 A
Oatfield Cl TN17 179 C
Oatfield Dr TN17 179 C
Oatfield Rd BR6 43 F
Occupation La SE18 12 B
Ocelot Ct 6 ME4 54 B
Ockham Dr BR5 30 A
Ockley Ct DA14 29 E
Ockley La TN18 189 A
Ockley Rd TN18 189 A

ctavia Ct ME5 68 B3
ctavia Way 12 SE28 3 B6
deon Ct 1 E16 1 A8
deon Par SE9 11 E3
diham Dr ME16 99 C7
ffen's Dr TN12 149 E3
ffenham Rd SE9 28 F4
ffham Prim Sch ME19 96 D8
ffham Rd ME19 97 A7
fficers Terr ME4 53 F7
fficers' Rd ME4 54 B8
gilby St SE18 1 F2
kehampton Cres DA16 13 C6
kemore Gdns BR5 44 C5
ld Ashford Rd ME17 120 E5
ld Bailey The ME17 119 E6
ld Barn Cl
Gillingham ME7 68 F6
Kemsing TN15 77 A2
Tonbridge TN9 142 F8
ld Barn Rd ME19 81 E2
ld Barn Way DA7 14 D4
ld Bexley Bsns Pk DA5 31 B8
ld Bexley CE Prim Sch
DA5 30 F7
ld Bexley La DA5 31 E6
ld Carriageway The
Gillingham ME7 68 F4
Sevenoaks TN13 91 C5
ld Castle Wlk ME8 69 D4
ld Chapel Rd BR8 45 C2
ld Chatham Rd
Kit's Coty ME20 83 D6
Sandling ME14 83 F1
ld Church La TN12 112 E4
ld Church Rd
Burham ME1 66 C1
Mereworth ME18,TN12 112 D5
Pembury TN2 144 D2
ld Clem Sq 12 SE18 12 A8
ld Coach Rd TN15 78 E5
ld Corn Stores The
ME14 101 C4
ld Court Ho The TN13 92 C3
ld Ctyd The BR1 42 B8
ld Dairy The TN12 129 E6
ld Dartford Rd DA4 46 F3
ld Dover Rd SE3 11 B7
ld Downs DA3 48 E4
ld Downs The DA3 48 E4
ld Dr ME15 115 F6
ld Farm Ave DA15 29 E6
ld Farm Gdns BR8 45 F6
ld Farm Rd E DA15 30 A6
ld Farm Rd W DA15 29 F6
ld Farmhouse The BR8 31 E1
ld Fire Sta The SE18 12 B7
ld Forge La ME9 86 F3
ld Forge Way DA14 30 B4
ld Gardens Cl TN2 173 B8
ld Gdn The TN13 91 D4
ld George Ct ME3 39 F4
ld Hadlow Rd TN10 127 F4
ld Ham La ME17 120 A4
ld Hill Chislehurst BR7 43 A8
Orpington BR6 57 E4
ld Ho The BR7 43 D8
ld Homesdale Rd BR2 42 C5
ld House La Hartlip ME9 70 E4
Langton Green TN3 157 D4
ld Kent Rd TN12 146 A6
ld La Ightham TN15 94 C4
Tatsfield TN16 88 D6
ld Lain ME17 119 F6
ld London Rd
Badgers Mount TN14 59 A1
Halstead TN14 74 E4
Tonbridge TN10 127 C3
Wrotham TN15 78 F4
ld Loose Cl ME15 115 F5
ld Loose Hill ME15 115 F4
ld Maidstone Rd
Keycol ME9 71 F5
Sidcup DA14 30 F1
ld Manor Dr DA12 36 C7
ld Manor Way
Bexley DA7 14 D5
Bromley BR7 28 F3
ld Mill Cl DA4 46 E1
ld Mill La ME20 83 C3
ld Mill Rd
Maidstone ME17 101 F1
Woolwich SE18 12 D8
ld Oast Bsns Ctr The
ME20 83 A1
ld Orch Charcott TN11 125 A3
Sandhurst TN18 196 B5
d Orch The ME8 70 A8
d Orchard La ME19 81 D1
d Otford Rd TN14 76 B1
d Park Rd SE2 3 A1
d Parsonage Ct ME19 97 C7
d Pattens La ME4 53 D2
d Perry St
Chislehurst BR7 29 E1
Northfleet DA11 35 E6
d Polhill TN14 75 D4
d Post Office La SE3 11 B4
d Rd Chatham ME4 53 F4
Crayford DA1,DA7 14 D3
East Peckham TN12 130 A6
Wateringbury ME18 113 C7
d Rd E DA12 36 D7
d Rd W DA11 36 A7
d Regent Dr TN17 191 E3
d Riding School The
TN3 171 B2
d Saw Mill The TN15 95 D5
Old Sch The BR6 57 B5
Old School Cl ME17 120 D4
Old School Ct
Chattenden ME3 39 F4
Egerton TN27 137 F3
Swanley BR8 45 E7
Old School Ho The 3
TN8 122 C1
Old School La ME19 80 F4
Old School Pl ME14 100 A5
Old School The
Goudhurst TN17 177 E8
Maidstone ME16 98 E1
Old School Yd DA12 36 E8
Old Soar Manor* TN15 95 B1
Old Soar Rd TN15 95 C1
Old Station Rd TN5 184 E6
Old Tannery Cl TN30 192 F7
Old Terry's Lodge Rd
TN15 78 A4
Old Timber Top Cotts The
TN13 92 C4
Old Tovil Rd ME15 100 A2
Old Trafford Cl ME16 99 B6
Old Tramyard SE18 2 E2
Old Tree La ME17 116 D3
Old Tye Ave TN16 72 E3
Old Vicarage The DA13 50 A1
Old Wardsdown TN5 187 B3
Old Watling St
Gravesend DA11 36 A3
Rochester ME2 52 B8
Old Weavers Cotts
TN17 190 D5
Old Whetsted Rd TN12 130 A2
Old White Hart Cotts
TN16 90 C3
Old Wlk The TN14 76 C2
Old Yard The TN16 90 C3
Old Yews The DA3 49 B6
Oldborough Manor Com Sch
ME15 116 B6
Oldbury Cl Oldbury TN15 94 B5
Orpington BR5 44 D5
Oldbury Cotts TN15 94 B6
Oldbury La TN15 94 B6
Oldchurch Ct 3 ME16 99 E3
Oldfield Cl Bromley BR1 42 F5
Gillingham ME8 69 D8
Maidstone ME15 100 E1
Oldfield Dr ME1 66 C5
Oldfield Rd Bexley DA7 13 E5
Bromley BR1 42 F5
Oldman Ct SE12 28 B6
Oleander Cl BR6 57 D5
Olive Rd DA1 32 D7
Oliver Cl Chatham ME4 54 B2
West Thurrock RM20 16 F7
Oliver Cres DA4 46 F2
Oliver Ct SE18 2 C2
Oliver Gdns E6 1 E8
Oliver North Ho ME15 114 E7
Oliver Rd
Staplehurst TN12 149 E4
Swanley BR8 45 D6
West Thurrock RM20 16 F7
West Thurrock RM20 17 A7
Oliver Twist Cl ME1 53 B4
Olivers Mill DA3 62 E8
Olivers Row ME14 101 C4
Olivier Dr ME2 39 B2
Olivine Cl ME5 84 A8
Olliffe Cl ME5 67 F2
Olron Cres DA6 13 E2
Olven Rd SE18 12 C8
Olyffe Ave DA16 13 A5
Onslow Cres BR7 43 B8
Onslow Dr DA14 30 D6
Onslow Rd ME1 53 D3
Opal Cl E16 1 D7
Opal Gn ME5 68 B2
Openshaw Rd SE2 3 B2
Orache Dr ME14 100 E5
Orange Court La BR6 57 A2
Orange Terr ME1 53 D5
Orangery La SE9 11 F2
Orbit Cl ME5 84 A8
Orbital One DA1 33 B6
Orchard Ave
Aylesford ME20 82 E1
Bexley DA17 3 F1
Dartford DA1 32 B7
Gravesend DA11 36 B3
Rochester ME2 38 F1
Orchard Bank ME17 117 B1
Orchard Bsns Ctr
Maidstone ME16 99 C8
Paddock Wood TN12 146 A8
Royal Tunbridge Wells
TN2 159 D8
Tonbridge TN9 127 E1
Orchard Cl Bexley DA7 13 E6
Coxheath ME17 115 C3
Edenbridge TN8 122 B2
Horsmonden TN12 162 F6
Langley Heath ME17 117 E4
New Barn DA3 49 B7
Royal Tunbridge Wells
TN2 159 D6
Sevenoaks TN14 92 C7
Orchard Cotts
Chislehurst BR7 29 E2
East Farleigh ME16 115 A8
Nettlestead Green ME18 113 C1
Orchard Cres
Horsmonden TN12 163 A6
Wateringbury ME18 113 D6
Orchard Ct
Benenden TN17 190 D6
Sidcup DA15 12 F2
Orchard Dr
Edenbridge TN8 122 B2
Maidstone ME14 100 E4
Meopham Sta DA13 49 F4
Newington ME9 71 A5
Tonbridge TN10 127 E5
Orchard Glade TN27 151 E5
Orchard Gn Bromley BR1 42 C8
Orpington BR6 57 E8
Orchard Gr Larkfield ME20 82 B2
Orpington BR6 43 F1
Royal Tunbridge Wells
TN1 159 B5
Orchard Hill DA1 14 E2
Orchard Ho DA8 14 F6
Orchard Ind Est ME15 116 F3
Orchard Lea TN11 126 F5
Orchard Pl Keston BR2 56 D2
2 Maidstone ME16 99 E3
Orpington BR5 44 C6
Sundridge TN14 90 D3
Orchard Prim Sch DA14 30 B3
Orchard Rd Bexley DA16 13 B4
Bromley BR1 42 C8
East Peckham TN12 130 A6
Erith DA17 4 A2
Northfleet DA11 35 C6
Orpington BR6 57 B5
Otford TN14 75 F3
Pratt's Bottom BR6 58 C1
Sevenoaks TN13 91 E5
Sidcup DA14 29 E4
Swanscombe DA10 17 E2
Tenterden TN30 183 A3
Orchard Rise TN3 171 B7
Orchard Rise E DA15 12 F2
Orchard Rise W DA15 12 E2
Orchard St Dartford DA1 15 E1
Gillingham ME8 69 E8
Maidstone ME15 100 A3
Orchard Terr DA9 16 E2
Orchard The
Maidstone ME14 101 B4
Sevenoaks TN13 91 E6
Swanley BR8 45 D7
Orchard View
Detling ME14 101 A8
Tenterden TN30 193 C8
Orchard Villas
Chainhurst TN12 132 A4
1 Chatham ME4 53 F3
Chislehurst BR7 29 E2
Sidcup DA14 30 C2
Orchard Way
Cranbrook TN17 179 B4
Dartford DA2 32 D5
Horsmonden TN12 163 A6
Kemsing TN15 77 A2
Oxted RH8 104 A2
Snodland ME6 81 F7
Orchardlea DA13 34 F3
Orchards Sh Ctr The DA1 15 E1
Orchid Cl 1 Newham E6 1 E8
Rochester ME2 52 C6
Orchidhurst TN2 159 D7
Ordnance Rd
Gravesend DA12 19 C1
Woolwich SE18 12 A8
Ordnance St ME4 53 E3
Ordnance Terr 9 ME4 53 E4
Oregon Sq BR6 43 D1
Orford Ct 7 DA2 16 B1
Oriental Rd E16 1 D5
Oriole Way Larkfield ME20 81 F2
Woolwich SE28 3 B6
Orion Rd ME1 67 C7
Orissa Rd SE18 2 E1
Orlestone Gdns BR6 58 E5
Orlick Rd DA12 37 B7
Ormesby Cl SE28 3 D6
Ormiston Rd SE10 1 A1
Ormonde Ave BR6 57 C8
Ormsby Gn ME8 69 E3
Ormsby Point 8 SE18 2 B2
Orpines The ME18 113 F7
Orpington By-Pass TN14 59 A2
Orpington Coll of Further
Education BR6 44 A1
Orpington Hospl BR6 57 F6
Orpington Rd BR7 43 E6
Orpington Sta BR6 57 E8
Orpington Trad Est 10
BR5 44 C5
Orwell Cl Lunsford ME20 81 F3
Rainham RM13 4 D8
Orwell Spike ME19 97 A5
Osberton Rd SE12 11 A2
Osborne Rd Bexley DA17 13 F8
Gillingham ME7 54 C5
Osbourne Rd DA2 16 B1
Osgood Ave BR6 57 F5
Osgood Gdns 1 BR6 57 F5
Oslin Wlk ME18 97 C2
Osmers Hill TN5 184 F7
Osmunda Ct TN2 159 C4
Osney Ho 4 SE2 3 D4
Osney Way DA12 36 F6
Osprey Ave ME5 54 E2
Osprey Cl E6 1 E8
Osprey Wlk ME20 81 F1
Ospringe Ct SE9 12 D1
Ospringe Pl TN2 159 F6
Osterberg Rd DA1 15 F3
Osterley Cl BR5 44 A8
Ostlers Ct 2 ME6 82 A8
Otford Cl Bromley BR1 43 A6
Sidcup DA5 14 B1
Otford Court (St Michael's
Sch) TN14 76 E4
Otford La TN14 75 B6
Otford Prim Sch TN14 76 B3
Otford Rd TN14 92 B7
Otford Sta TN14 76 C3
Otham La ME15 101 C2
Otham St
Maidstone ME15 101 C2
Otham ME15 117 B7
Otley Rd E16 1 C7
Otlinge Rd BR5 44 D5
Ottawa Rd RM18 19 A5
Otterbourne Pl ME15 100 E1
Otterden Cl BR6 57 E6
Otterham Quay La ME8 70 B8
Otteridge Rd ME14 101 A3
Otters Cl BR5 44 D5
Ottershaw Ho BR5 44 B8
Otway St Chatham ME4 54 A3
Gillingham ME7 54 D6
Otway Terr 1 ME4 54 A3
Oulton Cl SE28 3 C7
Our Lady of Grace RC Prim
Sch SE7 11 B8
Our Lady of Hartley RC Prim
Sch DA3 48 F4
Our Lady of the Rosary RC
Prim Sch DA15 12 E1
Our Lady's RC Prim Sch
DA1 15 D1
Oval The New Barn DA3 49 C6
Sidcup DA15 30 A8
Ovenden Rd
Sevenoaks TN14 90 F6
Sundridge TN14 90 D6
Over Minnis DA3 62 F7
Overcliffe DA11 19 A1
Overcourt Cl DA15 13 B1
Overdale TN14 108 B2
Overmead Eltham DA15 29 D8
Swanley BR8 45 E4
Overton Rd SE2 3 D3
Overy Liberty DA1 32 E8
Overy St DA1 15 E1
Owen Cl East Malling ME19 97 F8
Woolwich SE28 3 C5
Owenite St SE2 3 B2
Owens Way ME7 55 A6
Owl House Gdns* TN3 175 E7
Owletts* DA12 50 F6
Owletts Cl ME15 116 D8
Ox La TN30 183 B2
Ox Lea TN3 158 A3
Oxenden Wood Rd BR6 58 C4
Oxenhill Rd TN15 76 E2
Oxenhoath Rd TN11 111 D4
Oxfield TN8 122 D3
Oxford Cl DA12 36 F6
Oxford Ct DA14 29 F4
Oxford Mews DA5 31 A8
Oxford Rd Gillingham ME7 54 D3
Maidstone ME15 116 D8
Sidcup DA14 30 B3
Oxford St ME6 82 A8
Oxhawth Cres BR2 43 B3
Oxleas E6 2 B7
Oxleas Cl DA16 12 D5
Oxleas Wood Nature
Reserve* SE18 12 C4
Oxley Shaw La ME19 81 E2
Oyster Catchers Cl E16 1 B7
Ozolins Way E16 1 A7

P

Pacific Cl DA10 17 E2
Pacific Rd E16 1 A7
Packer Pl ME5 68 A8
Packham Cl BR6 58 C7
Packham Rd DA11 35 F5
Packhorse Rd TN13 91 C4
Packmores Rd SE9 12 E2
Pad's Hill ME15 100 A4
Padbrook RH8 104 A6
Padbrook Cl RH8 104 B6
Paddlesworth Rd ME6 65 D1
Paddock Cl
Fordcombe TN3 157 B5
Greenwich SE3 11 A5
Limpsfield RH8 104 A4
Orpington BR6 57 B6
Platt TN15 95 C6
Sutton at H DA4 47 C8
Paddock Rd DA6 13 E3
Paddock The
Ashurst TN3 156 F5
Chatham ME4 53 F4
Dartford DA2 33 E6
Farthing Street BR2 56 E2
Hadlow TN11 111 E1
Pembury TN2 160 C6
Vigo Village DA13 79 F7
Westerham TN16 89 C1
Paddock Way BR7 29 D1
Paddock Wood Bsns Ctr
TN12 146 A7
Paddock Wood Prim Sch
TN12 146 A6
Paddock Wood Sta
TN12 146 A7
Paddocks Cl BR5 58 D8
Paddocks The
Cowden TN8 155 B7
Gillingham ME7 69 A5
Paddocks The *continued*
Sevenoaks TN13 92 D3
Padsole La ME15 100 A4
Padstow Cl 3 BR6 57 F6
Padstow Manor 1 ME7 54 C6
Page Cl DA2 34 C5
Page Cres DA8 14 F7
Page Heath La BR1 42 D6
Page Heath Villas BR1 42 D6
Pageant Cl RM18 19 C6
Pagehurst Rd TN12 149 B3
Paget Gdns BR7 43 B8
Paget Rise SE18 12 A7
Paget Row ME7 54 C5
Paget St ME7 54 C5
Paget Terr SE18 12 B8
Pagitt St ME4 53 E3
Paiges Farm Cl TN14 108 C2
Pains Hill RH8 104 C4
Painters Ash La DA11 35 D5
Painters Ash Prim Sch
DA11 35 D5
Palace Ave ME15 100 A4
Palace Ct 5 Bromley BR1 42 B8
Eltham SE9 11 F1
Gillingham ME5 54 D2
Palace Gr BR1 42 B8
Palace Ind Est ME15 116 F4
Palace Rd Bromley BR1 42 B8
Hill Park TN16 89 A6
Palace View Bromley BR1 42 B6
Lewisham SE12 28 A6
Palace Wood Inf Sch
ME16 99 C6
Palace Wood Jun Sch
ME16 99 C6
Palewell Cl BR5 44 B7
Pallant Way BR6 57 A7
Pallet Way SE18 11 E6
Palm Ave DA14 30 D2
Palmar Cres DA7 14 A5
Palmar Rd Bexley DA7 14 A5
Maidstone ME16 99 D6
Palmarsh Rd BR5 44 D5
Palmeira Rd DA7 13 D4
Palmer Ave DA12 36 D4
Palmers Brook TN11 111 F2
Palmers Green La TN12 146 D1
Palmers Orch TN14 75 F8
Palmers Yd TN27 151 E5
Palmerston Cres SE18 12 C8
Palmerston Rd
Chatham ME4 53 F1
Grays RM20 17 D8
Orpington BR6 57 C5
Pamela Ct ME7 54 D5
Panbro Ho SE18 11 F6
Panfield Rd SE2 3 A3
Pankhurst Ave E16 1 B5
Pankhurst Ho SE18 12 A7
Pankhurst Rd ME3 40 D6
Pannell Rd ME3 27 A6
Panter's BR8 31 F1
Pantiles The Bexley DA7 13 F7
Bromley BR1 42 E6
20 Royal Tunbridge Wells
TN2 159 A2
Panton Cl ME5 68 C4
Pantyles The TN14 107 B5
Papillons Wlk SE3 11 A4
Papion Gr ME5 67 E2
Parade The Crayford DA1 14 F2
Gravesend DA12 36 D6
Kemsing TN15 76 E2
Meopham Sta DA13 50 A2
Rochester ME2 52 E8
Staplehurst TN12 149 F3
Swanscombe DA10 17 F2
Paradise Cotts ME9 70 E5
Paradise Path SE28 3 A5
Paradise Pl 14 SE18 1 E2
Paragon Cl E16 1 A7
Paragon The SE3 11 A5
Parbrook Rd ME3 24 B2
Parham Rd ME4 53 F2
Parish CE Prim Sch BR1 28 A1
Parish Gate Dr DA15 12 E1
Parish Wharf 5 SE18 1 E2
Park App DA16 13 B3
Park Ave Bromley BR1 28 A2
Edenbridge TN8 122 B2
Gillingham ME7 54 D3
Gravesend DA12 36 C7
Maidstone ME17 115 E2
Maidstone, Penenden Heath
ME14 100 B6
Northfleet DA11 35 E7
Orpington BR6 58 B7
Orpington BR6 57 A8
Tonbridge TN11 126 F5
West Thurrock RM20 17 B8
Park Barn Rd ME17 118 C5
Park Cliff Rd DA9 17 C3
Park Corner Rd DA13 34 F4
Park Cotts
8 Hawkhurst TN18 189 A2
Sevenoaks TN13 92 C2
Park Cres Chatham ME4 67 F8
Erith DA8 14 D8
Park Crescent Rd DA8 14 D8
Park Dr Longfield DA3 48 E6
Woolwich SE7 11 E8
Park Farm Houses ME20 98 B8
Park Farm Rd
Bromley BR1 42 D8

Park Farm Rd *continued*
Ryarsh ME19 80 F6
Park Gdns DA8 4 D2
Park Gr Bexley DA7 14 C3
Bromley BR1 42 B8
Park Hill Bromley BR1 42 F5
Meopham Sta DA13 49 F5
Park Hill Rd TN14 76 E2
Park Ho Maidstone ME14 100 B6
Sevenoaks TN13 92 C5
Sidcup DA14 30 A3
Park House Cotts DA4 60 F5
Park House Gdns TN4 143 A2
Park La
Gill's Green TN17,TN18 188 D7
Godden Green TN15 93 A4
Kemsing TN15 77 A1
Maidstone, Cock Stone ME17 116 D2
Maidstone, Ringlestone ME14 99 F7
Sevenoaks TN13 92 C3
Swanley Village BR8 46 C7
Park Manor ME7 54 B5
Park Mead DA15 13 B1
Park Mews BR7 29 B2
Park Pl 8 Bromley BR1 42 B8
Gravesend DA12 36 C8
Hever TN8 139 D4
Sevenoaks TN13 91 D4
Park Rd Addington ME19 80 C3
Bromley BR1 42 B8
Chislehurst BR7 29 B2
Dartford DA1 33 A8
Dunk's Green TN11 111 C5
Gravesend DA11 36 B7
Leybourne ME19 81 D3
Limpsfield RH8 104 A8
Marden Thorn TN12 149 A4
Mereworth TN12 112 F5
Orpington BR5 44 C4
Royal Tunbridge Wells TN4 159 B5
Royal Tunbridge Wells, Southborough TN4 143 A2
Swanley BR8 45 F5
Swanscombe DA10 17 E1
Park Road Ind Est BR8 45 F6
Park St TN2 159 C3
Park Terr Sundridge TN14 90 D3
Swanscombe DA9 17 B2
Park The DA14 30 A3
Park View
Hodsoll Street TN15 63 C2
Sevenoaks TN13 92 C3
Park View Cl TN8 122 B2
Park View Ct
2 Lewisham SE12 28 C5
Maidstone ME15 100 E1
Park View Rd DA16 13 C4
Park View Terr 2 TN30 193 A7
Park Villas ME14 100 E4
Park Way Coxheath ME17 115 D3
Joyden's Wood DA5 31 E5
Maidstone ME15 100 B1
Park Way Prim Sch ME15 100 B1
Park Wood Gn ME8 69 D5
Park Wood La TN12 150 C1
Park Wood Par ME15 116 F5
Park Wood Trad Est
Maidstone ME15 116 F4
Otham ME15 117 A4
Parkdale Rd SE18 2 E1
Parker Ave RM18 19 C6
Parker Cl Gillingham ME8 69 E5
Newham E16 1 E5
Parker Ho 4 SE18 2 B1
Parker Ind Ctr DA1 33 C7
Parker Rd RM17 17 F8
Parker St E16 1 E5
Parker's Cnr ME3 9 C2
Parkfield Hartley DA3 48 E5
Sevenoaks TN15 92 F4
Parkfield Rd ME8 55 F1
Parkfield Way BR2 42 F4
Parkfields ME2 52 C7
Parkgate Cotts BR6 59 C6
Parkgate Rd BR6 59 C6
Parkhill Rd Sidcup DA15 29 E5
Sidcup, Old Bexley DA5 30 F8
Parkhurst Gdns 2 DA5 31 A8
Parkhurst Rd DA5 31 A8
Parkland Cl TN13 108 D6
Parklands TN4 158 E8
Parkmore BR7 29 B1
Parkside Cliffe Woods ME3 39 B7
Halstead TN14 74 F6
Sidcup DA14 30 B6
Parkside Ave
Bexley DA1,DA7 14 E5
Bromley BR1 42 E5
Tilbury RM18 19 B5
Parkside Cotts TN16 88 E6
Parkside Cross DA7 14 E5
Parkside Ct TN30 192 F7
Parkside Lodge DA17 4 C1
Parkside Par DA1 14 F5
Parkside Rd DA17 4 C2
Parkview TN2 159 D4
Parkview Ct DA11 36 A6
Parkview Rd SE9 29 B6
Parkway Erith DA18 3 E3
Tonbridge TN10 127 D5
Parkway Prim Sch DA18 3 E3
Parkwood Cl TN2 159 C6
Parkwood Hall Sch BR8 46 B6
Parkwood Inf Sch ME8 69 E5
Parkwood Jun Sch ME8 69 E5
Parkwood Rd
Biggin Hill TN16 88 F6
Sidcup DA5 30 F8
Paroma Rd DA17 4 A3
Parr Ave ME7 54 D6
Parr Ct DA10 34 E8
Parrock Ave DA12 36 C7
Parrock Rd DA12 36 C7
Parrock St DA12 36 B8
Parrock The DA12 36 C7
Parrs Head Mews ME1 53 C6
Parry Ave E6 1 F7
Parry Pl SE18 2 B2
Parson's Croft TN8 139 C5
Parsonage Cl TN4 158 B5
Parsonage La
Cold Harbour ME9 71 F8
Lamberhurst TN3 176 B6
Rochester ME2 53 C8
Sidcup DA14 30 F4
Sutton at H DA4 33 B2
Parsonage Manorway DA17 14 A8
Parsonage Rd
Rusthall TN4 158 B5
West Thurrock RM20 17 C8
Parsons La Dartford DA2 32 B5
Stansted TN15 62 E1
Partridge Ave ME20 81 F3
Partridge Cl 1 E16 1 D8
Partridge Dr
Orpington BR6 57 C7
St Mary's Island ME4 40 B1
Partridge Gn SE9 29 A5
Partridge Rd DA14 29 E4
Partridge Sq 3 E6 1 E8
Pasadena Cvn Pk TN15 61 B1
Pasley Rd ME4,ME7 54 A7
Pasley Rd E ME7 54 B7
Pasley Rd N ME4 54 B7
Pasley Rd W ME7 54 A7
Passey Pl SE9 11 F1
Passfield Ho SE18 2 D2
Passfield Path 13 SE28 3 B6
Pastens Rd RH8 104 C4
Paston Cres SE12 28 B8
Pat Bassant Row DA10 34 E8
Pat Drew Ho BR1 42 C8
Patagonia Ho TN2 159 C3
Patch The TN13 91 E5
Patience Cotts TN14 108 B2
Patricia Ct Bexley SE2 13 B7
Chislehurst BR7 43 D8
Patrixbourne Ave ME8 55 C2
Pattenden Gdns TN12 130 A7
Pattenden La TN12 148 C7
Pattens Gdns ME1 53 E2
Pattens La ME1,ME4 53 E1
Pattens Pl ME1 53 D2
Patterdale Rd DA2 33 D7
Patterson Ct DA1 16 A2
Pattinson Point 14 E16 1 A8
Pattison Wlk SE18 2 C1
Paulinus Cl BR5 44 C6
Pavement The TN30 183 B3
Pavilion Gdns TN13 92 C3
Pavilion La ME18 113 A8
Pavilion The 5 TN9 127 B1
Pavings The ME17 102 C2
Paxton Ct 5 SE12 28 C5
Paxton Rd BR1 28 A1
Payne's La ME15 116 B7
Paynes Cotts TN13 75 D1
Paynesfield Rd
Tatsfield TN16 88 D7
Tatsfield TN16 88 D8
Peace Cotts ME15 131 D7
Peace St SE18 12 A8
Peach Croft DA11 35 E4
Peach Hall TN10 127 C6
Peacock Mews 7 ME16 99 E4
Peacock Rise ME5 68 A4
Peacock St DA12 36 C8
Peacock Wlk E16 1 B7
Peal Cl ME3 40 E5
Pear Tree Ave ME20 82 C1
Pear Tree Cl
Cranbrook TN17 179 D3
Swanley BR8 45 D7
Pear Tree La
Gillingham ME7 68 E7
Loose ME15 116 B6
Pear Tree Pl ME3 38 B3
Pear Tree Row ME17 117 B5
Pear Tree Wlk ME9 71 A5
Peareswood Rd DA8 14 F6
Pearl Cl E6 2 A7
Pearl Way ME18 97 C3
Pearse Pl TN3 176 B5
Pearson Way DA1 32 F6
Pearson's Green Rd TN12 146 D5
Pearson's Green Rd TN12 146 F3
Peartree Cl DA8 14 D6
Peartree Cotts ME8 70 B8
Peartree La DA12 38 A2
Peartree Way SE10 1 A2
Pease Hill TN15 62 F4
Peasley La TN17 177 D6
Peat Way ME3 10 D1
Peatfield Cl DA15 29 E5
Pebble Hill Cotts RH8 104 B6
Peckham Cl ME2 53 C8
Peckham Ct TN12 129 F6
Peckham Ho 6 BR5 44 D1
Peckham Hurst Rd TN11 111 E7
Pedham Place Est BR8 46 A4
Peel Rd BR6 57 C5
Peel St ME14 100 A6
Peel Yates Ho 12 SE18 1 E2
Peens La ME17 133 C7
Pegasus Ct DA12 36 C5
Peggoty Cl ME3 38 B3
Pegley Gdns SE12 28 A6
Pegwell St SE18 12 E7
Pelham Cotts DA5 31 B7
Pelham Ct 19 DA14 30 A5
Pelham Prim Sch DA7 14 A4
Pelham Rd Bexley DA7 14 A4
Gravesend DA11 36 A8
Pelham Rd S DA11 35 F7
Pelham Terr 4 DA11 35 F8
Pelican Cl ME2 52 C6
Pelican Ct ME18 113 E7
Pell Cl TN5 185 A6
Pellipar Gdns SE18 1 F1
Pellipar Rd SE18 1 F1
Pells La TN15 78 A7
Pemberton Gdns BR8 45 E7
Pemberton Sq 4 ME2 53 C8
Pemble Cl TN12 145 A7
Pembroke ME4 54 B8
Pembroke Cl DA8 4 D2
Pembroke Ct ME4 54 A4
Pembroke Gdns ME8 69 E4
Pembroke Par DA8 4 C1
Pembroke Pl DA4 47 B8
Pembroke Rd
Bromley BR1 42 D7
Coxheath ME17 115 C3
Erith DA8 4 D2
Newham E6 1 F8
Sevenoaks TN13 92 B2
Tonbridge TN9 127 A1
Pembroke Rise ME4 54 A7
Pembury Cl TN2 160 D7
Pembury Cres DA14 30 E6
Pembury Gdns ME16 99 D3
Pembury Gr TN9 143 C8
Pembury Grange TN2 160 A6
Pembury Hall Rd TN11, TN2 144 C3
Pembury Hospl TN2 160 B7
Pembury Rd Bexley DA7 13 E8
Pembury TN11 144 A2
Royal Tunbridge Wells TN2 159 E4
Tonbridge TN11,TN9 143 D7
Pembury Sch TN2 160 D8
Pembury Vineyard* TN2 144 F1
Pembury Way ME8 55 E2
Pembury Wlks TN11, TN2 144 C2
Pen Way TN10 127 E5
Pencroft Dr DA1 32 C8
Penda Rd DA8 14 B7
Pendant Ct BR6 58 A5
Pendennis Rd
Orpington BR6 58 C8
Sevenoaks TN13 92 B4
Penderel Mews TN30 193 B8
Pendlebury Gn SE18 11 E6
Pendragon Rd BR1,SE12 28 A5
Pendragon Sch BR1 28 A5
Pendrell St SE18 12 D8
Pendrill Pl TN5 184 F5
Penenden DA3 62 F8
Penenden Ct ME14 100 B7
Penenden Heath Rd ME14 100 C7
Penenden St ME14 100 A6
Penfold Cl Chatham ME5 68 B7
Maidstone ME15 116 E5
Penfold Hill ME17 118 B8
Penfold Ho 14 SE18 12 B8
Penfold La DA5 30 D7
Penfold Way ME15 115 F6
Penfolds Cl TN10 127 C5
Penford Gdns SE9 11 D4
Pengarth Rd DA5 13 D1
Penguin Cl ME2 52 D6
Penhale Cl BR6 58 A6
Penhall Rd SE7 1 D2
Penhill Rd DA5 30 C8
Penhurst Cl ME14 100 F5
Peninsular Park Rd SE7 1 A2
Penlee Cl TN8 122 C2
Penmon Rd SE2 3 A3
Penn Gdns BR7 43 B7
Penn La Bexley DA5 13 D1
Ide Hill TN14 106 E8
Penn Yd TN2 160 C6
Pennant Rd ME1 67 C7
Penney Cl DA1 32 D8
Pennine Way Bexley DA7 14 E6
Maidstone ME15 101 A1
Northfleet DA11 35 E5
Pennine Wlk TN2 159 D5
Pennington Manor 1 TN4 142 F2
Pennington Pl TN4 143 B1
Pennington Rd TN4 143 A2
Pennington Way SE12 28 B6
Penns Yd TN2 160 C6
Penny Cress Gdns ME16 99 C3
Penny Spring Farm (Cvn Pk) ME14 85 B2
Pennyfields TN17 179 D4
Pennyroyal Ave E6 2 A7
Penpool La DA16 13 B4
Penrith Ct ME7 55 A5
Penryn Manor 4 ME7 54 C6
Penshurst Ave DA15 13 A1
Penshurst CE Prim Sch TN11 141 A4
Penshurst Cl
Gillingham ME8 55 E2
New Barn DA3 49 D7
West Kingsdown TN15 61 E4
Penshurst Enterprise Ctr TN11 141 C4
Penshurst Pl* TN11 141 B4
Penshurst Rd Bexley DA7 13 F6
Penshurst TN3,TN11 141 A5
Poundsbridge TN11,TN3 157 E8
Penshurst Sta TN11 124 F1
Penshurst Vineyard* TN11 140 F2
Penshurst Way BR5 44 C5
Penstocks The ME15 99 D2
Pentagon Sh Ctr ME4 53 F4
Penton Ho 3 SE2 3 D4
Pentstemon Dr DA10 17 E2
Penventon Ct 3 RM18 19 A5
Pepingstraw Cl ME19 96 D7
Pepper Cl E6 1 F8
Pepper Hill DA11 35 C5
Pepperhill La DA11 35 C5
Pepy's Way ME2 52 F8
Pepys Cl 4 Dartford DA1 16 A3
Northfleet DA11 35 D5
Tilbury RM18 19 C6
Pepys Cres E16 1 A5
Pepys Rise BR6 43 F1
Perch La TN3 161 D1
Percival Rd BR6 57 B8
Percy Rd DA7 13 E5
Percy St 13 RM17 18 C8
Percy Terr TN4 159 A6
Peregrine Ct DA16 12 F6
Peregrine Rd ME19 97 A2
Peridot Ct ME15 116 E5
Peridot St E6 1 E8
Perie Row 9 ME7 54 A6
Perimeter Rd ME20 82 C3
Periton Rd SE9 11 D3
Perkins Cl DA9 16 F2
Perpins Rd SE9 12 E1
Perran Cl DA3 48 F5
Perry Gr DA1 16 A3
Perry Hall Cl BR6 44 A2
Perry Hall Prim Sch BR6 43 F3
Perry Hall Rd BR6 44 A2
Perry Hill ME3 22 C1
Perry Ho DA14 30 A3
Perry St Chatham ME4 53 E3
Chislehurst BR7 29 E2
Crayford DA1 14 E4
Maidstone ME14 99 F6
Northfleet DA11 35 F7
Perry Street Gdns BR7 29 E2
Perryfield St ME14 99 F6
Perrys La BR6,TN14 74 C6
Perth Ho 4 RM18 19 A5
Pescot Ave DA3 49 B6
Pested Bars Rd ME17 116 D5
Petchart Cl ME2 52 C3
Peter St 3 DA12 36 B8
Peterborough Gdns ME2 52 C6
Peters Cl DA16 12 E5
Petersfield TN2 160 E7
Petersfield Dr DA13 63 F1
Petersham Dr BR5 44 A6
Petersham Gdns BR5 43 F7
Peterstone Rd SE2 3 B4
Petham Court Cotts BR8 45 F4
Petham Gn ME8 55 C2
Petlands ME17 116 D5
Petrie Ho 3 SE18 12 A8
Pett La ME9 87 B7
Pett St SE18 1 E2
Petten Cl BR5 44 D1
Petten Gr BR5 44 D1
Petteridge La TN12 161 F7
Pettits Row TN12 147 D8
Pettman Cres SE28,SE18 2 D3
Petts Wood Rd BR5 43 D4
Petts Wood Sta BR5 43 C4
Petworth Rd DA6 14 A2
Peverel E6 2 A7
Peverel Dr ME14 101 A5
Peverel Gn ME8 69 D4
Peveril Ct 15 DA2 16 B1
Phalarope Way ME4 40 C2
Pheasant Cl E16 1 B7
Pheasant La ME15 116 B8
Pheasant Rd ME4 54 C2
Phelps Cl TN15 61 E4
Philimore Cl SE18 2 E1
Philip Ave BR8 45 D5
Philipot Almshouse SE9 11 F1
Philipot Path SE9 11 F1
Philippa Gdns SE9 11 D2
Phillips Cl DA1 15 B1
Phillips Ct ME8 55 B2
Philpots La TN11 125 E6
Philpott's Cross TN18 188 E2
Phineas Pett Rd SE9 11 E4
Phipps Ho 1 SE7 1 B1
Phoenix Cotts ME18 113 D6
Phoenix Ct 11 ME7 54 C6
Phoenix Dr Orpington BR2 56 D7
Wateringbury ME18 113 E7
Phoenix Ind Est ME2 53 D7
Phoenix Pk ME15 116 F4
Phoenix Pl DA1 32 D8
Phoenix Rd ME5 68 B2
Phoenix Yard Cotts ME18 97 F
Picardy Manorway DA17 4 B
Picardy Rd DA17 4 A
Picardy St DA17 4 A
Piccadilly Apartments 4 ME5 54 B
Pickering Ct 20 DA2 16 B
Pickering Ho 4 SE18 2 A
Pickering St ME15 116 B
Pickford Cl DA7 13 E
Pickford La DA7 13 E
Pickford Rd DA7 13 E
Pickforde La TN5 186 D
Pickhill Oast TN30 193 B
Pickhurst La BR2 42 A
Pickle's Way ME3 22 A
Pickmoss La TN14 76 A
Pickwick Cres ME1 53 C
Pickwick Ct SE9 28 F
Pickwick Gdns DA11 35 D
Pickwick Ho DA11 35 D
Pickwick Way BR7 29 C
Piedmont Rd SE18 2 D
Pier Approach Rd ME7 54 D
Pier Par 3 E16 2
Pier Pl ME2 40 A
Pier Rd Erith DA8 14 F
Gillingham ME7 54 E
Newham E16 2 A
Northfleet DA11 18 F
Swanscombe DA9 17 B
Pier Rd Ind Est ME7 54 D
Pier Way SE28 2 D
Pierce Mill La TN11 129 C
Piermont Pl BR1 42 E
Pigdown La TN8 139 D
Piggott's Cross TN8 123 D
Pigsdean Rd DA13 51 E
Pike Cl Bromley BR1 28 E
New Hythe ME20 82
Pikefields ME8 55 C
Pikefish La TN12,ME18 130 F
Pikey La ME19 97 E
Pile La TN12 150
Pilgrim's Way Cotts TN15 77
Pilgrims Ct Dartford DA1 16
Greenwich SE3 11
Pilgrims La RH8 88 D
Pilgrims Lakes ME17 119 E
Pilgrims Rd
Upper Halling ME2 65
Wouldham ME1 66
Pilgrims View
Sandling ME14 83
Swanscombe DA9 17 C
Pilgrims Way Boxley ME14 84
Broad Street ME14,ME17 102
Cuxton ME2 52
Dartford DA1 33
Detling ME14 85
Eccles ME20 83
Hollingbourne ME17 102
Lenham ME17 120
Thurnham ME14 101
Upper Halling ME2,ME6, ME19 65
Vigo Village ME19 80
Wrotham TN15 79
Wrotham TN15 79
Pilgrims Way E TN14 76
Pilgrims Way W TN14 75
Pilgrims' Rd DA10 17
Pilgrims' Way TN16 89
Pilgrims' Way TN14,TN15 77
Pilkington Rd BR6 57
Pillar Box La
Crouch TN11 111
Oldbury TN15 93
Pilot Rd ME1 67
Pilots Pl DA12 19
Pimp's Court Cotts ME15 115
Pimp's Court Farm Ctr ME15 115
Pimpernel Cl ME14 101
Pimpernel Way ME5 67
Pinchbeck Rd BR6 57
Pincott Rd DA6 14
Pincroft Wood DA3 49
Pine Ave DA12 36
Pine Cl Larkfield ME20 82
Swanley BR8 45
Pine Cotts ME14 99
Pine Glade BR6 56
Pine Gr Edenbridge TN8 122
Gillingham ME7 69
Maidstone ME14 100
Pine Ho 3 Chatham ME5 67
5 Maidstone ME14 100
Pine Lodge ME16 99
Pine Lodge Touring Pk ME17 101
Pine Pl ME15 99
Pine Rd ME2 52
Pine Ridge TN10 127
Pine Rise DA13 50
Pine Tree La TN15 94
Pine View TN15 95
Pinecrest Gdns BR6 57
Pinecroft DA16 13
Pinehurst Chislehurst BR7 29
Sevenoaks TN14 92
Pinehurst Wlk 4 BR6 43
Pineneedle La TN13 92
Pines Rd BR1 42
Pinesfield La ME19 80
Pinewood BR7 29

inewood Ave
Sevenoaks TN13 ... 92 D6
Sidcup DA15 ... 29 E7
inewood Cl
Orpington BR6 ... 43 D1
Paddock Wood TN12 ... 145 F6
inewood Ct TN4 ... 143 A1
inewood Dr
Chatham ME5 ... 84 D8
Orpington BR6 ... 57 E5
inewood Gdns TN4 ... 143 A1
inewood Pl DA2 ... 31 E6
inewood Rd Bexley SE2 ... 13 D8
Bromley BR2 ... 42 A5
Royal Tunbridge Wells
TN2 ... 159 D5
inkham TN12 ... 130 A5
inkham Gdns TN12 ... 130 A6
inks Hill BR8 ... 45 E4
innacle Hill DA7 ... 14 B3
innacle Hill N DA7 ... 14 B3
innacles The ME4 ... 40 C1
innell Rd SE9 ... 11 D3
innock La TN12 ... 149 E1
innock's Ave DA11 ... 36 B7
intail Cl Grain ME3 ... 27 B6
Newham E6 ... 1 E8
intails The ME4 ... 40 B1
into Way SE3 ... 11 B3
inton Hill TN5 ... 186 B3
ioneer Cotts TN11 ... 141 A1
ioneer Ct 5 DA11 ... 19 A1
ioneer Way BR8 ... 45 E6
ip's View ME3 ... 22 F5
iper's Green Rd TN16 ... 106 B7
ipers Cl TN5 ... 185 A4
ipers La TN16 ... 106 A8
ippenhall SE9 ... 12 B1
ippin Cl ME17 ... 115 B2
ippin Croft ME7 ... 69 A6
ippin Rd TN12 ... 129 F6
ippin Way ME19 ... 97 A2
ippins The DA13 ... 50 A3
irbright Cl ME5 ... 68 D2
irie St E16 ... 1 B5
irrip Cl DA12 ... 36 F6
it La TN8 ... 122 C4
itchfont La RH8 ... 104 B8
itfield DA3 ... 48 F5
itfield Cres SE28 ... 3 A5
itfield Dr DA13 ... 63 F7
itfold Cl SE12 ... 11 B1
itfold Rd SE12 ... 11 A1
itt Rd
Chartway Street ME17 ... 118 A2
Maidstone ME16 ... 99 B1
Orpington BR6 ... 57 C6
ittlesden TN30 ... 193 A7
ittlesden Pl 1 TN30 ... 193 A7
ittsmead Ave BR2 ... 42 A2
ittswood Cotts TN11 ... 128 A8
ix's La TN17 ... 192 A3
ixot Hill TN12 ... 146 B2
izien Well Rd ME18 ... 113 B7
lace Farm Ave BR6 ... 43 D1
lace La ME9 ... 70 D4
lain Rd TN12 ... 148 C4
lain The TN17 ... 177 E8
lains Ave ME15 ... 100 C1
laistow Gr BR1 ... 28 B1
laistow La BR1 ... 42 C8
laistow Sq ME14 ... 100 C6
lane Ave DA11 ... 35 D8
lane Tree Ho SE7 ... 1 D1
lane Wlk TN10 ... 127 C7
lantagenet Ho SE18 ... 1 F3
lantation Cl DA9 ... 16 F1
lantation Dr BR5 ... 44 D1
lantation La ME14 ... 101 A3
lantation Rd Erith DA8 ... 15 A6
Gillingham ME7 ... 55 A6
Hextable BR8 ... 32 A2
lantation The SE3 ... 11 A5
lat The TN8 ... 122 D1
latt CE Prim Sch TN15 ... 95 C7
latt Comm TN15 ... 95 C7
latt House La TN15 ... 79 C6
latt Ind Est TN15 ... 95 C8
latt Mill Cl TN15 ... 95 B7
latt Mill Terr TN15 ... 95 B7
latt The Frant TN3 ... 173 B1
Sutton Valence ME17 ... 134 E7
latt's Heath Prim Sch
ME17 ... 119 F2
latters The ME8 ... 69 C7
laxdale Green Rd TN15 ... 78 D7
laxtol Cl BR1 ... 42 C8
laxtol La TN15,TN11 ... 110 D8
laxtol Prim Sch TN15 ... 110 E7
laxtol Rd DA8 ... 14 A7
laystool Cl ME9 ... 71 B6
laystool Rd ME9 ... 71 A6
leasance Rd BR5 ... 44 B6
leasant Row 10 ME7 ... 54 A6
leasant Valley La
ME15 ... 115 B4
leasant View 15 Erith DA8 ... 4 E1
Orpington BR6 ... 57 C5
leasaunce Ct SE9 ... 11 F3
leasure House La
ME17 ... 135 A8
lewis Ho ME7 ... 54 E7
lomley Cl ME8 ... 69 D4
lough Cotts ME17 ... 117 D2
lough Hill TN15 ... 94 F4
lough Wents Rd ME17 ... 117 B2
lough Wlk TN8 ... 122 C3

Ploughmans Way
Chatham ME5 ... 68 A1
Gillingham ME8 ... 69 E6
Plover Cl Chatham ME5 ... 68 D1
Marlpit Hill TN8 ... 122 C3
Plover Rd ME20 ... 81 F2
Plowenders Cl ME19 ... 80 D2
Pluckley Cl ME8 ... 55 C3
Pluckley Rd TN27 ... 153 D2
Plug La DA13 ... 64 D5
Plum La SE18 ... 12 C7
Plum Tree Cotts TN18 ... 194 E8
Plum Tree La ME9 ... 86 B8
Plumcroft Prim Sch
SE18 ... 12 C8
Plumey Feather Cotts
TN6 ... 170 E3
Plummer La TN30 ... 192 F6
Plummers Croft TN13 ... 91 E6
Plumpton Wlk 9 ME15 ... 116 F6
Plumstead Common Rd
SE18 ... 12 C8
Plumstead High St SE18,
SE2 ... 2 E2
Plumstead Manor Sch
SE18 ... 12 D8
Plumstead Rd SE18 ... 2 C2
Plumstead Sta SE18 ... 2 D2
Plumtree Gr ME7 ... 69 A4
Plumtree Rd TN27 ... 150 F7
Plumtrees ME16 ... 99 A2
Plymouth Dr TN13 ... 92 C3
Plymouth Pk TN13 ... 92 C3
Plymouth Rd Bromley BR1 ... 42 B8
Newham E16 ... 1 A8
Plympton Cl 8 DA17 ... 3 E3
Plymstock Rd DA16 ... 13 C7
Poachers Cl ME5 ... 68 C5
Pochard Cl ME4 ... 40 B1
Pocket Hill TN13 ... 108 A7
Pococks Bank TN8 ... 123 C3
Podkin Wood ME5 ... 83 F8
Pointer Cl SE28 ... 3 D7
Pointer Sch The SE3 ... 11 A7
Polebrook Rd SE3 ... 11 C4
Polegate Cotts RM17 ... 17 E8
Polesden Rd TN2 ... 159 D2
Polesteeple Hill TN16 ... 72 D2
Polhill TN13,TN14 ... 75 C4
Polhill Dr ME5 ... 67 F2
Police Station Rd ME19 ... 97 C8
Pollard Cl E16 ... 1 A6
Pollard Ct ME7 ... 54 C5
Pollard Wlk DA14 ... 30 C2
Pollards Oak Cres RH8 ... 104 A3
Pollards Oak Rd RH8 ... 104 A3
Pollards Wood Hill RH8 ... 104 B5
Pollards Wood Rd RH8 ... 104 B4
Polley Cl TN2 ... 160 D7
Pollyhaugh DA4 ... 60 E7
Polperro Cl BR6 ... 43 F3
Polthorne Gr SE18 ... 2 D2
Polytechnic St 14 SE18 ... 2 A2
Pond Cl SE3 ... 11 A5
Pond Farm Rd
Hucking ME17 ... 86 D1
Oad Street ME9 ... 71 F1
Pond Hill ME3 ... 22 B6
Pond La TN15 ... 93 E2
Pond Path BR7 ... 29 B2
Pondfield La DA12 ... 37 E1
Pondfield Rd BR6 ... 57 B7
Pondwood Rise BR6 ... 43 E2
Pontefract Rd BR1 ... 28 A3
Pontoise Cl TN13 ... 91 F5
Pook La TN27 ... 168 D3
Poona Rd TN1 ... 159 B2
Pootings Rd TN8 ... 122 E7
Pope Dr TN12 ... 149 E4
Pope House La TN30 ... 183 B4
Pope Rd BR2 ... 42 D4
Pope St ME16 ... 99 C2
Pope Street Ct SE9 ... 28 F7
Popes La RH8 ... 121 A8
Popes Row Cotts TN17 ... 176 F2
Popes Wood ME14 ... 100 F6
Poplar Ave
Gravesend DA12 ... 36 C4
Orpington BR6 ... 57 B8
Poplar Cl
Hoo St Werburgh ME3 ... 40 E3
Rochester ME2 ... 52 F5
Poplar Field TN30 ... 199 D4
Poplar Gr ME16 ... 99 C5
Poplar Mount DA17 ... 4 C2
Poplar Pl SE28 ... 3 C6
Poplar Rd Rochester ME2 ... 52 E5
Wittersham TN30 ... 199 D4
Poplar Wlk DA13 ... 50 B3
Poplars Cl DA3 ... 49 C6
Poplars The DA12 ... 36 E8
Poplicans Rd ME2 ... 52 B3
Poppy Cl Erith DA17 ... 4 B4
Gillingham ME7 ... 54 E5
Maidstone ME16 ... 99 D3
Porchester Cl Hartley DA3 ... 48 F5
Loose ME15 ... 116 A6
Porchfield Cl DA12 ... 36 C6
Porcupine Cl SE9 ... 28 E6
Porrington Cl BR7 ... 43 A8
Port Ave DA9 ... 17 B1
Port Cl Chatham ME5 ... 68 B3
Maidstone ME14 ... 101 A5
Port Hill BR6 ... 74 B7
Port Rise ME4 ... 53 F3
Port Victoria Rd ME3 ... 27 C4
Porter Cl RM20 ... 17 C8
Porter Rd E6 ... 1 F7

Porters Cl TN12 ... 161 F6
Porters Wlk ME17 ... 117 E4
Porters Wood TN12 ... 161 E6
Porteus Ct DA1 ... 32 D6
Porthkerry Ave DA16 ... 13 A3
Portland Ave
Gravesend DA12 ... 36 B6
Sidcup DA15 ... 13 A1
Portland Cl TN10 ... 127 D7
Portland Cres SE9 ... 28 E6
Portland Pl 1 ME6 ... 82 A8
Portland Rd
Bromley,Mottingham SE9 ... 28 E6
Bromley,Sundridge BR1 ... 28 C3
Gillingham ME7 ... 54 E6
Gravesend DA12 ... 36 B7
Northfleet DA11 ... 18 D1
Wouldham ME1 ... 66 C4
Portland St 1 ME4 ... 54 B2
Portland Villas DA12 ... 36 B7
Portman Cl Bexley DA7 ... 13 E4
Maypole DA5 ... 31 E7
Portman Pk TN9 ... 127 C3
Portmeadow Wlk SE2 ... 3 D4
Portobello Par TN15 ... 62 A2
Portree Mews ME7 ... 54 E3
Portsdown Cl ME16 ... 99 B2
Portsea Rd RM18 ... 19 C6
Portsmouth Cl ME2 ... 52 D6
Portsmouth Mews E16 ... 1 B5
Portway Gdns SE18 ... 11 D7
Portway Rd ME3 ... 39 B7
Post Barn Rd ME4 ... 53 F2
Post Office Rd 12 TN18 ... 188 F2
Post Office Sq TN1 ... 159 A3
Postern La TN9,TN11 ... 127 E1
Postley Commercial Ctr
ME15 ... 100 A2
Postley Rd ME15 ... 100 A1
Postmill Dr ME15 ... 99 F1
Pot Kiln La TN26 ... 169 E4
Potash La TN15 ... 95 C6
Potter's La TN18 ... 189 A6
Pottery Rd Coldblow DA5 ... 31 C6
Hoo St Werburgh ME3 ... 40 D5
Potyn Ho ME1 ... 53 C4
Poulters Wood BR2 ... 56 D5
Pound Bank Cl TN15 ... 61 F2
Pound Cl BR6 ... 57 D8
Pound Court Dr BR6 ... 57 D8
Pound Green Ct 4 DA5 ... 31 A8
Pound Ho TN11 ... 128 E8
Pound La Halstead TN14 ... 74 D4
Sevenoaks TN13 ... 92 C3
Pound Park Rd SE7 ... 1 D2
Pound Pl SE9 ... 12 A1
Pound Rd TN12 ... 129 F6
Poundfield Rd TN18 ... 196 B5
Poundsbridge Hill TN11,
TN3 ... 157 D7
Poundsbridge La TN11 ... 141 D2
Pounsley Rd TN13 ... 91 E6
Pout Rd ME6 ... 81 F7
Poverest Prim Sch BR5 ... 44 A4
Poverest Rd BR5 ... 44 A4
Povey Ave ME2 ... 39 C2
Powder Mill La
Dartford DA1 ... 32 F6
Leigh TN11 ... 126 B1
Royal Tunbridge Wells
TN4 ... 159 B8
Tonbridge TN11 ... 126 E2
Powdermill Cl TN4 ... 159 C8
Powell Ave DA2 ... 33 E6
Powell Cl ME20 ... 83 A3
Power Ind Est DA8 ... 15 A6
Power Station Rd ME3 ... 27 B4
Powerscroft Rd DA14 ... 30 C2
Powis St SE18 ... 2 A3
Powlett Rd ME2 ... 39 C1
Powster Rd BR1 ... 28 B3
Powys Cl DA7 ... 13 D8
Poynder Rd RM18 ... 19 B6
Poynings Cl BR6 ... 58 C8
Poyntell Cres BR7 ... 43 D8
Poyntell Rd TN12 ... 149 F4
Pragnell Rd SE12 ... 28 B6
Prall's La TN12 ... 145 E2
Pratling St ME20 ... 83 C4
Pratts Bottom Prim Sch
TN14 ... 74 C8
Premier Bsns Ctr ME4 ... 54 C1
Premier Par ME20 ... 82 E1
Prentiss Ct SE7 ... 1 D2
Prescott Ave BR5 ... 43 B3
Presentation Ho 9 DA12 ... 36 B8
Prestbury Sq SE9 ... 28 F4
Preston Ave ME7 ... 54 E1
Preston Ct DA14 ... 29 F4
Preston Dr DA7 ... 13 D6
Preston Hall Hospl ME20 ... 82 F1
Preston Ho
Sutton at H DA4 ... 47 D7
1 Woolwich SE18 ... 2 A2
Preston Rd
Northfleet DA11 ... 35 E7
Tonbridge TN9 ... 127 A1
Preston Way ME8 ... 55 B2
Prestons Rd BR2 ... 56 A8
Prestwood Cl SE18 ... 13 A8
Pretoria Ho 4 Erith DA8 ... 14 E7
8 Maidstone ME15 ... 116 E5
Pretoria Rd Chatham ME4 ... 53 F2
Gillingham ME7 ... 54 D3
Prettymans La TN8 ... 122 F4
Pridmore Rd ME6 ... 81 F8
Priest Hill RH8 ... 104 B6
Priest's Wlk DA12 ... 37 A6

Priestdale Ct ME4 ... 53 E3
Priestfield Rd ME7 ... 54 E5
Priestfield Stad (Gillingham
FC) ME7 ... 54 E5
Priestfields ME1 ... 53 B3
Priestlands Park Rd
DA15 ... 29 F5
Priestley Dr
Lunsford ME20 ... 81 F4
Tonbridge TN10 ... 127 E7
Priestwood Rd DA13 ... 64 C5
Primmett Cl TN15 ... 61 E4
Primrose Ave ME8 ... 69 B5
Primrose Cl ME4 ... 67 E7
Primrose Dr ME20 ... 82 D1
Primrose Ho 10 ME15 ... 116 E7
Primrose Rd ME2 ... 65 E5
Primrose Terr DA12 ... 36 C7
Primrose Wlk TN12 ... 146 A5
Prince Arthur Rd ME7 ... 54 B6
Prince Charles Ave
Chatham ME5 ... 68 B4
Sutton at H DA4 ... 47 D7
Prince Consort Dr BR7 ... 43 D8
Prince Henry Rd SE7 ... 11 D7
Prince Imperial Rd
Chislehurst BR7 ... 29 B1
Woolwich SE18 ... 11 F6
Prince John Rd SE9 ... 11 E2
Prince Michael of Kent Ct
DA1 ... 15 A5
Prince Of Wales Rd SE3 ... 11 A6
Prince Phillip Lodge The
ME20 ... 82 F1
Prince Regent La E16 ... 1 C7
Prince Regent Sta E16 ... 1 C6
Prince Rupert Rd SE9 ... 11 F3
Prince's Plain BR2 ... 42 E1
Prince's St Rochester ME1 ... 53 C4
Royal Tunbridge Wells
TN2 ... 159 C3
Princes Ave Chatham ME5 ... 68 B5
Dartford DA2 ... 33 B7
Orpington BR5 ... 43 E4
Princes Cl DA14 ... 30 D5
Princes Plain Prim Sch
BR2 ... 42 E2
Princes Rd Dartford DA1 ... 32 D7
Dartford,Fleet-Downs DA1 ... 33 C7
Gravesend DA12 ... 36 C5
Hextable BR8 ... 32 A2
Princes St
Gravesend DA11 ... 19 B1
Maidstone ME14 ... 100 A5
Princes View DA1 ... 33 A7
Princes Way ME14 ... 85 A1
Princess Alice Way SE28 ... 2 D4
Princess Cl SE28 ... 3 D7
Princess Margaret Rd
RM18 ... 20 D7
Princess Mary Ave ME4 ... 54 B7
Princess Par BR6 ... 57 A7
Princess Royal University
Hospl BR6 ... 57 A6
Princess St DA7 ... 13 F4
Prinys Dr ME8 ... 69 C4
Priolo Rd SE7 ... 1 C1
Prior's Way TN8 ... 155 A6
Prioress Cres DA9 ... 17 C3
Priors Heath TN17 ... 177 C2
Priorsdean Cl ME16 ... 98 E1
Priorsford Ave BR5 ... 44 B5
Priory Ave BR5 ... 43 D3
Priory Cl Bromley BR7 ... 42 F8
Dartford DA1 ... 15 D2
East Farleigh ME15 ... 115 B8
Priory Ct 5 Dartford DA1 ... 15 D1
Gillingham ME8 ... 55 A2
Rochester ME1 ... 53 D5
Priory Ctr The DA1 ... 32 E8
Priory Dr SE2 ... 3 D1
Priory Fields DA4 ... 60 F8
Priory Gate 4 ME14 ... 100 A5
Priory Gdns Dartford DA1 ... 15 D2
* Orpington BR6 ... 44 B2
Priory Gr Aylesford ME20 ... 82 D1
Tonbridge TN9 ... 143 B8
Priory Hill DA1 ... 15 D1
Priory Ho 4 SE7 ... 11 C8
Priory Hospl Hayes Grove
The BR2 ... 56 A8
Priory La DA4 ... 46 F1
Priory Leas SE9 ... 28 E7
Priory Mews DA2 ... 33 C8
Priory Pl DA1 ... 15 D1
Priory Rd Dartford DA1 ... 15 D1
Dartford DA1 ... 15 D2
Gillingham ME8 ... 55 A2
Maidstone ME15 ... 100 A3
Rochester ME2 ... 53 A6
Tonbridge TN9 ... 143 C8
Priory Retail Pk DA1 ... 15 D2
Priory Sch The BR5 ... 44 C1
Priory St TN9 ... 143 B8
Priory Way TN30 ... 193 C7
Priory Wlk TN9 ... 143 B8
Pristling La TN12 ... 165 B8
Pritchard Ct ME7 ... 54 C3
Progress Est The ME15 ... 117 A4
Prospect Ave ME2 ... 53 B8
Prospect Cl DA17 ... 4 A2
Prospect Cotts
Lamberhurst TN3 ... 176 A3
Pratt's Bottom BR6 ... 58 C2
Prospect Gr DA12 ... 36 D8
Prospect Pk TN4 ... 142 F1
Prospect Pl Bromley BR2 ... 42 B6
Collier Street TN12 ... 131 C2

Prospect Pl *continued*
Dartford DA1 ... 15 F1
Gravesend DA12 ... 36 D8
Grays RM17 ... 18 B8
Maidstone ME16 ... 99 E3
Prospect Rd
Royal Tunbridge Wells
TN4 ... 158 F8
Royal Tunbridge
Wells,Camden Park TN2 ... 159 C3
Sevenoaks TN13 ... 92 C4
Prospect Row
Chatham ME4 ... 54 A3
Chatham ME7 ... 54 A6
Prospect Vale SE18 ... 1 E2
Prospero Ho 7 DA17 ... 4 A1
Provender Way ME14 ... 100 E5
Providence Chapel
TN12 ... 148 C6
Providence Cotts
Groombridge TN3 ... 171 C7
Higham ME3 ... 38 B2
Providence Pl TN27 ... 151 A7
Providence St DA9 ... 17 A2
Prudhoe Ct 27 DA2 ... 16 B1
Pucknells Cl BR8 ... 45 C8
Pudding La
Maidstone ME14 ... 99 F4
Seal TN15 ... 92 F6
Pudding Rd ME8 ... 69 F8
Puddingcake La TN17 ... 192 C5
Puddledock La
Hextable BR8,DA2 ... 31 F2
Toy's Hill TN16 ... 106 A3
Puffin Rd ME3 ... 27 B5
Pullington Cotts TN17 ... 190 E6
Pullman Mews SE12 ... 28 B5
Pullman Pl SE9 ... 11 E2
Pump Cl ME19 ... 81 D1
Pump La Chelsfield BR6 ... 59 B5
Gillingham ME7,ME8 ... 55 D3
Pump Terr TN1 ... 159 B4
Punch Croft DA3 ... 62 E7
Purbeck Rd ME4 ... 53 E2
Purcell Ave TN10 ... 127 F6
Purfleet By-Pass RM19 ... 16 D8
Purland Rd SE28 ... 2 F4
Purneys Rd SE9 ... 11 D3
Purrett Rd SE18 ... 2 F1
Purser Way ME7 ... 54 C7
Pursey Cl TN15 ... 61 E4
Puttenden Rd TN11 ... 110 F3
Pym Orch TN16 ... 90 C3
Pynham Cl SE2 ... 3 B3
Pyrus Cl ME5 ... 84 A8

Q

Quadrant The DA7 ... 13 D7
Quaggy Wlk SE3 ... 11 A3
Quaker Cl TN13 ... 92 D4
Quaker Dr TN17 ... 179 D6
Quaker La TN17 ... 179 D6
Quaker's Hall La TN13 ... 92 C5
Quakers Cl DA3 ... 48 E6
Quantock Cl TN2 ... 159 D5
Quantock Rd DA1 ... 14 E5
Quarries The ME17 ... 116 C4
Quarry Bank TN9 ... 143 A7
Quarry Cotts
Rockrobin TN5 ... 184 D7
Sevenoaks TN13 ... 92 A4
Quarry Hill TN15 ... 92 D4
Quarry Hill Par 3 TN9 ... 143 B8
Quarry Hill Rd
Borough Green TN15 ... 94 F6
Tonbridge TN9 ... 143 B8
Quarry Rd
Maidstone ME15 ... 100 A2
Royal Tunbridge Wells
TN1 ... 159 B5
Quarry Rise TN9 ... 143 A7
Quarry Sq ME14 ... 100 A5
Quarry Wood Ind Est
ME20 ... 98 E8
Quay La DA9 ... 17 B3
Quayside ME4 ... 54 B8
Quebec Ave TN16 ... 89 D1
Quebec Cotts 9 TN16 ... 89 D1
Quebec Ho* TN16 ... 89 D1
Quebec Rd RM18 ... 19 A5
Quebec Sq 10 TN16 ... 89 D1
Queen Anne Ave BR2 ... 42 A6
Queen Anne Gate DA7 ... 13 D4
Queen Anne Rd ME14 ... 100 B4
Queen Borough Gdns
BR7 ... 29 D2
Queen Elizabeth Military
Hospl The SE18 ... 11 E7
Queen Elizabeth Sq
ME15 ... 116 D6
Queen Mary's Hospl
DA14 ... 30 A2
Queen Mother Ct The
ME1 ... 53 B4
Queen St Bexley DA7 ... 13 F4
Chatham ME4 ... 54 A4
Erith DA8 ... 14 E8
Gravesend DA12 ... 19 B1
Kings Hill ME18 ... 97 B3
Paddock Wood TN12 ... 146 D7
Rochester ME1 ... 53 C4
Sandhurst TN18 ... 196 B5

Queen's Ave
Maidstone ME16 .....99 D5
Snodland ME6 .....82 A8
Queen's Dr TN14 .....92 C7
Queen's Farm Rd DA12 ...37 E7
Queens Gdns TN4 .....159 B6
Queen's Mews 12 TN18 .189 A2
Queen's Pas BR7 .....29 B2
Queen's Rd Bexley DA16 ...13 B5
Bromley BR1 .....42 A7
Chatham ME5 .....54 D1
Chislehurst BR7 .....29 B2
Gillingham ME7 .....54 C4
Hawkhurst TN18 .....189 A2
Maidstone ME16 .....99 C4
Royal Tunbridge Wells TN4 .....159 B6
Snodland ME6 .....82 A8
Queensborough Ind Pk RM20 .....17 A8
Queendown Ave ME8 ....69 D5
Queens Cotts TN5 .....184 E6
Queens Ct
Edenbridge TN8 .....122 D1
Gillingham ME8 .....70 A8
11 Hawkhurst TN18 .....189 A2
1 Sidcup DA14 .....30 A4
Queens Gate Gdns BR7 ...43 D8
Queens Gdns DA2 .....33 B7
Queens Ho ME16 .....99 B3
Queens Rd Erith DA8 .....14 E8
Gravesend DA12 .....36 C5
Queens Way ME14 .....85 A1
Queenscroft Rd SE9 .....11 D1
Queensland Ct RM18 .....18 F5
Queensland Ho 2 E16 ....2 A5
Queensway
Allhallows-on-S ME3 .....9 D3
Hayes BR2,BR4 .....56 A6
Orpington BR5 .....43 C3
Queenswood Rd
Kit's Coty ME20 .....83 D7
Sidcup DA15 .....12 F1
Quentins Rd TN16 .....73 B3
Quern The ME15 .....99 E1
Quernmore Cl BR1 .....28 A2
Quernmore Rd BR1 .....28 A2
Quested Way ME17 .....119 C6
Questor DA1 .....32 F6
Quickrells Ave ME3 .....22 B5
Quickthorn Cres ME5 .....67 E5
Quiet Nook BR2 .....56 D7
Quilter Rd BR5 .....44 D1
Quilter St SE18 .....2 F1
Quincewood Gdns TN10 .127 B7
Quinion Cl ME5 .....84 A8
Quinnell St ME8 .....55 E1
Quixote Cres ME2 .....39 B1

R

Rabbits Rd DA4 .....47 E7
Rablus Pl DA4 .....46 F3
Racefield Cl DA12 .....37 E1
Rackham Cl DA16 .....13 B5
Radburn Pl DA10 .....17 E2
Radfield Way DA15 .....29 D8
Radland Rd E16 .....1 A7
Radleigh Gdns ME1 .....53 E1
Radley Ho 13 SE2 .....3 D4
Radnor Ave DA16 .....13 B2
Radnor Cl Chislehurst BR7 .29 E2
Maidstone ME14 .....99 E7
Radnor Cres SE18 .....13 A7
Radzan Cl DA2 .....31 E6
Raeburn Ave DA1 .....15 B2
Raeburn Cl TN10 .....127 E6
Raeburn Rd DA15 .....12 E1
Rafford Way BR1 .....42 B6
Rag Hill TN16 .....88 E6
Rag Hill Cl TN16 .....88 E6
Rag Hill Rd TN16 .....88 E6
Raggatt Pl ME15 .....100 B2
Ragge Way TN15 .....92 F7
Raggleswood BR7 .....43 A8
Raglan Ct SE12 .....11 A2
Raglan Prim Sch BR2 ....42 D5
Raglan Rd Bromley BR2 ...42 C5
Erith DA17 .....3 F2
Woolwich SE18 .....2 C1
Ragstone Ct ME20 .....98 C8
Ragstone Rd ME15 .....101 A2
Railway Cotts
Cowden TN8 .....155 D8
Marden TN12 .....148 D6
Railway Pl Erith DA17 .....4 A3
21 Gravesend DA12 .....19 B1
Railway Sidings The DA13 .....50 A4
Railway St Chatham ME4 ...53 F4
Gillingham ME7 .....54 D6
Northfleet DA11 .....18 A2
Railway St Ind Pk ME7 ...54 D6
Railway Terr TN16 .....89 D1
Rainham Cl
Maidstone ME15 .....100 A1
Sidcup SE9 .....12 E1
Rainham Mark Gram Sch ME8 .....55 D2
Rainham Rd ME5 .....54 C3
Rainham Sch for Girls ME8 .....69 C8
Rainham Sh Ctr 2 ME8 ....55 F1
Rainham Sta ME8 .....55 F1
Rainton Rd SE7 .....1 A1
Raleigh Cl Chatham ME5 ..68 A6
Erith DA8 .....14 F8
Raleigh Mews 6 BR6 ....57 F5
Ramac Ind Est SE7 .....1 B1
Ramac Way SE7 .....1 B1
Ramillies Cl ME5 .....68 A6
Ramillies Rd DA15 .....13 B1
Rammell Mews TN17 ...179 D4
Rampion Cl ME14 .....100 E5
Ramsden Cl BR5 .....44 C1
Ramsden La TN17 .....190 F4
Ramsden Rd Erith DA8 ....14 D7
Orpington BR5 .....44 B1
Ramsgate Cl E16 .....1 B5
Ramslye Rd TN4 .....172 E8
Ramus Wood Ave BR6 ....57 E5
Rance Ho 11 SE18 .....1 E2
Rancliffe Gdns SE9 .....11 E3
Randall Cl DA8 .....14 C8
Randall Hill Rd TN15 .....78 F3
Randall Rd ME4 .....53 E1
Randall St ME14 .....99 F6
Randalls Row ME15 .....115 F5
Randle's La TN14 .....74 D5
Randolph App E16 .....1 C7
Randolph Cl DA7 .....14 C4
Randolph Cotts ME2 .....39 B1
Randolph Ho ME7 .....54 C5
Randolph Rd
Gillingham ME7 .....54 C5
Orpington BR2 .....42 F1
Ranelagh Gdns DA11 .....35 F8
Range Rd DA12 .....36 E8
Rangefield Rd BR1 .....28 A3
Rangeworth Pl DA15 .....29 F5
Rankine Rd TN2 .....159 D7
Ranleigh Gdns DA7 .....13 F7
Ranmore Path BR5 .....44 A5
Ranscombe Cl ME2 .....52 D5
Ranscombe Farm Cotts ME2 .....52 C4
Ransom Rd 1 SE7 .....1 C1
Ranters La TN17 .....177 C7
Ranworth Cl DA7,DA8 .....14 E5
Raphael Ave RM18 .....19 B7
Raphael Ct TN11 .....126 E7
Raphael Rd DA12 .....36 D8
Rashleigh Way DA4 .....47 C5
Ratcliffe Cl SE12 .....28 A8
Ratcliffe Highway
High Halstow ME3 .....24 D5
Hoo St Werburgh ME3 .....40 C6
Rathmore Rd
Gravesend DA11 .....36 B8
Greenwich SE7 .....1 B1
Raven Cl ME20 .....82 A1
Raven's Hoe DA14 .....30 A3
Ravens Dane Cl ME15 ...101 A1
Ravens Knowle ME1 .....66 D4
Ravens Way SE12 .....11 A2
Ravens Wood Sch for Boys BR2 .....56 D7
Ravensbourne Coll of Design & Communication BR7 ..28 F3
Ravensbourne Ct 23 BR5 .44 D1
Ravensbourne Rd
Bromley BR1 .....42 A6
Crayford DA1 .....15 A4
Ravensbourne Sch The BR2 .....42 B5
Ravensbury Rd BR5 .....44 A5
Ravenscourt Rd BR5 .....44 B7
Ravenscroft Cl 5 E16 .....1 A8
Ravenscroft Cres SE9 ....28 F5
Ravenscroft Rd E16 .....1 A8
Ravenshill BR7 .....43 B8
Ravensleigh Gdns BR1 ...28 B3
Ravensquay Bsns Ctr BR5 .....44 B4
Ravenswood DA5 .....30 E7
Ravenswood Ave
Rochester ME2 .....39 B1
Royal Tunbridge Wells TN2 .....159 D6
Ravensworth Rd SE9 .....28 F4
Ravine Gr SE18 .....12 E8
Rawdon Rd ME15 .....100 A3
Rawlings Cl 3 BR6 .....57 F5
Rawsthorne Cl E16 .....1 F5
Ray Lamb Way DA8 .....15 B7
Rayfield Cl BR2 .....42 E3
Rayfield Ct ME6 .....66 B1
Rayford Cl DA1 .....15 C2
Rayleas Cl SE18 .....12 B6
Rayleigh Cl ME16 .....99 D7
Rayleigh Ho 2 ME15 ....116 D8
Rayleigh Rd E16 .....1 B5
Raymer Rd ME14 .....100 B8
Raymere Gdns SE18 .....12 E7
Raymond Postgate Ct 5 SE28 .....3 B6
Raynehurst Jun & Inf Sch DA12 .....36 F5
Rayners Ct DA11 .....18 B1
Raynham Villas TN12 ....132 A4
Rays Hill DA4 .....47 C4
Read Way DA12 .....36 E3
Reader's Bridge Rd TN30 .....182 E4
Readers Ct ME18 .....114 A8
Reading Ho 4 ME15 .....116 F5
Readscroft Rd ME8 .....69 D5
Rebecca Ct DA14 .....30 B4
Recreation Ave ME6 .....82 A8
Recreation Cl ME14 .....100 B6
Recreation Ground Rd TN30 .....193 B7
Rectory Bsns Ctr 2 DA14 .....30 B4
Rectory Cl Crayford DA1 ...14 E3
Sidcup DA14 .....30 B4
Snodland ME6 .....82 A8
Wouldham ME1 .....66 C5
Rectory Ct 3 RM17 .....18 D8
Rectory Dr TN3 .....142 D3
Rectory Field Cres SE7 ...11 C7
Rectory Fields TN17 .....179 D5
Rectory Grange ME1 .....53 C2
Rectory La Brasted TN16 ...90 C3
Harrietsham ME17 .....119 E5
Ightham TN15 .....94 C5
Maidstone ME16 .....99 A1
Sevenoaks TN13 .....92 C1
Sidcup DA14 .....30 C4
Sutton Valence ME17 .....134 C6
Sutton Valence ME17 .....134 F7
Titsey TN16 .....88 E4
Rectory La N ME19 .....81 E2
Rectory La S ME19 .....81 E1
Rectory Mdw DA13 .....35 A2
Rectory Paddock Sch BR5 .....44 C7
Rectory Park Rd TN12 ..163 A2
Rectory Pl SE18 .....2 A2
Rectory Rd Cliffe ME3 .....22 A3
4 Grays RM17 .....18 D8
New Ash Green TN15 .....63 C5
Orpington BR2 .....56 D3
Swanscombe DA10 .....34 E8
West Tilbury RM18 .....19 D8
Reculver Wlk ME15 .....116 F7
Red Barracks Rd 4 SE18 ..1 F2
Red Cedars Rd BR6 .....43 E2
Red Hill Chislehurst BR7 ...29 B3
Red Hill ME18 .....97 F1
Red Hill Prim Sch BR7 ...29 B3
Red Ho* DA6 .....13 E3
Red Ho The RH8 .....104 C5
Red House Gdns ME18 ..113 C7
Red House La DA6 .....13 E3
Red La Limpsfield RH8 ...121 B7
Oxted RH8 .....104 B2
Red Lion Cl BR5 .....44 C3
Red Lion La SE18 .....12 A6
Red Lion Pl SE18 .....12 A6
Red Lion Sq TN15 .....110 E8
Red Lodge Cres DA5 .....31 E5
Red Lodge Rd DA5 .....31 D5
Red Oak TN18 .....194 E8
Red Oak Cl BR6 .....57 B8
Red Oast Cotts TN5 .....187 C3
Red Robin Cotts ME9 .....71 B6
Red St DA13 .....35 B2
Redbank ME19 .....81 E2
Redbourne Dr SE28 .....3 D7
Redbridge Cl ME5 .....68 C4
Redcliffe La ME14 .....100 B7
Redding Cl DA2 .....33 E6
Redding Ho SE18 .....1 E3
Reddy Rd DA8 .....14 F8
Rede Court Rd ME2 .....52 E8
Rede Wood Rd ME16 .....98 F3
Redfern Ave ME7 .....54 E5
Redfern Ho ME2 .....65 F5
Redgate Dr BR2 .....56 B8
Redhill Rd DA3 .....62 F6
Redhill Wood DA3 .....63 A7
Redhouse Rd TN16 .....88 C6
Redland Shaw ME4 .....53 E1
Redlands Rd TN13 .....91 F3
Redlane Cotts RH8 .....104 B2
Redleaf Cl Erith DA17 .....14 A8
Royal Tunbridge Wells TN2 .....159 D6
Redmans Ind Est RM18 ...20 A8
Redmans La BR6,TN14 .....59 E4
Redpoll Way DA18 .....3 D3
Redpoll Wlk TN12 .....146 A5
Redruth Manor 3 ME7 ....54 C6
Redsells Cl ME15 .....101 A1
Redshank Rd ME4 .....40 B1
Redstart Cl E6 .....1 E8
Redvers Rd ME4 .....54 A2
Redwall La ME15,ME17 ..132 C6
Redwell Gr ME18 .....97 C2
Redwell La TN15 .....94 B4
Redwing Cl ME20 .....82 A2
Redwing Path SE28 .....2 D4
Redwing Rd ME5 .....68 B7
Redwings La TN2 .....144 E2
Redwood Cl Chatham ME5 .68 B2
Sidcup DA15 .....30 A7
Redwood Ct DA1 .....16 A1
Redwood Pk TN12 .....145 A5
Reed Ave BR6 .....57 E7
Reed Cl Eltham SE12 .....11 A2
New Hythe ME20 .....82 A5
Newham E16 .....1 A8
Reed Court Cotts TN12 ..132 A5
Reed Court Farm Trail* TN12 .....132 A5
Reed St ME3 .....22 B6
Reedham Cres ME3 .....39 C7
Reeds La TN11 .....110 E5
Reeves Cl TN12 .....149 E4
Reeves Cres BR8 .....45 D6
Reeves Ct Ditton ME19 ....82 A1
Fordcombe TN3 .....157 B5
Reeves Rd SE18 .....12 B8
Reeves Terr TN5 .....186 E1
Reflection The E16 .....2 B4
Reform Rd ME4 .....54 B2
Regency Cl
Gillingham ME8 .....69 C3
West Kingsdown TN15 .....61 E4
Regency Hall 21 TN2 ....159 A2
Regency Ho TN2 .....159 B2
Regency Way DA6 .....13 E4
Regent Dr ME15 .....116 A8
Regent Pl TN2 .....159 D3
Regent Rd ME7 .....54 C4
Regent Sq DA17 .....4 B2
Regent St TN17 .....191 E4
Regent Way ME18 .....97 C3
Regent's Pl SE3 .....11 A5
Regents Ct 3 DA11 .....19 B1
Regents Dr BR2 .....56 D5
Regina Ct TN4 .....158 F4
Reginald Ave ME2 .....52 C3
Reginald Rd ME16 .....99 E3
Reidhaven Rd SE18 .....2 E2
Reigate Rd BR1,SE12 .....28 A5
Reinckendorf Ave SE9 ....12 D1
Reinden Gr ME15 .....100 F1
Rembrandt Cl TN10 .....127 E6
Rembrandt Dr DA11 .....35 E5
Remington Rd E6 .....1 E7
Rendlebury Ho 12 SE18 ....1 F2
Renfrew Cl E6 .....2 A6
Rennets Cl SE9 .....12 E2
Rennets Wood Ho SE9 ...12 D2
Rennets Wood Rd SE9 ...12 D2
Renovation The E16 .....2 B4
Renown Rd ME5 .....68 C2
Renshaw Cl 7 DA17 .....13 F8
Renton Dr BR5 .....44 D2
Repository Rd SE18 .....1 F1
Repton Rd BR6 .....58 A6
Repton Way ME5 .....67 F4
Reservoir Cl DA9 .....17 C1
Resolution Cl ME5 .....68 A6
Resolution Wlk SE18 .....1 F3
Restavon Cvn Pk TN16 ....73 B3
Restharrow Rd ME14 ....100 E4
Restharrow Way ME4 ....40 C1
Restmore Cl ME3 .....22 A4
Restons Cres SE9 .....12 E1
Retreat Cvn Pk The ME18 .....113 D6
Retreat The Grays RM17 ...18 B8
Orpington BR6 .....58 B4
Platt TN15 .....95 D8
Revell Rise SE18 .....12 F8
Revenge Rd ME5 .....84 C8
Reventlow Rd SE9 .....29 C7
Reynard Cl BR1 .....43 A6
Reynolah Gdns 3 SE7 .....1 B1
Reynolds Cl TN10 .....127 E6
Reynolds Fields ME3 .....38 C6
Reynolds La TN4 .....158 F7
Reynolds Pl SE3 .....11 B7
Rhode St ME4 .....54 A4
Rhodes Ho 5 ME5 .....54 C2
Rhodewood Cl ME15 ....101 A1
Rhododendron Ave DA13 .64 A2
Ribblesdale Rd DA2 .....33 C7
Ribston Cl BR2 .....42 F1
Ribston Gdns TN12 .....145 F7
Ricardo Path 5 SE28 .....3 C5
Rice Par BR5 .....43 D4
Richard Beau Nash Apartments 4 TN1 ....159 B4
Richard Cl SE18 .....1 E2
Richard House Dr E16 .....1 E7
Richard Neve Ho SE18 ....2 E2
Richard St Chatham ME4 ...53 F4
Rochester ME1 .....53 C3
Richard's Cl TN11 .....124 F2
Richardson Cl 7 DA9 ....17 A2
Richardson Rd TN4 .....159 A5
Richborough Cl BR5 .....44 D5
Richborough Drive ME2 ...39 A1
Richings Ho BR5 .....44 A8
Richmer Rd DA8 .....15 A7
Richmond Cl
Biggin Hill TN16 .....88 B8
Chatham ME5 .....68 B4
Rochester ME2 .....39 F1
Richmond Ct Bromley BR1 .28 B1
Sevenoaks TN13 .....92 B4
Richmond Dr DA12 .....36 E6
Richmond Inf Sch ME7 ....54 C6
Richmond Pl
Royal Tunbridge Wells TN2 .....159 B1
Woolwich SE18 .....2 C2
Richmond Rd
Gillingham ME7 .....54 C7
1 Grays RM17 .....18 C8
Richmond Way ME15 ....116 A8
Richmount Gdns SE3 .....11 A4
Ricketts Hill Rd TN16 .....88 E7
Rickyard Path SE9 .....11 E3
Riddlesdale Ave TN4 ....159 A6
Riddons Rd SE12 .....28 C4
Rideout St SE18 .....1 F2
Rider Cl DA15 .....12 E1
Ridge Ave DA1 .....14 F1
Ridge Cl SE28 .....2 D4
Ridge La DA13 .....64 A2
Ridge Meadow Prim Sch ME5 .....67 F6
Ridge The
Groombridge TN3 .....171 A6
Orpington BR6 .....57 D8
Sidcup DA5 .....30 F8
Ridge View Sch TN10 ....127 D5
Ridge Way Crayford DA1 ...14 F1
Marlpit Hill TN8 .....122 D4
Ridgebrook Rd SE3 .....11 D4
Ridgecroft Cl DA5 .....31 C7
Ridgelands TN3 .....142 C4
Ridgeway Dartford DA2 ....33 E3
Ridgeway *continued*
Hayes BR2 .....56 A
Hurst Green TN19 .....194 A
Pembury TN2 .....160 D
The Moor TN18 .....194 E
Ridgeway Ave DA12 .....36 E
Ridgeway Bglws DA12 ....37 F
Ridgeway Cres
Orpington BR6 .....57 E
Tonbridge TN10 .....127 D
Ridgeway Crescent Gdns BR6 .....57 E
Ridgeway Dr BR1 .....28 E
Ridgeway E DA15 .....12 F
Ridgeway The
Chatham ME4 .....67 E
Gillingham ME7 .....54 C
Shorne DA12 .....37 E
Tonbridge TN10 .....127 D
Ridgeway W DA15 .....12 E
Ridgewaye The TN4 .....143 E
Ridgewood DA3 .....49 C
Ridgway ME16 .....99 E
Ridgwell Rd E16 .....1 C
Ridgy Field Cl TN15 .....79 A
Riding La TN11 .....109 D
Riding Pk TN11 .....126 D
Ridings The
Biggin Hill TN16 .....72 B
Paddock Wood TN12 .....146 A
Royal Tunbridge Wells TN2 .....159 B
Ridlands Gr RH8 .....104 E
Ridlands La RH8 .....104 E
Ridlands Rise RH8 .....104 E
Ridley Ct BR6 .....57 C
Ridley Rd Bexley DA16 .....13 B
Bromley BR2 .....42 A
Rochester ME1 .....53 B
Riefield Rd SE9 .....12 C
Riggall Ct ME2 .....52 A
Riggs Way TN15 .....78 B
Ring Cl BR1 .....28 B
Ringden Ave TN12 145
Ringer's Ct 5 BR1 .....42 A
Ringer's Rd BR1 .....42 A
Ringle Gn TN18 196
Ringlestone Cres ME14 ...99
Ringlestone Rd ME17 ...103 B
Ringlet Cl E16 .....1 B
Ringlet Rd ME4 .....40 B
Ringmer Way BR1 42
Rings Hill TN11 126
Ringshall Rd BR5 44
Ringside TN8 122
Ringwood Ave BR6 58
Ringwood Cl ME8 69
Ringwood Rd ME15 116
Ripley Cl BR1 42
Ripley Rd Erith DA17 4
Newham E16 1
Ripleys Market DA1 32
Ripon Cl ME8 55
Ripon Rd SE18 12
Rippersley Rd DA16 13
Rippolson Rd SE18 2
Risden La TN18 195
Rise The Chatham ME4 54
Crayford DA1 14
Gillingham ME7 69
Gravesend DA12 36
Rochester ME1 53
Sevenoaks TN13 108
Sidcup DA5 30
Risedale Rd DA7 14
Riseden Rd TN5 184
Ritch Rd ME6 81
Ritter St SE18 12
Ritz Blgs TN1 159
Rivendell Cl ME3 27
River Bank Cl 8 ME15 ...100
River Cl ME15 115
River Cotts BR5 44
River Ct TN13 91
River Dr ME2 52
River Lawn Rd TN9 127
River Park View BR6 44
River Rd IG11 3
River St 6 ME7 54
River View Gillingham ME8 .55
Greenwich SE7 1
Maidstone ME15 99
River View Cl 6 ME4 53
River Way ME20 82
River Wlk TN9 127
Riverbank Rd BR1 28
Riverdale Est TN9 143
Riverdale Rd Erith DA8 4
Sidcup DA5 13
Woolwich SE18 2
Riverhead Cl ME16 99
Riverhead Ho TN13 91
Riverhead Inf Sch TN13 ..91
Riverhead Mews TN13 91
Riverhill TN15 108
Riverhill Cotts TN15 108
Riverhill House Gdns* TN15 108
Riverhope Mans SE18 1
Rivermead ME4 40
Rivermead Sch ME7 54
Rivers Cl ME18 113
Rivers Wlk ME17 120
Riversdale DA11 35
Riverside Edenbridge TN8 .122
Eynsford DA4 60
Greenwich SE7 1
Riverside Cl BR5 44

iverside Cotts TN14 ... 59 F1
iverside Ct
2 Orpington BR5 ... 44 C4
Tonbridge TN9 ... 127 C1
iverside Ctry Pk & Visitor
Ctr* ME7 ... 55 D5
iverside East Rd ME4 ... 40 C1
iverside Ind Est DA1 ... 15 E2
iverside Pk ME16 ... 115 A8
iverside Rd DA14 ... 30 E6
iverside Ret Pk TN14 ... 92 C8
iverside Way DA1 ... 15 E2
iverston Sch SE12 ... 11 A2
iverview 6 DA1 ... 16 A3
iverview Ct 16 Erith DA17 ... 4 A1
Stone DA9 ... 16 F1
iverview Hts SE18 ... 12 B7
iverview Inf Sch DA12 ... 36 E4
iverview Jun Sch DA12 ... 36 E4
iverview Rd DA9 ... 17 A2
iverwood La BR7 ... 43 D8
ixon Ho SE18 ... 12 B8
oach St ME2 ... 53 A7
oan Ct ME2 ... 52 F8
obert Napier Sch The
ME7 ... 54 E3
obert St Newham E16 ... 2 B5
Woolwich SE18 ... 2 D2
oberton Dr BR1 ... 42 C8
oberts Cl Eltham SE9 ... 29 D7
8 Orpington BR5 ... 44 C4
oberts Ho SE18 ... 11 E6
oberts Mews BR6 ... 44 A1
oberts Orchard Rd
ME16 ... 98 F3
oberts Rd Erith DA17 ... 4 A1
Gillingham ME8 ... 69 E8
Snodland ME6 ... 81 F8
obertson Ho SE18 ... 11 F6
obin Cres E6 ... 1 D8
obin Ct 6 ME1 ... 53 D4
obin Hill Dr BR7 ... 28 E2
obin Ho 5 ME16 ... 99 E4
obin Hood Gn BR5 ... 44 A4
obin Hood La
Bexley DA6 ... 13 E2
Chatham ME5 ... 67 D1
obin Hood Lane (Lower)
ME5 ... 67 F2
obin Hood Lane (Upper)
ME5 ... 67 E1
obin Way BR5 ... 44 B6
obina Cl DA6 ... 13 D3
obina Ct BR8 ... 46 A5
obinia Ave DA11 ... 35 D8
obins Ave ME17 ... 120 C5
obins Cl ME17 ... 120 C4
obins Ct Lewisham SE12 ... 28 C5
Maidstone ME14 ... 100 B7
obins Gr BR4 ... 56 A7
obinwood Dr TN15 ... 92 F8
obson Cl E6 ... 1 E7
obson Dr Aylesford ME20 ... 82 D2
Hoo St Werburgh ME3 ... 40 D6
obson Ho SE18 ... 12 A7
obyn Cotts TN26 ... 183 E8
obyns Croft 6 DA11 ... 35 E5
obyns Way
Edenbridge TN8 ... 138 D8
Sevenoaks TN13 ... 91 F5
ocfort Rd ME6 ... 82 A8
ochdale Ho TN1 ... 159 C5
ochdale Rd
Royal Tunbridge Wells
TN1 ... 159 C6
Woolwich SE2 ... 3 B2
ochester Airport ME1,
ME5 ... 67 C6
ochester Airport Ind Est
ME1 ... 67 C5
ochester Ave
Bromley BR1 ... 42 B7
Rochester ME1 ... 53 C4
ochester Castle* ME1 ... 53 C6
ochester Cath* ME1 ... 53 C6
ochester Cl 1 DA15 ... 13 B1
ochester Cres ME3 ... 40 D6
ochester Ct ME2 ... 53 E8
ochester Dr DA5 ... 14 A1
ochester Gate ME1 ... 53 D5
ochester Gram Sch for Girls
The ME1 ... 53 C2
ochester Ho 1 ME15 ... 116 D7
ochester Ind Coll ME1 ... 53 D4
ochester Rd
Burham ME1 ... 66 E2
Chalk DA12 ... 37 B6
Chatham ME1,ME5 ... 67 C4
Dartford DA1 ... 33 A8
Pratling Street ME20 ... 83 B4
Rochester ME2 ... 52 D4
Tonbridge TN10 ... 127 D4
ochester St ME4 ... 53 E3
ochester Sta ME1 ... 53 D5
ochester Way
Dartford DA1 ... 31 F8
Eltham SE9 ... 12 B4
Eltham,Kidbrooke SE3,SE9 ... 11 D4
ock Ave ME7 ... 54 C3
ock Cotts TN3 ... 173 B1
ock Farm Oasthouse
ME18 ... 113 C6
ock Hill BR6 ... 59 B4
ock Hill Rd TN27 ... 137 E2
ock Rd
Borough Green TN15 ... 94 F7
Maidstone ME14 ... 100 A6
ock Villa Rd TN1 ... 159 A4
Rockdale TN13 ... 92 B2
Rockdale Rd TN13 ... 92 C2
Rockliffe Manor Prim Sch
SE18 ... 12 F8
Rockmount Rd SE18 ... 2 F1
Rocks Cl ME19 ... 98 A6
Rocks Hill TN17 ... 166 A4
Rocks Rd The ME19 ... 98 B6
Rocky Hill ME16 ... 99 E4
Rocky Hill Terr 2 ME16 ... 99 E4
Rodeo Cl DA8 ... 15 B6
Roding Rd E6 ... 2 B8
Rodmell Rd TN2 ... 159 A2
Rodney Ave TN10 ... 127 E4
Rodney Gdns BR4 ... 56 A6
Rodway Rd BR1 ... 42 B8
Roebourne Way E16 ... 2 A5
Roebuck Ho ME1 ... 53 E5
Roebuck Rd ME1 ... 53 C5
Roedean Cl BR6 ... 58 B6
Roedean Rd TN2 ... 159 A1
Roehampton Cl DA12 ... 36 E8
Roehampton Dr BR7 ... 29 C2
Roethorne Gdns TN30 ... 193 B8
Roffen Rd ME1 ... 53 C2
Rogers Ct BR8 ... 46 A5
Rogers Rough Rd TN17 ... 177 B2
Rogers Wood La DA3 ... 62 B6
Rogersmead TN30 ... 193 A7
Rogley Hill TN27 ... 181 B6
Rogues Hill TN11 ... 141 C3
Rokesby Cl DA16 ... 12 D5
Rolinsden Way BR2 ... 56 D6
Rollesby Way SE28 ... 3 C7
Rolleston Ave BR5 ... 43 B3
Rolleston Cl BR5 ... 43 B2
Rollo Rd BR8 ... 31 F1
Rolvenden Ave ME8 ... 55 C3
Rolvenden Gdns BR1 ... 28 D1
Rolvenden Hill TN17 ... 192 C5
Rolvenden Prim Sch
TN17 ... 191 E3
Rolvenden Rd
Rochester ME2 ... 39 C2
Tenterden TN30 ... 192 E7
Rolvenden Sta* TN17 ... 192 D6
Roman Cl ME5 ... 67 D1
Roman Hts ME14 ... 100 C6
Roman Rd
Edenbridge TN8 ... 138 D5
Northfleet DA11 ... 35 C5
Snodland ME6 ... 81 F8
Roman Sq SE28 ... 3 A5
Roman Villa Rd DA2,DA4 ... 33 C2
Roman Way Crayford DA1 ... 14 E2
Rochester ME2 ... 52 F4
Romany Ct ME5 ... 54 D1
Romany Rd ME8 ... 55 C2
Romany Rise BR5 ... 43 C1
Romden Rd
Smarden,Haffenden Quarter
TN27 ... 169 B8
Smarden,Romden TN27 ... 153 D1
Rome Terr ME4 ... 53 F4
Romero Sq SE3 ... 11 C3
Romford Rd TN2 ... 160 F7
Romney Cl ME14 ... 101 A3
Romney Dr BR1 ... 28 D1
Romney Gdns DA7 ... 13 F6
Romney Pl ME15 ... 100 A4
Romney Rd Chatham ME5 ... 68 B5
Northfleet DA11 ... 35 E5
Woolwich SE18 ... 2 C3
Romney St TN15 ... 77 A7
Romney Street Cvn Pk
TN15 ... 77 A7
Romney Way TN10 ... 127 E5
Romsey Cl Orpington BR6 ... 57 C6
Rochester ME2 ... 52 E8
Ron Green Ct DA8 ... 14 D8
Ronald Ho SE3 ... 11 C3
Ronalds Rd BR1 ... 42 A8
Ronaldstone Rd DA15 ... 12 E1
Ronfearn Ave BR5 ... 44 D4
Ronver Rd SE12 ... 28 A7
Roodlands La TN8 ... 123 D6
Rook La ME9 ... 71 F6
Rook Wlk 2 E6 ... 1 E7
Rookdean TN13 ... 91 C5
Rookery Cres ME3 ... 22 B6
Rookery Ct RM20 ... 17 A8
Rookery Dr BR7 ... 43 A8
Rookery Gdns BR5 ... 44 C4
Rookery Hill ME6 ... 81 F8
Rookery La BR2 ... 42 D3
Rookery Lodge ME3 ... 22 C5
Rookery Rd BR6 ... 57 A1
Rookery The RM20 ... 17 A8
Rookery View RM17 ... 18 D8
Rookesley Rd BR5 ... 44 D2
Rookley Cl TN2 ... 159 D2
Rooks Hill TN15 ... 109 D6
Roopers TN3 ... 158 A7
Roosevelt Ave ME5 ... 68 A8
Rope Wlk Chatham ME4 ... 53 F5
Cranbrook TN17 ... 179 C5
Rope Wlk The TN18 ... 196 B5
Rope Yard Rails SE18 ... 2 B3
Ropemakers Ct ME4 ... 54 A1
Roper Cl ME8 ... 69 C3
Roper St 1 SE9 ... 12 A1
Roper's Gate TN2 ... 158 E1
Roper's Green La ME3 ... 24 B2
Roper's La ME3 ... 40 F8
Ropery Bsns Pk SE7 ... 1 C2
Rose Ave DA12 ... 36 E7
Rose Bruford Coll DA15 ... 30 B7
Rose Cotts
Lamberhurst TN3 ... 176 A5
Rochester ME2 ... 52 B8
St Mary Hoo ME3 ... 24 E6
Rose Ct ME17 ... 115 D1
Rose Dale BR6 ... 57 B8
Rose Hill Sch TN4 ... 158 E5
Rose St Northfleet DA11 ... 18 B1
Rochester ME1 ... 53 D3
Tonbridge TN9 ... 143 C8
Rose Terr ME19 ... 96 D7
Rose Way SE12 ... 11 A2
Rose Yd ME14 ... 100 A4
Roseacre RH8 ... 104 A1
Roseacre Gdns ME14 ... 101 A3
Roseacre Jun Sch
ME14 ... 101 A4
Roseacre La ME14 ... 101 A4
Roseacre Rd DA16 ... 13 B4
Rosebank Gdns DA11 ... 35 E7
Rosebank Wlk 13 SE18 ... 1 E2
Roseberry Gdns
Dartford DA1 ... 32 C8
Orpington BR6 ... 57 E7
Rosebery Ave DA15 ... 29 E8
Rosebery Ct DA11 ... 35 F7
Rosebery Rd
Chatham ME4 ... 53 E2
Gillingham ME7 ... 54 D7
Grays RM17 ... 17 E8
Rosecroft Cl
Biggin Hill TN16 ... 72 F1
Orpington BR5 ... 44 C3
Rosedale Cl Dartford DA2 ... 33 B8
Woolwich SE2 ... 3 B3
Rosedale Cnr BR7 ... 42 F8
Rosedene Ct DA1 ... 32 C8
Rosefield Sevenoaks TN13 ... 92 A3
15 Sidcup DA14 ... 30 A4
Rosegarth DA13 ... 49 E8
Rosehill Rd TN16 ... 72 C2
Rosehill Wlk TN1 ... 159 A3
Roseholme ME16 ... 99 D2
Roselare Cl TN16 ... 89 D1
Roseleigh Ave ME16 ... 99 C5
Rosemary Cl
4 Chatham ME5 ... 67 F4
Oxted RH8 ... 104 A2
Rosemary Ct 1 ME1 ... 53 D4
Rosemary La
Flimwell TN5 ... 187 A5
Hodsoll Street TN15 ... 63 D3
Swift's Green TN27 ... 152 F5
Rosemary Rd Bexley DA16 ... 12 F6
Maidstone ME15 ... 101 A3
West Malling ME19 ... 81 F1
Rosemead Gdns TN27 ... 151 B7
Rosemount Cl ME15 ... 115 F4
Rosemount Ct ME2 ... 39 A1
Rosemount Dr BR1 ... 42 F5
Rosenheath Cl BR6 ... 58 C3
Rosetta Prim Sch E16 ... 1 B8
Roseveare Rd SE12 ... 28 C4
Rosewood DA2 ... 31 E4
Rosewood Cl DA14 ... 30 C5
Rosewood Ct BR1 ... 42 D8
Rosher Ho DA11 ... 18 F1
Rosherville CE Prim Sch
DA11 ... 18 E1
Rosherville Way DA11 ... 18 E1
Roslin Way BR1 ... 28 A3
Ross Ct BR7 ... 28 F1
Ross Ho SE18 ... 11 E6
Ross Rd DA1 ... 15 A1
Ross St ME1 ... 53 D4
Ross Way SE9 ... 11 E4
Rossdale TN2 ... 159 D5
Rosse Mews SE3 ... 11 B6
Rossland Cl DA6 ... 14 B2
Rosslyn Gn ME16 ... 99 B5
Rossmore DA14 ... 30 A3
Rother Ct 24 BR5 ... 44 D1
Rother Rd TN10 ... 127 C5
Rother Vale ME5 ... 68 C3
Rothermere Cl TN17 ... 190 E6
Rothesay Ct 6 SE12 ... 28 B5
Rothley Cl TN30 ... 193 B8
Rouge La DA12 ... 36 B7
Rougemont ME18 ... 97 C2
Roughetts Rd ME19 ... 80 F3
Roughway La TN11 ... 111 C7
Round Ash Way DA3 ... 48 E3
Round Green Cotts
TN17 ... 164 F4
Round St DA12,DA13 ... 50 D5
Round Wood Cl ME5 ... 68 A1
Roundel Way TN12 ... 148 D5
Roundhay ME19 ... 81 E1
Roundhill Rd TN2 ... 159 D1
Roundlyn Gdns BR5 ... 44 B5
Roundtable Rd BR1 ... 28 A5
Roundway TN16 ... 72 D4
Roundwell ME14 ... 101 D3
Roundwood BR7 ... 43 B7
Routh St E6 ... 1 F8
Rover Rd ME5 ... 68 B2
Row The DA3 ... 62 F8
Rowan Cl Aylesford ME20 ... 82 E1
Meopham Sta DA13 ... 50 B3
Paddock Wood TN12 ... 145 F5
Rowan Cres DA1 ... 32 C7
Rowan Ct 2 SE12 ... 28 A8
Rowan Ho
4 Chatham ME5 ... 67 F5
7 Maidstone ME16 ... 99 A3
Royal Tunbridge Wells
TN4 ... 158 E4
Sidcup DA14 ... 29 F5
Rowan Lea ME5 ... 54 B1
Rowan Rd Bexley DA7 ... 13 E4
Swanley BR8 ... 45 D6
Rowan Shaw TN10 ... 127 D6
Rowan Tree Rd TN2 ... 158 E1
Rowan Wlk Chatham ME4 ... 53 E3
Orpington BR2 ... 56 F7
Rowans Cl DA3 ... 48 D7
Rowanwood Ave DA15 ... 30 A7
Rowbrocke Cl ME8 ... 69 D3
Rowdow La TN14,TN15 ... 76 E5
Rowe Pl ME20 ... 82 F6
Rowenden Vineyard*
TN17 ... 191 B2
Rowfield 6 TN8 ... 122 D3
Rowhill Cotts DA2 ... 31 E2
Rowhill Rd DA2 ... 32 A3
Rowhill Sch DA2 ... 32 C4
Rowland Ave ME7 ... 54 E2
Rowland Cl
Gillingham ME7 ... 54 E1
Maidstone ME16 ... 99 E3
Rowlands Manor BR5 ... 44 C3
Rowlatt Cl DA2 ... 32 C4
Rowlatt Rd DA2 ... 32 C5
Rowley Ave DA15 ... 30 B8
Rowley Hill TN2 ... 144 D1
Rowmarsh Cl DA11 ... 35 D4
Rowntree Path 1 SE28 ... 3 B5
Rowton Rd SE18 ... 12 C7
Rowzill Rd BR8 ... 31 F2
Royal Albert Sta E16 ... 1 E6
Royal Albert Way
Newham E16 ... 1 E6
Newham,Cyprus E6 ... 2 A6
Royal Ave TN9 ... 143 D8
Royal Chase TN4 ... 158 F4
Royal Cl BR6 ... 57 B6
Royal Connaught Apartments
E16 ... 1 D5
Royal Ct SE9 ... 28 F7
Royal Docks Com Sch The
E16 ... 1 C7
Royal Docks Rd E6 ... 2 B7
Royal Eagle Cl ME2 ... 53 E7
Royal Engineers Mus*
ME7 ... 54 B6
Royal Engineers' Rd
ME14 ... 99 F7
Royal Oak Cotts TN8 ... 105 C2
Royal Oak Rd DA6 ... 13 F3
Royal Oak Terr DA12 ... 36 C7
Royal Par BR7 ... 29 C1
Royal Parade Mews BR7 ... 29 C1
Royal Park Prim Sch
DA14 ... 30 E5
Royal Pier Rd DA12 ... 19 C1
Royal Rd Newham E16 ... 1 D7
Sidcup DA14 ... 30 D5
Sutton at H DA2 ... 33 A3
Royal Rise TN9 ... 143 C8
Royal Sch of Military
Engineering ME3 ... 39 C4
Royal Sovereign Ave
ME4 ... 54 B7
Royal Star Arc 5 ME14 ... 99 F4
Royal Tunbridge Wells Bsns
Pk TN2 ... 143 D1
Royal Victoria Pl
Newham E16 ... 1 B5
Royal Tunbridge Wells
TN1 ... 159 B4
Royal Victoria Sq E16 ... 1 B6
Royal Victoria Sta E16 ... 1 A6
Royal West Kent Ave
TN10 ... 127 D4
Roydene Rd SE18 ... 2 E1
Roydon Hall* TN12 ... 112 F4
Roydon Hall Rd TN12 ... 112 F4
Royston Rd Crayford DA1 ... 14 F1
Maidstone ME15 ... 101 A3
Roystons Cl ME8 ... 55 F2
Royton Ave ME17 ... 120 D5
Rubin Pl ME19 ... 97 B3
Ruck La TN12 ... 162 E3
Ruckinge Way ME8 ... 55 C3
Ruddstreet Cl SE18 ... 2 C2
Rudge Cl ME5 ... 68 D2
Rudland Rd DA7 ... 14 B4
Ruegg Ho 5 SE18 ... 12 A8
Ruffet Ct TN2 ... 158 E1
Ruffets Wood DA12 ... 36 C2
Rugby Cl ME5 ... 67 F4
Ruggles Cl ME23 ... 23 E3
Rumania Wlk DA12 ... 36 F5
Rumstead La ME17,ME9 ... 86 D4
Rumstead Rd ME9 ... 86 E4
Rumwood Ct ME17 ... 117 B5
Runciman Cl BR6 ... 58 C1
Runham La ME17 ... 119 E3
Running Horse Rdbt The
ME14 ... 83 E1
Runnymede Ct DA2 ... 33 C7
Runnymede Gdns ME15 ... 116 A8
Rural Vale DA11 ... 35 E8
Ruscombe Cl TN4 ... 142 F2
Rush Cl ME5 ... 68 A3
Rushbrook Rd SE9 ... 29 C6
Rushdean Rd ME2 ... 52 D5
Rushdene SE2 ... 3 D3
Rushdene Wlk TN16 ... 72 D2
Rushes The ME20 ... 82 B4
Rushet Rd BR5 ... 44 A7
Rushetts TN3 ... 157 F4
Rushetts Rd TN15 ... 61 E3
Rusheymead Ho 5 SE18 ... 2 F1
Rushford Cl TN27 ... 151 D5
Rushgrove St SE18 ... 1 F2
Rushley Cl BR2 ... 56 E6
Rushlye Cl TN3 ... 173 F5
Rushmead Dr ME15 ... 116 A7
Rushmere Ct TN15 ... 94 D7
Rushmore Cl BR1 ... 42 E6
Rushmore Hill BR6,TN14 ... 74 D6
Rushymead TN15 ... 77 A1
Ruskin Ave DA16 ... 13 A5
Ruskin Cl ME19 ... 97 F8
Ruskin Ct SE9 ... 11 F1
Ruskin Dr Bexley DA16 ... 13 A4
Orpington BR6 ... 57 E7
Ruskin Gr Bexley DA16 ... 13 A5
Dartford DA1 ... 16 A2
Ruskin Rd DA17 ... 4 A2
Ruskin Wlk BR2 ... 42 F3
Rusland Ave BR6 ... 57 D7
Russell Cl Bexley DA7 ... 14 A3
Crayford DA1 ... 15 A3
Greenwich SE7 ... 11 C7
Russell Ct ME4 ... 54 B3
Russell House Sch TN14 ... 76 C3
Russell Pl DA4 ... 47 A8
Russell Quay 2 DA11 ... 19 A1
Russell Rd
Gravesend DA12 ... 19 D1
Kit's Coty ME20 ... 83 D7
Newham E16 ... 1 B7
Tilbury RM18 ... 18 F5
Tilbury RM18 ... 18 F6
Russell Sq DA3 ... 48 D6
Russell Terr DA4 ... 47 C5
Russells Ave ME8 ... 70 A8
Russells Yd TN17 ... 179 D4
Russet Cl ME2 ... 52 E8
Russet Ct Coxheath ME17 ... 115 C3
17 Erith DA17 ... 4 A1
Russet Ho RM17 ... 18 C7
Russet Way ME19 ... 96 F2
Russets The
Maidstone ME16 ... 99 B5
Meopham Sta DA13 ... 50 A3
Russett Cl Ditton ME20 ... 98 E8
Orpington BR6 ... 58 B5
Russett Rd TN12 ... 129 F6
Russett Way BR8 ... 45 D8
Rusthall Grange TN4 ... 158 D4
Rusthall Pk TN4 ... 158 D4
Rusthall Rd TN4 ... 158 D4
Rustic Wlk E16 ... 1 B7
Ruston Rd SE18 ... 1 E3
Rustwick TN4 ... 158 D4
Ruth Ho 2 ME16 ... 99 E5
Ruth St ME4 ... 54 A2
Rutherford Way TN10 ... 127 D7
Rutherglen Rd SE2 ... 13 A8
Ruthin Rd SE3 ... 11 A8
Rutland Ave DA15 ... 30 A8
Rutland Cl Dartford DA1 ... 32 D8
Sidcup DA5 ... 30 D7
Rutland Ct Chislehurst BR7 ... 43 A8
Sidcup SE9 ... 29 C6
Rutland Gate DA17 ... 4 B1
Rutland Ho 10 SE18 ... 1 F2
Rutland Pl ME8 ... 69 C3
Rutland Way
Maidstone ME15 ... 116 E8
Orpington BR5 ... 44 C3
Ruxley Cl DA14 ... 30 E2
Ruxley Cnr DA14 ... 30 E2
Ruxley Corner Ind Est
DA14 ... 30 D2
Ruxley Ct 1 BR1 ... 42 C7
Ruxton Cl BR8 ... 45 E6
Ruxton Ct 5 BR8 ... 45 E6
Ryan Cl SE3 ... 11 C3
Ryan Dr ME15 ... 101 A2
Ryarsh Cres BR6 ... 57 E6
Ryarsh La ME19 ... 81 B1
Ryarsh Pk ME19 ... 80 F4
Ryarsh Prim Sch ME19 ... 81 A4
Ryarsh Rd ME19 ... 81 B5
Rycault Cl 4 ME16 ... 99 E3
Rycaut Cl ME8 ... 69 D3
Rycroft La TN14 ... 107 E5
Rydal Cl TN4 ... 158 E5
Rydal Dr Bexley DA7 ... 14 A6
Royal Tunbridge Wells
TN4 ... 158 E5
Rydal Ho ME15 ... 116 E7
Ryde Cl ME5 ... 68 B8
Rydens Ho SE9 ... 28 C5
Ryder Cl BR1 ... 28 B3
Ryders TN3 ... 158 A3
Rydons Cl SE9 ... 11 E4
Rye Cl DA5 ... 14 B1
Rye Cres BR5 ... 44 D1
Rye Field 25 BR5 ... 44 D1
Rye La Otford TN14 ... 76 A2
Sevenoaks TN13,TN14 ... 91 F7
Rye Rd Four Throws TN18 ... 195 D8
Hawkhurst TN18 ... 189 B1
Rye Wood Cotts TN14 ... 91 F7
Ryecroft Gravesend DA12 ... 36 E3
New Barn DA3 ... 49 D5
Ryecroft Rd
Orpington BR5 ... 43 D3
Otford TN14 ... 76 A2
Ryedale Ct TN13 ... 91 E6
Ryegrass Cl ME5 ... 68 C6
Ryelands Cres SE12 ... 11 C1
Rymers Cl TN2 ... 159 D7
Rymill St E16 ... 2 A5
Rysted La TN16 ... 89 D1

S

Sabre Ct ME7 55 A1
Sackville Ave BR2 42 A1
Sackville Cl TN13 92 B5
Sackville Rd DA2 32 E6
Sackville Sch TN11 126 C6
Sacred Heart Sch TN5 184 D5
Saddington St DA12 36 C8
Saddler's Pk DA4 60 D7
Saddlers Cl ME14 100 E5
Sadlers Cl ME5 67 D2
Saffron Cl ME16 99 B3
Saffron Way 1 ME5 67 F5
Sage Cl 7 E6 1 F8
Sage Rd ME1 53 B3
Saigasso Cl E16 1 D7
Sailfield Ct ME4 53 F7
Sailmakers Ct 5 ME4 54 B2
Saint Mary Magdalene CE Prim Sch SE18 2 A2
Saints Hill TN11 157 A8
St Aidan's Way DA12 36 E5
St Alban's Cl DA12 36 D5
St Alban's Gdns DA12 36 D5
St Alban's Rd DA1 15 F1
St Alban's Rd Inf Sch DA1 15 F1
St Albans Cl ME7 54 E7
St Albans Rd ME2 52 D6
St Alfege Rd SE7 11 D8
St Andrew's Cl ME16 99 A2
St Andrew's Ct 4 BR8 45 E6
St Andrew's Rd
10 Gravesend DA12 36 B8
Maidstone ME16 99 A3
Tilbury RM18 18 E5
St Andrew's Wlk ME3 9 D2
St Andrews Cl Erith SE28 3 D7
Paddock Wood TN12 146 A6
St Andrews Ct
26 Gravesend DA12 19 B1
Royal Tunbridge Wells TN4 143 A1
St Andrews Dr BR5 44 B2
St Andrews Ho BR1 28 B2
St Andrews Mews SE3 11 A7
St Andrews Park Rd TN4 143 A1
St Andrews Pk ME16 99 A3
St Andrews Rd
Gillingham ME7 54 D7
Paddock Wood TN12 146 A6
Sidcup DA14 30 D5
St Andrews Sch ME1 53 C4
St Andrews Way RH8 104 F4
St Ann's Green La TN12 148 F8
St Annes Ct ME16 99 E4
St Anns Way TN16 73 B3
St Anselm's RC Prim Sch DA1 16 A2
St Anthony's Ct BR6 57 B8
St Aubyns Cl BR6 57 F7
St Aubyns Gdns BR6 57 F8
St Audrey Ave DA7 14 A5
St Augustine Ho 1 TN9 143 B8
St Augustine of Canterbury RC Prim Sch ME8 69 D3
St Augustine's Ave BR2 42 E4
St Augustine's of Canterbury CE Prim Sch DA17 3 F2
St Augustine's RC Prim Sch TN4 159 A7
St Augustine's Rd DA17 3 F2
St Barnabas CE Prim Sch TN1 159 B5
St Barnabas Cl
Gillingham ME7 54 D3
Maidstone ME16 99 C8
St Barnabas' Cl TN1 159 B5
St Bartholomew's Hospl ME1 53 E4
St Bartholomew's La 4 ME1 53 E4
St Bartholomew's Terr 2 ME1 53 E4
St Bartholomews RC Prim Sch BR8 45 E6
St Benedict Rd ME6 81 E8
St Benedict's Ave DA12 36 E6
St Benedicts RC Prim Sch ME5 68 C2
St Benets Ct TN30 193 B8
St Benets Way TN30 193 B8
St Benjamins Dr BR6 58 C2
St Bernards Rd TN10 127 C6
St Blaise Ave BR1 42 B7
St Boltophs Ct TN13 92 B3
St Botolph Rd DA11 35 D5
St Botolph's Ave TN13 92 A3
St Botolph's CE Prim Sch DA11 35 D8
St Botolph's Rd TN13 92 B3
St Brelade's Ct TN8 122 A3
St Brides Cl DA18 3 D4
St Catherine's Hospl ME1 53 D4
St Catherine's RC Sch for Girls DA6 14 B2
St Catherines Ct ME1 53 D5
St Chad's Dr DA12 36 E5
St Chad's Rd RM18 19 A7
St Chad's Sch RM18 19 A6
St Clement's Ave RM20 17 B8
St Clement's Ho ME1 53 D5
St Clement's Rd RM20 17 C7
St Clement's Way RM20 16 F8
St Clements Cl DA11 35 F5
St Clements Ct RM17 17 F8
St Clere Hill Rd TN15 77 F7
St Columba's Cl DA12 36 E5
St Columba's RC Boys Sch DA6 14 B2
St David's Bridge TN17 179 D4
St David's Cres DA12 36 D4
St David's Rd
Allhallows ME3 9 D2
Hextable BR8 31 F1
Royal Tunbridge Wells TN4 159 B6
St Davids Gate ME16 99 A2
St Domingo Ho SE18 1 F3
St Dunstan's Dr DA12 36 E5
St Dunstans Wlk TN17 179 D4
St Edith's Rd TN15 77 A2
St Edmund Ho SE2 13 D8
St Edmund's Cotts TN15 62 A2
St Edmund's Ct TN15 62 A2
St Edmunds Cl DA18 3 D4
St Edmunds Rd DA1 16 A3
St Faith's La ME14 101 B4
St Faith's St ME14 99 F4
St Fidelis RC Prim Sch DA8 14 C8
St Fidelis' Rd DA8 4 D1
St Francis Ave DA12 36 E4
St Francis Cl
Maidstone ME14 100 B7
Orpington BR6 43 E3
Rochester ME2 52 E6
St Francis RC Prim Sch ME15 99 C4
St Francis Rd DA13 64 B3
St Francis' Rd DA8 4 D2
St George's Bickley CE Prim Sch BR1 42 D7
St George's CE Prim Sch TN15 78 F3
St George's CE Sch DA11 36 A6
St George's Cres DA12 36 D4
St George's Ct TN15 78 F3
St George's Ctr DA11 19 B1
St George's Pk TN2 172 F8
St George's Rd
Gillingham ME7 54 C6
Sevenoaks TN13 92 B5
Sidcup DA14 30 D2
St George's Sq ME16 99 E3
St George's Wlk ME3 9 D2
St Georges Cl SE28 3 D7
St Georges Ct TN4 159 A5
St Georges Mews 11 TN9 143 B8
St Georges Rd
Bromley BR1 42 F6
Orpington BR5 43 D3
Swanley BR8 45 F5
St Georges Rd W BR1 42 E7
St Georges Sq DA3 48 E6
St German's Pl SE3 11 A6
St Giles Cl BR6 57 D5
St Gregory's Cres DA12 36 E6
St Gregory's Ct DA12 36 E6
St Gregory's RC Comp Sch TN4 159 A7
St Helens DA14 30 B5
St Helens CE Prim Sch ME3 22 B5
St Helens Cotts ME15 114 E8
St Helens La ME15 114 E8
St Helens Rd Cliffe ME3 22 B5
7 Erith DA18 3 D4
St Helier's Cl ME16 99 B2
St Hilary Ho SE2 13 D8
St Hilda's Way DA12 36 E5
St Hildas TN15 110 F8
St James Cl
East Malling ME19 97 F8
Grain ME3 27 B6
Tonbridge TN10 127 D7
St James Ct
3 Bromley BR2 42 A7
Greenwich SE3 11 B6
Stone DA9 16 F1
St James Oaks DA11 36 A8
St James Pl DA1 15 D1
St James RC Prim Sch BR5 43 B4
St James Rd ME3 27 B5
St James Sq DA3 48 E6
St James Way DA14 30 E3
St James' CE Inf Sch TN2 159 C4
St James' CE Jun Sch TN2 159 C4
St James' CE Prim Sch ME3 27 B6
St James' Inf Sch ME19 97 F8
St James' La DA9 33 E8
St James' Pk TN1 159 C5
St James' Rd TN1 159 C5
St James's Ave DA11 36 A8
St James's Cl SE18 2 C1
St James's Ct TN1 159 B4
St James's Rd
Gravesend DA11 19 A1
Sevenoaks TN13 92 B5
St James's St DA11 19 A1
St Joachim's RC Prim Sch E16 1 C7
St John Fisher RC Comp (Lower) Sch ME4 53 F2
St John Fisher RC Comp Sch ME4 53 E3
St John Fisher RC Prim Sch DA18 3 E3
St John's CE Inf Sch ME4 53 E3
St John's CE Prim Sch ME14 100 E4
St John's CE Prim Sch TN4 159 B7
St John's CE Prim Sch TN13 92 D4
St John's Cl ME3 38 C4
St John's Ct TN13 92 C5
St John's Hill TN13,TN14 92 C5
St John's Jerusalem* DA4 33 B1
St John's La DA3 48 F3
St John's Par 4 DA14 30 B4
St John's Pk
Greenwich SE3 11 A7
Royal Tunbridge Wells TN4 159 A8
St John's RC Comp Sch DA12 36 D7
St John's RC Prim Sch DA12 36 E7
St John's Rd Bexley DA16 13 B4
Dartford DA2 33 C8
Erith DA8 4 D1
Gillingham ME7 54 C3
Gravesend DA12 36 D8
Higham ME3 38 C4
Newham E16 1 A7
Orpington BR5 43 E3
Royal Tunbridge Wells TN4 159 A6
Sevenoaks TN13 92 C5
Sidcup DA14 30 B4
St John's Terr SE18 12 D8
St Johns Ct DA8 4 D1
St Johns Rd ME3 40 E6
St Johns Way
Edenbridge TN8 122 C3
Rochester ME1 53 A2
St Joseph's RC Prim Sch
Bromley BR1 28 B1
Crayford DA1 14 E3
Northfleet DA11 35 D8
St Josephs Cl BR6 57 F6
St Josephs Ct 4 SE12 28 B5
St Josephs Prep Sch DA12 36 C6
St Justin Cl BR5 44 D6
St Katharine's Knockholt CE Prim Sch TN14 74 B2
St Katherine's La ME6 81 F7
St Katherine's Sch ME6 81 F7
St Katherines Cotts DA12 37 E4
St Katherines Rd DA18 3 D4
St Keverne Rd SE9 28 E4
St Kilda Rd BR6 43 F1
St Laurence Ave ME16 99 C8
St Laurence Cl BR5 44 D6
St Lawrence Ave TN4 142 D3
St Lawrence CE Prim Sch TN15 93 E3
St Lenard's Twr* ME19 97 A7
St Leonard's St ME19 97 B7
St Leonards Ave ME4 53 F2
St Leonards Cl
4 Bexley DA16 13 A4
Grays RM17 17 F8
St Leonards Rd ME16 99 C8
St Leonards Rise BR6 57 E6
St Luke's Ave ME14 100 B5
St Luke's CE Inf Sch TN4 159 C7
St Luke's Rd
Maidstone ME14 100 B5
Royal Tunbridge Wells TN4 159 B6
St Luke's Way ME3 9 D2
St Lukes Cl Dartford DA2 33 E3
Swanley BR8 45 D7
St Lukes Cotts BR8 45 D7
St Lukes Ct ME14 100 A6
St Margaret Clitherow RC Prim Sch
Tonbridge TN10 127 B6
Woolwich SE28 3 B5
St Margaret's at Troy Town CE Prim Sch ME1 53 C4
St Margaret's Banks ME1 53 D5
St Margaret's CE Jun Sch ME8 69 E8
St Margaret's CE Prim Sch SE18 2 C1
St Margaret's Cl DA2 33 D6
St Margaret's Cres DA12 36 E5
St Margaret's Ct 6 ME8 69 F8
St Margaret's Ct ME23 23 E3
St Margaret's Gr SE18 12 C8
St Margaret's Inf Sch ME8 69 E8
St Margaret's Mews ME1 53 C5
St Margaret's Rd
Dartford DA2,DA4 33 E2
Northfleet DA11 35 E7
St Margaret's St ME1 53 C5
St Margaret's Terr SE18 2 C1
St Margarets Ave DA15 29 D5
St Margarets CE Prim Sch TN12 131 D1
St Margarets Cl
Maidstone ME16 99 B2
St Margarets Cl *continued*
Orpington BR6 58 B6
St Margarets Dr ME8 69 C5
St Margarets Villas TN12 147 D8
St Mark's Ave DA11 35 F8
St Mark's CE Prim Sch
Bromley BR2 42 A6
Royal Tunbridge Wells TN4 158 D1
St Mark's Rd Bromley BR2 42 B6
Royal Tunbridge Wells TN2 172 F7
St Marks CE Prim Sch ME20 82 F6
St Marks Ct ME20 82 F6
St Marks Ho ME7 54 C5
St Marks Ind Est E16 1 D5
St Martin's Cl ME14 85 A1
St Martin's Dr DA4 60 D7
St Martin's Rd DA1 15 F1
St Martins Cl Erith DA18 3 D4
Newington ME9 71 C7
St Martins Mdw TN16 90 C4
St Mary & St Joseph's RC Sch DA14 30 A3
St Mary Cray Prim Sch BR5 44 C3
St Mary Cray Sta BR5 44 B5
St Mary St SE18 2 A2
St Mary's ME3 24 D5
St Mary's Abbey ME19 97 C8
St Mary's CE Prim Sch BR8 45 E5
St Mary's Church Rd TN14 90 F2
St Mary's Cl
Gravesend DA12 36 C6
Grays RM17 18 D8
Laddingford ME18 130 E4
Orpington BR5 44 C7
Platt TN15 95 C7
Ticehurst TN5 186 D1
St Mary's Ct Erith DA17 3 D2
5 Westerham TN16 89 D1
St Mary's Dr TN13 91 E4
St Mary's Gdns ME4 54 B7
St Mary's Gn TN16 72 C1
St Mary's Gr TN16 72 C1
St Mary's Island CE Prim Sch ME4 40 B2
St Mary's La
Speldhurst TN3 158 A8
Ticehurst TN5 186 D1
St Mary's Pl Eltham SE9 12 A1
Newington ME9 71 C7
St Mary's Prim Sch ME2 53 B7
St Mary's RC Prim Sch
Eltham SE9 12 A2
Gillingham ME7 54 D6
Tilbury RM18 18 F5
St Mary's Rd
Coldblow DA5 31 C7
Gillingham ME7 54 C6
Rochester ME2 53 B7
Stone DA9 16 E2
Swanley BR8 45 E5
Tonbridge TN9 143 B7
Wrotham TN15 79 A2
St Mary's View ME9 71 C7
St Mary's Wlk ME1 66 F1
St Marys Ct SE7 11 D7
St Marys Way DA3 48 E6
St Matthew's CE Inf Sch ME1 53 A2
St Matthew's Cl ME9 71 C7
St Matthew's High Brooms CE Prim Sch TN4 159 B8
St Matthew's Way ME3 9 D2
St Matthews Dr
Bromley BR1 42 F6
Rochester ME1 53 A2
St Mellion Cl SE28 3 D7
St Merryn Cl SE18 12 D7
St Michael's CE Inf Sch ME16 99 E3
St Michael's CE Prim Sch TN30 183 A3
St Michael's Cl
Chatham ME4 53 F3
Erith DA18 3 D4
St Michael's Ct 6 ME2 53 B8
St Michael's East Wickham CE Prim Sch DA16 13 C6
St Michael's Prim Sch TN7 170 B5
St Michael's RC Prim Sch ME4 53 F3
St Michael's Rd
Bexley DA16 13 B4
Maidstone ME16 99 D3
Royal Tunbridge Wells TN4 159 B7
St Michael's Rise DA16 13 B6
St Michael's Terr TN30 183 A3
St Michaels RH8 104 A5
St Michaels Cl
Bromley BR1 42 E6
4 Newham E16 1 D8
Pratling Street ME20 83 C3
St Michaels Ct TN11 126 E7
St Michaels Dr TN14 76 E3
St Mildred's Cl 4 TN30 193 A7
St Mildreds Rd 5 SE12 28 A8
St Nicholas CE Inf Sch ME2 53 A7
St Nicholas Ct TN13 92 B2
St Nicholas Dr TN13 92 C1
St Nicholas Gdns ME2 52
St Nicholas Rd SE18 2
St Nicolas La BR7 42
St Olave's & St Saviour's Gram Sch BR6 58
St Olaves Prep Sch SE9 29
St Patrick's Gdns DA12 36
St Patrick's RC Prim Sch SE18 2
St Paul's CE Prim Sch BR8 46
St Paul's Cl Greenwich SE7 1
Rochester ME2 52
Swanscombe DA10 34
St Paul's Cray CE Prim Sch BR5 44
St Paul's Cray Rd BR5, BR7 43
St Paul's Ct TN4 158
St Paul's RC Sch SE2 13
St Paul's Rd DA8 14
St Paul's Sq BR2 42
St Paul's St TN4 158
St Paul's Wood Hill BR5 43
St Paulinus Ct DA1 14
St Paulinus' CE Prim Sch DA1 14
St Pauls CE Inf Sch TN4 158
St Pauls CE Jun Sch TN4 158
St Pauls Cl TN10 127
St Pauls Inf Sch ME14 100
St Peter & St Paul RC Prim Sch BR5 43
St Peter Ave TN16 73
St Peter Chanel RC Prim Sch DA14 30
St Peter St ME1 53
St Peter's Bridge ME14 99
St Peter's CE Prim Sch
Aylesford ME20 83
Royal Tunbridge Wells TN2 159
St Peter's Cl DA10 34
St Peter's Ct ME20 82
St Peter's Inf Sch ME1 53
St Peter's Path ME1 53
St Peter's RC Prim Sch SE18 2
St Peter's St TN2 159
St Peters Cl
Chislehurst BR7 29
Ditton ME20 82
St Peters La BR5 44
St Peters Pl ME20 82
St Peters Rd ME20 82
St Peters Row TN3 157
St Peters St ME16 99
St Philip's Ave ME15 100
St Philips Ct TN2 159
St Philomena's RC Prim Sch BR5 44
St Quentin Rd DA16 12
St Ronan's Cl ME15 116
St Ronan's Sch TN18 189
St Saviours Rd ME15 116
St Simon Stock Sch ME16 99
St Stephen's Cl ME9 71
St Stephen's Cotts TN1 159
St Stephen's Ct TN1 159
St Stephen's Prim Sch TN9 143
St Stephen's RC Prim Sch DA16 13
St Stephen's Sq ME15 99
St Stephen's St TN9 143
St Stephens Mews ME1 67
St Thomas Ct DA5 31
St Thomas More RC Prim Sch
Bexley DA7 13
Chatham ME5 68
Eltham SE9 11
St Thomas More RC Sec Sch SE9 12
St Thomas of Canterbury RC Prim Sch ME8 55
St Thomas RC Prim Sch TN13 92
St Thomas Rd Erith DA17 4
Newham E16 1
Northfleet DA11 35
St Thomas' Dr BR5 43
St Thomas' RC Prim Sch RM17 18
St Thomas's Almshouses DA11 36
St Thomas's Ave DA11 36
St Thomas's Pl 15 RM17 18
St Thomas-a-Becket RC Prim Sch SE2 3
St Timothy's Mews 3 BR1 42
St Vincents Ave DA1 16
St Vincents La ME19 80
St Vincents RC Prim Sch SE9 28
St Vincents Rd DA1 16
St Welcume's Way ME17 119
St Werburgh Cres ME3 40
St Werburgh Ct ME3 40
St William of Perth RC Prim Sch ME1 53
St William's Way ME1 53
St Winifred's Rd TN16 72
Sala Ho SE3 11

alamons Way RM13 ... 4 E7
alcote Rd DA12 ... 36 E3
alem Pl DA11 ... 35 D8
alem St ME15 ... 100 A3
alhouse Cl SE28 ... 3 C7
alisbury Ave
Gillingham ME8 ... 69 D8
Swanley BR8 ... 46 A5
alisbury Cl TN10 ... 127 D5
alisbury Ho 4 ME15 ... 116 D7
alisbury Mews BR2 ... 42 E4
alisbury Rd Bromley BR2 ... 42 E4
Chatham ME4 ... 54 A3
Dartford DA2 ... 33 C7
2 Grays RM17 ... 18 C8
Kit's Coty ME20 ... 83 D7
Langton Green TN3 ... 157 F3
Maidstone ME14 ... 100 A6
Northfleet DA11 ... 35 F7
Royal Tunbridge Wells
TN4 ... 159 C8
Sidcup DA5 ... 31 A7
Tonbridge TN10 ... 127 D4
alix Rd RM17 ... 18 D8
allow Cl ME4 ... 40 C1
allows Shaw DA13 ... 50 C4
ally Port ME7 ... 54 A6
ally Port Gdns ME7 ... 54 B6
almon Rd Dartford DA1 ... 15 F4
Erith DA17 ... 4 A1
alomons Rd Newham E13 ... 1 C8
Rusthall TN4 ... 158 C4
alt La ME3 ... 21 F4
alt's Ave ME15 ... 115 F3
altash Rd DA16 ... 13 C6
altbox Hill TN16 ... 72 B6
altcote Cl DA1 ... 14 E1
alter's Cross ME18 ... 114 A1
altford Cl 2 DA8 ... 4 E1
altings Rd ME6 ... 82 A7
altley Cl E6 ... 1 E7
alts La ME15 ... 116 A4
altwood Cl BR6 ... 58 C6
altwood Rd ME15 ... 99 F1
alvadori Ct TN2 ... 160 D6
am Bartram Cl SE7 ... 1 C1
amara Cl ME5 ... 68 A1
amphire Cl ME14 ... 100 E4
amphire Ct RM17 ... 18 E8
amphire Way ME4 ... 40 A2
ampson Cl DA17 ... 3 D3
amson Ho SE18 ... 2 C2
amuel Cl SE18 ... 1 E2
amuel Palmer Ct BR6 ... 44 A2
amuel St SE18 ... 1 F2
anctuary Cl DA1 ... 15 D1
anctuary Rd ME8 ... 55 A3
anctuary The DA5 ... 13 D1
and La TN17 ... 166 F4
and Rd TN3 ... 176 A4
andalwood Ho DA15 ... 29 F5
andbach Pl SE18 ... 2 C1
andbanks Hill DA2 ... 34 B2
andbourne Dr ME14 ... 83 F1
andby Gn SE9 ... 11 E4
andcliff Rd DA8 ... 4 D1
anderling Ct SE28 ... 3 C6
anderling Way DA9 ... 17 A1
anderson Way TN9 ... 127 E1
andersons Ave TN14 ... 59 B1
anderstead Rd BR5 ... 44 B3
andfield Rd TN11 ... 157 A7
andford Rd
Bexley DA7,DA6 ... 13 E4
Bromley BR2 ... 42 A5
andgate Ct ME8 ... 69 F4
andgate Rd DA16 ... 13 C7
andham Point SE18 ... 2 B2
andhill La ME3 ... 38 D6
andhole Cotts TN12 ... 161 C4
andhurst Ave TN2 ... 160 E5
andhurst Cl
Gillingham ME8 ... 55 C3
Royal Tunbridge Wells
TN2 ... 159 C6
Sandhurst Cross TN18 ... 196 A4
andhurst Cross TN12 ... 150 F1
andhurst Ho TN2 ... 159 D5
andhurst La TN17 ... 191 B2
andhurst Pk TN2 ... 159 C6
andhurst Prim Sch
TN18 ... 196 C5
Sandhurst Rd Bexley DA5 ... 13 D2
Orpington BR6 ... 58 A6
Royal Tunbridge Wells
TN2 ... 159 D6
Sidcup DA15 ... 30 A5
Tilbury RM18 ... 19 C5
Sandhurst Vineyards*
TN18 ... 196 E5
Sandilands TN13 ... 91 D5
Sandling Ct ME14 ... 100 B7
Sandling La ME14 ... 100 A8
Sandling Prim Sch
ME14 ... 100 B8
Sandling Rd
Maidstone ME14 ... 99 F6
Maidstone,Ringlestone
ME14 ... 99 F7
Sandling Rise SE9 ... 29 A5
Sandling Way ME4 ... 40 B1
Sandown Cl TN2 ... 159 F6
Sandown Dr ME8 ... 69 D7
Sandown Gr TN2 ... 159 F6
Sandown Pk TN2 ... 159 F6
Sandown Rd
Gravesend DA12 ... 36 C2
West Malling ME19 ... 97 B8
Sandpiper Cl DA9 ... 17 A1
Sandpiper Dr DA8 ... 15 B7
Sandpiper Rd ME5 ... 68 D2
Sandpiper Way BR5 ... 44 D6
Sandpipers The DA12 ... 36 D6
Sandpit Pl SE7 ... 1 E1
Sandpit Rd DA1 ... 15 C3
Sandra Ct 5 ME2 ... 53 B8
Sandringham Ct ME19 ... 97 A1
Sandringham Dr
Bexley DA16 ... 12 E5
Maypole DA2 ... 31 E6
Sandringham Ho ME1 ... 53 B4
Sandringham Mews
TN4 ... 159 A5
Sandringham Rd
Bromley BR1 ... 28 A3
Gillingham ME8 ... 69 E3
Sandrock Ho TN2 ... 159 D4
Sandrock Rd TN2 ... 159 C4
Sandrock Villas TN18 ... 188 F3
Sandshaw Ct DA3 ... 48 E4
Sandstone La E16 ... 1 B6
Sandstone Rd SE12 ... 28 B6
Sandstone Rise ME5 ... 84 C8
Sandtoft Rd SE7 ... 11 B8
Sandway Path 6 BR5 ... 44 C5
Sandway Rd
Harrietsham ME17 ... 119 F4
Orpington BR5 ... 44 C5
Sandy Bank Rd DA12 ... 36 B7
Sandy Bury BR6 ... 57 D7
Sandy Dell ME7 ... 69 A3
Sandy Hill Ave SE18 ... 2 B1
Sandy Hill La SE18 ... 2 B2
Sandy Hill Rd SE18 ... 2 B1
Sandy La Bean DA13,DA2 ... 34 D5
Ightham TN15 ... 94 B3
Limpsfield RH8 ... 104 B7
Maidstone,Harbourland
ME14 ... 100 C8
Maidstone,Penenden Heath
ME14 ... 100 C7
Maidstone,Ware Street
ME14 ... 101 B5
New Town ME19 ... 81 A1
Orpington BR6 ... 44 A2
Ruxley BR5 ... 44 D8
Sevenoaks TN13 ... 92 C4
Snodland ME6,ME19 ... 81 E6
Tenterden TN30 ... 193 B7
Tilbury RM16 ... 19 B8
West Thurrock RM20 ... 17 B8
Westerham TN16 ... 89 D2
Wrotham Heath TN15,ME19 ... 79 F1
Sandy Mount ME14 ... 101 B5
Sandy Ridge
Borough Green TN15 ... 95 A7
Chislehurst BR7 ... 29 A2
Sandycroft SE2 ... 13 A8
Sandycroft Rd ME2 ... 38 F1
Santana Ho SE18 ... 12 B7
Santer Ho TN18 ... 194 E8
Sapho Pk DA12 ... 36 F4
Saphora Cl BR6 ... 57 D5
Sappers Wlk ME7 ... 54 C5
Sapphire Cl E6 ... 2 A7
Sara Cres DA9 ... 17 B3
Sara Ho 1 DA8 ... 14 E7
Sara Pk DA12 ... 36 E4
Sara Turnbull Ho 3 SE18 ... 1 F2
Saracen Cl ME7 ... 55 A1
Saracen Fields ME5 ... 84 C8
Sarafand Ho ME1 ... 53 B4
Sarah Ct 7 DA6 ... 13 E3
Sark Wlk E16 ... 1 B7
Sarsen Hts ME5 ... 67 F1
Sarsens Cl DA12 ... 50 F6
Sassoon Cl ME20 ... 82 A4
Satanita Cl E16 ... 1 D7
Saunder's Cross TN14 ... 59 B2
Saunders Cl DA11 ... 35 E6
Saunders Rd
Royal Tunbridge Wells
TN4 ... 158 E1
Woolwich SE18 ... 2 F1
Saunders St
7 Chatham ME4 ... 53 F3
Gillingham ME7 ... 54 C6
Saunders Way
Dartford DA1 ... 32 F6
Woolwich SE28 ... 3 B6
Savage Gdns E6 ... 1 F7
Savage Rd ME5 ... 68 B3
Saville Cl TN10 ... 127 D7
Saville Ho E16 ... 2 B5
Saville Rd E16 ... 1 E5
Savoy Rd DA1 ... 15 D2
Sawyers Ct ME4 ... 54 B2
Saxby Wood TN11 ... 125 F1
Saxbys Rd TN15 ... 93 D5
Saxon Cl Kings Hill ME19 ... 96 F2
Northfleet DA11 ... 35 C5
Otford TN14 ... 75 F2
Rochester ME2 ... 38 F1
Saxon Pl Horton Kirby DA4 ... 47 C4
Rochester ME2 ... 52 F5
Saxon Rd Bromley BR1 ... 28 A1
Hawley DA2 ... 32 E4
Saxon Way Prim Sch
ME7 ... 54 E6
Saxon Wlk DA14 ... 30 C2
Saxons Dr ME14 ... 100 B7
Saxton St ME7 ... 54 C5
Saxville Rd BR5 ... 44 B6
Sayer Cl DA9 ... 17 A2
Sayers La 6 TN30 ... 193 A7
Sayes Court Rd BR5 ... 44 B5
Scabharbour Rd TN14 ... 108 C1
Scadbury Gdns BR5 ... 44 A7
Scadbury Park Nature
Reserve* BR7 ... 29 F2
Scads Hill Cl BR6 ... 43 F3
Scarborough Cl TN16 ... 72 C1
Scarborough La ME1 ... 66 D2
Scarlet Cl BR5 ... 44 B5
Scarlett Cl ME5 ... 68 C5
Scarsbrook Rd SE3 ... 11 D4
Schofield Wlk SE3 ... 11 A7
Scholars Rise ME2 ... 52 D7
Scholey Cl ME2 ... 66 B4
School App TN15 ... 94 F7
School Ave ME7 ... 54 E4
School Cl DA13 ... 50 A2
School Cotts Bromley BR1 ... 28 A1
Crockenhill BR8 ... 45 D2
Seal TN15 ... 92 F6
Sidcup DA14 ... 30 C3
School Cres DA1 ... 14 F3
School Field TN8 ... 122 C2
School Hill TN3 ... 176 B6
School House La TN12 ... 163 E7
School La Bean DA2 ... 34 C5
Bexley DA16 ... 13 B4
Chestnut Street ME9 ... 71 F4
Culverstone Green DA13 ... 64 A2
Hadlow TN11 ... 128 E8
Hextable BR8 ... 32 B1
Higham ME3 ... 38 C5
Horton Kirby DA3,DA4 ... 47 E4
Knockmill TN15 ... 77 F8
Maidstone ME15 ... 100 E1
Newington ME9 ... 71 B7
Platt's Heath ME17 ... 119 F2
Plaxtol TN11,TN15 ... 110 E6
Seal TN15 ... 92 F6
Sutton Valence ME17 ... 134 E7
Trottiscliffe ME19 ... 80 A5
Wouldham ME1 ... 66 D5
School Rd Chislehurst BR7 ... 29 C1
Gravesend DA12 ... 36 C5
School Rise TN2 ... 158 F1
School Terr 6 TN18 ... 188 F2
School Villas ME18 ... 113 D5
Schoolfield Rd RM20 ... 17 A8
Schooner Ct DA2 ... 16 C3
Schooner Ho 11 DA8 ... 4 E1
Schooner Wlk ME2 ... 39 F3
Schrieber Mews ME7 ... 54 D5
Scilla Ct 11 RM17 ... 18 D8
Scimitar Cl ME7 ... 55 A1
Scords La TN16 ... 106 C4
Scotby Ave ME5 ... 68 B4
Scotland La DA12 ... 50 F6
Scotney Castle* TN3 ... 176 D3
Scotney Castle Gdns*
TN3 ... 176 D3
Scotney Cl BR6 ... 57 A6
Scotney Ho ME2 ... 39 C1
Scotsdale Cl BR5 ... 43 E5
Scotsdale Rd SE12 ... 11 B2
Scott Ave ME8 ... 70 A8
Scott Cl ME20 ... 98 C8
Scott Cres DA8 ... 14 F6
Scott Ho 4 DA17 ... 3 F1
Scott Rd Gravesend DA12 ... 36 D3
Tonbridge TN9 ... 142 F7
Scott St ME14 ... 99 F6
Scott Wilkie Prim Sch
E16 ... 1 C7
Scott's Terr ME4 ... 53 F3
Scotteswood Ave ME4 ... 53 F2
Scotts Ho DA16 ... 13 C6
Scotts Park Prim Sch
BR1 ... 42 C8
Scotts Pas 11 SE18 ... 2 B2
Scotts Rd BR1 ... 28 A1
Scotts Terr SE9 ... 28 E6
Scotts Way
Royal Tunbridge Wells
TN2 ... 172 E8
Sevenoaks TN13 ... 91 E5
Scoulding Rd E16 ... 1 A7
Scragged Oak Cvn Pk
ME14 ... 85 B2
Scragged Oak Rd
Detling ME14 ... 85 C5
Hucking ME17 ... 86 C1
Scratchers La DA3 ... 61 E7
Scratton Fields DA12 ... 50 D4
Scrubbs La ME16 ... 99 D4
Scudders Hill DA3 ... 48 C3
Seabrook Rd TN10 ... 127 A3
Seabrooke Rise RM17 ... 18 B8
Seacourt Rd SE2 ... 3 D4
Seaford Ct ME1 ... 53 B5
Seagull La E16 ... 1 A6
Seagull Rd ME2 ... 52 D6
Seal CE Prim Sch TN15 ... 92 F7
Seal Dr TN15 ... 92 F6
Seal Ho TN15 ... 92 F6
Seal Hollow Rd TN13 ... 92 D4
Seal Rd TN13,TN14,TN15 ... 92 D6
Sealand Ct ME1 ... 53 B5
Sealcroft Cotts TN15 ... 92 F8
Seamew Ct ME2 ... 52 C7
Searles Dr E6 ... 2 B8
Seaton Rd Bexley DA16 ... 13 C7
Dartford DA1 ... 32 A8
Gillingham ME7 ... 54 E3
Seaview ME3 ... 27 B5
Seaview Rd ME7 ... 54 C4
Second Ave Chatham ME4 ... 54 C1
Gillingham ME7 ... 54 E3
West Thurrock RM20 ... 17 A8
Secretan Rd ME1 ... 53 B1
Sedcombe Cl DA14 ... 30 C4
Sedge Cres ME5 ... 67 E4
Sedge Ct RM17 ... 18 E7
Sedgebrook Rd SE3 ... 11 D4
Sedgemere Rd SE2 ... 3 C3
Sedgemoor Ho ME1 ... 53 E5
Sedley DA13 ... 35 A2
Sedley Cl Aylesford ME20 ... 82 F2
Cliffe Woods ME3 ... 39 C7
Gillingham ME8 ... 69 C3
Sedley's CE Prim Sch
DA13 ... 35 A3
Sefton Cl BR5 ... 43 F5
Sefton Rd BR5 ... 43 F5
Sejant Ho 4 RM17 ... 18 B8
Selah Dr BR8 ... 45 C8
Selborne Ave DA5 ... 30 E7
Selborne Rd DA14 ... 30 B4
Selbourne Cl DA3 ... 49 D6
Selbourne Rd ME7 ... 54 D7
Selbourne Wlk ME15 ... 116 F6
Selby Cl Chislehurst BR7 ... 29 A2
14 Newham E6 ... 1 E8
Selby Rd Maidstone ME15 ... 116 F4
Newham E13 ... 1 B8
Select Bsns Ctr TN12 ... 149 E5
Selkirk Dr DA8 ... 14 E6
Sellbourne Pk TN3 ... 173 C4
Sellinge Gn ME8 ... 55 C3
Sellwood Ct DA1 ... 33 B7
Selsey Cres DA16 ... 13 D6
Selstead Cl ME8 ... 55 C2
Selwood Ho BR7 ... 29 C2
Selwyn Cres DA16 ... 13 B3
Selwyn Pl 1 BR5 ... 44 B6
Selwyn Rd RM18 ... 18 F5
Semple Gdns ME4 ... 53 E3
Senacre La ME15 ... 116 E6
Senacre Sq ME15 ... 116 F7
Senacre Tech Coll
ME15 ... 116 D6
Senacre Wood Prim Sch
ME15 ... 116 F7
Senator Wlk 4 SE28 ... 2 D3
Sencler Ho Bexley SE2 ... 13 D8
Erith SE2 ... 3 D1
Senlac Pl TN3 ... 171 C7
Senlac Rd SE12 ... 28 B7
Sennen Wlk SE9 ... 28 E5
Sennocke Ct TN13 ... 92 B2
Sequoia Gdns BR6 ... 43 F2
Sermon Dr BR8 ... 45 C6
Serpentine Ct TN13 ... 92 D5
Serpentine Rd TN13 ... 92 D4
Serviden Dr BR1 ... 42 D8
Sessions House Sq ME14 ... 99 F5
Setford Rd ME5 ... 68 C6
Settington Ave ME5 ... 54 C1
Seven Acres
Crockenhill BR8 ... 45 D3
New Ash Green DA3 ... 62 E7
Seven Mile La
Kings Hill TN15,ME18 ... 96 A3
Mereworth TN11,TN12 ... 112 E3
Wrotham Heath TN15 ... 95 F7
Seven Wents TN15 ... 94 A4
Sevenoaks Bsns Ctr
TN14 ... 92 C6
Sevenoaks By-Pass
TN13,TN14 ... 107 F7
Sevenoaks Cl DA7 ... 14 B3
Sevenoaks Hospl TN13 ... 92 C6
Sevenoaks Mus & Gallery*
TN13 ... 92 C2
Sevenoaks Prep Sch
TN15 ... 93 A1
Sevenoaks Prim Sch
TN13 ... 92 B5
Sevenoaks Rd
Borough Green TN15 ... 94 F7
Ightham TN15 ... 94 A4
Orpington BR6 ... 57 F6
Otford TN14 ... 76 B3
Pratt's Bottom BR6,TN14 ... 58 C2
Sevenoaks Sch TN13 ... 92 C1
Sevenoaks Sch Int Ctr
TN13 ... 92 B1
Sevenoaks Sta TN13 ... 92 A3
Sevenoaks Way BR5 ... 44 C7
Sevenoaks Way Ind Est 1
BR5 ... 44 C6
Sevenoaks Wildfowl
Reserve* TN14 ... 92 A7
Severn Cl TN10 ... 127 C5
Severn Rd ME5 ... 68 C5
Sevington Pk ME15 ... 115 F6
Sewell Rd SE2 ... 3 B4
Sextant Pk ME2 ... 53 E6
Sexton Rd RM18 ... 18 F6
Seymour Dr BR2 ... 42 F1
Seymour Rd
1 Chatham ME5 ... 54 B3
Gillingham ME8 ... 70 C8
Northfleet DA11 ... 35 F6
Tilbury RM18 ... 18 F6
Seymour St SE18 ... 2 C3
Seymour Wlk DA10 ... 34 E8
Shacklands Rd TN14 ... 59 D1
Shackleton Cl ME5 ... 68 B6
Shades The ME2 ... 52 C7
Shaftesbury Cl ME19 ... 81 F1
Shaftesbury Ct Erith DA8 ... 14 F6
3 Woolwich SE28 ... 3 C5
Shaftesbury Dr ME16 ... 99 C4
Shaftesbury La DA1 ... 16 B3
Shaftesbury Rd TN4 ... 159 A5
Shaftsbury Ct E6 ... 2 A7
Shakespeare Ave RM18 ... 19 B6
Shakespeare Farm Rd
ME3 ... 24 F7
Shakespeare Ho 1 DA17 ... 3 F1
Shakespeare Rd
Bexley DA7 ... 13 E6
Dartford DA1 ... 16 A3
Gillingham ME7 ... 54 C3
Tonbridge TN9 ... 142 F8
Shalder Ho ME7 ... 54 D7
Shalfleet Cl 1 ME5 ... 68 A7
Shalford Cl BR6 ... 57 C6
Shallons Rd SE9 ... 29 B4
Shambles The TN13 ... 92 C2
Shamel Bsns Ctr ME2 ... 53 C7
Shamley Rd ME5 ... 68 D2
Shamrock Rd DA12 ... 36 F8
Shandon Cl TN2 ... 159 C4
Shanklin Cl ME5 ... 68 C8
Shannon Ct BR6 ... 44 A2
Sharfleet Dr ME2 ... 52 B7
Sharland Rd DA12 ... 36 C6
Sharman Ct DA14 ... 30 A4
Sharnal La ME6 ... 82 A7
Sharnal St ME3 ... 24 A2
Sharnbrooke Cl DA16 ... 13 C4
Sharon Cres ME5 ... 67 F4
Sharon Ct 10 DA14 ... 30 B4
Sharp Way DA1 ... 15 F4
Sharp's Field TN27 ... 151 E5
Sharps Gn ME8 ... 55 D5
Sharsted Way
Gillingham ME7 ... 69 A3
Maidstone ME14 ... 101 B5
Shaw Cl Cliffe Woods ME3 ... 39 B8
Maidstone ME14 ... 100 C7
Woolwich SE28 ... 3 B5
Shaw Cres RM18 ... 19 B6
Shaw Ho 6 Erith DA17 ... 3 F1
5 Newham E16 ... 2 A5
Shaw Rd TN16 ... 88 C7
Shaw The TN2 ... 159 C2
Shawbrooke Rd SE9 ... 11 D3
Shawfield Pk BR1 ... 42 D7
Shawhill Ho ME19 ... 80 B1
Shaws Way ME1 ... 53 C3
Shawstead Rd ME7,ME7 ... 68 D5
Sheafe Dr TN17 ... 179 C5
Sheal's Cres ME15 ... 100 A2
Sheals Ct ME15 ... 100 A2
Shearers Cl ME14 ... 100 E4
Shears Cl DA2 ... 32 C6
Shears Green Ct DA11 ... 36 A6
Shears Green Inf Sch
DA11 ... 35 F5
Shears Green Jun Sch
DA11 ... 35 F5
Shearwater
Maidstone ME16 ... 99 B5
New Barn DA3 ... 49 B6
Shearwater Cl ME2 ... 52 C7
Shearwood Cres DA1 ... 15 A4
Sheen Rd BR5 ... 43 F5
Sheepbarn La TN16 ... 72 A7
Sheepcote La BR5,BR8 ... 44 F4
Sheephurst La TN12 ... 147 E5
Sheerness Harbour Est
ME12 ... 27 F3
Sheerness Mews E16 ... 2 B4
Sheerwater Rd E16 ... 1 D8
Sheet Hill TN15 ... 94 D2
Sheffield Rd 4 TN4 ... 142 F2
Sheilings The TN15 ... 92 F7
Shelbury Cl DA14 ... 30 A5
Shelden Dr ME8 ... 69 F8
Sheldon Bsns Ctr ME2 ... 53 D8
Sheldon Cl SE12 ... 11 B2
Sheldon Rd DA7 ... 13 F6
Sheldon Way ME20 ... 82 B3
Sheldrake Cl E16 ... 1 F5
Sheldwich Terr BR2 ... 42 E3
Shell Cl BR2 ... 42 E3
Shellbank La DA2 ... 34 B4
Shelldrake Cl ME3 ... 27 B5
Shelley Cl BR6 ... 57 E7
Shelley Dr DA16 ... 12 E6
Shelley Ho DA1 ... 14 E2
Shelley Pl RM18 ... 19 B6
Shelley Rd ME16 ... 99 C2
Shelley Rise ME1 ... 53 A3
Shelleys La TN14 ... 74 A3
Shelton Cl TN10 ... 127 C5
Shenden Cl TN13 ... 108 C7
Shenden Way TN13 ... 108 C7
Shenfield Ho SE18 ... 11 D7
Shenley Gr ME14 ... 83 F2
Shenley Rd DA1 ... 33 A8
Shenstone Cl DA1 ... 14 D3
Shenstone Sch DA1 ... 14 D3
Shepherd St DA11 ... 35 D8
Shepherds Cl BR6 ... 57 F7
Shepherds Gate ME7 ... 68 F5
Shepherds Gate Dr
ME14 ... 100 E6
Shepherds Gn BR7 ... 29 D1
Shepherds La
Dartford DA1 ... 32 B8
Woolwich SE28 ... 2 E5
Shepherds Leas SE9 ... 12 D3
Shepherds Way
Langley Heath ME17 ... 117 E4
Lower Stoke ME3 ... 25 C4
Shepherds Wlk TN2 ... 159 D4
Shepherdsgrove La
RH19 ... 154 A4
Sheppards Coll 8 BR1 ... 42 A8

Shepperton Cl ME5 ..68 C4
Shepperton Rd BR5 ..43 C3
Sheppey Cl DA8 ..15 B7
Sheppey Rd ME15 ..116 A7
Sheppy Ho 1 BR1 ..28 B1
Sheppy Pl DA12 ..36 B8
Shepway Ct ME15 ..116 C8
Shepway Inf Sch ME15 ..116 E8
Shepway Jun Sch ME15 ..116 E8
Sherard Mans SE9 ..11 F2
Sherard Rd SE9 ..11 E2
Sheraton Ct ME5 ..67 F1
Sherborne Gr TN15 ..77 A2
Sherborne Rd BR5 ..43 F4
Sherbourne Cl
Royal Tunbridge Wells TN2 ..159 D2
West Kingsdown TN15 ..61 E4
Sherbourne Dr
Maidstone ME16 ..99 B2
Rochester ME2 ..39 A1
Sherbrooke Cl DA7 ..14 A3
Sherenden La TN12 ..164 D8
Sherenden Pk TN11 ..129 A5
Sherenden Rd TN11 ..144 D7
Sherfield Rd RM17 ..18 B8
Sheridale Bsns Ctr ME2 ..53 A6
Sheridan Cl Chatham ME5 ..68 C7
Maidstone ME14 ..99 E8
Swanley BR8 ..45 F6
Sheridan Cres BR7 ..43 B7
Sheridan Ct Dartford DA1 ..16 A3
Rochester ME1 ..53 A2
Sheridan Lodge 1 BR2 ..42 C5
Sheridan Rd Bexley DA7 ..13 E4
Erith DA17 ..4 A2
Sheriff Dr ME5 ..68 A2
Sheringham Cl ME16 ..99 D7
Sheringham Ho 5 ME15 ..116 D8
Sherington Prim Sch SE7 ..11 B8
Sherington Rd SE7 ..11 B8
Sherlies Ave BR6 ..57 E8
Sherman Cl ME7 ..55 B1
Sherman Rd BR1 ..42 A8
Shernden La TN8 ..138 C4
Shernold Sch ME16 ..99 D5
Shernolds ME15 ..116 B7
Sherway Cl TN27 ..151 E5
Sherway Rd TN27 ..152 D6
Sherwin Knight Inf Sch ME2 ..52 E5
Sherwin Knight Jun Sch ME2 ..52 E5
Sherwood Ave ME5 ..68 A2
Sherwood Cl DA5 ..13 C1
Sherwood Ho
Chatham ME5 ..68 A3
Erith DA8 ..14 E8
Sherwood Park Ave DA15 ..13 B1
Sherwood Park Com Prim Sch TN2 ..159 D6
Sherwood Park Prim Sch DA15 ..13 B1
Sherwood Pl TN3 ..157 E3
Sherwood Rd Bexley DA16 ..12 E4
Royal Tunbridge Wells TN2 ..159 E5
Sherwood Way TN2 ..159 D6
Shieldhall St SE2 ..3 C2
Shillingheld Cl ME14 ..100 F5
Shinecroft TN14 ..76 A3
Shingle Barn La ME15 ..114 C3
Shinglewell Rd DA8 ..14 A7
Ship Field Cl TN16 ..88 C6
Ship Hill TN16 ..88 D6
Ship La Rochester ME1 ..53 E4
Sutton at H BR8,DA4 ..46 E8
Shipbourne Rd
Shipbourne TN11 ..110 D2
Tonbridge TN10 ..127 C5
Shipbourne Sch TN11 ..110 C4
Shipley Ct ME14 ..100 A4
Shipley Hills Rd DA13 ..49 E1
Shipman Rd E16 ..1 C7
Shipwrights Ave ME4 ..54 B2
Shire Ct DA18 ..3 D3
Shire La
Farthing Street BR6 ..57 C3
Orpington BR6 ..57 E5
Shirebrook Rd SE3 ..11 D4
Shirehall Rd DA2 ..32 E4
Shires The TN12 ..146 A7
Shirley Ave Chatham ME5 ..67 D5
Sidcup DA5 ..30 D7
Shirley Cl Chalk DA12 ..37 B6
Dartford DA1 ..15 C3
Shirley Ct ME15 ..116 E5
Shirley Gdns TN4 ..158 C5
Shirley Gr TN4 ..158 C5
Shirley House Dr SE7 ..11 C7
Shirley Hts 5 DA6 ..13 E3
Shirley Rd DA15 ..29 E5
Shirley Way ME15 ..101 A3
Sholden Gdns BR5 ..44 C4
Sholden Rd ME2 ..39 C1
Shooters Hill SE18 ..12 A6
Shooters Hill Rd SE18, SE3 ..11 D6
Shore The Northfleet DA11 ..18 C2
Northfleet,Rosherville DA11 ..18 F1
Shoreham Aircraft Mus* TN14 ..75 F8
Shoreham Cl DA5 ..30 D7
Shoreham Ho TN14 ..76 A8
Shoreham La
Badgers Mount TN14 ..75 A7
Chelsfield BR6 ..59 A3
Sevenoaks TN13 ..91 F4
Tenterden TN30 ..183 A3
Shoreham Pl TN14 ..76 A7
Shoreham Rd
Orpington BR5 ..44 B7
Otford TN14 ..76 B5
Shoreham Sta TN14 ..76 B8
Shoreham Village Sch TN14 ..75 F8
Shoreham Way BR2 ..42 A3
Shoreham Wlk ME15 ..116 F7
Shorehill Ct TN15 ..76 F2
Shorehill La TN15 ..76 F4
Shorland Ct ME1 ..53 B5
Shorne CE Prim Sch DA12 ..37 E3
Shorne Cl Orpington BR5 ..44 D5
3 Sidcup DA15 ..13 B1
Shorne Ifield Rd DA12 ..37 C2
Shorne Wood Ctry Pk* DA12 ..37 C1
Shornefield Cl BR1 ..43 A6
Shornells Way SE2 ..3 C1
Short La RH8 ..104 B3
Short Path SE18 ..12 B8
Short St 3 ME4 ..54 B3
Shortlands Cl DA17 ..3 F3
Shortlands Gn ME15 ..116 F5
Shorts Way ME1 ..53 A3
Shortway SE9 ..11 E4
Shottenden Rd ME7 ..54 D7
Shottery Cl SE9 ..28 E5
Showfields Rd TN2 ..158 F1
Shrapnel Cl SE18 ..11 E7
Shrapnel Rd SE9 ..11 F4
Shrewsbury La SE18 ..12 B6
Shroffold Rd BR1 ..28 A5
Shropshire Terr 1 ME15 ..116 E7
Shrubbery Rd
Gravesend DA12 ..36 C7
Sutton at H DA4 ..47 D8
Shrubcote TN30 ..193 C7
Shrublands Ct
Royal Tunbridge Wells TN2 ..159 C4
1 Tonbridge TN9 ..127 C2
Shrubsall Cl SE9 ..28 E7
Shrubshall Mdw TN15 ..111 A8
Shrubsole Dr ME14 ..83 F3
Shurlock Ave BR8 ..45 D7
Shurlock Dr BR6 ..57 C6
Shuttle Cl
Biddenden TN27 ..168 A2
Sidcup DA15 ..29 F8
Shuttle Rd DA1 ..15 A4
Shuttlemead DA5 ..30 F8
Sibley Cl DA6 ..13 E2
Sibthorpe Rd SE12 ..28 C8
Sidcup By Pass Rd
Orpington BR5,BR7,DA14 ..30 B1
Sidcup DA14 ..29 E4
Sidcup Hill DA14 ..30 B3
Sidcup Hill Gdns DA14 ..30 C3
Sidcup Pl DA14 ..30 A3
Sidcup Rd SE12,SE9 ..28 D7
Sidcup Sta DA15 ..30 A6
Sidcup Tech Ctr DA14 ..30 D2
Sidewood Rd SE9 ..29 D7
Sidmouth Ct DA1 ..33 B7
Sidmouth Rd Bexley DA16 ..13 C7
Orpington BR5 ..44 B5
Sidney Cl TN2 ..172 F8
Sidney Gdns TN14 ..76 C2
Sidney Ho SE18 ..11 F6
Sidney Rd Gillingham ME7 ..54 C7
Rochester ME1 ..53 A2
Sidney St ME16 ..99 C2
Siebert Rd SE3 ..11 A8
Siedle Ho 9 SE18 ..12 A8
Siemens Rd SE18 ..1 D3
Signal Ct 6 ME8 ..55 F1
Silchester Ct ME14 ..100 C7
Silecroft Rd DA7 ..14 A6
Silk Cl SE12 ..11 A1
Silk Mills Cl TN13 ..92 C6
Silver Bank ME5 ..68 A6
Silver Birch Ave DA13 ..63 F1
Silver Birch Cl
Joyden's Wood DA2 ..31 E4
Woolwich SE28 ..3 A5
Silver Birch Wlk ME18 ..113 D6
Silver Birches ME5 ..68 A3
Silver Cl TN9 ..143 B6
Silver Hill Chatham ME4 ..53 F3
Hurst Green TN19 ..194 B1
Rochester ME1 ..52 F2
Tenterden TN30 ..183 B1
Silver Hill Gdns 4 ME4 ..53 F3
Silver Rd DA12 ..36 E6
Silver Spring Cl DA8 ..14 B8
Silver St ME9 ..87 F5
Silver Tree ME5 ..68 B1
Silverdale Hartley DA3 ..48 F5
Maidstone ME16 ..99 A2
Silverdale Dr Bromley SE9 ..28 E6
Gillingham ME8 ..69 F7
Silverdale La
Royal Tunbridge Wells TN4 ..159 B6
Sandhurst Cross TN18 ..195 F5
Silverdale Rd Bexley DA7 ..14 B5
Orpington,Petts Wood BR5 ..43 C5
Silverdale Rd *continued*
Orpington,St Paul's Cray BR5 ..44 A6
Royal Tunbridge Wells TN4 ..159 B6
Silverden Cotts TN18 ..195 F4
Silverhurst Dr TN10 ..127 C7
Silverland St E16 ..1 F5
Silverlocke Rd RM17 ..18 D8
Silverspot Cl ME8 ..69 F7
Silversted La TN16 ..89 D6
Silverstone Ct 10 BR1 ..42 C7
Silvertown Sta E16 ..1 E5
Silvertown Way E16 ..1 A5
Silverweed Rd ME5 ..67 F4
Silwood Cl TN2 ..159 E7
Simmonds Ct TN4 ..158 B4
Simmonds Dr DA3 ..49 A4
Simmonds La ME15 ..117 B6
Simmons Rd SE18 ..2 B1
Simnel Rd SE12 ..28 B8
Simon Ct 5 SE28 ..3 B5
Simone Cl BR1 ..42 D8
Simpson Rd ME6 ..82 A6
Simpson's Cotts BR2 ..56 C7
Simpson's Rd BR1,BR2 ..42 A6
Simpsons Pl 6 BR1 ..42 A6
Sinclair Cl ME8 ..69 E5
Sinclair Way DA2 ..33 D4
Sindal Shaw Ho ME5 ..67 E4
Singapore Dr ME7 ..54 B5
Single St TN16 ..73 B4
Single's Cross TN14 ..74 D4
Single's Cross La TN14 ..74 C5
Singlewell Prim Sch DA12 ..36 D2
Singlewell Rd DA11 ..36 B4
Sinkertweazel TN17 ..179 E2
Sion Wlk 8 TN1 ..159 A2
Sir David's Pk TN4 ..142 E1
Sir Evelyn Rd ME1 ..53 B1
Sir John Hawkins Hospl ME4 ..53 E4
Sir John Hawkins Way ME4 ..53 F4
Sir Joseph Williamson's Mathematical Sch ME1 ..53 C1
Sir Martin Bowes Ho 11 SE18 ..2 A2
Sir Thomas Longley Rd ME2 ..53 E6
Sirdar Strand DA12 ..36 F3
Siscup Rd SE9 ..29 B6
Siskin Gdns TN12 ..146 A5
Siskin Wlk ME20 ..81 F2
Sissinghurst Castle Gdns* TN17 ..166 D1
Sissinghurst CE Prim Sch TN17 ..180 B8
Sissinghurst Dr ME16 ..99 B4
Sissinghurst Rd
Biddenden TN27 ..167 C2
Sissinghurst TN17,TN27 ..180 D8
Sittingbourne Rd
Maidstone,Detling ME14 ..100 E8
Maidstone,Penenden Heath ME14 ..100 B6
Siward Rd BR2 ..42 C6
Six Bells La TN13 ..92 C1
Six Fields Path TN30 ..193 A7
Six Penny Cl TN8 ..138 C8
Skeet Hill La BR5,BR6 ..58 E8
Skeffington St SE18 ..2 C3
Skeynes Rd TN8 ..122 B1
Skibbs La BR5,BR6 ..58 E7
Skinner Gdns TN17 ..180 A8
Skinner St Chatham ME4 ..53 F3
Gillingham ME7 ..54 C5
Skinner Street Prim Sch ME7 ..54 C6
Skinner's Terr 13 TN9 ..143 B8
Skinner's Way ME17 ..117 E4
Skinners Cl ME20 ..83 A6
Skinners La TN8 ..122 D2
Skinners' Sch The TN4 ..159 A6
Skinney La DA4 ..47 D6
Skippers Cl DA9 ..17 B2
Skua Ct ME2 ..52 C7
Sky Studios E16 ..2 A4
Skye Cl ME15 ..116 A7
Slade Cl ME5 ..68 B2
Slade Gdns DA8 ..14 F6
Slade Green Inf Sch DA8 ..15 A7
Slade Green Jun Sch DA8 ..15 A7
Slade Green Rd DA8 ..15 B7
Slade Green Sta DA8 ..15 A6
Slade Prim Sch TN9 ..127 B2
Slade The
Lamberhurst TN3 ..176 A3
Tonbridge TN9 ..127 B2
Woolwich SE18 ..12 E8
Sladebrook Rd SE3 ..11 D4
Sladedale Rd SE18 ..2 E1
Slades Dr BR7 ..29 C4
Slaney Rd TN12 ..149 F4
Slater Cl 9 SE18 ..2 A2
Slaters TN8 ..123 F2
Slatin Rd ME2 ..53 B8
Sleeches Cross TN3 ..173 B2
Sleepers Stile Rd TN5 ..175 B1
Slicketts Hill ME4 ..54 A4
Slip Mill Rd TN18 ..188 E4
Slip The TN16 ..89 C1
Slipway Rd ME12 ..27 F3
Sloane Gdns BR6 ..57 C7
Sloane Sq DA3 ..48 E6
Slocum Cl SE28 ..3 C6
Small Bridge Cotts TN17 ..163 B2
Small Bridge Rd TN12, TN17 ..163 B2
Small Grains DA3 ..62 B7
Small Hythe Cl ME15 ..101 B2
Small Hythe Rd TN30 ..193 B4
Small Profits ME15, ME18 ..114 A4
Smallhythe Pl* TN30 ..193 C1
Smallhythe Place (Mus)* TN30 ..199 C8
Smarden Bsns Est TN27 ..168 D7
Smarden Cl 8 DA17 ..4 A1
Smarden Gr SE9 ..28 F4
Smarden Prim Sch TN27 ..153 A1
Smarden Rd
Standen TN27 ..168 B6
Swift's Green TN27 ..152 B4
Smarts Cotts ME14 ..101 C4
Smarts Hill TN11 ..141 A1
Smarts Rd DA12 ..36 C6
Smetham Gdns ME2 ..39 B1
Smith Rd ME5 ..68 B3
Smith St ME2 ..53 A6
Smith's Hill ME15 ..114 C5
Smithers Cl TN11 ..111 E1
Smithers Ct TN12 ..130 A7
Smithers La TN12 ..130 A7
Smithfield Rd ME3 ..27 C5
Smithies Rd SE2 ..3 B2
Smiths La TN8 ..105 C2
Smiths Orch ME9 ..87 F5
Smithy Field 7 TN8 ..122 D3
Smithy The TN5 ..184 A3
Smugglers TN18 ..189 A1
Smugglers Wlk DA9 ..17 B2
Smythe Cl TN4 ..142 E3
Smythe Rd DA4 ..47 A8
Snag La TN14 ..73 D7
Snape La TN5 ..184 D1
Snape View TN5 ..184 F4
Snelling Ave DA11 ..35 F6
Snipe Cl Erith DA8 ..15 B7
Pembury TN2 ..160 E8
Snipe Ct ME2 ..52 C7
Snoad La TN12 ..165 A8
Snodhurst Ave ME5 ..67 E5
Snodhurst Ho 2 ME5 ..68 A7
Snodland CE Prim Sch ME6 ..81 F8
Snodland Rd ME19 ..81 D7
Snodland Sta ME6 ..82 B8
Snodlands Cl BR6 ..57 A1
Snoll Hatch Rd TN12 ..129 F5
Snow Ho ME7 ..54 E7
Snowdon Ave ME14 ..100 B5
Snowdon Cl ME5 ..68 B7
Snowdon Par ME14 ..100 C5
Snughorne La TN27 ..168 D8
Sobraon Villas TN15 ..95 C7
Sole Fields TN13 ..108 C8
Sole St DA12,DA13 ..50 D4
Sole Street Farm ME3 ..39 B3
Sole Street Sta DA13 ..50 D4
Solefield Prep Sch TN13 ..108 C8
Solefields Rd TN13 ..108 C8
Solent Gdns ME5 ..68 B8
Soleoak Dr TN13 ..108 B8
Solomon Rd
Gillingham ME8 ..70 A8
Rainham ME8 ..55 F1
Solomons Rd ME4 ..53 F4
Somerden Rd BR5 ..44 D2
Somerfield Cl ME16 ..99 D5
Somerfield Hospl The ME16 ..99 E5
Somerfield La ME16 ..99 D4
Somerfield Rd ME16 ..99 D4
Somerhill Ave DA15 ..30 B8
Somerhill Rd Bexley DA16 ..13 B5
Tonbridge TN9 ..143 D8
Somerset Ave DA16 ..12 F3
Somerset Cl ME5 ..68 C8
Somerset Rd Dartford DA1 ..32 B8
Maidstone ME15 ..116 C8
Orpington BR6 ..44 A2
Royal Tunbridge Wells TN4 ..159 A6
Somerset Villas TN3 ..171 C7
Somersham Rd DA7 ..13 E5
Somertrees Ave SE12 ..28 B6
Somerville Gdns TN4 ..158 F4
Somerville Rd DA1 ..15 F1
Somner Wlk ME15 ..116 F4
Sonnet Wlk TN16 ..72 C1
Soper's La TN18 ..188 D4
Sophia Rd E16 ..1 B7
Sophurst La TN12 ..161 C5
Sopurst Wood TN12 ..161 D5
Sopwith Cl TN16 ..72 D3
Sorrel Cl SE28 ..3 A5
Sorrel Ct 8 RM17 ..18 D8
Sorrel Gdns E6 ..1 E8
Sorrell Cl 4 TN8 ..122 D3
Sorrell Rd ME5 ..67 F4
Sorrell Way DA11 ..35 E4
Sortmill Rd ME6 ..82 B7
Sounds Lodge BR8 ..45 C3
South Ash Rd TN15 ..62 E4
South Ave ME8 ..55 B2
South Aylesford Ret Pk ME20 ..98 E8
South Bank Cliffe ME3 ..22 B2
Staplehurst TN12 ..149 E2
Sutton Valence ME17 ..134 E7
South Bank *continued*
Westerham TN16 ..89
South Borough Prim Sch ME15 ..100
South Brook La TN8 ..123
South Bush La ME8 ..70
South Cl DA6 ..13
South Cres ME17 ..115
South Ct TN4 ..159
South Dr BR6 ..57
South Eastern Rd ME2 ..53
South Frith TN4 ..143
South Gipsy Rd DA16 ..13
South Glade The DA5 ..30
South Gr TN1 ..159
South Green La ME9 ..86
South Hall Cl DA4 ..46
South Hill BR7 ..28
South Hill Rd DA12 ..36
South Kent Ave DA11 ..18
South La ME17 ..134
South Molton Rd E16 ..1
South Park Bsns Village ME15 ..100
South Park Rd ME15 ..100
South Pk TN13 ..92
South Pondside Rd ME4 ..54
South Rd Chatham ME4 ..54
Chatham ME4,ME7 ..54
Erith DA8 ..14
Marden TN12 ..148
South Ridge BR2 ..42
South Rise Prim Sch SE18 ..2
South Rise Way SE18 ..2
South Row Greenwich SE3 ..11
Penshurst TN8 ..140
South Side Three Rd ME4 ..54
South St Bromley BR1 ..42
Gravesend DA12 ..36
Maidstone ME16 ..98
South Street Rd ME9 ..86
South Terr
Chattenden ME3 ..39
Farningham DA4 ..46
South View Bromley BR1 ..42
Oxted RH8 ..104
South View Cl DA5 ..13
South View Ct 11 BR1 ..42
South View Rd
Dartford DA2 ..32
Royal Tunbridge Wells TN4 ..159
Turner's Green TN5 ..184
West Thurrock RM20 ..17
South View Terr TN17 ..177
Southampton Mews E16 ..1
Southborough CE Prim Sch & Tunbridge Wells Language Unit TN4 ..158
Southborough Ct TN4 ..143
Southborough La BR2 ..42
Southborough Prim Sch BR2 ..43
Southborough Rd BR1 ..42
Southbourne BR2 ..42
Southbourne Gdns SE12 ..11
Southbourne Gr ME5 ..68
Southcroft Ave DA16 ..12
Southcroft Rd BR6 ..57
Southdene TN14 ..74
Southend Cl SE9 ..12
Southend Cres SE9 ..12
Southern Pl BR8 ..45
Southernden Rd TN27 ..136
Southey Mews E16 ..1
Southey Way 1 ME20 ..81
Southey Wlk RM18 ..19
Southfield Ct DA1 ..15
Southfield Rd
Orpington BR7 ..44
Royal Tunbridge Wells TN4 ..159
Southfield Shaw DA13 ..64
Southfields Hextable BR8 ..31
Rochester ME1 ..53
Speldhurst TN3 ..158
Turner's Green TN5 ..184
Southfields Rd TN15 ..61
Southfields Sch DA11 ..36
Southfields Way TN4 ..159
Southfleet Ave DA3 ..49
Southfleet Rd Bean DA2 ..34
8 Northfleet DA11 ..35
Orpington BR6 ..57
Swanscombe DA10 ..35
Southgate TN4 ..158
Southgate Rd TN30 ..193
Southill Rd Bromley BR7 ..28
Chatham ME4 ..53
Southland Rd SE18 ..12
Southlands Ave BR6 ..57
Southlands Ct BR2 ..42
Southlands Gr BR1 ..42
Southlands Rd BR1,BR2 ..42
Southlees La ME9 ..86
Southold Rise SE9 ..28
Southover BR1 ..28
Southport Rd SE18 ..2
Southspring DA15 ..29
Southview Ave RM18 ..19
Southview Cl BR8 ..46
Southview Hts RM20 ..17
Southwark Pl BR1 ..42
Southwark Rd ME2 ..52
Southway BR2 ..42
Southways ME17 ..134
Southwell Rd ME2 ..52

Sou – Sto 237

outhwold Rd DA5 14 B1
outhwood ME16 98 F2
outhwood Ave TN4 159 A6
outhwood Bldgs TN4 158 B4
outhwood Cl BR1 42 F5
outhwood Ho SE9 29 B6
outhwood Rd Eltham SE9 29 B6
Rusthall TN4 158 B5
Woolwich SE28 3 B5
overeign Bvd ME7,ME8 55 A2
overeign Ct Bromley BR2 42 F3
Sutton at H DA4 47 B8
overeign Ho SE18 1 F3
overeign Way TN9 127 C1
overeigns The ME16 99 D4
overeigns Way TN12 148 C6
overign Ho BR7 29 D1
owerby Cl SE9 11 F2
pa Ind Pk TN2 159 E8
pa Valley Rly* TN3 171 D7
pade La ME9 70 C6
par Cl TN11 111 F1
parepenny La DA4 46 E1
parkes Cl BR2 42 B5
parkeswood Ave TN17 191 F3
parkeswood Cl TN17 191 F3
parrow Dr BR5 43 D1
parrow's Farm L Ctr
SE9 29 C8
parrows Green Rd
TN5 184 F5
parrows La SE9 29 C7
pearhead Rd ME14 99 F7
pearman St 8 SE18 12 A8
pectrum Bsns Ctr ME2 53 E8
pectrum Bsns Est
ME15 116 F4
peedgate Farm DA3 61 F8
peedgate Hill DA3 62 A8
peedwell Ave ME5 67 F4
peedwell Cl
Gillingham ME7 54 E5
Maidstone ME14 100 E5
5 Marlpit Hill TN8 122 D3
peedwell Ct RM17 18 E7
pekehill SE9 28 F5
pekes Rd ME7 69 B6
peldhurst CE Prim Sch
TN3 158 A7
peldhurst Ct ME16 99 D4
peldhurst Hill TN3 158 B8
peldhurst Rd
Langton Green TN3 157 F5
Royal Tunbridge Wells
TN3,TN4 158 E8
pelmonden Rd TN12 162 F2
pembley Ct ME4 53 E4
pencer Cl Chatham ME5 68 A5
Orpington BR6 57 F8
pencer Ct 5 BR6 57 C5
pencer Flats ME5 68 B8
pencer Gdns SE9 11 F2
pencer Mews
10 Royal Tunbridge Wells
TN1 159 B4
6 Royal Tunbridge
Wells,Mount Sion TN1 159 A2
pencer St DA11 36 A8
pencer Way ME15 116 E7
pencer Wlk RM18 19 B5
penlow Dr ME5 84 A8
penny La TN12 147 B7
peranza St SE18 2 F1
peyside TN10 127 B5
pielman Rd DA1 15 F3
piers The ME7 55 C5
pillway The ME15 99 D2
pindle Cl SE18 1 E3
pindle Glade ME14 100 C5
pindle Ho 8 DA15 30 A5
pindles RM18 19 A7
pindlewood Cl ME5 68 B3
pinel Cl SE18 2 F1
pinnaker Ct 4 ME1 53 C1
pinnens Acre Com Jun Sch
ME5 68 C1
pinners Cl TN27 168 A2
pinners Wents TN11 111 D8
pinney Oak BR1 42 E7
pinney The Chatham ME5 68 B1
Maidstone ME15 100 B2
Sidcup DA14 30 E3
Swanley BR8 45 E7
Tonbridge TN9 143 A7
pinney Way TN14 73 D8
pinneys The BR1 42 F7
pire Cl DA12 36 B7
pires The Dartford DA1 32 D6
Maidstone ME16 99 D4
Rochester ME2 52 D5
pital St DA1 15 D1
pitfire Cl ME5 68 B6
pitfire Rd ME19 96 F3
pode La TN8 155 A7
ponden La TN18 196 A7
pongs La TN17 166 A1
portsfield ME14 100 B5
portsmans Cotts ME19 97 B5
pot La ME15 101 A2
pout La Brenchley TN12 162 C5
Crockham Hill TN8 105 C1
pray Hill TN3 176 B4
pray St SE18 2 B2
prig The ME14 101 A4
pring Cott DA1 32 D8
pring Cross DA3 63 A7
pring Ct 17 DA15 30 A5
Spring Gdns
Biggin Hill TN16 72 C1
Orpington BR6 58 B4
Rusthall TN4 158 B4
Spring Gr DA12 36 B7
Spring Head Rd TN15 76 F2
Spring Hill TN11,TN3 157 A7
Spring La
Bidborough TN3 142 D3
Oldbury TN15 94 B5
Spring Lodge 3 BR5 44 C4
Spring Shaw Rd BR5 44 A8
Spring Vale Bexley DA7 14 B3
Dartford DA1 32 D8
Maidstone ME16 99 E4
Swanscombe DA9 17 C1
Spring Vale Cl BR8 45 F8
Spring Vale N DA1 32 D8
Spring Vale S DA1 32 D8
Springcroft DA3 49 A4
Springdale Cotts ME3 39 A3
Springett Almshouses
TN18 194 E8
Springett Cl ME20 82 F6
Springett Way ME17 115 D3
Springfield Ave
Maidstone ME14 99 F7
Swanley BR8 45 F5
Tenterden TN30 183 C2
Springfield Cotts TN12 162 F5
Springfield Gdns BR1 42 F5
Springfield Gr SE7 11 C8
Springfield Ind Est
TN18 188 F3
Springfield Rd
Bexley,Bexleyheath DA7 14 B3
Bexley,Welling DA16 13 B4
Bromley BR1 42 F5
Edenbridge TN8 122 B1
Gillingham ME7 54 E6
Groombridge TN3 171 C7
Lunsford ME20 81 F4
Royal Tunbridge Wells
TN4 142 F1
Springfield Terr 7 ME4 53 F4
Springfield Wlk 3 BR6 43 D1
Springfields TN5 186 E1
Springhead TN2 159 D5
Springhead Ent Pk DA11 35 C7
Springhead Rd Erith DA8 14 F8
Northfleet DA11 35 C7
Springholm Cl TN16 72 C1
Springrove Cotts TN12 148 B5
Springshaw Cl TN13 91 D4
Springvale ME8 69 C6
Springvale Ct Eltham SE12 11 A3
Northfleet DA11 35 C6
Springvale Ret Pk 2
BR5 44 C6
Springvale Way BR5 44 C6
Springview Apartments
TN2 159 D6
Springwater Cl SE18 12 A6
Springwell Rd TN9 143 B8
Springwood Cl 1 ME16 99 A3
Springwood Hall TN11 110 D1
Springwood Rd ME16 99 A3
Sprivers Gdns* TN12 162 E4
Spruce Cl ME20 82 B2
Spruce Ho TN4 158 E4
Spruce Rd TN16 72 D3
Sprucedale Cl BR8 45 E7
Spur Rd BR6 58 A8
Spurgeon Cl RM17 18 C8
Spurgeons Cotts ME17 115 E2
Spurrell Ave DA5 31 D4
Spurway ME14 101 A4
Square Hill ME15 100 B4
Square Hill Rd ME15 100 B4
Square The Cowden TN8 155 B6
Hadlow TN11 128 E8
Hunton ME15 131 D7
Leigh TN11 125 F1
Lenham ME17 120 D5
Sevenoaks TN13 91 E5
Swanley BR8 45 D6
Tatsfield TN16 88 C7
Wadhurst TN5 185 A4
Squerryes Ct* TN16 105 C7
Squerryes Mede TN16 105 C8
Squires Cl ME2 52 B7
Squires Field BR8 45 F8
Squires Ho 3 SE18 12 B8
Squires Way DA2 31 D4
Squires Wood Dr BR7 28 F1
Squirrel Way TN2 159 E5
Stable Cl ME5 68 C5
Stabledene Way TN2 160 D6
Stables End BR6 57 C7
Stables The TN18 194 E8
Stace Cl TN30 193 C8
Stacey Cl DA12 36 E3
Stacey Rd TN10 127 A4
Staceys St ME14 99 F5
Stack La DA3 48 F4
Stack Rd DA4 47 D5
Stackfield 1 TN8 122 D3
Stacklands Cl TN15 61 E4
Stadium Rd SE18 11 F8
Stadium Way DA1 14 E2
Stadler Cl ME16 99 D7
Staffa Rd ME15 116 A7
Staffhurst Wood Rd
TN8,RH8 121 C6
Stafford Cl DA9 16 F2
Stafford Rd
Royal Tunbridge Wells
TN2 159 E4
Stafford Rd *continued*
Sidcup DA14 29 E4
Tonbridge TN9 127 B2
Stafford St ME7 54 C5
Stafford Way TN13 108 C8
Stag Rd Chatham ME5 68 B5
Royal Tunbridge Wells
TN2 159 D8
Stagshaw Cl ME15 100 A2
Stainer Ho SE3 11 C3
Stainer Rd TN10 127 F6
Staines Wlk DA14 30 C2
Stainmore Cl BR7 43 D8
Stair Rd TN10 127 F4
Stairfoot La TN13 91 C5
Stake La ME2 66 A6
Staleys Rd TN15 94 F7
Stalham Ct ME7 69 B4
Stalin Ave ME5 68 B8
Stalisfield Pl BR6 57 A1
Stampers The ME15 99 D2
Stan La ME18 112 A7
Stanam Rd TN2 160 E6
Stanbridge Rd TN8 122 B2
Stanbrook Rd
Northfleet DA11 35 F8
Woolwich SE2 3 B4
Standard Ind Est E16 1 F4
Standard Rd Bexley DA6 13 E3
Erith DA17 4 A1
Farthing Street BR6 57 A1
Standen Cl ME8 69 E4
Standen St
Benenden TN17,TN18 190 D2
Royal Tunbridge Wells
TN4 159 A5
Standen Street TN17 196 E8
Standings Cross TN12 145 E1
Standish Ho SE3 11 B3
Stane Way SE18 11 E7
Stanford Dr ME16 99 C3
Stanford La TN11 112 C2
Stanford Way ME2 52 C2
Stangate Rd Birling ME19 81 B8
Rochester ME2 52 C7
Stangrove Rd TN8 122 C1
Stanham Pl DA1 15 A3
Stanham Rd DA1 15 C2
Stanhill Cotts DA2 31 D2
Stanhope Ave BR2 42 A1
Stanhope Cl ME14 99 E7
Stanhope Rd Bexley DA7 13 E5
Rochester ME2 53 A7
Royal Tunbridge Wells
TN1 159 C5
Sidcup DA15 30 A4
Swanscombe DA10 17 F1
Stanhope Way TN13 91 D5
Stanhopes RH8 104 B7
Stanley Cl
Staplehurst TN12 149 E4
Stone DA9 16 E2
Stanley Cotts DA2 33 E3
Stanley Cres DA12 36 D3
Stanley Glyn Ct BR7 29 A3
Stanley Holloway Ct E16 1 A7
Stanley Rd Bromley BR2 42 C5
Chatham ME5 68 C6
Gillingham ME7 54 C6
Grays RM17 18 B8
Marden TN12 148 D5
Northfleet DA11 35 E7
Orpington BR6 43 F1
Royal Tunbridge Wells
TN1 159 B5
Sidcup DA14 30 A5
Swanscombe DA10 17 F1
Stanley Way BR5 44 B4
Stanmore Ho SE12 28 B7
Stanmore Rd DA17 4 C2
Stansfeld Rd E16 1 D7
Stansted CE Prim Sch
TN15 62 F1
Stansted Cl ME16 99 D7
Stansted Cres DA5 30 D7
Stansted Hill TN15 63 A1
Stansted La TN15 62 C1
Stanton Cl BR5 44 C2
Stanton Ct
9 Bromley BR1 42 C7
5 Sidcup DA15 30 A5
Staple Cl DA5 31 D5
Staple Dr TN12 149 F4
Stapleford Ct TN13 91 F4
Staplehurst Ho BR5 44 C4
Staplehurst Rd
Bogden TN12 133 C2
Frittenden TN12,TN17 150 D1
Gillingham ME8 55 B3
Staplehurst Sch TN12 149 E3
Staplehurst Sta TN12 149 E5
Staplers Ct ME14 100 B8
Staples Ho E6 2 A7
Staples The BR8 46 B8
Stapleton Rd Bexley DA7 13 F8
Orpington BR6 57 F7
Stapley Rd DA17 4 A1
Star Bsns Ctr RM13 4 D8
Star Hill Crayford DA1 14 E2
Rochester ME1 53 D5
Star Hill Rd TN14 75 A2
Star Ho TN3 176 B5
Star La Gillingham ME7 69 A7
Orpington BR5,BR8 44 E5
Star Mill Ct ME5 54 D2
Star Mill La ME5 54 D2
Starboard Ave DA9 17 B1
Starling Cl DA3 49 B6
Starnes Ct 5 ME14 100 A5
Starr Cotts TN12 131 C2
Starts Cl BR6 57 A7
Starts Hill Ave BR6 57 B6
Starts Hill Rd BR6 57 B6
Starve Goose La TN17 178 E4
State Farm Ave BR6 57 C6
Stately Pk ME18 113 C1
Station App
Bexley,Barnehurst DA7 14 C5
Bexley,Bexleyheath DA7 13 E5
Bexley,Welling DA16 13 A5
Borough Green TN15 94 F7
Bromley BR7 28 E2
Chelsfield BR6 58 B5
Chislehurst BR7 43 A7
Dartford DA1 15 E1
Edenbridge TN8 122 C2
Grays RM17 18 A8
Greenwich SE3 11 B4
Halling ME2 66 A5
Hayes BR2 42 A1
Maidstone ME16 99 F3
Orpington BR6 57 F8
Orpington,St Mary Cray BR5 44 B5
Otford TN14 76 C3
Paddock Wood TN12 146 A7
Staplehurst TN12 149 E5
Swanley BR8 45 E5
Station Cotts
Gill's Green TN18 188 F5
Hartley TN17 178 E2
Horsmonden TN12 163 B5
Station Cres SE3 1 A1
Station Ct TN15 94 F7
Station Hill
Chiddingstone Causeway
TN11 141 A8
Hayes BR2 56 A8
Station Hill Cotts ME15 115 A7
Station Mews 3 TN30 193 A7
Station Par
Sevenoaks TN13 92 A3
Sidcup DA15 30 A6
Station Rd Aylesford ME20 82 E2
Betsham DA13 35 A4
Bexley DA7 13 E4
Borough Green TN15 94 F7
Brasted TN16 90 B4
Bromley BR1 42 A8
Cliffe ME3 22 B3
Crayford DA1 14 F1
Cuxton ME2 52 C2
East Farleigh ME15 115 A7
East Tilbury RM18 20 B7
Edenbridge TN8 122 C2
Erith DA17 4 A3
Eynsford DA4 60 D7
Goudhurst TN17 177 C7
Groombridge TN3 171 C7
Halstead TN14 74 F8
Harrietsham ME17 119 D6
Headcorn TN27 151 D5
Hurst Green TN19 194 A3
Longfield DA3 48 E6
Maidstone ME14 99 F5
Meopham Sta DA13 50 A4
Nettlestead Green ME18 113 C1
Newington ME9 71 B6
Northfleet DA11 18 B1
Northiam TN31 197 C1
Orpington BR6 57 F8
Orpington,St Mary Cray BR5 44 C5
Otford TN14 76 C3
Paddock Wood TN12 145 F7
Rainham ME8 55 F1
Rochester ME2 53 C7
Rockrobin TN5 184 C6
Sevenoaks TN13 91 E7
Shoreham TN14 76 A7
Sidcup DA14,DA15 30 A5
Staplehurst TN12 149 F5
Stone DA9 17 A2
Sutton at H DA4 47 B7
Swanley BR8 45 E5
Tenterden TN30 193 A7
Withyham TN7 170 B5
Station Rd N DA17 4 B3
Station Sq BR5 43 C4
Station St E16 2 B5
Steadman Cl ME3 38 C6
Stede Hill ME17 103 F3
Stedley 17 DA14 30 A4
Stedman Cl DA5 31 E5
Steele Ave DA9 17 A2
Steele St ME2 53 A8
Steele Wlk DA8 14 B7
Steele's La DA13 64 A6
Steellands Rise TN5 186 F1
Steep Cl BR6 57 F4
Steephill Sch DA3 48 D5
Steeple Heights Dr TN16 72 D2
Steerforth Cl ME1 53 C2
Steers Pl TN11 111 E2
Stella Cl TN12 148 D5
Stelling Rd DA8 14 D7
Stenning Ct TN10 127 C4
Stephen Cl BR6 57 F7
Stephen Rd DA7 14 C4
Stephen's Rd TN4 159 B6
Stephenson Ave RM18 19 A6
Stephenson Ho SE2 3 D1
Stepneyford La TN17 191 C7
Steps Hill Rd ME9 86 D6
Sterling Ave ME16 99 C5
Sterling Ho SE3 11 B3
Sterndale Rd DA1 32 F8
Sterry Gdns ME15 116 E7
Stevanne Ct 1 DA17 4 A1
Stevedale Rd DA16 13 C5
Steven Cl ME4 54 A3
Stevens Cl Dartford DA2 33 E3
Egerton TN27 137 F3
Joyden's Wood DA5 31 D4
Snodland ME6 82 A8
Stevens Cotts TN30 193 A7
Stevens Rd ME20 82 F6
Stevenson Cl Erith DA8 15 B7
Maidstone ME15 99 F3
Stevenson Way ME20 81 F4
Stewart Cl BR7 29 B4
Stewart Ho ME3 39 F6
Stewart Rd TN4 159 C7
Steyning Gr SE9 28 F4
Steynton Ave DA5 30 D6
Stickens La ME19 97 E7
Stickfast La ME17 135 D3
Stickland Rd 2 DA17 4 A2
Stilebridge La
Underling Green ME17 133 A5
Underling Green TN12 132 E3
Stiles Cl Bromley BR2 42 F3
Erith DA8 4 B1
Still La TN4 142 F2
Stillwater Mews ME4 40 B2
Stirling Cl Gillingham ME8 69 E4
Rochester ME1 53 A3
Sidcup DA14 29 F4
Stirling Dr BR6 58 B5
Stirling Ho 5 SE18 2 B1
Stirling Rd ME19 96 F3
Stisted Way TN27 137 F3
Stock Hill TN16 72 D2
Stock La DA2 32 C4
Stockbury Dr ME16 99 D7
Stockbury Ho 7 BR5 44 D1
Stockenbury TN12 129 F6
Stockett La ME15 115 D6
Stockland Green Rd
TN3 158 B8
Stocks Green Prim Sch
TN11 126 E5
Stocks Green Rd TN11 126 C5
Stocks Rd TN30 199 F3
Stockton Cl ME14 100 B8
Stockwell Cl BR1 42 B7
Stofield Gdns SE9 28 D5
Stoke Com Sch ME3 25 C5
Stoke Rd Allhallows ME3 9 C1
Hoo St Werburgh ME3 40 F6
Kingsnorth ME3 41 C8
Lower Stoke ME3 24 E1
Stokesay Ct 14 DA2 16 B1
Stone Cotts TN3 175 F4
Stone Court La TN2 160 E8
Stone Cross Rd TN5 185 A4
Stone Crossing Halt DA9 16 E2
Stone Ct DA8 4 F1
Stone Hill Rd TN27 137 F2
Stone House Hospl DA2 16 C1
Stone Lake Ind Pk SE7 1 C2
Stone Lake Ret Pk SE7 1 C2
Stone Lodge Farm Pk*
DA2 16 D1
Stone Pit La TN18 196 E5
Stone Place Rd DA9 16 E2
Stone Rd BR2 42 A5
Stone Row TN3 157 B5
Stone Row Cotts TN3 157 D1
Stone St Cranbrook TN17 179 D5
Gravesend DA11 19 B1
Royal Tunbridge Wells
TN1 159 B4
Stone Street Rd TN15 93 E2
Stone Wood DA2 34 C5
Stone, St Mary's CE Prim Sch
DA9 33 E8
Stoneacre* ME15 117 B7
Stoneacre Cl ME8 69 D5
Stoneacre Ct 7 ME15 100 A1
Stoneacre La ME15 117 B7
Stonebridge Green Rd
TN27 137 F4
Stonebridge Rd DA11 18 B2
Stonechat Sq 6 E6 1 E8
Stonecroft DA13 80 A8
Stonecroft Rd DA8 14 C7
Stonecrop Cl ME4 40 C1
Stonecross Lea ME5 54 C1
Stonefield Cl DA7 14 A4
Stonefield Way SE7 11 D7
Stonegate Cl BR5 44 C6
Stonegate Rd TN5 185 C1
Stonehill Woods Pk
DA14 31 B2
Stonehorse Ct ME3 39 A3
Stonehorse La ME2 39 A2
Stonehouse Cnr RM19 16 E8
Stonehouse La
Halstead TN14 74 E8
Pratt's Bottom TN14 58 E1
Purfleet RM19 16 E8
Stonehouse Rd BR6,TN14 58 D1
Stoneings La TN14 89 F8
Stoneleigh Rd RH8 104 E5
Stoneness Rd RM20 17 C7
Stones Cross Rd BR8 45 C4
Stones Rdbt ME4 40 B1
Stonestile Bsns Pk
TN27 151 A7
Stonestile Rd TN27 151 A7
Stoneswood Rd RH8 104 B5
Stonewall E6 2 A8

Stonewall Park Rd TN3 .157 F3
Stonewood Cl TN4 159 A8
Stonewood Rd DA8 4 E1
Stoney Alley SE18 12 A5
Stoney Bank ME7 54 F1
Stony Cnr DA13 49 E6
Stony La ME1 67 C5
Stonyfield TN8 122 D3
Stopford Rd ME7 54 D4
Store Rd E16 2 A4
Storehouse Wharf ME12 27 F3
Storey St E16 2 A4
Stornaway Strand DA12 36 F4
Stotfold BR1 42 E8
Stour Cl Orpington BR2 56 C6
Rochester ME2 52 F7
Tonbridge TN10 127 B5
Stour Ct 22 BR5 44 D1
Stour Rd DA1 15 A4
Stow Ct DA2 33 C8
Stowe Rd BR6 58 B6
Stowting Rd BR6 57 E6
Strait Rd E6 1 F6
Strand Approach Rd ME7 54 E7
Strand Cl DA13 50 A3
Strand Ct SE18 2 E1
Strand Rdbt The ME7 54 E7
Strandfield Cl SE18 2 E1
Stratfield Ho SE12 28 A6
Stratford Ave ME8 69 D8
Stratford Dr ME15 116 D6
Stratford House Ave BR1 42 E6
Stratford La 2 ME8 69 F8
Stratford Rd ME19 97 A8
Stratford St TN1 159 C5
Strathaven Rd SE12 11 B1
Stratheden Par SE3 11 A7
Stratheden Rd SE3 11 A7
Stratton Cl DA7 13 E4
Stratton Rd DA7 13 E4
Stratton Terr TN16 105 C8
Straw Mill Hill ME15 99 E1
Strawberry Cl TN2 172 E7
Strawberry Fields BR8 45 E7
Strawberry Vale TN9 127 C1
Stream La TN18 195 A7
Stream Pit La TN18 196 B5
Stream Side TN10 127 D6
Stream The ME20 82 C1
Stream Way DA17 14 A8
Streamdale SE2 13 B8
Streamside ME20 82 B1
Streamside Cl BR2 42 A5
Streatfield TN8 122 D1
Streatfield Ho TN16 89 C1
Street End Rd ME5 54 B1
Street Farm Cotts ME3 40 F6
Street The Ash TN15 62 E5
Benenden TN17 190 D6
Boxley ME14 84 C3
Bredhurst ME7 69 B1
Cobham DA12 50 F6
Detling ME14 85 A1
Egerton TN27 137 F3
Frittenden TN17 166 E7
Hartlip ME9 70 D5
High Halstow ME23 23 E3
Horton Kirby DA4 47 C5
Ightham TN15 94 D6
Maidstone ME14 101 C4
Meopham DA13 50 A1
Mereworth ME18 112 D8
Plaxtol TN15 110 F7
Ryarsh ME19 80 F4
Shorne DA12 37 E3
Silver Street ME9 87 F5
Sissinghurst TN17 180 B8
Smarden TN27 153 A1
Stockbury ME9 86 E8
Teston ME18 114 A7
Trottiscliffe ME19 80 A5
Ulcombe ME17 135 F7
Upper Halling ME2 65 E5
Wittersham TN30 199 D3
Wormshill ME9 103 F7
Streetfield ME17 135 F7
Streetfield Mews SE3 11 A4
Streetfield Rd ME8 55 F1
Strettitt Gdns TN12 129 F5
Strickland Ave DA1 15 F4
Strickland Way 5 BR6 57 F6
Strongbow Cres SE9 11 F2
Strongbow Rd SE9 11 F2
Strood Ret Pk ME2 53 B7
Strood Sta ME2 53 C7
Strover St ME7 54 C7
Struttons Ave DA11 35 F6
Stuart Ave BR2 42 A1
Stuart Cl Hextable BR8 32 A1
Maidstone ME14 100 C6
Royal Tunbridge Wells TN2 172 F8
Stuart Evans Cl DA16 13 C4
Stuart Mantle Way DA8 14 E7
Stuart Rd Bexley DA16 13 B6
Gillingham ME7 54 D3
Gravesend DA11 19 A1
Stubbs Hill BR6,TN14 74 C6
Studios The DA3 62 F8
Studland Cl DA15 29 F5
Studley Cres DA3 49 C7
Studley Ct DA14 30 B3
Stumble Hill TN11 110 C5
Sturdee Ave ME7 54 E4
Sturdee Cotts ME3 41 A6
Sturges Field BR7 29 D2
Sturla Rd ME4 54 A3
Sturmer Ct ME19 97 A2
Sturry Way ME8 55 C2
Styants Bottom Rd TN15 93 F5
Style Cl ME8 69 E4
Styles Cl TN8 123 B5
Styles Cotts TN8 123 B5
Styles Ct TN12 145 F7
Styles La ME14 84 C3
Sudbury E6 2 A7
Sudbury Cres BR1 28 A3
Suffolk Ave ME8 55 F1
Suffolk Ct 7 ME8 55 F1
Suffolk Mews 1 TN1 159 A4
Suffolk Rd Dartford DA1 15 E1
Gravesend DA12 19 D1
Maidstone ME15 116 D8
Sidcup DA14 30 C2
Suffolk Way TN13 92 C2
Sullivan Ave E16 1 D8
Sullivan Cl DA1 32 C8
Sullivan Rd Tilbury RM18 19 A6
Tonbridge TN10 127 E5
Sultan Mews ME5 68 C2
Sultan Rd ME5 68 C2
Summer Cl TN30 183 C1
Summer Hill BR7 43 A7
Summerfield
6 Bromley BR1 42 B8
Marden TN17 164 B6
Summerfield St 9 SE12 28 A8
Summerhill TN27 151 A6
Summerhill Ave TN4 142 F1
Summerhill Cl BR6 57 E7
Summerhill Rd
Bogden TN12 133 C1
Dartford DA1 32 D8
Summerhill Villas BR7 43 B8
Summerhouse Dr DA2, DA5 31 D4
Summerlands Lodge BR6 57 A6
Summerton Way SE28 3 D7
Summervale Rd TN4 158 E1
Sumner Cl Orpington BR6 57 C6
Rolvenden TN17 191 F3
Sun Ct DA8 14 F5
Sun Hill DA3 62 A8
Sun La Gravesend DA12 36 C6
Greenwich SE3 11 B7
Sun Rd DA10 17 F1
Sun Terr ME5 68 B4
Sunburst Cl TN12 148 D5
Sunbury St SE18 1 F3
Sunderland Cl ME1 53 A3
Sunderland Dr ME8 70 A8
Sunderland Ho 3 ME7 54 C7
Sunderland Point E16 2 C5
Sundew Ct 9 RM17 18 D8
Sundorne Rd SE7 1 C1
Sundridge & Brasted CE Prim Sch TN14 90 E2
Sundridge Ave
Bexley DA16 12 D4
Bromley BR1 42 D8
Sundridge Cl DA1 16 A1
Sundridge Ct 10 BR1 28 B1
Sundridge Dr ME5 68 A4
Sundridge Hill
Cuxton ME2 52 C3
Halstead TN14 74 C1
Sundridge Ho BR1 28 B3
Sundridge La TN14 74 C2
Sundridge Park Sta BR1 28 B1
Sundridge Rd TN14 91 B8
Sunfields Pl SE3 11 B7
Sunhill Ct TN2 160 C6
Sunland Ave DA6 13 E3
Sunningdale Cl Erith SE28 3 E7
Gillingham ME8 69 D6
Sunningdale Ct ME15 100 B4
Sunningdale Dr ME8 69 D6
Sunningdale Rd BR1 42 E4
Sunninghill DA11 35 E6
Sunningvale Ave TN16 72 D3
Sunningvale Cl TN16 72 D3
Sunnybank TN5 187 E3
Sunnydale BR6 57 A8
Sunnydale Rd SE12 11 B2
Sunnyfield Rd BR7 44 A6
Sunnyfields Cl ME8 69 E8
Sunnymead Ave ME7 54 E5
Sunnyside TN8 122 B3
Sunnyside Rd TN4 158 C4
Sunray Ave BR2 42 F3
Sunset Cl DA8 15 B7
Sunset Rd SE28 3 A5
Sunshine Ct 1 ME8 69 F8
Superabbey Est ME20 83 B2
Superior Dr 4 BR6 57 F4
Surlingham Cl SE28 3 D6
Surrenden Rd TN12 149 E3
Surrey Cl TN2 172 F8
Surrey Rd ME15 116 D8
Susan Rd SE3 11 B5
Susan Wood BR7 43 A8
Sussex Cl TN2 159 C1
Sussex Dr ME5 68 A4
Sussex Mews 19 TN2 159 A2
Sussex Rd Dartford DA1 33 A8
Erith DA8 14 B7
Maidstone ME15 116 D8
Orpington BR5 44 C3
Sidcup DA14 30 B3
Tonbridge TN9 143 A8
Sussex Road Prim Sch TN9 143 A8
Sutcliffe Rd Bexley DA16 13 C5
Woolwich SE18 12 E8
Sutherland Ave
Bexley DA16 12 E3
Biggin Hill TN16 72 E1
Orpington BR5 43 F4
Sutherland Cl Chalk DA12 37 B6
Stone DA9 16 F2
Sutherland Gdns ME8 69 E6
Sutherland Ho SE18 11 F6
Sutherland Rd Erith DA17 4 A3
Royal Tunbridge Wells TN1 159 B3
Sutlej Rd SE7 11 C7
Sutton at Hone CE Prim Sch DA4 33 A1
Sutton Cl ME8 70 A8
Sutton Ct TN12 148 C5
Sutton Forge TN12 148 D5
Sutton Rd Langley ME17 117 C5
Maidstone ME15 116 D6
Sutton St ME14 101 D4
Sutton Valence Castle* ME17 134 F7
Sutton Valence Prep Sch ME17 134 C7
Sutton Valence Prim Sch ME17 134 E7
Sutton Valence Sch ME17 134 E7
Swadelands Cl ME17 120 C5
Swadelands Sch ME17 120 C5
Swaffield Rd TN13 92 C5
Swain Cl ME2 52 F8
Swain Rd Gillingham ME8 69 B6
Tenterden TN30 183 D3
Swaisland Rd DA1 15 B1
Swaislands Dr DA1 14 F2
Swale Rd Crayford DA1 15 A3
Rochester ME2 52 C7
Swaledale Rd DA2 33 C7
Swallow Cl Bexley DA8 14 E6
Stone DA9 16 F2
Swallow Ct 3 SE12 28 A8
Swallow Dr TN2 159 F6
Swallow Ho 4 ME16 99 E4
Swallow Rd ME20 81 F2
Swallow Rise ME5 68 A5
Swallow St E6 1 E8
Swallowfield Rd SE7 1 B1
Swallowfields 2 DA11 35 E5
Swallowtail Cl BR5 44 D5
Swan Apartments 12 ME15 116 E5
Swan App E6 1 E8
Swan Bsns Pk DA1 15 C3
Swan Cl BR5 44 A6
Swan Cotts TN30 199 D3
Swan La Brandfold TN17 163 F3
Dartford DA1 31 F8
Marlpit Hill TN8 122 C4
Swan Rd SE18 1 D3
Swan Ridge TN8 122 D4
Swan St
West Malling ME19 97 C8
Wittersham TN30 199 C3
Swan Valley Com Sch DA10 34 F8
Swanbridge Rd DA7 14 B6
Swanland Dr TN9 142 F7
Swanley Ctr BR8 45 E6
Swanley La BR8 45 F6
Swanley New Barn Rly* BR8 45 E8
Swanley Rd DA16 13 C6
Swanley Sch BR8 45 E6
Swanley Sta BR8 45 D5
Swanley Village Rd BR8 46 B8
Swanmead Way TN9 127 D2
Swanscombe Bsns Ctr DA10 17 E2
Swanscombe Ho 1 BR5 44 B7
Swanscombe Inf Sch DA10 34 F8
Swanscombe St DA10 17 F1
Swanscombe Sta DA10 17 F2
Swansea Ct E16 2 B4
Swanton Rd Erith DA8 14 B7
Mereworth ME18 112 A8
Swanzy Rd TN14 92 C7
Sward Rd BR5 44 A3
Swattenden La TN17 179 B1
Swaylands Rd DA17 14 A8
Swaynesland Rd RH8 104 F1
Sweeps Hill Cl TN2 160 D7
Sweeps La BR5 44 D5
Sweet Briar Ct ME16 99 D5
Sweetings La TN3,TN5 175 D1
Sweetlands La TN12 150 A5
Sweets La ME19 98 A4
Swetenham Wlk SE18 2 C1
Sweyn Pl SE3 11 A5
Sweyne Jun Sch The DA10 34 F8
Sweyne Rd DA10 17 E1
Swievelands Rd TN16 72 C1
Swift Cl Larkfield ME20 82 A2
Woolwich SE28 3 B6
Swift Cres ME5 68 C6
Swift Ho 6 ME16 99 E4
Swifts View TN17 179 D6
Swiller's La DA12 37 E3
Swinburne Gdns RM18 19 B5
Swingate Ave ME3 22 B6
Swingate Cl ME5 68 B2
Swingate Inf Sch ME5 68 C1
Swingate La SE18 12 E7
Swingfield Ct BR2 42 D4
Swinton Ave ME3 39 F5
Swires Shaw BR2 56 D6
Swithland Gdns SE9 29 A4
Syamore Mews DA8 4 D1
Sycamore Ave DA15 12 F1
Sycamore Cl Eltham SE9 28 E6
Gravesend DA12 36 D8
Tilbury RM18 19 A5
Sycamore Cotts
Bidborough TN3 142 D3
Pembury TN2 160 C6
Sycamore Cres ME16 99 C5
Sycamore Ct Erith DA8 4 D1
Stone DA9 33 E8
Sycamore Dr
Aylesford ME20 82 E1
Swanley BR8 45 E7
Sycamore Gdns TN12 145 F5
Sycamore Lodge BR6 57 F8
Sycamore Rd
Dartford DA1 32 D7
Rochester ME2 52 E5
Sychem La TN12 145 A6
Sychem Pl TN12 145 A7
Sydenham Cotts SE12 28 C6
Sydney Cotts 11 BR5 44 C6
Sydney Rd Bexley DA6 13 D3
Chatham ME4 54 A3
Erith SE2 3 D3
Sidcup DA14 29 E4
Tilbury RM18 19 A5
Sydney Terr TN18 188 F3
Sylewood Cl ME1 67 B8
Sylvan Cl RH8 104 B6
Sylvan Glade ME5 84 A8
Sylvan Mews DA9 17 B3
Sylvan Rd ME8 69 C8
Sylvan Wlk BR1 42 F6
Sylvester Ave BR7 28 F2
Sylvestre Cl ME2 66 A4
Sylvestres TN13 91 E6
Symonds Cl TN15 61 E5
Symonds La ME18 130 F6
Symonds Rd ME3 22 A4
Symons Ave ME4 54 A2
Syon Lodge 11 SE12 28 A8
Syringa Ct 10 RM17 18 D8

T

Tabor Ct TN12 163 A6
Tadburn Gn ME5 68 B4
Taddington Wood La ME5 67 E2
Tadley Ct Gillingham ME7 54 F6
Rochester ME1 67 C8
Tail Race The ME15 99 E2
Tainter Rd TN11 111 E1
Talbot Pk TN2 159 D5
Talbot Rd Maidstone ME16 99 C6
The Moor TN18 194 F8
Tall Trees Cl ME17 118 D2
Tallents Cl DA4 33 B1
Tallis Cl E16 1 B7
Tallis Gr SE7 11 B8
Tally Rd RH8 104 E4
Tamar Dr ME2 52 F7
Tamar Rd TN10 127 B5
Tamar St SE7 1 E2
Tamarind Cl ME7 69 A4
Tamesis Strand DA12 36 E3
Tan Yard La DA5 31 A8
Tandridge Dr BR6 43 D1
Tandridge Pl 2 BR6 43 D1
Tangier La TN3 173 B6
Tangleberry Cl BR1 42 F5
Tanglewood Cl ME8 69 C6
Tanglewood Ct BR5 44 C6
Tangmere Cl ME7 54 F5
Tanhurst Wlk SE2 3 D3
Tanker Hill ME8 69 D6
Tanners Mead TN8 122 C1
Tannery Rd TN9 127 C1
Tansy Cl E6 2 A7
Tanyard Rolvenden TN17 191 E4
Sandhurst TN18 196 B5
Tanyard Cotts DA12 37 E1
Tanyard Hill DA12 37 E2
Tanyard La TN4 142 F1
Tanyard The TN17 179 D4
Tappan Dr ME4 40 B2
Tapsell's La TN5 184 D5
Tarbutts TN17 179 D4
Target Bsns Ctr ME15 116 F4
Tarland Ho TN2 159 D3
Tarling Cl DA14 30 B5
Tarnwood Pk SE9 28 F7
Tarragon Rd ME16 99 B3
Tasker Cl ME15 101 B3
Tasman Wlk E16 1 D7
Tasmania Ho RM18 19 A6
Tassell Cl ME19 82 A1
Tate Rd E16 1 F5
Tates TN18 189 A1
Tates Orch DA3 48 F3
Tatler Cl ME5 68 D2
Tatsfield Cl ME8 55 A2
Tatsfield La
Biggin Hill TN16 88 F6
Hill Park TN16 89 A6
Tatsfield Prim Sch TN16 88 D6
Tattersall Cl SE9 11 E2
Tattershall Ct 22 DA2 16 B1
Tattershall Rd ME15 100 A1
Tattlebury La TN17 163 F1
Tattlebury Rd TN27 151 C8
Taunton Cl Bexley DA7 14 D5
Taunton Cl *continued*
Maidstone ME15 116 F
Taunton Rd DA11 18 A
Taunton Vale DA12 36 D
Tavern Cl TN15 94 F
Tavern Cotts TN15 93 A
Taverners Rd ME8 69 E
Tavistock Cl Chatham ME5 67 F
Gillingham ME8 69 E
Tavistock Rd Bexley DA16 13 C
2 Bromley BR2 42 A
Tavy Bridge SE2 3 C
Tawney Rd SE28 3 B
Tay Cl ME5 68 B
Tayfields TN12 150 C
Taylor Cl
Harrietsham ME17 119 D
4 Orpington BR6 57 F
Taylor Ct 1 TN2 159 C
Taylor Rd ME6 81 F
Taylor Row DA2 32 C
Taylor St TN4 159 A
Taylor's Bldgs SE18 2 B
Taylor's La Higham ME3 38 B
Rochester ME2 53 B
Taylors Cl DA14 29 F
Taylors La ME19 79 F
Taylors Pl ME19 79 E
Tea Garden La TN3 158 C
Teakcroft Ctr RM13 4 D
Teal Ave BR5 44 D
Teal Cl Grain ME3 27 B
Newham E16 1 D
Teapot La ME20 82 E
Teardrop Ctr BR8 46 C
Teasaucer Hill ME15 115 F
Teasel Cl ME14 100 F
Teasel Cres SE28 2 E
Teasel Rd ME5 67 F
Teasels TN27 168 A
Teasley Mead TN3 156 C
Tebbs Way TN15 94 C
Tedder Ave ME5 68 A
Tedder Rd TN4 159 B
Teesdale Rd DA2 33 C
Teeswater Ct DA18 3 D
Teign Mews SE9 28 E
Teignmouth Rd DA16 13 C
Teise Cl TN2 159 D
Telegraph Hill ME3 38 C
Telemann Sq SE3 11 B
Telford Ho 2 Erith DA17 4 A
1 Maidstone ME14 100 A
Telford Rd SE9 29 D
Tellson Ave SE18 11 E
Telscombe Cl BR6 57 E
Telston La TN14 75 F
Temeraire Manor 2 ME7 54 A
Tempest Rd ME19 96 F
Templar Dr Erith SE28 3 D
Gravesend DA11 36 A
Templars Ct 11 TN8 122 D
Temple Cl SE28 2 C
Temple Gdns ME2 53 A
Temple Hill DA1 15 F
Temple Hill Com Prim Sch DA1 16 A
Temple Hill Sq DA1 15 F
Temple Manor* ME2 53 A
Temple Mill Prim Sch ME2 39 B
Temple Rd TN16 72 D
Temple Sch ME2 39 B
Temple Way ME19 81 F
Templemore DA14 30 B
Tenby Rd DA16 13 D
Tenchley's La
Limpsfield RH8 104 D
The Chart RH8 104 E
Tenney Ho RM17 18 B
Tennyson Ave ME3 39 B
Tennyson Cl DA16 12 F
Tennyson Ho 2 DA17 3 F
Tennyson Rd
Dartford DA1 16 A
Gillingham ME7 54 C
Tennyson Wlk
Northfleet DA11 35 D
Tilbury RM18 19 B
Tensing Ave DA11 35 E
Tent Peg La BR5 43 C
Tenterden & District Mus* TN30 193 A
Tenterden CE Jun Sch TN30 193 B
Tenterden Cl SE9 28 F
Tenterden Inf Sch TN30 193 B
Tenterden Rd
Biddenden TN27 182 B
Chatham ME5 68 B
Fosten Green TN27 181 F
Rolvenden TN17 192 A
Tenterden Station Est TN30 193 A
Tenterden Town Sta* TN30 193 A
Tenterden Vineyard* TN30 193 C
Tenzing Ct SE9 28 E
Terance Butler Ave ME2 53 E
Terence Cl Chatham ME4 54 A
Gravesend DA12 36 F
Terence Ct 6 DA17 13 F
Terminus Rd ME16 99 A
Tern Cres ME2 52 C
Terrace Rd ME16 99 E
Terrace St DA12 19 B

errace The
25 Gravesend DA12 ....19 B1
Rochester ME1 ....53 C5
Sevenoaks TN13 ....91 D5
erraces The DA2 ....33 C8
erry Wlk ME19 ....81 E2
erry's Lodge Rd TN15 ....78 C6
esters Cl RH8 ....104 B3
eston Ho ME18 ....114 A7
eston La ME15,ME18 ....114 C7
eston Rd Kings Hill ME19 ....97 B5
Offham ME19 ....96 C7
Red Hill ME18 ....97 E2
West Malling ME19 ....97 A6
etty Way BR1,BR2 ....42 A7
eviot Cl DA16 ....13 B6
ewson Rd SE18 ....2 E1
eynham Gn
Gillingham ME8 ....55 A4
Hayes BR2 ....42 A4
eynham Ho SE9 ....12 D1
eynham Rd DA2 ....33 C8
hackeray Ave RM18 ....19 B6
hackeray Rd ME20 ....81 F3
hames Ave
Gillingham ME8 ....69 E8
High Halstow ME23 ....23 E4
hames Barrier Visitor Ctr*
SE18 ....1 D3
hames Gate DA1 ....16 A3
hames Rd Crayford DA1 ....15 A4
Grays RM17 ....18 B7
Newham E16 ....1 D5
Tonbridge TN10 ....127 C5
hames Road Ind Est E16 ....1 D4
hames Terr ME3 ....22 B6
hames View ME3 ....39 C7
hames View Cotts ME3 ....38 D3
hames View Inf Sch
ME8 ....55 D2
hames View Jun Sch
ME8 ....55 D2
hames Way
Gravesend DA11 ....19 A1
Northfleet DA11 ....35 E7
hamesbank Pl SE28 ....3 C7
hamesgate Sh Ctr 20
DA11 ....19 B1
hameside Ind Est E16 ....1 D4
hameside Inf & Jun Schs
RM17 ....18 C8
hamesmead Sh Ctr SE28 ....3 A6
hamesmere Dr SE28 ....3 A6
hamesview DA9 ....17 C2
hamesview Sch DA12 ....36 F5
hanet Dr BR2 ....56 D7
hanet Ho
7 Maidstone ME15 ....116 F5
7 Northfleet DA11 ....35 F7
hanet Rd Erith DA8 ....14 E7
Sidcup DA5 ....31 A8
hanington Ct SE9 ....12 E1
hatch Barn Rd TN27 ....151 D6
hatcher Ct DA1 ....32 D8
hatcher Rd TN12 ....149 E4
hatchers La ME3 ....22 B5
hatchers The ME16 ....99 B5
haxted Rd SE9 ....29 C6
heaker Ho DA4 ....47 D7
heatre Sq 7 TN30 ....193 A7
helma Cl DA12 ....36 F3
helma Gdns SE3 ....11 E6
heobalds TN18 ....188 F2
heobalds Cl TN15 ....77 A1
heodore Cl TN2 ....159 E7
heodore Pl ME7 ....54 C5
hicketts TN13 ....92 C4
hird Ave Chatham ME5 ....54 C1
Gillingham ME7 ....54 F4
West Thurrock RM20 ....17 A8
hird St TN3 ....157 F3
hirlemere Cl ME16 ....99 D8
hirlmere Cl
Gillingham ME7 ....55 A5
Rochester ME2 ....39 C1
hirlmere Rd Bexley DA7 ....14 C6
Royal Tunbridge Wells
TN4 ....158 E5
hirsk Ho 6 ME15 ....116 F6
hirza Rd DA1 ....15 F1
histle Ct DA1 ....33 B7
histle Rd DA12 ....36 E8
histlebank ME5 ....68 A3
histlebrook SE2 ....3 C4
histlebrook Ind Est SE2 ....3 C4
histledown
Gravesend DA12 ....36 D2
Maidstone ME14 ....100 F4
histledown Cl ME7 ....69 A4
histlefield Cl DA5 ....30 D7
histlemead BR7 ....43 B7
homas Aveling Sch The
ME1 ....67 C8
homas Cotts DA13 ....35 B1
homas Cribb Mews E6 ....2 A7
homas Dinwiddy Rd
SE12 ....28 B6
homas Dr DA12 ....36 D6
homas Dunk Almshouses 13
TN18 ....189 A2
homas Shearley Ct DA5 ....31 B8
homas St Rochester ME1 ....53 C3
Royal Tunbridge Wells
TN4 ....159 A5
Woolwich SE18 ....2 B2
homas Tallis Sch SE3 ....11 B4
homas Wyatt Way TN15 ....78 F3
hompson Cl ME8 ....70 A8
Thomson Cl ME6 ....66 A1
Thong La Basted TN15 ....94 F5
Gravesend DA12 ....37 A2
Thorn Cl Bromley BR2 ....43 A3
Chatham ME5 ....67 D1
Thorn Rd TN12 ....148 E4
Thorn's Mdw TN16 ....90 C4
Thorndale BR7 ....28 F1
Thorndale Cl ME5 ....67 D4
Thornden Ct TN17 ....198 A8
Thornden La
Rolvenden TN17 ....192 A1
Rolvenden Layne TN17 ....198 A8
Thorndike Cl ME4 ....67 F8
Thorndike Ho ME4 ....67 F8
Thorndon Cl BR5 ....43 F7
Thorndon Rd BR5 ....43 F7
Thorndyke Way TN15 ....78 F3
Thorne Cl Erith DA8 ....14 B8
Newham E16 ....1 A7
Thornet Wood Rd BR1 ....43 A6
Thorney Croft Cl ME17 ....118 D2
Thornfield Gdns TN2 ....159 F5
Thornham Rd ME8 ....55 C3
Thornhill Ave SE18 ....12 E7
Thornhill Pl ME14 ....100 A6
Thornton Dene DA14 ....30 A3
Thornton Rd Bromley BR1 ....28 A3
Erith DA17 ....4 B2
Thorntree Prim Sch SE7 ....1 D1
Thorntree Rd SE7 ....1 D1
Thorold Rd ME5 ....54 B3
Thorpe Ave TN10 ....127 C5
Thorpe Cl BR6 ....57 E8
Thorpe Wlk ME8 ....69 D3
Thrale Way ME8 ....69 E4
Three Corners DA7 ....14 B5
Three Elm La TN11 ....128 D5
Three Gates Rd DA3 ....48 A2
Three Leg Cross Rd
TN5 ....186 D3
Three Oaks La TN5 ....184 D7
Thresher Field TN8 ....140 A6
Threshers Dr ME14 ....100 E5
Thrift The DA2 ....34 C5
Throckmorten Rd E16 ....1 B7
Throwley Cl SE2 ....3 C3
Thrush Cl ME5 ....68 B7
Thunderer Rd RM9 ....3 F8
Thurnham CE Inf Sch
ME14 ....101 A4
Thurnham Ho 5 BR5 ....44 D1
Thurnham La ME14 ....101 C7
Thurrock Bsns Ctr RM20 ....16 F8
Thurrock Ent Ctr RM18 ....18 A8
Thurrock Park Way
RM17 ....18 D7
Thursland Rd DA14 ....30 E3
Thursley Rd SE9 ....28 F5
Thurston Dr ME2 ....52 D7
Thurstone Ct ME14 ....99 F6
Thwaite Cl DA8 ....14 C8
Thyer Cl BR6 ....57 C6
Thyme Cl SE3 ....11 C4
Thyme Wlk ME16 ....99 B3
Tibbs Court La TN12 ....162 A6
Ticehurst Cl BR5 ....30 A1
Tichborne Cl ME16 ....99 C6
Tickford Cl SE2 ....3 C4
Tidal Basin Rd E16 ....1 A6
Tidebrook Ct 4 BR5 ....44 C5
Tidelock Ho SE28 ....2 D4
Tideside Ct SE18 ....1 E3
Tideway The ME1 ....67 C8
Tidford Rd DA16 ....12 F5
Tiger La BR2 ....42 B5
Tilbrook Rd SE3 ....11 D4
Tilbury Cl BR5 ....44 B7
Tilbury Fort* RM18 ....19 C3
Tilbury Manor Inf Sch
RM18 ....19 B7
Tilbury Manor Jun Sch
RM18 ....19 B7
Tilbury PRU RM18 ....18 F6
Tilbury Town Sta RM18 ....18 F5
Tilden Cl TN26 ....183 D7
Tilden Ct TN26 ....183 E7
Tilden Gill Rd TN30 ....193 C7
Tilden La TN12 ....132 C3
Tilden Rd ME17,TN27 ....135 E2
Tile Farm Rd BR6 ....57 D7
Tile Fields ME17 ....102 D2
Tile Kiln La Coldblow DA5 ....31 C6
Dartford DA2,DA5 ....31 F5
Tilebarn Cnr TN10 ....127 E4
Tilehurst Point 2 SE2 ....3 C4
Tilghman Way ME6 ....66 B1
Till Ave DA4 ....46 F2
Tilley Cl ME3 ....40 D5
Tillingbourne Gn BR5 ....44 A5
Tillmans TN15 ....95 A7
Tilmans Mead DA4 ....47 A2
Tilsden La TN17 ....179 E3
Tilt Yard App SE9 ....11 F1
Tilton Rd TN15 ....94 F7
Timber Bank DA13 ....79 F8
Timber Cl BR7 ....43 A7
Timber Ct RM17 ....18 A8
Timber Tops ME5 ....84 D8
Timberbank ME5 ....68 A6
Timbercroft La SE18 ....12 E7
Timbercroft Prim Sch
SE18 ....12 E7
Timbertop Rd TN16 ....72 C1
Timothy Cl DA6 ....13 E3
Timothy Ho DA18 ....3 E4
Tinker Pot La TN15 ....77 D6
Tinker's Alley ME4 ....53 F7
Tinkerpot Rise TN15 ....77 C5
Tinkers La TN5 ....186 E3
Tintagel Gdns ME2 ....52 F7
Tintagel Manor 6 ME7 ....54 C6
Tintagel Rd BR5 ....44 C1
Tintern Rd ME16 ....99 D7
Tippens Cl TN17 ....179 D4
Titan Rd RM17 ....18 B8
Titchfield Cl 5 ME15 ....116 F6
Titchfield Rd ME15 ....116 F6
Tithe Yd ME17 ....120 D5
Titmuss Ave SE28 ....3 B6
Titsey Cnr RH8 ....104 B7
Titsey Hill CR6,RH8 ....88 B4
Titsey Pl* RH8 ....88 B3
Titsey Rd Limpsfield RH8 ....104 B8
Titsey RH8 ....88 B1
Tiverton Dr SE9 ....29 C7
Tivoli Gdns
Gravesend DA12 ....36 B7
Woolwich SE18 ....1 E2
Tobruk Way ME5 ....67 F6
Toby Gdns TN11 ....128 E8
Tockwith Ct TN13 ....92 D4
Toddington Cres ME5 ....67 D1
Toke Pl ME17 ....132 E8
Tolcairn Ct 2 DA17 ....4 A1
Tolgate La ME2 ....53 B7
Tolgate Way ME14 ....83 E4
Tolhurst Rd TN12 ....145 A7
Tollgate Mews TN15 ....95 A8
Tollgate Pl TN27 ....151 E5
Tollgate Rd Dartford DA2 ....33 D8
Newham E6 ....1 E8
Tolsey Mead TN15 ....95 A8
Tom Coombs Cl SE9 ....11 E3
Tom Cribb Rd SE28 ....2 D3
Tom Jenkinson Rd E16 ....1 A5
Tom Joyce Cl ME6 ....81 F7
Tomlin Cl Snodland ME6 ....82 A8
Staplehurst TN12 ....149 E4
Tonbridge By-Pass
Tonbridge TN4,TN9,TN11 ....143 C6
Tonbridge,Stocks Green
TN11,TN9,TN4,TN14,TN15 ....126 B5
Tonbridge Castle* TN9 ....127 B2
Tonbridge Chambers 10
TN9 ....143 B8
Tonbridge Cottage Hospl
TN11 ....143 C6
Tonbridge Ct ME16 ....99 D3
Tonbridge Gram Sch for Girls
TN9 ....143 C7
Tonbridge Ho ME2 ....39 C1
Tonbridge Rd
Hadlow TN11 ....128 C7
Ightham TN15 ....94 C3
Little Mill TN11,TN12 ....129 D4
Maidstone,East Barming
ME16 ....98 E1
Maidstone,Upper Fant
ME16 ....99 C3
Pembury TN2 ....160 A7
Sevenoaks TN13,TN15 ....108 D7
Tonbridge TN11 ....126 E5
Wateringbury ME18 ....113 C8
Tonbridge Sch TN10 ....127 C3
Tonbridge Sta TN9 ....127 B1
Tong La TN12 ....162 B2
Tong Rd TN12,TN3 ....162 A4
Tongswood Dr TN18 ....189 C1
Tony Law Ho SE12 ....11 A2
Tooley St DA11 ....35 D8
Top Dartford Rd BR8,DA2 ....32 A2
Topcliffe Dr BR6 ....57 D6
Topley Dr ME23 ....23 E3
Topley St SE9 ....11 D3
Tor Gr SE28 ....2 E5
Tor Rd DA16 ....13 C6
Torbay Rd TN12 ....130 B5
Torbrook Cl DA5 ....13 E1
Tormount Rd SE18 ....12 E8
Toronto Rd
Gillingham ME7 ....54 E4
Tilbury RM18 ....19 A5
Torrens Wlk DA12 ....36 E3
Torrington Cl ME18 ....112 D8
Torver Way BR6 ....57 D7
Totnes Rd DA16 ....13 C7
Tovil Gn ME15 ....99 E2
Tovil Green Bsns Pk
ME15 ....99 E1
Tovil Hill ME15 ....99 E2
Tovil Rd ME15 ....99 F2
Tovil, St Stephen's CE Inf Sch
ME15 ....99 E2
Tower Cl Gravesend DA12 ....36 E3
Orpington BR6 ....57 F7
Tower Croft DA4 ....60 E8
Tower Gdns ME14 ....101 B4
Tower Hill ME19 ....96 D7
Tower Ind Est TN15 ....78 D5
Tower La ME14 ....101 B4
Tower Park Rd DA1 ....14 F2
Tower Rd Bexley DA7 ....14 A3
Dartford DA1 ....15 C1
Erith DA17 ....4 C2
Orpington BR6 ....57 F7
Tower Ret Pk DA1 ....14 F2
Tower View ME19 ....97 B3
Towerfields BR2 ....56 E6
Towers Point ME1 ....53 B4
Towers Wood DA4 ....47 D8
Town Acres TN10 ....127 C4
Town Hill
Lamberhurst TN3 ....176 A4
West Malling ME19 ....81 C1
Town Hill Cl ME19 ....81 C1
Town Lock Ho 4 TN9 ....127 C2
Town Mdw TN17 ....179 D4
Town Pier Sq 5 DA11 ....19 B1
Town Rd ME3 ....39 A6
Town Sq DA8 ....14 E8
Town Square Cres DA9 ....33 F8
Town Station Cotts
TN8 ....122 D1
Towncourt Cres BR5 ....43 D5
Towncourt La BR5 ....43 D2
Townfield Cnr DA12 ....36 D7
Towngate Wood Pk Mobile
Home Pk TN10 ....127 E7
Townland Cl TN27 ....168 A2
Townlands Rd TN5 ....184 F4
Townley Gram Sch for Girls
DA6 ....13 F2
Townley Rd DA6 ....13 F2
Townsend Rd ME6 ....81 F8
Townsend Sq ME19 ....97 A2
Townshend Cl DA14 ....30 C2
Townshend Ho 14 SE18 ....1 F2
Townshend Rd BR7 ....29 B3
Toy's Hill TN16,TN8 ....106 C3
Toynbec Cl BR7 ....29 B4
Tracies The ME9 ....71 C6
Trader Rd E6 ....2 B7
Tradescant Dr DA13 ....50 B3
Trafalgar Rd Dartford DA1 ....32 E6
Gravesend DA11 ....36 A8
Wouldham ME1 ....66 C5
Trafalgar St ME7 ....54 C5
Tramways ME5 ....54 C2
Tranquil Rise DA8 ....4 E1
Transfesa Rd TN12 ....146 A7
Transmere Cl BR5 ....43 C3
Transmere Rd BR5 ....43 C3
Transom Ho 3 ME1 ....53 C1
Trapfield Cl ME14 ....101 C4
Trapfield La ME14 ....101 C4
Trapham Rd ME16 ....99 D5
Trasa Ct 10 RM17 ....18 C8
Travers Gdns ME9 ....87 F5
Travertine Rd ME5 ....68 B1
Trebble Rd DA10 ....17 E1
Trebilco Cl TN2 ....159 D7
Tredegar Rd DA2 ....32 A5
Tredwell Cl BR1 ....42 E5
Tree La TN15 ....110 E8
Tree Rd E16 ....1 C7
Treebourne Rd TN16 ....72 C1
Treetops Gravesend DA12 ....36 B4
Kemsing TN15 ....77 A2
Tonbridge TN9 ....143 B7
Treetops Cl SE2 ....3 E1
Treewall Gdns BR1 ....28 B4
Trefoil Ho Erith DA18 ....3 E4
Grays RM17 ....18 B7
Tregony Rd BR6 ....57 F6
Trelawn Cres ME5 ....68 B2
Trellyn Cl ME16 ....98 F2
Trench Rd TN10 ....127 C6
Trenear Cl BR6 ....58 A6
Trent Rd ME5 ....68 B5
Trentham Dr BR5 ....44 A5
Trenton Cl ME16 ....99 B7
Trevale Rd ME1 ....53 B1
Trevelyan Cl DA1 ....15 F3
Trevereux Hill RH8 ....104 F4
Trevino Dr ME5 ....67 F2
Trevithick Dr DA1 ....15 F3
Trevor Cl BR2 ....42 A2
Trevor Dr ME16 ....99 C5
Trewin Cl ME20 ....82 D2
Trewsbury Ho 2 SE2 ....3 D4
Triangle Ct E16 ....1 C8
Triangle The DA15 ....30 A8
Tricorn Ho SE28 ....2 D5
Trident Cl ME2 ....53 E7
Trinity Cl Orpington BR2 ....42 E1
Royal Tunbridge Wells
TN2 ....159 D4
Trinity Ct Aylesford ME20 ....83 A3
Dartford DA1 ....33 B7
Eltham SE9 ....12 B1
Trinity Gdns DA1 ....15 D1
Trinity Mews SE9 ....12 D1
Trinity Pl DA6 ....13 F3
Trinity Rd Gillingham ME7 ....54 C6
Gravesend DA12 ....36 C8
Trinity Sch ME1 ....53 D4
Trinity Sch, Belvedere
DA17 ....4 C2
Trinity St 12 E16 ....1 A8
Tristan Gdns TN4 ....158 D4
Triton Lodge 9 DA8 ....4 E1
Triumph Rd E6 ....1 F7
Trivett Cl DA9 ....17 A2
Trolling Down Hill DA2 ....33 C6
Troodos Hill ME14 ....99 F8
Troon Cl SE28 ....3 D7
Trosley Ave DA11 ....36 B6
Trosley Ctry Pk* ME19,
DA13 ....80 A7
Trosley Ctry Pk Visitor Ctr*
DA13 ....79 E7
Trosley Rd DA17 ....14 A8
Trottiscliffe CE Prim Sch
ME19 ....80 A5
Trottiscliffe Rd ME19 ....80 D3
Trotts La TN16 ....105 C8
Trotwood Cl ME5 ....84 A8
Troughton Rd SE7 ....1 B1
Troutbeck Ho ME20 ....82 C1
Troy Ct 6 SE18 ....2 B2
Troy La TN8 ....121 F4
Troy Mews ME1 ....53 C4
Troys Mead ME17 ....102 D2
Trubridge Rd ME3 ....40 E5
Truro Cl ME8 ....55 D3
Truro Rd DA12 ....36 D5
Truro Wlk TN10 ....127 D5
Trusedale Rd E6 ....1 F7
Trycewell La TN15 ....94 D6
Tuam Rd SE18 ....12 D8
Tubbenden Cl BR6 ....57 E7
Tubbenden Dr BR6 ....57 D6
Tubbenden Inf & Jun Sch
BR6 ....57 D6
Tubbenden La BR6 ....57 E7
Tubbenden La S BR6 ....57 D5
Tubs Hill TN13 ....92 B3
Tubs Hill Par TN13 ....92 A3
Tudeley La
Tonbridge TN9 ....143 D7
Tonbridge, Tudeley TN11,
TN9 ....144 B8
Tudor Ave ME14 ....100 B6
Tudor Cl Bromley BR7 ....42 F8
Dartford DA1 ....15 B1
Northfleet DA11 ....35 E7
Tudor Cres TN14 ....76 D3
Tudor Ct Biggin Hill TN16 ....72 E2
Crockenhill BR8 ....45 C2
Royal Tunbridge Wells
TN2 ....158 E1
Sidcup DA14 ....30 A5
Tudor Dr TN14 ....76 C3
Tudor Gr Chattenden ME3 ....39 F4
Gillingham ME8 ....69 F8
Tudor Par SE9 ....11 E3
Tudor Way BR5 ....43 D3
Tudor Wlk DA5 ....13 E1
Tudway Rd SE3 ....11 C3
Tufa Cl ME5 ....68 B1
Tuffs Cotts ME3 ....25 C3
Tufnail Rd DA1 ....15 F1
Tufton Rd ME8 ....55 F1
Tufton St ME14 ....100 A4
Tugboat St SE28 ....2 E4
Tugmutton Cl BR6 ....57 B6
Tulip Cl 5 E6 ....1 F8
Tulip Tree Cl TN9 ....143 B8
Tumblefield Est TN15 ....78 F8
Tumblefield Rd TN15 ....78 E7
Tumblers Hill ME17 ....134 F7
Tunbridge Wells Girls' Gram
Sch TN4 ....159 A6
Tunbridge Wells Gram Sch
for Boys TN4 ....159 A7
Tunbridge Wells High Sch
TN2 ....159 F5
Tunbridge Wells Ind Hospl
The TN3 ....157 B3
Tunbridge Wells Mus &
Gall* TN1 ....159 B4
Tunbridge Wells Sta
TN1 ....159 A3
Tunbridge Wells Trad Pk
TN2 ....159 D8
Tunbridge Wells West Sta*
TN2 ....158 F1
Tunbury Ave ME5 ....67 F1
Tunbury Ave S ME5 ....67 F1
Tunbury Prim Sch ME5 ....67 F1
Tunnan Leys E6 ....2 A7
Tunnel Ave 1 SE10 ....1 A1
Tunnel Cotts RM20 ....17 A8
Tunnel Est RM20 ....16 F8
Tunnel Rd TN1 ....159 B4
Tunstall Cl BR6 ....57 E6
Tunstock Way DA17 ....3 E3
Tupman Cl ME1 ....53 B4
Tuppy St SE28 ....2 C3
Turgis Cl ME17 ....117 E4
Turks Hall Pl ME2 ....65 E5
Turley Cotts TN3 ....158 A8
Turnberry Way BR6 ....43 D1
Turnbull Cl DA9 ....33 E8
Turnbury Cl SE28 ....3 D7
Turnden Rd TN17 ....179 A3
Turner Ave TN17 ....179 D3
Turner Cl TN16 ....72 C7
Turner Ct DA1 ....15 C2
Turner Ho
Gravesend DA12 ....36 C6
5 Greenwich SE7 ....11 B8
Turner Rd Bean DA2 ....34 B5
Tonbridge TN10 ....127 E5
Turner St ME3 ....22 B5
Turner's Oak DA3 ....62 E7
Turners Ave TN30 ....193 B8
Turners Gdns TN13 ....108 C7
Turners Green La TN5 ....184 F6
Turners Green Rd TN5 ....184 F6
Turners Pl DA4 ....47 C8
Turnpike Ct DA6 ....13 D3
Turnpike Dr BR6 ....58 D2
Turnpike La RM18 ....19 D8
Turnstone DA3 ....49 A7
Turnstone Rd ME5 ....68 C1
Turnstones The DA12 ....36 D6
Turpin La DA8 ....15 A8
Turpington Cl BR2 ....42 E2
Turpington La BR2 ....42 E3
Turton Ho 5 SE18 ....12 B8
Tuscan Dr ME5 ....68 C1
Tuscan Rd SE18 ....2 D1
Tutsham Way TN12 ....145 F6
Tuxford Rd TN4 ....158 B5
Tweed Rd TN10 ....127 C5
Tweedy Rd BR1 ....42 A8
Twigg Cl DA8 ....14 E7

Twin Tumps Way SE28 ...3 A6
Twisden Rd ME19 ...97 F8
Twiss Ho 6 SE18 ...2 B1
Twistleton Ct DA1 ...15 D1
Twitton La TN14 ...75 E3
Twitton Mdws TN14 ...75 E3
Two Gates Hill ME3 ...38 F5
Twydall Ent Ctr ME8 ...55 C4
Twydall Gn ME8 ...55 B3
Twydall Inf Sch ME8 ...55 B2
Twydall Jun Sch ME8 ...55 B2
Twydall La ME8 ...55 B2
Twyford Ct ME14 ...100 D6
Twyford Rd TN11 ...111 E1
Twysden Cotts TN18 ...196 A4
Tydeman Rd ME15 ...100 F2
Tye La BR6 ...57 C5
Tyeshurst Cl SE2 ...3 E1
Tyland Barn Wildlife Conservation Ctr* ME14 ...83 E3
Tyland La ME14 ...83 F3
Tyler Cl East Malling ME19 ..97 F8
Erith DA8 ...14 B7
Tyler Dr ME8 ...69 E4
Tyler Gr DA1 ...15 F3
Tylers Green Rd BR8 ...45 C2
Tylney Rd BR1 ...42 D7
Tyndall Rd DA16 ...12 F4
Tyne Cl ME5 ...68 C5
Tyne Rd TN10 ...127 B5
Tynedale Cl DA2 ...33 D7
Tynemouth Cl E6 ...2 B7
Tynemouth Rd SE18 ...2 E1
Typhoon Rd ME19 ...96 F3
Tyron Way DA14 ...29 F3
Tyrrell Ave DA16 ...13 B2
Tyrrells Hall Cl 5 RM17 ..18 D8
Tyrwhitt-Drake Mus of Carriages* ME15 ...100 A3

U

Uckfield La TN8 ...139 D4
Udall Cotts DA15 ...29 E5
Ufton Cl ME15 ...100 E1
Ulcombe CE Prim Sch ME17 ...135 F6
Ulcombe Hill ME17 ...118 F1
Ulcombe Rd
Headcorn TN27 ...151 C6
Langley Heath ME17 ...117 E3
Ullswater Ho 5 ME15 ...116 E7
Underdown Ave ME4 ...53 F1
Underlyn Ind Est TN12 ..132 F2
Underlyn La TN12 ...132 D1
Underriver House Rd TN15 ...109 D5
Underwood ME19 ...96 D7
Underwood Cl ME15 ...99 F2
Underwood The SE9 ...28 F6
Unicorn Wlk DA9 ...16 F2
Unicumes La ME16 ...99 C2
Union Pk ME15 ...116 F4
Union Pl ME4 ...54 A4
Union Rd BR2 ...42 D4
Union Sq 22 TN2 ...159 A2
Union St Chatham ME4 ...54 A3
Flimwell TN5 ...187 B3
Maidstone ME14 ...100 A5
Rochester ME1 ...53 C5
Unity Way SE18 ...1 D3
Univ of East London E16 ..2 A6
Univ of Greenwich ME4 ..54 B8
Univ of Greenwich Avery Hill Campus (Mansion Site) SE9 ...12 C1
Univ of Greenwich Avery Hill Campus (Southwood Site) SE9 ...12 D1
Univ of Greenwich Avery Hill Campus Southwood Site SE9 ...29 D8
University Gdns DA5 ...30 F8
University Pl DA8 ...14 C7
University Way
Dartford DA1 ...15 E4
Woolwich E16 ...2 B6
Unwin Cl ME20 ...83 A3
Upbury Arts Coll ME7 ...54 B4
Upbury Way ME4 ...54 A4
Upchat Rd ME2,ME3 ...39 F3
Updale Rd DA14 ...29 F4
Upland Prim Sch DA7 ...13 F4
Upland Rd DA7 ...13 F4
Uplands SE18 ...2 B1
Uplands Cl Rochester ME2 .52 D6
Sevenoaks TN13 ...91 F4
Uplands Com Tech Coll TN5 ...185 A4
Uplands Rd BR6 ...44 B1
Uplands Way TN13 ...91 F4
Upnor Castle* ME2 ...39 F2
Upnor Ho ME15 ...116 E8
Upnor Rd ME2 ...39 E2
Upper Abbey Rd DA17 ...4 A2
Upper Austin Lodge Farm Cotts DA4 ...60 E3
Upper Austin Lodge Rd DA4 ...60 D4
Upper Ave DA13 ...49 E8
Upper Barn Hill ME15 ..114 E3
Upper Britton Pl ME7 ...54 B5
Upper Bush Rd ME2 ...51 F2
Upper Church Hill DA9 ..16 E2
Upper Cumberland Wlk TN1 ...159 B1
Upper Dr TN16 ...72 C1
Upper Dunstan Rd TN4 ..159 B6
Upper East Rd ME4 ...54 B8
Upper Fant Rd ME16 ...99 D2
Upper Green La TN11 ..110 D5
Upper Green Rd TN11 ..110 D5
Upper Grosvenor Rd TN1,TN4 ...159 B6
Upper Grove Rd DA17 ...13 F8
Upper Haysden La TN11, TN9 ...142 E6
Upper Holly Hill Rd DA17 ..4 B1
Upper Hunton Hill ME15 ...115 A3
Upper Luton Rd ME5 ...54 C2
Upper Mill ME18 ...113 D8
Upper Nellington TN3 ..158 B4
Upper Park Rd
Bromley BR1 ...42 C8
Erith DA17 ...4 B2
Upper Platts TN5 ...186 F1
Upper Profit TN3 ...158 A3
Upper Rd ME15 ...100 B2
Upper Ruxley Cotts DA14 .31 A1
Upper Sheridan Rd DA17 ..4 A2
Upper Spring La TN15 ...94 B5
Upper St
Hollingbourne ME17 ...102 E3
Leeds ME17 ...117 F5
Rusthall TN4 ...158 D4
Upper Stephens TN3 ...158 A3
Upper Stone St ME15 ..100 A3
Upper Street N DA3 ...62 F8
Upper Street S DA3 ...62 F8
Upper Wickham La DA16 .13 B6
Upperton Rd DA14 ...29 F3
Upton Cl DA5 ...13 F1
Upton Day Hospl DA6 ...13 E3
Upton Prim Sch DA6 ...13 F2
Upton Quarry TN3 ...157 F3
Upton Rd Bexley DA5,DA6 ..13 E2
Woolwich SE18 ...12 C8
Upton Rd S DA5 ...13 F1
Upton Villas 4 DA6 ...13 E3
Uptons TN27 ...151 C6
Upwood Rd SE12 ...11 A1
Uridge Cres TN10 ...127 C4
Uridge Rd TN10 ...127 C4
Urquhart Cl ME5 ...68 A5
Ursula Lodges DA14 ...30 B3
Usborne Cl TN12 ...149 E3

V

Vaizeys Wharf SE7 ...1 B3
Vale Ave
Royal Tunbridge Wells,Mount Sion TN1 ...159 A3
Royal Tunbridge Wells,Southborough TN4 ..142 F1
Vale Cl BR6 ...57 A6
Vale Cotts ME9 ...87 A8
Vale Ct TN4 ...143 A2
Vale Dr ME5 ...67 E6
Vale Rd Bromley BR1 ...43 A7
Dartford DA1 ...32 B8
Hawkhurst TN18 ...188 F3
Maidstone ME15 ...115 E4
Northfleet DA11 ...35 E7
Royal Tunbridge Wells,Mount Sion TN1 ...159 A3
Royal Tunbridge Wells,Southborough TN4 ..142 F1
Tonbridge TN9 ...127 C1
Vale Rise TN9 ...143 E8
Valence Ho ME15 ...116 C7
Valence Rd DA8 ...14 D7
Valence Sch TN16 ...89 F1
Valence View TN17 ...166 E7
Valenciennes Ho ME4 ...54 A4
Valentine Ave DA5 ...30 E7
Valentine Cl ME7 ...55 A1
Valentine Dr ME23 ...23 E4
Valentine Rd ME15 ...116 E7
Valerian Cl ME5 ...67 E4
Valetta Way ME1 ...53 B4
Valiant Ho 5 SE7 ...1 C1
Valiant Rd ME5 ...68 C2
Valiant Way E6 ...1 F8
Valley (Charlton Athletic FC) The SE7 ...1 C1
Valley Cl DA1 ...14 F1
Valley Dr
Gravesend,Riverview Park DA12 ...36 D4
Gravesend,Singlewell DA12 .36 E1
Maidstone ME15 ...115 F6
Sevenoaks TN13 ...92 B1
Valley Forge Cl TN10 ...127 F4
Valley Gdns DA9 ...17 B1
Valley Gr SE7 ...1 C1
Valley Hts DA1 ...15 F3
Valley Industries TN11 ..128 B7
Valley L Ctr SE9 ...29 C8
Valley La DA13 ...64 B2
Valley Mushroom Farm TN16 ...72 D1
Valley Park Com Sch ME14 ...100 C4
Valley Rd Crayford DA1 ...14 F1
Erith DA8 ...4 D2
Fawkham Green DA3 ...48 C2
Gillingham ME7 ...54 E4
Orpington BR5 ...44 B8
Valley Rd *continued*
Rusthall TN4 ...158 D4
Valley Rise ME5 ...67 F1
Valley The ME17 ...115 D3
Valley View
Biggin Hill TN16 ...72 D1
Royal Tunbridge Wells TN4 ...143 A2
Swanscombe DA9 ...17 B1
Valley View Rd ME1 ...53 B1
Valley View Terr DA4 ...46 F1
Valleyside SE7 ...1 D1
Valliers Wood Rd DA15 ...29 E7
Vambery Rd SE18 ...12 C8
Vanbrugh Cl 2 E16 ...1 D8
Vanbrugh Pk SE3 ...11 A7
Vanburgh Cl BR6 ...43 E1
Vancouver Cl BR6 ...58 A6
Vancouver Dr ME8 ...55 C1
Vandome Cl E16 ...1 B7
Vandyke Cross SE9 ...11 E2
Vanessa Cl DA17 ...4 A1
Vanessa Way DA5 ...31 D5
Vanessa Wlk DA12 ...36 F3
Vange Cottage Mews ME1 ...53 B4
Vanguard Cl E16 ...1 A8
Vanguard Way ME2 ...53 E8
Vanity La ME17 ...115 D1
Vanoc Gdns BR1 ...28 A4
Vanquisher Wlk DA12 ...36 F5
Varley Rd E16 ...1 B7
Varnes St ME20 ...82 F6
Vaughan Ave TN10 ...127 E6
Vaughan Rd DA16 ...12 F5
Vauxhall Cl DA11 ...35 F8
Vauxhall Cres ME6 ...82 A6
Vauxhall Gdns TN9 ...143 C7
Vauxhall La
Bidborough TN11,TN4 ...143 B4
Tonbridge TN11 ...143 D6
Vauxhall Pl DA1 ...32 E8
Veitchil Barn BR8 ...45 F8
Veles Rd ME6 ...81 F8
Venmead Ct 4 DA17 ...4 A2
Venners Cl DA7 ...14 E5
Ventnor Cl ME5 ...68 C8
Venture Cl DA5 ...30 E8
Venture Ct SE12 ...28 A8
Venus Rd SE18 ...1 F3
Verdun Rd SE18,SE2 ...13 A8
Vermont Rd TN4 ...158 C4
Vernham Rd SE18 ...12 C8
Vernon Cl Orpington BR5 ...44 B6
West Kingsdown TN15 ...61 F2
Vernon Rd
Royal Tunbridge Wells TN1 ...159 C6
Swanscombe DA10 ...17 F1
Veroan Rd DA7 ...13 E5
Verona Gdns DA12 ...36 E4
Verona Ho DA8 ...14 F7
Vert Ho RM17 ...18 C7
Veryan Cl BR5 ...44 C5
Vesper Ct TN27 ...153 A1
Vestry Cotts
New Barn DA3 ...49 C5
Sevenoaks TN14 ...92 C8
Vestry Rd TN14 ...92 C8
Via Romana DA12 ...37 B7
Viaduct Terr DA4 ...47 C7
Vicarage Ave SE3 ...11 A7
Vicarage Cl
Aylesford ME20 ...82 F3
Erith DA8 ...14 C8
Halling ME2 ...66 A5
Stoke ME3 ...25 A3
Vicarage Ct Chalk DA12 ...37 A7
Newington ME9 ...71 B7
Vicarage Dr DA11 ...18 C1
Vicarage Hill TN16 ...89 D1
Vicarage La Chalk DA12 ...37 A6
East Farleigh ME15 ...115 B6
Hoo St Werburgh ME3 ...40 E4
Sevenoaks TN13 ...91 D8
Vicarage Pk SE18 ...2 C1
Vicarage Rd Coldblow DA5 .31 B7
Gillingham ME7 ...54 C5
Halling ME2 ...65 F5
Rochester ME2 ...53 B8
Royal Tunbridge Wells TN4 ...142 F2
Woolwich SE18 ...2 C1
Yalding ME18 ...114 A1
Vicarage Row ME3 ...38 C4
Vicarage Sq RM17 ...18 A8
Vicarage Way TN19 ...194 A3
Vicary Way ME16 ...99 D5
Vickers Rd DA8 ...4 D1
Victor Mills Cotts DA14 ...31 A1
Victoria Ave 3 DA12 ...36 B8
Victoria Bglws DA14 ...30 F1
Victoria Bsns Ctr DA16 ...13 B5
Victoria Cl Chatham ME5 ..67 D2
Edenbridge TN8 ...138 C8
Victoria Cotts
Cranbrook TN17 ...179 D5
Edenbridge TN8 ...138 C8
Victoria Ct 6 ME16 ...99 E3
Victoria Dock Rd E16 ...1 B6
Victoria Dr Kings Hill ME19 .96 F1
Sutton at H DA4 ...47 D7
Victoria Gdns TN16 ...72 C4
Victoria Hill Rd BR8 ...46 A8
Victoria Ind Pk DA1 ...15 E2
Victoria Orch ME16 ...99 B3
Victoria Rd Bexley DA6 ...14 A3
Bromley BR2 ...42 D4
Victoria Rd *continued*
Chatham,Luton ME4 ...54 B2
Chatham,Walderslade ME5 ..67 E3
Chislehurst BR7 ...29 A3
Dartford DA1 ...15 E2
Edenbridge TN8 ...138 C8
Erith DA8 ...14 E8
Golden Green TN11 ...128 F6
Northfleet DA11 ...35 F7
Royal Tunbridge Wells TN1 ...159 B4
Royal Tunbridge Wells,Southborough TN4 ..142 E1
Sevenoaks TN13 ...92 B2
Sidcup DA15 ...30 A5
Victoria Scott Ct DA1 ...14 F4
Victoria St Eccles ME20 ...82 F6
Erith DA17 ...3 F1
Gillingham ME7 ...54 D6
Maidstone ME16 ...99 E3
Rochester ME1 ...53 D5
Rochester,Strood ME2 ...53 B7
Victoria Terr ME1 ...53 A2
Victoria Way SE7 ...1 B1
Victoria Wharf DA1 ...15 E2
Victory Cotts TN14 ...108 C2
Victory Lodge 10 DA8 ...4 E1
Victory Manor 1 ME7 ...54 A6
Victory Pk ME2 ...53 E7
Victory Terr ME17 ...134 E8
Victory Way DA2 ...16 C3
Vidal Manor ME7 ...54 C5
Vidgeon Ave ME3 ...40 D6
View Cl TN16 ...72 C3
View Rd ME3 ...39 B7
View The SE2 ...3 E1
Viewfield Rd DA5 ...30 C7
Viewland Rd SE18 ...2 F1
Viewlands ME5 ...54 C3
Viewlands Ave TN16 ...89 F7
Viewpoint ME14 ...100 C8
Viewpoint Ct DA3 ...48 F5
Vigilant Way DA12 ...36 F3
Vigo Hill ME19,TN15 ...79 E6
Vigo Rd TN15 ...79 C7
Vigo Village Sch DA13 ...80 A8
Viking Cl ME2 ...52 F4
Viking Ho 3 SE18 ...1 E2
Viking Rd DA11 ...35 C5
Viking Way Erith DA8 ...4 C3
West Kingsdown TN15 ...61 E5
Villa Cl DA12 ...37 B6
Villa Ct DA1 ...32 E6
Villa Rd ME3 ...38 B3
Villacourt Rd SE18,SE2 ...13 A8
Village Green Ave TN16 ..72 E2
Village Green Rd DA1 ...15 A3
Village Green Way TN16 ..72 E2
Village The SE7 ...11 D8
Village View ME5 ...54 C2
Villas Rd SE18 ...2 C2
Vincent Cl Bromley BR2 ...42 B5
Sidcup DA15 ...29 E7
Vincent Rd
Kit's Coty ME20 ...83 C7
Woolwich SE18 ...2 B2
Vincent Sq TN16 ...72 C6
Vincent St 13 E16 ...1 A8
Vine Ave TN13 ...92 B3
Vine Court Rd TN13 ...92 C4
Vine Ct
16 Gravesend DA11 ...19 B1
Staplehurst TN12 ...149 F3
Wateringbury ME18 ...113 D8
Vine Lodge TN13 ...92 C3
Vine Rd BR6 ...57 F4
Vine The TN13 ...92 C3
Vine Wlk TN12 ...149 E3
Vineries The ME7 ...54 E5
Vines La
Hildenborough TN11 ...109 C1
Rochester ME1 ...53 C5
Viney's Gdns TN30 ...183 C1
Vineyard La TN5 ...186 C2
Vinson Cl BR6 ...44 A1
Vinson Ct DA15 ...30 A6
Vinters Rd ME14 ...100 B4
Vintners Way ME14 ...100 E4
Viola Ave SE2 ...3 B1
Violet Cl ME5 ...84 A8
Violets The TN12 ...146 A5
VIP Trad Est SE7 ...1 C2
Virginia Rd ME7 ...54 C7
Virginia Wlk DA12 ...36 E2
Viscount Dr E6 ...1 F8
Vista The Eltham SE9 ...28 E8
Sidcup DA14 ...29 F3
Vixen Cl ME5 ...68 C6
Voce Rd SE18 ...12 D7
Vogue Ct 11 BR1 ...42 B8
Voyagers Cl SE28 ...3 C7
Vulcan Cl Chatham ME5 ...68 B7
Newham E6 ...2 A7
Vyne The DA7 ...14 B4
Vyvyan Cotts TN17 ...190 C3
Vyvyan Ho SE18 ...12 A6

W

Wadard Terr BR8 ...46 C4
Wade Ave BR5 ...44 D2
Wadeville Cl DA17 ...4 A1
Wadhurst Bsns Pk TN5 ..184 B7
Wadhurst CE Prim Sch TN5 ...184 F5
Wadhurst Rd TN3 ...173 D1
Wadhurst Sta TN5 ...184 C6
Wadlands Rd ME3 ...22 B
Waghorn Rd ME6 ...82 A
Waghorn St ME4 ...54 B
Wagon La TN12 ...130 C
Wagoners Cl ME14 ...100 E
Wagtail Way BR5 ...44 D
Waid Cl DA1 ...15 F
Wainhouse Cl TN8 ...122 D
Wainscott Prim Sch ME2 .39 D
Wainscott Rd ME2 ...39 D
Wainscott Wlk ME2 ...39 D
Waite Davies Rd 8 SE12 .28 A
Wake Rd ME1 ...67 C
Wakefield Cl ME2 ...52 D
Wakefield Rd DA9 ...17 C
Wakehurst Cl ME17 ...115 B
Wakeleys Cotts ME8 ...70 B
Wakely Cl TN16 ...72 C
Wakerley Cl 6 E6 ...1 F
Waldair Ct E16 ...2 B
Waldeck Rd DA1 ...16 A
Waldegrave Rd BR1 ...42 F
Walden Ave BR7 ...28 F
Walden Cl DA17 ...3 F
Walden Par BR7 ...28 F
Walden Rd BR7 ...28 F
Waldenhurst Rd BR5 ...44 D
Waldens Cl BR5 ...44 D
Waldens Rd BR5 ...44 E
Waldens The ME17 ...118 E
Walderslade Ctr ME5 ...68 A
Walderslade Girls Sch ME5 ...67 F
Walderslade Prim Sch ME5 ...68 A
Walderslade Rd ME5 ...67 F
Walderslade Woods ME5 .67 E
Waldo Ind Est BR1 ...42 D
Waldo Rd BR1 ...42 D
Waldrist Way DA18 ...3 F
Waldron Dr ME15 ...115 F
Waldstock Rd SE28 ...3 A
Walk The ME17 ...118 E
Walkden Rd BR7 ...29 A
Walker Cl Crayford DA1 ...14 F
Woolwich SE18 ...2 C
Walker Pl TN15 ...94 D
Walkhurst Cotts TN17 ..190 F
Walkhurst Rd TN17 ...190 F
Walkley Rd DA1 ...15 B
Walks The TN3 ...171 C
Wall Cl ME3 ...40 D
Wallace Cl Erith SE28 ...3 D
Royal Tunbridge Wells TN2 ...173 A
Wallace Gdns DA10 ...17 E
Wallace Rd ME1 ...67 E
Wallace Terr TN15 ...62 E
Waller Hill TN17 ...166 B
Wallers TN3 ...158 A
Wallhouse Rd DA8 ...15 C
Wallis Ave ME15 ...116 E
Wallis Cl DA2 ...31 F
Wallis Field TN3 ...171 B
Wallis Pk DA11 ...18 B
Walmer Cl BR6 ...57 D
Walmer Ct 3 ME14 ...100 A
Walmer Ho ME2 ...39 C
Walmer Terr SE18 ...2 D
Walmers Ave ME3 ...38 A
Walnut Cl Chatham ME5 ..68 B
Eynsford DA4 ...60 D
Paddock Wood TN12 ...146 A
Yalding ME18 ...113 F
Walnut Hill Rd DA13 ...49 E
Walnut Tree Ave
Dartford DA1 ...32 E
Loose ME15 ...116 A
Walnut Tree Cl
Chislehurst BR7 ...43 C
Westerham TN16 ...89 D
Walnut Tree Ct ME20 ...82 B
Walnut Tree La ME15 ..116 A
Walnut Tree Rd DA8 ...4 E
Walnut Tree Way DA13 ..50 B
Walnut Way
Royal Tunbridge Wells TN4 ...159 D
Swanley BR8 ...45 D
Walnuts Rd BR6 ...44 B
Walnuts The BR6 ...44 A
Walpole Cl ME19 ...81 F
Walpole Ho 4 BR7 ...43 D
Walpole Pl SE18 ...2 B
Walpole Rd BR2 ...42 D
Walsham Cl SE28 ...3 D
Walsham Rd ME5 ...67 F
Walshaw Ho 2 ME14 ..100 A
Walsingham Cl ME8 ...69 D
Walsingham Ho 3 ME14 ...100 A
Walsingham Pk BR7 ...43 D
Walsingham Rd BR5 ...44 B
Walsingham Wlk DA17 ..14 A
Walter Burke Ave ME1 ..66 C
Walter's Farm Rd TN9 .127 C
Walters Green Rd TN11 .156 F
Walters Ho SE18 ...12 A
Walters Rd ME3 ...40 E
Walters Yd BR1 ...42 A
Walterstown Ct DA1 ...32 D
Waltham Cl Dartford DA1 .15 A
27 Orpington BR5 ...44 D
Waltham Rd ME8 ...55 C
Walthamstow Hall TN13 ..92 C
Walthamstow Hall (Nursery Unit) TN13 ...92 B
Walton Rd Sidcup DA14 ...30 C

Walton Rd continued
Tonbridge TN10 127 F6
Walwyn Ave BR1 42 D6
Wanden La TN27 153 C8
Wansbury Way BR8 46 A5
Wanstead Cl BR1 42 C7
Wanstead Rd BR1 42 C7
Wansunt Rd DA5 31 C7
Warberry Park Gdns TN4 158 E4
Warblers Cl 3 ME2 53 A7
Ward Cl Durgates TN5 184 E5
Erith DA8 14 D8
Ward's La TN5 185 E4
Warde's ME18 113 F2
Warden Cl ME16 99 C4
Warden Mill Cl ME18 113 E7
Warden Rd ME1 53 C2
Wardens Field Cl 2 BR6 57 F4
Wardona Ct DA10 17 F1
Wardour Ct 11 DA2 16 B1
Wards Wharf App E16 1 D4
Wardwell La ME9 71 C8
Ware St ME14 101 A5
Warepoint Dr SE28 2 D4
Warham Rd TN14 76 B3
Waring Cl BR6 58 A4
Waring Dr BR6 58 A4
Waring Rd DA14 30 C2
Warland Rd
West Kingsdown TN15 61 F2
Woolwich SE18 12 E7
Warmlake ME17 117 F1
Warmlake Bsns Est ME17 117 E1
Warmlake Rd ME17 117 C1
Warne Pl 4 DA15 13 B1
Warner St ME4 53 F3
Warnett Ct ME6 66 A1
Warnford Gdns ME15 116 A8
Warnford Rd BR6 57 F5
Warren Ave BR6 57 F5
Warren Cl DA6 14 A2
Warren Cotts TN11 141 A3
Warren Ct TN15 92 C3
Warren Dr BR6 58 B5
Warren Farm La TN3 172 B4
Warren Gdns BR6 58 A5
Warren Hastings Ct DA11 18 F1
Warren La Oxted RH8 104 A1
Woolwich SE18 2 B3
Yelsted ME9 70 C3
Warren Rd Bexley DA6 14 A2
Dartford DA1 32 E5
Hayes BR2 56 A8
Kit's Coty ME5 83 D7
Luddesdown ME2 51 D3
Northfleet DA13 35 B3
Orpington BR6 58 C5
Sidcup DA14 30 C5
Warren Ridge TN3 173 C3
Warren Road Prim Sch BR6 57 F6
Warren The
Gravesend DA12 36 D4
2 Greenwich SE7 11 C8
Penshurst TN11 141 A4
Ticehurst TN5 186 E1
Warren View DA12 37 E2
Warren Wlk 1 SE7 11 C8
Warren Wood Cl BR2 56 A8
Warren Wood Com Prim Sch & Language Unit ME1 67 C8
Warren Wood Rd ME1 67 C7
Warrens The DA3 48 F3
Warrington Rd TN12 146 A6
Warrior Ave DA12 36 C4
Warsop Trad Est TN8 138 D8
Warspite Rd SE18 1 E3
Warwall E6 2 B7
Warwick Cl Orpington BR6 58 A7
Sidcup DA5 30 F8
Warwick Cres ME1 52 F2
Warwick Ct 8 DA8 14 F7
Warwick Gdns DA13 64 A8
Warwick Pk TN2 159 B1
Warwick Pl
Maidstone ME16 99 E3
Northfleet DA11 18 B2
Warwick Rd Bexley DA16 13 C4
4 Royal Tunbridge Wells TN1 159 A2
Sidcup DA14 30 B3
Warwick Terr SE18 12 D8
Warwick Way DA1 32 E6
Washington Ho ME15 116 E5
Washneys Rd BR6 74 B6
Washwell La TN5 184 F3
Wassall La TN17 197 E7
Wat Tyler Way ME15 100 A4
Watchgate DA2 33 E3
Watchmans Terr 6 ME5 54 C2
Water La
Harrietsham ME17 119 B5
Hawkhurst TN18 189 B4
Headcorn TN17,TN27 151 A4
Hunton ME15 131 D6
Kingswood ME17 118 F3
Limpsfield RH8 104 A8
6 Maidstone ME15 100 A4
Maidstone,Bearsted ME14 101 E6
Shoreham TN14 75 F6
Sidcup DA14 30 F6
Smarden TN27 152 F2
West Malling ME19 97 C8
Water Mill Way DA4 47 B7
Water Slippe TN11 111 D1
Watercress Cl TN14 92 C7
Watercress Dr TN14 92 C7
Watercroft Rd TN14 58 F1
Waterdale Rd SE2 13 A8
Waterdales DA11 35 D7
Waterdown Rd TN4 158 E1
Waterfield TN2 173 A7
Waterfield Cl Erith DA17 4 A3
Woolwich SE28 3 B5
Waterfrets Cotts TN3 157 F5
Waterfront Studios Bsns Ctr E16 1 A5
Watergate Ho 5 SE18 2 A2
Waterglade Ind Pk RM20 16 F8
Waterhead Cl DA8 14 E7
Waterhouse Cl E16 1 D8
Wateringbury CE Prim Sch ME18 113 E6
Wateringbury Cl BR5 44 B7
Wateringbury Rd ME19 97 F3
Wateringbury Sta ME18 113 E6
Waterlakes TN8 138 C8
Waterloo Pl
Cranbrook TN17 179 D5
Tonbridge TN9 143 B8
Waterloo Rd
Cranbrook TN17 179 D6
Gillingham ME7 54 C4
Tonbridge TN9 143 B8
Waterloo St
1 Gravesend DA12 36 C8
Maidstone ME15 100 A3
Waterlow Rd
Maidstone ME14 100 A6
Vigo Village DA13 79 F7
Waterman's La TN12 146 B3
Watermans Way DA9 17 B3
Watermeadow Cl
Erith DA8 15 B6
Gillingham ME7 68 F6
Watermill Cl
Maidstone ME16 99 B5
Rochester ME2 53 C8
Watermint Cl BR5 44 D5
Waters Cotts TN5 185 A4
Waters Edge ME15 99 F2
Waters Edge Ct DA8 4 F1
Waters Pl ME7 69 A6
Waterside Crayford DA1 14 F2
Maidstone ME14 99 F5
Waterside Ct
Leybourne ME19 81 E2
Rochester ME2 53 E6
Waterside Gate ME16 99 F5
Waterside La ME7 54 F7
Waterside Mews ME18 113 D6
Waterside Sch SE18 2 D1
Watersmeet Cl ME15 100 A1
Watersmeet Way SE28 3 D7
Waterton BR8 45 D5
Waterton Ave DA12 36 E8
Waterworks Cotts TN14 92 B6
Watery La
Heaverham TN15 93 D7
Sidcup BR5,DA14 30 B2
Watford Rd E16 1 A8
Watkins Cl TN12 149 E5
Watling Ave ME5 54 D2
Watling Ho 10 SE18 12 A8
Watling St Bexley DA6,DA7 14 C3
Dartford DA1,DA2 33 C8
Gillingham ME5 54 D2
Gravesend DA11,DA12 36 C2
Northfleet DA11,DA13 35 C5
Rochester ME2 52 D7
Watson Ave ME5 67 D5
Watson Cl RM20 17 A6
Watt Ho SE2 3 C1
Watt's Cross Rd TN11 126 B6
Watt's La BR7 43 C8
Watts Cl Snodland ME6 82 B8
Wadhurst TN5 184 F4
Watts' Ave ME1 53 C4
Watts' St ME4 53 E3
Wavell Dr DA15 12 E1
Waveney Rd TN10 127 B5
Waverley Cl Bromley BR2 42 D4
Chatham ME5 68 D2
Coxheath ME17 115 C3
Waverley Cres
Woolwich SE18 12 D8
Woolwich SE18 2 D1
Waverley Dr TN2 159 F6
Waverley Gdns E6 1 E8
Waverley Rd SE18 2 D1
Way Volante DA12 36 E4
Wayfield Com Prim Sch ME5 68 A7
Wayfield Link SE9 12 D1
Wayfield Rd ME5 68 A7
Waylands BR8 45 F5
Waylands Cl TN14 74 E4
Wayne Cl BR6 57 F7
Wayne Ct ME2 39 D2
Wayside
3 Chislehurst BR7 43 D8
Tenterden TN30 183 B2
Wayside Ave TN30 183 B3
Wayside Dr TN8 122 D3
Wayside Flats TN30 183 B2
Wayside Gr SE9 28 F4
Wayville Rd DA1 33 B8
Weald Cl Istead Rise DA13 35 E1
Maidstone ME15 116 C6
Orpington BR2 56 E8
Sevenoaks Weald TN14 108 C2
Weald Com Prim Sch TN14 108 B2
Weald Ct TN11 126 D6
Weald of Kent Gram Sch for Girls The TN9 143 C7
Weald Rd TN13 108 B7
Weald The BR7 28 F2
Weald View
Frittenden TN17 166 E6
Paddock Wood TN12 146 E1
Turner's Green TN5 184 F6
Weald View Rd TN9 143 B7
Wealden Ave TN30 183 B1
Wealden Cl TN11 126 E5
Wealden Ct 5 ME5 54 B3
Wealden Pl TN13 92 D6
Wealden View TN17 177 E8
Wealden Way ME20 98 E7
Weardale Ave DA2 33 C7
Weare Rd TN4 159 C8
Weatherly Cl ME1 53 C4
Weathersfield Ct SE9 11 F1
Weaver Cl E6 2 B6
Weaver's Orch DA13 35 A2
Weavering Cl ME2 39 B2
Weavering Cotts ME14 100 E3
Weavering St ME14 100 F4
Weavers Cl
Gravesend DA11 36 A7
Staplehurst TN12 149 F4
Weavers Cotts TN17 177 E8
Weavers La TN14 92 C6
Weavers The
Biddenden TN27 168 A1
Maidstone ME16 99 B5
Webb Cl ME3 40 D6
Webb Ct 6 SE28 3 B6
Webb's Mdw TN15 92 C2
Webber Cl DA8 15 B7
Webster Rd ME8 55 F1
Wedgewood Cl ME16 99 B5
Wedgewood Ct DA5 30 F8
Wedgewood Dr ME5 68 A7
Wedgwoods TN16 88 C6
Weeds Wood Rd ME5 67 F4
Week St ME14 100 A4
Weeks La TN27 168 A5
Weigall Rd SE12,SE3 11 A3
Weir Mill ME19 97 F7
Weir Rd DA5 31 B8
Weird Wood DA3 49 C6
Welbeck Ave Bromley BR1 28 A4
Royal Tunbridge Wells TN4 159 C8
Sidcup DA15 30 A7
Welcombe Ct ME8 69 D8
Weld Cl TN12 149 F4
Weldstock Ho 2 SE28 2 D3
Well Cl TN11 125 F1
Well Field DA3 48 F5
Well Hall* SE9 11 E3
Well Hall Par SE9 11 F3
Well Hall Rd SE18,SE9 11 F5
Well Hill BR6 59 B5
Well Hill La BR6 59 B4
Well Hill Nursery BR6 59 C4
Well Penn Rd ME3 22 C3
Well Rd Maidstone ME14 100 A5
Otford TN14 76 C3
Well St East Malling ME19 97 E6
Maidstone ME15,ME17 115 E4
Wellan Cl DA16 13 B2
Welland Rd TN10 127 B4
Wellands Cl BR1 42 F7
Wellbrook Rd BR6 57 A6
Wellcome Ave DA1 15 E3
Weller Ave ME1 53 D2
Weller Pl BR6 73 A8
Weller Rd TN4 158 C4
Wellers Cl TN16 105 C8
Wellesley Cl 7 SE7 1 C1
Welling High St DA16 13 B3
Welling Sch DA16 13 B6
Welling Sta DA16 13 A5
Welling Way DA16 12 D4
Wellingfield Ct 1 DA16 13 A4
Wellington Ave
Sidcup DA15 13 A1
Woolwich SE18 2 B3
Wellington Cotts
Gill's Green TN18 188 E4
Meopham DA13 64 A7
Wellington Gdns SE7 1 C1
Wellington Ho 6 ME15 116 E5
Wellington Mews SE7 11 C8
Wellington Par DA15 13 A2
Wellington Pl
Maidstone ME14 99 F6
Sparrow's Green TN5 184 F5
Wellington Rd Bexley DA5 13 D2
Bromley BR2 42 C5
Dartford DA1 15 C1
Erith DA17 3 F1
Gillingham ME7 54 C4
Orpington BR5 44 C3
Tilbury RM18 19 A5
Wellington St
Gravesend DA12 36 C8
Woolwich SE18 2 A2
Wellington Way ME19 96 F3
Wellingtonia Way TN8 122 C2
Wellmeade Dr TN13 108 B8
Wells Cl
Royal Tunbridge Wells TN1 159 A3
Tenterden TN30 193 B8
Tonbridge TN10 127 D4
Westerham TN16 105 C8
Wells Cotts ME18 113 C2
Wells Ct ME2 52 D5
Wells Ho Bromley BR1 28 B3
Wells Ho continued
Royal Tunbridge Wells TN4 158 F4
Wells Rd Bromley BR1 42 F7
Rochester ME2 52 D5
Wellsmoor Gdns BR1 43 A6
Welton Cl TN9 142 F7
Welton Rd SE18 12 E7
Wemmick Cl ME1 67 D7
Wendover Cl ME2 66 B5
Wendover Ct BR2 42 B6
Wendover Rd
Bromley BR1,BR2 42 B6
Eltham SE9 11 D4
Wendover Way
Bexley DA16 13 A3
Orpington BR6 44 A3
Wensley Cl SE9 11 F1
Wents Wood ME14 100 F5
Wentworth Cl Erith SE28 3 D7
Gravesend DA11 36 A3
Hayes BR2 56 A8
Orpington BR6 57 E5
Wentworth Dr
Cliffe Woods ME3 39 B8
Dartford DA1 15 A1
Gillingham ME8 69 E7
Wentworth Ho 3 SE3 11 A7
Wentworth Prim Sch DA1 32 A8
Wenvoe Ave DA7 14 B5
Wernbrook St SE18 12 C8
Wesley Ave E16 1 B5
Wesley Cl Maidstone ME16 98 F3
Orpington BR5 44 C6
Wesley Ho BR1 42 D6
Wessex Dr DA8 14 E6
Wessex Wlk DA2 31 E6
West App BR5 43 C4
West Borough Prim Sch ME16 99 B3
West Brow BR7 29 B3
West Common Rd BR2 56 B7
West Crescent Rd DA12 19 C1
West Cross TN30 192 F7
West Cross Gdns TN30 192 F7
West Ct 3 ME15 100 A1
West Dr Chatham ME5 67 D5
Sutton Valence ME17 135 B7
West End Brasted TN16 90 B2
Kemsing TN15 77 A2
Marden TN12 148 C6
West Hallowes SE9 28 E7
West Heath Cl DA1 14 F1
West Heath La TN13 108 B7
West Heath Rd
Bexley SE2 13 D8
Crayford DA1 14 F1
West Hill Biggin Hill BR6 72 F7
Dartford DA1 15 D1
West Hill Dr DA1 15 C1
West Hill Prim Sch DA1 15 C1
West Hill Rise DA1 15 D1
West Holme DA8 14 C6
West Kent Ave DA11 18 C1
West Kent Coll TN9 143 A7
West Kingsdown CE Prim Sch TN15 62 A2
West Kingsdown Ind Est TN15 61 F2
West La ME3 26 F6
West Lodge Prep Sch DA14 30 A5
West Malling CE Prim Sch ME19 97 B8
West Malling Ind Pk ME19 80 E2
West Malling Sta ME19 97 D8
West Mersea Cl E16 1 B5
West Mill DA11 18 F1
West Mill Rd ME20 82 C4
West Motney Way ME8 55 F3
West Park Ave TN4 142 F1
West Park Rd ME15 100 B2
West Parkside SE10 1 A2
West Pk SE9 28 E7
West Rd Chatham ME4 54 A7
Goudhurst TN17 177 E8
Kilndown TN17 176 F3
West Shaw DA3 48 D7
West St Bexley DA7 13 F4
Bromley BR1 42 A7
Erith DA8 4 E1
Gillingham ME7 54 D6
Gravesend DA11 19 B1
Grays RM17 18 A8
Harrietsham ME17 119 C6
Hunton ME15 131 D7
Rochester ME2 39 B1
West Malling ME19 97 B8
Woodside Green ME17 120 E8
Wrotham TN15 78 F3
West Terr DA15 29 E7
West Thurrock Prim Sch RM20 17 A8
West Thurrock Way RM20 17 B8
West View Hospl TN30 192 E6
West View Rd
Crockenhill BR8 45 D3
Dartford DA1 15 F1
Swanley BR8 46 A5
West Way BR5 43 D4
West Wlk ME16 99 B3
West Wood Cott BR6 59 B4
West Wood Rd ME9 86 B8
West Woodside DA5 30 E7
West Yoke TN15 62 D7
Westbere Ho BR5 44 C4
Westbourne Rd DA7 13 E7
Westbrook Ct SE3 11 B6
Westbrook Dr BR5 44 D1
Westbrook Rd SE3 11 B6
Westbrook Terr TN2 159 D1
Westbrooke Cl ME4 54 A2
Westbrooke Cres DA16 13 C4
Westbrooke Rd
Bexley DA16 13 C4
Sidcup DA15 29 D6
Westbrooke Sch DA16 13 D4
Westbury Ct 5 DA14 30 A4
Westbury Rd BR1 42 D8
Westbury Terr TN16 105 C8
Westcombe Hill SE3 11 A8
Westcombe Park Rd SE3 11 A7
Westcombe Park Sta SE3 1 A1
Westcott Ave DA11 36 A5
Westcott Cl BR1 42 F4
Westcourt Prim Sch DA12 36 E6
Westcourt Rd ME7 54 A6
Westdale Rd SE18 12 B8
Westdean Ave SE12 28 C7
Wested Farm Cotts BR8 45 F2
Wested La BR8 46 A3
Westerdale Rd 5 SE10 1 A1
Westergate Rd Bexley SE2 13 E8
Rochester ME2 38 F1
Westerham Cl ME8 55 B3
Westerham Dr DA15 13 C1
Westerham Hill TN16 89 B5
Westerham Rd
Brasted TN16 90 A2
Limpsfield RH8,TN16 104 C6
Orpington BR2 56 D4
Sevenoaks TN13 91 C4
Westerham TN16 105 A8
Westerhill Rd ME17 115 C1
Western Ave
Chatham ME4 54 A8
7 Hawkhurst TN18 188 F2
Western Beach Apartments E16 1 A5
Western Cross Cl DA9 17 C1
Western Gateway E16 1 A6
Western Rd
Borough Green TN15 94 F7
Hawkhurst TN18 188 F2
Maidstone ME16 99 C2
Royal Tunbridge Wells TN1 159 C5
Royal Tunbridge Wells,Southborough TN4 143 A1
Turner's Green TN5 184 F6
Western Way SE28 2 E4
Westfield
New Ash Green DA3 62 F6
1 Orpington BR6 57 C5
Sevenoaks TN13 92 C5
Westfield Bsns Ctr ME2 53 C7
Westfield Cl DA12 36 C2
Westfield Cotts
Cudham TN14 73 D3
West Kingsdown TN15 61 F4
Westfield Gdns ME9 71 C3
Westfield Ho TN30 192 F7
Westfield Rd DA7 14 C4
Westfield Sole Rd ME5, ME14 84 D8
Westfield St SE18 1 D3
Westfield Terr TN17 178 F1
Westfield Villas TN12 148 B5
Westgate Ct SE12 28 A7
Westgate Ho 6 DA1 15 D1
Westgate Prim Sch DA1 32 D8
Westgate Rd DA1 15 D1
Westharold BR8 45 D6
Westhill Cl DA12 36 B7
Westholme BR6 43 F2
Westhorne Ave SE12,SE9 11 C2
Westhurst Dr BR7 29 B3
Westland Ho 1 E16 2 A5
Westland Lodge 2 BR1 42 C7
Westleigh Dr BR1 42 E8
Westmarsh Cl ME15 116 F7
Westmead ME20 82 C4
Westminster Ind Est SE18 1 D3
Westminster Sq ME16 99 B4
Westmoor St SE7 1 D3
Westmore Rd TN16 88 C7
Westmoreland Ave DA16 12 E3
Westmoreland Pl 9 BR1 42 A6
Westmoreland Rd BR2 42 A5
Westmorland Cl ME15 116 E7
Westmorland Gn ME15 116 E7
Westmorland Rd ME15 116 E7
Westmount Ave ME4 53 F3
Westmount Rd SE9 12 A3
Weston Ave RM20 16 F8
Weston Rd ME2 53 A8
Westree Ct 7 ME16 99 E3
Westree Rd ME16 99 E3
Westrise TN9 143 A7
Westview ME4 40 B2
Westway Coxheath ME17 115 C3
Pembury TN2 160 D7
Westways
Edenbridge TN8 122 C2
Westerham TN16 89 C1
Westwell Cl BR5 44 D1
Westwell Ct TN30 192 F7
Westwell Ho TN30 192 F7
Westwood Cl BR1 42 D6

Westwood Farm DA13 ....34 D2
Westwood La DA16 ....12 F4
Westwood Rd
Betsham DA13 ....34 E2
East Peckham TN12 ......129 E6
Loose ME15 ....116 A7
Rusthall TN4 ....158 C5
Westwood Tech Coll
DA16 ....12 E3
Westwood Way TN13 .....91 F5
Westwood Wlk ME9 ......71 B7
Wetheral Dr ME5 ....68 B4
Wey Cl ME5 ....68 C5
Weybridge Cl ME5 ....68 C4
Weyhill Cl ME14 ....100 C6
Weyman Rd SE3 ....11 C6
Weymouth Cl E6 ....2 B7
Wharf La ME3 ....22 B6
Wharf Rd Gillingham ME7 ..54 C7
Gravesend DA12 ....19 E1
Grays RM17 ....17 F8
Maidstone ME15 ....99 E2
Wharf Rd S RM17 ....17 F8
Wharfedale Rd DA2 ......33 C7
Wharfside Cl DA8 ....4 F1
Wharnecliffe Ho DA9 .....17 B1
Wharton Rd BR1 ....42 B8
Whatcote Cotts TN15 ....95 C7
Whatman Cl ME14 ....100 C6
Wheatcroft DA12 ....36 C7
Wheatcroft Gr ME8 ....69 F7
Wheatear Way ME5 ....68 B7
Wheatfield ME19 ....81 E1
Wheatfield Cl TN17 .....179 C5
Wheatfield Dr TN17 .....179 C5
Wheatfield Lea TN17 ....179 C5
Wheatfield Way TN17 ...179 C5
Wheatfields Chatham ME5 .68 D2
Maidstone ME14 ....100 D4
Newham E6 ....2 B7
Wheatley Cl DA9 ....17 A2
Wheatley Terrace Rd
DA8 ....14 F8
Wheatsheaf Cl ME15 ....116 B8
Wheatsheaf Hill
Chelsfield TN14 ....58 F2
Ide Hill TN14 ....106 F4
Wheatsheaf Way TN10 ..127 D6
Wheatstone Rd DA8 ....4 D1
Wheelbarrow Park Est
TN12 ....148 B7
Wheeler Pl ME18 ....97 A2
Wheeler St
Headcorn TN27 ....151 E5
Maidstone ME14 ....100 A5
Wheeler's La ME17 .....132 E7
Wheelers The ME8 ....69 B6
Wheelock Cl DA8 ....14 B7
Wheelwrights The
ME17 ....119 D6
Wheelwrites TN15 ......110 E7
Whenman Ave DA5 ....31 C5
Whernside Cl SE28 ....3 C6
Whetsted Rd
Five Oak Green TN12 ....145 C8
Whetsted TN12 ....129 F1
Whetstone Rd SE3 ....11 D6
Whiffen Wlk ME19 ....82 B1
Whiffen's Ave ME4 ....53 F5
Whiffen's Ave W ME4 ....53 F5
Whimbrel Cl SE28 ....3 C6
Whimbrel Gn ME20 ....81 F2
Whimbrel Wlk ME5 ....68 C1
Whimbrels The ME4 ......40 B1
Whinchat Rd SE28 ....2 D3
Whinfell Way DA12 ......36 F4
Whinyates Rd SE9 ....11 E4
Whippendell Cl BR5 .....44 B8
Whippendell Way BR5 ....44 B7
Whistler Rd TN10 ....127 D6
Whitby Cl Biggin Hill TN16 ..72 B1
Stone DA9 ....17 A2
Whitby Rd SE18 ....1 F2
Whitchurch Cl ME16 .....99 E4
Whitcombe Cl ME5 ......68 C3
White Ave DA11 ....35 F5
White Bear Pas [3] TN1 ..159 A2
White Cottage Rd TN10 .127 D6
White Gate ME2 ....52 F8
White Gates DA14 ....30 A3
White Hart Cl TN13 .....108 C7
White Hart Par TN13 .....91 E5
White Hart Rd
Orpington BR6 ....44 A2
Woolwich SE18 ....2 E2
White Hart Wood TN13 ..108 C6
White Hart Yd [10] DA11 ...19 B1
White Hill Rd ME9,ME14 ..69 D1
White Horse Hill BR7,SE9 .29 A4
White Horse La
Harvel DA13 ....64 C2
Otham Hole ME15 ....117 A6
White Horse Rd DA13 ....64 E1
White House Cl ME3 .....40 E4
White House La TN14 ...107 F5
White House Rd TN14 ...107 F5
White La RH8,TN16 ....88 B3
White Lodge TN1 ....159 C4
White Lodge Cl TN13 .....92 B4
White Oak Cl [13] TN9 ....143 B8
White Oak Gdns DA15 ....29 F8
White Oak Prim Sch BR8 .45 E7
White Oak Sq [3] BR8 .....45 E6
White Post
Four Elms TN8 ....123 A6
White Post continued
Hollingbourne ME17 ......103 B5
White Post Cnr TN11 ....110 F5
White Post Hill DA4 ......47 A2
White Post La
Culverstone Green DA13 ....63 F2
Sole Street DA13 ....50 B5
White Rd ME4 ....54 A2
White Rock Ct ME16 .....99 E3
White Rock Pl [5] ME16 ....99 E3
White's La TN18 ....189 B2
White's Mdw BR1 ....43 A5
Whitebeam Ave BR2 .....43 A3
Whitebeam Cl TN15 ......77 A2
Whitebeam Dr ME17 ....115 B3
Whitebine Gdns TN12 ...130 A6
Whitebread La TN31 ....197 D1
Whitecroft BR8 ....45 E7
Whitefield Cl BR5 ....44 C6
Whitefield Rd TN4 ......159 A6
Whitefriars TN13 ....108 A8
Whitefriars Wharf TN9 ..127 C1
Whitegate Cl TN4 ....159 A8
Whitegate Ct ME8 ....69 D5
Whitegates Ave TN15 ....61 E4
Whitegates La TN5 ......184 D8
Whitehall Dr ME17 ......118 D3
Whitehall La Erith DA8 ...14 F5
[6] Grays RM17 ....18 C8
Whitehall Rd
Broad Street ME14 ....102 A6
Bromley BR2 ....42 D5
Whitehaven Cl BR2 ......42 A5
Whitehaven Ct [6] DA6 ....13 E3
Whitehead Cl DA2 ....32 C5
Whiteheads La ME14 ....101 B4
Whitehill TN15 ....79 B3
Whitehill Inf Sch DA12 ...36 C5
Whitehill Jun Sch DA12 ..36 C5
Whitehill La DA12 ....36 D5
Whitehill Par DA12 ....36 C5
Whitehill Rd Dartford DA1 .15 A2
Gravesend DA12 ....36 C6
Longfield,Whitehill DA13 ...48 D8
Meopham DA13 ....64 B7
Whitehorse Hill ME5 .....54 B3
Whitehouse Cres ME1 ....83 A8
Whitelake Rd TN10 .....127 C5
Whiteleaves Rise ME2 ....52 B3
Whitelimes TN18 ....188 D8
Whiteoak Ct [1] BR8 ......45 E6
Whitepost La DA13 ....80 A8
Whites Cl DA9 ....17 C1
Whitewall Ctr ME2 ....53 D8
Whitewall Rd ME2 ....53 D7
Whitewall Way ME2 ......53 D7
Whitewebbs Way BR5 ....43 F8
Whitewell La TN17 ......179 D7
Whitewood Cotts TN16 ...88 C7
Whitfield Cres DA2 ....33 C8
Whitfield Rd DA7 ....13 F7
Whitings Way E6 ....2 A8
Whitmore St ME16 ....99 D2
Whitney Wlk DA14 ....30 E2
Whittaker St ME4 ....54 A4
Whitworth Rd SE18 ......12 A7
Whybourne Crest TN2 ..159 D1
Whyman Ave ME4 ....54 A1
Wichling Cl BR5 ....44 D1
Wicken Ho ME16 ....99 E4
Wickenden Rd TN13 .....92 C5
Wickens Pl ME19 ....97 C8
Wickets The TN14 ......108 C2
Wickham Cl ME9 ....71 B6
Wickham Common Prim Sch
BR4 ....56 A6
Wickham Ct DA16 ....12 E5
Wickham Field TN14 .....75 F3
Wickham Gdns TN4 .....158 D5
Wickham La SE2,SE18 ....13 A8
Wickham Pl ME17 ....120 D5
Wickham St Bexley DA16 ..13 A6
Rochester ME1 ....53 D3
Wickhams Way DA3 ......48 F4
Wickhurst Rd TN14 .....107 F3
Wicks Cl SE9 ....28 D4
Wicksteed Cl DA5 ....31 D5
Widbury TN3 ....157 F3
Widecombe Rd SE9 ....28 E5
Widgeon Cl E16 ....1 B7
Widgeon Path SE28 ....2 D3
Widgeon Rd Erith DA8 ....15 B7
Rochester ME2 ....52 D6
Widmore Lodge Rd BR1 ..42 D7
Widmore Rd BR1 ....42 C7
Wierton Hill ME17 ......133 D7
Wierton La ME17 ....116 E1
Wierton Rd ME17 ....133 E8
Wigmore Rd ME8 ....69 B4
Wilberforce Ct [2] SE28 ....3 C5
Wilberforce Rd ME17 ...115 D3
Wilberforce Way DA12 ...36 D3
Wilde Cl RM18 ....19 C5
Wilde Rd DA8 ....14 B7
Wilden Park Rd TN12 ...164 E7
Wilderness Rd BR7 ......29 B1
Wildernesse Ave TN15 ...92 F5
Wildernesse Mount
TN13 ....92 D5
Wildernesse Sch The
TN13 ....92 E6
Wildfell Cl ME5 ....84 C8
Wildman Cl ME8 ....69 D3
Wildwood Cl
Kingswood ME17 ....118 E2
[1] Lewisham SE12 ....28 A8
Wildwood Glade ME7 ....69 B4
Wilford Ho [3] SE18 ....2 B1
Wilfred St [23] DA12 ....19 B1
Wilkins Way TN16 ....90 B3
Wilkinson Cl [1] DA1 ......16 A3
Wilkinson Pl ME18 ....97 A2
Wilkinson Rd E16 ....1 C7
Wilks Ave DA1 ....32 F6
Will Adams Ct [9] ME7 ....54 C6
Will Adams Rdbt ME8 ....54 F2
Will Adams Way ME8 .....54 F1
Will Crooks Gdns SE9 ....11 D3
Will Thorne Pav The E16 ..1 E7
Willenhall Rd SE18 ....2 B1
Willersley Ave
Orpington BR6 ....57 D7
Sidcup DA15 ....29 F7
Willersley Cl DA15 ....29 F7
Willesley Gdns TN17 ....179 D6
Willett Cl BR5 ....43 E3
Willett Way BR5,BR6 .....43 E3
Willetts Cotts TN3 ......156 C4
Willetts La TN3 ....156 C4
William Baker Ho ME20 ...98 F8
William Barefoot Dr SE9 .29 A5
William Ho [4] DA12 ....36 B8
William Judge Cl TN30 ..193 D7
William Luck Cl TN12 ...129 E6
William Rd ME2 ....52 C2
William Smith Ho [10] DA17 .4 A3
William St
Gravesend DA12 ....36 B8
Grays RM17 ....18 C8
Royal Tunbridge Wells
TN4 ....159 A5
Williams Way DA2 ....31 D6
Willicombe Ho TN2 .....159 D4
Willicombe Pk TN2 .....159 D4
Willington Gn ME15 ....116 E7
Willington St ME15 .....100 F2
Willis Ho ME1 ....53 C4
Willis Rd DA8 ....4 D2
Willoughby Way SE7 ......1 B2
Willow Ave
Hoo St Werburgh ME3 ......40 E3
Sidcup DA15 ....13 A1
Swanley BR8 ....45 F5
Willow Cl Bromley BR2 ....42 F4
Orpington BR5 ....44 B2
Sidcup DA5 ....13 F1
Willow Cres
Five Oak Green TN12 .....145 B7
Staplehurst TN12 ....149 F5
Willow Ct Dartford DA1 ...32 C7
Loose ME15 ....116 A6
Willow Dene Sch SE18 ...12 E6
Willow Gr BR7 ....29 B2
Willow Grange DA14 .....30 B5
Willow Ho
[2] Chatham ME5 ....67 F5
[8] Maidstone ME16 ....99 A3
Willow La
Paddock Wood TN12 .....146 E6
Woolwich SE18 ....2 A2
Willow Lea TN10 ....127 C7
Willow Lodge TN4 ......158 E4
Willow Pk TN14 ....75 F2
Willow Rd Dartford DA1 ...32 C7
Erith DA8 ....15 A6
Larkfield ME20 ....81 F3
Rochester ME2 ....52 E6
Willow Rise ME15 ....100 F1
Willow Terr DA4 ....60 E8
Willow Tree Ct DA14 .....29 F3
Willow Tree Rd TN2 .....158 F1
Willow Tree Wlk BR1 ....42 B8
Willow Vale BR7 ....29 B2
Willow Way
Biddenden TN27 ....182 D7
Maidstone ME15 ....100 B3
Willow Wents ME18 ......96 D1
Willow Wlk
Culverstone Green DA13 ....63 F3
Orpington BR6 ....57 B7
Royal Tunbridge Wells
TN2 ....159 E8
Willow Wood Rd DA13 ....63 F2
Willowbank Ct [12] ME15 .100 B4
Willowbank Dr ME23 .....23 E4
Willowby Gdns ME8 .....69 E4
Willowfields Cl [1] SE18 ....2 E1
Willowherb Cl ME4 ....40 C1
Willowmead ME19 ....81 E2
Willows The
Gillingham ME8 ....55 E2
Grays RM17 ....18 D8
Newington ME9 ....71 B6
Willowside ME6 ....66 A1
Willrose Cres SE2 ....3 B1
Wilman Rd TN4 ....159 B7
Wilmar Way TN15 ....92 F7
Wilmecote Ct ME8 ....69 D8
Wilmington Ave BR6 .....58 C8
Wilmington Court Rd
DA2 ....32 A6
Wilmington Gram Sch for
Boys DA2 ....32 B5
Wilmington Hall Sch
DA2 ....32 B5
Wilmington Ho DA2 ......32 D6
Wilmington Prim Sch
DA2 ....32 B5
Wilmington Way ME8 ....55 B2
Wilmot Rd DA1 ....15 B2
Wilmount St SE18 ....2 B2
Wilson Ave ME1 ....67 E7
Wilson Cl
Maidstone ME15 ....116 E7
Tonbridge TN11 ....126 E5
Wilson Ct ME18 ....114 A1
Wilson Ho [3] SE7 ....11 C8
Wilson La DA4 ....47 F7
Wilson Rd TN10 ....127 E5
Wilsons La ME15 ....115 A5
Wilsons Way DA13 ....63 F3
Wilton Dr ME20 ....98 B8
Wilton Ho [2] BR7 ....43 D8
Wilton Rd SE2 ....3 C2
Wiltshire Cl Chatham ME5 .68 C8
Dartford DA2 ....33 D8
Wiltshire Rd BR6 ....44 A2
Wiltshire Way
[4] Maidstone ME15 ....116 E8
Royal Tunbridge Wells
TN2 ....159 D7
Wimborne [6] DA14 ....30 B4
Wimborne Ave BR7 ......43 F6
Wimborne Ho DA12 ......36 D5
Wimbourne Dr ME8 ......69 D6
Wimpole Cl BR2 ....42 C5
Win'freds Cl TN17 ......191 E3
Winch Cl TN17 ....179 D3
Winch's Garth TN12 ....149 F5
Winchcomb Gdns SE9 ...11 D4
Winchelsea Ave DA7 .....13 F7
Winchelsea Rd ME5 .....68 B5
Winchester Ave ME5 .....67 F4
Winchester Cl [11] E6 ....1 F7
Winchester Cres DA12 ...36 D5
Winchester Ct [14] DA17 ....4 A1
Winchester Gr TN13 .....92 B4
Winchester Ho
[3] Maidstone ME15 ....116 D7
Woolwich SE18 ....11 D7
Winchester Pl [9] ME14 ..100 A5
Winchester Rd
Bexley DA7 ....13 D5
Hawkhurst TN18 ....189 A2
Orpington BR6 ....58 C6
Tonbridge TN10 ....127 D5
Winchester Way ME8 ....70 A8
Wincliff Rd TN9 ....143 B8
Wincrofts Dr SE9 ....12 D3
Windermere Cl
Dartford DA1 ....32 B7
Orpington BR6 ....57 B7
Windermere Dr ME8 .....69 D7
Windermere Ho [4]
ME15 ....116 E7
Windermere Rd DA7 .....14 C5
Windhover Way DA12 ....36 E4
Windmill Cl ME2 ....39 B1
Windmill Cotts
Cranbrook TN17 ....179 D6
Lower Stoke ME3 ....25 C5
Windmill Ct
Maidstone ME17 ....116 B3
Royal Tunbridge Wells
TN2 ....159 C3
Windmill Dr BR2 ....56 C6
Windmill Grange TN15 ...61 F3
Windmill Hill
Brenchley TN12 ....146 B1
Platt TN15 ....95 D7
Pye Corner ME17 ....136 B7
Windmill Hts ME14 .....101 B4
Windmill La
Cousley Wood TN5 ......185 C8
Durgates TN5 ....184 E4
Wrotham Heath TN15 .....95 E8
Windmill La E ME19 .....97 C6
Windmill La W ME19 ....97 A6
Windmill Manor ME7 ....54 C4
Windmill Pk TN15 ....95 E7
Windmill Rd
Gillingham ME7 ....54 C4
Sevenoaks TN13 ....108 B6
Sevenoaks Weald TN14 ....108 B2
Windmill Row ME17 ....117 D2
Windmill St
Gravesend DA12 ....36 B7
Rochester ME2 ....39 B1
Royal Tunbridge Wells
TN2 ....159 C3
Windrush Ct [8] DA8 ......4 E1
Windrush Prim Sch SE28 ..3 B5
Windsor Ave ME4 ....53 F2
Windsor Cl
Chislehurst BR7 ....29 B3
Maidstone ME14 ....100 B6
Windsor Ct
[1] Bromley BR1 ....42 E6
Gillingham ME7 ....54 D5
[18] Sidcup DA14 ....30 A5
Windsor Dr Dartford DA1 ..15 A1
Orpington BR6 ....58 A4
Windsor Hall E16 ....1 B5
Windsor Rd Bexley DA6 ...13 E3
Gillingham ME7 ....54 D5
Gravesend DA12 ....36 B4
Windward Rd ME1 ......53 C1
Windy Ridge BR1 ....42 E8
Windyridge ME7 ....54 E1
Winfield La TN15 ....94 E3
Winford Mews ME1 ......53 A2
Wingate Rd DA14 ....30 C2
Wingfield Ct DA15 ....29 F7
Wingfield Prim Sch SE3 ..11 B4
Wingfield Rd DA12 ......36 B8
Wingham Cl
Gillingham ME8 ....55 C3
Maidstone ME15 ....116 F7
Wingrove Dr
Maidstone ME14 ....100 E5
Rochester ME2 ....53 C7
Winifred Rd Dartford DA1 ..15 B2
Erith DA8 ....4 E1
Maidstone ME15 ....100 F3
Winifred St E16 1
Winn Common Rd SE18 ..12
Winn Rd SE12,SE9 28
Winnipeg Dr [3] BR6 57
Winser Rd TN17 192
Winsor Prim Sch E6 2
Winsor Terr E6 2
Winston Ave ME18 97
Winston Cl DA9 16
Winston Ct [10] BR1 42
Winston Dr ME2 39
Winston Rd ME2 52
Winstone Scott Ave
TN3 157
Winterborne Ave BR6 57
Winterfield La ME19 97
Wintergarden Cres DA9 ..34
Wintergreen Cl
[8] Newham E16 1
St Mary's Island ME4 40
Winters Croft DA12 36
Winterton Ct [8] TN16 89
Winton Ct BR8 45
Winton Rd BR6 57
Wireless Rd TN16 72
Wirral Wood Cl BR7 29
Wirrals The ME5 68
Wise Ho SE18 12
Wise's La TN15 62
Wiseacre TN3 176
Wishart Rd SE3 11
Wisley Rd BR5 30
Wistaria Cl BR6 57
Wisteria Gdns BR8 45
Wisteria Ho [11] ME15 116
Witches La TN13 91
Witham Way ME2 52
Withens Cl BR5 44
Witherston Way SE9 29
Withyham Rd TN3 171
Wittersham CE Prim Sch
TN30 199
Wittersham Cl ME5 68
Wittersham Ho [2] BR5 44
Wittersham Rd
Wittersham TN30 199
Wittersham,Potman's Heath
TN17,TN30 198
Wittersham Road Sta*
TN17 198
Wixom Ho SE3 11
Woburn Cl SE28 3
Woburn Ct [1] DA6 13
Wodehouse Cl ME20 81
Wodehouse Rd DA1 16
Woldham Pl BR2 42
Woldham Rd BR2 42
Wolds Dr BR6 57
Wolf Ho ME4 54
Wolf's Cnr RH8 104
Wolf's Hill RH8 104
Wolf's Rd RH8 104
Wolf's Row RH8 104
Wolfe Cl BR2 42
Wolfe Cres SE7 1
Wolfe Rd ME16 99
Wolfs Wood RH8 104
Wollaston Cl ME8 69
Wolseley Rd TN4 159
Wolsey Ct SE9 11
Wolsey Mews BR6 57
Wolsley Cl DA1 14
Wolsley Ho DA1 14
Wolvercote Rd SE2 3
Wombwell Gdns DA11 35
Wood Cl Ditton ME20 98
Joyden's Wood DA5 31
Wood Dr Bromley BR7 28
Sevenoaks TN13 91
Wood End BR8 45
Wood La Dartford DA2 33
East End TN17 181
Wood Lodge Gdns BR1 ...28
Wood Lodge Grange
TN13 92
Wood Pl DA14 30
Wood Point [10] E16 1
Wood Rd TN16 72
Wood Retreat SE18 12
Wood Ride BR5 43
Wood St Chatham ME7 54
Cuxton ME2 52
[9] Grays RM17 18
Royal Tunbridge Wells
TN1 159
Swanley Village BR8 46
Wood View Cl TN15 61
Wood Way BR6 57
Woodberry Gr DA5 31
Woodbine Cotts ME2 65
Woodbine Rd DA15 29
Woodbridge Dr ME15 99
Woodbrook Rd SE2 13
Woodbury Cl
Biggin Hill TN16 ....72 F1
Royal Tunbridge Wells
TN4 ....159 A5
Woodbury Gdns SE12 ....28 B4
Woodbury La TN30 .....193 A7
Woodbury Park Gdns
TN4 ....159 B5
Woodbury Park Rd TN4 .159 B5
Woodbury Rd
Chatham ME5 ....67 F1
Hawkhurst TN18 ....189 A2
Woodchurch Cl
Chatham ME5 ....68 B5
Sidcup DA14 ....29 D5

oodchurch Cres ME8 ....55 C2
oodchurch Ct 🔲 BR5 ..44 C4
oodchurch Dr BR1 ....28 D1
oodchurch Rd TN30 ..193 D8
oodcut ME14 ....100 A8
oodcock La
oodcock La
rafty Green ME17 ......136 E5
en Green TN17 ....190 E3
oodcocks
eadcorn TN27 ....151 D5
ewham E16 ....1 D8
oodcote Dr BR6 ....43 D2
oodcroft SE9 ....28 F5
oodcut ME14 ....100 A8
oodfall Dr DA1 ....14 F3
oodfalls Ind Est ME18 .130 D6
oodfield Ave
ravesend DA11 ....36 B6
onbridge TN11 ....126 E5
oodfield Rd TN9 .....143 B8
oodfield Way ME3 ....39 E4
oodfields TN13 ....91 D4
oodford Gr ME18 ......97 B3
oodford Ho 🔲 SE18 ....12 B8
oodford Rd ME16 ......99 B2
oodgate La ME9 ......71 C2
oodgate Rd ME19 ....80 D4
oodgate Way TN9,
TN11 ....143 E7
oodgates Cl TN26 ....183 D7
oodgers Gr BR8 ......45 F7
oodget Cl E6 ....1 E7
oodhatch Cl E6 ....1 E8
oodhayes BR7 ....29 B2
oodhead Dr BR6 ......57 E8
oodhill SE18 ....1 C2
oodhill Pk TN2 ......160 C6
oodhill Prim Sch SE18 ..1 E2
oodhurst ME5 ....67 D4
oodhurst Ave BR5 ....43 C3
oodhurst La ME2 ......52 B2
oodhurst Rd SE2 ......3 A2
oodington Cl SE9 ......12 A1
oodknoll Dr BR7 ......42 F8
oodland Ave DA3 ......48 F5
oodland Cl
New Barn DA3 ....49 C6
Royal Tunbridge Wells
TN4 ....159 C7
West Malling ME19 ....97 A8
oodland Dr TN8 .....122 D3
oodland Rd TN4 ....159 C7
oodland Rise TN15 ....92 E4
oodland Terr SE7 ......1 E2
oodland View TN30 ..199 E4
oodland Way
Bidborough TN4 ......142 D3
Erith SE2 ....3 D2
Maidstone ME14 ....100 B7
Orpington BR5 ....43 C4
Swanscombe DA9 ......17 A3
oodlands Bexley DA6 ..14 B8
Chatham ME5 ....68 A2
Coxheath ME17 ......115 B3
Cranbrook TN17 .....179 D6
Paddock Wood TN12 ..145 F7
Pembury TN2 ....160 F7
Royal Tunbridge Wells
TN4 ....143 A2
oodlands Ave
Sidcup DA15 ....29 E7
Snodland ME6 ....81 F8
oodlands Cl
Bromley BR1 ....42 F7
Maidstone ME14 ....100 B7
Swanley BR8 ....45 F7
Teston ME18 ....114 B8
oodlands Ct ME5 ......67 F3
oodlands Farm DA16 ..12 C5
oodlands Inf & Jun Schs
TN10 ....127 E6
oodlands La DA12 ....37 E1
oodlands Par ME20 ....98 D8
oodlands Pk DA5 ......31 D4
oodlands Pk (Cvn Pk)
TN27 ....182 D7

Woodlands Prim Sch
ME7 ....54 F4
Woodlands Rd Bexley DA7 .13 E4
Bromley BR1 ....42 F7
Ditton ME20 ....98 D8
Gillingham ME7 ......54 F4
Orpington BR6 ....58 A4
Tonbridge TN9 ......143 A7
Woodlands Rise BR8 ....45 F7
Woodlands Terr
Crockenhill BR8 ......45 B3
Gillingham ME7 ......54 F3
Woodlands The BR6 ....58 B4
Woodlands View TN14 ..59 A1
Woodlark Rd ME4 ....40 B1
Woodlea Leybourne ME19 ..81 F2
New Barn DA3 ....49 C6
Woodleas ME16 ....98 F2
Woodley Rd BR6 ......58 C8
Woodman Par 🔲 E16 ..2 A5
Woodman St E16 ......2 A5
Woodmere SE9 ....28 F7
Woodmount BR8 ......45 D2
Woodpecker Cl 🔲 TN8 ..122 D3
Woodpecker Glade ME8 .69 D6
Woodpecker Rd
Larkfield ME20 ....81 F1
Woolwich SE28 ....3 C6
Woodrow SE18 ....1 F2
Woodrush Pl ME4 ......40 B1
Woods Green Cotts TN5 .184 F7
Woodsgate Way TN2 ..160 B6
Woodside Gillingham ME8 ..69 C6
Kilndown TN17 ......176 F2
Orpington BR6 ....58 B5
Vigo Village DA13 ....79 F8
Woodside Ave BR7 ....29 C3
Woodside Cl Crayford DA7 ..14 D3
Pembury TN2 ....160 E6
Woodside Cres DA15 ..29 E5
Woodside Dr DA2 ......31 E4
Woodside Gn ME3 ....39 B7
Woodside La DA5 ......13 D1
Woodside Par DA15 ..29 E5
Woodside Rd Bromley BR1 .42 E4
Crayford DA7 ....14 D3
Maidstone ME15 ....116 C7
Pembury TN2 ....160 E6
Rusthall TN4 ....158 D4
Sevenoaks TN13 ......92 B4
Sidcup DA15 ....29 E5
Sundridge TN14 ......90 E3
Tonbridge TN9 ......143 B7
Woodside Sch DA17 ....4 B2
Woodstock Cl DA5 ......30 F7
Woodstock Ct SE12 ....11 A1
Woodstock Rd ME2 ....53 A7
Woodvale Ct BR1 ......42 B8
Woodview Cl BR6 ......57 C8
Woodview Cres TN11 ..126 F5
Woodview Rd BR8 ......45 D7
Woodview Rise ME2 ....38 F1
Woodville SE3 ....11 B6
Woodville Cl SE12 ......11 A2
Woodville Gr 🔲 DA16 ..13 A4
Woodville Pl DA12 ......36 B8
Woodville Rd ME15 ..100 A2
Woodville St 🔲 SE18 ....1 E2
Woodward Terr DA9 ..16 E1
Woodyates Rd
Eltham SE12 ....28 B8
Lewisham SE12 ......11 A1
Woolacombe Rd SE3 ..11 C5
Woolaston Ct ME15 ....99 F1
Woolbrook Rd DA1 ....14 E1
Wooldeys Rd ME8 ......55 F2
Woolf Cl SE28 ....3 B5
Woolf Wlk RM18 ......19 C5
Woollett Cl DA1 ....15 A3
Woollett St ME14 ....100 A5
Woolley Cl TN4 ......142 F1
Woolley Rd
Maidstone ME15 ....116 F7
Royal Tunbridge Wells
TN4 ....142 F1
Woolpack Cnr TN27 ..182 A7
Woolpack Cotts TN27 ..182 A7

Woolwich Arsenal Sta
SE18 ....2 B2
Woolwich Church St SE18 ..1 E3
Woolwich Cl ME5 ......68 A7
Woolwich Comm SE18 ..12 A8
Woolwich Dockyard Ind Est
SE18 ....1 E3
Woolwich Dockyard Sta
SE18 ....1 F2
Woolwich High St SE18 ..2 A3
Woolwich Manor Way E6 ..2 A7
Woolwich Manorway E16 ..2 B4
Woolwich New Rd SE18 ..2 B2
Woolwich Polytechnic Sch
for Boys SE28 ....3 A5
Woolwich Rd Bexley DA7 .14 A4
Erith SE2 ....3 E1
Greenwich SE10,SE7 ....1 C2
Wootton Gn SE18 ......55 D3
Wootton Ho SE9 ......12 D1
Wopsle Cl ME1 ....67 D7
Worcester Ave ME19 ..97 A2
Worcester Cl
Istead Rise DA13 ......35 F1
Rochester ME2 ....52 E8
Swanscombe DA9 ......17 B3
Worcester Rd ME15 ..116 D7
Wordsworth Cl
Chatham ME5 ....68 C7
Tilbury RM18 ....19 C5
Wordsworth Ho 🔲 SE18 .12 A8
Wordsworth Rd
Bexley DA16 ....12 E6
Maidstone ME14 ....100 B7
Wordsworth Way
Dartford DA1 ....16 A3
New Hythe ME20 ......82 A4
Workhouse La
Coxheath ME15 .....115 C4
Sutton Valence ME17 .115 A8
Workhouse Rd ME19 ..80 F4
World of Silk* DA1 ....14 C2
Worlds End La BR6 ....58 B3
Wormdale Hill ME9 ....71 B3
Wormdale Rd ME9 ....71 B4
Worsenden TN27 .....167 E1
Worsfold Ct ME15 ....100 A1
Worships Hill TN13 ....91 E4
Worth Cl BR6 ....57 E6
Worthing Ct RM17 ....17 E8
Wotton Cl ME15 ......116 E5
Wotton Gn BR5 ....44 D5
Wouldham All Saints CE Prim
Sch ME1 ....66 C5
Wouldham Rd
Grays RM17,RM20 ....17 E8
Rochester ME1 ....52 E1
Wouldham Terr 🔲 BR5 ..44 B6
Wrangleden Cl ME15 ..116 E5
Wrangleden Rd ME15 .116 E5
Wrangling La DA13 ....64 F3
Wrekin Rd SE18 ......12 C7
Wren Cl Larkfield ME20 ..81 F1
Orpington BR5 ....44 D6
Wren Ind Est ME15 ..116 A3
Wren Path SE28 ....2 D4
Wren Rd DA14 ....30 C5
Wren Way ME5 ....68 B6
Wren Wlk RM18 ......19 B7
Wren's Cross ME15 ..100 A3
Wrens Croft DA11 ....35 E4
Wrens Rd ME9 ....87 F6
Wricklemarsh Rd
Greenwich SE3 ....11 B6
Greenwich SE3 ....11 B5
Wright Cl Gillingham ME8 ..55 C2
Swanscombe DA10 ....17 D1
Wrights Cl TN5 ......193 A8
Wrotham Hill Rd TN15 ..79 A6
Wrotham Rd Bexley DA16 .13 C6
Borough Green TN15 ..95 A8
Culverstone Green DA13 ..63 F4
Gravesend DA11,DA13 ..36 A4
Meopham Sta DA13 ....50 A3
Wrotham Road Prim Sch
DA11 ....36 B8
Wrotham Sch TN15 ....79 A1

Wrotham Water La ME19,
TN15 ....79 E5
Wrotham Water Rd TN15,
ME19 ....79 E4
Wrott & Hill Ct DA4 ....47 B8
Wrottesley Rd SE18 ....12 C8
Wroxham Rd SE28 ......3 D6
Wulfred Way TN15 ....77 B1
Wyatt Cl TN15 ....94 F7
Wyatt Ho 🔲 ME2 ......53 A7
Wyatt Pl ME2 ....53 A7
Wyatt Rd DA1 ....14 F4
Wyatt St ME14 ......100 A4
Wyborne Prim Sch SE9 ..29 B7
Wybourne Rise TN2 ..173 B8
Wybournes La ME23 ..23 C3
Wycliffe Cl DA16 ......12 F6
Wycliffe Ho 🔲 DA11 ..35 F7
Wycliffe Row DA11 ....35 F7
Wycombe Ct SE3 ......11 A7
Wydeville Manor Rd
SE12 ....28 B4
Wye Cl BR6 ....43 F2
Wye Rd
Borough Green TN15 ..95 A8
Gravesend DA12 ......36 D6
Tonbridge TN10 ......127 C5
Wyfold Rd 🔲 SE2 ......3 C1
Wyke Manor Rd ME14 .100 A4
Wykeham Cl DA12 ....36 E2
Wykeham Cotts ME17 .115 F2
Wykeham Ct BR7 ......29 E2
Wykeham Gr ME17 ..118 A7
Wykeham Rd ME2 ....53 B8
Wyles Rd ME4 ....53 E2
Wyles St ME7 ....54 E2
Wylie Ho ME3 ....39 F6
Wylie Rd ME3 ....40 D6
Wyncham Ave DA15 ..29 E7
Wyncroft Cl BR1 ......42 F6
Wyndcliff Rd SE3,SE7 ..11 B8
Wyndham Ave TN11 ..125 F1
Wyndham Cl Leigh TN11 .125 F1
Orpington BR6 ....43 C1
Wyndham Rd ME4 ....53 E2
Wynford Gr BR5 ......44 B6
Wynford Pl DA17 ......14 A8
Wynford Way SE9 ....28 F5
Wynn's Ave DA15 ......13 A2
Wytchlings The ME17 ..118 D2
Wythens Wlk SE9 ......12 B1
Wytherling Cl ME14 ..100 F5
Wythes Cl BR1 ....42 F7
Wythes Rd E16 ....1 A5
Wythfield Rd SE9 ......11 F1
Wyvern Cl Dartford DA1 ..32 C8
Orpington BR6 ....58 B7
Snodland ME6 ....82 A7
Wyvern Ho 🔲 RM17 ..18 B8
Wyvill Cl ME8 ....69 E5

Y

Yalding Cl ME2 ....39 B1
Yalding Gr BR5 ....44 D5
Yalding Hill ME18 ....114 A3
Yalding Organic Gdns*
ME18 ....130 F7
Yalding St Peter & St Paul CE
Prim Sch ME18 .....114 A1
Yalding Sta ME18 ....113 D1
Yantlet Dr ME2 ....52 C7
Yard The ME5 ....68 B3
Yardley Cl TN9 ......127 D3
Yardley Court Prep Sch
TN11 ....143 F7
Yardley Park Rd TN9 ..127 D3
Yarnton Way SE2,DA18 ..3 E4
Yarrow Cres E6 ....1 E8
Yarrow Rd ME14 ....100 F5
Yarrow Rd ME5 ....67 F4
Yateley St SE18 ....1 D3
Yaugher La ME9 ......70 C3
Ye Olde Tudor Cr ME7 ..29 B3
Yelsted La Chatham ME14 ..84 D7
Yelsted ME9 ....70 A1

Yelsted Rd ME9 ....86 A7
Yeoman Cl E6 ....2 B6
Yeoman Ct ME14 ....101 B3
Yeoman Dr ME7 ......54 F1
Yeoman Gdns TN12 ..145 F6
Yeoman Ho ME1 ......53 D4
Yeoman La ME14 ....101 A2
Yeoman Pk ME15 ....101 A2
Yeoman Way ME15 ..101 A2
Yeoman's Mdws TN13 ..92 A1
Yeovil Cl BR6 ....57 E8
Yester Dr BR7 ....28 E1
Yester Pk BR7 ....28 F2
Yester Rd BR7 ....28 E1
Yew Rd ME3 ....40 E3
Yew Tree Cl
Aylesford ME20 ....82 E1
Bexley DA6 ....13 A6
Chatham ME5 ....68 D1
New Barn DA3 ....49 D7
Sevenoaks TN13 ......91 D4
Yew Tree Cotts
Groombridge TN3 ....171 F8
Halstead TN14 ....74 F7
Sandling ME14 ....83 F1
Yew Tree Green Rd
TN12 ....147 A1
Yew Tree Mews TN16 .105 D8
Yew Tree Pl ME7 ......69 B1
Yew Tree Rd TN4 ....159 B8
Yews The DA12 ....36 D7
Yewtree Ho 🔲 ME1 ....53 B8
Yewtree Ind Est ME20 ..82 D2
Yoke Cl ME2 ....53 B8
Yokosuka Way ME14,ME8 ..55 A7
Yolande Gdns SE9 ......11 E2
Yopps Gn TN15 ....94 E1
York Ave Chatham ME5 ..67 F3
Gillingham ME7 ......54 C4
Sidcup DA15 ....29 C6
York Cl E6 ....1 F7
York Hill ME5 ....54 C2
York Par TN10 ......127 C6
York Pl RM17 ....18 A8
York Rd Biggin Hill TN16 ..88 B8
Dartford DA1 ....32 F8
Gravesend DA12 ......36 C5
Maidstone ME15 ....100 C6
Northfleet DA11 ......35 D8
Rochester ME1 ....53 C3
Royal Tunbridge Wells
TN1 ....159 A4
Tonbridge TN10 ....127 D5
York Rise BR6 ....57 E8
York Road Jun Sch DA1 .32 F8
York Terr DA8 ....12 F3
Yorkland Ave DA16 ....12 F3
Youens Pl ME3 ....38 B3
Young Rd E16 ....1 C7

Z

Zambra Way TN15 ....92 F7
Zangwill Rd SE18,SE3 ..11 D6
Zealand Ho SE18 ....1 E2
Zelah Rd BR5 ....44 C2
Zetland Ave ME7 ......54 E2
Zillah Gdns ME8 ......69 C6
Zion Pl DA12 ....36 B8
Zion St TN15 ....92 F6

Addresses

Name and Address	Telephone	Page	Grid reference

Name and Address	Telephone	Page	Grid reference

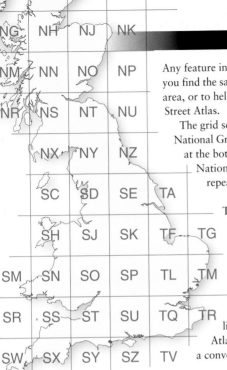

Any feature in this atlas can be given a unique reference to help you find the same feature on other Ordnance Survey maps of the area, or to help someone else locate you if they do not have a Street Atlas.

The grid squares in this atlas match the Ordnance Survey National Grid and are at 500 metre intervals. The small figures at the bottom and sides of every other grid line are the National Grid kilometre values (**00** to **99** km) and are repeated across the country every 100 km (see left).

To give a unique National Grid reference you need to locate where in the country you are. The country is divided into 100 km squares with each square given a unique two-letter reference. Use the administrative map to determine in which 100 km square a particular page of this atlas falls.

The bold letters and numbers between each grid line (**A** to **F**, **1** to **8**) are for use within a specific Street Atlas only, and when used with the page number, are a convenient way of referencing these grid squares.

Example   The railway bridge over DARLEY GREEN RD in grid square B1

Step 1: Identify the two-letter reference, in this example the page is in **SP**

Step 2: Identify the 1 km square in which the railway bridge falls. Use the figures in the southwest corner of this square: Eastings **17**, Northings **74**. This gives a unique reference: **SP 17 74**, accurate to 1 km.

Step 3: To give a more precise reference accurate to 100 m you need to estimate how many tenths along and how many tenths up this 1 km square the feature is (to help with this the 1 km square is divided into four 500 m squares). This makes the bridge about **8** tenths along and about **1** tenth up from the southwest corner.

This gives a unique reference: **SP 178 741**, accurate to 100 m.

Eastings (read from left to right along the bottom) come before Northings (read from bottom to top). If you have trouble remembering say to yourself "Along the hall, THEN up the stairs"!

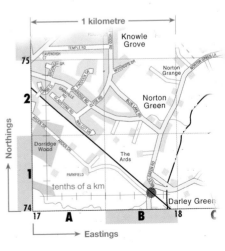

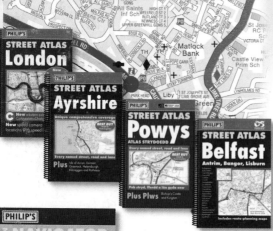